A 17 HAR 2008

# Collins
# STREETFINDER
# GLASGOW

## Contents

| | |
|---|---|
| Key to street map symbols | 1 |
| Key to street map pages | 2-3 |
| City centre map | 4-5 |
| Street maps | 6-145 |
| Local information | 146-165 |
| Rail & subway network map | 166-167 |
| Key to route planning map symbols | 168 |
| Key to route planning maps | 169 |
| Route planning maps | 170-173 |
| Index to place names | 174-175 |
| Index to street names | 176-270 |

D0273474

# ⊙ Collins

Published by Collins
*An imprint of* HarperCollins Publishers
77-85 Fulham Palace Road, Hammersmith, London W6 8JB

www.collinsworld.com

Copyright © HarperCollins Publishers Ltd 2008

Collins® is a registered trademark of HarperCollins Publishers Limited

Mapping generated from Collins Bartholomew digital databases

This product uses map data licensed from Ordnance Survey ® with the permission of the Controller of Her Majesty's Stationery Office. © Crown copyright. Licence number 399302

The British city and town population figures are derived from the 2001 census.
Source: National Statistics website: www.statistics.gov.uk
Crown copyright material is reproduced with the permission of the Controller of HMSO.

Printed in China

ISBN 978-0-00-725458-3   Imp 001       UI12278   LDL

e-mail: roadcheck@harpercollins.co.uk

| | | | |
|---|---|---|---|
| M73 | Motorway/under construction or proposed | Toll → | One-way street/Toll |
| A74 | Primary road dual/single | | Restricted access street |
| A89 | A Road dual/single | | Pedestrian street |
| B763 | B Road dual/single | | Minor road/Track |
| | Other road dual/single | FB | Footpath/Footbridge |
| | Road under construction | | Unitary authority boundary |
| | Road tunnel | | Postcode boundary |

| | | | |
|---|---|---|---|
| | Railway/tunnel/level crossing | | Subway station |
| | Main/Other railway station | | Bus/Coach station |
| P&R P&R | Park & Ride bus/rail | | Pedestrian ferry |

| | | | |
|---|---|---|---|
| | Leisure/Tourism | | Hospital |
| | Shopping/Retail | | Industry/Commerce |
| | Administration/Law | | Notable building |
| | Education | | Major religious building |

| | | | |
|---|---|---|---|
| | Health centre | + ☾ ✡ | Church/Mosque/Synagogue |
| Pol | Police station | | Cinema/Theatre |
| PO | Post Office | | Hotel |
| Lib | Library | | Tourist information centre (all year/seasonal) |
| | Fire station/Crematorium/Ambulance station/Community centre | P | Car park |

| | | | |
|---|---|---|---|
| | Wood/Forest | | Golf course |
| | Park/Garden/Recreation ground | | Cemetery |
| | Public open space | | Built up area |

| | | | |
|---|---|---|---|
| 271 | National Grid number | 16 | Page continuation number |

For general map abbreviations see list on page 176

SCALE 1:15,840 4 inches to 1 mile (6.3 cm to 1 km)

| 0 | 1/4 | 1/2 | 3/4 | 1 mile |
|---|---|---|---|---|

| 0 | 1/4 | 1/2 | 3/4 | 1 | 1 1/4 | 1 1/2 kilometres |

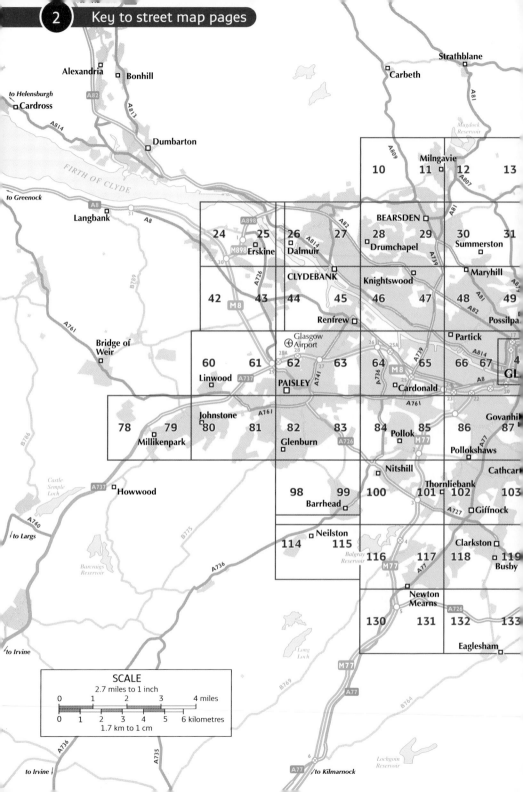

Strathblane

Alexandria □ Bonhill
Carbeth

to Helensburgh
□ Cardross

Mugdock
Reservoir

Dumbarton

Milngavie

FIRTH OF CLYDE

to Greenock
Langbank

**10** **11** **12** **13**

BEARSDEN □

**24** **25** **26** **27** **28** **29** **30** **31**
Erskine Dalmuir Drumchapel Summerston

Maryhill

CLYDEBANK Knightswood

**42** **43** **44** **45** **46** **47** **48** **49**
Possilpa

Renfrew

Partick

Glasgow
Airport

**60** **61** **62** **63** **64** **65** **66** **67** **4**
Linwood GL.

PAISLEY Cardonald

Govanhil

**78** **79** **80** **81** **82** **83** **84** **85** **86** **87**
Millikenpark Glenburn Pollok
Pollokshaws

Bridge of
Weir

Nitshill
Cathcar

Castle
Semple
Loch
Howwood
Thornliebank

**98** **99** **100** **101** **102** **103**
Barrhead Giffnock

to Largs

Neilston
Clarkston

**114** **115** **116** **117** **118** **119**
Busby

Balgray
Reservoir

Barcraigs
Reservoir

Newton
Mearns

to Irvine
**130** **131** **132** **133**
Eaglesham

Long
Loch

### SCALE
2.7 miles to 1 inch

0 1 2 3 4 miles

0 1 2 3 4 5 6 kilometres
1.7 km to 1 cm

Lochgoin
Reservoir

to Irvine
to Kilmarnock

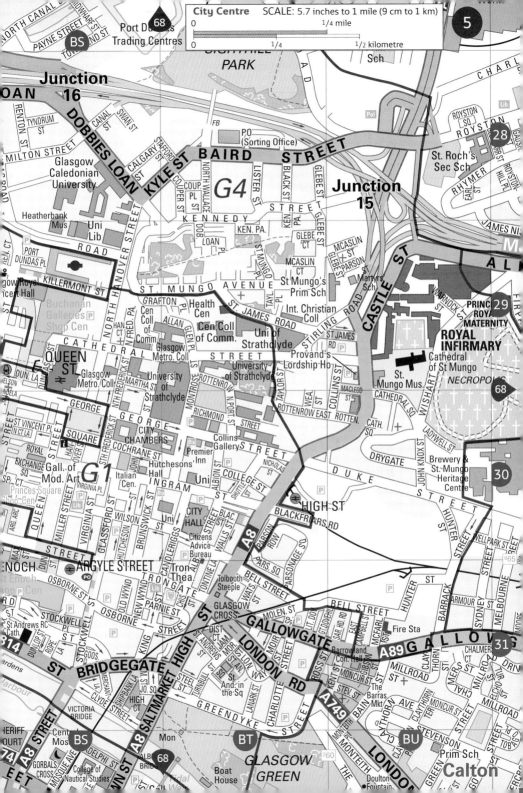

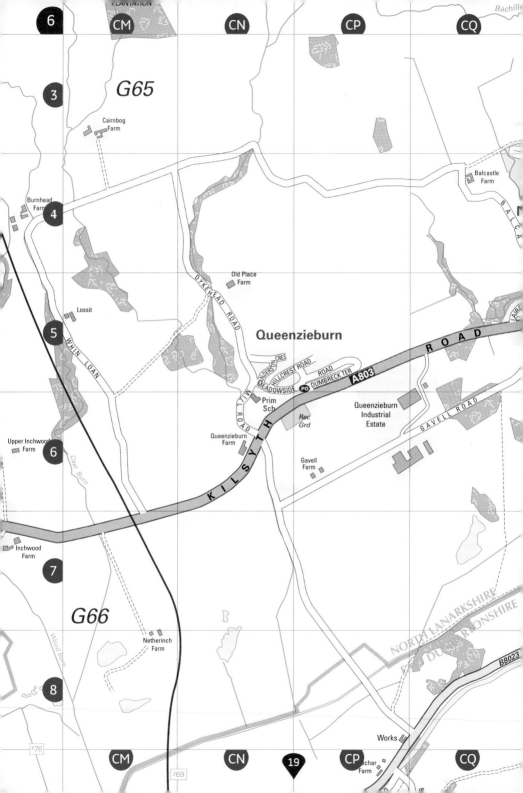

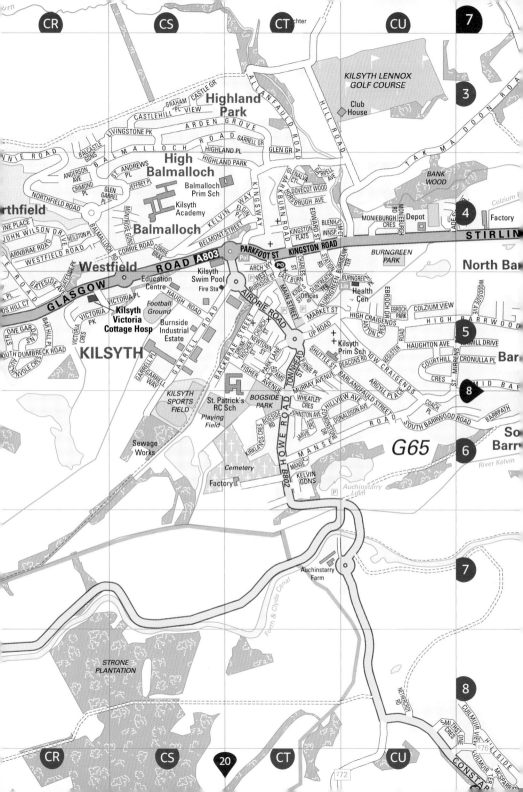

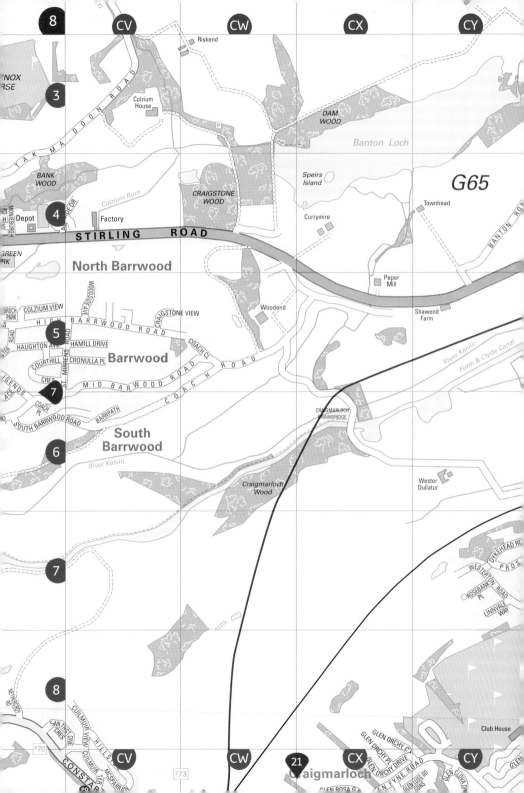

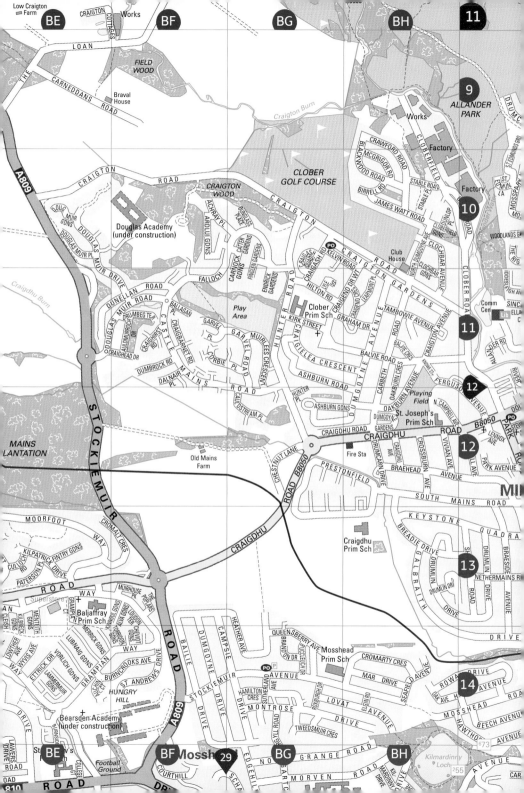

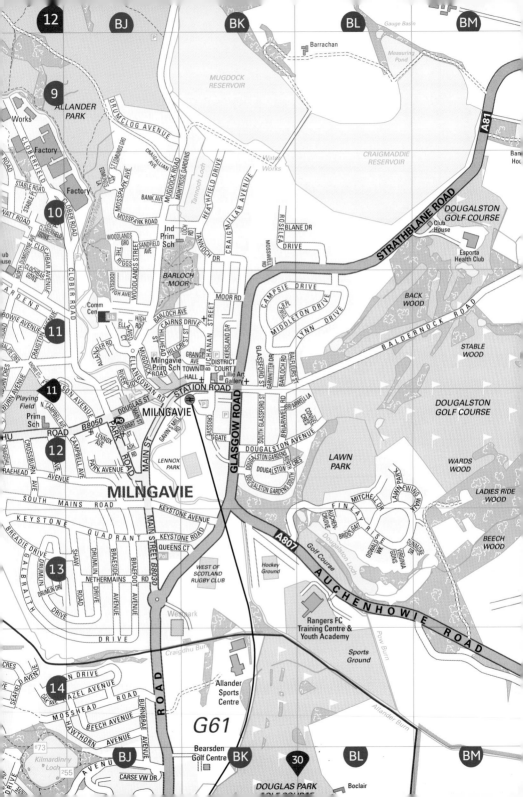

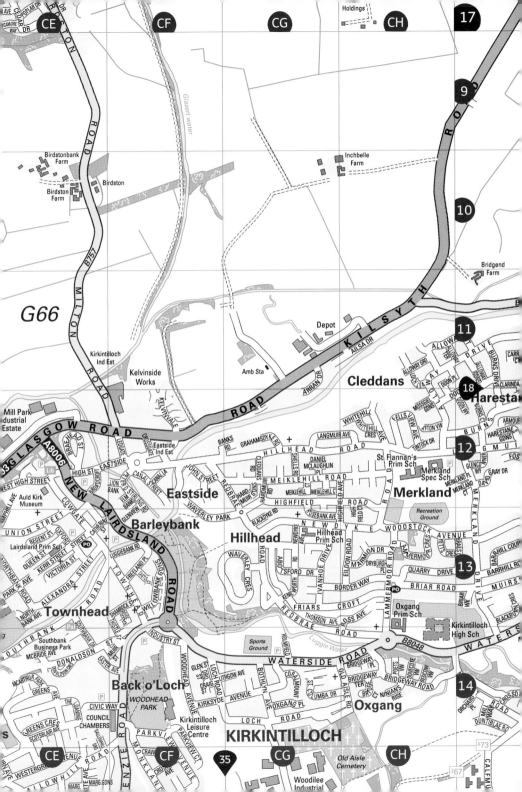

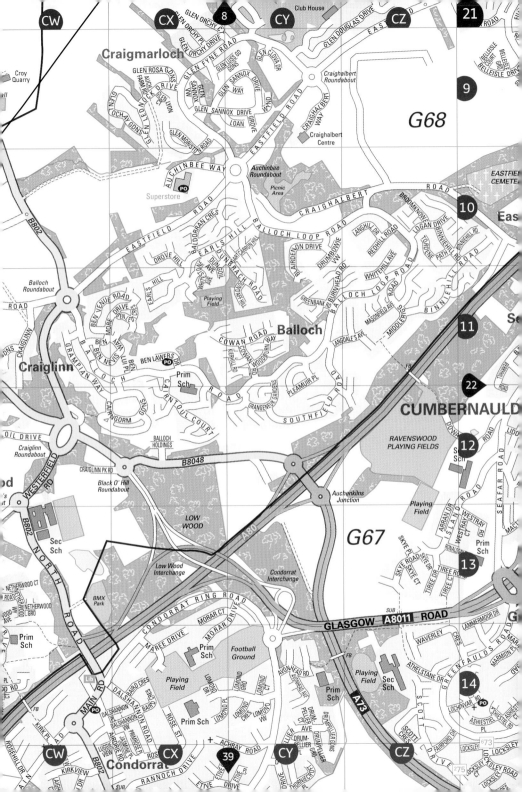

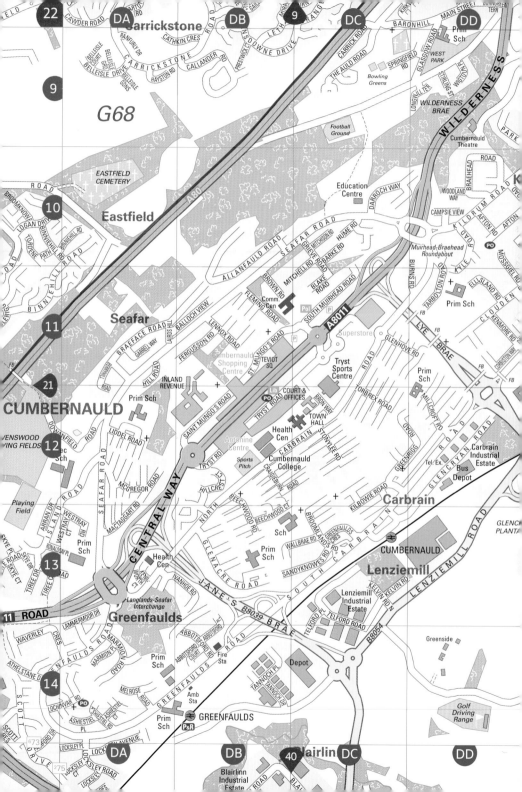

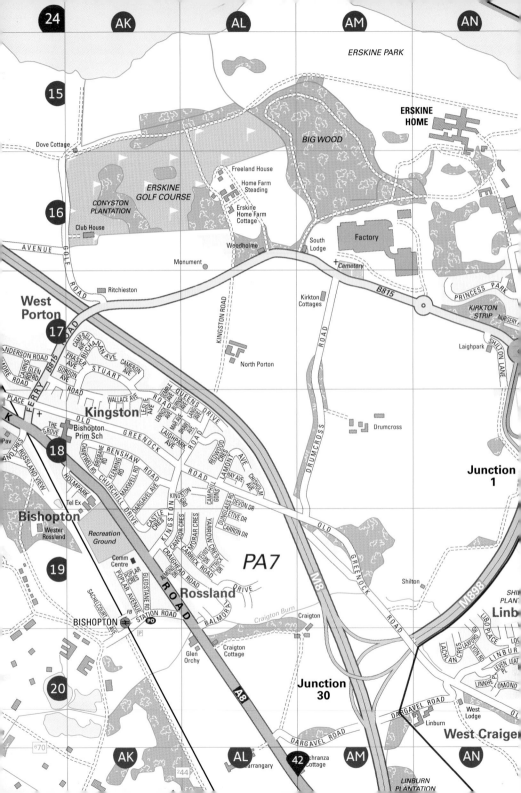

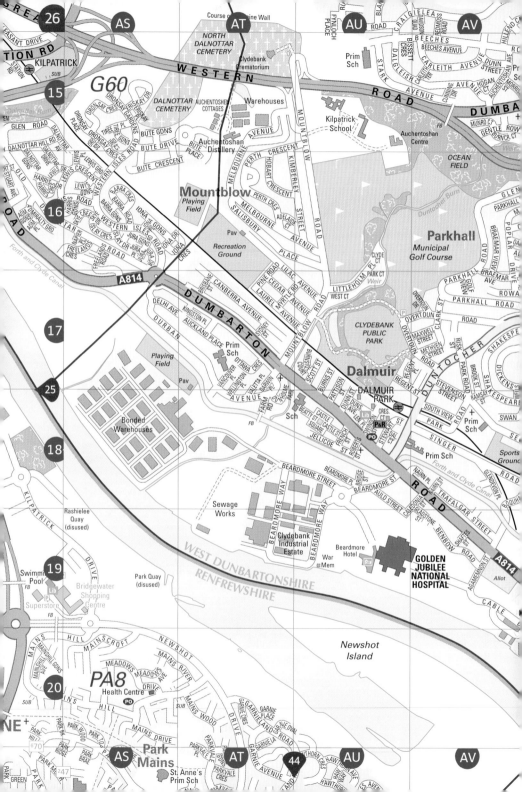

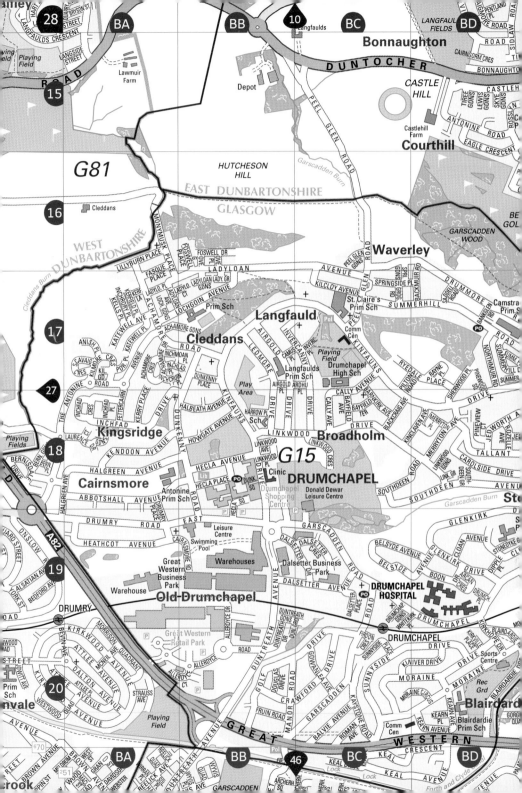

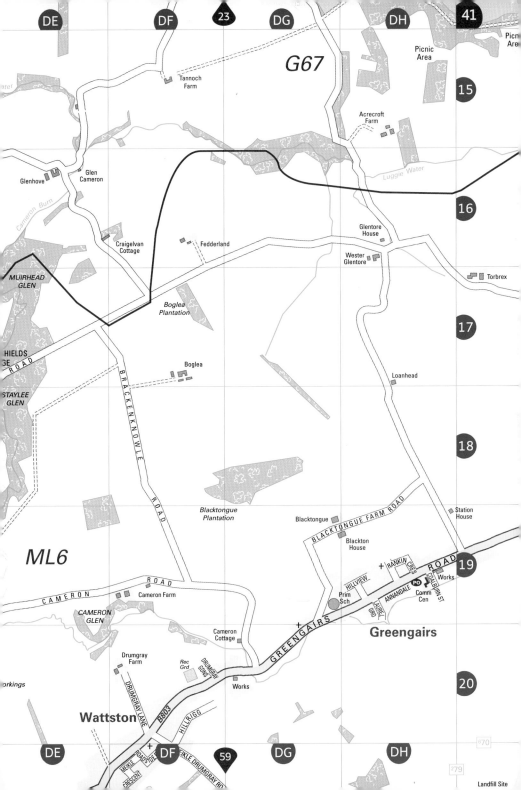

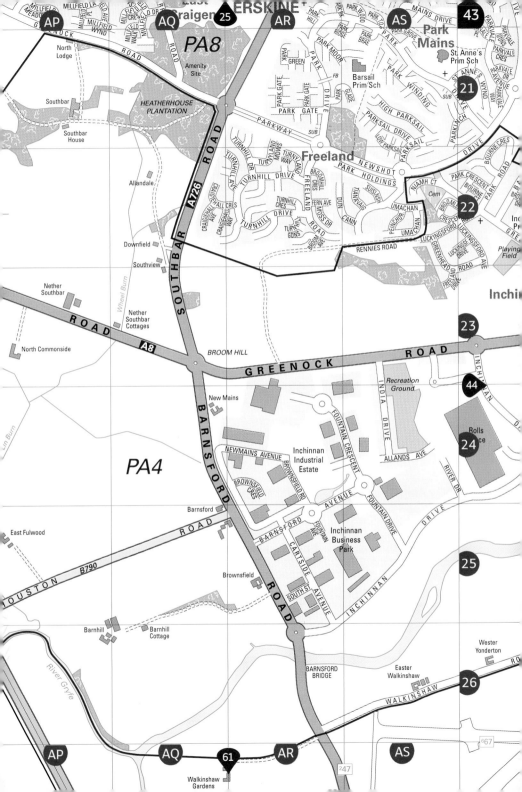

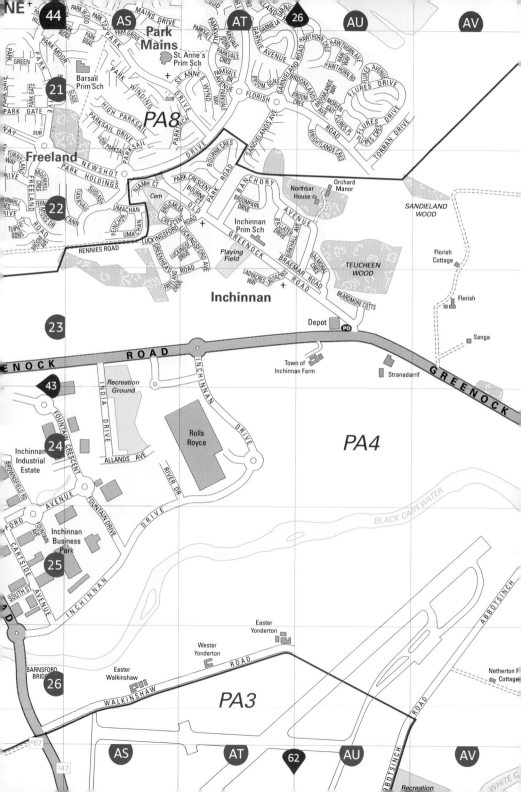

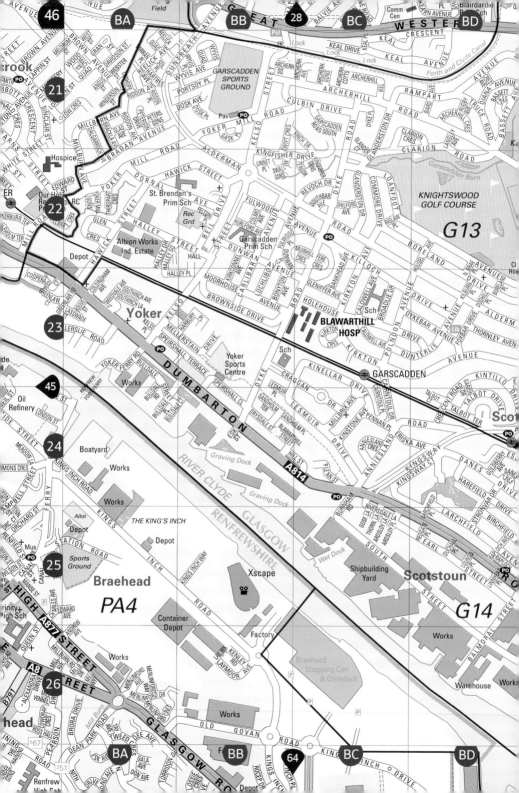

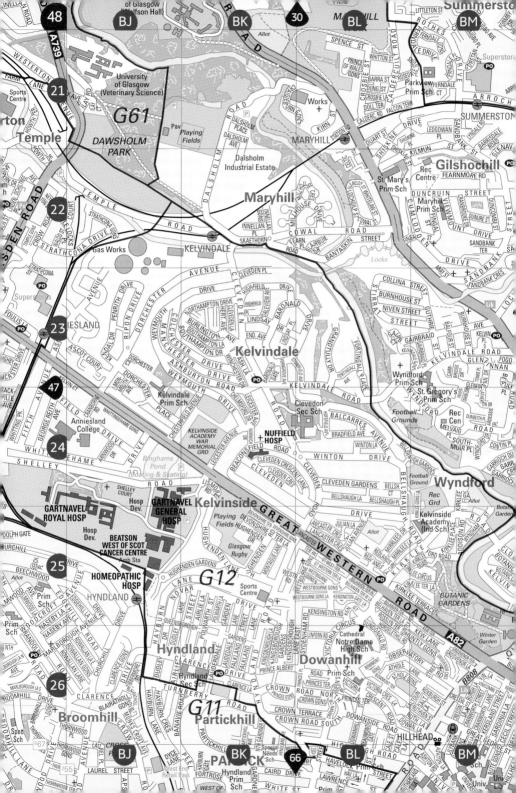

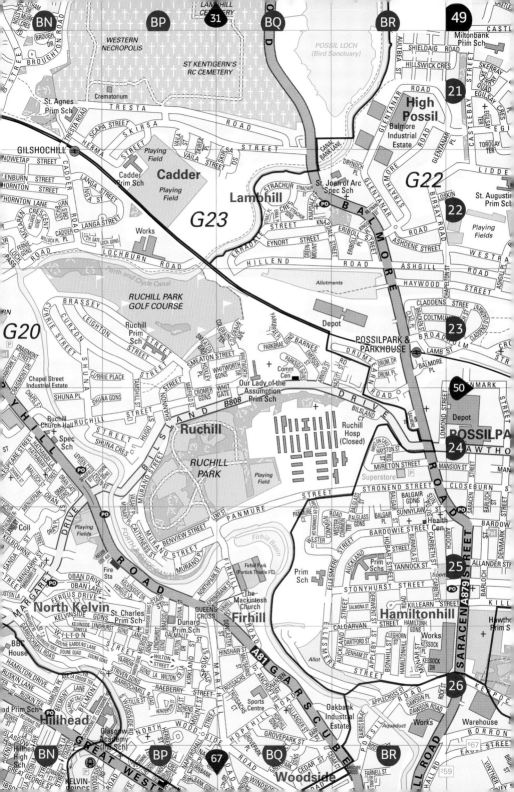

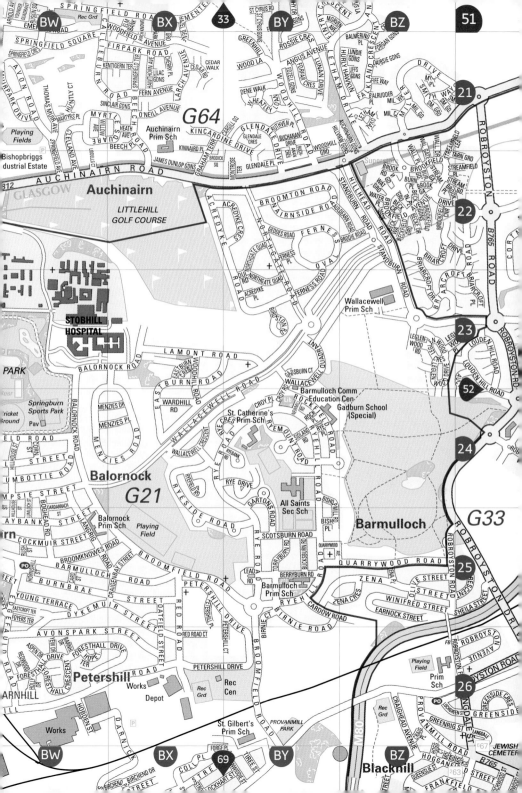

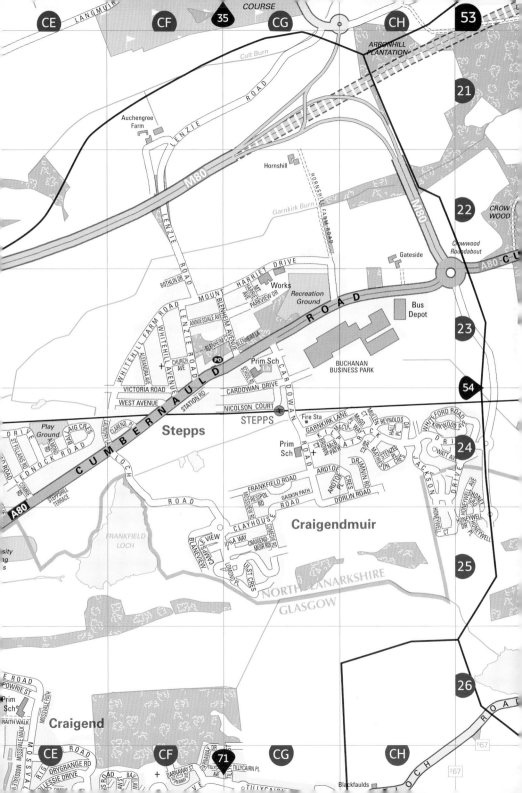

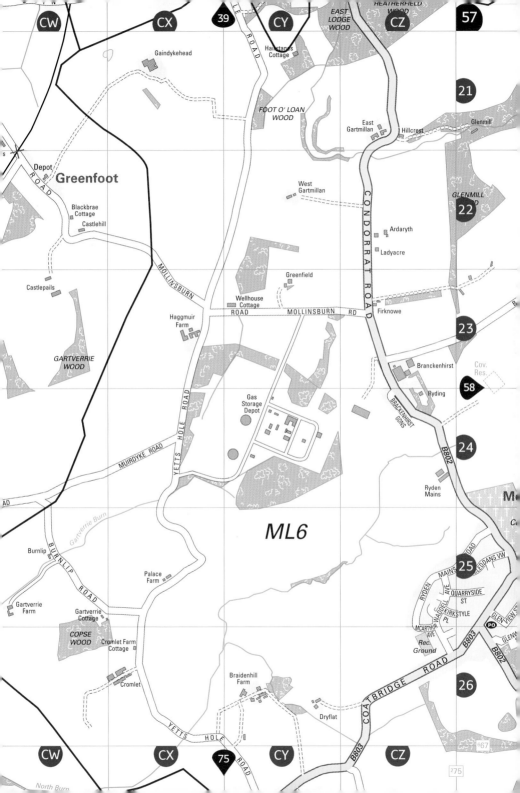

Wattston

DE
DF
**41**
DG
DH
**59**

MEIKLE DRUMGRAY ROAD

MEIKLE ROAD CLYDE PL
CRESCENT

GAIRS ROAD

Landfill Site

**21**

Works

Meikle
Drumgray
Farm

**22**

Opencast Workings

Drumshangie

DARNGAVIL ROAD

**23**

ML6

**24**

Drumshangie Moss

Whiterigg
Farm

**25**

ROAD

DYKEHEAD

Dykehead
Farm

Airdriehill
Farm

**26**

BALLOCHNEY

Meadowhead

North Burn

rling Road
Ind Est

Meadowhead
House

BALLOCHNEY ROAD

The Shambles

ARDRIE AVE
ARKLE AVE
ARKANE AVE
ARNDALE RD
GOLDEN SILVER
PL
SPRING CRANGE A
BANK
KINTYRE CRESCENT
AIRK LANE
ANTRIM LANE
BELLAS
ARNSHILL VIEW

ANNIESHILL VIEW

BALLOCHNIE DRIVE

LIVINGSTON DRIVE
EAST AVE

MW
MW

AIRDRIEHILL ROAD

DE
DF
**77**
DG
DH

Opencast Workings

MEADOWHEAD

Plains

Playing
Fields

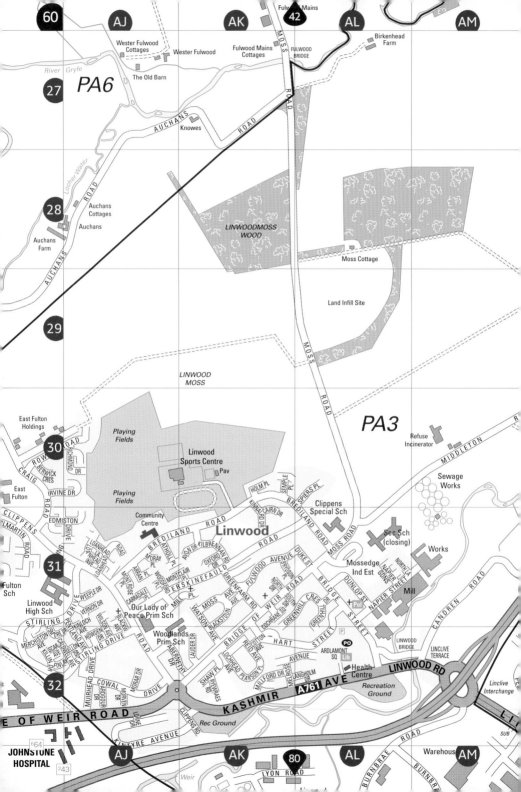

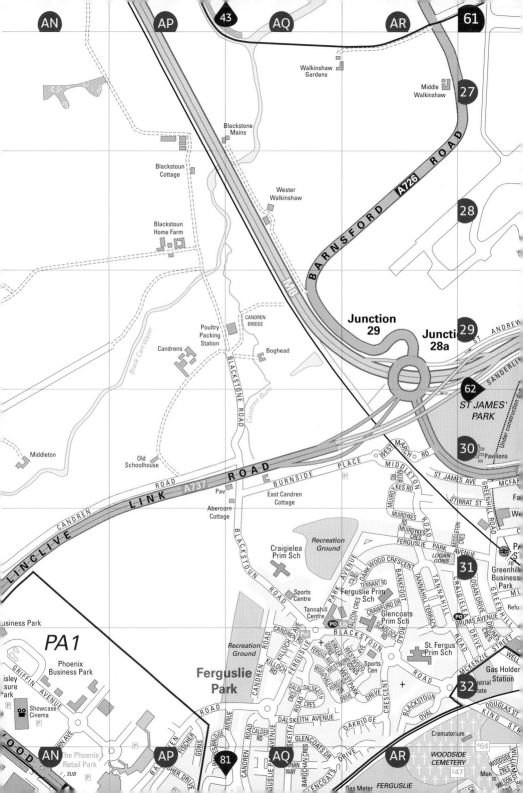

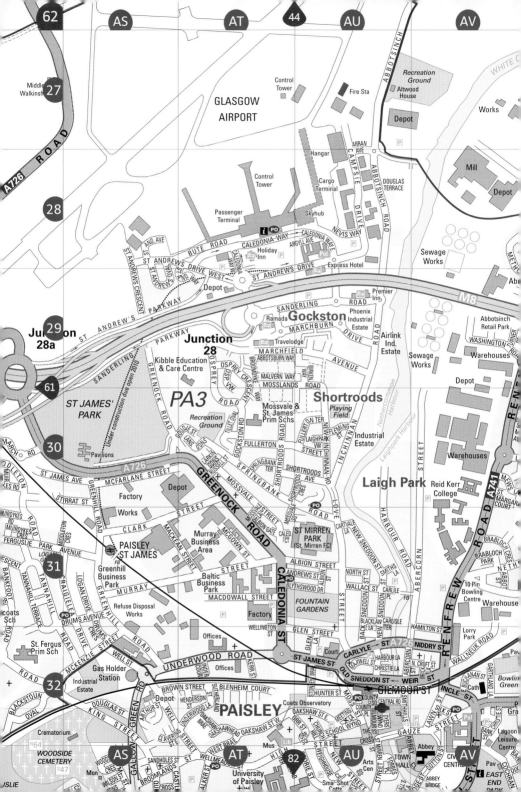

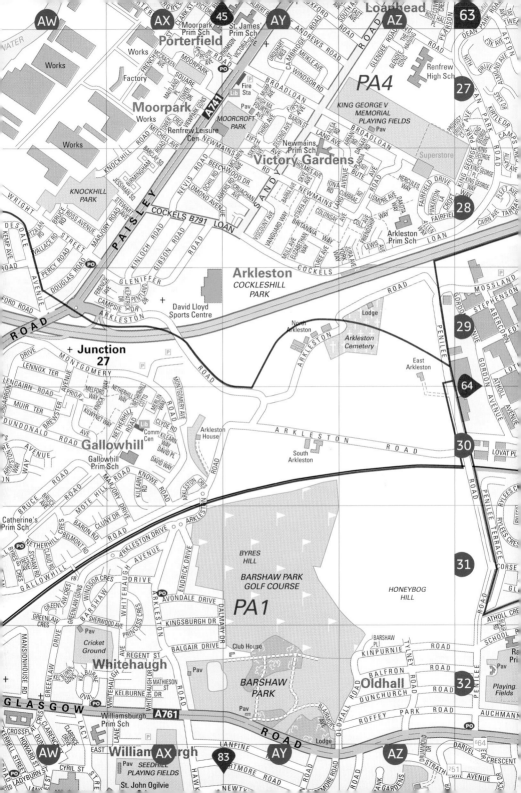

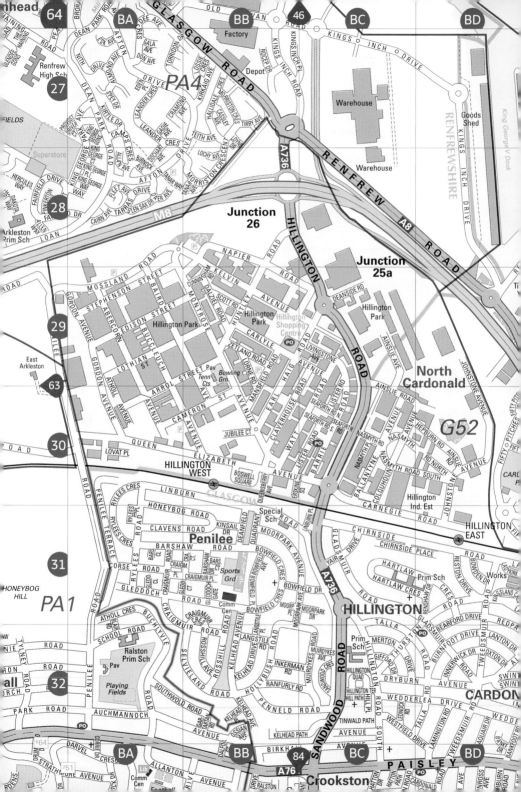

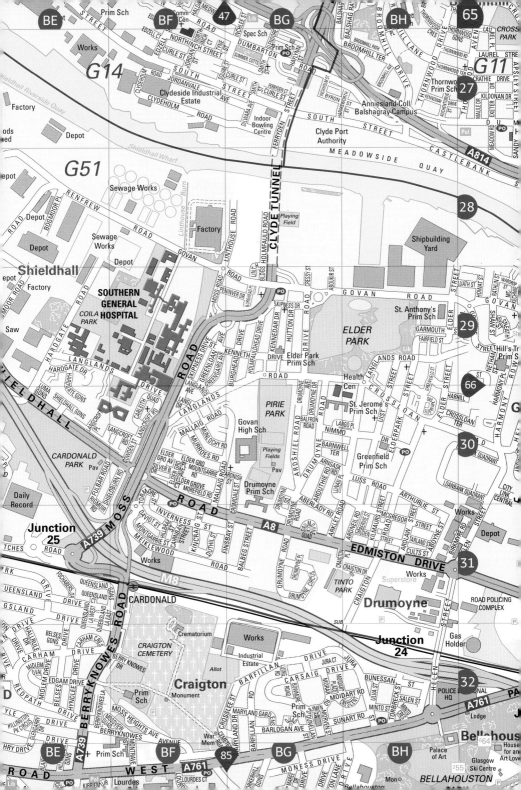

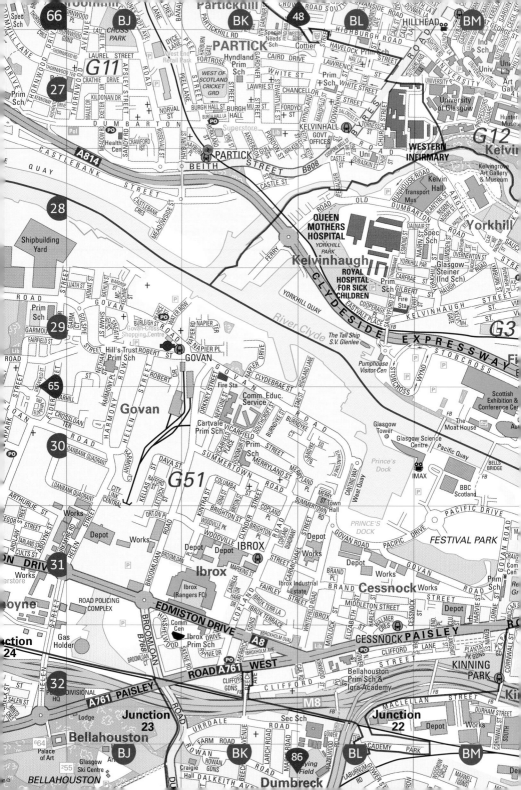

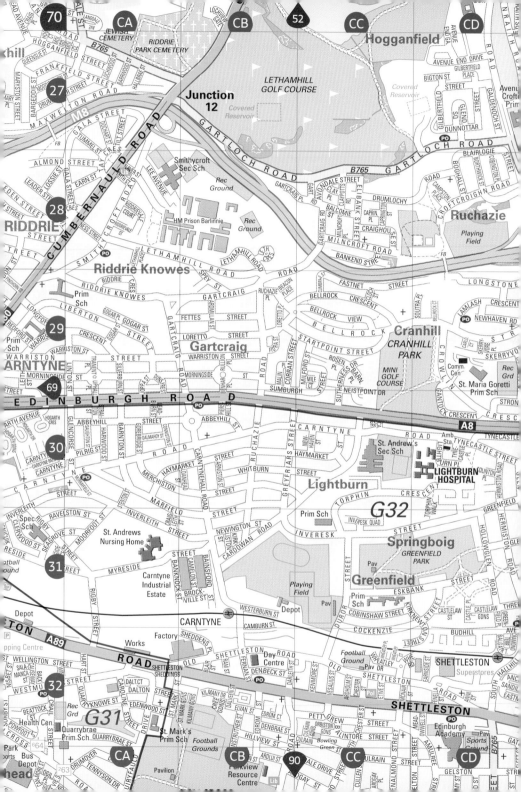

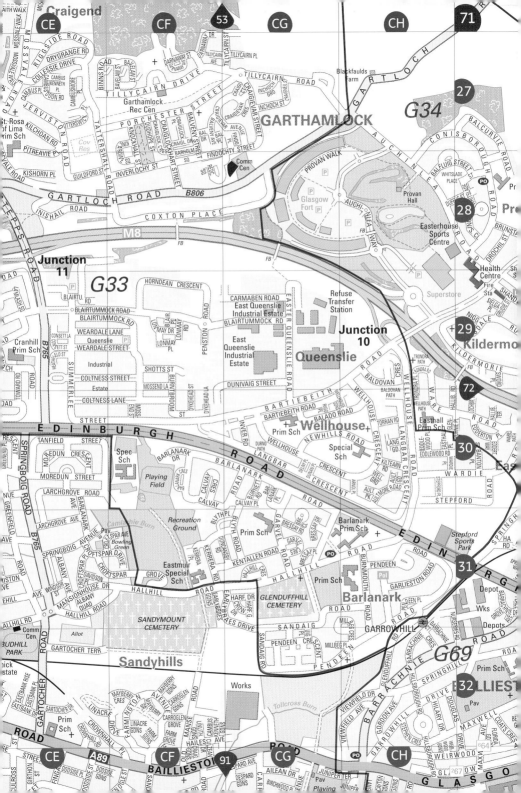

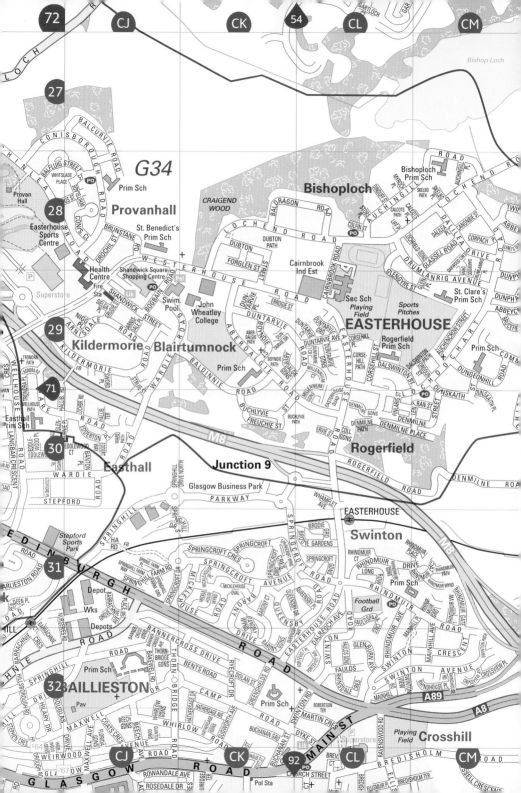

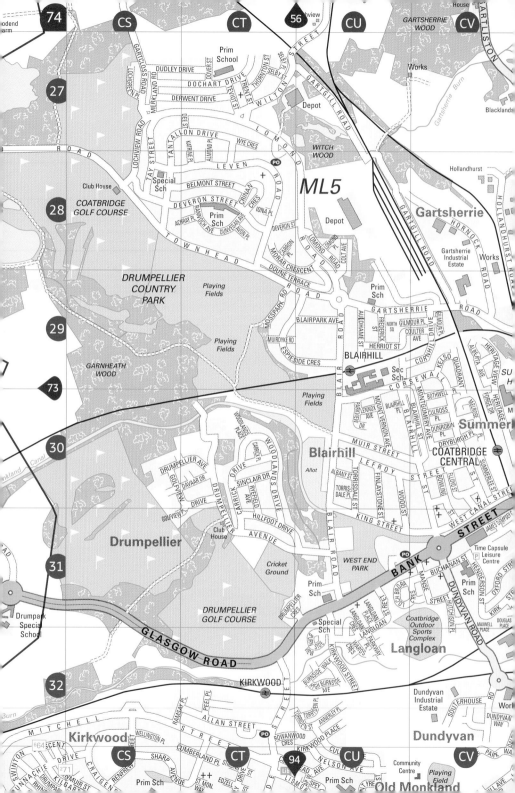

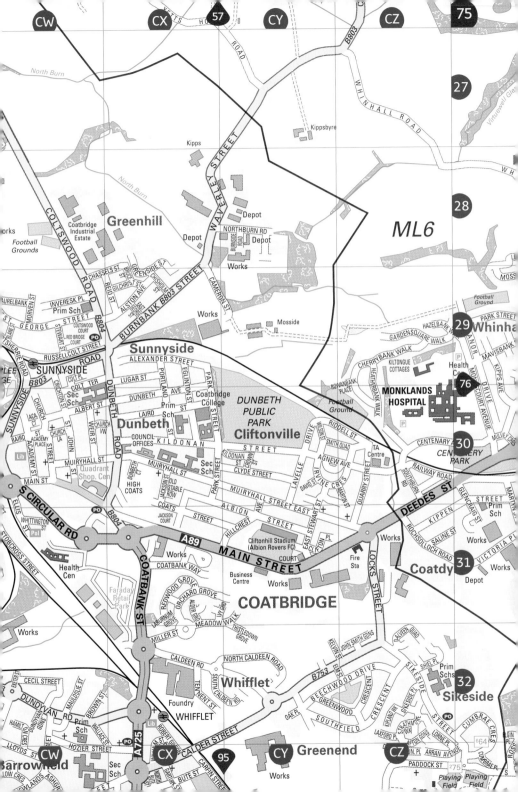

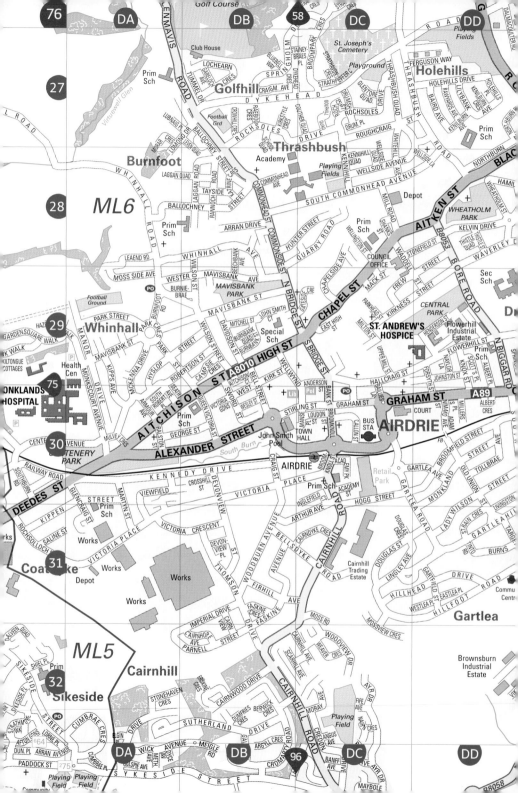

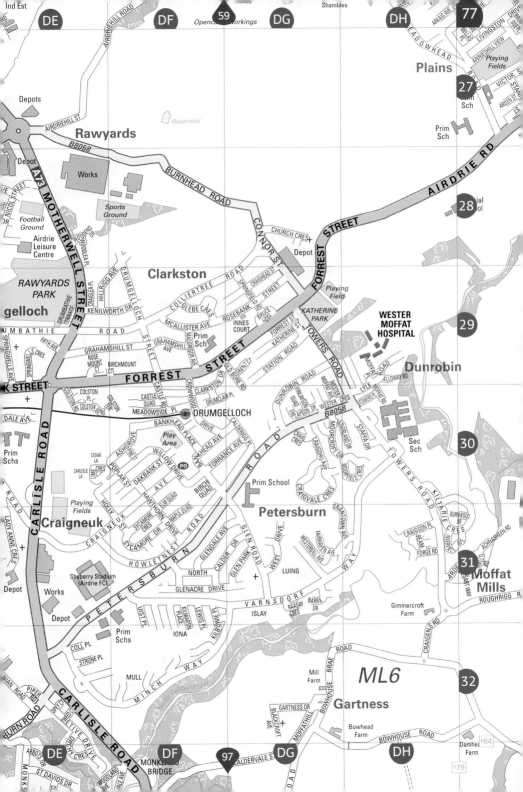

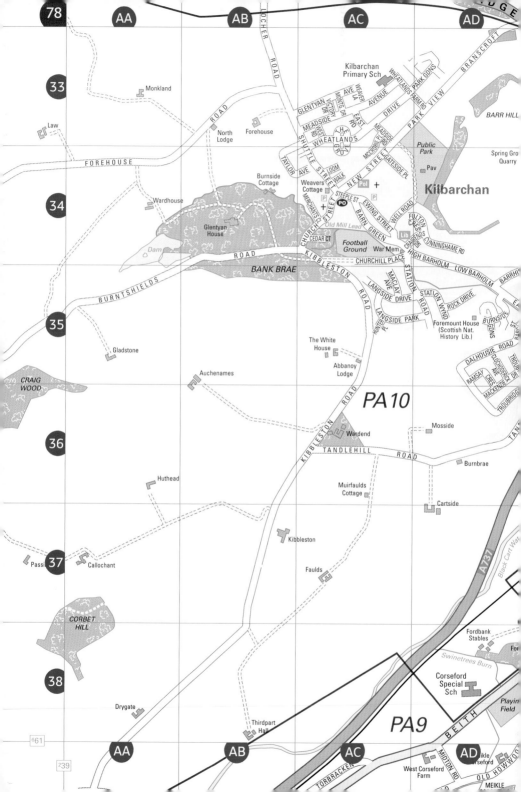

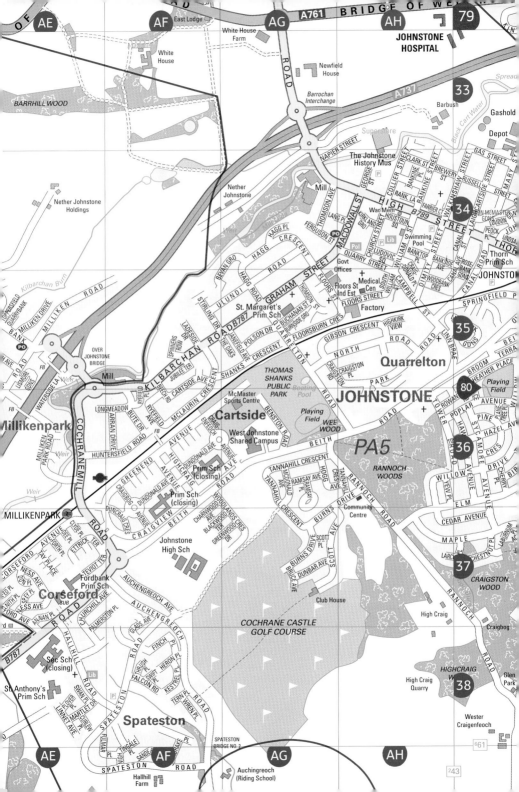

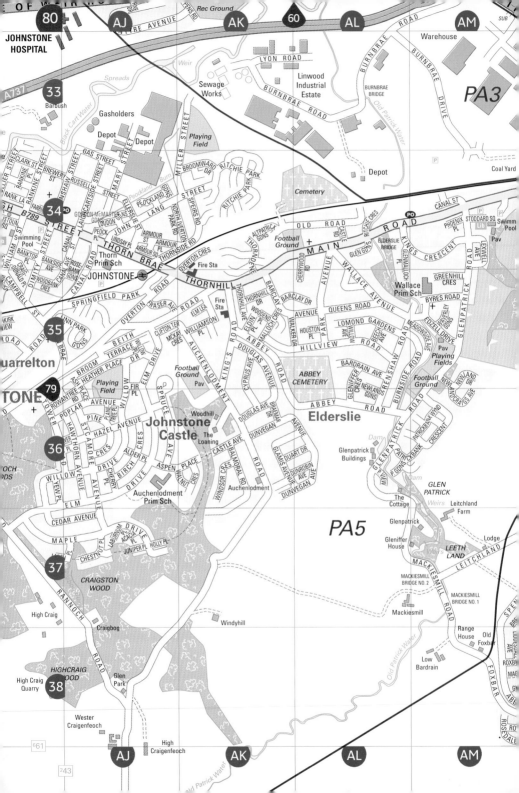

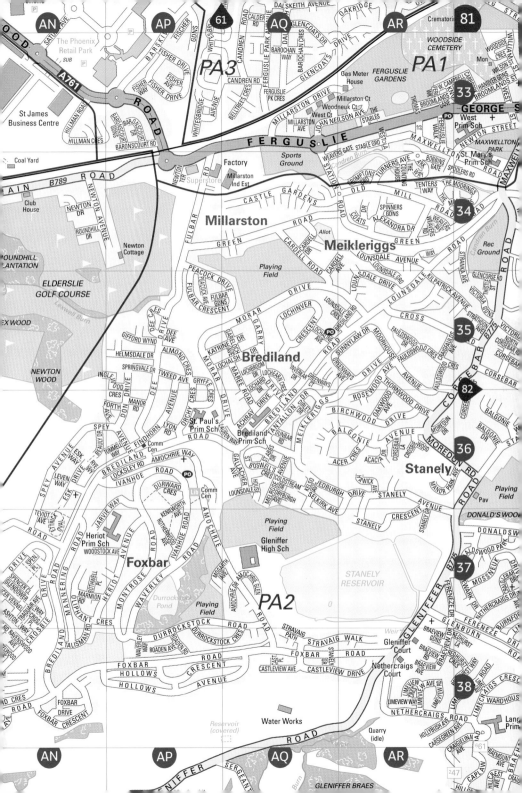

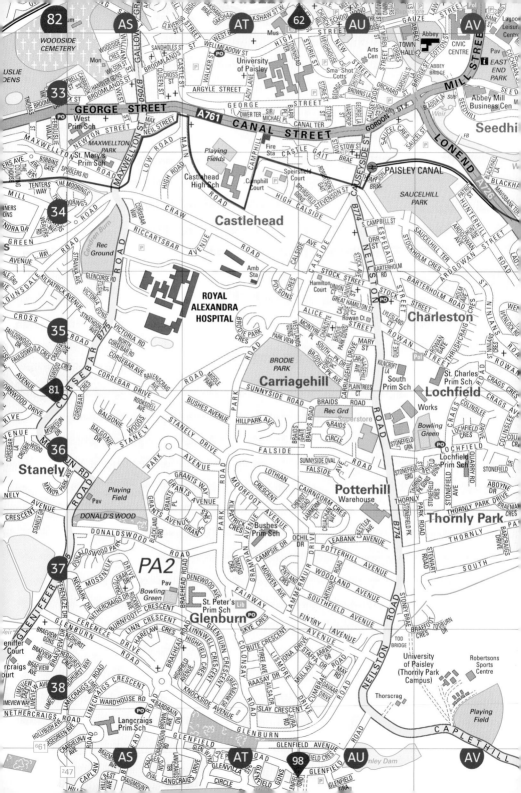

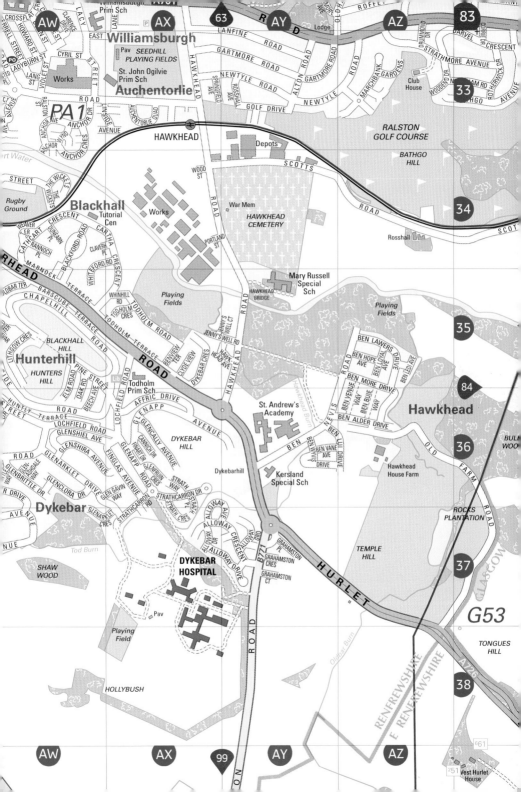

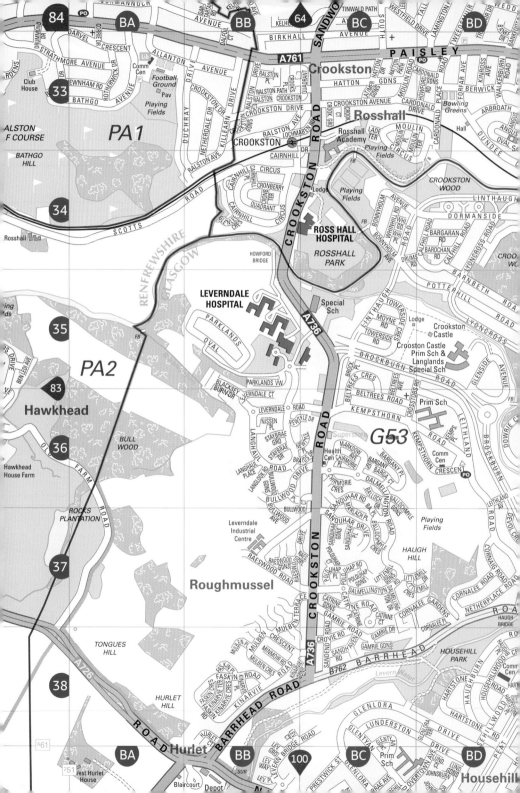

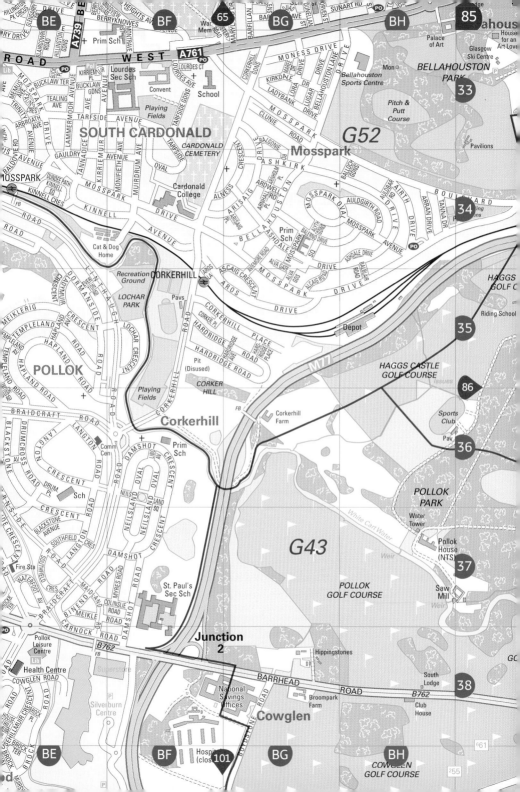

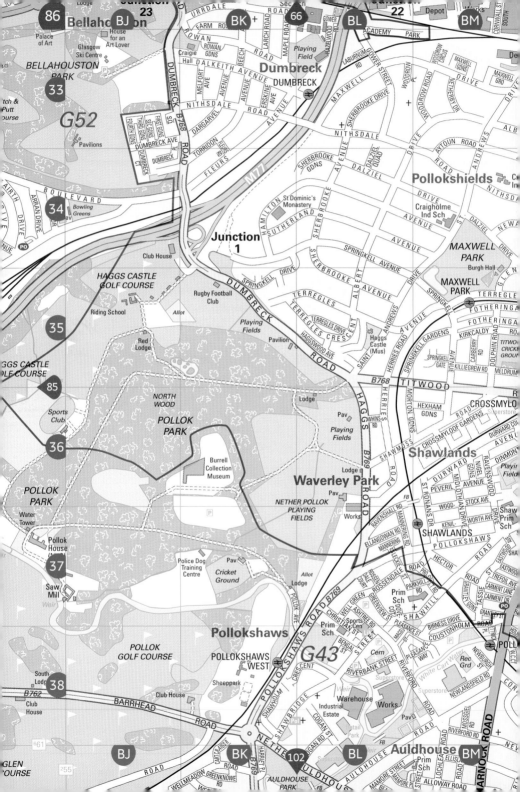

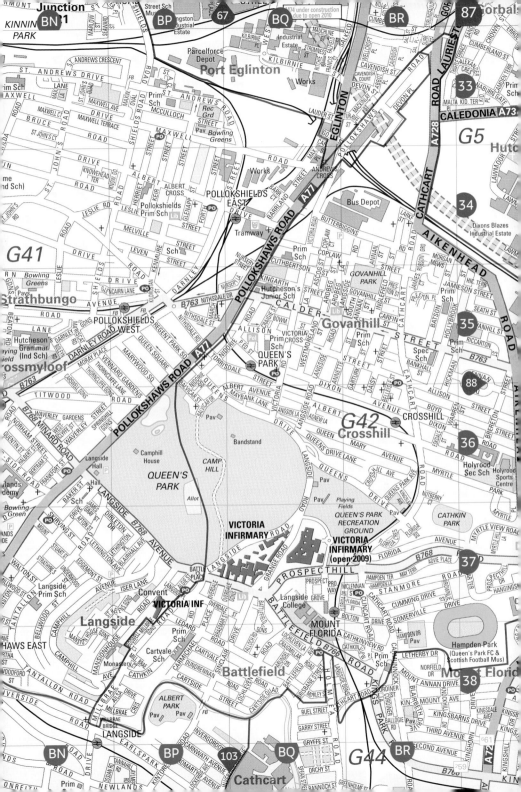

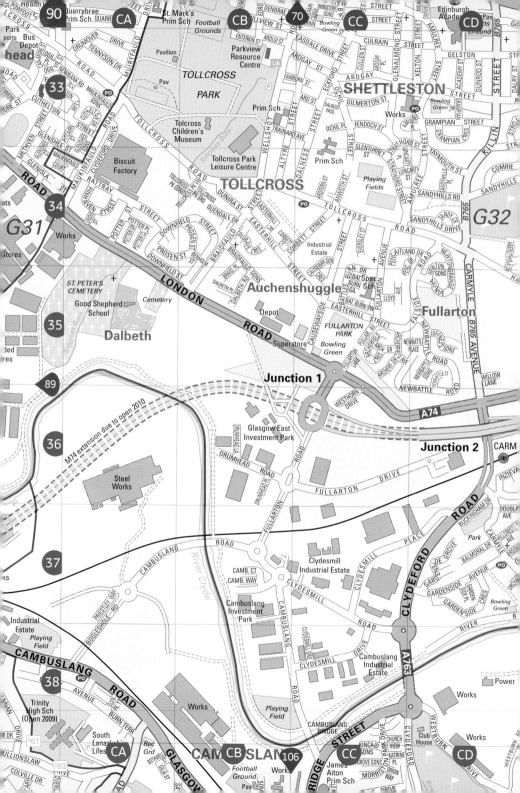

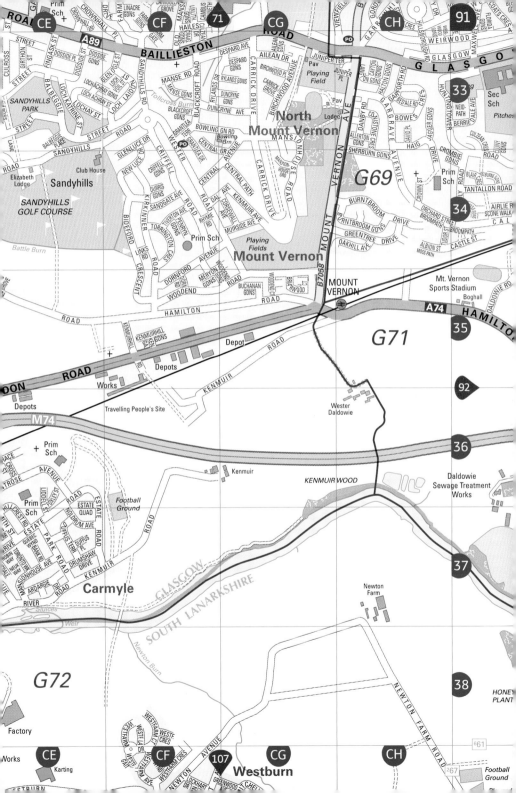

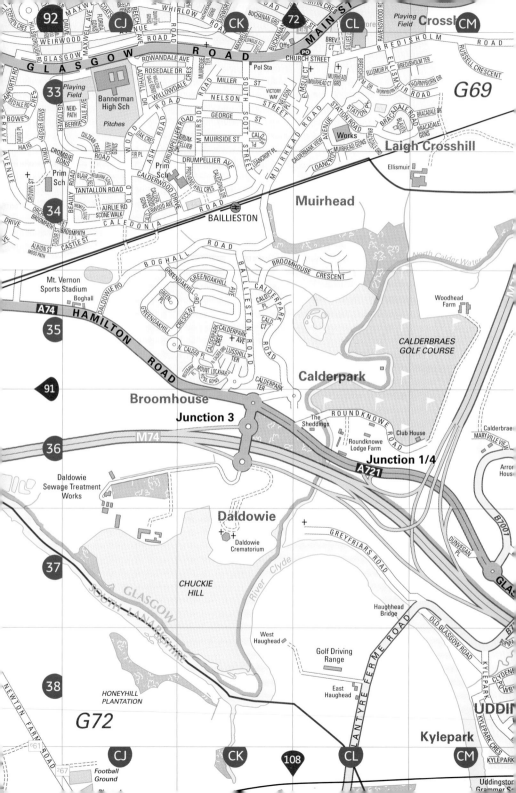

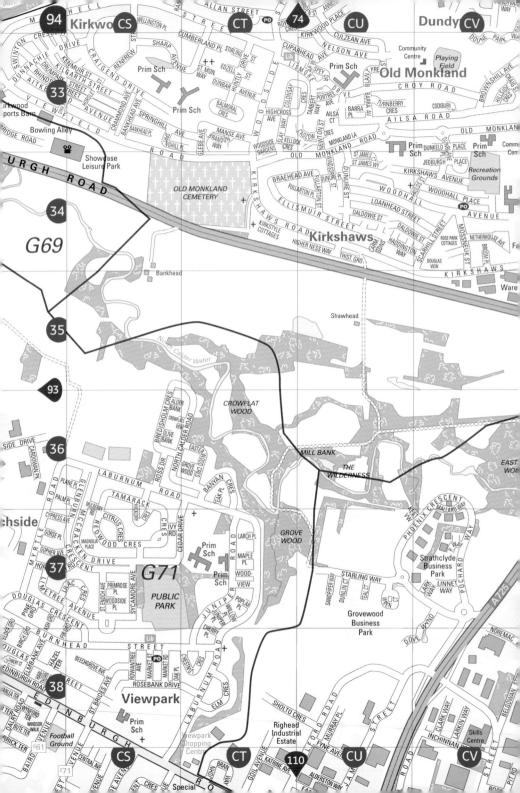

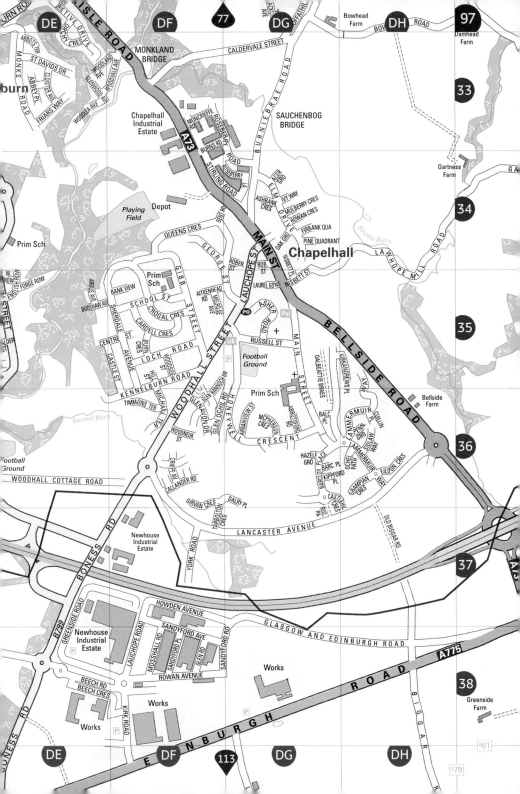

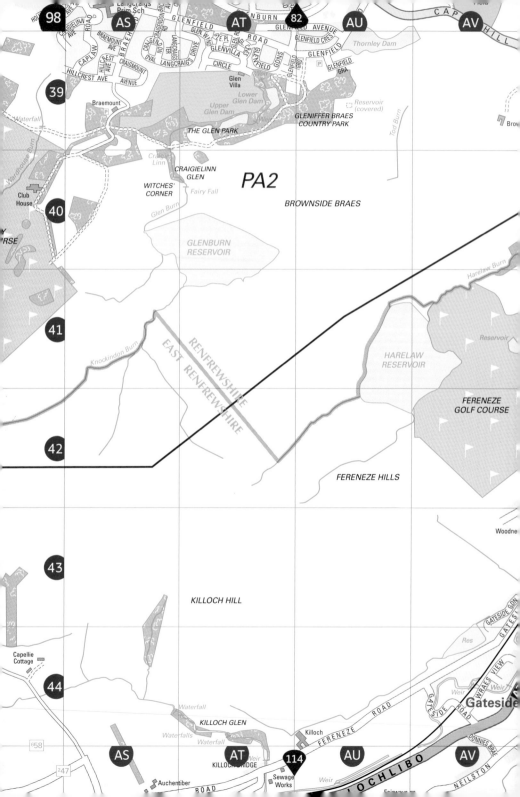

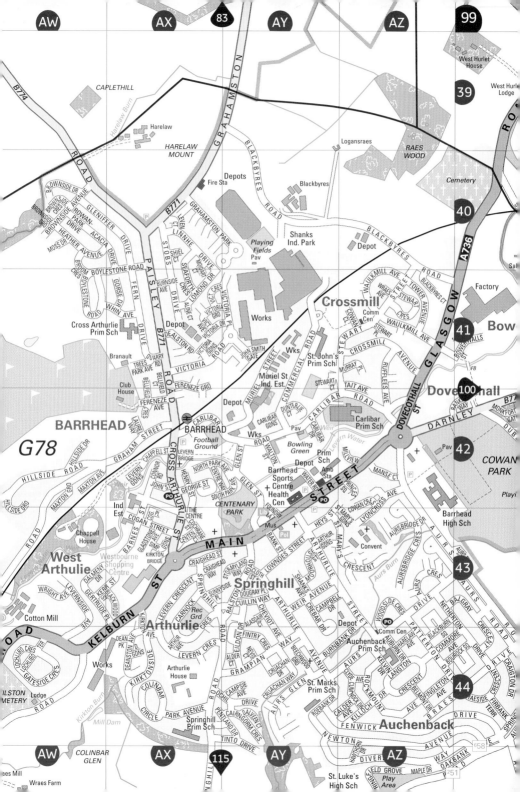

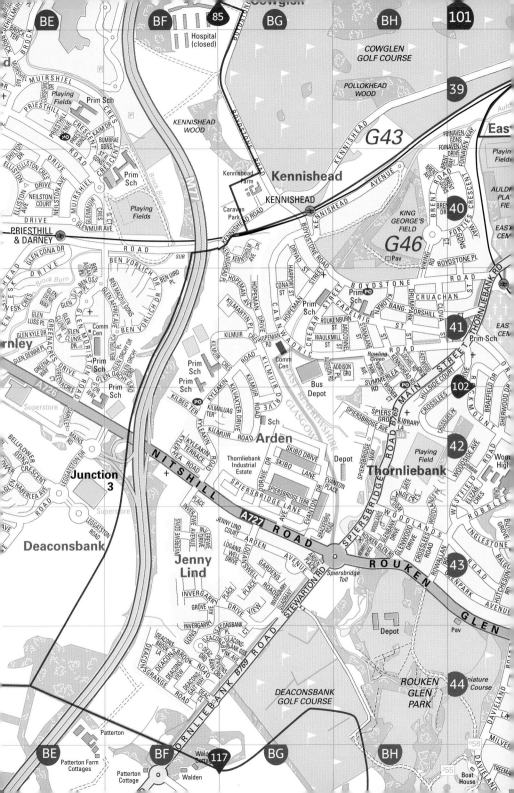

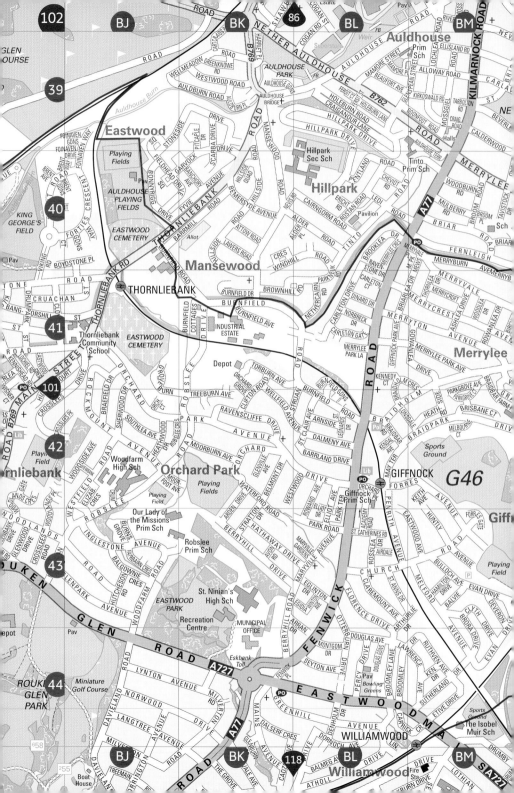

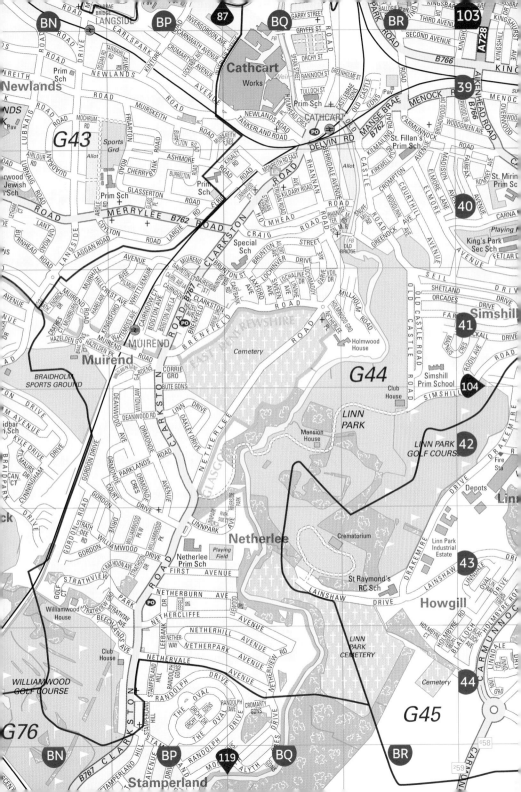

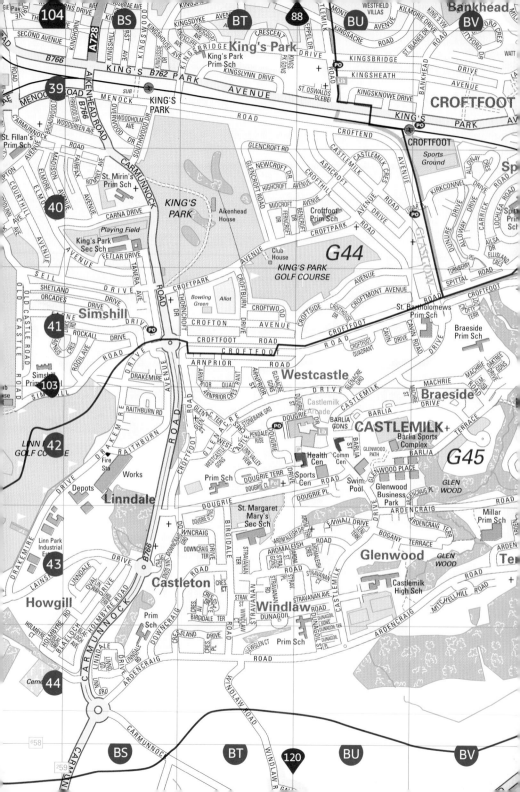

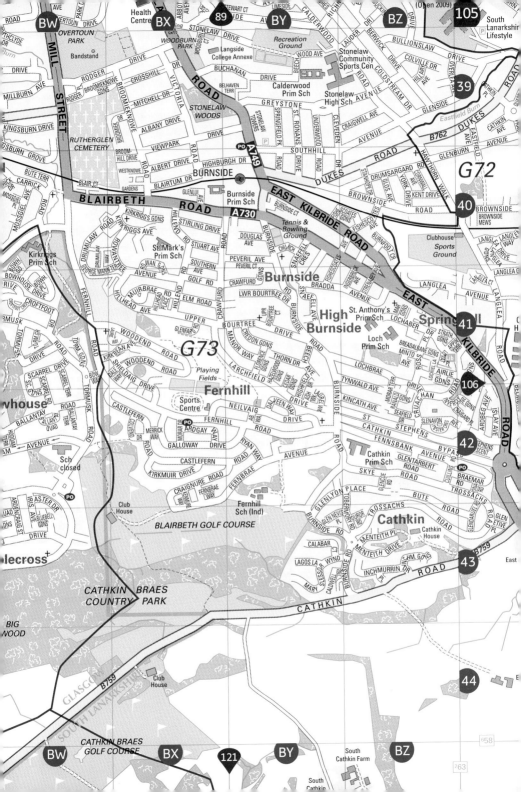

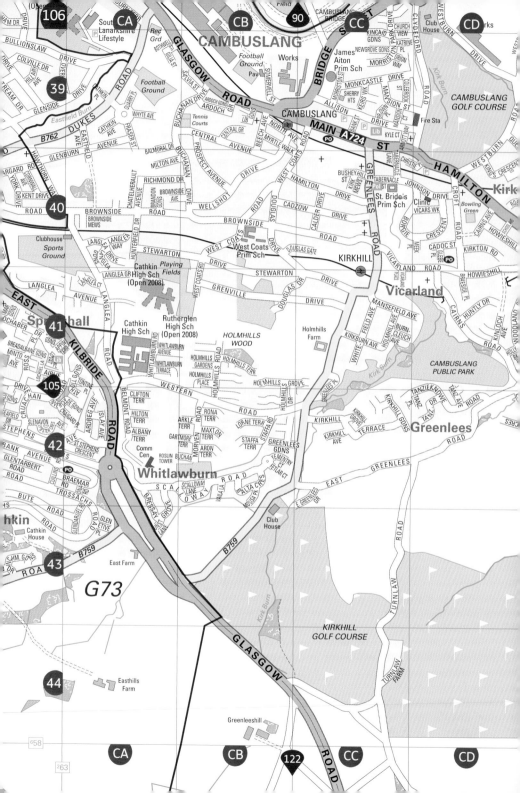

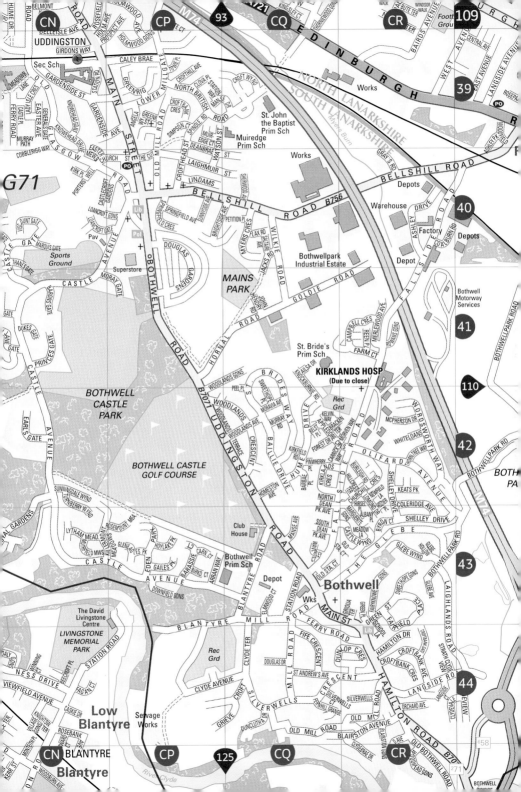

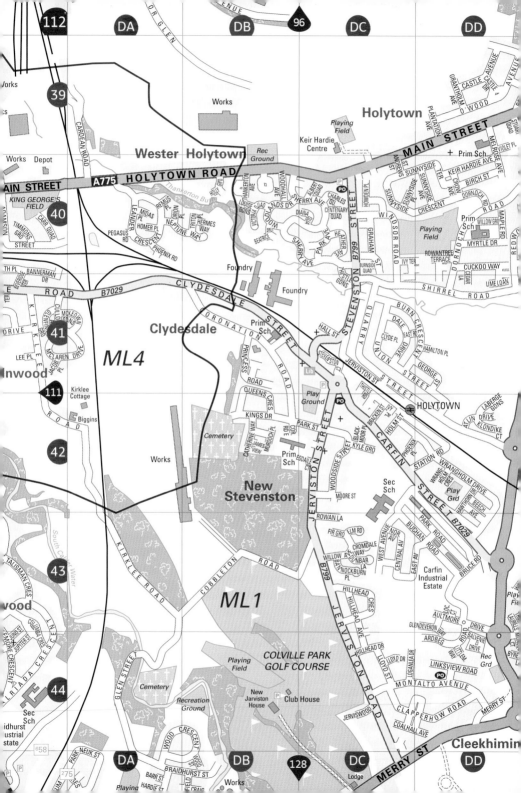

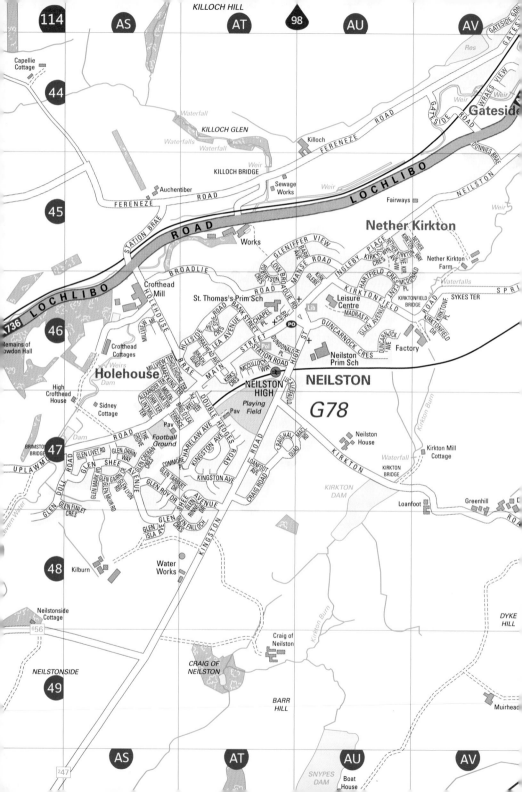

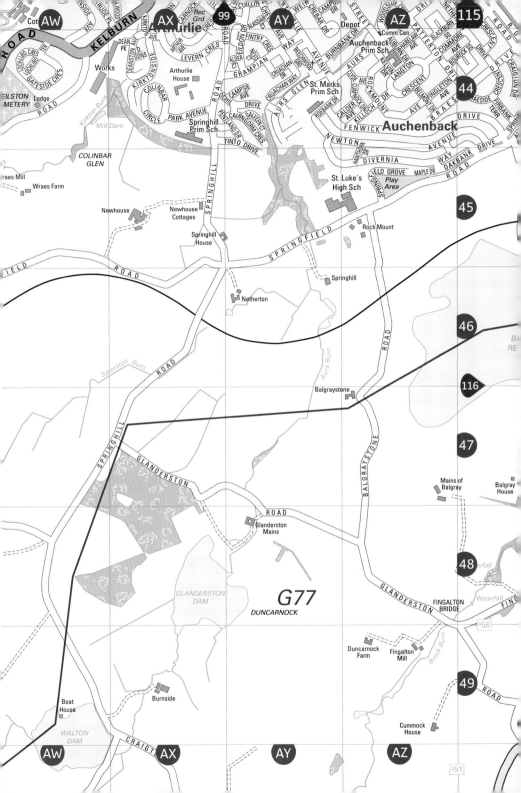

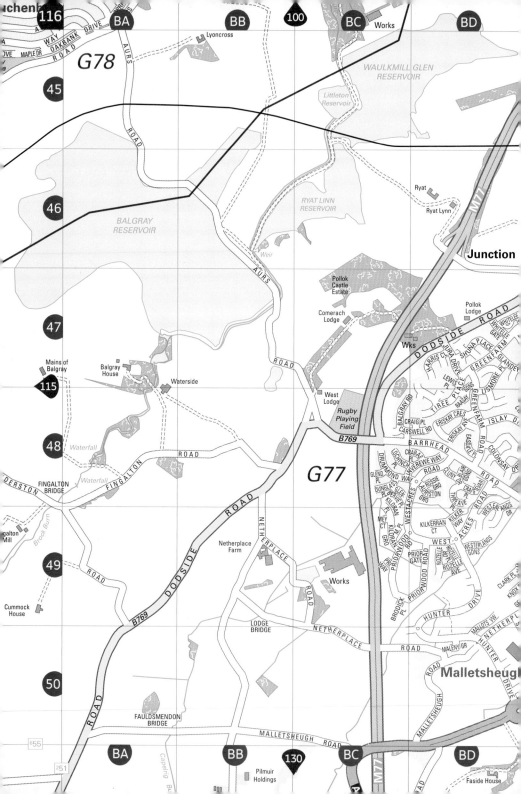

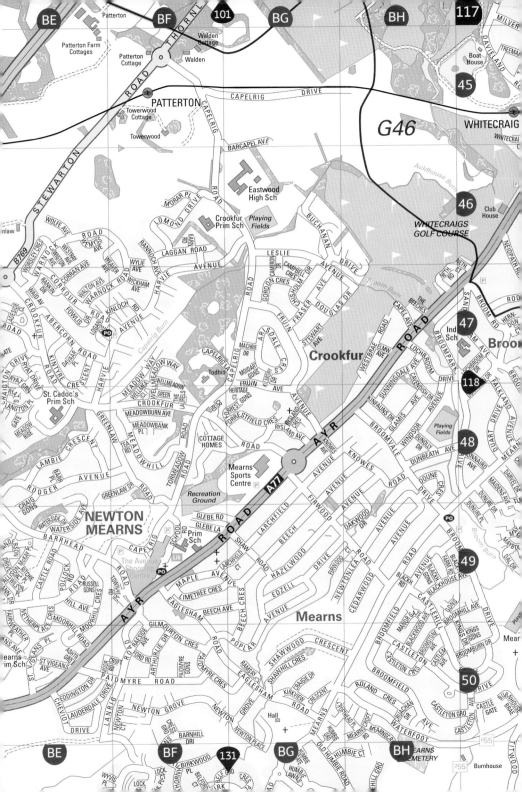

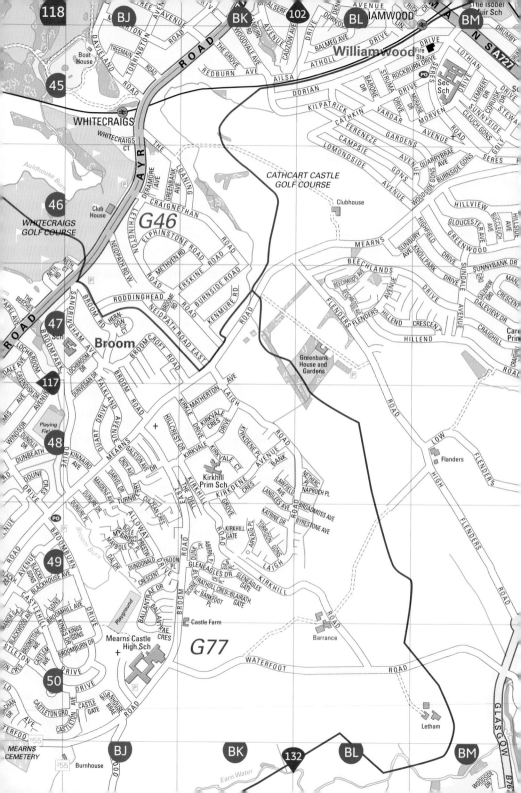

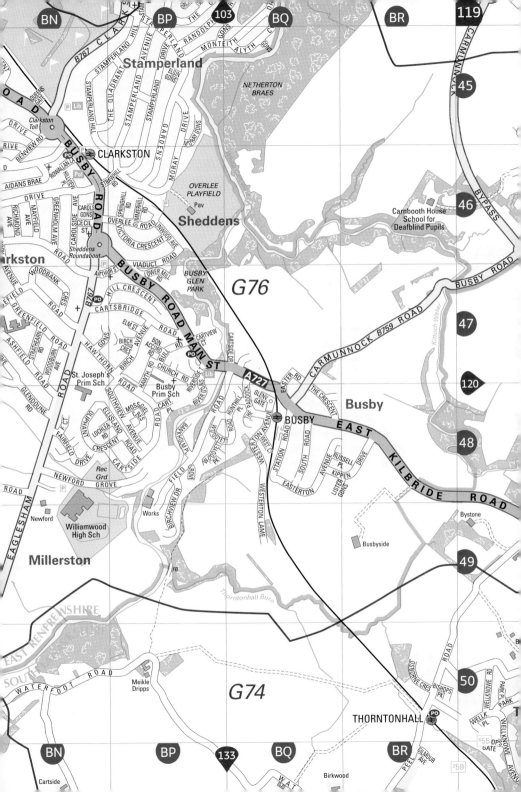

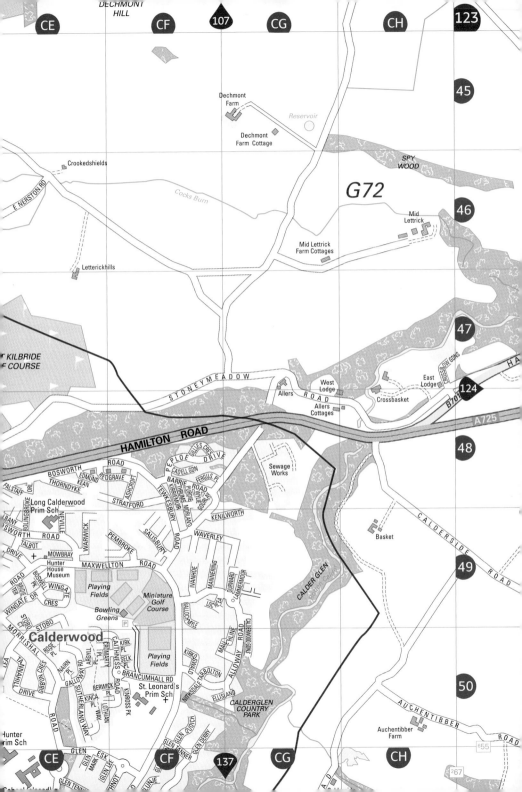

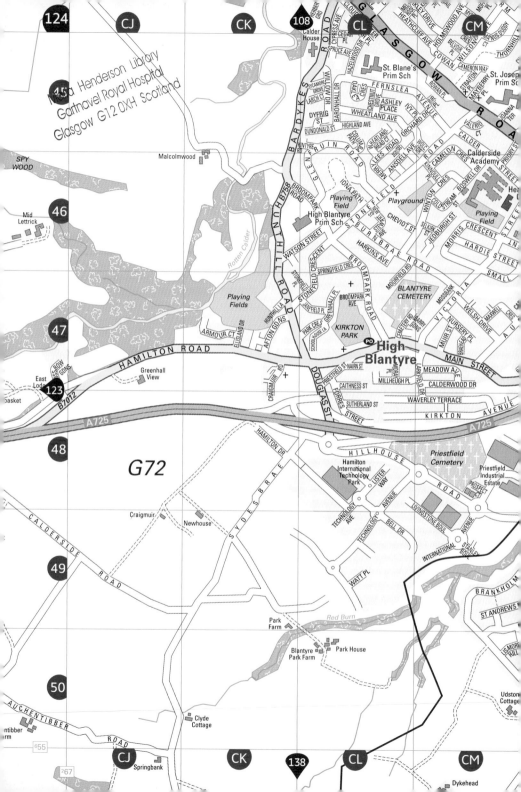

**124** CJ CK **108** CL CM

**45**

SPY WOOD

Malcolmwood

Mid Lettrick **46**

Rotten Calder

**47**

Playing Fields

East Lodge
**123**

Greenhall View

HAMILTON ROAD

Basket

B7012

A725

**48**

*G72*

Craigmuir

Newhouse

CALDERSIDE ROAD

**49**

SYDES BRAE

HAMILTON DR

Hamilton International Technology Park

HILLHOUSE ROAD

Priestfield Cemetery

Priestfield Industrial Estate

LISTER WAY
TECHNOLOGY AVE
BELL DR
WATT PL

TECHNOLOGY AVE

AVENUE

LIVINGSTONE BOUL

INTERNATIONAL AVENUE

BRANKHOLM

ST ANDREWS

LISMORE HILL

**50**

AUCHENTIBBER

Park Farm

Blantyre Park Farm

Park House

Red Burn

Clyde Cottage

ibber
rm

Springbank

ROAD

655

267

Udston Cottage

Dykehead

CJ CK **138** CL CM

BARDYKES ROAD
Calder House
Calder House Rd

GLASGOW ROAD

CJ
CEDAR PL
SYCAMORE PL
CYPRESS AVE
HAZELWOOD DR
SPRUCE AVE
LARCH CT

HOLMSWOOD AVE
HEATHCLIFFE AVE
COWAN PL
WILSON

RUNIAN PL
FERNSLEA AVENUE

St. Blane's Prim Sch
CAMERON WAY

St. Joseph's Prim Sch

ASHLEY PLACE
ORCHARD DRIVE
CALDER ROAD

Calderside Academy

WHEATLAND AVE
HIGHLAND AVE
LEES ROAD
ANSDELL AVE

CAMELON CRES
WINTON ST
COLDSTREAM
BOSWELL DR

Playground

Playing Field

HARDIE STREET
MORRIS CRESCENT

HARKINS AVE

BLANTYRE CEMETERY

MOSSBANK

VICTORIA ST

WELSH DRIVE
MAXWELL CRES

NURSERY PL

MUIR ST

MAIN STREET

High Blantyre

KIRKTON PARK

MEADOW AVE
CALDERWOOD DR

WAVERLEY TERRACE

KIRKTON AVENUE

A725

GLENFRUIN ROAD
UNTHANK ROAD B758
BROOMPARK ROAD

High Blantyre Prim Sch

WATSON STREET
STONEFIELD CRESCENT
SPRINGFIELD CRES
HUNTHILL RD
AFTON GDNS
ELLISLAND DR
ARMOUR CT
CRAIGMUIR RD

BROOMPARK ROAD
BURNBRAE ROAD
CHEVIOT ST

BROOMPARK AVE

PARK CRES
SCHOOL LA

DOUGLAS ST
FORREST STREET
PRIESTFIELD ST
NAIRN ST
CAITHNESS ST
MILLHEUGH PL
SUTHERLAND ST

PO High Blantyre

HILLHOUSE ROAD
PROSPECT

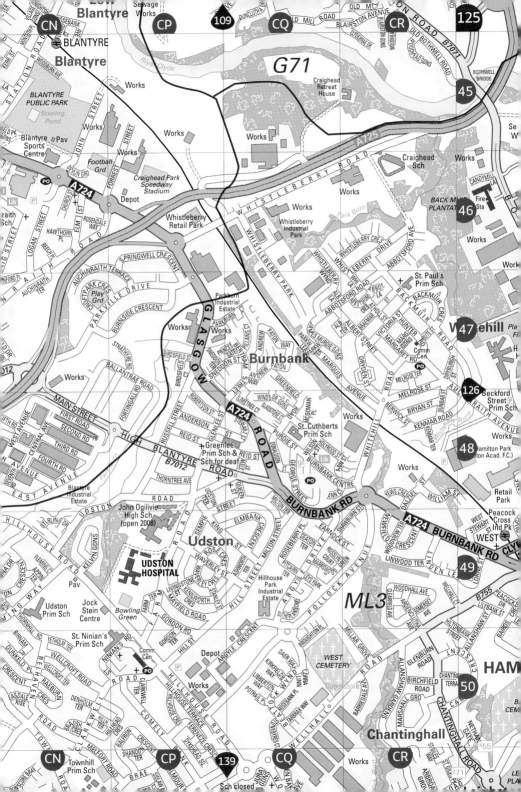

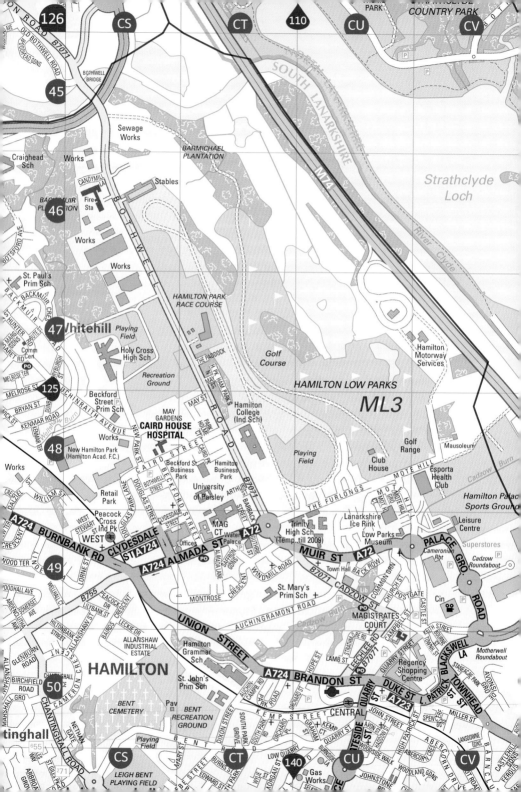

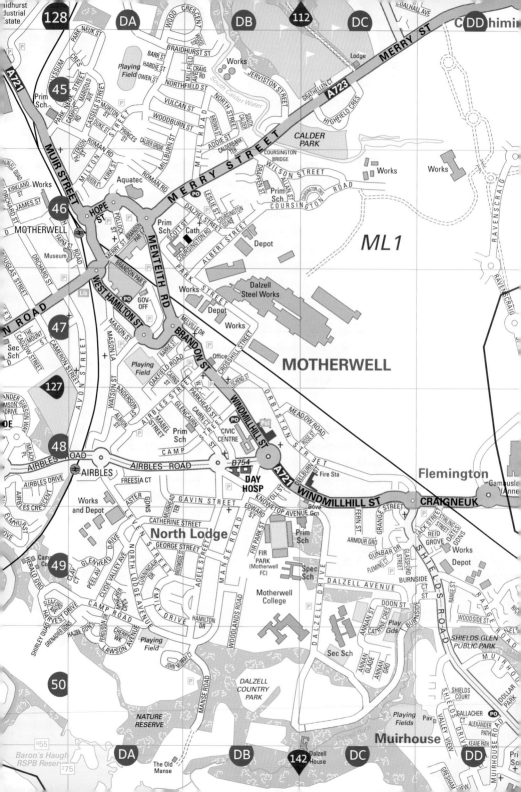

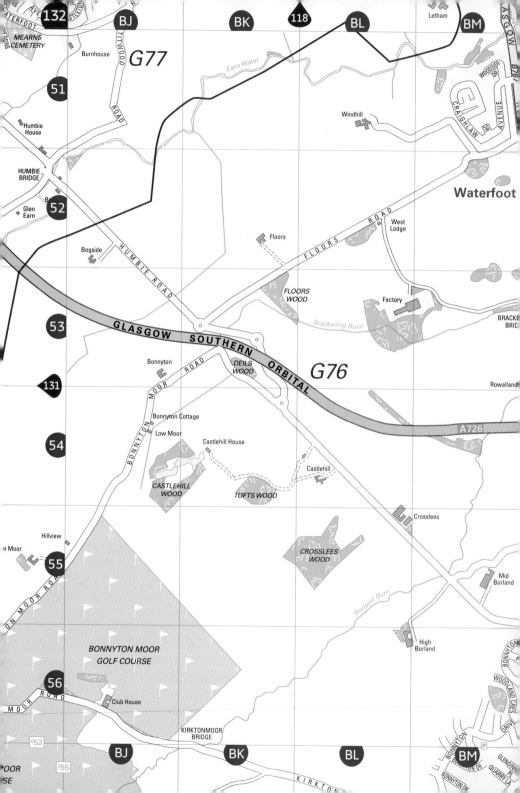

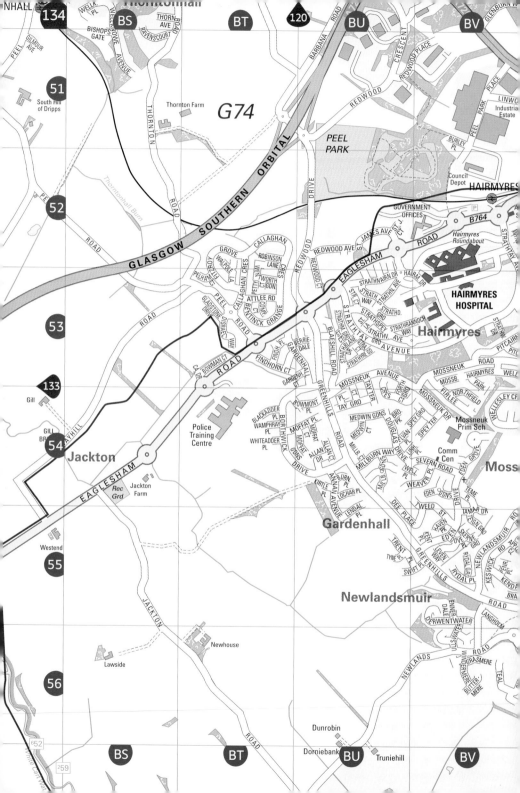

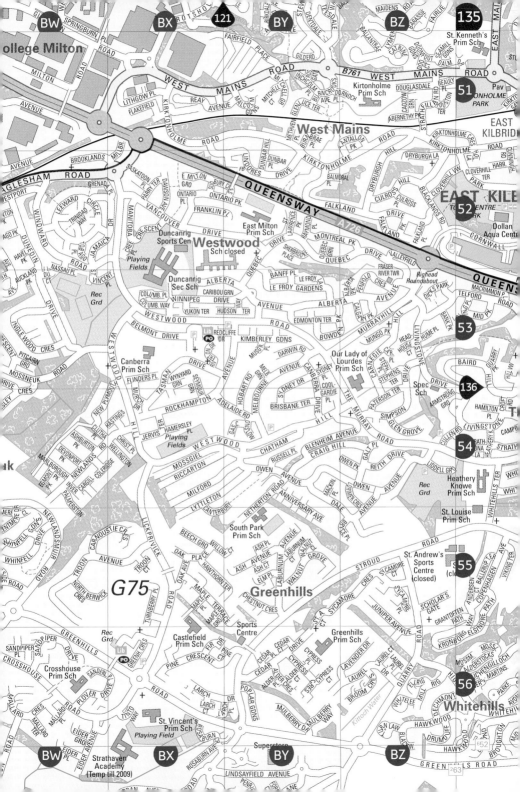

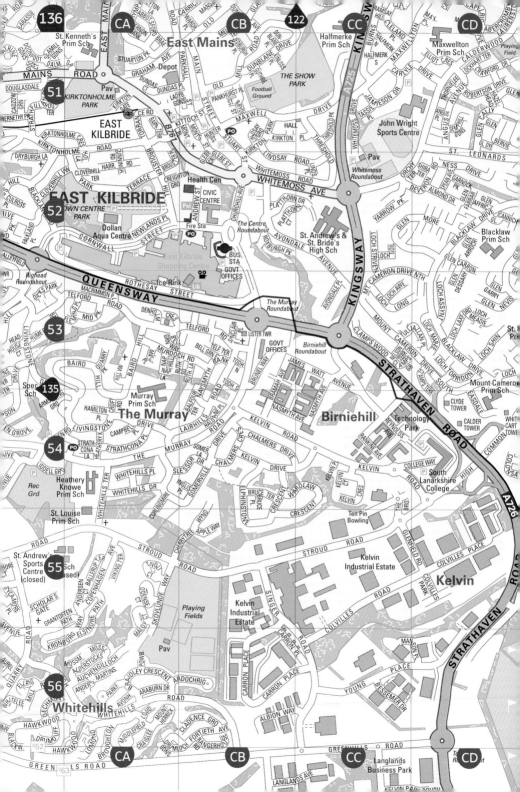

**WISHAW**

EXCELSIOR PARK

SHIELDS ROAD

BARONS ROAD

CLYDE TER

TON ROAD

CANYON ROAD

NETHERTON ROAD

B754

NETHERBANK RD

NETHERHALL ROAD

NETHERDALE ROAD

Works

MARSHALL STREET

ALEXANDER STREET

DUNIVAIG LA

STATION

Pav

Bowl Grn

Indoor Bowling

Football Grd

WISHAW

BELTANE REC GRD

51

Sports Grd

Football Grd

Prim Sch

ATTERCLIFFE AVE

COVENANT PL

DALE CT

INGLIS

NETHAN AVENUE

STENTON

THOMSON TER

PRIOR TER

McMILLAN RD

Netherton Industrial Estate

PO

Greyhound Race Track

HALLINAN GDNS

MILLBANK ROAD

CALEDONIAN

SUNART PL

TARBE

T. MICHAEL ROAD

Upper Muirhouse Farm

**Netherton**

KIRKHILL ROAD

KIRKNETHAN

CLYDESDALE AVE

SHAW CR

NETHERTON ROAD

SAFFRON WOOD

BEECH WOOD

MAPLE WOOD

ELM WOOD

ASHW

Prim Sch

CLARENDON PL

DR RD

DAKBA AVE

Factory

Factory

**Pather**

+

Playing Field

Kirkhill House

Kirkhill Orchard

**ML2**

CARBARNS RD

CARBARNS

STUART QUAD

CAM OR

MARG CR

KYLE QUAD

GRANGE AVENUE

CURRAN AVE

CARBARNS ISLAY QUAD

OLD MANSE ROAD

Works

Works

RANDALLS ORCHARD

CARBARNS EAST

WAY

WITCUTT

CARBA QUAD

CALA SONA

MONTGOMERY CRES

**Gowkthrapple**

B754

ALLERSHAW ROAD

ALLERSHAW PL

BIRKSHAW BRAE

STANHOPE PL

Playing Field

Sewage Works

CARBARNS ORCHARD

CAP PL

NVL

North Lodge

53

CASTLEH

STANHOPE

Lower Carbarns

CARBARNS WOOD

Hall Gill

Castlehill

54

Upper Carbarns

Cambusnethan House

NORTH LANARKSHIRE

SOUTH LANARKSHIRE

Prince's Lodge

**HIGHMAINSHEAD WOOD**

55

Lucindabank

Wemysshill Orchard

West Belmont

Wes Belmo

56

Sewage Works

**LANARK ROAD**

River Clyde

279

652

LANARK

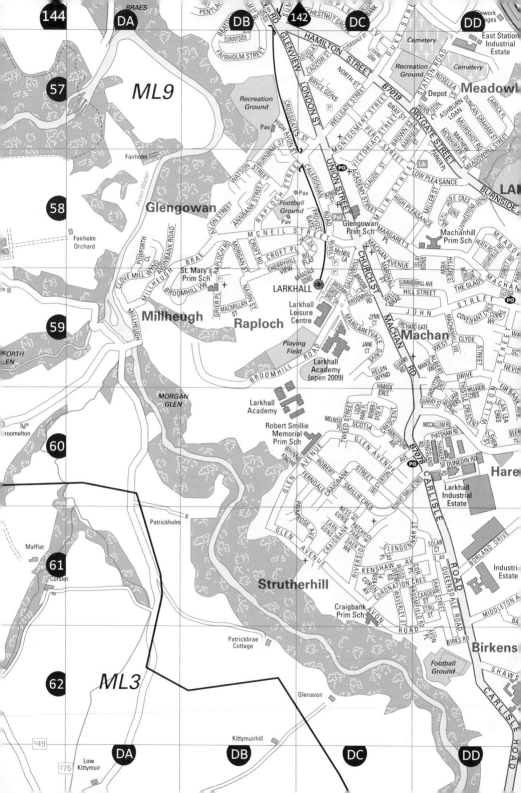

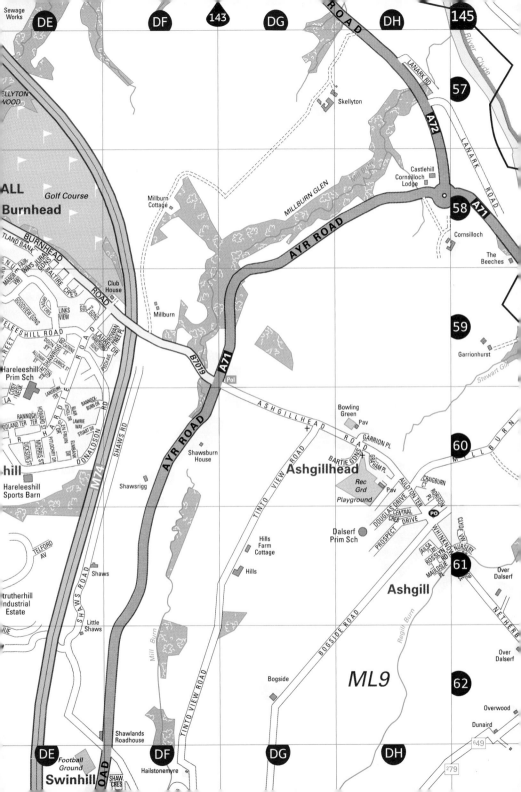

146

# Glasgow information

### Contents

| | |
|---|---|
| History & development | 147 |
| Local information | 148-151 |
| Places of worship | 151 |
| Architecture, museums & shops | 152-153 |
| Sport & recreation | 154-156 |
| Entertainment | 156-157 |
| Strathclyde further education | 157-158 |
| Hospitals | 158-160 |
| Visitor information | 160-162 |
| Weather | 162 |
| Parks & gardens | 163 |
| Transport | 164 |
| Glasgow International Airport | 165 |
| Rail & subway map | 166-167 |

The City of Glasgow began life as a makeshift hamlet of huts huddled round a 6thC church, built by St. Mungo on the banks of a little salmon river – the Clyde. It was called Gleschow, meaning 'beloved green place' in Celtic. The cathedral was founded in 1136; the university, the second oldest in Scotland, was established in the 15thC; and in 1454 the flourishing medieval city wedged between the cathedral and the river was made a Royal burgh. The city's commercial prosperity dates from the 17thC when the lucrative tobacco, sugar and cotton trade with the New World flourished. The River Clyde, Glasgow's gateway to the Americas, was dredged, deepened and widened in the 18thC to make it navigable to the city's heart

By the 19thC, Glasgow was the greatest shipbuilding centre in the world. From the 1820s onwards, it grew in leaps and bounds westwards along a steep ridge of land running parallel with the river. The hillside became encased in an undulating grid of streets and squares. Gradually the individualism, expressed in one-off set pieces characteristic of the 18thC and early 19thC, gave way to a remarkable coherent series of terraced squares and crescents of epic proportions – making Glasgow one of the finest of Victorian cities. But the price paid for such rapid industrialisation, the tremendous social problems manifest in the squalor of some of the worst of the 19thC slums, was high. Today the city is still the commercial and industrial capital of the West of Scotland. The most notorious of the slums have been cleared but the new buildings lack that sparkling clenchfisted Glaswegian character of the 19thC. Ironically, this character was partially destroyed when the slums were cleared for it wasn't the architecture that had failed, only the bureaucrats, who designated such areas as working class ghettos.

## Districts

Little remains of medieval Glasgow, which stood on the wedge of land squeezed between the Cathedral and the River Clyde. Its business centre was The Cross, a space formed by the junction of several streets with the tall, square Tolbooth Steeple, 1626, in the middle. Opposite is Trongate, an arch astride a footpath, complete with tower and steeple salvaged from 17thC St. Mary's Church which was destroyed by fire in 1793.

The centre of 21stC Glasgow is George Square, a tree-lined piazza planned in 1781 and pinned down by more than a dozen statues including an 80 foot high Doric column built in 1837 to carry a statue of Sir Walter Scott. Buildings of interest include the monumental neo-Baroque City Chambers 1883-88 which takes up the east side and the Merchants' House 1874, on the west. To the south of the square, in a huddle of narrow streets, is the old Merchant City. Of interest here is the elegant Trades Hall, 85 Glassford Street, built by Robert Adam in 1794.

An elegant Ionic portico stands on a rusticated ground storey flanked by domed towers. Hutcheson's Hall, 158 Ingram Street, is a handsome Italianate building designed by David Hamilton in 1805. Nearby is the Gallery of Modern Art (GOMA), previously Stirling's Library, but originally an 18thC private residence, it became the Royal Exchange in 1827 when the Corinthian portico was added. To the north west is Kelvingrove, Victorian Glasgow at its best. This area is built around a steep saddle of land, landscaped by Paxton in 1850 and lined along its edge with handsome terraces.

Last but not least are the banks of the River Clyde. From Clyde Walkway on the north bank in Glasgow Green you can see: the Suspension Bridge of 1871 with its pylons in the form of triumphal arches; 17thC Merchants' Steeple; the Gothic Revival St. Andrew's R.C. Cathedral of 1816; the church, built 1739, in nearby St. Andrew's Square is a typical copy of London's St. Martin-in-the-Fields.

## Useful information
**Area of City** 79 sq. miles (approx)

**Population (Glasgow City)** 629,501

**Electricity** 240 volts A.C.

### Emergency Services
Police, Fire and Ambulance. Dial 999 on any telephone.

## Licensing Hours
Public houses in the city centre are generally licensed Monday to Saturday from 11am to 12 midnight and on Sunday from 12.30pm to 6.30pm, with many open on Sunday evening up to 11pm or midnight.

Restaurants, hotels and public houses with catering facilicities; same as above but can be extended for drinks with meals.

## Tourist Information Centres (Visit Scotland)
11 George Square, G2 1DY
0141 204 4400

Paisley, 9a Gilmour Street,
Paisley, PA1 1DD
0141 889 0711

Glasgow International Airport (Abbotsinch),
Paisley, PA3 2ST
0141 848 4440

## Help & advice
### Chamber of Commerce
30 George Square, G2 1EQ
0141 204 2121

### Citizens Advice Bureaus
Citizens advice Direct 0844 848 9600
(telephone advice and information)

Airdrie
Resource Centre,
14 Anderson Street, Airdrie, ML6 0AA
01236 754 109

Barrhead
216 Main Street, Barrhead, G78 1SN
0141 881 2032

Bellshill
6 Hamilton Road, Bellshill, ML4 1AQ
01698 748 615

Coatbridge
Unit 10 Fountain Business Park,
Ellis Street, Coatbridge, ML5 3AA
01236 421 447/ 8

Cumbernauld
3rd Floor, 2 Annan House, Annan Way,
Cumbernauld, G67 1DP
01236 723 201

East Dunbartonshire
11 Alexandra Street,
Kirkintilloch, G66 1HB
0141 775 3220

East Kilbride
9 Olympia Way, East Kilbride, G74 1JT
01355 263698

Glasgow Bridgeton
35 Main Street, Bridgeton, G40 1QB
0141 554 0336

Glasgow Castlemilk
27 Dougrie Drive, Castlemilk,
G45 9AD
0141 634 0338

Glasgow Drumchapel
195c Drumry Road East,
Drumchapel, G15 8NS
0141 944 2612 / 0205

Glasgow Easterhouse
46 Shandwick Square, Easterhouse, G34 9DS
0141 771 2328

Glasgow Greater Pollok
6 Haughburn Road,
Greater Pollock, G53 6AE
0141 876 4401

Glasgow Maryhill
25 Avenuepark Street, G20 8TS
0141 946 6373

Glasgow Parkhead
1361-1363 Gallowgate, G31 4DN
0141 554 0004

Hamilton
Almada Tower, 67 Almada Street,
Hamilton, ML3 0HQ
01698 283 477

Motherwell & Wishaw
32 Civic Square, Motherwell, ML11 1TP
01698 251981/ 259389

Paisley
45 George Street, Paisley, PA1 2JY
0141 889 2121

Rutherglen & Cambuslang
Kyle Court, 17 Main Street,
Cambuslang, G72 7EX
0141 646 3191

**Consumer Advice Centre**
231 George Street, G1 1RX
0141 287 6681

**Customs and Excise**
21 India Street, G2 4PZ
0141 221 3828

**Enable**
(Organisation for people with learning
disabilities)
6th Floor
7 Buchanan Street, G1 3HL
0141 226 4541

**Border and Immigration Agency**
Festival Court,
200 Brand Street, Govan, G51 1DH
0870 606 7766

**Housing aid and advice**
Shelter, First Floor Suite 2,
Breckenridge House,
274 Sauchiehall Street, G2 3EH
0844 893 5560

**Lost property**
Trains – There is a railway switchboard
number that will put you through to Lost
Property (at any station). 0141 335 3276
Buses – Office of bus company
Elsewhere in City – Strathclyde Police.
Lost Property Department,
173 Pitt Street, G2 4JS
0141 532 2000

**Registrar of Births, Deaths and Marriages**
1 Martha Street, G1 1JJ
0141 287 7677

Marriages only:
22 Park Circus,  G3 6BE
0141 287 8350
Hours:  Monday  9.15am – 5.00pm
Tuesday to Friday 9.15am – 4.00pm
Births must be registered within twenty one
days, deaths within eight days and
marriages within three days.  The Registrar
should be consulted at least one month
before intended date of marriage.

**Children 1st**
61 Sussex Street,
G41 1DY
0141 418 5690

**RNID - Royal National Institute for the
Deaf**
Empire House,
131 West Nile Street, G1 2RX
0141 341 5330
0141 341 5347 (textphone)

**Shopmobility**
Book a battery powered wheelchair or
scooter, or request a guide at the following:
Braehead Shopping Centre 0141 885 4630
Buchanan Galleries 0141 332 8017
East Kilbride Shopping Centre 01355 571300
Hamilton, Newcross Centre 01698 459955
Motherwell, 89 Merry Street 01698 303199
Paisley Centre, The 0141 889 0441

## Helplines

**Childline**  0800 1111
**Missing Persons**  0500 700 700
**NSPCC** Child Protection  0808 800 5000
**ParentLine Scotland**  0808 800 2222

**Rape Crisis Scotland**  08088 01 03 02
**SSPCA**  0870 73 77722
**Samaritans**  08457 90 90 90
**Victim Support Scotland**  0845 603 9213

## Media

**British Broadcasting Corporation**
40 Pacific Quay, G51 1DA
0141 422 6000

**Scottish Television (stv)**
Pacific Quay, G51 1PQ
0141 300 3000

*Morning Daily Newspapers*
**Daily Record**
1 Anderston Quay, G3 8DA
0141 309 3000

**The Herald**
200 Renfield Street, G2 3PR
0141 302 7000

**Scottish Daily Express**
4th Floor, Citypoint 2,
25 Tyndrum Street, G4 0JY
0141 332 9600

**The Scotsman**
80 St. Vincent Street, G2 5UB
0141 236 6400

*Evening Daily Newspapers*
**Evening Times**
200 Renfield Street, G2 3PR
0141 302 7000

*Sunday Newspapers*
**Scotland on Sunday**
80 St. Vincent Street, G2 5UB
0141 236 6400

**Sunday Herald**
200 Renfield Street, G2 3PR
0141 302 7800

**Scottish Sunday Express**
4th Floor, Citypoint 2,
25 Tyndrum Street, G4 0JY
0141 332 9600

**Sunday Mail**
1 Anderston Quay, G3 8DA
0141 309 3000

**Sunday Post**
144 Port Dundas Road, G4 0HZ
0141 332 9933

## Post Offices

City Branch Office
87 Bothwell Street, G2 7AA
Monday – Friday 9.00am – 5.30pm
except Tuesday 9.30am – 5.30pm

Post Office Customer Services
0845 722 3344

St. Vincent Street Branch Office
47 St. Vincent Street, G2 5QX
Monday to Friday 9am – 5.45pm
except Tuesday 9.30am – 5.45pm
Saturdays 9am – 5.30pm

## Local Government

**East Dunbartonshire**
Tom Johnston House,
Civic Way, Kirkintilloch, G66 4TJ
0845 045 4510

**East Renfrewshire**
Eastwood Park,
Rouken Glen Road, Giffnock, G46 6UG
0141 577 3000

**Glasgow City**
City Chambers, George Square, G2 1DU
0141 287 2000

**North Lanarkshire**
Civic Centre, Motherwell, ML1 1TW
01698 302222

**Renfrewshire**
North Building, Cotton Street, Paisley,
PA1 1BU
0141 842 5000

**South Lanarkshire**
Almada Street,
Hamilton, ML3 0AA
01698 454444

**West Dunbartonshire**
Garshake Road
Dumbarton
G82 3PU
01389 737000

Maria Henderson Library
Gartnavel Royal Hospital
Glasgow G12 0XH Scotland

## Places of worship

Glasgow Cathedral is a perfect example of pre-Reformation Gothic architecture. Begun in 1238, it has a magnificent choir and handsome nave with shallow projecting transepts. On a windy hill to the east is the Necropolis, a cemetery with a spiky skyline of Victoriana consisting of pillars, temples and obelisks, dominated by an 1825 Doric column carrying the statue of John Knox. Other churches of interest: Landsdowne Church built by J. Honeyman in 1863; St. George's Tron Church by William Stark 1807; Caledonian Road Church, a temple and tower on top of a storey-high base, designed by Alexander Thomson in 1857; a similar design is to be found at the United Presbyterian Church, St. Vincent Street, 1858, but on a more impressive scale; Queen's Cross Church 1897 is an amalgam of Art Nouveau and Gothic Revival by the brilliant Charles Rennie Mackintosh.

### Churches within central Glasgow:
**Church of Scotland**
Glasgow Cathedral- St. Mungo,
Cathedral Square G4 0QZ

Renfield St. Stephen's Church,
260 Bath Street, G2 4JP

St. Columba Church (Gaelic),
300 St. Vincent Street, G2 5RU

St. George's Tron Church,
165 Buchanan Street, G1 2JX

**Baptist**
Adelaide Place Church,
209 Bath Street, G2 4HZ

**Episcopal Church in Scotland**
Cathedral Church of St. Mary,
300 Great Western Road, G4 9JB

**First Church of Christ, Scientist**
87 Berkeley Street, G3 7DX

**Free Church of Scotland**
265 St. Vincent Street, G2 7LA

**German Speaking Congregation**
Emanuel House,
7 Hughenden Terrace, G12 9XR

**Greek Orthodox**
St. Luke's Cathedral,
27 Dundonald Road, G12 9LL

**Islamic Centre**
Glasgow Central Mosque,
Mosque Avenue, G5 9TA

**Jewish Orthodox Synagogue**
Garnethill Hebrew Congregation,
129 Hill Street, G3 6UB

**Methodist**
Woodlands Church,
229 Woodlands Road, G3 6LW

**Quaker**
38 Elmbank Crescent, G2 4PS

**Roman Catholic**
St. Andrew's Cathedral,
186 Clyde Street, G1 4JY

St. Aloysius' Church,
25 Rose Street, G3 6RE

**Unitarian Church**
72 Berkeley Street, G3 7DS

**United Free**
Candlish Wynd, 62 Daisy Street, G42 8HF

## Interesting Buildings

Victorian Glasgow was extremely eclectic architecturally. Good examples of the Greek Revival style are Royal College of Physicians 1845, by W.H. Playfair and the Custom House 1840, by G.L. Taylor. The Queen's Room 1857, by Charles Wilson, is a handsome temple used now as a Christian Science church. The Gothic style is seen at its most exotic in the Stock Exchange 1877, by J. Burnet.

The new Victorian materials and techniques with glass, wrought and cast iron were also ably demonstrated in the buildings of the time. Typical are: Gardener's Stores 1856, by J. Baird; the Buck's Head, Argyle Street, an amalgam of glass and cast iron; and the Egyptian Halls of 1873, in Union Street, which has a masonry framework. Both are by Alexander Thomson. The Templeton Carpet Factory 1889, Glasgow Green, by William Leiper, is a Venetian Gothic building complete with battlemented parapet.

The great genius of Scottish architecture is Charles Rennie Mackintosh whose major buildings are in Glasgow. In the Scotland

*University of Glasgow*

Street School 1904–6, he punctuated a 3-storey central block with flanking staircase towers in projecting glazed bays. His most famous building – Glasgow School of Art 1897–9 – is a magnificent Art Nouveau building of taut stone and glass; the handsome library, with its gabled facade, was added later in 1907–9.

## Galleries & Museums

Scotland's largest tourist attraction, The Burrell Collection, is situated in Pollok Country Park, Haggs Road and has more than 8,000 objects, housed in an award winning gallery. The Museum and Art Gallery, Kelvingrove Park, Argyle Street, a palatial sandstone building with glazed central court, has one of the best municipal collections in Britain; superb Flemish, Dutch and French paintings, drawings, prints, also ceramics, silver, costumes and armour, as well as a natural history section.

*The Clyde Auditorium at the SECC*

The Gallery of Modern Art, Royal Exchange Square, houses the city's contemporary art collection in an elegant neo-classical building. Provand's Lordship c1471, in Castle Street, is Glasgow's oldest house and is now a museum of furniture and household items dating from the 16th – 18thC. Pollok House, Pollok Country Park, a handsome house designed by William Adam in 1752, has paintings by William Blake and a notable collection of Spanish paintings, including works by El Greco.

*Kelvingrove Art Gallery and Museum*

The Museum of Transport, housed in Kelvin Hall, Bunhouse Road, has a magnificent collection of trams, cars, model ships, bicycles, horse-drawn carriages and steam locomotives. The People's Palace, Glasgow Green built 1898 with a huge glazed Winter Garden, has a lively illustrated history of the city. But the oldest museum in Glasgow is the Hunterian Museum, University of Glasgow, University Avenue, opened in 1807, it has a fascinating collection of manuscripts, early painted books, as well as some fine archaeological and geological exhibits.

*Princes Square Shopping Centre*

## Streets & Shopping

The Oxford Street of Glasgow is Sauchiehall (meaning 'willow meadow') Street. This together with Buchanan Street, The Buchanan Galleries Shopping Centre, Argyle Street, Princes Square and St. Enoch Centre form the main shopping area. Here you will find the department stores, boutiques and general shops. All three streets are largely pedestrianised, but the most exciting is undoubtedly Buchanan Street. Of particular interest is the spatially elegant Argyll Arcade 1828, the Venetian Gothic-style Stock Exchange 1877, the picturesque Dutch gabled Buchanan Street Bank building 1896 and the Glasgow Royal Concert Hall (opened 1990). In Glasgow Green is The Barras, the city's famous street market, formed by the junction of London Road and Kent Street.

## East Dunbartonshire
**The Allander Sports Complex**
Milngavie Road, Bearsden, G61 3DF
0141 578 8222

**Kirkintilloch Leisure Centre**
Woodhead Park, Kirkintilloch, G66 3HD
0141 578 8222

**Leisuredrome**
147 Balmuildy Road, Bishopbriggs, G64 3HD
0141 772 6391

## East Renfrewshire
**Barrhead Sports Centre**
Main Street, Barrhead, G78 1SW
0141 580 1174

**Eastwood Recreational Centre**
Eastwood Park, Rouken Glen Road,
Giffnock, G46 6UG
0141 577 4956

**Neilston Leisure Centre**
Main Street, Neilston, G78 3NN
0141 577 4811

## Glasgow City
**Alexandra Sports Hall**
Alexandra Parade, G31
0141 556 1695

**Auchinlea Recreation Centre**
Auchinlea Road, G34 9PQ
0141 771 7600

**Barlia Sports Complex**
Barlia Drive, G45 9UD
0141 634 5474

**Bellahouston Leisure Centre**
Bellahouston Drive, G52 1HH
0141 427 9090

**Castlemilk Pool**
137 Castlemilk Drive, G45 9UG
0141 634 8254

**Castlemilk Sports Centre**
10 Dougrie Road, G45 9NH
0141 634 8187

**Crownpoint Road Sports Complex**
183 Crownpoint Road, G40 2AL
0141 554 8274

**Donald Dewar Leisure Centre**
220 Garscadden Road, G15 8SX
0141 944 9710

**Drumchapel Pool**
199 Drumry Road East, G15 8NS
0141 944 5812

**Easterhouse Pool**
5 Bogbain Road, G34 9DU
0141 771 7978

**Easterhouse Sports Centre**
Auchinlea Road, G34 9PQ
0141 771 1963

**Glasgow Green Football Centre**
Kings Drive, G40 1HB
0141 554 7547

**Gorbals Leisure Centre**
275 Ballater Street, G5 0YP
0141 429 5556

**Holyrood Sports Centre**
600 Aikenhead Road, G42 0PD
0141 423 9431

**Kelvin Hall International Sports Arena**
1445 Argyle Street, G3 8AW
0141 357 2525

**North Woodside Leisure Centre**
Braid Square, G4 9YQ
0141 332 8102

**Palace of Art** (Bellahouston Park)
Paisley Road West, G52 1EQ
0141 427 5180

**Pollok Leisure Centre**
27 Cowglen Road, G53 6EW
0141 881 3313

**Scotstoun Leisure Centre**
72 Danes Drive, G14 9HD
0141 959 4000

**Springburn Leisure Centre**
10 Kay Street, G21 1JY
0141 557 5878

**Springburn Sports Park**
Broomfield Road, G21 1JY
0141 557 1692

**Tollcross Park Leisure Centre**
Wellshot Road, G32 7QR
0141 763 2345

**Whitehill Pool**
240 Onslow Drive, G31 2QU
0141 551 9969

**Yoker Sports Centre**
2 Speirshall Terrace, G14 0LN
0141 959 8386

## North Lanarkshire
**Airdrie Leisure Centre**
Motherwell Street, Airdrie, ML6 7HU
01236 762871

**Aquatec,**
Menteith Road, Motherwell, ML1 1AZ
01698 332828

**Birkenshaw Sports Barn**
Fourth Street, Tannochside, G71 6AU
01698 815872

**Broadwood Stadium,**
1 Ardgoil Drive, Cumbernauld, G68 9NE
01236 451351

**Coatbridge Outdoor Sports Centre**
Langloan Street, Coatbridge, ML5 1ER
01236 812472

**Iain Nicolson Recreation Centre**
Chryston Road, Chryston, G69 9NA
0141 779 2835

**John Smith Pool**
Stirling Street, Airdrie, ML6 0AH
01236 750130

**Keir Hardie Centre**
Main Street, Holytown, ML1 4TP
01698 833803

**Kilsyth Swimming Pool**
1 Airdrie Street, Kilsyth, G65 9JE
01236 828166

**Kirkwood Sports Barn**
Viewfield Road,
Coatbridge, M5 5GB
01236 420122

**Sir Matt Busby Sports Complex**
50 Main Street, Bellshill, ML4 3DP
01698 747466

**Time Capsule**
100 Buchanan Street, Coatbridge, ML5 1DL
01236 449572

**Tryst Sports Centre**
Tryst Walk, Cumbernauld, G67 1EW
01236 728138

## Renfrewshire
**Elderslie Leisure Centre**
Stoddard Square, Elderslie, PA 9AS
01505 328133

**Erskine Community Sports Centre
and Swimming Pool**
Bridgewater Shopping Centre,
Erskine, PA8 7AA
0141 812 0044 (swimming pool)
0141 812 7722 (sports centre)

**Johnstone Swimming Pool**
Ludovic Square, Johnstone, PA5 8EE
01505 322 954

**Lagoon Leisure Centre**
11 Christie Street, Paisley, PA1 1NB
0141 889 4000

**Linwood Sports Centre**
Brediland Road, Linwood, PA3 3RA
01505 329461

**McMaster Sports Centre**
Thomas Shanks Park, Greenend Avenue,
Johnstone, PA5 0LE
01505 335 171

**Renfrew Leisure Centre**
Paisley Road, Renfrew, PA4 8LJ
0141 886 6916

**Renfrew Victory Baths**
Inchinnan Road, Renfrew, PA4 8ND
0141 886 2088

## South Lanarkshire
**Blantyre Sports Centre**
Glasgow Road, Blantyre, G72 0JS
01698 727800

**Burnhill Sports Centre**
Toryglen Road, Rutherglen, G73 1JH
0141 643 0327

**Dollan Aqua Centre**
Brouster Hill, East Kilbride, G74 1AF
01355 260000

**Duncanrig Sports Centre**
Alberta Avenue, East Kilbride, G75 8HY
01355 248922

**Eddlewood Sports Barn**
Devonhill Avenue, Hamilton, ML3 7RP
01648 422991

**Hamilton Palace Sports Ground**
Motehill, Hamilton, ML3 6BY
01698 424101

**Hamilton Water Palace**
35 Almada Street, Hamilton, ML3 0HQ
01698 459950

**Hareleeshill Sports Barn**
Donaldson Road,
Larkhall, ML9 2SS
01698 887917

**Jock Stein Centre**
Hillhouse Road, Hamilton, ML3 9TB
01698 828488

**John Wright Sports Centre**
Calderwood Road, East Kilbride, G74 3EU
01355 237731

**Larkhall Leisure Centre**
Broomhill Road, Larkhall, ML9 1QP
01698 881742

**St Andrew's Sports Centre**
Scholar's Gate, Whitehills,
East Kilbride, G75 9JL
01355 230020

**South Lanarkshire Lifestyle**
Glenside Drive, Rutherglen, G73 3LH
0141 642 9500

**Stewartfield Community Sports Centre**
3 MacNeish Way, Stewartfield,
East Kilbride, G74 4TT
01355 227 888

**Stonelaw Community Sports Centre**
Calderwood Road, Rutherglen, G73 3SE
0141 647 6779

## West Dunbartonshire
**Antonine Sports Centre**
Roman Road, Duntocher,
Clydebank, G81 6BT
01389 878972

**The Play Drome**
2 Abbotsford Road, Clydebank, G81 1PA
0141 951 4321

## Entertainment

As Scotland's commercial and industrial capital, Glasgow offers a good choice of leisure activities. The city now has many theatres where productions include serious drama, pantomime, pop and musicals. Glasgow is home to Scottish Opera, Scotland's national opera company and the largest performing arts company in Scotland. They have regular performances at the Theatre Royal, Hope Street which has been completely restored to its full Victorian splendour. Also performing at the Theatre Royal, across Scotland and abroad is Scottish Ballet, Scotland's national dance company.

The Royal Scottish National Orchestra (RSNO) gives classical music concerts at the Glasgow Royal Concert Hall between October and April. Cinemas are still thriving in Glasgow, as are the many public houses, some of which provide meals and live entertainment. In the city centre and Byres Road, West End, there is a fair number of restaurants where traditional home cooking, as well as international cuisines, can be sampled. More night life can be found at the city's nightclubs, discos and dance halls.

### Cinemas
**Cineworld** 7 Renfrew Street,
G2 3AB. 0871 200 2000

**Cineworld** The Forge Shopping Centre,
1221 Gallowgate,
G31 4EB. 0871 200 2000

**Empire** 23 Britannia Way, Clydebank,
G81 2RZ. 0871 471 471 4

**Glasgow Film Theatre** 12 Rose Street,
G3 6RB. 0141 332 8128

**Grosvenor** Ashton Lane, Hillhead,
G12 8SJ. 0141 339 8444

**IMAX Glasgow Science Centre**
50 Pacific Quay, G51 1EA
0871 540 1000

**Odeon** Olympia Shopping Centre,
Rothesay Street, East Kilbride,
G74 1PG.  0871 2244 007

**Odeon** Springfield Quay, Paisley Road,
G5 8NP.  0871 2244 007

**Odeon** Xscape Braehead, Kings Inch Road,
Braehead PA4 8XQ.  0871 2244 007

**Showcase** Barrbridge Leisure Centre,
Coatbridge, G69 7TZ.  0871 220 1000

**Showcase** Phoenix Business Park, Paisley,
PA1 2BH.  0871 220 1000

---

# Theatres
**The Arches**
253 Argyle Street, G2 8DL
0870 240 7528

**Citizens' Theatre**
119 Gorbals Street, G5 9DS
0141 429 0022

**King's Theatre**
297 Bath Street, G2 4JN
0870 060 6648

**Mitchell Theatre**
Granville Street, G3 7DR
0141 287 2805

**New Athenaeum Theatre (R.S.A.M.D.)**
100 Renfrew Street, G2 3DB
0141 332 5057

**Pavilion Theatre**
121 Renfield Street, G2 3AX
0141 332 1846

**Theatre Royal**
282 Hope Street, G2 3QA
0870 0606 647

**Tramway**
25 Albert Drive, G41 2PE
0845 330 3511

**Tron Theatre**
63 Trongate, G1 5HB
0141 552 4267

---

# Halls
**City Halls,** Candleriggs, G1 1NQ
0141 353 8000

**Glasgow Royal Concert Hall**
2 Sauchiehall Street, G2 3NY
0141 353 8000

**Scottish Exhibition Conference Centre
(SECC),** Exhibition Way, G3 8YW
0141 248 3000

For more information about the following
Glasgow City Council halls contact;
Cultural and Leisure Services,
3rd Floor, 20 Trongate, G1 5ES
0141 287 4350
**Couper Institute,** 86 Clarkston Road,
G44 3DA
**Langside Hall**, 5 Langside Avenue, G41 2QR
**Partick Burgh Hall**,
9 Burgh Hall Street, G11 5LN
**Shettleston Hall**, Wellshot Road, G32 7AX
**Woodside Hall**, Glenfarg Street, G20 7QF

## Strathclyde further education

**Anniesland College**
19 Hatfield Drive, G12 OYE
0141 357 3969

**Cardonald College of Further Education**
690 Mosspark Drive, G52 3AY
0141 272 3333

**Central College of Commerce**
300 Cathedral Street, G1 2TA
0141 552 3941

**Clydebank College**
Kilbowie Road, Clydebank, G81 2AA
0141 952 7771

**Coatbridge College**
Kildonan Street, Coatbridge, ML5 3LS
01236 422316

**Cumbernauld College**
Tryst Road, Town Centre, Cumbernauld,
G67 1HU
01236 731811

**Glasgow Caledonian University**
70 Cowcaddens Road, G4 0BA
0141 331 3000

**Glasgow Metropolitan College:**
North Hanover Street Campus,
60 North Hanover Street, G1 2BP
0141 566 6222
Cathedral Street Campus,
230 Cathedral Street, G1 2TG
0141 552 3751

**Glasgow College of Nautical Studies**
21 Thistle Street, G5 9XB
0141 565 2500

**Glasgow School of Art**
167 Renfrew Street, G3 6RQ
0141 353 4500

**John Wheatley College**
East End Campus,
2 Haghill Road, G31 3SR
0141 588 1500
Easterhouse Campus,
1200 Westerhouse Road,
G34 9HZ
0141 588 1500

**Langside College**
50 Prospecthill Road, G42 9LB
0141 649 4991

**North Glasgow College**
110 Flemington Street, G21 4BX
0141 558 9001

**Motherwell College**
Dalzell Drive, Motherwell, ML1 2DD
01698 232 425

**Reid Kerr College,**
Renfrew Road, Paisley, PA3 4DR
0141 581 2222

**Royal Scottish Academy of Music & Drama,**
100 Renfrew Street, G2 3DB
0141 332 4101

**Scotus College**
2 Chesters Road, Bearsden, G61 4AG
0141 942 8384

**South Lanarkshire College**
College Way, East Kilbride, G75 0NE
0141 641 6600

**Stow College**
43 Shamrock Street, G4 9LD
0141 332 1786

**University of Glasgow**
University Avenue, G12 8QQ
0141 330 2000

**University of Paisley**
Paisley Campus, High St, Paisley, PA1 2BE
0141 848 3000
Hamilton Campus, Almada Street, Hamilton
ML3 0JB.  01698 283100

**University of Strathclyde**
16 Richmond Street, G1 1XQ
0141 552 4400

## Hospitals

**Airbles Road Hospital**
49 Airbles Road, Motherwell, ML1 2TP
01698 269336

**Beatson West of Scotland Cancer Centre**
1053 Great Western Road, G12 0YN
0141 301 7000

**Blawarthill Hospital**
129 Holehouse Drive, Blawarthill, G13 3TG
0141 211 9000

**Caird House Hospital**
Caird Street, Hamilton, ML3 0AL
01698 540182

**Coathill Hospital**
Hospital Street, Coatbridge, ML5 4DN
01236 707706

**Drumchapel Hospital**
129 Drumchapel Road, G15 6PX
0141 211 6000

**Dykebar Hospital**
Grahamston Road, Paisley, PA2 7DE
0141 884 5122

**Gartnavel General Hospital**
1053 Great Western Road, G12 0YN
0141 211 3000

**Gartnavel Royal Hospital**
1055 Great Western Road, G12 0XH
0141 211 3600

**Glasgow Dental Hospital and School**
378 Sauchiehall Street, G2 3JZ
0141 211 9600

**Glasgow Nuffield Hospital**
25 Beaconsfield Road, G12 0PJ
0141 334 9441

**Glasgow Royal Infirmary**
82-84 Castle Street, G4 0SF
0141 211 4000

**Golden Jubilee National Hospital**
Beardmore Street, Clydebank, G81 4HX
0141 951 5000

**Hairmyres Hospital**
Eaglesham Road, East Kilbride, G75 8RG
01355 585000

**Homeopathic Hospital**
1053 Great Western Road, G12 0XQ
0141 211 1600

**Johnstone Hospital**
Bridge of Weir Road, Johnstone, PA5 8YX
01505 331471

**Kilsyth Victoria Cottage Hospital**
Glasgow Road, Kilsyth, G65 9AG
01236 822172

**Kirklands Hospital** (Due to close)
Fallside Road, Bothwell, G71 8BB

**Leverndale Hospital**
510 Crookston Road, G53 7TU
0141 211 6400

**Lightburn Hospital**
966 Carntyne Road, G32 6ND
0141 211 1500

**Mansionhouse Unit** (Victoria Infirmary)
100 Mansionhouse Road, G41 3DX
0141 201 6161

**Mearnskirk House**
Old Mearns Road, Newton Mearns, G77 5RZ
0141 616 3742

**Monklands Hospital**
Monkscourt Avenue, Airdrie, ML6 0JS
01236 748748

**Parkhead Hospital**
81 Salamanca Street, G31 5ES
0141 211 8300

**Parkview Resource Centre/Shettleston Day Hospital**
152 Wellshot Road, G32 7AX
0141 303 8800

**Princess Royal Maternity Hospital**
16 Alexandra Parade, G31 2ER
0141 211 5400

**Queen Mother's Hospital**
Dalnair Street, Yorkhill, G3 8SJ
0141 201 0550

**Ross Hall Hospital** (BMI)
221 Crookston Road, G52 3NQ
0141 810 3151

**Royal Alexandra Hospital**
Corsebar Road, Paisley, PA2 9PN
0141 887 9111

**Royal Hospital for Sick Children**
Dalnair Street, Yorkhill, G3 8SJ
0141 201 0000

**St Andrew's Hospice**
Henderson Street, Airdie, ML6 6DJ
01236 766951

**Southern General Hospital**
1345 Govan Road, G51 4TF
0141 201 1100

**Victoria Infirmary**
Langside Road, G42 9TY
0141 201 6000

**Strathclyde Hospital**
Airbles Road, Motherwell, ML1 3BW
01236 748 748

**Wester Moffat Hospital**
Towers Road, Airdrie, ML6 8LW
01236 763377

**Stobhill Hospital**
133 Balornock Road, G21 3UW
0141 201 3000

**Western Infirmary**
Dumbarton Road, Partick, G11 6NT
0141 211 2000

**Udston Hospital**
Farm Road, Burnbank, Hamilton, ML3 9LA
01698 723200

## Visitor information

**Botanic Garden**
730 Great Western Road. 0141 334 2422.
The gardens were formed in 1817 to provide a source of plant material for use in teaching medicine and botany. Today specialist plant collections include exotic Australian tree and ferns, orchids and tropical begonias.

**Burrell Collection, The**
Pollok Country Park. 0141 287 2550
This award winning building houses a world-famous collection gifted to Glasgow by Sir William Burrell. Visitors can see art objects from Iraq, Egypt, Greece and Italy. Tapestries, furniture, textiles, ceramics, stained glass and sculptures from medieval Europe, and drawings from the 15th to 19th centuries.

**City Chambers**
George Square. 0141 287 2000.
The City Chambers is the headquarters of Glasgow City Council and arguably Glasgow's finest example of Victorian architecture. The building was opened in 1888 by Queen Victoria and to this day has preserved all its original features.

**Fossil Grove**
Victoria Park. 0141 950 1448.
Uncovered by accident in 1887, Glasgow's discovery is now designated a Site of Special Scientific Interest. Fossil tree trunks from around 330 million years ago are preserved in situ.

**Gallery of Modern Art**
Royal Exchange Square. 0141 229 1996.
The elegant Royal Exchange building displays works by living artists from across the world. A wide range of temporary exhibitions plus a programme of events including music, drama, dance and workshops.

**Glasgow Cathedral** (St. Mungo)
Cathedral Square. 0141 552 6891.
The only Scottish mainland medieval cathedral to have survived the Reformation complete. Notable features are the elaborately vaulted crypt, the stone screen and the unfinished Blackadder Aisle.

**Glasgow School of Art**
167 Renfrew Street. 0141 353 4526.
Glasgow School of Art is Charles Rennie Mackintosh's architectural masterpiece. The Mackintosh Building continues to be admired and respected and has taken its place as one of the most influential and significant structures of the 20th century.

**Glasgow Science Centre**
Pacific Quay. 0871 540 1000.
Features exhibits devoted to modern science,

a planetarium and IMAX cinema. The centre highlights Glasgow's past, present and future. The Glasgow Tower is the highest free-standing structure in Scotland.

### House for an Art Lover
Bellahouston Park. 0141 353 4770.
A house designed in 1901 by Charles Rennie Mackintosh but only built between 1989 and 1996. Exhibition and film showing the construction. Sculpture park. Situated in parkland adjacent to magnificent Victorian walled gardens.

### Hunterian Art Gallery
82 Hillhead Street. 0141 330 5431.
A prestigious art gallery housing many important works by old masters, impressionists and Scottish paintings from the 18th century to present. Also houses the Mackintosh House, a reconstructed interior of the architect's own house in Glasgow using original furniture, prints and designs.

### Hunterian Museum
University of Glasgow. 0141 330 4221.
Scotland's first public museum was established in 1807 based on the vast collections of Dr William Hunter (1718 – 83). Many items from his valuable collections are on display together with new and exciting additions. See displays of dinosaurs from Scotland, Romans in Scotland, geology, archaeology, medicine and anatomy, the history of science and coins.

### Kelvingrove Art Gallery and Museum
Kelvingrove. 0141 287 2700.
This fine national art collection contains superb paintings and sculptures, silver and ceramic, European armour, weapons and firearms, clothing, and furniture.

### Lighthouse, The
11 Mitchell Lane. 0141 221 6362.
The Lighthouse, Scotland's Centre for Architecture, Design and the City, is the long-term legacy of Glasgow 1999 UK City of Architecture and Design. It is the imaginative conversion of Charles Rennie Mackintosh's first public commission and is located in the heart of the city centre.

### Museum of Transport
Kelvin Hall. 0141 287 2720.
The history of transport on land and sea with vehicles from horse-drawn carriages to motor cycles, fire engines, railway engines, steam and motor cars. Also a re-creation of a typical 1938 Glasgow street.

### National Piping Centre
30–34 McPhater Street. 0141 353 0220.
A national and international centre of excellence of the bagpipes and its music. Housed in a fine listed building.

### Necropolis
Behind Glasgow Cathedral. 0141 287 3961.
Remarkable and extensive burial ground laid out in 1833, with numerous elaborate tombs of 19th century illustrious Glaswegians and others.

### People's Palace
Glasgow Green. 0141 271 2962.
Opened in 1898, this collection displays the story of Glasgow and its people, and its impact on the world from 1175 to the present day. A number of important collections, photographs, film sequences and reminiscences bring to life the city's past.

### Pollok House
Pollok Country Park. 0141 616 6410.
The house was built in 1740 and extended in 1890 by Sir John Stirling Maxwell. The house contains a renowned collection of paintings and furnishings appropriate for an Edwardian country house.

### Provand's Lordship
3 Castle Street. 0141 552 8819.
The oldest dwelling in Glasgow, built in 1471 as a manse for the St Nicholas Hospital.

**St Mungo Museum of Religious Life & Art**
2 Castle Street. 0141 553 2557.
A unique museum exploring the universal themes of life, death and the hereafter through beautiful and evocative art objects associated with different religious faiths.

**Scotland Street School**
(Museum & Education)
225 Scotland Street. 0141 287 0500.
A magnificent building with twin leaded towers and Glasgow-style stone carving designed by Charles Rennie Mackintosh in 1904. Now housing a permanent exhibition on the history of education.

**Tall Ship at Glasgow Harbour**
Stobcross Road. 0141 222 2513.
The principal attraction is an opportunity to board the 103-year-old restored sailing ship Glenlee, the only Clyde-built sailing ship afloat in the UK. The Pumphouse Building (1877) also houses exhibitions. .

**Tenement House**
145 Buccleuch Street. 0141 333 0183.
A typical late Victorian Glasgow tenement flat, retaining many original features and possessions of the woman who lived here for 50 years give a fascinating glimpse of life in the early 20th century.

## Weather

The City of Glasgow is on the same latitude as the City of Moscow, but because of its close proximity to the warm Atlantic shores, and the prevailing westerly winds, it enjoys a more moderate climate. Summers are generally cool and winters mostly mild, this gives Glasgow fairly consistent summer and winter temperatures. Despite considerable cloud the city is sheltered by hills to the south-west and north and the average rainfall for Glasgow is usually less than 40 inches per year. The following table shows the approximate average figures for sunshine, rainfall and temperatures to be expected in Glasgow throughout the year.

### Weather forecasts
For the central Scotland and Strathclyde: Weathercall 09068 500 421 (60p per min)

| Month | Hours of Sunshine | Inches of Rainfall | Temperature C Ave. Max. | Ave. Min. | High/Low |
|---|---|---|---|---|---|
| January | 36 | 3.8 | 5.5 | 0.8 | -18 |
| February | 62 | 2.8 | 6.3 | 0.8 | -15 |
| March | 94 | 2.4 | 8.8 | 2.2 | 21 |
| April | 147 | 2.4 | 11.9 | 3.9 | 22 |
| May | 185 | 2.7 | 15.1 | 6.2 | 26 |
| June | 181 | 2.4 | 17.9 | 9.3 | 30 |
| July | 159 | 2.9 | 18.6 | 10.8 | 29 |
| August | 143 | 3.5 | 18.5 | 10.6 | 31 |
| September | 106 | 4.1 | 16.3 | 9.1 | -4 |
| October | 76 | 4.1 | 13.0 | 6.8 | -8 |
| November | 47 | 3.7 | 8.7 | 3.3 | -11 |
| December | 30 | 4.2 | 6.5 | 1.9 | -12 |

There are over 70 public parks within the city. The most famous is Glasgow Green. Abutting the north bank of the River Clyde, it was acquired in 1662. Of interest are the Winter Gardens attached to the People's Palace. Kelvingrove Park is an 85-acre park laid out by Sir Joseph Paxton in 1852. On the south side of the city is the 148-acre Queen's Park, Victoria Road, established 1857–94. Also of interest: Rouken Glen, Thornliebank, with a spectacular waterfall, walled garden, nature trail and boating facilities; Victoria Park, Victoria Park Drive, with its famous Fossil Grove, flower gardens and yachting pond. In Great Western Road are the Botanic Gardens. Founded in 1817, the gardens' 42 acres are crammed with natural attractions, including the celebrated Kibble Palace glasshouse with its fabulous tree ferns, exotic plants and white marble Victorian statues.

*University tower from Kelvingrove Park*

**Alexandra Park**
10 Sannox Gardens, G31 3JE.

**Botanic Gardens**
730 Great Western Road, G12 OUE.

**Cathkin Braes County Park**
Cathkin Road, G73.

**Chatelherault County Park**
Hamilton, ML3 7UE.

**Hogganfield Park**
Cumbernauld Road, G33.

**Glasgow Green**
Greendyke Street, G1 5DB.

**Kelvingrove Park**
Otago Street, G3 6BY.

**King's Park**
325 Carmunnock Road, G44.

**Linn Park**
Clarkston Road, G44 5TA.

**Pollok Country Park**
Pollokshaws Road, G43.

**Queen's Park**
520 Langside Road, G42.

**Rouken Glen Park**
Rouken Glen Road, G46.

**Springburn Park**
Balgrayhill Road, G21.

**Strathclyde County Park**
Hamilton Road, Motherwell, ML1 3ED.

**Tollcross Park**
254B Wellshot Road, G32 7AX.

**Victoria Park**
Victoria Park Drive North, G14.

The City of Glasgow has one of the most advanced, fully integrated public transport systems in the whole of Europe. The Strathclyde Partnership for Transport (SPT) is responsible for planning the network: local railways, local bus services, local passenger ferries and the Glasgow Subway (with links to Glasgow International Airport, the Steamer and car ferry services). Contact them on 0141 332 6811. For general travel enquiries contact Traveline on 0871 200 22 33.

The rail network map is on pages 166-167.

## Bus Services
### Long Distance Coach Service
Citylink  08705 505050
National Express  08705 808080
Scottish Citylink Coaches Ltd and National Express provide rapid services to London and most parts of Scotland.

A comprehensive network of local bus services is provided by a variety of operators within the City of Glasgow and also direct to a number of surrounding towns. These services depart from City Centre bus stops or from Buchanan Bus Station, Killermont Street, G2.  0141 333 3708

### Local Bus Services
Traveline Scotland (timetable only)
0870 608 2 608

## Railway Services
National Rail (timetable only):
08457 484 950
ScotRail (telesales only): 08457 550033
Northern: 08706 023322
G.N.E.R. (timetable & telesales):
08457 225225
Virgin (timetable & telesales):
08457 222333

ScotRail trains serve over 170 stations in Glasgow and Strathclyde (see map on pages 166-167) and operate to most destinations in Scotland.
Northern, G.N.E.R. & Virgin operate services to England.
Use Glasgow Queen Street station for services to the north and east of Glasgow and use Glasgow Central station for services to the west and south of Glasgow and England.

## Parking
Car Parking in the central area of Glasgow is controlled. Parking meters are used extensively and signs indicating restrictions are displayed at kerbsides and on entry to the central area. Traffic Wardens are on duty.

There are a large number of car parks throughout the city centre, many of which are open 24 hours a day. See the mapping section for locations. General parking enquiries 0141 287 4040

## Taxis
Glasgow has around 1500 traditional London type taxis, all licensed by the Glasgow City Council. At the time of publishing, a three mile journey costs approximately £7. The total price of each journey is shown on the meter at all times and is calculated by distance or time or a combination of both. The major taxi companies offer City tours at fixed prices, listing the places of interest to be visited, leaflets are available at all major hotel reception areas. Tours vary from 1 to 3 hours and in price between £25 and £45.

Any passenger wishing to travel to a destination outside the Glasgow District Boundary should ascertain from the driver the fare to be charged.
### Complaints
Any complaints regarding the conduct of a taxi driver should be addressed to:
Taxi Enforcement Unit,
231 George Street, G1 1RX
0141 287 4294

Located eight miles (13km) west of Glasgow alongside the M8 motorway at Junction 28 & 28A this airport is linked to Buchanan Bus Station by the Glasgow Flyer with services running up to every 15 minutes from 6.00am – 11.00pm Monday to Saturday and up to every 30 minutes at off peak times. There is a frequent coach service linking the Airport with all major bus and rail terminals in the city. Coach and bus tickets along with rail information can be obtained from the SPT travel desk, door 5 on the ground floor. Car parking is available with a graduated scale of charges.

The Airport telephone number 0870 040 008

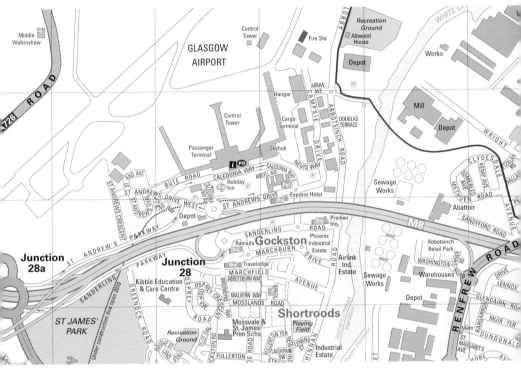

## Airlines (with telephone reservations)

**Aer Lingus** 0870 876 5000

**Air Transat** 0207 616 9187

**BMI** 0870 607 0555

**BMI Baby** 0870 264 2229

**British Airways** 0870 850 9850

**Continental** 0845 607 6760

**Easy Jet** 0905 821 0905

**Flybe** 0871 700 0123

**Fly Globespan** 0870 556 1522

**Icelandair** 0870 787 4020

**KLM Cityhopper** 08705 074 074

**Zoom Airlines** 0870 240 0055

## Prestwick International Airport

Access to Glasgow via a 45 minute train journey. Flights from and to scheduled destinations across Europe. Discounted rail fares to Glasgow Central station are available for air passengers.
Prestwick International Airport
0871 223 0700

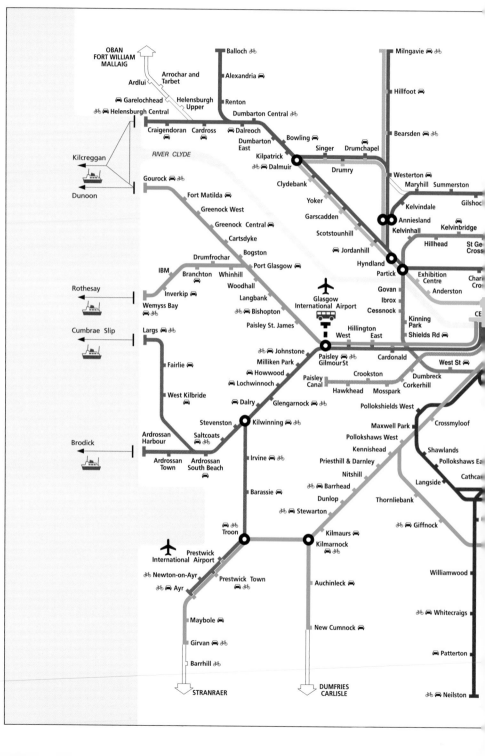

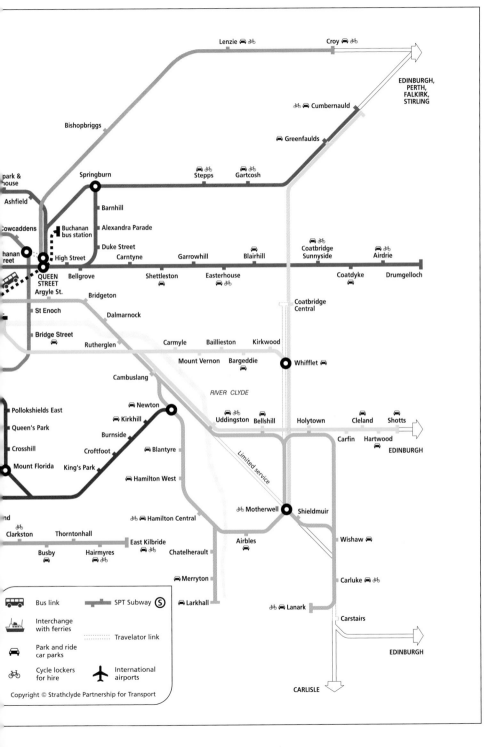

Lenzie  Croy

EDINBURGH,
PERTH,
FALKIRK,
STIRLING

Cumbernauld

Bishopbriggs

Greenfaulds

Springburn      Stepps    Gartcosh

park &
house

Ashfield

Barnhill

Cowcaddens

Buchanan
bus station      Alexandra Parade

Duke Street          Coatbridge       Airdrie
hanan                             Sunnyside
reet    High Street    Carntyne    Garrowhill    Blairhill

QUEEN    Bellgrove      Shettleston    Easterhouse       Coatdyke    Drumgelloch
STREET
Argyle St.

Bridgeton                                      Coatbridge
Central
St Enoch

Bridge Street
Carmyle    Baillieston    Kirkwood
Rutherglen

Carmyle    Baillieston    Kirkwood    Whifflet

Mount Vernon    Bargeddie

Cambuslang

RIVER CLYDE

Pollokshields East    Newton

Queen's Park    Kirkhill          Uddingston  Bellshill    Holytown    Cleland    Shotts

Burnside                                            Carfin  Hartwood
Crosshill    Croftfoot    Blantyre                                    EDINBURGH

Mount Florida    King's Park

Hamilton West

nd

Clarkston    Thorntonhall          Hamilton Central    Motherwell    Shieldmuir

East Kilbride    Airbles            Wishaw
Busby    Hairmyres
Chatelherault

Merryton                    Carluke

Larkhall              Lanark

Carstairs

EDINBURGH

CARLISLE

Bus link          SPT Subway  S

Interchange
with ferries          Travelator link

Park and ride
car parks

Cycle lockers      International
for hire          airports

Copyright © Strathclyde Partnership for Transport

| | |
|---|---|
| M8 — Motorway | Road proposed or under construction |
| Motorway junctions (full, limited access) | Multi-level junction with full/ limited access |
| Stirling / Harthill — Motorway service areas (off road, full, limited access) | Roundabout |
| Hamilton | |
| A80 — Primary route dual / single | Road distance in miles |
| A89 — 'A' road dual / single | Road tunnel |
| B806 — 'B' road dual / single | Steep hill (arrows point downhill) |
| Minor road | |
| Roads with restricted access | Level crossing / Toll |

| | |
|---|---|
| Zeebrugge — Car ferry | (H) Heliport |
| Railway line / station / tunnel | P&R P&R — Park and Ride site operated by bus / rail |
| ✈ Airport with scheduled services | Canal / Dry canal / Canal tunnel |

| | |
|---|---|
| Built up area | **Peterhead** Primary route destination |
| Town / Village / Other settlement | Seaside destination |

| | |
|---|---|
| County / Unitary Authority boundary | Woodland |
| National Park boundary | Beach / Lighthouse |
| Regional / Forest Park boundary | 468 Spot height (metres) |
| Danger Zone — Military range | ▲ 941 Summit height (metres) |
| 172 — Page continuation number | Lake / Dam / River / Waterfall |

More details of selected places of interest shown on the mapping can be found on pages 160-162

| | | |
|---|---|---|
| ℹ Tourist information office (all year / seasonal) | Event venue | Nature reserve (NNR indicates a National Nature Reserve) |
| m Ancient monument | Garden | Racecourse |
| Aquarium | Golf course | Rail Freight Terminal |
| Aqueduct / Viaduct | Historic house | Ski slope (artificial) |
| 1643 Battlefield | Historic ship | Steam railway centre / Preserved railway |
| Blue flag beach | Major football club | University |
| Camp site / Caravan site | Major shopping centre / Outlet village | Wildlife park / Zoo |
| Castle | Major sports venue | Other interesting feature |
| Country park | Motor racing circuit | (NTS) National Trust for Scotland property |
| Ecclesiastical building | Museum / Art gallery | |

SCALE

0    4    8    12    16 miles

0    5    10    15    20    25 kilometres

1:250,000  4 miles to 1 inch (2.5cm) / 2.5km to 1cm

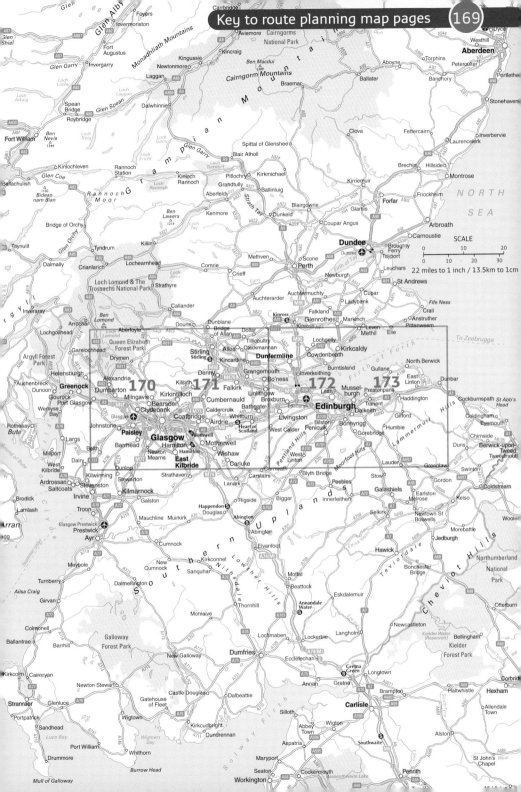

SCALE

0   10   20
0   10   20   30

22 miles to 1 inch / 13.5km to 1cm

N O R T H

S E A

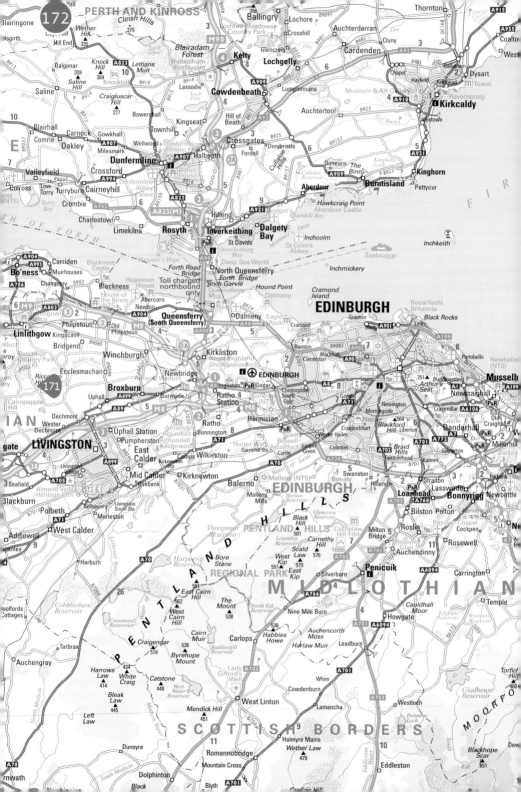

Macduff's Castle
Wemyss
Vemyss
ss

H OF FORTH

**North Berwick**
Fidra
Yellowcraig
Lamb
Craigleith
Bass Rock
Scottish Seabird Centre

Gullane Bents
Muirfield
Dirleton
Tantallon Castle
Auldhame
St Baldred's Boat
Scoughall

Gullane Point
**Gullane**
Dirleton Castle & Gardens
187
North Berwick Law
Kingston
Whitekirk
St Baldred's Cradle

A198
Aberlady Bay
Luffness
Fenton Barns
B1345

Aberlady
Craigielaw
Drem
8
Tyninghame House
Belhaven Bay
**Dunbar**

Craigielaw Point
Luffness
Mungoswells
East Fortune
A198
Tyninghame
John Muir
West Barns
A1087

Gosford Bay
Ballencrieff
Chesters Hill Fort
Museum of Flight
B1407
Preston Mill & Phantassie (NTS)
A199
Dunbar
A650
Broxbu

A198
Gosford House
5
Church of Plague
B1343
Athelstaneford
Preston
East Linton
A199
Dunbar 1296
Spott
Doonhill Homestea
Inr

Longniddry Bents
7
Spittal
B1377
Garleton Hills
St Mary's Church
Hailes
Traprain
9
Bield Pitcox
Brunt Hill
225

Seton Collegiate Church
**Longniddry**
Elvingston
A1
Luggate
Luggate Burn
Stenton

Cockenzie and Port Seton
Preston Tower & Hamilton House (NTS)
7
**Haddington**
Traprain Law Fort
Pressmennan Lake
Halls
Deuchrie Dod
Dre Burn

Preston pans 1745
Meadowmill
A6093
Lennoxlove
Bransly Hill
397

**Prestonpans**
Pinkie 1547
**Tranent**
Gladsmuir
Whitelaw Hill
Garvald

Levenhall
A199
Macmerry
B6369
Carfrae
Nunraw Abbey
Dunbar Common

Wallyford
B6415
Penston
New Winton
New Town
Samuelston
Bolton
Gifford Church
Clints Dod
White
398

6
Elphinstone
B6371
Winton House
Pencaitland
B6355
Gifford
B6355
Danskine
400
Rangely Kip

Carberry Tower
Market Cross
West Saltoun
B6355
Sportleton Edge
Gamelshiel

Crossgatehall
**Ormiston**
A6093
5
East Saltoun
Longyester
Newlands Hill
423
Whiteadder Reservoir
Penshiel Hill

th
4
A6124
Cousland
Peastonbank
Gilchriston
B6368
Cranshaws Hill
379
Crans

Whitehill
Oxenford
Peaston
Faseny Water
27

sthouses
Edgehead
B6371
Humbie
Meikle Says Law
535
Meikle Law
467
Wrunk Law
364

Mayfield
Ford
Pathhead
Lammer Law
528
Hopes Reservoir
Seenes Law
513
Lam

grange
Vogrie
Crichton
A68
Fala Dam
West Hill
451
Crib Law
509
Hunt Law
495
Blythe Edge
Longformacus

Newlandrig
Crichton Castle
Fala
B6457
Soutra Hill
Watch Water Reservoir

rebridge
B6458
13
394
363
Hogs Law
448
Dirringt Great La
398

wick
Borthwick
Tynehead
Fala Moor
Dun Law
Turf Law
A68
Southern Upland Way
Dirrington Little Law
363

North Middleton
6
A7
Gilston
B6368
Scoured Rig
363

B7007
Falahill
Heriot Water
Oxton
Carfraemill
**SCOTTISH BORDERS**

HILLS
Dun Law
Heriot
Collie Law
381
Edgarhope Wood
Westruther
B6456

Ladyside Height
Fountainhall
A7
9
Inchkeith Hill
365
Thirlestane Castle
Thirlestane
Whiteburn
A697
Houndslow
8

tside
Torquhan
B709
**Lauder**
Lauder Common
A6089
Eden

LAMMERMUIR HILLS

E A S T   L O T H I A N

LAUDER

Blackadder Water

## A

| | | |
|---|---|---|
| Abronhill | 23 | DF9 |
| Acre | 30 | BK20 |
| Airdrie | 76 | DC30 |
| Anderston | 4 | BP30 |
| Annathill | 38 | CU19 |
| Anniesland | 47 | BG23 |
| Arden | 101 | BG42 |
| Arkleston | 63 | AY29 |
| Arthurlie | 99 | AX44 |
| Ashgillhead | 145 | DG60 |
| Auchenback | 99 | AZ44 |
| Auchenshuggle | 90 | CB35 |
| Auchentorlie | 83 | AX33 |
| Auchinairn | 51 | BW22 |
| Auchinloch | 35 | CE19 |
| Auldhouse | 102 | BL39 |

## B

| | | |
|---|---|---|
| Back o'Loch | 17 | CF14 |
| Baillieston | 71 | CH32 |
| Balgrayhill | 50 | BV23 |
| Balloch | 21 | CY11 |
| Balmalloch | 7 | CS4 |
| Balmore | 14 | BU13 |
| Balmore Haughs | 14 | BT14 |
| Balornock | 51 | BW24 |
| Bankhead | 88 | BV38 |
| Bardowie | 13 | BR14 |
| Bargarran | 25 | AP18 |
| Bargeddie | 73 | CN32 |
| Barlanark | 71 | CH31 |
| Barleybank | 17 | CF13 |
| Barmulloch | 51 | BZ25 |
| Barnellan | 13 | BQ12 |
| Barrhead | 99 | AW42 |
| Barrowfield | 95 | CW33 |
| Barrwood | 8 | CV5 |
| Battlefield | 87 | BP38 |
| Bearsden | 29 | BF17 |
| Bellahouston | 66 | BJ32 |
| Bellshill | 111 | CW41 |
| Birkenshaw, G71 | 93 | CP36 |
| Birkenshaw, ML9 | 144 | DD62 |
| Birniehill | 136 | CC54 |
| Bishopbriggs | 32 | BV19 |
| Bishoploch | 72 | CL28 |
| Blackhall | 83 | AW34 |
| Blackhill | 69 | BZ27 |
| Blackwood | 20 | CT12 |
| Blairdardie | 28 | BD20 |
| Blairhill | 74 | CU30 |
| Blairlinn | 40 | DC15 |
| Blairtummock | 72 | CJ29 |
| Blantyre | 125 | CM56 |
| Blochairn | 69 | BW28 |
| Blysthwood | 45 | AY24 |
| Boclair | 30 | BK17 |
| Bonnaughton | 28 | BC15 |
| Bothwell | 109 | CQ43 |
| Bothwellhaugh | 110 | CU44 |
| Bowerwalls | 100 | BA41 |
| Bowhouse | 104 | BV42 |
| Braedale | 127 | CX47 |
| Braehead | 46 | BA25 |
| Braeside | 104 | BV42 |
| Brediland | 81 | AQ35 |
| Bridgend | 37 | CN18 |
| Bridgeton | 68 | BV32 |
| Broadholm | 28 | BC18 |
| Broadwood | 20 | CV12 |
| Broom | 118 | BJ47 |
| Broomhill | 47 | BH26 |

| | | |
|---|---|---|
| Broomhouse | 92 | CJ36 |
| Brownsburn | 96 | DD33 |
| Burnbank | 125 | CQ47 |
| Burnfoot | 76 | DA28 |
| Burnhead | 145 | DE58 |
| Burnside | 105 | BY41 |
| Busby | 119 | BR48 |

## C

| | | |
|---|---|---|
| Cadder, G23 | 49 | BP22 |
| Cadder, G64 | 33 | BX16 |
| Cadzow | 140 | CU53 |
| Cairnhill | 76 | DA32 |
| Cairnsmore | 28 | BA18 |
| Calderbank | 96 | DC34 |
| Calderbraes | 93 | CN37 |
| Calderpark | 92 | CL35 |
| Calderwood | 123 | CE50 |
| Calton | 68 | BU32 |
| Cambuslang | 106 | CB39 |
| Camlachie | 69 | BX31 |
| Canniesburn | 29 | BH18 |
| Carbrain | 22 | DC12 |
| Cardonald | 64 | BD32 |
| Carfin | 113 | DE43 |
| Carmunnock | 120 | BU45 |
| Carmyle | 91 | CE37 |
| Carnbroe | 95 | CY34 |
| Carntyne | 69 | BZ29 |
| Carriagehill | 82 | AT35 |
| Carrickstone | 22 | DA9 |
| Cartside | 79 | AF36 |
| Castlehead | 82 | AT34 |
| Castlemilk | 104 | BU42 |
| Castleton | 104 | BS43 |
| Cathcart | 103 | BQ39 |
| Cathkin | 105 | BZ43 |
| Ceekhimin | 112 | DD44 |
| Cessnock | 66 | BL31 |
| Chantinghill | 125 | CR50 |
| Chapelhall | 97 | DG34 |
| Charleston | 82 | AU35 |
| Chryston | 54 | CL21 |
| Claddens | 35 | CH16 |
| Clarkston, G76 | 118 | BM46 |
| Clarkston, ML6 | 77 | DF29 |
| Cleddans, G15 | 28 | BB17 |
| Cleddans, G66 | 17 | CH11 |
| Cliftonville | 75 | CY30 |
| Clydebank | 27 | AW20 |
| Clydesdale | 112 | DA41 |
| Coatbridge | 75 | CY31 |
| Coatdyke | 75 | CZ31 |
| College Milton | 135 | BW51 |
| Colston | 50 | BV22 |
| Commonhead | 73 | CN29 |
| Condorrat | 39 | CW15 |
| Coresford | 79 | AE37 |
| Corkerhill | 85 | BF36 |
| Courthill | 28 | BC15 |
| Cowcaddens | 4 | BR28 |
| Cowglen | 85 | BG38 |
| Cowlairs | 50 | BT25 |
| Craigend | 53 | CZ26 |
| Craigendmuir | 53 | CG25 |
| Craiglinn | 21 | CW11 |
| Craigmarloch | 21 | CW9 |
| Craigneuk, ML2 | 129 | DF49 |
| Craigneuk, ML6 | 77 | DE31 |
| Craigton | 65 | BF32 |
| Craigton Village | 10 | BD9 |
| Cranhill | 70 | CC29 |
| Cranston Hill | 67 | BN30 |
| Croftfoot | 104 | BV39 |
| Crookfur | 117 | BG47 |
| Crookston | 84 | BC33 |

| | | |
|---|---|---|
| Crosshill, G42 | 87 | BQ36 |
| Crosshill, G69 | 72 | CM32 |
| Crossmill | 99 | AY41 |
| Crossmyloof | 87 | BN35 |
| Croy | 20 | CV9 |
| Cumbernauld | 21 | CZ12 |

## D

| | | |
|---|---|---|
| Dalbeth | 90 | CA35 |
| Daldowie | 92 | CK37 |
| Dalmarnock | 89 | BW35 |
| Dalmuir | 26 | AU17 |
| Dalshannon | 39 | CW15 |
| Dalton | 107 | CH42 |
| Darnley | 101 | BE41 |
| Deaconsbank | 101 | BE43 |
| Dennistoun | 69 | BW29 |
| Dovecothall | 99 | AZ42 |
| Dowanhill | 48 | BL26 |
| Drumchapel | 28 | BB18 |
| Drumgelloch | 76 | DD29 |
| Drumoyne | 65 | BH31 |
| Drumpellier | 74 | CS31 |
| Drumry | 27 | AY19 |
| Dullatur | 9 | CZ7 |
| Dumbreck | 86 | BK33 |
| Dunbeth | 75 | CX30 |
| Dundyvan | 74 | CV32 |
| Dunrobin | 77 | DH29 |
| Duntiblane | 18 | CJ14 |
| Duntocher | 27 | AX15 |
| Dykebar | 83 | AW37 |

## E

| | | |
|---|---|---|
| Eaglesham | 133 | BN56 |
| Earnock | 139 | CN52 |
| East Balgrochan | 15 | BY11 |
| East Craigend | 25 | AQ20 |
| East Kilbride | 135 | BZ52 |
| East Mains | 136 | CA51 |
| East Shawhead | 95 | CX35 |
| Easterhouse | 72 | CL29 |
| Eastfield | 22 | DA10 |
| Easthall | 72 | CJ30 |
| Eastside | 17 | CF12 |
| Eastwood | 102 | BJ39 |
| Eddlewood | 140 | CT54 |
| Elderslie | 80 | AL36 |
| Erskine | 25 | AR20 |
| Erskine Harbour | 25 | AQ17 |

## F

| | | |
|---|---|---|
| Fairhill | 140 | CS53 |
| Fallside | 110 | CS40 |
| Ferguslie Park | 61 | AP32 |
| Fernhill | 105 | BX42 |
| Finnieston | 66 | BM29 |
| Firhill | 49 | BQ25 |
| Flemington, G72 | 107 | CF42 |
| Flemington, ML1 | 128 | DD48 |
| Fluchter | 13 | BR11 |
| Forgewood | 111 | CZ43 |
| Foxbar | 81 | AP37 |
| Freeland | 43 | AR22 |
| Fullarton | 90 | CD35 |

## G

| | | |
|---|---|---|
| Gallowhill | 63 | AW30 |
| Gardenhall | 134 | BU55 |
| Garnethill | 4 | BQ28 |
| Garnkirk | 54 | CJ23 |

| | | |
|---|---|---|
| Gartcosh | 55 | CP24 |
| Gartcraig | 70 | CB29 |
| Garthamlock | 71 | CG27 |
| Gartlea | 76 | DD31 |
| Gartness | 77 | DD32 |
| Gartsherrie | 74 | CV28 |
| Gateside | 98 | AV44 |
| Germiston | 69 | BX27 |
| Giffnock | 102 | BM43 |
| Gilshochill | 48 | BM22 |
| Glenboig | 56 | CU23 |
| Glenburn | 82 | AT37 |
| Glengowan | 144 | DA58 |
| Glenmavis | 58 | DA25 |
| Glenwood | 104 | BU43 |
| Gockston | 62 | AY19 |
| Golfhill | 76 | DB27 |
| Gorbals | 68 | BS32 |
| Govan | 66 | BJ30 |
| Govanhill | 87 | BQ35 |
| Greenend | 95 | CY33 |
| Greenfaulds | 22 | DA13 |
| Greenfield | 70 | CC31 |
| Greenfoot | 57 | CW22 |
| Greengairs | 41 | DH20 |
| Greenhill | 75 | CX28 |
| Greenhills | 135 | BY55 |
| Greenlees | 106 | CD42 |
| Greens, The | 16 | CD14 |

## H

| | | |
|---|---|---|
| Haghill | 69 | BY30 |
| Hairmyres | 134 | BV53 |
| Halfway | 107 | CF41 |
| Haltonrig | 111 | CX39 |
| Hamilton | 126 | CS50 |
| Hamiltonhill | 49 | BR25 |
| Hangingshaw | 88 | BS37 |
| Hardgate | 27 | AY15 |
| Hareleeshill | 144 | DD60 |
| Harestanes | 18 | CJ12 |
| Hawkhead | 83 | AZ36 |
| Hayston | 16 | CC13 |
| High Balmalloch | 7 | CS4 |
| High Blantyre | 124 | CL47 |
| High Burnside | 105 | BY41 |
| High Gallowhill | 34 | CC15 |
| High Knightswood | 47 | BG21 |
| High Possil | 49 | BR21 |
| Highland Park | 7 | CS3 |
| Hillhead, G12 | 49 | BN26 |
| Hillhead, G66 | 17 | CG13 |
| Hillington | 64 | BC31 |
| Hillpark | 102 | BL40 |
| Hogganfield | 70 | CC27 |
| Holehills | 76 | DD27 |
| Holehouse | 114 | AS46 |
| Holytown | 112 | DC39 |
| Househillwood | 100 | BD39 |
| Howgill | 103 | BR43 |
| Hunt Hill | 20 | CS12 |
| Hunterhill | 83 | AW35 |
| Hurlet | 100 | BA39 |
| Hutchesontown | 88 | BS34 |
| Hyndland | 48 | BJ26 |

## I

| | | |
|---|---|---|
| Ibrox | 66 | BK31 |
| Inchinnan | 44 | AT23 |

## J

| | | |
|---|---|---|
| Jackton | 134 | BS54 |
| Jenny Lind | 101 | BF43 |
| Johnstone | 79 | AH36 |

Johnstone Castle 80 AJ36
Jordanhill 47 BG24

**K**

Kelvin 136 CD55
Kelvindale 48 BK23
Kelvingrove 66 BM28
Kelvinhaugh 66 BK28
Kelvinside 48 BK24
Kennishead 101 BG40
Kessington 30 BJ17
Kilbarchan 78 AD34
Kilbowie 27 AX19
Kildermorie 72 CJ29
Kildrum 22 DD10
Killermont 30 BK19
Kilsyth 7 CR5
King's Park 104 BT39
Kingsridge 28 BA18
Kingston, G5 67 BP32
Kingston, PA7 24 AK18
Kinning Park 66 BM32
Kirkhill 106 CD40
Kirkintilloch 17 CG14
Kirklandneuk 45 AW26
Kirkshaws 94 CU34
Kirkwood 74 CS32
Knightswood 47 BE22
Kylepark 92 CM38

**L**

Laigh Crosshill 92 CL33
Laigh Park 62 AU30
Laighstonehall 140 CS51
Lambhill 49 BQ22
Langfauld 28 BB17
Langloan 74 CU32
Langmuir, G66 18 CK12
Langmuir, G69 93 CP33
Langside 87 BN37
Larkhall 144 DD58
Laurieston 67 BR32
Lenzie 35 CF16
Lenziemill 22 DC13
Lightburn 70 CC30
Linburn 24 AN19
Linndale 104 BS42
Linnvale 27 AZ20
Linwood 60 AK31
Little Earnock 139 CQ52
Loanhead 45 AZ26
Lochfield 82 AV36
Low Blantyre 109 CN44
Low Waters 140 CU52
Luggiebank 40 DC15

**M**

Machan 144 DC59
Malletsheugh 116 BD50
Mansewood 102 BK40
Marnoch 56 CS22
Maryhill 48 BK22
Meadowhill 144 DD57
Mearns 117 BG49
Meikle Earnock 140 CS54
Meiklerigs 81 AQ34
Merkland 17 CH12
Merrylee 102 BM41
Millarston 81 AP34
Millerston, G33 52 CC25
Millerston, G76 119 BN49
Millheugh 144 DA59
Millikenpark 79 AE36
Milngavie 12 BJ12

Milnwood 111 CZ41
Milton 50 BS22
Milton of Campsie 16 CD9
Mollinsburn 38 CT17
Moodiesburn 36 CM19
Moorpark 63 AX27
Mosshead 29 BF15
Mossneuk 134 BV54
Mosspark 85 BG34
Motherwell 128 DB47
Mount Ellen 55 CN23
Mount Florida 87 BR38
Mount Vernon 91 CG34
Mountblow 26 AT16
Muirend 103 BN41
Muirhead, G69
    (Baillieston) 92 CL34
Muirhead, G69
    (Chryston) 54 CM22
Muirhouse 128 DC50
Murray, The 136 CA54

**N**

Neilston 114 AU46
Nerston 122 CB49
Nether Kirkton 114 AU45
Netherlee 103 BQ43
Netherton, G13 47 BH21
Netherton, ML2 143 DE52
New Monkland 58 DA24
New Stevenston 112 DB42
Newarthill 113 DH41
Newlands 103 BN39
Newlandsmuir 134 BU55
Newton 107 CH39
Newton Mearns 117 BE49
Nitshill 100 BB40
North Barr 25 AQ18
North Barrwood 8 CV4
North Cardonald 64 BD29
North Haugh 127 CW48
North Kelvin 49 BN25
North Lodge 128 DA49
North Motherwell 127 CX45
North Mount
    Vernon 91 CG33
Northfield 6 CQ4

**O**

Old Drumchapel 28 BA19
Old Kilpatrick 25 AQ15
Old Monkland 94 CU33
Oldhall 63 AZ32
Orbiston 111 CW42
Orchard Park,
    G46 102 BJ42
Orchard Park,
    G66 35 CG17
Oxgang 17 CH14

**P**

Paisley 62 AT32
Park Mains 44 AS21
Parkhall 26 AV16
Parkhead 89 BZ33
Parkhouse 50 BT23
Partick 66 BK27
Partickhill 48 BK26
Penilee 64 BB31
Petersburn 77 DG31
Petershill 51 BW26
Philipshill 120 BU49
Pinewood 29 BE18
Pollok 85 BE35

Pollokshaws 86 BK38
Pollokshields 86 BM34
Polmadie 88 BT35
Port Dundas 67 BR27
Port Eglinton 87 BP33
Porterfield 63 AX27
Possilpark 50 BS24
Potterhill 82 AU36
Priesthill 100 BD39
Provanhall 72 CJ28
Provanmill 69 BY27

**Q**

Quarrelton 79 AH35
Queenslie 71 CG29
Queenzieburn 6 CN5

**R**

Radnor Park 27 AW18
Raploch 144 DB59
Rashielee 25 AQ19
Ravenscraig 129 DE47
Rawyards 77 DE27
Renfrew 45 AY26
Riddrie 69 BZ28
Riddrie Knowes 70 CA29
Riggend 40 DD20
Robroyston 52 CA23
Rogerfield 72 CL30
Rosehall 95 CX33
Rosshall 84 BC33
Rossland 24 AL19
Roughmussel 84 BB37
Roystonhill 68 BV29
Ruchazie 70 CD28
Ruchill 49 BP24
Rutherglen 89 BX37

**S**

St. Leonards 137 CE52
Sandyhills 71 CF32
Scotstoun 46 BD25
Scotstounhill 46 BD24
Seafar 22 DA11
Seedhill 82 AV33
Shawfield 88 BV36
Shawhead 95 CW34
Shawlands 86 BL36
Sheddens 119 BP46
Shettleston 90 CC33
Shieldhall 65 BE29
Shirrel 95 CX38
Shortroods 62 AU30
Sighthill 68 BU27
Sikeside 75 CZ32
Silvertonhill 140 CV51
Simshill 104 BS41
South Barrwood 8 CV6
South Cardonald 85 BE33
South Claddens 35 CH17
South Haugh 127 CW50
South Nitshill 100 BC41
South Westerton 29 BF19
Spateston 79 AF38
Spittal 104 BV40
Springboig 70 CC31
Springburn 50 BV25
Springhall 105 BZ41
Springhill 99 AY43
Stamperland 119 BP45
Stand 58 DD23
Stanely 81 AR36
Stepps 53 CF24
Stewartfield 121 BY49

Stonedyke 28 BD18
Strathbungo 87 BN35
Strutherhill 144 DB61
Summerlee 74 CV30
Summerston 30 BM20
Sunnyside 75 CX29
Swinton 72 CL31

**T**

Tannochside 93 CR37
Temple 47 BH21
Templecross 104 BV43
Thornliebank 101 BH42
Thornly Park 82 AV37
Thorntonhall 120 BS50
Thrashburn 76 DB28
Tintock 18 CL11
Tollcross 90 CB34
Torrance 15 BY12
Toryglen 88 BT37
Townhead 17 CE13
Tradeston 67 BQ32
Twechar 19 CP10

**U**

Uddingston 92 CM38
Udston 125 CP49

**V**

Vicarland 106 CC41
Victory Gardens 63 AY28
Viewpark 94 CS38

**W**

Wardlawhill 89 BY38
Waterfoot 132 BM52
Wattston 41 DE20
Waverley 28 BC16
Waverley Park 86 BL36
Wellhouse 71 CG30
Welside 107 CF42
West Arthurlie 99 AW43
West Balgrochan 15 BW12
West Craigend 24 AN20
West Mains 135 BY51
Westburn 107 CG39
Westcastle 104 BT41
Wester Holytown 112 DA40
Westermains 16 CC13
Westerton 29 BG19
Westerwood 9 DB7
Westfield, G65 7 CR4
Westfield, G68 38 CU15
Westwood 135 BX52
Whifflet 75 CY32
Whinhall 76 DA29
Whitecrook 45 AZ21
Whitehaugh 63 AW32
Whitehill 125 CR47
Whitehills 135 BZ56
Whiteinch 47 BG26
Whitlawburn 106 CA42
Williamsburgh 83 AX33
Williamwood 118 BL45
Windlaw 104 BT43
Wishaw 129 DG50
Woodside 67 BQ27
Wyndford 48 BM24

**Y**

Yoker 46 BA23
Yorkhill 66 BM28

## General abbreviations

| | | | | | | | | | | | |
|---|---|---|---|---|---|---|---|---|---|---|---|
| All | Alley | Comm | Community | Gdn | Garden | Mt | Mount | Shop | Shopping |
| Allot | Allotments | Conv | Convent | Gdns | Gardens | Mus | Museum | Sq | Square |
| Amb | Ambulance | Cor | Corner | Govt | Government | N | North | St. | Saint |
| App | Approach | Coron | Coroners | Gra | Grange | NTS | National Trust | St | Street |
| Arc | Arcade | Cors | Corners | Grd | Ground | | for Scotland | Sta | Station |
| Av | Avenue | Cotts | Cottages | Grds | Grounds | Nat | National | Sts | Streets |
| Ave | Avenue | Cov | Covered | Grn | Green | PH | Public House | Sub | Subway |
| Bdy | Broadway | Crem | Crematorium | Grns | Greens | PO | Post Office | Swim | Swimming |
| Bk | Bank | Cres | Crescent | Gro | Grove | Par | Parade | TA | Territorial |
| Bldgs | Buildings | Ct | Court | Gros | Groves | Pas | Passage | | Army |
| Boul | Boulevard | Cts | Courts | Gt | Great | Pav | Pavilion | TH | Town Hall |
| Bowl | Bowling | Ctyd | Courtyard | Ho | House | Pk | Park | Tenn | Tennis |
| Br | Bridge | Dep | Depot | Hos | Houses | Pl | Place | Ter | Terrace |
| Bus | Business | Dev | Development | Hosp | Hospital | Pol | Police | Thea | Theatre |
| C of S | Church of | Dr | Drive | Hts | Heights | Prec | Precinct | Trd | Trading |
| | Scotland | Dws | Dwellings | Ind | Industrial | Prim | Primary | Twr | Tower |
| Cath | Cathedral | E | East | Int | International | Prom | Promenade | Twrs | Towers |
| Cem | Cemetery | Ed | Education | Junct | Junction | Pt | Point | Uni | University |
| Cen | Central, | Elec | Electricity | La | Lane | Quad | Quadrant | Vil | Villas |
| | Centre | Embk | Embankment | Las | Lanes | RC | Roman | Vil | Villa |
| Cft | Croft | Est | Estate | Lib | Library | | Catholic | Vw | View |
| Cfts | Crofts | Ex | Exchange | Ln | Loan | Rbt | Roundabout | W | West |
| Ch | Church | Exhib | Exhibition | Lo | Lodge | Rd | Road | Wd | Wood |
| Chyd | Churchyard | FB | Footbridge | Lwr | Lower | Rds | Roads | Wds | Woods |
| Cin | Cinema | FC | Football Club | Mag | Magistrates | Rec | Recreation | Wf | Wharf |
| Circ | Circus | Fld | Field | Mans | Mansions | Res | Reservoir | Wk | Walk |
| Cl | Close | Flds | Fields | Mem | Memorial | Ri | Rise | Wks | Works |
| Clo | Close | Fm | Farm | Mkt | Market | S | South | Yd | Yard |
| Co | County | Gall | Gallery | Mkts | Markets | Sch | School | | |
| Coll | College | Gar | Garage | Ms | Mews | Sec | Secondary | | |

## Locality abbreviations

| | | | | | |
|---|---|---|---|---|---|
| Abbots. | Abbotsinch | Deac. | Deaconsbank | Linw. | Linwood |
| Baill. | Baillieston | Dunt. | Duntocher | M. of Cam. | Milton of Campsie |
| Barr. | Barrhead | E.Kil. | East Kilbride | Millik. | Millikenpark |
| Bears. | Bearsden | Eagle. | Eaglesham | Miln. | Milngavie |
| Birk. | Birkenshaw | Elder. | Elderslie | Mood. | Moodiesburn |
| Bishop. | Bishopbriggs | Gart. | Gartcosh | Muir. | Muirhead |
| Blan. | Blantyre | Giff. | Giffnock | Neil. | Neilston |
| Both. | Bothwell | Glenb. | Glenboig | New Stev. | New Stevenston |
| Calder. | Calderbank | Glenm. | Glenmavis | New. | Newarthill |
| Camb. | Cambuslang | Green. | Greengairs | Newt. M. | Newton Mearns |
| Carm. | Carmunnock | Hous. | Houston | Old Kil. | Old Kilpatrick |
| Chap. | Chapelhall | How. | Howwood | Ruther. | Rutherglen |
| Chry. | Chryston | Inch. | Inchinnan | Thornlie. | Thornliebank |
| Clark. | Clarkston | Kilb. | Kilbarchan | Thornton. | Thorntonhall |
| Cumb. | Cumbernauld | Kirk. | Kirkintilloch | Torr. | Torrance |
| Cumb.V. | Cumbernauld Village | Lenz. | Lenzie | Udd. | Uddingston |

## Post town abbreviations

| | | | | | |
|---|---|---|---|---|---|
| Air. | Airdrie | Ersk. | Erskine | Pais. | Paisley |
| Bell. | Bellshill | Ham. | Hamilton | Renf. | Renfrew |
| Bish. | Bishopton | John. | Johnstone | Wis. | Wishaw |
| Clyde. | Clydebank | Lark. | Larkhall | | |
| Coat. | Coatbridge | Moth. | Motherwell | | |

This index contains streets that are not named on the map due to insufficient space. For each of these cases the nearest street that does appear on the map is listed in *italics*.

### A

| | | |
|---|---|---|
| Abbey Cl, Pais. PA1 | 62 | AU32 |
| Abbeycraig Rd, G34 | 72 | CM28 |
| Abbeydale Way, (Ruther.) G73 | 105 | BY42 |
| Abbey Dr, G14 | 47 | BG25 |
| Abbeygreen St, G34 | 73 | CN28 |
| Abbeyhill St, G32 | 70 | CA30 |
| Abbey Mill Business Cen, | | |
| Pais. PA1 | 82 | AV33 |
| Abbey Pl, Air. ML6 | 97 | DE33 |
| Abbey Rd, (Elder.) John. PA5 | 80 | AK35 |
| Abbey Wk, (Baill.) G69 | | |
| *off Sunnyside Dr* | 73 | CP32 |

| | | |
|---|---|---|
| Abbey Wk, Lark. ML9 | | |
| *off Carrick Pl* | 144 | DD57 |
| Abbotsburn Way, Pais. PA3 | 62 | AT29 |
| Abbotsford, (Bishop.) G64 | 33 | BY19 |
| Abbotsford Av, (Ruther.) G73 | 89 | BX38 |
| Abbotsford Av, Ham. ML3 | 125 | CR46 |
| Abbotsford Av, Lark. ML9 | 144 | DC60 |
| Abbotsford Brae, (E.Kil.) G74 | 122 | CA50 |
| Abbotsford Ct, (Cumb.) G67 | 22 | DB14 |
| Abbotsford Cres, Ham. ML3 | 125 | CR47 |
| Abbotsford Cres, Pais. PA2 | 80 | AM38 |
| Abbotsford Dr, (Kirk.) G66 | 17 | CG13 |
| Abbotsford La, Bell. ML4 | | |
| *off Cochrane St* | 110 | CV39 |

| | | |
|---|---|---|
| Abbotsford La, Ham. ML3 | 125 | CR47 |
| Abbotsford Pl, G5 | 67 | BR32 |
| Abbotsford Pl, (Cumb.) G67 | 22 | DB14 |
| Abbotsford Pl, Moth. ML1 | | |
| *off Ivy Ter* | 112 | DD40 |
| Abbotsford Rd, (Bears.) G61 | 29 | BE15 |
| Abbotsford Rd, (Cumb.) G67 | 22 | DB14 |
| Abbotsford Rd, (Chap.) Air. ML6 | 97 | DG36 |
| Abbotsford Rd, Clyde. G81 | 27 | AX20 |
| Abbotsford Rd, Ham. ML3 | 125 | CQ47 |
| Abbotshall Av, G15 | 28 | BA18 |
| Abbotsinch Retail Pk, Pais. PA3 | 62 | AV29 |
| Abbotsinch Rd, Pais. PA3 | 62 | AU27 |
| Abbotsinch Rd, Renf. PA4 | 44 | AV25 |

| Name | Pg | Ref | Name | Pg | Ref | Name | Pg | Ref |
|---|---|---|---|---|---|---|---|---|
| Abbots Ter, Air. ML6 | 97 | DE33 | Acre Valley Rd, (Torr.) G64 | 15 | BX11 | Airbles Dr, Moth. ML1 | 127 | CZ48 |
| Abbot St, G41 | | | Adam Av, Air. ML6 | 76 | DD30 | Airbles Fm Rd, Moth. ML1 | 127 | CY48 |
| off Frankfort St | 87 | BN36 | Adams Ct La, G1 | 4 | BR31 | Airbles Rd, Moth. ML1 | 127 | CZ48 |
| Abbot St, Pais. PA3 | 62 | AV31 | Adamslie Cres, (Kirk.) G66 | 16 | CC13 | Airbles St, Moth. ML1 | 128 | DA48 |
| Abbott Cres, Clyde. G81 | 45 | AZ21 | Adamslie Dr, (Kirk.) G66 | 16 | CC13 | Airdale Av, (Giff.) G46 | 102 | BL43 |
| Aberconway St, Clyde. G81 | 45 | AY21 | Adamson St, Bell. ML4 | 111 | CZ40 | Airdriehill Rd, Air. ML6 | 77 | DE27 |
| Abercorn Av, G52 | 64 | BA29 | Adams Pl, (Kilsyth) G65 | 7 | CT5 | Airdriehill St, Air. ML6 | 77 | DE27 |
| Abercorn Cres, Ham. ML3 | 140 | CU51 | Adamswell St, G21 | 50 | BU26 | Airdrie Rd, (Kilsyth) G65 | 7 | CT5 |
| Abercorn Dr, Ham. ML3 | 126 | CV50 | Adamswell Ter, (Mood.) G69 | 37 | CQ19 | Airdrie Rd, (Cumb.) G67 | 38 | CT17 |
| Abercorn Pl, G23 | 31 | BN20 | Addie St, Moth. ML1 | 128 | DB45 | Airdrie Rd, Air. ML6 | 77 | DH28 |
| Abercorn Rd, (Newt. M.) G77 | 117 | BE47 | Addiewell Pl, Coat. ML5 | 95 | CW33 | Aird's La, G1 | | |
| Abercorn St, Pais. PA3 | 62 | AV31 | Addiewell St, G32 | | | off Bridgegate | 5 | BS31 |
| Abercrombie Cres, (Baill.) G69 | 73 | CP32 | off Cardowan Rd | 70 | CC30 | Airgold Dr, G15 | 28 | BB17 |
| Abercrombie Dr, (Bears.) G61 | 10 | BD13 | Addison Gro, (Thornlie.) G46 | 101 | BH41 | Airgold Pl, G15 | 28 | BB17 |
| Abercrombie Pl, (Kilsyth) G65 | 7 | CR4 | Addison Pl, (Thornlie.) G46 | 101 | BH41 | Airlie Av, (Bears.) G61 | | |
| Abercromby Cres, (E.Kil.) G74 | 122 | CD50 | Addison Rd, G12 | 48 | BM25 | off Montrose Dr | 11 | BG14 |
| Abercromby Dr, G40 | 68 | BV31 | Addison Rd, (Thornlie.) G46 | 101 | BG41 | Airlie Dr, Bell. ML4 | 111 | CW39 |
| Abercromby Pl, (E.Kil.) G74 | 122 | CD50 | Adelaide Ct, Clyde. G81 | 26 | AT16 | Airlie Gdns, (Ruther.) G73 | 105 | BZ41 |
| Abercromby Sq, G40 | 68 | BV31 | Adelaide Rd, (E.Kil.) G75 | 135 | BX54 | Airlie La, G12 | 48 | BK25 |
| Abercromby St, G40 | 68 | BV32 | Adele St, Moth. ML1 | 128 | DB49 | Airlie Rd, (Baill.) G69 | 92 | CJ34 |
| Aberdalgie Gdns, G34 | 72 | CK29 | Adelphi St, G5 | 68 | BT32 | Airlie St, G12 | 48 | BJ26 |
| Aberdalgie Path, G34 | 72 | CK29 | Admiral St, G41 | 67 | BN32 | Airlink Ind Est, Pais. PA3 | 62 | AU29 |
| Aberdalgie Rd, G34 | 72 | CK29 | Admiralty Gdns, (Old Kil.) G60 | 25 | AR16 | Airlour Rd, G43 | 103 | BN40 |
| Aberdeen Rd, Air. ML6 | | | Admiralty Gro, (Old Kil.) G60 | 25 | AR16 | Airth Ct, Moth. ML1 | 111 | CZ44 |
| off Stirling Rd | 97 | DF33 | Admiralty Pl, (Old Kil.) G60 | 25 | AR16 | Airth Dr, G52 | 85 | BH34 |
| Aberdour St, G31 | 69 | BY30 | Advie Pl, G42 | 87 | BR37 | Airth La, G52 | | |
| Aberfeldy Av, (Plains) Air. ML6 | 59 | DH26 | Affric Dr, Pais. PA2 | 83 | AX36 | off Mosspark Dr | 85 | BH34 |
| Aberfeldy St, G31 | 69 | BY30 | Afton Cres, (Bears.) G61 | 30 | BK18 | Airth Pl, G52 | | |
| Aberfoyle St, G31 | 69 | BY30 | Afton Dr, Renf. PA4 | 64 | BA27 | off Mosspark Dr | 85 | BH34 |
| Aberlady Rd, G51 | 65 | BG30 | Afton Gdns, (Blan.) G72 | 124 | CK47 | Airthrey Av, G14 | 47 | BG26 |
| Abernethy Dr, (Linw.) Pais. PA3 | 60 | AJ32 | Afton Gdns, Coat. ML5 | 95 | CZ33 | Airthrey La, G14 | | |
| Abernethy Pk, (E.Kil.) G74 | 135 | BZ51 | Afton Rd, (Cumb.) G67 | 22 | DD10 | off Airthrey Av | 47 | BG25 |
| Abernethy Pl, (Newt. M.) G77 | 118 | BK49 | Afton St, G41 | 87 | BN37 | Airth Way, (Cumb.) G68 | 20 | CU13 |
| Abernethy St, G31 | 69 | BY30 | Afton St, Lark. ML9 | 145 | DE59 | Airyligg Dr, (Eagle.) G76 | 133 | BN56 |
| Aberuthven Dr, G32 | 90 | CD34 | Afton Vw, (Kirk.) G66 | 17 | CH12 | Aitchison Ct, Air. ML6 | 76 | DB29 |
| Abigail Pl, (Blan.) G72 | 108 | CM44 | Agamemnon St, Clyde. G81 | 26 | AV19 | Aitchison St, Air. ML6 | 76 | DA30 |
| Aboukir St, G51 | 65 | BG29 | Agate Ter, Bell. ML4 | 111 | CW41 | Aitkenhead Av, Coat. ML5 | 93 | CR33 |
| Aboyne Dr, Pais. PA2 | 82 | AV36 | Agnew Av, Air. ML6 | 75 | CY30 | Aitkenhead Rd, (Udd.) G71 | 93 | CQ36 |
| Aboyne St, G51 | 65 | BH31 | Agnew Av, Coat. ML5 | 75 | CY30 | Aitkenhead Rd, (Chap.) Air. | | |
| Acacia Dr, (Barr.) G78 | 99 | AW40 | Agnew Gro, Bell. ML4 | 110 | CT40 | ML6 | 97 | DF35 |
| Acacia Dr, Pais. PA2 | 81 | AR36 | Agnew La, G42 | 87 | BQ36 | Aitken Rd, Ham. ML3 | 140 | CU54 |
| Acacia Pl, John. PA5 | 80 | AJ37 | Aidans Brae, (Clark.) G76 | 119 | BN46 | Aitken St, G31 | 69 | BY30 |
| Acacia Way, (Camb.) G72 | 107 | CG40 | Aigas Cotts, G13 | | | Aitken St, Air. ML6 | 76 | DD28 |
| Academy Ct, Coat. ML5 | | | off Fern La | 47 | BH24 | Alasdair Ct, (Barr.) G78 | 99 | AY43 |
| off Academy St | 75 | CW30 | Aikenhead Rd, G42 | 87 | BR34 | Albans Cres, Moth. ML1 | 127 | CX45 |
| Academy Pk, G51 | 86 | BL33 | Aikenhead Rd, G44 | 104 | BS39 | Albany, (E.Kil.) G74 | 123 | CE49 |
| Academy Pk, Air. ML6 | 76 | DC30 | Aikman Pl, (E.Kil.) G74 | 122 | CD50 | Albany Av, G32 | 71 | CE31 |
| Academy Pl, Coat. ML5 | | | Aikman Rd, Moth. ML1 | 127 | CX48 | Albany Cotts, G13 | | |
| off Baird St | 75 | CW30 | Ailean Dr, G32 | 91 | CG33 | off Fern La | 47 | BH24 |
| Academy Rd, (Giff.) G46 | 102 | BL43 | Ailean Gdns, G32 | 91 | CG33 | Albany Cres, Moth. ML1 | | |
| Academy St, G32 | 90 | CD33 | Aillort Pl, (E.Kil.) G74 | 122 | CA50 | off Thankerton Av | 112 | DB40 |
| Academy St, Air. ML6 | 76 | DC30 | Ailort Av, G44 | | | Albany Dr, (Ruther.) G73 | 105 | BX39 |
| Academy St, Coat. ML5 | 75 | CW30 | off Lochinver Dr | 103 | BQ40 | Albany Pl, (Both.) G71 | | |
| Academy St, Lark. ML9 | 144 | DC58 | Ailsa Av, (Ashgill) Lark. ML9 | 145 | DH61 | off Marguerite Gdns | 109 | CR43 |
| Academy Ter, Bell. ML4 | 111 | CX40 | Ailsa Av, Moth. ML1 | 127 | CX46 | Albany Quad, G32 | 71 | CE31 |
| Acer Cres, Pais. PA2 | 81 | AQ36 | Ailsa Ct, Coat. ML5 | 94 | CU33 | Albany Rd, Ham. ML3 | | |
| Acer Gro, (Chap.) Air. ML6 | 97 | DG34 | Ailsa Ct, Ham. ML3 | 138 | CM52 | off Annsfield Rd | 140 | CS53 |
| Achamore Cres, G15 | 28 | BA17 | Ailsa Cres, Moth. ML1 | 127 | CX46 | Albany St, G40 | 89 | BW33 |
| Achamore Dr, G15 | 28 | BA17 | Ailsa Dr, G42 | 87 | BP38 | Albany St, Coat. ML5 | 74 | CU30 |
| Achamore Rd, G15 | 28 | BA17 | Ailsa Dr, (Giff.) G46 | 118 | BK45 | Albany Ter, (Camb.) G72 | 106 | CA42 |
| Achray Dr, Pais. PA2 | 81 | AQ36 | Ailsa Dr, (Kirk.) G66 | 17 | CH11 | Albany Way, Pais. PA3 | | |
| Achray Pl, (Miln.) G62 | 11 | BF10 | Ailsa Dr, (Both.) G71 | 109 | CQ41 | off Abbotsburn Way | 62 | AU29 |
| Achray Pl, Coat. ML5 | 74 | CS28 | Ailsa Dr, (Ruther.) G73 | 104 | BV40 | Albany Wynd, Lark. ML9 | | |
| Achray Rd, (Cumb.) G67 | 21 | CX14 | Ailsa Dr, Clyde. G81 | 27 | AX15 | off Duncan Graham St | 144 | DD57 |
| Acorn Ct, G40 | 88 | BV33 | Ailsa Dr, Pais. PA2 | 82 | AT38 | Alba Way, Ham. ML3 | 140 | CS55 |
| Acorn St, G40 | 88 | BV33 | Ailsa Pl, Coat. ML5 | 94 | CV33 | Alberta Av, (E.Kil.) G75 | 135 | BX53 |
| Acre Dr, G20 | 30 | BK20 | Ailsa Rd, (Bishop.) G64 | 33 | BX19 | Alberta Av, Coat. ML5 | 74 | CV29 |
| Acredyke Cres, G21 | 51 | BY22 | Ailsa Rd, Coat. ML5 | 94 | CU33 | Alberta Cres, (E.Kil.) G75 | | |
| Acredyke Pl, G21 | 51 | BY23 | Ailsa Rd, Renf. PA4 | 63 | AY27 | off Alberta Av | 135 | BY53 |
| Acredyke Rd, G21 | 51 | BX22 | Ainslie Av, G52 | 64 | BC29 | Alberta Pk, (E.Kil.) G75 | 135 | BZ53 |
| Acredyke Rd, (Ruther.) G73 | 88 | BV37 | Ainslie Rd, G52 | 64 | BC29 | Alberta Pl, (E.Kil.) G75 | | |
| Acre Rd, G20 | 30 | BK20 | Ainslie Rd, (Cumb.) G67 | 23 | DE10 | off Alberta Av | 135 | BZ53 |
| Acres, The, Lark. ML9 | 144 | DD59 | Airbles Cres, Moth. ML1 | 127 | CZ48 | Albert Av, G42 | 87 | BP36 |

| | | | |
|---|---|---|---|
| Albert Br, G1 | 68 | BS32 | |
| Albert Br, G5 | 68 | BS32 | |
| Albert Cres, Air. ML6 | 76 | DD30 | |
| Albert Cross, G41 | 87 | BP34 | |
| Albert Dr, G41 | 86 | BL35 | |
| Albert Dr, (Bears.) G61 | 30 | BK18 | |
| Albert Dr, (Ruther.) G73 | 105 | BX40 | |
| Albert La, Lark. ML9 | 144 | DD59 | |
| Albert La, Ham. ML3 | 125 | CQ47 | |
| Albert Pl, Air. ML6 | 76 | DD29 | |
| Albert Quad, Moth. ML1 | | | |
| _off Sherry Av_ | 112 | DC40 | |
| Albert Rd, G42 | 87 | BQ36 | |
| Albert Rd, (Lenz.) G66 | 35 | CE18 | |
| Albert Rd, Clyde. G81 | 27 | AW18 | |
| Albert Rd, Renf. PA4 | 45 | AY26 | |
| Albert St, Coat. ML5 | 75 | CW30 | |
| Albert St, Ham. ML3 | 125 | CR47 | |
| Albert St, Moth. ML1 | 128 | DB46 | |
| Albert Ter, Ham. ML3 | 125 | CQ47 | |
| Albion Gate, G1 | | | |
| _off Albion St_ | 5 | BT30 | |
| Albion Gate, Pais. PA3 | 62 | AT31 | |
| Albion St, G1 | 5 | BT31 | |
| Albion St, (Baill.) G69 | 91 | CH34 | |
| Albion St, Coat. ML5 | 75 | CX30 | |
| Albion St, Moth. ML1 | 128 | DA48 | |
| Albion St, Pais. PA3 | 62 | AT31 | |
| Albion Way, (E.Kil.) G75 | 136 | CB56 | |
| Albion Wks Ind Est, G13 | 46 | BA22 | |
| Alcaig Rd, G52 | 85 | BG35 | |
| Alder Av, (Kirk.) G66 | 34 | CD16 | |
| Alder Av, Ham. ML3 | 140 | CU52 | |
| Alder Bk, (Udd.) G71 | 94 | CS36 | |
| Alder Ct, (E.Kil.) G75 | 135 | BY56 | |
| Alder Ct, (Barr.) G78 | 99 | AY44 | |
| Alder Cres, (E.Kil.) G75 | 135 | BY56 | |
| Alder Gate, (Camb.) G72 | 107 | CG40 | |
| Alder Gro, Coat. ML5 | 75 | CX31 | |
| Alder La, (Holytown) Moth. ML1 | | | |
| _off Elm Rd_ | 113 | DE40 | |
| Alder La, (New Stev.) Moth. ML1 | | | |
| _off Jerviston St_ | 112 | DC42 | |
| Alderman Pl, G13 | 47 | BE23 | |
| Alderman Rd, G13 | 46 | BB21 | |
| Alder Pl, G43 | 102 | BK40 | |
| Alder Pl, (E.Kil.) G75 | 135 | BY56 | |
| Alder Pl, John. PA5 | 80 | AJ36 | |
| Alder Rd, G43 | 102 | BL40 | |
| Alder Rd, (Cumb.) G67 | 23 | DF11 | |
| Alder Rd, Clyde. G81 | 26 | AV16 | |
| Alderside Pl, (Both.) G71 | | | |
| _off Churchill Cres_ | 109 | CR42 | |
| Alderstocks, (E.Kil.) G75 | 136 | CA56 | |
| Alderston Pl, Bell. ML4 | 110 | CU41 | |
| Alderston Way, | | | |
| (Righead Ind. Est.) Bell. ML4 | 110 | CU39 | |
| Aldersyde Av, Wis. ML2 | 129 | DF49 | |
| Aldersyde Gdns, (Udd.) G71 | 93 | CN38 | |
| Aldersyde Pl, (Blan.) G72 | 108 | CL44 | |
| Alexander Av, (Kilsyth) G65 | 19 | CN9 | |
| Alexander Av, (Udd.) G71 | 110 | CS39 | |
| Alexander Av, (Eagle.) G76 | 133 | BN55 | |
| Alexander Balfour Gdns, | | | |
| Ham. ML3 _off Morris St_ | 140 | CT52 | |
| Alexander Cres, G5 | 88 | BS33 | |
| Alexander Gdns, Ham. ML3 | 141 | CW51 | |
| Alexander Gibson Way, | | | |
| Moth. ML1 | 127 | CZ47 | |
| Alexander Path, Moth. ML1 | 128 | DD50 | |
| Alexander Pl, (Kirk.) G66 | 18 | CK14 | |
| Alexander St, Air. ML6 | 76 | DA30 | |
| Alexander St, Clyde. G81 | 27 | AX20 | |
| Alexander St, Coat. ML5 | 75 | CX29 | |
| Alexander St, Wis. ML2 | 129 | DH50 | |
| Alexander Ter, (Neil.) G78 | 114 | AS47 | |
| Alexandra Av, (Stepps) G33 | 53 | CF23 | |
| Alexandra Av, (Lenz.) G66 | 35 | CE17 | |
| Alexandra Ct, G31 | 69 | BX29 | |
| Alexandra Cross, G31 | 69 | BX30 | |
| Alexandra Dr, Pais. PA2 | 81 | AR34 | |
| Alexandra Dr, Renf. PA4 | 45 | AZ26 | |
| Alexandra Gdns, (Kirk.) G66 | 35 | CE17 | |
| Alexandra Gate, G31 | 69 | BW29 | |
| Alexandra Par, G31 | 5 | BU29 | |
| Alexandra Pk, (Kirk.) G66 | 35 | CE17 | |
| Alexandra Pk St, G31 | 69 | BX30 | |
| Alexandra Rd, (Lenz.) G66 | 35 | CE17 | |
| Alexandra St, (Kirk.) G66 | 17 | CE13 | |
| Alexandria Quad, Moth. ML1 | | | |
| _off Main St_ | 112 | DC40 | |
| Alford Av, (Kirk.) G66 | 16 | CD13 | |
| Alford St, G21 | 50 | BT26 | |
| Alfred La, G12 | 48 | BM26 | |
| Alfred Ter, G12 | 49 | BN26 | |
| Algie St, G41 | 87 | BP37 | |
| Algoma Pl, (E.Kil.) G75 | | | |
| _off Winnipeg Dr_ | 135 | BX53 | |
| Alice Av, Bell. ML4 | 111 | CW41 | |
| Alice St, Pais. PA2 | 82 | AU35 | |
| Aline Ct, (Barr.) G78 | | | |
| _off Lomond Dr_ | 99 | AX41 | |
| Alisa Rd, Clyde. G81 | 45 | AX21 | |
| Alison Lea, (E.Kil.) G74 | 122 | CD50 | |
| Allan Av, Renf. PA4 | 64 | BA28 | |
| Allan Ct, (E.Kil.) G75 | 134 | BU54 | |
| Allandale Av, Moth. ML1 | 113 | DH40 | |
| Allandale Path, (Blan.) G72 | | | |
| _off Winton Cres_ | 124 | CM46 | |
| Allander Av, (Miln.) G62 | 13 | BQ14 | |
| Allander Dr, (Torr.) G64 | 15 | BW13 | |
| Allander Gdns, (Bishop.) G64 | 32 | BV17 | |
| Allander Rd, (Bears.) G61 | 29 | BF18 | |
| Allander Rd, (Miln.) G62 | 12 | BJ11 | |
| Allander St, G22 | 50 | BS25 | |
| Allander Wk, (Cumb.) G67 | | | |
| _off Cumbernauld Shop Cen_ | 22 | DB12 | |
| Allan Dr, (E.Kil.) G75 | 134 | BU54 | |
| Allands Av, (Inch.) Renf. PA4 | 44 | AS24 | |
| Allanfauld Rd, (Kilsyth) G65 | 7 | CT3 | |
| Allanfauld Rd, (Cumb.) G67 | 22 | DB11 | |
| Allan Glen Gdns, (Bishop.) G64 | 33 | BX17 | |
| Allan Glen Pl, G4 | 5 | BT29 | |
| Allan Pl, G40 | 89 | BX34 | |
| Allanshaw Gdns, Ham. ML3 | 125 | CR50 | |
| Allanshaw Gro, Ham. ML3 | | | |
| _off Allanshaw Gdns_ | 139 | CR51 | |
| Allanshaw Ind Est, Ham. ML3 | 126 | CS50 | |
| Allanshaw St, Ham. ML3 | 126 | CS50 | |
| Allan St, G40 | 89 | BX35 | |
| Allan St, Coat. ML5 | 74 | CT32 | |
| Allan St, Moth. ML1 | 128 | DB46 | |
| Allanton Av, Pais. PA1 | 84 | BA33 | |
| Allanton Dr, G52 | 64 | BD32 | |
| Allanton Lea, Ham. ML3 | 140 | CS53 | |
| Allendale, (E.Kil.) G74 | 135 | BY51 | |
| Allen Way, Renf. PA4 | 63 | AZ28 | |
| Allerdyce Ct, G15 | 28 | BA20 | |
| Allerdyce Dr, G15 | 28 | BB20 | |
| Allerdyce Rd, G15 | 28 | BB20 | |
| Allershaw Pl, Wis. ML2 | 143 | DH53 | |
| Allershaw Rd, Wis. ML2 | 143 | DH53 | |
| Allerton Gdns, (Baill.) G69 | 91 | CH33 | |
| Alleysbank Rd, (Ruther.) G73 | 89 | BX36 | |
| Allison Av, Ersk. PA8 | 25 | AP19 | |
| Allison Dr, (Camb.) G72 | 106 | CC39 | |
| Allison Pl, G42 | | | |
| _off Prince Edward St_ | 87 | BQ35 | |
| Allison Pl, (Gart.) G69 | 55 | CN25 | |
| Allison Pl, (Newt. M.) G77 | 117 | BE49 | |
| Allison St, G42 | 87 | BQ35 | |
| Allnach Pl, G34 | 73 | CN29 | |
| Alloway Av, Pais. PA2 | 83 | AX37 | |
| Alloway Ct, (Kirk.) G66 | 17 | CH11 | |
| Alloway Cres, (Ruther.) G73 | 104 | BV40 | |
| Alloway Cres, Pais. PA2 | 83 | AX37 | |
| Alloway Dr, (Kirk.) G66 | 17 | CH12 | |
| Alloway Dr, (Ruther.) G73 | 104 | BV40 | |
| Alloway Dr, (Newt. M.) G77 | 118 | BJ49 | |
| Alloway Dr, Clyde. G81 | 27 | AY18 | |
| Alloway Dr, Pais. PA2 | 83 | AX37 | |
| Alloway Gdns, (Kirk.) G66 | 18 | CJ11 | |
| Alloway Gdns, Ham. ML3 | 138 | CM52 | |
| Alloway Gro, (Kirk.) G66 | 17 | CH11 | |
| Alloway Gro, Pais. PA2 | 83 | AY37 | |
| Alloway Quad, (Kirk.) G66 | 18 | CJ12 | |
| Alloway Rd, G43 | 102 | BM39 | |
| Alloway Rd, (E.Kil.) G74 | 123 | CG50 | |
| Alloway Rd, Air. ML6 | 77 | DH29 | |
| Alloway St, Lark. ML9 | 145 | DE59 | |
| Alloway Ter, (Kirk.) G66 | 17 | CH11 | |
| Alloway Wynd, Moth. ML1 | | | |
| _off Kirkoswald Rd_ | 113 | DG41 | |
| Almada Gro, Ham. ML3 | | | |
| _off Almada La_ | 126 | CT49 | |
| Almada La, Ham. ML3 | 126 | CT49 | |
| Almada St, Ham. ML3 | 126 | CS49 | |
| Alma St, G40 | 69 | BW32 | |
| Almond Av, Renf. PA4 | 64 | BA27 | |
| Almond Bk, (Bears.) G61 | 29 | BE19 | |
| Almondbank, (Plains) Air. ML6 | | | |
| _off Arondale Rd_ | 59 | DH26 | |
| Almond Cres, Pais. PA2 | 81 | AP35 | |
| Almond Dr, (Kirk.) G66 | 34 | CD16 | |
| Almond Dr, (E.Kil.) G74 | 136 | CD52 | |
| Almond Dr, Bish. PA7 | 24 | AK19 | |
| Almond Pl, Coat. ML5 | 74 | CT28 | |
| Almond Pl, Moth. ML1 | | | |
| _off Cuckoo Way_ | 112 | DD40 | |
| Almond Rd, G33 | 53 | CE24 | |
| Almond Rd, (Bears.) G61 | 29 | BF19 | |
| Almond St, G33 | 69 | BZ28 | |
| Almond Vale, (Udd.) G71 | | | |
| _off Hamilton Vw_ | 93 | CQ38 | |
| Almond Way, Moth. ML1 | | | |
| _off Ferguson Dr_ | 128 | DA50 | |
| Alness Cres, G52 | 85 | BF34 | |
| Alness St, Ham. ML3 | 140 | CT52 | |
| Alness Ter, Ham. ML3 | 140 | CT51 | |
| Aloa Way, Lark. ML9 | | | |
| _off Blair Atholl Dr_ | 145 | DE60 | |
| Alpine Gro, (Udd.) G71 | 93 | CP38 | |
| Alsatian Av, Clyde. G81 | 27 | AZ19 | |
| Alsh Ter, Ham. ML3 | 139 | CQ52 | |
| Alston Av, Coat. ML5 | 75 | CX29 | |
| Alston Gdns, (Bears.) G61 | 10 | BD13 | |
| Alston La, G40 | | | |
| _off Claythorn St_ | 5 | BU31 | |
| Altnacreag Gdns, (Mood.) G69 | 37 | CQ18 | |
| Alton Rd, Pais. PA1 | 83 | AY33 | |
| Altpatrick Gdns, (Elder.) | | | |
| John. PA5 | 80 | AK34 | |
| Altyre St, G32 | 90 | CB34 | |
| Alva Gdns, G52 | 85 | BG35 | |
| Alva Gdns, (Bears.) G61 | 11 | BF13 | |
| Alva Gate, G52 | 85 | BG34 | |
| Alva Pl, (Lenz.) G66 | 35 | CG17 | |
| Alwyn Ct, (E.Kil.) G74 | 122 | CA50 | |

| Name | Page | Grid |
|---|---|---|
| Alwyn Dr, (E.Kil.) G74 | 122 | CA50 |
| Alyssum Cres, Moth. ML1 | 127 | CZ45 |
| Alyth Cres, (Clark.) G76 | 119 | BQ45 |
| Alyth Gdns, G52 | 85 | BG34 |
| Alyth Gdns, (Clark.) G76 | 119 | BQ45 |
| Ambassador Way, Renf. PA4 | | |
| *off Cockels Ln* | 63 | AZ28 |
| Amber Ter, Bell. ML4 | 111 | CW41 |
| Ambleside, (E.Kil.) G75 | 134 | BV55 |
| Ambleside Ri, Ham. ML3 | 140 | CS55 |
| Amethyst Av, Bell. ML4 | 111 | CW41 |
| Amisfield St, G20 | 49 | BN24 |
| Amochrie Dr, Pais. PA2 | 81 | AQ37 |
| Amochrie Glen, Pais. PA2 | 81 | AQ37 |
| Amochrie Rd, Pais. PA2 | 81 | AP37 |
| Amochrie Way, Pais. PA2 | 81 | AP36 |
| Amulree Pl, G32 | 90 | CC33 |
| Amulree St, G32 | 70 | CD32 |
| Ancaster Dr, G13 | 47 | BH23 |
| Ancaster La, G13 | | |
| *off Great Western Rd* | 47 | BH23 |
| Anchor Av, Pais. PA1 | 83 | AW33 |
| Anchor Cres, Pais. PA1 | 83 | AW34 |
| Anchor Dr, Pais. PA1 | 83 | AW33 |
| Anchor La, G1 | | |
| *off St. Vincent Pl* | 5 | BS30 |
| Anchor Wynd, Pais. PA1 | 83 | AW34 |
| Ancroft St, G20 | 49 | BQ26 |
| Ancrum St, G32 | 70 | CD32 |
| Andersen Ct, (E.Kil.) G75 | 136 | CA55 |
| Anderside, (E.Kil.) G75 | 136 | CA56 |
| Anderson Av, (Kilsyth) G65 | 7 | CR4 |
| Anderson Ct, Bell. ML4 | 111 | CX40 |
| Anderson Cres, (Kilsyth) G65 | 6 | CN5 |
| Anderson Dr, (Newt. M.) G77 | 117 | BE49 |
| Anderson Dr, Renf. PA4 | 45 | AZ25 |
| Anderson Gdns, (Blan.) G72 | | |
| *off Station Rd* | 109 | CN44 |
| Anderson La, Air. ML6 | | |
| *off Chapel St* | 76 | DC29 |
| Anderson St, G11 | 66 | BK27 |
| Anderson St, Air. ML6 | 76 | DC29 |
| Anderson St, Ham. ML3 | 125 | CP48 |
| Anderson St, Moth. ML1 | 128 | DA48 |
| Anderston Cross Cen, G2 | 4 | BQ30 |
| Anderston Quay, G3 | 4 | BP31 |
| Andrew Av, (Lenz.) G66 | 35 | CF18 |
| Andrew Av, Renf. PA4 | 46 | BA26 |
| Andrew Dr, Clyde. G81 | 45 | AY21 |
| Andrew Patton Way, Ham. ML3 | 125 | CQ47 |
| Andrew Sillars Av, (Camb.) G72 | 106 | CD40 |
| Andrews St, Pais. PA3 | 62 | AT31 |
| Andrew St, (E.Kil.) G74 | 136 | CB52 |
| Anford Pl, (Blan.) G72 | 125 | CN47 |
| Angela Way, (Udd.) G71 | 109 | CP39 |
| Angle Gate, G14 | 47 | BF25 |
| Angus Av, G52 | 84 | BD33 |
| Angus Av, (Bishop.) G64 | 51 | BY21 |
| Angus Av, (E.Kil.) G74 | 136 | CD51 |
| Angus Av, Air. ML6 | 76 | DC32 |
| Angus Av, Ham. ML3 | 127 | CW50 |
| Angus Av, Moth. ML1 | 127 | CY45 |
| Angus Gdns, (Udd.) G71 | 93 | CP37 |
| Angus La, (Bishop.) G64 | 33 | BZ20 |
| Angus Oval, G52 | 84 | BD33 |
| Angus Pl, G52 | 84 | BD33 |
| Angus Pl, (E.Kil.) G74 | 136 | CD51 |
| Angus St, G21 | 50 | BU25 |
| Angus St, Clyde. G81 | 46 | BA21 |
| Angus Wk, (Udd.) G71 | 93 | CR38 |
| Anish Pl, G15 | 28 | BA17 |
| Annan Av, (E.Kil.) G75 | 134 | BU54 |
| Annan Ct, Coat. ML5 | | |
| *off Kirk St* | 74 | CV31 |
| Annan Cres, (Chap.) Air. ML6 | | |
| *off Callander Rd* | 97 | DF36 |
| Annandale, (Green.) Air. ML6 | 41 | DH19 |
| Annandale St, G42 | 87 | BR34 |
| Annandale Ter, (Old Kil.) G60 | | |
| *off Dalnottar Av* | 26 | AS15 |
| Annan Dr, (Bears.) G61 | 29 | BE18 |
| Annan Dr, (Ruther.) G73 | 89 | BZ38 |
| Annan Glade, Moth. ML1 | 128 | DC50 |
| Annan Gro, Moth. ML1 | 128 | DC50 |
| Annan Pl, John. PA5 | 79 | AE37 |
| Annan St, Moth. ML1 | 128 | DC49 |
| Annan Way, (Cumb.) G67 | | |
| *off Cumbernauld Shop Cen* | 22 | DB12 |
| Annathill Gdns, (Annathill) Coat. ML5 | 38 | CU19 |
| Annbank Pl, G31 | 68 | BV31 |
| Annbank St, G31 | 68 | BV31 |
| Annbank St, Lark. ML9 | 144 | DB58 |
| Ann Ct, Ham. ML3 | 125 | CQ48 |
| Anne Av, Renf. PA4 | 45 | AZ25 |
| Anne Cres, (Lenz.) G66 | 35 | CF18 |
| Annerley Ct, Coat. ML5 | | |
| *off Torriden Pl* | 74 | CU32 |
| Annerley Pl, Coat. ML5 | 74 | CU32 |
| Annette St, G42 | 87 | BQ35 |
| Annfield Gdns, (Blan.) G72 | 108 | CK44 |
| Annfield Pl, G31 | 68 | BV30 |
| Annick Dr, (Bears.) G61 | 29 | BE18 |
| Annick Ind Est, G32 | 71 | CE32 |
| Annick St, G32 | 70 | CD32 |
| Annick St, (Camb.) G72 | 107 | CF40 |
| Anniesdale Av, (Stepps) G33 | 53 | CF23 |
| Anniesland Cres, G14 | 46 | BC24 |
| Anniesland Ind Est, G13 | 47 | BG21 |
| Anniesland Mans, G13 | | |
| *off Ancaster Dr* | 47 | BH23 |
| Anniesland Rd, G13 | 46 | BD24 |
| Anniesland Rd, G14 | 46 | BC24 |
| Annieston, (Kilsyth) G65 | 19 | CP9 |
| Anniversary Av, (E.Kil.) G75 | 135 | BY54 |
| Annsfield Rd, Ham. ML3 | 140 | CS54 |
| Ann St, Ham. ML3 | 125 | CQ48 |
| Ansdell Av, (Blan.) G72 | 124 | CL46 |
| Anson St, G40 | 88 | BV33 |
| Anson Way, Renf. PA4 | | |
| *off Britannia Way* | 63 | AY28 |
| Anstruther St, G32 | 90 | CB33 |
| Anthony St, G2 | 4 | BQ30 |
| Antigua Way, (E.Kil.) G75 | | |
| *off Leeward Circle* | 135 | BW52 |
| Anton Cres, (Kilsyth) G65 | 7 | CU5 |
| Antonine, (Kirk.) G66 | 18 | CK11 |
| Antonine Av, Moth. ML1 | 127 | CY45 |
| Antonine Gdns, Clyde. G81 | 27 | AW15 |
| Antonine Rd, (Bears.) G61 | 28 | BD15 |
| Antonine Rd, (Dullatur) G68 | 9 | CZ7 |
| Antonine Rd, The, G15 | 28 | BA18 |
| Antrim La, Lark. ML9 | | |
| *off Roselea St* | 144 | DD57 |
| Anwoth St, G32 | 90 | CC34 |
| Apartments, The, (Giff.) G46 | | |
| *off Milverton Rd* | 102 | BK44 |
| Apollo Path, Moth. ML1 | | |
| *off Maple Rd* | 112 | DD40 |
| Appin Ct, (Kirk.) G66 | | |
| *off Moray Pl* | 18 | CK12 |
| Appin Cres, G31 | 69 | BX30 |
| Appin Rd, G31 | 69 | BX30 |
| Appin Ter, (Ruther.) G73 | 105 | BZ41 |
| Appin Ter, Ham. ML3 | 125 | CN49 |
| Appin Way, (Both.) G71 | | |
| *off Bracken Ter* | 109 | CQ42 |
| Appin Way, (Glenm.) Air. ML6 | 58 | DA25 |
| Appin Way, Coat. ML5 | 94 | CU33 |
| Appleby Cl, (E.Kil.) G75 | 134 | BV55 |
| Appleby St, G22 | 49 | BR26 |
| Applecross Gdns, (Mood.) G69 | 37 | CP18 |
| Applecross Rd, (Kirk.) G66 | 18 | CK12 |
| Applecross St, G4 | 49 | BR26 |
| Appledore Cres, (Both.) G71 | 109 | CQ42 |
| Apple Way, (E.Kil.) G75 | 136 | CB55 |
| Appleyard Ct, Bell. ML4 | | |
| *off Busby Rd* | 110 | CV42 |
| Apsley La, G11 | | |
| *off Apsley St* | 66 | BJ27 |
| Apsley St, G11 | 66 | BJ27 |
| Aqua Av, Ham. ML3 | 139 | CN51 |
| Aqua Ct, Ham. ML3 | | |
| *off Aqua Av* | 139 | CN51 |
| Araburn Dr, (E.Kil.) G75 | 136 | CA56 |
| Aranthrue Cres, Renf. PA4 | 45 | AY25 |
| Aranthrue Dr, Renf. PA4 | | |
| *off Aranthrue Cres* | 45 | AY25 |
| Aray St, G20 | 48 | BM22 |
| Arbroath Av, G52 | 84 | BD33 |
| Arbroath Gro, Ham. ML3 | 139 | CR51 |
| Arcadia Pl, G40 | 68 | BU32 |
| Arcadia St, G40 | 68 | BU32 |
| Arcadia St, Bell. ML4 | | |
| *off Primrose Av* | 95 | CW38 |
| Arcan Cres, G15 | 28 | BD19 |
| Archamore Gdns, G15 | 28 | BA17 |
| Archerfield Av, G32 | 90 | CC35 |
| Archerfield Cres, G32 | 90 | CC35 |
| Archerfield Dr, G32 | 90 | CC35 |
| Archerfield Gro, G32 | 90 | CC35 |
| Archerhill Av, G13 | 46 | BC21 |
| Archerhill Cotts, G13 | 46 | BC21 |
| Archerhill Cres, G13 | 46 | BD21 |
| Archerhill Gdns, G13 | 46 | BC21 |
| Archerhill Rd, G13 | 46 | BC21 |
| Archerhill Sq, G13 | 46 | BB21 |
| Archerhill Ter, G13 | 46 | BC21 |
| Archibald Pl, Bell. ML4 | 111 | CZ41 |
| Arch Way, (Kilsyth) G65 | 7 | CT4 |
| Ardargie Dr, G32 | 91 | CE37 |
| Ardargie Gro, G32 | | |
| *off Ardargie Dr* | 91 | CE37 |
| Ardargie Pl, G32 | | |
| *off Ardargie Dr* | 91 | CE37 |
| Ardbeg Av, (Bishop.) G64 | 33 | BY20 |
| Ardbeg Av, (Ruther.) G73 | 106 | CA42 |
| Ardbeg La, G42 | 87 | BQ35 |
| Ardbeg Rd, (Carfin) Moth. ML1 | 112 | DD44 |
| Ardbeg St, G42 | 87 | BQ35 |
| Ardconnel St, (Thornlie.) G46 | 101 | BH41 |
| Arden Av, (Thornlie.) G46 | 101 | BG43 |
| Ardenclutha Av, Ham. ML3 | 125 | CR49 |
| Arden Ct, Air. ML6 | | |
| *off Monkscourt Av* | 75 | CZ29 |
| Arden Ct, Ham. ML3 | 140 | CT52 |
| Ardencraig Dr, G45 | 104 | BV43 |
| Ardencraig Gdns, G51 | 105 | BW43 |
| Ardencraig Pl, G45 | 104 | BU42 |
| Ardencraig Quad, G45 | 104 | BV43 |
| Ardencraig Rd, G45 | 104 | BS44 |
| Ardencraig St, G45 | 105 | BW42 |
| Ardencraig Ter, G45 | 104 | BV43 |
| Arden Dr, (Giff.) G46 | 102 | BK43 |
| Arden Gro, (Kilsyth) G65 | 7 | CS3 |
| Ardenlea, (Udd.) G71 | 93 | CP38 |

| Name | Page | Grid |
|---|---|---|
| Ardenlea St, G40 | 89 | BX34 |
| Arden Pl, (Thornlie.) G46 | 101 | BG43 |
| Arden Rd, Ham. ML3 | 140 | CS51 |
| Arden Ter, Ham. ML3 | 140 | CS51 |
| Ardery St, G11 | | |
| off Apsley St | 66 | BJ27 |
| Ardessie Pl, G20 | 48 | BM24 |
| Ardessie St, G23 | | |
| off Torrin Rd | 30 | BM20 |
| Ardfern Rd, Air. ML6 | 77 | DH31 |
| Ardfern St, G32 | 90 | CC34 |
| Ardgay Pl, G32 | 90 | CC33 |
| Ardgay St, G32 | 90 | CC33 |
| Ardgay Way, (Ruther.) G73 | 105 | BX42 |
| Ardgoil Dr, (Cumb.) G68 | 20 | CV12 |
| Ardgour Ct, (Blan.) G72 | | |
| off Ballantrae Rd | 125 | CP47 |
| Ardgour Dr, (Linw.) Pais. PA3 | 60 | AJ32 |
| Ardgour Par, Moth. ML1 | 113 | DE43 |
| Ardgowan Av, Pais. PA2 | 82 | AV34 |
| Ardgowan Ct, Pais. PA2 | | |
| off Cartha Cres | 83 | AX34 |
| Ardgowan Dr, (Udd.) G71 | 93 | CP38 |
| Ardgowan St, Pais. PA2 | 82 | AV35 |
| Ardholm St, G32 | 70 | CC32 |
| Ardhu Pl, G15 | 28 | BC17 |
| Ardlamont Sq, (Linw.) | | |
| Pais. PA3 | 60 | AL32 |
| Ardlaw St, G51 | 65 | BH31 |
| Ardle Rd, G43 | 103 | BN40 |
| Ard Ln, Moth. ML1 | | |
| off Howden Pl | 112 | DC40 |
| Ardlui Gdns, (Miln.) G62 | 11 | BF10 |
| Ardlui St, G32 | 90 | CB33 |
| Ardmaleish Cres, G45 | 104 | BU43 |
| Ardmaleish Dr, G45 | 104 | BT43 |
| Ardmaleish Rd, G45 | 104 | BT43 |
| Ardmaleish St, G45 | 104 | BT43 |
| Ardmaleish Ter, G45 | 104 | BU43 |
| Ardmay Cres, G44 | 88 | BS38 |
| Ardmillan St, G33 | 70 | CB29 |
| Ardmory Av, G42 | 88 | BT38 |
| Ardmory La, G42 | 88 | BU38 |
| Ardmory Pl, G42 | 88 | BU38 |
| Ardnahoe Av, G42 | 88 | BT37 |
| Ardnahoe Pl, G42 | 88 | BT37 |
| Ardneil Rd, G51 | 65 | BH31 |
| Ardnish St, G51 | 65 | BG30 |
| Ardoch Gdns, (Camb.) G72 | 106 | CB39 |
| Ardoch Gro, (Camb.) G72 | 106 | CB39 |
| Ardochrig, (E.Kil.) G75 | 136 | CA56 |
| Ardoch Rd, (Bears.) G61 | 30 | BK16 |
| Ardoch St, G22 | 50 | BS25 |
| Ardoch Way, (Chry.) G69 | | |
| off Braeside Av | 37 | CP19 |
| Ardo Gdns, G51 | | |
| off Hinshelwood Dr | 66 | BJ32 |
| Ard Rd, Renf. PA4 | 45 | AX25 |
| Ardshiel Rd, G51 | 65 | BG30 |
| Ardsloy La, G14 | 46 | BC25 |
| Ardsloy Pl, G14 | 46 | BC25 |
| Ard St, G32 | 90 | CC33 |
| Ardtoe Cres, G33 | 53 | CG24 |
| Ardtoe Pl, G33 | 53 | CG24 |
| Arduthie Rd, G51 | 65 | BG30 |
| Ardwell Rd, G52 | 85 | BG34 |
| Argosy Way, Renf. PA4 | | |
| off Britannia Way | 63 | AY28 |
| Argus Av, (Chap.) Air. ML6 | 97 | DE35 |
| Argyle Cres, (Hillhouse | | |
| Ind. Est.) Ham. ML3 | 125 | CP50 |
| Argyle Dr, Ham. ML3 | 125 | CQ49 |
| Argyle St, G2 | 4 | BQ30 |
| Argyle St, G3 | 66 | BM28 |
| Argyle St, Pais. PA1 | 82 | AT33 |
| Argyll Arc, G2 | 5 | BS30 |
| Argyll Av, (Abbots.) Pais. PA3 | 62 | AT28 |
| Argyll Av, Renf. PA4 | 45 | AX25 |
| Argyll Cres, Air. ML6 | 96 | DB33 |
| Argyll Gdns, Lark. ML9 | 144 | DD58 |
| Argyll Pl, (Kilsyth) G65 | 7 | CU5 |
| Argyll Pl, (E.Kil.) G74 | 123 | CE50 |
| Argyll Pl, Bell. ML4 | 110 | CV42 |
| Argyll Rd, (Bears.) G61 | 29 | BG15 |
| Argyll Rd, Clyde. G81 | 27 | AY20 |
| Arisaig Dr, G52 | 85 | BG34 |
| Arisaig Dr, (Bears.) G61 | 30 | BK18 |
| Arisaig Pl, G52 | 85 | BG34 |
| Arisdale Cres, (Newt. M.) G77 | 117 | BG47 |
| Arkaig Av, (Plains) Air. ML6 | 59 | DH26 |
| Arkaig Pl, (Newt. M.) G77 | 118 | BK49 |
| Ark La, G31 | 68 | BV30 |
| Arkleston Ct, Pais. PA3 | | |
| off Montgomery Rd | 63 | AX29 |
| Arkleston Cres, Pais. PA3 | 63 | AX30 |
| Arkleston Dr, Pais. PA1 | 63 | AX31 |
| Arkleston Rd, Pais. PA1 | 63 | AX31 |
| Arkleston Rd, Pais. PA3 | 63 | AY30 |
| Arkleston Rd, Renf. PA4 | 63 | AW29 |
| Arkle Ter, (Camb.) G72 | 106 | CB42 |
| Arklet Rd, G51 | 65 | BG31 |
| Arkwrights Way, Pais. PA1 | | |
| off Turners Av | 81 | AR34 |
| Arlington Pl, G3 | 4 | BP28 |
| Arlington St, G3 | 4 | BP28 |
| Armadale Ct, G31 | 69 | BW29 |
| Armadale Path, G31 | 69 | BW29 |
| Armadale Pl, G31 | 69 | BW29 |
| Armadale St, G31 | 69 | BW30 |
| Armine Path, Moth. ML1 | | |
| off Glenburn Av | 113 | DE41 |
| Armour Av, Air. ML6 | 76 | DA30 |
| Armour Ct, (Kirk.) G66 | 18 | CJ12 |
| Armour Ct, (Blan.) G72 | 124 | CK47 |
| Armour Dr, (Kirk.) G66 | 18 | CJ12 |
| Armour Gdns, (Kirk.) G66 | | |
| off Armour Ct | 18 | CJ12 |
| Armour Gro, Moth. ML1 | 128 | DC49 |
| Armour Pl, (Kirk.) G66 | 18 | CJ12 |
| Armour Pl, John. PA5 | 80 | AJ34 |
| Armour Pl, Moth. ML1 | | |
| off Glenburn Av | 113 | DE41 |
| Armour Sq, John. PA5 | 80 | AJ34 |
| Armour St, G31 | 5 | BU31 |
| Armour St, John. PA5 | 80 | AJ34 |
| Armstrong Cres, (Udd.) G71 | 93 | CQ37 |
| Armstrong Gro, (E.Kil.) G75 | 135 | BZ54 |
| Arnbrae Rd, (Kilsyth) G65 | 7 | CR4 |
| Arngask Rd, G51 | 65 | BG30 |
| Arnhall Pl, G52 | 85 | BG34 |
| Arnhem St, (Camb.) G72 | 107 | CF40 |
| Arnholm Pl, G52 | 85 | BG34 |
| Arnisdale Pl, G34 | 72 | CJ29 |
| Arnisdale Rd, G34 | 72 | CJ29 |
| Arnisdale Way, (Ruther.) G73 | | |
| off Shieldaig Dr | 105 | BX42 |
| Arniston St, G32 | 70 | CB30 |
| Arniston Way, Pais. PA3 | 63 | AW30 |
| Arnold Av, (Bishop.) G64 | 33 | BW20 |
| Arnold St, G20 | 49 | BQ23 |
| Arnol Pl, G33 | 71 | CH30 |
| Arnott Dr, Coat. ML5 | 95 | CW33 |
| Arnott Quad, Moth. ML1 | | |
| off Frood St | 111 | CY44 |
| Arnott Way, (Camb.) G72 | 106 | CC39 |
| Arnprior Cres, G45 | 104 | BT42 |
| Arnprior Gdns, (Chry.) G69 | | |
| off Braeside Av | 37 | CP19 |
| Arnprior Quad, G45 | 104 | BT41 |
| Arnprior Rd, G45 | 104 | BT41 |
| Arnprior St, G45 | 104 | BT41 |
| Arnside Av, (Giff.) G46 | 102 | BL42 |
| Arnwood Dr, G12 | 48 | BJ24 |
| Arondale Rd, Air. ML6 | 59 | DH26 |
| Aron Ter, (Camb.) G72 | 106 | CB42 |
| Aros Dr, G52 | 85 | BF35 |
| Aros La, G52 | 85 | BF35 |
| Arran, (E.Kil.) G74 | 137 | CE52 |
| Arran Av, Coat. ML5 | 95 | CZ33 |
| Arran Av, (Abbots.) Pais. PA3 | 62 | AU27 |
| Arran Dr, (Giff.) G46 | 102 | BK43 |
| Arran Dr, G52 | 85 | BH34 |
| Arran Dr, (Kirk.) G66 | 17 | CG12 |
| Arran Dr, (Cumb.) G67 | 21 | CZ13 |
| Arran Dr, Air. ML6 | 76 | DB28 |
| Arran Dr, (Glenm.) Air. ML6 | 58 | DB24 |
| Arran Dr, John. PA5 | 79 | AF36 |
| Arran Dr, Pais. PA2 | 82 | AU38 |
| Arran Gdns, Ham. ML3 | 140 | CU52 |
| Arran La, (Chry.) G69 | 37 | CQ19 |
| Arran Path, Lark. ML9 | | |
| off Bannockburn Dr | 145 | DE60 |
| Arran Pl, Clyde. G81 | 27 | AY19 |
| Arran Pl, (Linw.) Pais. PA3 | 60 | AJ31 |
| Arran Rd, Moth. ML1 | 127 | CY46 |
| Arran Rd, Renf. PA4 | 63 | AZ27 |
| Arran Ter, (Ruther.) G73 | | |
| off Carrick Rd | 104 | BV40 |
| Arran Vw, (Kilsyth) G65 | | |
| off Murray Av | 7 | CT5 |
| Arranview St, (Chap.) Air. ML6 | 97 | DG36 |
| Arran Way, (Both.) G71 | 109 | CP43 |
| Arrochar Ct, G23 | 48 | BM21 |
| Arrochar Dr, G23 | 30 | BM20 |
| Arrochar Path, G23 | | |
| off Chatton St | 30 | BM20 |
| Arrochar St, G23 | 48 | BM21 |
| Arrol Pl, G40 | 89 | BX33 |
| Arrol Rd, G40 | 89 | BW33 |
| Arrol St, G52 | 64 | BA30 |
| Arrotshole Ct, (E.Kil.) G74 | 121 | BX49 |
| Arrotshole Rd, (E.Kil.) G74 | 121 | BX50 |
| Arrowsmith Av, G13 | 47 | BF21 |
| Arthur Av, (Barr.) G78 | 99 | AX44 |
| Arthur Av, Air. ML6 | 76 | DB31 |
| Arthurlie Av, (Barr.) G78 | 99 | AY43 |
| Arthurlie Dr, (Giff.) G46 | 102 | BL44 |
| Arthurlie Dr, (Newt. M.) G77 | 117 | BF50 |
| Arthurlie Gdns, (Barr.) G78 | 99 | AY43 |
| Arthurlie St, G51 | 65 | BH30 |
| Arthurlie St, (Barr.) G78 | 99 | AY43 |
| Arthur Pl, (Clark.) G76 | | |
| off Eaglesham Rd | 119 | BN47 |
| Arthur Rd, Pais. PA2 | 82 | AU37 |
| Arthur St, G3 | 66 | BM28 |
| Arthur St, (Clark.) G76 | 119 | BN47 |
| Arthur St, Ham. ML3 | 126 | CT48 |
| Arthur St, Pais. PA1 | 62 | AS32 |
| Arundel Dr, G42 | 87 | BQ38 |
| Arundel Dr, (Bishop.) G64 | 33 | BX17 |
| Asbury Ct, (Linw.) Pais. PA3 | | |
| off Melrose Av | 60 | AL32 |
| Ascaig Cres, G52 | 85 | BF35 |
| Ascog Rd, (Bears.) G61 | 29 | BH19 |
| Ascog St, G42 | 87 | BQ35 |
| Ascot Av, G12 | 47 | BH23 |
| Ascot Ct, G12 | 48 | BJ23 |
| Ash Av, (E.Kil.) G75 | 135 | BY55 |
| Ashbank Cres, (Chap.) Air. ML6 | 97 | DG34 |

| Name | Page | Grid |
|---|---|---|
| Ashburn Gdns, (Miln.) G62 | 11 | BG12 |
| Ashburn Ln, Lark. ML9 | 144 | DD57 |
| Ashburn Rd, (Miln.) G62 | 11 | BG11 |
| Ashburton La, G12 | 48 | BK23 |
| Ashburton Pk, (E.Kil.) G75 | 135 | BW54 |
| Ashburton Rd, G12 | 48 | BJ23 |
| Ashby Cres, G13 | 29 | BG20 |
| Ash Ct, (E.Kil.) G75 | 135 | BY55 |
| Ashcroft, (E.Kil.) G74 | 123 | CF48 |
| Ashcroft Dr, G44 | 104 | BU40 |
| Ashdale Dr, G52 | 85 | BG34 |
| Ashdene St, G22 | 49 | BR22 |
| Asher Rd, (Chap.) Air. ML6 | 97 | DG35 |
| Ashfield, (Bishop.) G64 | 33 | BW18 |
| Ashfield Rd, (Miln.) G62 | 12 | BJ12 |
| Ashfield Rd, (Clark.) G76 | 119 | BN47 |
| Ashfield St, G22 | 50 | BS25 |
| Ashgillhead Rd, (Ashgill) Lark. ML9 | 145 | DG60 |
| Ashgill Pl, G22 | 50 | BS23 |
| Ashgill Rd, G22 | 49 | BR22 |
| Ash Gro, (Bishop.) G64 | 33 | BX20 |
| Ash Gro, (Kirk.) G66 | 34 | CD16 |
| Ashgrove, (Mood.) G69 *off Deepdene Rd* | 37 | CP19 |
| Ash Gro, (Udd.) G71 | 93 | CR37 |
| Ashgrove, Air. ML6 | 77 | DF30 |
| Ashgrove, Coat. ML5 | 95 | CW33 |
| Ashgrove Rd, Bell. ML4 | 95 | CX38 |
| Ashgrove St, G40 | 89 | BW35 |
| Ashiestiel Ct, (Cumb.) G67 | 22 | DA14 |
| Ashiestiel Pl, (Cumb.) G67 | 22 | DA14 |
| Ashiestiel Rd, (Cumb.) G67 | 22 | DA14 |
| Ashkirk Dr, G52 | 85 | BG34 |
| Ashkirk Dr, (Ashgill) Lark. ML9 *off Rosslyn Rd* | 145 | DH61 |
| Ashland Av, Ham. ML3 | 140 | CT54 |
| Ashlea Dr, (Giff.) G46 | 102 | BM41 |
| Ashlea Gdns, (Plains) Air. ML6 | 59 | DH26 |
| Ashley Dr, (Both.) G71 | 109 | CR40 |
| Ashley La, G3 | 4 | BP28 |
| Ashley Pk, (Udd.) G71 | 110 | CS40 |
| Ashley Pl, (Blan.) G72 | 124 | CL45 |
| Ashley St, G3 | 4 | BP28 |
| Ashmore Rd, G43 | 103 | BP40 |
| Ashmore Rd, G44 | 103 | BP40 |
| Ash Pl, (E.Kil.) G75 | 135 | BY55 |
| Ash Pl, John. PA5 | 80 | AJ35 |
| Ash Rd, (Baill.) G69 | 92 | CJ34 |
| Ash Rd, Clyde. G81 | 26 | AV16 |
| Ashton Gdns, (Gart.) G69 | 55 | CQ23 |
| Ashton Grn, (E.Kil.) G74 *off Dalrymple Dr* | 136 | CA51 |
| Ashton La, G12 | 66 | BM27 |
| Ashton La N, G12 *off Ashton La* | 66 | BM27 |
| Ashton Rd, G12 | 66 | BM27 |
| Ashton Rd, (Ruther.) G73 | 89 | BW36 |
| Ashton St, Moth. ML1 | 111 | CZ43 |
| Ashton Way, Pais. PA2 | 81 | AN37 |
| Ashtree Ct, (Old Kil.) G60 | 25 | AQ15 |
| Ashtree Gro, (Newt. M.) G77 | 117 | BE50 |
| Ashtree Rd, G43 | 86 | BL37 |
| Ashvale Cres, G21 | 50 | BU24 |
| Ash Wk, (Ruther.) G73 | 105 | BY42 |
| Ash Wk, Moth. ML1 *off Elm Rd* | 112 | DD40 |
| Ashwood, Wis. ML2 | 143 | DG52 |
| Ashwood Gdns, G13 | 47 | BH24 |
| Ashworth Ter, Ham. ML3 | 125 | CQ49 |
| Ash Wynd, (Camb.) G72 | 107 | CG41 |
| Aspen Dr, G21 | 51 | BW26 |
| Aspen Pl, (Camb.) G72 | 107 | CG40 |
| Aspen Pl, John. PA5 | 80 | AJ36 |
| Aspen Way, Ham. ML3 | 140 | CU51 |
| Asquith Pl, Bell. ML4 | 111 | CZ40 |
| Aster Dr, G45 | 105 | BW42 |
| Aster Gdns, G53 *off Waukglen Cres* | 101 | BE42 |
| Aster Gdns, Moth. ML1 | 128 | DA48 |
| Athelstane Dr, (Cumb.) G67 | 21 | CZ14 |
| Athelstane Rd, G13 | 47 | BE22 |
| Athena Way, (Udd.) G71 | 93 | CQ38 |
| Athole Gdns, G12 | 48 | BL26 |
| Athole La, G12 | 48 | BL26 |
| Atholl Av, G52 | 64 | BA29 |
| Atholl Av, (Torr.) G64 | 15 | BX12 |
| Atholl Ct, (Kirk.) G66 | 18 | CK12 |
| Atholl Ct, (Blan.) G72 *off Ballantrae Rd* | 125 | CP47 |
| Atholl Cres, Pais. PA1 | 64 | BA31 |
| Atholl Dr, (Giff.) G46 | 118 | BL45 |
| Atholl Gdns, (Bears.) G61 | 11 | BG14 |
| Atholl Gdns, (Bishop.) G64 | 32 | BV18 |
| Atholl Gdns, (Ruther.) G73 | 106 | CA42 |
| Atholl La, (Mood.) G69 | 37 | CQ19 |
| Atholl Pl, Coat. ML5 | 95 | CX34 |
| Atholl Pl, (Linw.) Pais. PA3 | 60 | AJ31 |
| Atholl St, Ham. ML3 | 125 | CR47 |
| Atholl Ter, (Udd.) G71 | 93 | CP36 |
| Atlas Ind Est, G21 | 50 | BV25 |
| Atlas Pl, G21 | 50 | BV26 |
| Atlas Rd, G21 | 50 | BU25 |
| Atlas Sq, G21 *off Ayr St* | 50 | BV25 |
| Atlas St, Clyde. G81 | 45 | AX21 |
| Atlin Dr, (New Stev.) Moth. ML1 | 112 | DD42 |
| Attercliffe Av, Wis. ML2 | 143 | DE51 |
| Attlee Av, Clyde. G81 | 28 | BA20 |
| Attlee Pl, Clyde. G81 | 28 | BA20 |
| Attlee Rd, (E.Kil.) G74 | 134 | BT53 |
| Attow Rd, G43 | 102 | BK40 |
| Auburn Dr, (Barr.) G78 | 99 | AZ44 |
| Auchans Rd, (Hous.) John. PA6 | 60 | AJ27 |
| Auchenbothie Cres, G33 | 52 | CA23 |
| Auchenbothie Pl, G33 *off Auchenbothie Cres* | 52 | CA24 |
| Auchencrow St, G34 | 72 | CM29 |
| Auchencruive, (Miln.) G62 | 12 | BL13 |
| Auchendavie Rd, G66 | 18 | CK11 |
| Auchendavie Steading, (Kirk.) G66 | 18 | CL11 |
| Auchengeich Rd, (Mood.) G69 | 36 | CM17 |
| Auchengilloch, (E.Kil.) G75 | 136 | CA56 |
| Auchengreoch Av, John. PA5 | 79 | AF37 |
| Auchengreoch Rd, John. PA5 | 79 | AF37 |
| Auchengreoch Rd, (How.) John. PA9 | 79 | AF37 |
| Auchenhowie Rd, (Miln.) G62 | 12 | BL13 |
| Auchenkilns Holdings, (Cumb.) G67 | 39 | CZ15 |
| Auchenkilns Junct, (Cumb.) G67 | 21 | CY13 |
| Auchenlodment Rd, John. PA5 | 80 | AK35 |
| Auchentibber Rd, (Blan.) G72 | 123 | CH50 |
| Auchentorlie Quad, Pais. PA1 | 83 | AX33 |
| Auchentorlie St, G11 | 65 | BH27 |
| Auchentoshan Av, Clyde. G81 | 26 | AV15 |
| Auchentoshan Ter, G21 | 68 | BV27 |
| Auchentoshen Cotts, (Old Kil.) G60 | 26 | AT15 |
| Auchinairn Gdns, (Bishop.) G64 | 51 | BZ21 |
| Auchinairn Rd, (Bishop.) G64 | 51 | BW22 |
| Auchinbee Fm Rd, (Cumb.) G68 | 21 | CX9 |
| Auchinbee Rbt, (Cumb.) G68 | 21 | CY10 |
| Auchinbee Way, (Cumb.) G68 | 21 | CX10 |
| Auchincampbell Rd, Ham. ML3 | 126 | CT50 |
| Auchineden Ct, (Bears.) G61 | 11 | BE14 |
| Auchingill Path, G34 *off Auchingill Rd* | 72 | CM28 |
| Auchingill Pl, G34 | 72 | CM28 |
| Auchingill Rd, G34 | 72 | CL28 |
| Auchingramont Rd, Ham. ML3 | 126 | CT49 |
| Auchinlea Retail Pk, G34 *off Auchinlea Way* | 71 | CH28 |
| Auchinlea Rd, G34 | 71 | CH27 |
| Auchinlea Way, G34 | 71 | CH28 |
| Auchinleck Av, G33 | 52 | CA23 |
| Auchinleck Cres, G33 | 52 | CA23 |
| Auchinleck Dr, G33 | 52 | CA23 |
| Auchinleck Gdns, G33 | 52 | CA23 |
| Auchinleck Rd, G33 | 52 | CB22 |
| Auchinloch Rd, (Lenz.) G66 | 35 | CF17 |
| Auchinloch St, G21 | 50 | BV26 |
| Auchinraith Av, Ham. ML3 | 125 | CR47 |
| Auchinraith Rd, (Blan.) G72 | 124 | CM47 |
| Auchinraith Ter, (Blan.) G72 | 124 | CN47 |
| Auchintibber Ct, (Blan.) G72 *off Ballantrae Rd* | 125 | CN47 |
| Auchinvole Cres, (Kilsyth) G65 | 7 | CR5 |
| Auchmannoch Av, Pais. PA1 | 64 | BA32 |
| Auckland Pk, (E.Kil.) G75 | 135 | BW53 |
| Auckland Pl, Clyde. G81 | 26 | AT17 |
| Auckland St, G22 | 49 | BR26 |
| Auldbar Rd, G52 | 85 | BH34 |
| Auldbar Ter, Pais. PA2 | 83 | AW35 |
| Auldburn Pl, G43 | 102 | BK39 |
| Auldburn Rd, G43 | 102 | BK39 |
| Auldearn Rd, G21 | 51 | BY22 |
| Auldgirth Rd, G52 | 85 | BH34 |
| Auldhame St, Coat. ML5 | 74 | CU29 |
| Auldhouse Av, G43 *off Thornliebank Rd* | 102 | BK39 |
| Auldhouse Ct, G43 *off Stoneside Dr* | 102 | BK39 |
| Auldhouse Gdns, G43 | 102 | BK39 |
| Auldhouse Rd, G43 | 102 | BL39 |
| Auldhouse Ter, G43 | 102 | BM39 |
| Auld Kirk Rd, (Camb.) G72 | 107 | CE42 |
| Auldmurroch Dr, (Miln.) G62 | 11 | BF11 |
| Auld Rd, The, (Cumb.) G67 | 22 | DC9 |
| Aulds Brae, Air. ML6 *off Chapel St* | 76 | DC29 |
| Auld St, Clyde. G81 | 26 | AU18 |
| Auldton Ter, (Ashgill) Lark. ML9 | 145 | DH60 |
| Aultbea St, G22 | 49 | BR21 |
| Aultmore Dr, (Carfin) Moth. ML1 | 112 | DD43 |
| Aultmore Gdns, G33 | 71 | CH30 |
| Aultmore Pk, G33 | 71 | CH30 |
| Aultmore Rd, G33 | 71 | CH30 |
| Aurora Av, Clyde. G81 | 45 | AX21 |
| Aursbridge Cres, (Barr.) G78 | 99 | AZ43 |
| Aursbridge Dr, (Barr.) G78 | 99 | AZ43 |
| Aurs Cres, (Barr.) G78 | 99 | AZ43 |
| Aurs Dr, (Barr.) G78 | 99 | AZ44 |
| Aurs Glen, (Barr.) G78 | 99 | AY44 |
| Aurs Pl, (Barr.) G78 | 100 | BA43 |
| Aurs Rd, (Newt. M.) G77 | 116 | BB47 |
| Aurs Rd, (Barr.) G78 | 99 | AZ43 |
| Austen La, G13 *off Skaterig La* | 47 | BG24 |
| Austen Rd, G13 | 47 | BG24 |
| Austine Dr, Ham. ML3 | 140 | CU54 |
| Avenel Rd, G13 | 29 | BG20 |

| Name | Page | Grid |
|---|---|---|
| Avenue, The, (Kilb.) John. PA10 | | |
| *off Low Barholm* | 78 | AD35 |
| Avenue End Dr, G33 | 70 | CD27 |
| Avenue End Gate, G33 | 52 | CD26 |
| Avenue End Rd, G33 | 52 | CD25 |
| Avenuehead Rd, (Chry.) G69 | 37 | CQ20 |
| Avenuepark St, G20 | 49 | BN25 |
| Avenue Shop Cen, The, | | |
| (Newt. M.) G77 | 117 | BF49 |
| Avenue St, G40 | 69 | BW32 |
| Avenue St, (Ruther.) G73 | 89 | BX36 |
| Aviemore Gdns, (Bears.) G61 | 30 | BK16 |
| Aviemore Rd, G52 | 85 | BG35 |
| Avoch Dr, (Thornlie.) G46 | 101 | BG42 |
| Avoch St, G34 | | |
| *off Dubton St* | 72 | CK28 |
| Avon Av, (Bears.) G61 | 30 | BK18 |
| Avonbank Cres, Ham. ML3 | 140 | CU53 |
| Avonbank Rd, (Ruther.) G73 | 88 | BV38 |
| Avonbank Rd, Lark. ML9 | 144 | DA59 |
| Avonbrae Cres, Ham. ML3 | 140 | CU53 |
| Avonbridge Dr, Ham. ML3 | 126 | CV50 |
| Avondale Av, (E.Kil.) G74 | 136 | CB52 |
| Avondale Dr, Pais. PA1 | 63 | AX31 |
| Avondale Pl, (E.Kil.) G74 | 136 | CC53 |
| Avondale St, G33 | 70 | CC28 |
| Avon Dr, (Bishop.) G64 | | |
| *off Avon Rd* | 51 | BW21 |
| Avon Dr, Bell. ML4 | 111 | CY41 |
| Avon Dr, (Linw.) Pais. PA3 | 60 | AK31 |
| Avonhead, (E.Kil.) G75 | 136 | CA56 |
| Avonhead Av, (Cumb.) G67 | 21 | CY14 |
| Avonhead Gdns, (Cumb.) G67 | 21 | CY14 |
| Avonhead Pl, (Cumb.) G67 | | |
| *off Avonhead Av* | 21 | CY14 |
| Avonhead Rd, (Cumb.) G67 | 21 | CY14 |
| Avon Pl, Coat. ML5 | 74 | CT28 |
| Avon Pl, Lark. ML9 | 144 | DD62 |
| Avon Rd, (Giff.) G46 | 102 | BK43 |
| Avon Rd, (Bishop.) G64 | 51 | BW21 |
| Avon Rd, Lark. ML9 | 144 | DC61 |
| Avonside Gro, Ham. ML3 | 126 | CV50 |
| Avonspark St, G21 | 51 | BW26 |
| Avon St, Ham. ML3 | 126 | CU50 |
| Avon St, Lark. ML9 | 144 | DB58 |
| Avon St, Moth. ML1 | 128 | DA48 |
| Avon Wk, (Cumb.) G67 | | |
| *off Cumbernauld Shop Cen* | 22 | DB12 |
| Aylmer Rd, G43 | 103 | BP39 |
| Ayr Dr, Air. ML6 | 96 | DC33 |
| Ayr Rd, (Giff.) G46 | 118 | BJ46 |
| Ayr Rd, (Newt. M.) G77 | 117 | BG48 |
| Ayr Rd, Lark. ML9 | 145 | DF60 |
| Ayr St, G21 | 50 | BU26 |
| Ayton Pk N, (E.Kil.) G74 | 122 | CD50 |
| Ayton Pk S, (E.Kil.) G74 | 122 | CD50 |
| Aytoun Dr, Ersk. PA8 | 25 | AP18 |
| Aytoun Rd, G41 | 86 | BM34 |
| Azalea Gdns, (Camb.) G72 | 107 | CG40 |

**B**

| Name | Page | Grid |
|---|---|---|
| Babylon Av, Bell. ML4 | 111 | CW42 |
| Babylon Dr, Bell. ML4 | 111 | CW42 |
| Babylon Pl, Bell. ML4 | 111 | CW43 |
| Babylon Rd, Bell. ML4 | 110 | CV42 |
| Backbrae St, (Kilsyth) G65 | 7 | CS5 |
| Back Causeway, G31 | 69 | BZ32 |
| Backmuir Cres, Ham. ML3 | 125 | CR47 |
| Backmuir Pl, Ham. ML3 | | |
| *off Backmuir Rd* | 125 | CR47 |
| Backmuir Rd, G15 | 28 | BD17 |
| Backmuir Rd, Ham. ML3 | 125 | CR47 |

| Name | Page | Grid |
|---|---|---|
| Back o'Barns, Ham. ML3 | | |
| *off Church St* | 126 | CV49 |
| Back o'Hill Rd, (Torr.) G64 | 14 | BU11 |
| Back Row, Ham. ML3 | 126 | CU49 |
| Back Sneddon St, Pais. PA3 | 62 | AU32 |
| Badenheath Pl, (Cumb.) G68 | 38 | CT16 |
| Badenheath Ter, (Cumb.) G67 | 38 | CT17 |
| Badenoch Rd, (Kirk.) G66 | 18 | CK12 |
| Bagnell St, G21 | 50 | BV24 |
| Bahamas Way, (E.Kil.) G75 | | |
| *off Leeward Circle* | 135 | BW52 |
| Bailie Dr, (Bears.) G61 | 11 | BF14 |
| Baillie Dr, (Both.) G71 | 109 | CQ42 |
| Baillie Dr, (E.Kil.) G74 | 122 | CD49 |
| Baillie Pl, (E.Kil.) G74 | 122 | CD49 |
| Baillies La, Air. ML6 | | |
| *off Graham St* | 76 | DC29 |
| Baillieston Rd, G32 | 91 | CF33 |
| Baillieston Rd, (Udd.) G71 | 92 | CK34 |
| Baillie Wynd, (Udd.) G71 | 93 | CQ37 |
| Bainsford St, G32 | 70 | CB31 |
| Bain Sq, G40 | | |
| *off Bain St* | 5 | BU31 |
| Bain St, G40 | 5 | BU31 |
| Baird Av, G52 | 64 | BA29 |
| Baird Av, Air. ML6 | 76 | DD27 |
| Baird Av, (Strutherland Ind. Est.) | | |
| Lark. ML9 | 144 | DD61 |
| Baird Ct, Clyde. G81 | 27 | AW19 |
| Baird Cres, (Cumb.) G67 | 21 | CX14 |
| Baird Dr, (Bears.) G61 | 29 | BF16 |
| Baird Dr, Ersk. PA8 | 25 | AP18 |
| Baird Hill, (E.Kil.) G75 | 136 | CA53 |
| Baird Pl, Bell. ML4 | 95 | CW38 |
| Bairds Av, (Udd.) G71 | 109 | CR39 |
| Bairds Brae, G4 | 49 | BR26 |
| Bairds Cres, Ham. ML3 | 126 | CS50 |
| Bairdsland Vw, Bell. ML4 | 111 | CX40 |
| Baird St, G4 | 5 | BT28 |
| Baird St, Coat. ML5 | 75 | CW30 |
| Baker Pl, G41 | | |
| *off Baker St* | 87 | BN36 |
| Baker St, G41 | 87 | BN36 |
| Bakewell Rd, (Baill.) G69 | 72 | CJ32 |
| Balaclava St, G2 | 4 | BQ30 |
| Balado Rd, G33 | 71 | CG30 |
| Balbeggie Pl, G32 | 91 | CE33 |
| Balbeggie St, G32 | 91 | CE33 |
| Balbeg St, G51 | 65 | BG31 |
| Balblair Rd, G52 | 85 | BH34 |
| Balcarres Av, G12 | 48 | BL24 |
| Balcary Pl, (Chap.) Air. ML6 | 97 | DG36 |
| Balcastle Gdns, (Kilsyth) G65 | 7 | CR4 |
| Balcastle Rd, (Kilsyth) G65 | 6 | CQ4 |
| Balcomie St, G33 | 70 | CC28 |
| Balcomie Ter, Ham. ML3 | | |
| *off Balmore Dr* | 139 | CR53 |
| Balcurvie Rd, G34 | 72 | CJ27 |
| Baldernock Rd, (Miln.) G62 | 12 | BL11 |
| Baldinnie Rd, G34 | 72 | CK29 |
| Baldorran Cres, (Cumb.) G68 | 21 | CX10 |
| Baldovan Cres, G33 | 71 | CH29 |
| Baldovan Path, G33 | 71 | CH30 |
| Baldovie Rd, G52 | 85 | BE34 |
| Baldragon Rd, G34 | 72 | CK28 |
| Baldric Rd, G13 | 47 | BE23 |
| Baldwin Av, G13 | 47 | BF21 |
| Balerno Dr, G52 | 85 | BG34 |
| Balfearn Dr, (Eagle.) G76 | 133 | BN56 |
| Balfleurs St, (Miln.) G62 | 12 | BK11 |
| Balfluig St, G34 | 71 | CH28 |
| Balfour St, G20 | 48 | BM23 |
| Balfour Ter, (E.Kil.) G75 | 136 | CB54 |

| Name | Page | Grid |
|---|---|---|
| Balfour Wynd, Lark. ML9 | | |
| *off Fir Bk Av* | 144 | DD60 |
| Balfron Cres, Ham. ML3 | 125 | CP50 |
| Balfron Rd, G51 | 65 | BG30 |
| Balfron Rd, Pais. PA1 | 63 | AZ32 |
| Balgair Dr, Pais. PA1 | 63 | AX32 |
| Balgair Gdns, G22 | 49 | BR24 |
| Balgair Pl, G22 | 49 | BR25 |
| Balgair St, G22 | 49 | BR24 |
| Balgair Ter, G32 | 70 | CD32 |
| Balglass Gdns, G22 | 49 | BR25 |
| Balglass St, G22 | 49 | BR25 |
| Balgonie Av, Pais. PA2 | 81 | AQ36 |
| Balgonie Dr, Pais. PA2 | 82 | AS36 |
| Balgonie Rd, G52 | 85 | BG33 |
| Balgonie Wds, Pais. PA2 | 82 | AS36 |
| Balgownie Cres, (Thornlie.) | | |
| G46 | 102 | BJ43 |
| Balgraybank St, G21 | 50 | BV25 |
| Balgray Cres, (Barr.) G78 | 99 | AZ43 |
| Balgrayhill Rd, G21 | 50 | BV24 |
| Balgray Rd, (Newt. M.) G77 | 116 | BC48 |
| Balgraystone Rd, (Newt. M.) | | |
| G77 | 115 | AZ47 |
| Balintore St, G32 | 70 | CC32 |
| Baliol La, G3 | 4 | BP28 |
| Baliol St, G3 | 4 | BP28 |
| Baljaffray Rd, (Bears.) G61 | 10 | BC14 |
| Ballagan Pl, (Miln.) G62 | 11 | BF11 |
| Ballaig Av, (Bears.) G61 | 29 | BF16 |
| Ballaig Cres, (Stepps) G33 | 53 | CE24 |
| Ballantay Quad, G45 | 105 | BW42 |
| Ballantay Rd, G45 | 105 | BW42 |
| Ballantay Ter, G45 | 105 | BW42 |
| Ballantrae, (E.Kil.) G74 | 121 | BZ50 |
| Ballantrae Ct, G3 | 4 | BP30 |
| Ballantrae Cres, (Newt. M.) | | |
| G77 | 118 | BJ49 |
| Ballantrae Dr, (Newt. M.) G77 | 118 | BJ50 |
| Ballantrae Rd, (Blan.) G72 | 125 | CN47 |
| Ballantrae Wynd, Moth. ML1 | | |
| *off Ivy Ter* | 112 | DD40 |
| Ballantyne Av, G52 | 64 | BC30 |
| Ballater Dr, (Bears.) G61 | 29 | BH19 |
| Ballater Dr, Pais. PA2 | 82 | AV36 |
| Ballater Dr, (Inch.) Renf. PA4 | 44 | AT22 |
| Ballater Pl, G5 | 88 | BT33 |
| Ballater St, G5 | 68 | BS32 |
| Ballater Way, (Glenb.) Coat. ML5 | | |
| *off The Oval* | 56 | CS23 |
| Ballayne Dr, (Chry.) G69 | 37 | CQ18 |
| Ballerup Ter, (E.Kil.) G75 | 136 | CA55 |
| Ballindalloch Dr, G31 | 69 | BW29 |
| Ballindarroch La, G31 | | |
| *off Armadale St* | 69 | BW29 |
| Balloch Gdns, G52 | 85 | BH34 |
| Balloch Holdings, (Cumb.) G68 | 21 | CX12 |
| Balloch Loop Rd, (Cumb.) G68 | 21 | CY10 |
| Ballochmill Rd, (Ruther.) G73 | 89 | BZ37 |
| Ballochmyle, (E.Kil.) G74 | 123 | CF49 |
| Ballochmyle Cres, G53 | 84 | BC37 |
| Ballochmyle Dr, G53 | 84 | BC36 |
| Ballochmyle Gdns, G53 | 84 | BC36 |
| Ballochmyle Pl, G53 | 84 | BC37 |
| Ballochney La, Air. ML6 | | |
| *off Ballochney St* | 76 | DA27 |
| Ballochney Rd, Air. ML6 | 59 | DG26 |
| Ballochney St, Air. ML6 | 76 | DA28 |
| Balloch Rd, (Cumb.) G68 | 21 | CW11 |
| Balloch Rbt, (Cumb.) G68 | 21 | CW11 |
| Balloch Vw, (Cumb.) G67 | 22 | DB11 |
| Ballogie Rd, G44 | 87 | BR38 |
| Balmalloch Rd, (Kilsyth) G65 | 7 | CR4 |

| Street | No | Grid |
|---|---|---|
| Balmartin Rd, G23 | 30 | BM20 |
| Balmedie, Ersk. PA8 | 25 | AQ19 |
| Balmeg Av, (Giff.) G46 | 118 | BL45 |
| Balmerino Pl, (Bishop.) G64 | 51 | BZ21 |
| Balmoral Av, (Glenm.) Air. ML6 | 58 | DB24 |
| Balmoral Cres, Coat. ML5 | 94 | CT33 |
| Balmoral Cres, (Inch.) Renf. PA4 | 44 | AU22 |
| Balmoral Dr, G32 | 90 | CD37 |
| Balmoral Dr, (Bears.) G61 | 30 | BJ19 |
| Balmoral Dr, (Camb.) G72 | 106 | CA40 |
| Balmoral Dr, Bish. PA7 | 24 | AL19 |
| Balmoral Gdns, (Udd.) G71 | 93 | CP36 |
| Balmoral Gdns, (Blan.) G72 | 108 | CL43 |
| Balmoral Path, Lark. ML9 | | |
| *off Afton St* | 145 | DE59 |
| Balmoral Pl, (E.Kil.) G74 | 135 | BY52 |
| Balmoral Rd, (Elder.) John. PA5 | 80 | AK36 |
| Balmoral St, G14 | 46 | BD26 |
| Balmore Dr, Ham. ML3 | 139 | CQ53 |
| Balmore Pl, G22 | 49 | BR23 |
| Balmore Rd, G22 | 49 | BR22 |
| Balmore Rd, G23 | 31 | BQ18 |
| Balmore Rd, (Miln.) G62 | 31 | BP15 |
| Balmore Rd, (Torr.) G64 | 14 | BS13 |
| Balmore Sq, G22 | 49 | BR24 |
| Balmuildy Rd, G23 | 31 | BQ17 |
| Balmuildy Rd, (Bishop.) G64 | 32 | BV18 |
| Balornock Rd, G21 | 51 | BW24 |
| Balornock Rd, (Bishop.) G64 | 51 | BW23 |
| Balruddery Pl, (Bishop.) G64 | 51 | BZ21 |
| Balshagray Av, G11 | 47 | BG26 |
| Balshagray Cres, G14 | | |
| *off Dumbarton Rd* | 65 | BG27 |
| Balshagray Dr, G11 | 47 | BG26 |
| Balshagray La, G11 | 65 | BH27 |
| Balshagray Pl, G11 | | |
| *off Balshagray Dr* | 47 | BH26 |
| Balta Cres, (Camb.) G72 | 106 | CB42 |
| Baltic Business Pk, Pais. PA3 | 62 | AT31 |
| Baltic Ct, G40 | | |
| *off Baltic St* | 89 | BW34 |
| Baltic La, G40 | 89 | BW34 |
| Baltic Pl, G40 | 89 | BW33 |
| Baltic St, G40 | 89 | BW33 |
| Balvaird Cres, (Ruther.) G73 | 89 | BW38 |
| Balvaird Dr, (Ruther.) G73 | 89 | BW38 |
| Balvenie Dr, (Carfin) Moth. ML1 | | |
| *off Ardbeg Rd* | 112 | DD44 |
| Balvenie St, Coat. ML5 | 95 | CX34 |
| Balveny Av, G33 | 71 | CF27 |
| Balveny Dr, G33 | 71 | CF27 |
| Balveny Pl, G33 | 71 | CF27 |
| Balveny St, G33 | 71 | CF27 |
| Balvicar Dr, G42 | 87 | BP36 |
| Balvicar St, G42 | 87 | BP35 |
| Balvie Av, G15 | 28 | BC20 |
| Balvie Av, (Giff.) G46 | 102 | BM43 |
| Balvie Cres, (Miln.) G62 | 11 | BH11 |
| Balvie Rd, (Miln.) G62 | 11 | BH11 |
| Banavie La, G11 | | |
| *off Banavie Rd* | 48 | BK26 |
| Banavie Rd, G11 | 48 | BJ26 |
| Banchory Av, G43 | 102 | BK40 |
| Banchory Av, (Glenm.) Air. ML6 | 58 | DB24 |
| Banchory Av, (Inch.) Renf. PA4 | 44 | AT22 |
| Banchory Cres, (Bears.) G61 | 30 | BJ19 |
| Baneberry Path, (E.Kil.) G74 | 121 | BZ49 |
| Banff Av, Air. ML6 | 96 | DC33 |
| Banff Pl, (E.Kil.) G75 | 135 | BY53 |
| Banff St, G33 | | |
| *off Gilbertfield St* | 70 | CD27 |
| Bangorshill St, (Thornlie.) G46 | 101 | BH41 |
| Bank Av, (Miln.) G62 | 12 | BJ10 |
| Bankbrae Av, G53 | 100 | BC39 |
| Bankend St, G33 | 70 | CC28 |
| Bankfield Dr, Ham. ML3 | 140 | CT54 |
| Bankfoot Dr, G52 | 64 | BD32 |
| Bankfoot Pl, (Newt. M.) G77 | 118 | BK49 |
| Bankfoot Rd, G52 | 84 | BD33 |
| Bankfoot Rd, Pais. PA3 | 61 | AR31 |
| Bankglen Rd, G15 | 28 | BD17 |
| Bankhall St, G42 | 87 | BR35 |
| Bankhead Av, G13 | 46 | BC23 |
| Bankhead Av, Air. ML6 | 77 | DF30 |
| Bankhead Av, Bell. ML4 | 111 | CX42 |
| Bankhead Av, Coat. ML5 | 94 | CS33 |
| Bankhead Dr, (Ruther.) G73 | 89 | BW38 |
| Bankhead Pl, Air. ML6 | 77 | DF30 |
| Bankhead Pl, Coat. ML5 | 94 | CS33 |
| Bankhead Rd, (Kirk.) G66 | 18 | CJ14 |
| Bankhead Rd, (Ruther.) G73 | 104 | BV39 |
| Bankhead Rd, (Carm.) G76 | 120 | BT46 |
| Bankholm Pl, (Clark.) G76 | 119 | BP48 |
| Bankknock St, G32 | 70 | CA31 |
| Bank Pk, (E.Kil.) G75 | 135 | BZ53 |
| Bank Rd, G32 | 91 | CE37 |
| Bankside Av, John. PA5 | 79 | AH34 |
| Banks Rd, (Kirk.) G66 | 17 | CF12 |
| Bank St, G12 | 67 | BN27 |
| Bank St, (Camb.) G72 | 106 | CC39 |
| Bank St, (Barr.) G78 | 99 | AY43 |
| Bank St, (Neil.) G78 | 114 | AT46 |
| Bank St, Air. ML6 | 76 | DC30 |
| Bank St, Coat. ML5 | 74 | CU31 |
| Bank St, Pais. PA1 | 82 | AV33 |
| Banktop Pl, John. PA5 | 79 | AH34 |
| Bank Vw, (Chap.) Air. ML6 | 97 | DF35 |
| Bankview Cres, (Kirk.) G66 | 16 | CC13 |
| Bankview Dr, (Kirk.) G66 | 16 | CC13 |
| Bank Way, Lark. ML9 | | |
| *off Duncan Graham St* | 144 | DD57 |
| Bannatyne Av, G31 | 69 | BX30 |
| Bannercross Av, (Baill.) G69 | 72 | CJ32 |
| Bannercross Dr, (Baill.) G69 | 72 | CJ32 |
| Bannercross Gdns, (Baill.) G69 | 72 | CJ32 |
| Banner Dr, G13 | 29 | BE20 |
| Bannerman Dr, Bell. ML4 | 111 | CZ40 |
| Bannerman Pl, Clyde. G81 | 27 | AX19 |
| Banner Rd, G13 | 29 | BE20 |
| Bannockburn Dr, Lark. ML9 | 145 | DE60 |
| Bannockburn Pl, (New Stev.) | | |
| Moth. ML1 | 112 | DC43 |
| Bantaskin St, G20 | 48 | BL22 |
| Banton Pl, G33 | 72 | CJ30 |
| Banton Rd, G65 | 8 | CY4 |
| Banyan Cres, (Udd.) G71 | 94 | CT36 |
| Barassie, (E.Kil.) G74 | 121 | BZ50 |
| Barassie Ct, (Both.) G71 | 109 | CP43 |
| Barassie Cres, (Cumb.) G68 | 9 | DB7 |
| Barbados Grn, (E.Kil.) G75 | | |
| *off Leeward Circle* | 135 | BW52 |
| Barbae Pl, (Both.) G71 | 109 | CQ42 |
| Barbana Rd, (E.Kil.) G74 | 134 | BU51 |
| Barbegs Cres, (Kilsyth) G65 | 20 | CV9 |
| Barberry Av, G53 | 100 | BD43 |
| Barberry Gdns, G53 | 100 | BD43 |
| Barberry Pl, G53 | 101 | BE43 |
| Barbeth Gdns, (Cumb.) G67 | 39 | CX16 |
| Barbeth Pl, (Cumb.) G67 | 39 | CW15 |
| Barbeth Rd, (Cumb.) G67 | 39 | CW15 |
| Barbeth Way, (Cumb.) G67 | 39 | CW15 |
| Barbreck Rd, G42 | | |
| *off Pollokshaws Rd* | 87 | BQ35 |
| Barcaldine Av, (Chry.) G69 | 54 | CK21 |
| Barcapel Av, (Newt. M.) G77 | 117 | BG46 |
| Barclay Av, (Elder.) John. PA5 | 80 | AK35 |
| Barclay Dr, (Elder.) John. PA5 | 80 | AK35 |
| Barclay Rd, Moth. ML1 | 127 | CX47 |
| Barclay Sq, Renf. PA4 | 63 | AX28 |
| Barclay St, G21 | | |
| *off Lenzie St* | 50 | BV24 |
| Barclay St, (Old Kil.) G60 | 25 | AR16 |
| Barcloy Pl, (Chap.) Air. ML6 | 97 | DG36 |
| Barcraigs Dr, Pais. PA2 | 82 | AV37 |
| Bard Av, G13 | 46 | BD21 |
| Bardowie St, G22 | 49 | BR25 |
| Bardrain Av, (Elder.) John. PA5 | 80 | AL35 |
| Bardrain Rd, Pais. PA2 | 82 | AS38 |
| Bardrill Dr, (Bishop.) G64 | 32 | BU20 |
| Bardykes Rd, (Blan.) G72 | 124 | CK45 |
| Barefield St, Lark. ML9 | 144 | DC57 |
| Barfillan Dr, G52 | 65 | BG32 |
| Barfillan Rd, G52 | 85 | BG33 |
| Bargany Ct, G53 | 84 | BC36 |
| Bargany Pl, G53 | 84 | BC36 |
| Bargany Rd, G53 | 84 | BC36 |
| Bargaran Rd, G53 | 84 | BD34 |
| Bargarran Rd, Ersk. PA8 | 25 | AP19 |
| Bargarran Sq, Ersk. PA8 | | |
| *off Bargarran Rd* | 25 | AQ18 |
| Bargarron Dr, Pais. PA3 | 63 | AW30 |
| Bargeddie St, G33 | 69 | BZ27 |
| Bar Hill Pl, (Kilsyth) G65 | 7 | CR5 |
| Barholm Sq, G33 | 71 | CF27 |
| Barke Rd, (Cumb.) G67 | 22 | DC10 |
| Barkly Ter, (E.Kil.) G75 | | |
| *off Kimberley Gdns* | 135 | BY53 |
| Barlae Av, (Eagle.) G76 | 133 | BN53 |
| Barlanark Av, G32 | 71 | CE30 |
| Barlanark Cres, G33 | 71 | CF30 |
| Barlanark Dr, G33 | 71 | CF30 |
| Barlanark Pl, G32 | 70 | CD31 |
| Barlanark Pl, G33 | 71 | CG30 |
| Barlanark Rd, G33 | 71 | CF30 |
| Barlandfauld St, (Kilsyth) G65 | 7 | CT5 |
| Barlia Dr, G45 | 104 | BU42 |
| Barlia Gdns, G51 | 104 | BU42 |
| Barlia St, G45 | 104 | BU42 |
| Barlia Ter, G45 | 104 | BV42 |
| Barloch Av, (Miln.) G62 | 12 | BJ11 |
| Barloch Rd, G62 | 12 | BK11 |
| Barloch St, G22 | 50 | BS25 |
| Barlogan Av, G52 | 65 | BG32 |
| Barlogan Quad, G52 | 65 | BG32 |
| Barmulloch Rd, G21 | 51 | BW25 |
| Barnard Gdns, (Bishop.) G64 | 33 | BW17 |
| Barnbeth Rd, G53 | 84 | BD35 |
| Barncluith Rd, Ham. ML3 | 126 | CV50 |
| Barnes Rd, G20 | 49 | BQ23 |
| Barness Pl, G33 | 70 | CC29 |
| Barnes St, (Barr.) G78 | 99 | AX43 |
| Barnett Path, (Blan.) G72 | | |
| *off Selkirk St* | 124 | CM46 |
| Barnflat St, (Ruther.) G73 | 89 | BX36 |
| Barn Grn, (Kilb.) John. PA10 | 78 | AC34 |
| Barnhill Dr, G21 | | |
| *off Foresthall Dr* | 51 | BW26 |
| Barnhill Dr, (Newt. M.) G77 | 117 | BF50 |
| Barnhill Dr, Ham. ML3 | 138 | CM51 |
| Barnkirk Av, G15 | 28 | BC17 |
| Barnsford Av, (Inch.) Renf. PA4 | 43 | AR25 |
| Barnsford Rd, (Abbots.) | | |
| Pais. PA3 | 61 | AQ29 |
| Barnsford Rd, (Inch.) Renf. PA4 | 43 | AQ24 |
| Barns St, Clyde. G81 | 45 | AY21 |
| Barnswood Pl, (Both.) G71 | | |
| *off Burleigh Rd* | 109 | CR42 |
| Barnton St, G32 | 70 | CA30 |
| Barnwell Ter, G51 | 65 | BG30 |

| | | |
|---|---|---|
| Barochan Cres, Pais. PA3 | 81 | AQ33 |
| Barochan Pl, G53 | | |
| *off Barochan Rd* | 84 | BD34 |
| Barochan Rd, G53 | 84 | BD34 |
| Barochan Way, Pais. PA3 | 81 | AQ33 |
| Baronald Dr, G12 | 48 | BK23 |
| Baronald Gate, G12 | 48 | BK23 |
| Baronald St, (Ruther.) G73 | 89 | BX36 |
| Baron Ct, Ham. ML3 | 141 | CW51 |
| Barone Dr, (Clark.) G76 | 118 | BL45 |
| Baronhall Dr, (Blan.) G72 | 124 | CL45 |
| Baronhill, (Cumb.) G67 | 9 | DC8 |
| Baron Path, (Baill.) G69 | | |
| *off Campsie Vw* | 73 | CP32 |
| Baron Rd, Pais. PA3 | 63 | AW31 |
| Baronscourt Dr, Pais. PA1 | 81 | AP33 |
| Baronscourt Gdns, Pais. PA1 | 81 | AP33 |
| Baronscourt Rd, Pais. PA1 | 81 | AP33 |
| Barons Gate, (Both.) G71 | 109 | CN41 |
| Barons Rd, Moth. ML1 | 143 | DE51 |
| Baron St, Renf. PA4 | 63 | AY27 |
| Barony Ct, (Baill.) G69 | 72 | CK31 |
| Barony Dr, (Baill.) G69 | 72 | CK31 |
| Barony Gdns, (Baill.) G69 | 72 | CK32 |
| Barony Gro, (Camb.) G72 | 107 | CG41 |
| Barony Pl, (Cumb.) G68 | 20 | CU12 |
| Barony Wynd, (Baill.) G69 | 72 | CK31 |
| Barra Av, Coat. ML5 | 94 | CU33 |
| Barra Av, Renf. PA4 | 63 | AY28 |
| Barrachnie Av, (Baill.) G69 | 72 | CJ31 |
| Barrachnie Ct, (Baill.) G69 | 71 | CH31 |
| Barrachnie Cres, (Baill.) G69 | 71 | CH32 |
| Barrachnie Dr, (Baill.) G69 | 72 | CJ31 |
| Barrachnie Gro, (Baill.) G69 | 72 | CJ31 |
| Barrachnie Pl, (Baill.) G69 | 72 | CJ31 |
| Barrachnie Rd, (Baill.) G69 | 71 | CH32 |
| Barrack St, G4 | 5 | BU31 |
| Barrack St, Ham. ML3 | 126 | CT48 |
| Barra Cres, (Old Kil.) G60 | 26 | AS16 |
| Barra Dr, Air. ML6 | 77 | DG31 |
| Barra Gdns, (Old Kil.) G60 | 26 | AS16 |
| Barra Pl, Coat. ML5 | 94 | CU33 |
| Barra Rd, (Old Kil.) G60 | 26 | AS16 |
| Barraston Rd, (Torr.) G64 | 14 | BV10 |
| Barra St, G20 | 48 | BL21 |
| Barr Av, (Neil.) G78 | 114 | AU45 |
| Barrbridge Rd, (Baill.) G69 | 93 | CR33 |
| Barr Cres, Clyde. G81 | 27 | AX16 |
| Barr Gro, (Udd.) G71 | 93 | CQ37 |
| Barrhead Rd, G43 | 85 | BG38 |
| Barrhead Rd, G53 | 100 | BB39 |
| Barrhead Rd, (Newt. M.) G77 | 116 | BC48 |
| Barrhead Rd, Pais. PA2 | 82 | AV34 |
| Barrhill Ct, (Kirk.) G66 | 18 | CJ13 |
| Barrhill Cres, (Kilb.) John. PA10 | 78 | AD35 |
| Barrhill La, (Kilsyth) G65 | 19 | CP9 |
| Barrhill Rd, (Kirk.) G66 | 18 | CJ13 |
| Barrhill Rd, Ersk. PA8 | 25 | AQ20 |
| Barr Hill Ter, G65 | 19 | CQ9 |
| Barriedale Av, Ham. ML3 | 125 | CR50 |
| Barrie Quad, Clyde. G81 | 27 | AW17 |
| Barrie Rd, G52 | 64 | BC30 |
| Barrie Rd, (E.Kil.) G74 | 123 | CF48 |
| Barrie St, Moth. ML1 | 128 | DA47 |
| Barrington Dr, G4 | 67 | BP27 |
| Barrisdale Rd, G20 | 48 | BM21 |
| Barrisdale Way, (Ruther.) G73 | | |
| *off Shieldaig Dr* | 105 | BX41 |
| Barrland Dr, (Giff.) G46 | 102 | BL42 |
| Barrland St, G41 | 87 | BQ34 |
| Barrmill Rd, G43 | 102 | BJ40 |
| Barrochan Interchange, | | |
| John. PA5 | 79 | AG33 |

| | | |
|---|---|---|
| Barrowfield Gate, G40 | 89 | BX33 |
| Barrowfield Pl, G40 | 89 | BX33 |
| Barrowfield St, G40 | 69 | BW32 |
| Barrowfield St, Coat. ML5 | 95 | CW33 |
| Barrpath, (Kilsyth) G65 | 8 | CV6 |
| Barr Pl, (Newt. M.) G77 | 117 | BE48 |
| Barr Pl, Pais. PA1 | 82 | AT33 |
| Barr St, G20 | 49 | BQ26 |
| Barr St, Moth. ML1 | 128 | DA45 |
| Barr Ter, (E.Kil.) G74 | 136 | CA51 |
| Barrwood Pl, (Udd.) G71 | 93 | CQ37 |
| Barrwood St, G33 | 70 | CA27 |
| Barry Gdns, (Blan.) G72 | 124 | CM47 |
| Barscube Ter, Pais. PA2 | 83 | AW35 |
| Barshaw Cl, G52 | 64 | BA31 |
| Barshaw Ct, G52 | 64 | BB31 |
| Barshaw Dr, G52 | 64 | BB31 |
| Barshaw Dr, Pais. PA1 | 63 | AW31 |
| Barshaw Pl, Pais. PA1 | | |
| *off Kinpurnie Rd* | 63 | AZ32 |
| Barshaw Rd, G52 | 64 | BA31 |
| Barskiven Rd, Pais. PA1 | 81 | AP33 |
| Barterholm Rd, Pais. PA2 | 82 | AU35 |
| Bartholomew St, G40 | 89 | BW34 |
| Bartiebeith Rd, G33 | 71 | CG30 |
| Bartie Gdns, (Ashgillhead) | | |
| Lark. ML9 | 145 | DG60 |
| Barwood Dr, Ersk. PA8 | 25 | AQ17 |
| Barwood Rd, Ersk. PA8 | 25 | AQ17 |
| Bassett Av, G13 | 46 | BD21 |
| Bassett Cres, G13 | 46 | BD21 |
| Bathgate St, G31 | 69 | BW31 |
| Bathgo Av, Pais. PA1 | 84 | BA33 |
| Bath La, G2 | 4 | BQ29 |
| Bath La W, G3 | | |
| *off North St* | 4 | BP29 |
| Bath St, G2 | 4 | BQ29 |
| Batson St, G42 | 87 | BR35 |
| Battlefield Av, G42 | 87 | BQ38 |
| Battlefield Cres, G42 | | |
| *off Battlefield Gdns* | 87 | BQ38 |
| Battlefield Gdns, G42 | 87 | BQ37 |
| Battlefield Rd, G42 | 87 | BQ37 |
| Battle Pl, G41 | 87 | BP37 |
| Battles Burn Dr, G32 | 90 | CC35 |
| Battles Burn Gate, G32 | 90 | CC35 |
| Battles Burn Vw, G32 | 90 | CC35 |
| Bavelaw St, G33 | 71 | CF27 |
| Bayfield Av, G15 | 28 | BC18 |
| Bayfield Ter, G15 | 28 | BC18 |
| Beacon Pl, G33 | | |
| *off Bellrock St* | 70 | CB29 |
| Beaconsfield Rd, G12 | 48 | BK24 |
| Beard Cres, (Gart.) G69 | 55 | CP24 |
| Beardmore Cotts, (Inch.) | | |
| Renf. PA4 | 44 | AU23 |
| Beardmore Pl, Clyde. G81 | 26 | AU18 |
| Beardmore St, Clyde. G81 | 26 | AT18 |
| Beardmore Way, G31 | 69 | BX31 |
| Beardmore Way, Clyde. G81 | 26 | AT19 |
| Bearford Dr, G52 | 64 | BD32 |
| Bearsden Rd, G13 | 47 | BH23 |
| Bearsden Rd, (Bears.) G61 | 47 | BH23 |
| Bearsden Shop Cen, (Bears.) G61 | 30 | BJ17 |
| Beaton Rd, G41 | 87 | BN35 |
| Beaton St, Lark. ML9 | 144 | DB57 |
| Beatrice Dr, Moth. ML1 | 112 | DB40 |
| Beatson Wynd, (Udd.) G71 | | |
| *off Macmillan Gdns* | 93 | CQ36 |
| Beattock St, G31 | 69 | BZ32 |
| Beattock Wynd, Ham. ML3 | 125 | CQ50 |
| Beatty St, Clyde. G81 | 26 | AU18 |
| Beaufort Av, G43 | 102 | BL39 |

| | | |
|---|---|---|
| Beaufort Dr, (Kirk.) G66 | 16 | CD13 |
| Beaufort Gdns, (Bishop.) G64 | 32 | BU20 |
| Beauly Dr, Pais. PA2 | 81 | AN36 |
| Beauly Pl, G20 | 48 | BM23 |
| Beauly Pl, (Bishop.) G64 | 33 | BZ19 |
| Beauly Pl, (Chry.) G69 | 36 | CM20 |
| Beauly Pl, (E.Kil.) G74 | 135 | BZ51 |
| Beauly Pl, Coat. ML5 | 95 | CX34 |
| Beauly Rd, (Baill.) G69 | 92 | CJ34 |
| Beaumont Gate, G12 | 48 | BL26 |
| Beckfield Cres, G33 | | |
| *off Brookfield Av* | 51 | BZ22 |
| Beckfield Dr, G33 | 51 | BZ22 |
| Beckfield Gate, G33 | | |
| *off Brookfield Av* | 51 | BZ22 |
| Beckfield Gro, G33 | 51 | BZ22 |
| Beckfield Pl, G33 | | |
| *off Brookfield Av* | 51 | BZ22 |
| Beckfield Wk, G33 | | |
| *off Brookfield Av* | 51 | BZ22 |
| Beckford St, Ham. ML3 | 126 | CS48 |
| Beckford St Business Pk, | | |
| Ham. ML3 | 126 | CS48 |
| Bedale Rd, (Baill.) G69 | 91 | CH33 |
| Bedcow Vw, (Kirk.) G66 | 17 | CH14 |
| Bedford Av, Clyde. G81 | 27 | AZ19 |
| Bedford La, G5 | 67 | BR32 |
| Bedford St, G5 | 67 | BR32 |
| Bedlay Ct, (Chry.) G69 | 37 | CQ18 |
| Bedlay Pl, (Annathill) | | |
| Coat. ML5 | 38 | CV20 |
| Bedlay Vw, (Udd.) G71 | 93 | CR36 |
| Bedlay Wk, (Chry.) G69 | | |
| *off Bedlay Ct* | 37 | CQ18 |
| Beech Av, G41 | 86 | BK33 |
| Beech Av, (Bears.) G61 | 12 | BJ14 |
| Beech Av, (Camb.) G72 | 72 | CJ32 |
| Beech Av, (Camb.) G72 | 106 | CB39 |
| Beech Av, (Ruther.) G73 | 105 | BY41 |
| Beech Av, (Newt. M.) G77 | 117 | BF49 |
| Beech Av, (Elder.) John. PA5 | 80 | AL35 |
| Beech Av, Lark. ML9 | 145 | DE59 |
| Beech Av, Moth. ML1 | 112 | DD42 |
| Beech Av, Pais. PA2 | 83 | AW36 |
| Beechbank Av, Air. ML6 | 76 | DB29 |
| Beech Ct, Coat. ML5 | | |
| *off Ailsa Rd* | 94 | CV33 |
| Beech Cres, (Camb.) G72 | 107 | CG41 |
| Beech Cres, (Newt. M.) G77 | 117 | BG50 |
| Beech Cres, Moth. ML1 | 97 | DE38 |
| Beech Dr, Clyde. G81 | 27 | AW16 |
| Beeches, The, (Blan.) G72 | | |
| *off Burnbrae Rd* | 124 | CL46 |
| Beeches, The, (Newt. M.) G77 | 117 | BH47 |
| Beeches Av, Clyde. G81 | 26 | AV15 |
| Beeches Rd, Clyde. G81 | 26 | AV15 |
| Beeches Ter, Clyde. G81 | 27 | AW15 |
| Beech Gdns, (Baill.) G69 | 72 | CJ32 |
| Beechgrove, (Chry.) G69 | 37 | CP19 |
| Beech Gro, (Gart.) G69 | 55 | CQ24 |
| Beech Gro, (E.Kil.) G75 | 135 | BX55 |
| Beechgrove Av, (Udd.) G71 | 94 | CS38 |
| Beechgrove Quad, Moth. ML1 | | |
| *off Graham St* | 112 | DC40 |
| Beechgrove St, G40 | 89 | BX35 |
| Beechlands Av, G44 | 103 | BN43 |
| Beechlands Dr, (Clark.) G76 | 118 | BL46 |
| Beechmount Rd, (Lenz.) G66 | 35 | CE17 |
| Beech Pl, (Bishop.) G64 | 51 | BX21 |
| Beech Pl, (Blan.) G72 | 125 | CN46 |
| Beech Rd, (Bishop.) G64 | 51 | BX21 |
| Beech Rd, (Lenz.) G66 | 35 | CE15 |
| Beech Rd, John. PA5 | 79 | AF35 |

| | | |
|---|---|---|
| Beech Rd, Moth. ML1 | 97 | DE38 |
| Beech Ter, Lark. ML9 | 144 | DD60 |
| Beechwood, Lark. ML9 | 142 | DC56 |
| Beechwood, Wis. ML2 | 143 | DF52 |
| Beechwood Av, (Ruther.) G73 | 105 | BY39 |
| Beechwood Av, (Clark.) G76 | 118 | BL47 |
| Beechwood Av, Ham. ML3 | 139 | CR53 |
| Beechwood Ct, (Bears.) G61 | | |
| off Drymen Rd | 29 | BH18 |
| Beechwood Ct, (Cumb.) G67 | 22 | DB13 |
| Beechwood Dr, G11 | 47 | BH25 |
| Beechwood Dr, Coat. ML5 | 75 | CY32 |
| Beechwood Dr, Renf. PA4 | 63 | AX28 |
| Beechwood Gdns, (Mood.) G69 | 37 | CP20 |
| Beechwood Gdns, Bell. ML4 | 111 | CY41 |
| Beechwood Gro, (Barr.) G78 | 99 | AY44 |
| Beechwood La, (Bears.) G61 | 29 | BH18 |
| Beechwood Pl, G11 | 47 | BH25 |
| Beechwood Pl, Bell. ML4 | 111 | CY41 |
| Beechwood Rd, (Cumb.) G67 | 22 | DB12 |
| Beechworth Dr, Moth. ML1 | 113 | DF43 |
| Beecroft Pl, (Blan.) G72 | 109 | CN44 |
| Beil Dr, G13 | 46 | BB22 |
| Beith Dr, Air. ML6 | 96 | DC33 |
| Beith Rd, John. PA5 | 80 | AJ35 |
| Beith Rd, (How.) John. PA9 | 78 | AD38 |
| Beith Rd, (Kilb.) John. PA10 | 78 | AD38 |
| Beith St, G11 | 66 | BK28 |
| Belford Ct, (Newt. M.) G77 | 131 | BF51 |
| Belford Gro, (Newt. M.) G77 | 131 | BF51 |
| Belgowan St, (Bellshill Ind. Est.) | | |
| Bell. ML4 | 94 | CV38 |
| Belgrave La, G12 | 49 | BN26 |
| Belgrave St, (Bellshill Ind. Est.) | | |
| Bell. ML4 | 110 | CV39 |
| Belgrave Ter, G12 | 49 | BN26 |
| Belhaven Ct, (Newt. M.) G77 | 131 | BE51 |
| Belhaven Cres La, G12 | | |
| off Kensington Rd | 48 | BL25 |
| Belhaven Pk, (Muir.) G69 | 54 | CL22 |
| Belhaven Pl, (Newt. M.) G77 | 131 | BF51 |
| Belhaven Rd, Ham. ML3 | 125 | CN50 |
| Belhaven Ter, G12 | 48 | BL25 |
| Belhaven Ter, (Ruther.) G73 | 105 | BY39 |
| Belhaven Ter La, G12 | 48 | BL25 |
| Belhaven Ter W, G12 | 48 | BL25 |
| Belhaven Ter W La, G12 | 48 | BL25 |
| Bellahouston Dr, G52 | 85 | BG34 |
| Bellahouston La, G52 | 85 | BG33 |
| Bellairs Pl, (Blan.) G72 | 108 | CL44 |
| Bellcraig Ct, (Clark.) G76 | | |
| off Easterton Av | 119 | BR48 |
| Bell Dr, (Blan.) G72 | 124 | CL49 |
| Belleisle Av, (Udd.) G71 | 109 | CN39 |
| Belleisle Ct, (Cumb.) G68 | 22 | DA9 |
| Belleisle Dr, (Cumb.) G68 | 22 | DA9 |
| Belleisle Gdns, (Cumb.) G68 | 22 | DA9 |
| Belleisle Gro, (Cumb.) G68 | 22 | DA9 |
| Belleisle St, G42 | 87 | BR36 |
| Bellevue Av, (Kirk.) G66 | 16 | CD13 |
| Bellevue Pl, G21 | 68 | BV28 |
| Bellevue Rd, (Kirk.) G66 | 16 | CD13 |
| Bellfield Ct, (Barr.) G78 | | |
| off Bellfield Cres | 99 | AX41 |
| Bellfield Cres, (Barr.) G78 | 99 | AX41 |
| Bellfield Rd, (Kirk.) G66 | 16 | CD13 |
| Bellfield St, G31 | 69 | BW31 |
| Bellflower Av, G53 | 100 | BD42 |
| Bellflower Ct, (E.Kil.) G74 | 121 | BY50 |
| Bellflower Gdns, G53 | 101 | BE42 |
| Bellflower Gro, (E.Kil.) G74 | 121 | BY50 |
| Bellflower Pl, G53 | 101 | BE42 |
| Bell Grn E, (E.Kil.) G75 | 136 | CB53 |
| Bell Grn W, (E.Kil.) G75 | 136 | CA53 |
| Bellgrove St, G31 | 68 | BV31 |
| Bellisle Ter, Ham. ML3 | | |
| off Pitreavie Ct | 139 | CR53 |
| Bellrock Ct, G33 | 70 | CD29 |
| Bellrock Cres, G33 | 70 | CC29 |
| Bellrock Path, G33 | | |
| off Bellrock St | 70 | CD29 |
| Bellrock St, G33 | 70 | CC29 |
| Bellrock Vw, G33 | 70 | CC29 |
| Bellscroft Av, (Ruther.) G73 | 88 | BV38 |
| Bellsdyke Rd, Air. ML6 | 76 | DB31 |
| Bellsfield Dr, (Blan.) G72 | 124 | CM47 |
| Bellshaugh Ct, G12 | 48 | BL24 |
| Bellshaugh Gdns, G12 | 48 | BL24 |
| Bellshaugh La, G12 | 48 | BL24 |
| Bellshaugh Pl, G12 | 48 | BL24 |
| Bellshaugh Rd, G12 | 48 | BL24 |
| Bellshill N Ind Est, Bell. ML4 | 110 | CV39 |
| Bellshill Rd, (Both.) G71 | 110 | CT43 |
| Bellshill Rd, (Udd.) G71 | 109 | CP40 |
| Bellshill Rd, Bell. ML4 | 110 | CT43 |
| Bellshill Rd, Moth. ML1 | 111 | CV43 |
| Bellside Rd, (Chap.) Air. ML6 | 97 | DG35 |
| Bell St, G1 | 5 | BT31 |
| Bell St, G4 | 5 | BT31 |
| Bell St, Air. ML6 | 76 | DB29 |
| Bell St, Bell. ML4 | 95 | CX38 |
| Bell St, Clyde. G81 | 45 | AZ22 |
| Bell St, Renf. PA4 | 45 | AZ25 |
| Bell St, Wis. ML2 | 129 | DH50 |
| Belltrees Cres, Pais. PA3 | 81 | AQ33 |
| Bellview Ct, Renf. PA4 | 45 | AZ25 |
| Bellvue Cres, Bell. ML4 | 110 | CU41 |
| Bellvue Way, Coat. ML5 | 95 | CZ33 |
| Bellwood St, G41 | 87 | BN38 |
| Bellziehill Rd, Bell. ML4 | 110 | CU40 |
| Belmar Ct, (Linw.) Pais. PA3 | | |
| off Langholm Dr | 60 | AL32 |
| Belmont Av, (Udd.) G71 | 93 | CN38 |
| Belmont Ct, (Kirk.) G66 | | |
| off Willowbank Gdns | 17 | CF13 |
| Belmont Cres, G12 | 49 | BN26 |
| Belmont Dr, (Giff.) G46 | 102 | BK42 |
| Belmont Dr, (Ruther.) G73 | 89 | BX38 |
| Belmont Dr, (E.Kil.) G75 | 135 | BX53 |
| Belmont Dr, (Barr.) G78 | 99 | AZ44 |
| Belmont La, G12 | 49 | BN26 |
| Belmont Rd, G21 | 50 | BV23 |
| Belmont Rd, (Camb.) G72 | 106 | CA41 |
| Belmont Rd, Pais. PA3 | 63 | AW31 |
| Belmont St, G12 | 49 | BN26 |
| Belmont St, (Kilsyth) G65 | 7 | CS4 |
| Belmont St, Clyde. G81 | 45 | AX21 |
| Belmont St, Coat. ML5 | 74 | CT28 |
| Belses Dr, G52 | 65 | BE32 |
| Belses Gdns, G52 | 65 | BE32 |
| Belstane Pl, (Both.) G71 | 109 | CQ42 |
| Belstane Rd, G67 | 40 | DB16 |
| Belsyde Av, G15 | 28 | BC19 |
| Beltane St, G3 | 4 | BP29 |
| Beltrees Av, G53 | 84 | BC36 |
| Beltrees Cres, G53 | 84 | BC36 |
| Beltrees Rd, G53 | 84 | BC36 |
| Belvidere Av, G31 | 89 | BY35 |
| Belvidere Cres, (Bishop.) G64 | 33 | BX19 |
| Belvidere Cres, Bell. ML4 | 111 | CX41 |
| Belvidere Gate, G31 | 89 | BY33 |
| Belvidere Rd, Bell. ML4 | 111 | CW41 |
| Belvoir Pl, (Blan.) G72 | 124 | CM45 |
| Bemersyde, (Bishop.) G64 | 33 | BX19 |
| Bemersyde Av, G43 | 102 | BK40 |
| Bemersyde Pl, Lark. ML9 | 144 | DC60 |
| Bemersyde Rd, Pais. PA2 | 80 | AM37 |
| Ben Aigan Pl, G53 | 101 | BE40 |
| Ben Alder Dr, Pais. PA2 | 83 | AZ36 |
| Benalder St, G11 | 66 | BL28 |
| Benarty Gdns, (Bishop.) G64 | 33 | BX19 |
| Benbecula, (E.Kil.) G74 | 137 | CE52 |
| Benbow Rd, Clyde. G81 | 26 | AV19 |
| Ben Buie Way, Pais. PA2 | 83 | AZ36 |
| Bencroft Dr, G44 | 104 | BU40 |
| Ben Donich Pl, G53 | | |
| off Ben Vorlich Dr | 101 | BF41 |
| Ben Edra Pl, G53 | | |
| off Ben Vorlich Dr | 101 | BF41 |
| Benford Av, Moth. ML1 | 113 | DF41 |
| Benford Knowe, Moth. ML1 | 113 | DG41 |
| Bengairn St, G31 | 69 | BY30 |
| Bengal Pl, G43 | | |
| off Christian St | 86 | BL38 |
| Bengal St, G43 | 86 | BL38 |
| Ben Garrisdale Pl, G53 | | |
| off Ben Vorlich Dr | 101 | BF41 |
| Ben Glas Pl, G53 | | |
| off Ben Vorlich Dr | 101 | BF40 |
| Benhar Pl, G33 | 70 | CB30 |
| Benholm St, G32 | 90 | CB34 |
| Ben Hope Av, Pais. PA2 | 83 | AZ35 |
| Ben Laga Pl, G53 | | |
| off Ben Vorlich Dr | 101 | BF41 |
| Ben Lawers Dr, (Cumb.) G68 | 21 | CX11 |
| Ben Lawers Dr, Pais. PA2 | 83 | AZ35 |
| Ben Ledi Av, Pais. PA2 | 83 | AZ35 |
| Ben Ledi Cres, (Cumb.) G68 | 21 | CX11 |
| Ben Loyal Av, Pais. PA2 | 83 | AZ35 |
| Ben Lui Dr, Pais. PA2 | 83 | AY36 |
| Ben Lui Pl, G53 | | |
| off Ben Vorlich Dr | 101 | BF41 |
| Ben Lui Pl, (Cumb.) G68 | 21 | CX11 |
| Ben Macdui Gdns, G53 | 101 | BF41 |
| Ben More Dr, G68 | 21 | CW11 |
| Ben More Dr, Pais. PA2 | 83 | AZ35 |
| Benmore St, G21 | 50 | BV23 |
| Bennan Sq, G42 | 88 | BS35 |
| Benn Av, Pais. PA1 | 83 | AW33 |
| Ben Nevis Rd, Pais. PA2 | 83 | AY36 |
| Ben Nevis Way, (Cumb.) G68 | 21 | CW11 |
| Benny Lynch Ct, G5 | 68 | BS32 |
| Ben Oss Pl, G53 | 101 | BE41 |
| Benson St, Coat. ML5 | 95 | CW33 |
| Benston Rd, John. PA5 | 79 | AG36 |
| Bent Cres, (Udd.) G71 | 110 | CS39 |
| Benthall St, G5 | 88 | BT33 |
| Bentinck Gra, (E.Kil.) G74 | 134 | BT53 |
| Bentinck St, G3 | 67 | BN28 |
| Bent Rd, (Chap.) Air. ML6 | 97 | DF34 |
| Bent Rd, Ham. ML3 | 126 | CS50 |
| Bents Rd, (Baill.) G69 | 72 | CK32 |
| Ben Uird Pl, G53 | 101 | BF41 |
| Ben Vane Av, Pais. PA2 | 83 | AY36 |
| Ben Venue Rd, (Cumb.) G68 | 21 | CW11 |
| Ben Venue Way, Pais. PA2 | 83 | AZ36 |
| Benvie Gdns, (Bishop.) G64 | 33 | BX19 |
| Benview Rd, (Clark.) G76 | 119 | BN46 |
| Benview St, G20 | 49 | BP25 |
| Benview Ter, Pais. PA2 | 83 | AX35 |
| Ben Vorlich Dr, G53 | 101 | BF41 |
| Ben Vorlich Pl, G53 | 101 | BF41 |
| Ben Wyvis Dr, Pais. PA2 | 83 | AY36 |
| Berelands Cres, (Ruther.) G73 | 88 | BU38 |
| Berelands Pl, (Ruther.) G73 | 88 | BV38 |
| Beresford Av, G14 | 47 | BG25 |
| Berkeley St, G3 | 67 | BN29 |
| Berkeley Ter La, G3 | 4 | BP29 |
| Berkley Dr, (Blan.) G72 | 108 | CL44 |

| | | | | | | | |
|---|---|---|---|---|---|---|---|
| Bernadette Cres, Moth. ML1 | 113 | DF43 | Birch Pl, (Blan.) G72 | 124 | CM45 | Blackadder Pl, (E.Kil.) G75 | 134 | BT54 |
| Bernard Path, G40 | 89 | BW33 | Birch Pl, (Camb.) G72 | 107 | CH41 | Blackbog Rd, Air. ML6 | 40 | DB19 |
| Bernard St, G40 | 89 | BW33 | Birch Quad. Air. ML6 | 77 | DF30 | Blackbraes Av, (E.Kil.) G74 | 122 | CD49 |
| Bernard Ter, G40 | 89 | BW33 | Birch Rd, (Cumb.) G67 | 23 | DG10 | Blackbraes Rd, (E.Kil.) G74 | 122 | CD49 |
| Berneray St, G22 | 50 | BS22 | Birch Rd, Clyde. G81 | 27 | AW17 | Blackburn Cres, (Kirk.) G66 | 18 | CJ13 |
| Bernisdale Dr, G15 | 27 | AZ18 | Birch St, G5 | | | Blackburn Sq, (Barr.) G78 | 99 | AZ44 |
| Bernisdale Gdns, G15 | 27 | AZ18 | off Silverfir St | 88 | BT33 | Blackburn St, G51 | 66 | BM31 |
| Bernisdale Pl, G15 | 27 | AZ18 | Birch St, Moth. ML1 | 112 | DD40 | Blackbyres Ct, (Barr.) G78 | 99 | AZ41 |
| Berridale Av, G44 | 103 | BQ39 | Birch Vw, (Bears.) G61 | 30 | BJ16 | Blackbyres Rd, (Barr.) G78 | 99 | AY39 |
| Berriedale, (E.Kil.) G75 | 134 | BT53 | Birchview Dr, (Clark.) G76 | 119 | BP49 | Blackcraig Av, G15 | 28 | BC18 |
| Berriedale Av, (Baill.) G69 | 92 | CJ33 | Birchwood Av, G32 | 91 | CG33 | Blackcroft Av, Air. ML6 | 77 | DG32 |
| Berryburn Rd, G21 | 51 | BY25 | Birchwood Dr, Pais. PA2 | 81 | AQ36 | Blackcroft Gdns, G32 | 91 | CF33 |
| Berry Dyke, (Kirk.) G66 | | | Birchwood Pl, G32 | 91 | CG33 | Blackcroft Rd, G32 | 91 | CF33 |
| off Burnbrae Rd | 18 | CK14 | Birdsfield Ct, Ham. ML3 | | | Blackdyke Rd, (Kirk.) G66 | 17 | CG13 |
| Berryhill Dr, (Giff.) G46 | 102 | BK43 | off Birdsfield St | 125 | CP47 | Blackfarm Rd, (Newt. M.) G77 | 117 | BH49 |
| Berryhill Rd, (Giff.) G46 | 102 | BK44 | Birdsfield Dr, (Blan.) G72 | 124 | CM47 | Blackfaulds Rd, (Ruther.) G73 | 88 | BU37 |
| Berryhill Rd, (Cumb.) G67 | 22 | DA11 | Birdsfield St, Ham. ML3 | 125 | CP47 | Blackford Rd, Pais. PA2 | 83 | AW34 |
| Berryknowe, (Kirk.) G66 | | | Birdston Rd, G21 | 51 | BY23 | Blackfriars Rd, G1 | 5 | BT30 |
| off Alexander Pl | 18 | CK14 | Birgidale Rd, G45 | 104 | BT43 | Blackfriars St, G1 | 5 | BT30 |
| Berryknowe Av, (Chry.) G69 | 54 | CL22 | Birgidale Ter, G45 | 104 | BT43 | Blackhall Ct, Pais. PA2 | | |
| Berryknowes Av, G52 | 65 | BE32 | Birkdale, (E.Kil.) G74 | 121 | BY50 | off Cartha Cres | 83 | AX34 |
| Berryknowes Dr, G52 | 65 | BF32 | Birkdale Ct, (Both.) G71 | 109 | CP43 | Blackhall La, Pais. PA1 | 82 | AV34 |
| Berryknowes La, G52 | 65 | BE32 | Birkdale Cres, (Cumb.) G68 | 9 | DB7 | Blackhall St, Pais. PA1 | 82 | AV34 |
| Berryknowes Rd, G52 | 65 | BE32 | Birkdale Wd, (Cumb.) G68 | 9 | DC7 | Blackhill Cotts, G23 | 31 | BQ20 |
| Bertram St, G41 | 87 | BN36 | Birken Rd, (Lenz.) G66 | 35 | CG17 | Blackhill Ct, G23 | 30 | BM19 |
| Bertram St, Ham. ML3 | 125 | CQ47 | Birkenshaw Ind Est, (Udd.) G71 | 93 | CN35 | Blackhill Dr, G23 | 31 | BN19 |
| Bertram St, Lark. ML9 | | | Birkenshaw Rd, (Gart.) G69 | 56 | CS21 | Blackhill Gdns, G23 | 30 | BM19 |
| off Keir Hardie Rd | 145 | DE60 | Birkenshaw St, G31 | 69 | BX30 | Blackhill Pl, G33 | | |
| Bertrohill Ter, G33 | | | Birkenshaw Way, Pais. PA3 | 62 | AU29 | off Maxwelton Rd | 70 | CA27 |
| off Stepps Rd | 71 | CE30 | Birkhall Av, G52 | 84 | BB33 | Blackhill Rd, G23 | 31 | BN19 |
| Bervie St, G51 | 65 | BH31 | Birkhall Av, (Inch.) Renf. PA4 | 44 | AT22 | Blackhouse Av, (Newt. M.) |
| Berwick Cres, Air. ML6 | 76 | DB32 | Birkhall Dr, (Bears.) G61 | 29 | BH19 | G77 | 117 | BH49 |
| Berwick Dr, G52 | 84 | BD33 | Birkhill Av, (Bishop.) G64 | 33 | BX19 | Blackhouse Gdns, (Newt. M.) |
| Berwick Dr, (Ruther.) G73 | 105 | BZ39 | Birkhill Gdns, (Bishop.) G64 | 33 | BX19 | G77 | 117 | BH49 |
| Berwick Pl, (E.Kil.) G74 | 123 | CE50 | Birkhill Rd, Ham. ML3 | 140 | CT54 | Blackhouse Rd, (Newt. M.) |
| Berwick Pl, Coat. ML5 | 95 | CX34 | Birkmyre Rd, G51 | 65 | BH31 | G77 | 117 | BH49 |
| Berwick St, Coat. ML5 | 95 | CX34 | Birks Rd, Lark. ML9 | 144 | DD62 | Blackie St, G3 | 66 | BM29 |
| Berwick St, Ham. ML3 | 125 | CR48 | Birks Rd, Renf. PA4 | | | Blackland Gro, Pais. PA2 | 82 | AS37 |
| Bessemer Dr, (E.Kil.) G75 | 136 | CC56 | off Tower Dr | 63 | AX27 | Blacklands Pl, (Lenz.) G66 | 35 | CG17 |
| Betula Dr, Clyde. G81 | 27 | AW16 | Birkwood Pl, (Newt. M.) G77 | 131 | BF51 | Blacklands Rd, (E.Kil.) G74 | 135 | BZ52 |
| Bevan Gro, John. PA5 | 79 | AF35 | Birkwood St, G40 | | | Blacklaw Dr, (E.Kil.) G74 | 136 | CD52 |
| Beveridge Ter, Bell. ML4 | 111 | CZ41 | off Dalmarnock Rd | 89 | BX35 | Blacklaw La, Pais. PA3 | 62 | AU31 |
| Beverley Rd, G43 | 102 | BM39 | Birmingham Rd, Renf. PA4 | 63 | AX28 | Blackmoor Pl, Moth. ML1 | 112 | DC42 |
| Bevin Av, Clyde. G81 | 27 | AZ20 | Birnam Av, (Bishop.) G64 | 33 | BX19 | Blackmoss Dr, Bell. ML4 | | |
| Bideford Cres, G32 | 91 | CF34 | Birnam Cres, (Bears.) G61 | 30 | BK16 | off Hamilton Rd | 111 | CW41 |
| Biggar Rd, Moth. ML1 | 97 | DH38 | Birnam Gdns, (Bishop.) G64 | 33 | BX19 | Blackness St, Coat. ML5 | 95 | CX34 |
| Biggar St, G31 | 69 | BX31 | Birnam Pl, (Newt. M.) G77 | 118 | BK49 | Black O' Hill Rbt, (Cumb.) G68 | 21 | CW12 |
| Bigton St, G33 | 70 | CD27 | Birnam Pl, Ham. ML3 | 125 | CN50 | Blacksey Burn Dr, G53 | 84 | BB35 |
| Billings Rd, Moth. ML1 | 127 | CX48 | Birnam Rd, G31 | | | Blackstone Av, G53 | 85 | BE37 |
| Bilsland Ct, G20 | 49 | BR24 | off London Rd | 89 | BZ34 | Blackstone Cres, G53 | 85 | BE36 |
| Bilsland Dr, G20 | 49 | BP24 | Birness Dr, G43 | 86 | BM37 | Blackstone Rd, Pais. PA3 | 61 | AQ29 |
| Binend Rd, G53 | 85 | BE37 | Birness St, G43 | | | Blackstoun Av, (Linw.) |
| Binniehill Rd, (Cumb.) G68 | 21 | CZ11 | off Pleasance St | 86 | BM38 | Pais. PA3 | 60 | AK32 |
| Binnie Pl, G40 | 68 | BU32 | Birnie Ct, G21 | 51 | BY26 | Blackstoun Oval, Pais. PA3 | 61 | AR32 |
| Binns Rd, G33 | 71 | CE27 | Birniehill Rbt, (E.Kil.) G74 | 136 | CC53 | Blackstoun Rd, Pais. PA3 | 61 | AQ32 |
| Birch Av, (Clark.) G76 | 119 | BP47 | Birnie Rd, G21 | 51 | BY25 | Black St, G4 | 5 | BT28 |
| Birch Brae, Ham. ML3 | 140 | CU52 | Birnock Av, Renf. PA4 | 64 | BA28 | Black St, Air. ML6 | 76 | DD28 |
| Birch Ct, Coat. ML5 | | | Birrell Rd, (Miln.) G62 | 11 | BH10 | Blackswell La, Ham. ML3 | 126 | CV50 |
| off Ailsa Rd | 94 | CV33 | Birrens Rd, Moth. ML1 | 127 | CY45 | Blackthorn Av, (Kirk.) G66 | 34 | CC16 |
| Birch Cres, (Clark.) G76 | 119 | BP47 | Birsay Rd, G22 | 49 | BR22 | Blackthorn Gro, (Kirk.) G66 | 34 | CD16 |
| Birch Cres, John. PA5 | 80 | AJ36 | Bishopdale, (E.Kil.) G74 | 121 | BY50 | Blackthorn Rd, (Cumb.) G67 | 23 | DF9 |
| Birch Dr, (Lenz.) G66 | 35 | CF16 | Bishop Gdns, (Bishop.) G64 | 32 | BU19 | Blackthorn Rd, (Udd.) G71 | | |
| Birch Dr, (Camb.) G72 | 107 | CE39 | Bishop Gdns, Ham. ML3 | 140 | CU54 | off Redwood Cres | 94 | CS37 |
| Birchend Dr, G21 | 69 | BX27 | Bishopmill Pl, G21 | 51 | BY25 | Blackthorn St, G22 | 50 | BU24 |
| Birchend Pl, G21 | 69 | BW27 | Bishopmill Rd, G21 | 51 | BY24 | Blacktongue Fm Rd, (Green.) |
| Birchfield Dr, G14 | 46 | BD25 | Bishops Gate, (Thornton.) G74 | 134 | BS51 | Air. ML6 | 41 | DG19 |
| Birchfield Rd, Ham. ML3 | 125 | CR50 | Bishopsgate Dr, G21 | 50 | BU22 | Blackwood, (E.Kil.) G75 | 135 | BZ56 |
| Birch Gro, (Udd.) G71 | 93 | CR38 | Bishopsgate Gdns, G21 | 50 | BU22 | Blackwood Av, (Newt. M.) G77 | 117 | BH50 |
| Birchgrove, Lark. ML9 | 142 | DC56 | Bishopsgate Pl, G21 | 50 | BU22 | Blackwood Av, (Linw.) Pais. PA3 | 60 | AJ31 |
| Birch Knowe, (Bishop.) G64 | 51 | BX21 | Bishopsgate Rd, G21 | 50 | BU22 | Blackwood Rd, (Miln.) G62 | 11 | BH9 |
| Birchlea Dr, (Giff.) G46 | 102 | BM41 | Bishops Pk, (Thornton.) G74 | 119 | BR50 | Blackwood Rd, G68 | 20 | CT12 |
| Birchmount Ct, Air. ML6 | | | Bishop St, G3 | 4 | BQ30 | Blackwood Rbt, (Cumb.) G68 | 20 | CV11 |
| off Forrest St | 77 | DE29 | Bissett Cres, Clyde. G81 | 26 | AU15 | Blackwoods Cres, (Mood.) G69 | 37 | CP19 |

| | | |
|---|---|---|
| Blackwoods Cres, Bell. ML4 | 111 | CY41 |
| Blackwoods Gdns, Moth. ML1 | | |
| *off Frood St* | 111 | CY44 |
| Blackwood St, G13 | 47 | BG22 |
| Blackwood St, (Barr.) G78 | 99 | AX43 |
| Blackwood Ter, John. PA5 | 79 | AF37 |
| Bladda La, Pais. PA1 | 82 | AV33 |
| Blades Ct, (Gart.) G69 | 55 | CQ23 |
| Bladnoch Dr, G15 | 29 | BE19 |
| Blaeloch Av, G45 | 104 | BS44 |
| Blaeloch Dr, G45 | 103 | BR44 |
| Blaeloch Ter, G45 | 103 | BR44 |
| Blaeshill Rd, (E.Kil.) G75 | 134 | BU53 |
| Blairatholl Av, G11 | 48 | BJ26 |
| Blairatholl Cres, (Newt. M.) | | |
| G77 | 118 | BK49 |
| Blair Atholl Dr, Lark. ML9 | 145 | DE60 |
| Blairatholl Gdns, G11 | 48 | BJ26 |
| Blairatholl Gate, (Newt. M.) | | |
| G77 | 118 | BK49 |
| Blairbeth Ct, (Ruther.) G73 | 105 | BW40 |
| Blairbeth Dr, G44 | 87 | BR38 |
| Blairbeth Pl, (Ruther.) G73 | | |
| *off Drumilaw Rd* | 105 | BW40 |
| Blairbeth Rd, (Ruther.) G73 | 105 | BW40 |
| Blairbeth Ter, (Ruther.) G73 | | |
| *off Blairbeth Rd* | 105 | BY40 |
| Blairbuie Dr, G20 | 48 | BL22 |
| Blair Cres, (Baill.) G69 | 92 | CJ34 |
| Blairdardie Dr, G15 | 28 | BD20 |
| Blairdardie Rd, G13 | 28 | BD20 |
| Blairdardie Rd, G15 | 28 | BD20 |
| Blairdenan Av, (Mood.) G69 | 37 | CP18 |
| Blairdenon Dr, (Cumb.) G68 | 21 | CY11 |
| Blair Gdns, (Torr.) G64 | 15 | BX12 |
| Blair Gdns, (Newt. M.) G77 | 116 | BD48 |
| Blairgowrie Rd, G52 | 85 | BE33 |
| Blairgrove Ct, Coat. ML5 | 74 | CU31 |
| Blairhall Av, G41 | 87 | BP37 |
| Blairhill Av, (Kirk.) G66 | 36 | CJ15 |
| Blairhill Pl, Coat. ML5 | 74 | CU30 |
| Blairhill St, Coat. ML5 | 74 | CU30 |
| Blairholm Dr, Bell. ML4 | 111 | CX42 |
| Blairlinn Ind Est, (Cumb.) G67 | 40 | DB15 |
| Blairlinn Rd, (Cumb.) G67 | 40 | DB15 |
| Blairlinn Vw, (Cumb.) G67 | 40 | DC15 |
| Blairlogie St, G33 | 70 | CD28 |
| Blairmore Av, Pais. PA1 | 63 | AY32 |
| Blairpark Av, Coat. ML5 | 74 | CU29 |
| Blair Path, Moth. ML1 | | |
| *off Toll St* | 128 | DB48 |
| Blair Rd, Coat. ML5 | 74 | CU31 |
| Blair Rd, Pais. PA1 | 64 | BA31 |
| Blairston Av, (Both.) G71 | 109 | CQ44 |
| Blairston Gdns, (Both.) G71 | 109 | CR44 |
| Blair St, G32 | 70 | CB32 |
| Blairtum Dr, (Ruther.) G73 | 105 | BX40 |
| Blairtummock Pl, G33 | 71 | CF29 |
| Blairtummock Rd, G33 | 71 | CE29 |
| Blake Rd, (Cumb.) G67 | 22 | DC11 |
| Blane Dr, (Miln.) G62 | 12 | BK10 |
| Blanefield Gdns, G13 | 47 | BH21 |
| Blane St, Coat. ML5 | 75 | CW29 |
| Blaneview, (Stepps) G33 | 53 | CF25 |
| Blantyre Ct, Ersk. PA8 | 25 | AQ18 |
| Blantyre Ferme Rd, (Udd.) | | |
| G71 | 108 | CL39 |
| Blantyre Gdns, (Cumb.) G68 | 20 | CU12 |
| Blantyre Ind Est, (Blan.) G72 | 125 | CN48 |
| Blantyre Mill Rd, (Both.) G71 | 109 | CP44 |
| Blantyre Rd, (Both.) G71 | 109 | CQ43 |
| Blantyre St, G3 | 66 | BM28 |
| Blantyre St, Coat. ML5 | 94 | CU33 |
| Blaven Ct, (Baill.) G69 | 92 | CL33 |
| Blawarthill St, G14 | 46 | BB24 |
| Bleasdale Ct, Clyde. G81 | 27 | AX19 |
| Blenheim Av, (Stepps) G33 | 53 | CF23 |
| Blenheim Av, (E.Kil.) G75 | 135 | BY54 |
| Blenheim Ct, (Stepps) G33 | 53 | CF23 |
| Blenheim Ct, (Kilsyth) G65 | 7 | CT4 |
| Blenheim Ct, Pais. PA1 | 62 | AT32 |
| Blenheim La, (Stepps) G33 | 53 | CG23 |
| Blochairn Rd, G21 | 69 | BW28 |
| Bluebell Gdns, G45 | 105 | BW43 |
| Bluebell Gdns, Moth. ML1 | | |
| *off Malleable Gdns* | 111 | CY43 |
| Bluebell Wk, Moth. ML1 | | |
| *off Thistle Rd* | 112 | DC42 |
| Bluebell Way, Air. ML6 | 76 | DB27 |
| Bluevale St, G31 | 69 | BW31 |
| Blyth Pl, G33 | 71 | CF31 |
| Blyth Rd, G33 | 71 | CG31 |
| Blythswood Av, Renf. PA4 | 45 | AZ25 |
| Blythswood Ct, G2 | | |
| *off Cadogan St* | 4 | BQ30 |
| Blythswood Dr, Pais. PA3 | 62 | AT31 |
| Blythswood Retail Pk, | | |
| Renf. PA4 | 45 | AX25 |
| Blythswood Rd, Renf. PA4 | 45 | AY24 |
| Blythswood Sq, G2 | | |
| *off Blythswood St* | 4 | BQ29 |
| Blythswood St, G2 | 4 | BQ30 |
| Bobbins Gate, Pais. PA1 | 81 | AR34 |
| Boclair Av, (Bears.) G61 | 29 | BH17 |
| Boclair Cres, (Bears.) G61 | 30 | BJ17 |
| Boclair Cres, (Bishop.) G64 | 33 | BW20 |
| Boclair Rd, (Bears.) G61 | 30 | BJ17 |
| Boclair Rd, (Miln.) G62 | 30 | BM15 |
| Boclair Rd, (Bishop.) G64 | 33 | BW19 |
| Boclair St, G13 | 47 | BG21 |
| Boden Ind Est, G40 | 89 | BX33 |
| Boden Quad, Moth. ML1 | 111 | CX43 |
| Boden St, G40 | 89 | BW33 |
| Bodmin Gdns, (Chry.) G69 | | |
| *off Gartferry Rd* | 37 | CP18 |
| Bogany Ter, G45 | 104 | BU43 |
| Bogbain Rd, G34 | 72 | CJ29 |
| Boggknowe, (Udd.) G71 | 92 | CM37 |
| Boghall Rd, (Udd.) G71 | 92 | CJ34 |
| Boghall St, G33 | 70 | CD28 |
| Boghead Rd, G21 | 51 | BW24 |
| Boghead Rd, (Kirk.) G66 | 34 | CC16 |
| Bogleshole Rd, (Camb.) G72 | 90 | CA38 |
| Bogmoor Pl, G51 | 65 | BE28 |
| Bogmoor Rd, G51 | 65 | BE29 |
| Bogside Pl, (Baill.) G69 | | |
| *off Whamflet Av* | 72 | CL30 |
| Bogside Rd, G33 | 52 | CC24 |
| Bogside Rd, (Kilsyth) G65 | 7 | CT6 |
| Bogside Rd, (Ashgill) | | |
| Lark. ML9 | 145 | DG62 |
| Bogside St, G40 | 89 | BX33 |
| Bogs Vw, Bell. ML4 | 110 | CV42 |
| Bogton Av, G44 | 103 | BP41 |
| Bogton Av La, G44 | 103 | BP41 |
| Boleyn Rd, G41 | 87 | BN35 |
| Bolingbroke, (E.Kil.) G74 | 123 | CE49 |
| Bolivar Ter, G42 | 88 | BS37 |
| Bolton Dr, G42 | 87 | BQ37 |
| Bon Accord Rd, (Clark.) G76 | 119 | BP47 |
| Bon Accord Sq, Clyde. G81 | 45 | AX21 |
| Bonawe St, G20 | | |
| *off Kirkland St* | 49 | BP25 |
| Boness Rd, Moth. ML1 | 113 | DE39 |
| Boness St, G40 | 89 | BX33 |
| Bonhill St, G22 | 49 | BR26 |
| Bonnar St, G40 | 89 | BW34 |
| Bonnaughton Rd, (Bears.) | | |
| G61 | 28 | BD15 |
| Bonnyholm Av, G53 | 84 | BC34 |
| Bonnyrigg Dr, G43 | 102 | BJ40 |
| Bonnyton Dr, (Eagle.) G76 | 132 | BM56 |
| Bonnyton La, Ham. ML3 | | |
| *off Loch Grn* | 139 | CR54 |
| Bonnyton Moor Rd, (Eagle.) | | |
| G76 | 132 | BJ54 |
| Bonyton Av, G13 | 46 | BB23 |
| Boon Dr, G15 | 28 | BD19 |
| Boquhanran Pl, Clyde. G81 | 27 | AW18 |
| Boquhanran Rd, Clyde. G81 | 26 | AV18 |
| Borden La, G13 | 47 | BG24 |
| Borden Rd, G13 | 47 | BG24 |
| Border Way, (Kirk.) G66 | 17 | CG13 |
| Boreland Dr, G13 | 46 | BC22 |
| Boreland Dr, Ham. ML3 | 139 | CN51 |
| Boreland Pl, G13 | 46 | BD23 |
| Bore Rd, Air. ML6 | 76 | DD28 |
| Borgie Cres, (Camb.) G72 | 106 | CC40 |
| Borland Cres, (Eagle.) G76 | | |
| *off Pollock Av* | 133 | BN56 |
| Borland Dr, Lark. ML9 | 144 | DD61 |
| Borland Rd, (Bears.) G61 | 30 | BJ18 |
| Borron St, G4 | 50 | BS26 |
| Borrowdale, (E.Kil.) G75 | | |
| *off Ullswater* | 134 | BV56 |
| Borthwick Dr, (E.Kil.) G75 | 134 | BT54 |
| Borthwick St, G33 | 70 | CD28 |
| Bosfield Cor, (E.Kil.) G74 | 122 | CB50 |
| Bosfield Pl, (E.Kil.) G74 | 122 | CB50 |
| Bosfield Rd, (E.Kil.) G74 | 122 | CB50 |
| Boswell Ct, G42 | 87 | BP38 |
| Boswell Dr, (Blan.) G72 | 124 | CM46 |
| Boswell Pk, (E.Kil.) G74 | 123 | CE49 |
| Boswell Sq, G52 | 64 | BB30 |
| Bosworth Rd, (E.Kil.) G74 | 123 | CE48 |
| Botanic Cres, G20 | 48 | BM25 |
| Botanic Cres La, G20 | 48 | BM25 |
| Bothlin Dr, (Stepps) G33 | 53 | CF23 |
| Bothlyn Av, (Kirk.) G66 | 17 | CG14 |
| Bothlyn Cres, (Gart.) G69 | 55 | CN22 |
| Bothlyn Rd, (Chry.) G69 | 54 | CM21 |
| Bothwellhaugh Quad, Bell. ML4 | | |
| *off Strathview Rd* | 110 | CV42 |
| Bothwellhaugh Rd, Bell. ML4 | 110 | CV44 |
| Bothwellhaugh Rd, Moth. ML1 | 110 | CV44 |
| Bothwell La, G2 | 4 | BQ30 |
| Bothwellpark Ind Est, (Udd.) | | |
| G71 | 109 | CQ40 |
| Bothwellpark Pl, Bell. ML4 | | |
| *off Philip Murray Rd* | 110 | CT39 |
| Bothwellpark Rd, (Both.) G71 | 110 | CS42 |
| Bothwell Pl, Coat. ML5 | 74 | CV30 |
| Bothwell Pl, Pais. PA2 | 81 | AN37 |
| Bothwell Rd, (Udd.) G71 | 109 | CP40 |
| Bothwell Rd, Ham. ML3 | 126 | CS46 |
| Bothwell St, G2 | 4 | BQ29 |
| Bothwell St, (Camb.) G72 | 106 | CA39 |
| Bothwell St, Ham. ML3 | 126 | CS48 |
| Bothwick Way, Pais. PA2 | | |
| *off Crosbie Dr* | 81 | AN37 |
| Boulevard, The, G5 | 88 | BT34 |
| Boundary Rd, (Ruther.) G73 | | |
| *off Rutherglen Rd* | 88 | BU35 |
| Bourhill Ct, Wis. ML2 | | |
| *off Netherton Rd* | 143 | DF51 |
| Bourne Ct, (Inch.) Renf. PA4 | 44 | AT22 |
| Bourne Cres, (Inch.) Renf. PA4 | 44 | AT22 |
| Bourne St, Ham. ML3 | 126 | CV50 |
| Bourock Sq, (Barr.) G78 | 99 | AZ44 |

| Name | Page | Grid |
|---|---|---|
| Bourtree Rd, Ham. ML3 | 139 | CP52 |
| Bouverie St, G14 | 46 | BA23 |
| Bouverie St, (Ruther.) G73 | 88 | BV38 |
| Bowden Dr, G52 | 64 | BD31 |
| Bowden Pk, (E.Kil.) G75 | 135 | BY53 |
| Bower St, G12 | 49 | BN26 |
| Bowerwalls St, (Barr.) G78 | 100 | BA41 |
| Bowes Cres, (Baill.) G69 | 91 | CH33 |
| Bowfield Av, G52 | 64 | BB31 |
| Bowfield Cres, G52 | 64 | BB31 |
| Bowfield Dr, G52 | 64 | BB31 |
| Bowfield Path, G52 | | |
| *off Bowfield Av* | 64 | BB31 |
| Bowfield Pl, G52 | 64 | BB31 |
| Bowfield Ter, G52 | | |
| *off Bowfield Cres* | 64 | BB31 |
| Bowhousebrae Rd, Air. ML6 | 77 | DG32 |
| Bowhouse Dr, G45 | 105 | BW41 |
| Bowhouse Gdns, G45 | 105 | BW40 |
| Bowhouse Gro, G45 | 104 | BV41 |
| Bowhouse Pl, G45 | 105 | BW41 |
| Bowhouse Rd, Air. ML6 | 77 | DH32 |
| Bowhouse Way, (Ruther.) G73 | 105 | BW41 |
| Bowling Grn La, G14 | 47 | BF26 |
| Bowling Grn Rd, G14 | 47 | BF26 |
| Bowling Grn Rd, G32 | 91 | CF33 |
| Bowling Grn Rd, G44 | | |
| *off Clarkston Rd* | 103 | BQ40 |
| Bowling Grn Rd, (Chry.) G69 | 54 | CM21 |
| Bowling Grn St, Bell. ML4 | 111 | CX40 |
| Bowling St, Coat. ML5 | 74 | CV30 |
| Bowman Ct, (E.Kil.) G75 | 134 | BT53 |
| Bowman Flat, Lark. ML9 | 144 | DC58 |
| Bowman St, G42 | 87 | BQ35 |
| Bowmont Gdns, G12 | 48 | BL26 |
| Bowmont Hill, (Bishop.) G64 | 33 | BW17 |
| Bowmont Pl, (Camb.) G72 | 107 | CF40 |
| Bowmont Pl, (E.Kil.) G75 | 134 | BT54 |
| Bowmont Ter, G12 | 48 | BL26 |
| Bowmore Gdns, (Udd.) G71 | 93 | CN37 |
| Bowmore Gdns, (Ruther.) G73 | | |
| *off Ardbeg Av* | 106 | CA42 |
| Bowmore Rd, G52 | 65 | BG32 |
| Bowyer Vennel, Bell. ML4 | 110 | CV39 |
| Boyd Dr, Moth. ML1 | 127 | CX46 |
| Boydstone Pl, (Thornlie.) G46 | 101 | BH40 |
| Boydstone Rd, G43 | 101 | BG40 |
| Boydstone Rd, (Thornlie.) G46 | 101 | BG39 |
| Boydstone Rd, G53 | 101 | BG40 |
| Boyd St, G42 | 87 | BR36 |
| Boylestone Rd, (Barr.) G78 | 99 | AW41 |
| Boyle St, Clyde. G81 | 45 | AZ21 |
| Boyndie Path, G34 | 72 | CK29 |
| Boyndie St, G34 | 72 | CK29 |
| Brabloch Cres, Pais. PA3 | 62 | AV31 |
| Brabloch Pk, Pais. PA3 | 62 | AV31 |
| Bracadale Dr, (Baill.) G69 | 92 | CM33 |
| Bracadale Gdns, (Baill.) G69 | 92 | CM33 |
| Bracadale Gro, (Baill.) G69 | 92 | CL33 |
| Bracadale Rd, (Baill.) G69 | 92 | CL33 |
| Brackenbrae Av, (Bishop.) G64 | 32 | BU19 |
| Brackenbrae Rd, (Bishop.) G64 | 32 | BV20 |
| Brackenhill Dr, Ham. ML3 | 139 | CR54 |
| Brackenhirst Gdns, (Glenm.) Air. ML6 | 57 | CZ24 |
| Brackenhirst Rd, (Glenm.) Air. ML6 | 58 | DA23 |
| Brackenknowle Rd, Air. ML6 | 41 | DF17 |
| Brackenrig Cres, (Eagle.) G76 | 133 | BN52 |
| Brackenrig Rd, (Thornlie.) G46 | 101 | BG43 |
| Bracken St, G22 | 49 | BR23 |
| Bracken St, Moth. ML1 | 112 | DC42 |
| Bracken Ter, (Both.) G71 | 109 | CQ42 |
| Bracken Way, Lark. ML9 | | |
| *off Morris St* | 145 | DE60 |
| Brackla Av, G13 | 46 | BA21 |
| Brackla Av, Clyde. G81 | 46 | BA21 |
| Bradan Av, G13 | 46 | BA22 |
| Bradan Av, Clyde. G81 | 46 | BA22 |
| Bradda Av, (Ruther.) G73 | 105 | BY41 |
| Bradfield Av, G12 | 48 | BL24 |
| Bradley Ct, (Stepps) G33 | 53 | CH24 |
| Bradshaw Cres, Ham. ML3 | 125 | CN50 |
| Brady Cres, (Mood.) G69 | 37 | CQ18 |
| Braedale Av, Air. ML6 | 76 | DD30 |
| Braedale Av, Moth. ML1 | 127 | CX47 |
| Braeface Rd, (Cumb.) G67 | 22 | DA11 |
| Braefield Dr, (Thornlie.) G46 | 102 | BJ42 |
| Braefoot Av, (Miln.) G62 | 12 | BJ13 |
| Braefoot Cres, Pais. PA2 | 82 | AU38 |
| Braehead, (Blan.) G72 | 124 | CM47 |
| Braehead Av, (Miln.) G62 | 11 | BH12 |
| Braehead Av, (Neil.) G78 | 114 | AT46 |
| Braehead Av, Coat. ML5 | 94 | CT34 |
| Braehead Av, Lark. ML9 | | |
| *off Millheugh Brae* | 144 | DA59 |
| Braehead Dr, Bell. ML4 | 110 | CV41 |
| Braehead Pl, Bell. ML4 | 110 | CV41 |
| Braehead Quad, (Neil.) G78 | 114 | AT46 |
| Braehead Quad, Moth. ML1 | | |
| *off Hillside Cres* | 113 | DF41 |
| Braehead Rd, (Cumb.) G67 | 22 | DD10 |
| Braehead Rd, (Thornton.) G74 | 120 | BS50 |
| Braehead Rd, Pais. PA2 | 98 | AS39 |
| Braehead Shop Cen, G51 | 46 | BC26 |
| Braehead St, (Kirk.) G66 | 17 | CE12 |
| Braemar Av, Clyde. G81 | 26 | AV16 |
| Braemar Ct, G44 | 103 | BN41 |
| Braemar Cres, (Bears.) G61 | 29 | BH19 |
| Braemar Cres, Pais. PA2 | 82 | AV36 |
| Braemar Dr, (Elder.) John. PA5 | 80 | AK36 |
| Braemar Rd, (Ruther.) G73 | 106 | CA42 |
| Braemar Rd, (Inch.) Renf. PA4 | 44 | AT22 |
| Braemar St, G42 | 87 | BP38 |
| Braemar St, Ham. ML3 | 125 | CR47 |
| Braemar Vw, Clyde. G81 | 26 | AV16 |
| Braemore Gdns, G22 | 50 | BT25 |
| Braemount Av, Pais. PA2 | 98 | AS39 |
| Braes Av, Clyde. G81 | 27 | AZ20 |
| Braeside Av, (Miln.) G62 | 12 | BJ13 |
| Braeside Av, (Mood.) G69 | 37 | CP19 |
| Braeside Av, (Ruther.) G73 | 89 | BY38 |
| Braeside Cres, (Baill.) G69 | 73 | CP32 |
| Braeside Cres, (Barr.) G78 | 100 | BA44 |
| Braeside Dr, (Barr.) G78 | 99 | AZ44 |
| Braeside Gdns, Ham. ML3 | 140 | CU53 |
| Braeside La, Lark. ML9 | | |
| *off Meadowhill St* | 144 | DD57 |
| Braeside Pl, (Camb.) G72 | 106 | CD41 |
| Braeside Rd, Moth. ML1 | 113 | DF41 |
| Braeside St, G20 | 49 | BP26 |
| Braeside Way, Lark. ML9 | | |
| *off Fisher St* | 144 | DD60 |
| Braes O'Yetts, (Kirk.) G66 | 18 | CJ13 |
| Braeview Av, Pais. PA2 | 81 | AR38 |
| Braeview Dr, Pais. PA2 | 81 | AR38 |
| Braeview Gdns, Pais. PA2 | 81 | AR38 |
| Braeview Pl, (E.Kil.) G74 | 122 | CC49 |
| Braeview Rd, Pais. PA2 | 81 | AR38 |
| Braid Av, Moth. ML1 | 113 | DH44 |
| Braidbar Ct, (Giff.) G46 | | |
| *off Braidbar Rd* | 102 | BL42 |
| Braidbar Fm Rd, (Giff.) G46 | 102 | BM41 |
| Braidbar Rd, (Giff.) G46 | 102 | BL42 |
| Braidcraft Pl, G53 | | |
| *off Braidcraft Rd* | 85 | BE37 |
| Braidcraft Rd, G53 | 85 | BE36 |
| Braidcraft Ter, G53 | | |
| *off Braidcraft Rd* | 85 | BF36 |
| Braidfauld Gdns, G32 | 90 | CB34 |
| Braidfauld Pl, G32 | 90 | CB35 |
| Braidfauld St, G32 | 90 | CB34 |
| Braidfield Gro, Clyde. G81 | 27 | AX16 |
| Braidfield Rd, Clyde. G81 | 27 | AX16 |
| Braidholm Cres, (Giff.) G46 | 102 | BL42 |
| Braidholm Rd, (Giff.) G46 | 102 | BL42 |
| Braidhurst Ind Est, Moth. ML1 | 111 | CZ44 |
| Braidhurst St, Moth. ML1 | 128 | DA45 |
| Braidley Cres, (E.Kil.) G75 | 136 | CA56 |
| Braidpark Dr, (Giff.) G46 | 102 | BM42 |
| Braids Circle, Pais. PA2 | 82 | AU36 |
| Braids Ct, Pais. PA2 | 82 | AU36 |
| Braids Dr, G53 | 84 | BB36 |
| Braids Gait, Pais. PA2 | 82 | AT36 |
| Braid Sq, G4 | 67 | BQ27 |
| Braids Rd, Pais. PA2 | 82 | AU36 |
| Braid St, G4 | 67 | BQ27 |
| Bramah Av, (E.Kil.) G75 | 136 | CB54 |
| Bramley Pl, (Lenz.) G66 | 35 | CG17 |
| Bramley Pl, Air. ML6 | | |
| *off Fairhaven Av* | 77 | DH31 |
| Brampton, (E.Kil.) G75 | 134 | BV55 |
| Branchock Av, (Camb.) G72 | 107 | CF41 |
| Brancumhall Rd, (E.Kil.) G74 | 123 | CF50 |
| Brandon Arc, Moth. ML1 | 128 | DA47 |
| Brandon Ct, Moth. ML1 | | |
| *off Brandon Par S* | 128 | DA47 |
| Brandon Dr, (Bears.) G61 | 11 | BG14 |
| Brandon Gdns, (Camb.) G72 | 106 | CA40 |
| Brandon Par E, Moth. ML1 | 128 | DA46 |
| Brandon Par S, Moth. ML1 | 128 | DA47 |
| Brandon Pl, Bell. ML4 | 110 | CU42 |
| Brandon St, G31 | 68 | BV31 |
| Brandon St, Coat. ML5 | | |
| *off Lismore Dr* | 94 | CU33 |
| Brandon St, Ham. ML3 | 126 | CU50 |
| Brandon St, Moth. ML1 | 128 | DA47 |
| Brandon Way, Coat. ML5 | 94 | CT33 |
| Brand Pl, G51 | 66 | BL31 |
| Brand St, G51 | 66 | BL31 |
| Brankholm Brae, Ham. ML3 | 124 | CM49 |
| Branklyn Ct, G13 | 47 | BF23 |
| Branklyn Cres, G13 | 47 | BF23 |
| Branklyn Gro, G13 | 47 | BF23 |
| Branklyn Pl, G13 | 47 | BF23 |
| Brannock Av, Moth. ML1 | 113 | DF41 |
| Brannock Pl, Moth. ML1 | 113 | DF41 |
| Brannock Rd, Moth. ML1 | 113 | DF42 |
| Branscroft, (Kilb.) John. PA10 | 78 | AD33 |
| Brassey St, G20 | 49 | BN23 |
| Breadalbane Cres, Moth. ML1 | 111 | CZ44 |
| Breadalbane Gdns, (Ruther.) G73 | 105 | BZ41 |
| Breadalbane St, G3 | | |
| *off St. Vincent St* | 4 | BP29 |
| Breadie Dr, (Miln.) G62 | 11 | BH13 |
| Breamish Pl, (E.Kil.) G75 | | |
| *off Dove Pl* | 134 | BV55 |
| Brechin Rd, (Bishop.) G64 | 33 | BY20 |
| Brechin St, G3 | 67 | BN29 |
| Breck Av, Pais. PA2 | 80 | AM37 |
| Brediland Rd, Pais. PA2 | 81 | AN36 |
| Brediland Rd, (Linw.) Pais. PA3 | 60 | AJ31 |
| Bredin Way, Moth. ML1 | 127 | CX45 |
| Bredisholm Cres, (Udd.) G71 | 94 | CS36 |
| Bredisholm Dr, (Baill.) G69 | 92 | CL33 |
| Bredisholm Rd, (Baill.) G69 | 92 | CL33 |
| Bredisholm Ter, (Baill.) G69 | 92 | CL33 |
| Bremner Cotts, Clyde. G81 | 26 | AV15 |

| | | |
|---|---|---|
| Brenfield Av, G44 | 103 | BP41 |
| Brenfield Dr, G44 | 103 | BP41 |
| Brenfield Rd, G44 | 103 | BP41 |
| Brent Av, (Thornlie.) G46 | 101 | BH40 |
| Brent Ct, (E.Kil.) G74 | 122 | CA50 |
| Brent Dr, (Thornlie.) G46 | 101 | BH40 |
| Brent Gdns, (Thornlie.) G46 | 102 | BJ40 |
| Brent Rd, (Thornlie.) G46 | 101 | BH40 |
| Brent Rd, (E.Kil.) G74 | 122 | CA50 |
| Brent Way, (Thornlie.) G46 | 101 | BH40 |
| Brentwood Av, G53 | 100 | BC41 |
| Brentwood Dr, G53 | 100 | BC41 |
| Brentwood Sq, G53 | 100 | BD41 |
| Brereton St, G42 | 88 | BS36 |
| Bressay, (E.Kil.) G74 | 122 | CA50 |
| Bressay Cl, G33 | 71 | CG31 |
| Bressay Gro, G33 | 71 | CG31 |
| Bressay Gro, (Camb.) G72 | 106 | CA42 |
| Bressay Pl, G33 | 71 | CG31 |
| Bressay Rd, G33 | 71 | CG31 |
| Breval Ct, (Baill.) G69 | 92 | CL33 |
| Brewery St, John. PA5 | 79 | AH34 |
| Brewster Av, Pais. PA3 | 63 | AW30 |
| Briarbush Way, (Blan.) G72 | | |
| off Ansdell Av | 124 | CL46 |
| Briarcroft Dr, G33 | 51 | BZ22 |
| Briarcroft Pl, G33 | 52 | CA23 |
| Briarcroft Rd, G33 | 51 | BZ23 |
| Briar Dr, Clyde. G81 | 27 | AX17 |
| Briar Gdns, G43 | 102 | BM40 |
| Briar Gro, G43 | 102 | BM40 |
| Briarlea Dr, (Giff.) G46 | 102 | BL41 |
| Briar Neuk, (Bishop.) G64 | | |
| off Woodfield Av | 51 | BX21 |
| Briar Rd, G43 | 102 | BM40 |
| Briar Rd, (Kirk.) G66 | 17 | CH13 |
| Briar Wk, (Kirk.) G66 | 18 | CJ13 |
| Briarwell La, (Miln.) G62 | 12 | BK12 |
| Briarwell Rd, (Miln.) G62 | 12 | BK12 |
| Briarwood Ct, G32 | 91 | CG35 |
| Briarwood Gdns, G32 | | |
| off Woodend Rd | 91 | CG35 |
| Briarwood Rd, Wis. ML2 | 129 | DG49 |
| Brick La, Pais. PA3 | | |
| off Weir St | 62 | AV32 |
| Bridgebar St, (Barr.) G78 | 99 | AZ41 |
| Bridgeburn Dr, (Mood.) G69 | 37 | CN19 |
| Bridgeford Av, Bell. ML4 | | |
| off Rosebank Rd | 95 | CY38 |
| Bridgegait, (Miln.) G62 | 12 | BL13 |
| Bridgegate, G1 | 5 | BS31 |
| Bridgegate Path, G1 | | |
| off Bridgegate | 5 | BS31 |
| Bridge La, Pais. PA2 | | |
| off Tenters Way | 81 | AR34 |
| Bridgend Cres, (Mood.) G69 | 37 | CN19 |
| Bridgend Pl, (Mood.) G69 | 37 | CN19 |
| Bridge of Weir Rd, (Linw.) | | |
| Pais. PA3 | 60 | AK32 |
| Bridge St, G5 | 4 | BR31 |
| Bridge St, (Camb.) G72 | 106 | CC39 |
| Bridge St, Clyde. G81 | 26 | AU18 |
| Bridge St, Ham. ML3 | 140 | CS51 |
| Bridge St, Pais. PA1 | 82 | AU33 |
| Bridge St, (Linw.) Pais. PA3 | 60 | AL31 |
| Bridge St, Wis. ML2 | 129 | DG50 |
| Bridgeton Business Cen, G40 | 68 | BV32 |
| Bridgeton Cross, G40 | 68 | BV32 |
| Bridgewater Shop Cen, | | |
| Ersk. PA8 | 26 | AS19 |
| Bridgeway Ct, (Kirk.) G66 | 17 | CH14 |
| Bridgeway Pl, (Kirk.) G66 | 17 | CH14 |
| Bridgeway Rd, (Kirk.) G66 | 17 | CH14 |
| Bridgeway Ter, (Kirk.) G66 | 17 | CH14 |
| Bridie Ter, (E.Kil.) G74 | 123 | CE49 |
| Brigbrae Av, Bell. ML4 | 111 | CY42 |
| Brigham Pl, G23 | | |
| off Broughton Rd | 49 | BN21 |
| Brighton Pl, G51 | 66 | BK31 |
| Brighton St, G51 | 66 | BK31 |
| Brightside Av, (Udd.) G71 | 109 | CP40 |
| Bright St, G21 | 68 | BV28 |
| Brig O'Lea Ter, (Neil.) G78 | 114 | AS47 |
| Brigside Gdns, Ham. ML3 | 141 | CW51 |
| Brisbane Ct, (Giff.) G46 | 102 | BM42 |
| Brisbane Rd, Bish. PA7 | 24 | AK18 |
| Brisbane St, G42 | 87 | BQ38 |
| Brisbane St, Clyde. G81 | 26 | AT17 |
| Brisbane Ter, (E.Kil.) G75 | 135 | BY54 |
| Britannia Way, Clyde. G81 | | |
| off Sutherland Rd | 27 | AX19 |
| Britannia Way, Renf. PA4 | 63 | AY28 |
| Briton St, G51 | 66 | BK31 |
| Broadcroft, (Kirk.) G66 | 17 | CE12 |
| Broadford St, G4 | 68 | BS27 |
| Broadholm St, G22 | 49 | BR23 |
| Broadleys Av, (Bishop.) G64 | 32 | BV18 |
| Broadlie Ct, (Neil.) G78 | 114 | AT46 |
| Broadlie Dr, G13 | 46 | BC23 |
| Broadlie Rd, (Neil.) G78 | 114 | AS46 |
| Broadloan, Renf. PA4 | 63 | AY27 |
| Broadmoss Av, (Newt. M.) | | |
| G77 | 118 | BL49 |
| Broad Sq, (Blan.) G72 | 124 | CL45 |
| Broad St, G40 | 68 | BV32 |
| Broadwalk, The, (E.Kil.) G75 | 136 | CC55 |
| Broadway, The, Wis. ML2 | 129 | DG49 |
| Broadwood Business Pk, | | |
| (Cumb.) G68 | 20 | CV13 |
| Broadwood Dr, G44 | 103 | BR39 |
| Broadwood Rbt, (Cumb.) G68 | 20 | CV13 |
| Brockburn Cres, G53 | 84 | BD37 |
| Brockburn Pl, G53 | 84 | BC35 |
| Brockburn Rd, G53 | 84 | BC35 |
| Brockburn Ter, G53 | 85 | BE37 |
| Brocklinn Pk, (E.Kil.) G75 | 134 | BU54 |
| Brock Oval, G53 | 101 | BE39 |
| Brock Pl, G53 | 85 | BE38 |
| Brock Rd, G53 | 101 | BE39 |
| Brock Ter, G53 | 85 | BE38 |
| Brockville St, G32 | 70 | CB31 |
| Brock Way, (Cumb.) G67 | | |
| off North Carbrain Rd | 22 | DB12 |
| Brodick Av, Moth. ML1 | 127 | CX46 |
| Brodick Dr, (E.Kil.) G74 | 121 | BZ50 |
| Brodick Pl, (Newt. M.) G77 | 116 | BC49 |
| Brodick Sq, (Bishop.) G64 | 51 | BX22 |
| Brodick St, G21 | 69 | BW28 |
| Brodie Gdns, (Baill.) G69 | 72 | CL31 |
| Brodie Gro, (Baill.) G69 | 72 | CL31 |
| Brodie Pk Av, Pais. PA2 | 82 | AU35 |
| Brodie Pk Cres, Pais. PA2 | 82 | AT35 |
| Brodie Pk Gdns, Pais. PA2 | 82 | AU35 |
| Brodie Pl, (E.Kil.) G74 | 121 | BZ50 |
| Brodie Rd, G21 | 51 | BZ22 |
| Brogan Cres, Moth. ML1 | 127 | CX46 |
| Bron Way, (Cumb.) G67 | 22 | DC12 |
| Brookfield Av, G33 | 51 | BZ22 |
| Brookfield Cor, G33 | 51 | BZ22 |
| Brookfield Dr, G33 | 51 | BZ22 |
| Brookfield Gdns, G33 | | |
| off Brookfield Av | 51 | BZ22 |
| Brookfield Gate, G33 | | |
| off Brookfield Av | 51 | BZ22 |
| Brookfield Pl, G33 | 51 | BZ22 |
| Brookfield Rd, G33 | 51 | BZ22 |
| Brooklands, (E.Kil.) G74 | 135 | BW52 |
| Brooklands Av, (Udd.) G71 | 93 | CN38 |
| Brooklea Dr, (Giff.) G46 | 102 | BL40 |
| Brooklime Dr, (E.Kil.) G74 | 121 | BY49 |
| Brooklime Gdns, (E.Kil.) G74 | 121 | BY50 |
| Brookside St, G40 | 69 | BW32 |
| Brook St, G40 | 68 | BV32 |
| Brook St, Clyde. G81 | 26 | AV17 |
| Broom Av, Ersk. PA8 | 43 | AR22 |
| Broomburn Dr, (Newt. M.) G77 | 117 | BH49 |
| Broom Cliff, (Newt. M.) G77 | | |
| off Castleton Dr | 117 | BH50 |
| Broom Cres, (E.Kil.) G75 | 135 | BZ56 |
| Broom Cres, (Barr.) G78 | 99 | AW40 |
| Broomcroft Rd, (Newt. M.) G77 | 118 | BJ47 |
| Broom Dr, Clyde. G81 | 27 | AW17 |
| Broom Dr, Lark. ML9 | | |
| off Maple Dr | 142 | DC56 |
| Broomdyke Way, Pais. PA3 | 62 | AT29 |
| Broomfield Av, (Camb.) G72 | | |
| off Cambuslang Rd | 89 | BZ38 |
| Broomfield Av, (Newt. M.) G77 | 117 | BH50 |
| Broomfield La, G21 | 50 | BV24 |
| Broomfield Pl, G21 | 50 | BV24 |
| Broomfield Rd, G21 | 50 | BV24 |
| Broomfield Rd, (Giff.) G46 | 118 | BJ47 |
| Broomfield Rd, Lark. ML9 | 144 | DC61 |
| Broomfield St, Air. ML6 | 76 | DD30 |
| Broomfield Ter, (Udd.) G71 | 93 | CP36 |
| Broomfield Wk, (Kirk.) G66 | | |
| off Willowbank Gdns | 17 | CF13 |
| Broom Gdns, (Kirk.) G66 | 34 | CD15 |
| Broomhill Av, G11 | 65 | BH27 |
| Broomhill Av, G32 | 90 | CD37 |
| Broomhill Av, (Newt. M.) G77 | 117 | BH50 |
| Broomhill Ct, Lark. ML9 | 144 | DC59 |
| Broomhill Cres, Bell. ML4 | | |
| off Crofthead Cres | 110 | CV42 |
| Broomhill Cres, Ersk. PA8 | 43 | AR22 |
| Broomhill Dr, G11 | 47 | BH26 |
| Broomhill Dr, (Ruther.) G73 | 105 | BX40 |
| Broomhill Dr, Lark. ML9 | 144 | DC59 |
| Broomhill Fm Ms, (Kirk.) G66 | | |
| off Kilsyth Rd | 17 | CG12 |
| Broomhill Gdns, G11 | 47 | BH26 |
| Broomhill Gdns, (Newt. M.) | | |
| G77 | 117 | BH49 |
| Broomhill Gate, Lark. ML9 | 144 | DC59 |
| Broomhill La, G11 | 47 | BH26 |
| Broomhill Path, G11 | 65 | BH27 |
| Broomhill Pl, G11 | 65 | BH27 |
| Broomhill Rd, Lark. ML9 | 144 | DB59 |
| Broomhill Ter, G11 | 65 | BH27 |
| Broomhill Vw, Lark. ML9 | 144 | DA59 |
| Broomhouse Cres, (Udd.) G71 | 92 | CK34 |
| Broomieknowe Dr, (Ruther.) | | |
| G73 | 105 | BX39 |
| Broomieknowe Gdns, (Ruther.) | | |
| G73 | 105 | BW39 |
| Broomieknowe Rd, (Ruther.) | | |
| G73 | 105 | BX39 |
| Broomielaw, G1 | 4 | BQ31 |
| Broomielaw, G2 | 4 | BQ31 |
| Broomknoll St, Air. ML6 | 76 | DC30 |
| Broomknowe, (Cumb.) G68 | 21 | CZ10 |
| Broomknowes Av, (Kirk.) G66 | 35 | CG17 |
| Broomknowes Rd, G21 | 51 | BW25 |
| Broomlands Av, Ersk. PA8 | 44 | AT21 |
| Broomlands Cres, Ersk. PA8 | 44 | AT21 |
| Broomlands Gdns, Ersk. PA8 | 44 | AT21 |
| Broomlands La, Pais. PA1 | 81 | AR33 |
| Broomlands Rd, (Cumb.) G67 | 22 | DC13 |
| Broomlands St, Pais. PA1 | 82 | AS33 |

Broomlands Way, Ersk. PA8   44   AU21
Broomlea Cres, (Inch.) Renf.
  PA4   44   AS22
Broomlee Rd, (Cumb.) G67   40   DB15
Broomley Dr, (Giff.) G46   102   BL44
Broomley La, (Giff.) G46   102   BL44
Broomloan Ct, G51   66   BJ32
Broomloan Pl, G51   66   BJ31
Broomloan Rd, G51   66   BJ31
Broompark Av, (Blan.) G72
  *off Broompark Rd*   124   CL47
Broompark Circ, G31   68   BV29
Broompark Cres, Air. ML6   76   DC27
Broompark Dr, G31   68   BV30
Broompark Dr, (Newt. M.) G77   117   BH47
Broompark Dr, (Inch.) Renf.
  PA4   44   AT22
Broompark La, G31   68   BV30
Broompark Rd, (Blan.) G72   124   CL46
Broompark Rd, Wis. ML2   129   DF49
Broompark St, G31   68   BV30
Broompath, (Baill.) G69   91   CH34
Broom Pl, G43   102   BM40
Broom Pl, Coat. ML5   94   CV34
Broom Pl, Moth. ML1   113   DE41
Broom Rd, G43   102   BM40
Broom Rd, (Newt. M.) G77   118   BJ47
Broom Rd E, (Newt. M.) G77   118   BK49
Broomside Cres, Moth. ML1
  *off Adele St*   128   DB49
Broomside St, Moth. ML1   128   DA49
Broomstone Av, (Newt. M.)
  G77   117   BH50
Broom Ter, John. PA5   80   AJ35
Broomton Rd, G21   51   BY22
Broomvale Dr, (Newt. M.) G77   117   BH48
Broomward Dr, John. PA5   80   AK34
Brora Cres, Ham. ML3
  *off Sherry Dr*   139   CQ53
Brora Dr, (Giff.) G46   102   BM43
Brora Dr, (Bears.) G61   30   BK17
Brora Dr, Renf. PA4   46   BA26
Brora Gdns, (Bishop.) G64   33   BX20
Brora La, G33
  *off Brora St*   69   BZ28
Brora Rd, (Bishop.) G64   33   BX20
Brora St, G33   69   BZ28
Broughton Dr, G23   49   BN21
Broughton Gdns, G23
  *off Broughton Rd*   31   BP20
Broughton Pl, Coat. ML5   95   CX34
Broughton Pl, Ham. ML3   125   CQ50
Broughton Rd, G23   49   BN21
Brouster Gate, (E.Kil.) G74
  *off East Kilbride Shop Cen*   136   CB52
Brouster Hill, (E.Kil.) G74   136   CA51
Brouster Pl, (E.Kil.) G74   136   CA52
Brown Av, Clyde. G81   46   BA21
Brown Ct, (Stepps) G33   53   CG24
Brownhill Rd, G43   102   BK41
Brownlie St, G42   87   BR37
Brown Pl, (Camb.) G72   106   CC39
Brown Rd, (Cumb.) G67   22   DB11
Brownsburn Ind Est, Air. ML6   76   DD32
Brownsburn Rd, Air. ML6   96   DD33
Brownsdale Rd, (Ruther.) G73   88   BV38
Brownsfield Cres, (Inch.)
  Renf. PA4   43   AR24
Brownshill Av, Coat. ML5   94   CV33
Brownside Av, (Camb.) G72   106   CA40
Brownside Av, (Barr.) G78   99   AW40
Brownside Av, Pais. PA2   82   AS38
Brownside Cres, (Barr.) G78   99   AW40

Brownside Dr, G13   46   BB23
Brownside Dr, (Barr.) G78   99   AW40
Brownside Gro, (Barr.) G78   99   AW40
Brownside Ms, (Camb.) G72   106   CA40
Brownside Rd, (Camb.) G72   106   CA40
Brownside Rd, (Ruther.) G73   105   BZ40
Brownsland Ct, (Gart.) G69   55   CP23
Browns La, Pais. PA1   82   AU33
Brown St, G2   4   BQ30
Brown St, Coat. ML5   75   CW32
Brown St, Lark. ML9   144   DC57
Brown St, Moth. ML1   128   DB45
Brown St, Pais. PA1   62   AS32
Brown St, Renf. PA4   45   AX26
Bruce Av, John. PA5   79   AG37
Bruce Av, Moth. ML1   127   CZ46
Bruce Av, Pais. PA3   63   AW30
Bruce Ct, Air. ML6   77   DG29
Brucefield Pl, G34   72   CM29
Bruce Pl, (E.Kil.) G75   136   CB54
Bruce Rd, G41   87   BN33
Bruce Rd, Moth. ML1   112   DD43
Bruce Rd, Pais. PA3   63   AW31
Bruce Rd, Renf. PA4   63   AW28
Bruce's Ln, Lark. ML9
  *off Wallace Dr*   145   DE59
Bruce St, Bell. ML4   111   CX40
Bruce St, Clyde. G81   27   AX20
Bruce St, Coat. ML5   75   CX29
Bruce Ter, (Blan.) G72   109   CN44
Bruce Ter, (E.Kil.) G75   136   CB54
Brunel Way, (E.Kil.) G75   136   CB53
Brunstane Rd, G34   72   CJ28
Brunswick Ho, Clyde. G81
  *off Perth Cres*   26   AT15
Brunswick St, G1   5   BS30
Brunton St, G44   103   BQ40
Brunton Ter, G44   103   BP41
Bruntsfield Av, G53   100   BD42
Bruntsfield Gdns, G53   100   BD42
Bryan St, Ham. ML3   125   CR48
Bryce Gdns, Lark. ML9   144   DC57
Bryce Pl, (E.Kil.) G75   135   BZ55
Brydson Pl, (Linw.) Pais. PA3   60   AK31
Bryson Ct, Ham. ML3   140   CT54
Bryson St, Clyde. G81   10   BA14
Buccleuch Av, G52   64   BA29
Buccleuch Av, (Clark.) G76   118   BM46
Buccleuch Dr, (Bears.) G61   11   BG14
Buccleuch La, G3   4   BQ28
Buccleuch St, G3   4   BQ28
Buchanan Av, Bish. PA7   24   AK17
Buchanan Business Pk,
  (Stepps) G33   53   CG23
Buchanan Cres, (Bishop.) G64   51   BY22
Buchanan Cres, Ham. ML3   139   CR51
Buchanan Dr, (Bears.) G61   30   BJ17
Buchanan Dr, (Bishop.) G64   51   BY21
Buchanan Dr, (Lenz.) G66   35   CF18
Buchanan Dr, (Camb.) G72   106   CA39
Buchanan Dr, (Ruther.) G73   105   BX39
Buchanan Dr, (Newt. M.) G77   117   BG46
Buchanan Gdns, G32   91   CG35
Buchanan Gro, (Baill.) G69   72   CK32
Buchanan Pl, (Torr.) G64   15   BX12
Buchanan St, G1   4   BR30
Buchanan St, (Miln.) G62   12   BK11
Buchanan St, (Baill.) G69   92   CK33
Buchanan St, Air. ML6
  *off Graham St*   76   DC30
Buchanan St, Coat. ML5   74   CV31
Buchanan St, John. PA5   79   AG35
Buchandyke Rd, (E.Kil.) G74   122   CD50

Buchan Grn, (E.Kil.) G74   122   CD50
Buchan Rd, Moth. ML1   112   DC43
Buchan St, G5
  *off Norfolk St*   67   BR32
Buchan St, Ham. ML3   140   CS53
Buchan Ter, (Camb.) G72   106   CA42
Buchlyvie Gdns, (Bishop.) G64   50   BV21
Buchlyvie Path, G34   72   CK30
Buchlyvie Rd, Pais. PA1   64   BA31
Buchlyvie St, G34   72   CK30
Buckie, Ersk. PA8   25   AQ18
Buckie Wk, Bell. ML4
  *off Hattonrigg Rd*   111   CW39
Buckingham Ct, Ham. ML3
  *off Stirling Dr*   125   CN49
Buckingham Dr, G32   90   CD37
Buckingham Dr, (Ruther.) G73   89   BZ38
Buckingham St, G12   48   BM26
Buckingham Ter, G12   48   BM26
Bucklaw Gdns, G52   85   BE33
Bucklaw Pl, G52   85   BE33
Bucklaw Ter, G52   85   BE33
Buckley St, G22   50   BT23
Bucksburn Rd, G21   51   BY25
Buckthorne Pl, G53   100   BD42
Buddon St, G40   89   BY33
Budhill Av, G32   70   CD32
Budshaw Av, (Chap.) Air. ML6   97   DE35
Bulldale Ct, G14   46   BA24
Bulldale Pl, G14   46   BA24
Bulldale Rd, G14   46   BA24
Bulldale St, G14   46   BA23
Buller Cres, (Blan.) G72   108   CL43
Bullionslaw Dr, (Ruther.) G73   105   BZ39
Bulloch Av, (Giff.) G46   102   BM43
Bull Rd, (Clark.) G76   119   BP47
Bullwood Av, G53   84   BB35
Bullwood Ct, G53   84   BB37
Bullwood Dr, G53   84   BB36
Bullwood Gdns, G53   84   BB36
Bullwood Pl, G53   84   BB36
Bunbury Ter, (E.Kil.) G75
  *off Kimberley Gdns*   135   BY53
Bunessan St, G52   65   BH32
Bunhouse Rd, G3   66   BL28
Burghead Dr, G51   65   BG30
Burghead Pl, G51   65   BG29
Burgher St, G31   69   BY32
Burgh Hall La, G11   66   BK27
Burgh Hall St, G11   66   BK27
Burgh La, G12   48   BM26
Burleigh Pl, Coat. ML5   95   CY34
Burleigh Rd, (Both.) G71   109   CR42
Burleigh St, G51   66   BJ29
Burleigh St, Coat. ML5   95   CX34
Burley Pl, (E.Kil.) G74   134   BV51
Burlington Av, G12   48   BK23
Burmola St, G22   49   BR25
Burnacre Gdns, (Udd.) G71   93   CN38
Burnawn Gdns, G33
  *off Brookfield Dr*   51   BZ22
Burnawn Gro, G33
  *off Brookfield Av*   51   BZ22
Burnawn Pl, G33
  *off Brookfield Av*   51   BZ22
Burnbank Cen, Ham. ML3   125   CQ48
Burnbank Dr, (Barr.) G78   99   AY44
Burnbank Gdns, G20   67   BP27
Burnbank Gdns, Ham. ML3
  *off George St*   125   CQ48
Burnbank La, G20
  *off Napiershall St*   67   BP27
Burnbank Pl, G4   5   BU30

Burnbank Pl, G20
*off Burnbank Ter* 67 BQ27
Burnbank Quad, Air. ML6 76 DB29
Burnbank Rd, Ham. ML3 125 CQ48
Burnbank St, Air. ML6 76 DB29
Burnbank St, Coat. ML5 75 CX29
Burnbank Ter, G20 67 BP27
Burnbank Ter, (Kilsyth) G65 7 CU4
Burnblea Gdns, Ham. ML3 140 CU51
Burnblea St, Ham. ML3 140 CT51
Burnbrae, (Kilsyth) G65 19 CP9
Burnbrae, Clyde. G81 27 AW15
Burnbrae Av, (Bears.) G61 12 BJ14
Burnbrae Av, (Mood.) G69 37 CQ19
Burnbrae Av, (Linw.) Pais. PA3
*off Bridge St* 60 AL32
Burnbrae Dr, (Ruther.) G73
*off East Kilbride Rd* 105 BZ40
Burnbrae Dr, (Linw.) Pais. PA3 80 AM33
Burnbrae Gdns, G53 101 BF39
Burnbrae Pl, (E.Kil.) G74 135 BY51
Burnbrae Rd, (Kirk.) G66 18 CK14
Burnbrae Rd, (Lenz.) G66 35 CG19
Burnbrae Rd, (Chry.) G69 36 CK19
Burnbrae Rd, (Blan.) G72 124 CL46
Burnbrae Rd, (Linw.) Pais. PA3 80 AK33
Burnbrae St, G21 51 BW25
Burnbrae St, Lark. ML9 144 DB58
Burncleuch Av, (Camb.) G72 106 CC41
Burn Cres, (Chap.) Air. ML6 97 DF35
Burn Cres, Moth. ML1 112 DC41
Burncrooks Av, (Bears.) G61 11 BE14
Burncrooks Av, (E.Kil.) G74 135 BY51
Burncrooks Ct, Clyde. G81 26 AV15
Burndyke Ct, G51 66 BK30
Burndyke Sq, G51 66 BL30
Burndyke St, G51 66 BK30
Burnet Rose Ct, (E.Kil.) G74 121 BY49
Burnet Rose Gdns, (E.Kil.) G74 121 BY49
Burnet Rose Pl, (E.Kil.) G74 121 BY49
Burnett Rd, G33 71 CG30
Burnfield Av, (Thornlie.) G46 102 BK41
Burnfield Cotts, (Thornlie.)
G46 102 BK41
Burnfield Dr, G43 102 BK41
Burnfield Gdns, (Giff.) G46 102 BL41
Burnfield Rd, G43 102 BJ40
Burnfield Rd, (Thornlie.) G46 102 BK41
Burnfoot Cres, (Ruther.) G73 105 BZ40
Burnfoot Cres, Pais. PA2 82 AS38
Burnfoot Dr, G52 64 BD32
Burnfoot Rd, Air. ML6 76 DA29
Burngreen, (Kilsyth) G65 7 CT5
Burngreen Pk, (Kilsyth) G65 7 CU5
Burnham Rd, G14 46 BC25
Burnham Ter, G14
*off Burnham Rd* 46 BC25
Burnhaven, Ersk. PA8 25 AQ19
Burnhead Rd, G43 103 BN40
Burnhead Rd, (Cumb.) G68 21 CY11
Burnhead Rd, Air. ML6 77 DF28
Burnhead Rd, Lark. ML9 145 DE58
Burnhead St, (Udd.) G71 93 CR38
Burnhill Quad, (Ruther.) G73 88 BV37
Burnhill St, (Ruther.) G73 88 BV37
Burnhouse Brae, (Newt. M.)
G77 118 BJ50
Burnhouse Cres, Ham. ML3 139 CR52
Burnhouse Rd, Ham. ML3 139 CR52
Burnhouse St, G20 48 BM23
Burniebrae, Air. ML6 76 DA29
Burniebrae Rd, (Chap.) Air.
ML6 97 DG34

Burn La, Moth. ML1
*off Quarry St* 112 DC41
Burnlip Rd, Air. ML6 57 CW25
Burnmouth Ct, G33
*off Pendeen Rd* 71 CH31
Burnmouth Pl, (Bears.) G61 30 BJ16
Burnmouth Rd, G33 71 CH31
Burnock Pl, (E.Kil.) G75 134 BU54
Burnpark Av, (Udd.) G71 92 CM38
Burn Pl, (Camb.) G72
*off Burn Ter* 90 CA38
Burns Av, Bish. PA7 24 AK18
Burns Ct, (Kirk.) G66 18 CJ12
Burns Cres, Air. ML6 76 DD31
Burns Dr, (Kirk.) G66 18 CJ11
Burns Dr, John. PA5 79 AG37
Burns Gdns, (Blan.) G72 108 CL44
Burns Gro, (Thornlie.) G46 102 BJ43
Burnside, (Bears.) G61 11 BE14
Burnside Av, (Kirk.) G66 16 CD14
Burnside Av, (Barr.) G78 99 AX41
Burnside Av, (Calder.) Air. ML6 96 DD35
Burnside Av, Bell. ML4 111 CY41
Burnside Ct, (Bears.) G61
*off Burnside* 11 BE14
Burnside Ct, (Ruther.) G73 105 BY40
Burnside Ct, Clyde. G81 26 AU17
Burnside Ct, Coat. ML5
*off Kirk St* 74 CV32
Burnside Ct, Moth. ML1 128 DD49
Burnside Cres, (Blan.) G72 125 CP47
Burnside Gdns, (Clark.) G76 118 BM46
Burnside Gdns, (Kilb.)
John. PA10 78 AD35
Burnside Gate, (Ruther.) G73
*off Burnside Rd* 105 BY40
Burnside Gro, John. PA5 79 AG35
Burnside Ind Est, (Kilsyth) G65 7 CS5
Burnside La, Ham. ML3 126 CU50
Burnside Pl, Lark. ML9 144 DD58
Burnside Pl, Pais. PA3 61 AQ30
Burnside Quad, Moth. ML1
*off Graham St* 112 DC40
Burnside Rd, (Giff.) G46 118 BK47
Burnside Rd, (Ruther.) G73 105 BY40
Burnside Rd, Coat. ML5 75 CY28
Burnside Rd, (Elder.)
John. PA5 80 AL36
Burnside Rd, Moth. ML1 113 DF41
Burnside St, Moth. ML1 128 DC49
Burn Side Vw, Coat. ML5 74 CU32
Burnside Wk, (Bears.) G61
*off Burnside* 11 BE14
Burnside Wk, Coat. ML5 74 CU32
Burns La, Air. ML6
*off Stirling Rd* 97 DF34
Burns Ln, Lark. ML9
*off Duncan Graham St* 144 DD57
Burns Pk, (E.Kil.) G74 136 CC51
Burns Path, Bell. ML4
*off Bell St* 95 CX38
Burns Rd, (Kirk.) G66 18 CJ12
Burns Rd, (Cumb.) G67 22 DD10
Burns Rd, Air. ML6 97 DF34
Burns St, G4 67 BR27
Burns St, Clyde. G81 26 AU18
Burns St, Ham. ML3 140 CT51
Burns Way, Moth. ML1
*off Glenburn Av* 113 DE41
Burntbroom Dr, (Baill.) G69 91 CH34
Burntbroom Gdns, (Baill.) G69 91 CH34
Burntbroom St, G33 71 CF29
Burn Ter, (Camb.) G72 90 CA38

Burntshields Rd, (Kilb.)
John. PA10 78 AA35
Burn Vw, (Cumb.) G67 23 DE10
Burnwood Dr, Air. ML6 77 DH31
Burra Gdns, (Bishop.) G64 33 BZ18
Burrells La, G4 5 BU30
Burrelton Rd, G43 103 BP39
Burton La, G42
*off Langside Rd* 87 BQ36
Busby Rd, (Carm.) G76 120 BS46
Busby Rd, (Clark.) G76 119 BP46
Busby Rd, Bell. ML4 110 CV42
Bushes Av, Pais. PA2 82 AT36
Busheyhill St, (Camb.) G72 106 CC40
Bute, (E.Kil.) G74 137 CE52
Bute Av, Moth. ML1 127 CY46
Bute Av, Renf. PA4 63 AZ28
Bute Cres, (Old Kil.) G60 26 AS16
Bute Cres, (Bears.) G61 29 BH19
Bute Cres, Pais. PA2 82 AT38
Bute Dr, (Old Kil.) G60 26 AS15
Bute Dr, John. PA5 79 AF36
Bute Gdns, G12 66 BM27
Bute Gdns, G44 103 BP41
Bute Gdns, (Old Kil.) G60 26 AS15
Bute La, G12
*off Great George St* 66 BM27
Bute Pl, (Old Kil.) G60 26 AT15
Bute Rd, (Kirk.) G66 18 CK13
Bute Rd, (Ruther.) G73 105 BZ42
Bute Rd, (Abbots.) Pais. PA3 62 AT28
Bute St, Coat. ML5 95 CX33
Bute St, Ham. ML3 125 CR47
Bute Ter, (Udd.) G71 93 CR38
Bute Ter, (Ruther.) G73 105 BW40
Butler Wynd, Bell. ML4
*off Cochrane St* 110 CV40
Butterbiggins Rd, G42 87 BQ34
Butterburn Pk, Ham. ML3 140 CT51
Butterfield Pl, G41
*off Pollokshaws Rd* 87 BQ34
Buttermere, (E.Kil.) G75 134 BV56
Byars Rd, (Kirk.) G66 16 CD13
Byrebush Rd, G53 85 BE36
Byres Av, Pais. PA3 63 AW31
Byres Cres, Pais. PA3 63 AW31
Byresknowe La, Moth. ML1 112 DD44
Byres Rd, G11 66 BL27
Byres Rd, G12 66 BL27
Byres Rd, (Elder.) John. PA5 80 AM35
Byres Rd, Moth. ML1 113 DG41
Byrestone Av, (Newt. M.) G77 118 BL49
Byron Ct, (Both.) G71 109 CR43
Byron St, G11 65 BQ27
Byron St, Clyde. G81 27 AW17
Byshot St, G22 50 BT25

# C

Cable Dep Rd, Clyde. G81 26 AV19
Cadder Ct, (Bishop.) G64 33 BX16
Cadder Gro, G20
*off Cadder Rd* 49 BN22
Cadder Pl, G20 49 BN22
Cadder Rd, G20 49 BN22
Cadder Rd, G23 49 BN22
Cadder Rd, (Bishop.) G64 33 BX16
Cadder Way, (Bishop.) G64 33 BX16
Cadell Gdns, (E.Kil.) G74 123 CF48
Cadoc St, (Camb.) G72 106 CD40
Cadogan St, G2 4 BQ30
Cadsaw Rbt, Ham. ML3 126 CV49
Cadzow Av, (Giff.) G46 118 BK45

| | | | | | | | | |
|---|---|---|---|---|---|---|---|---|
| Cadzow Cres, Coat. ML5 | 94 | CU33 | Cairn Vw, Air. ML6 | 76 | DB31 | Caledonian Cres, G12 | | |
| Cadzow Dr, (Camb.) G72 | 106 | CB40 | Cairnwood Dr, Air. ML6 | 76 | DB32 | *off Great Western Rd* | 67 | BN27 |
| Cadzow Dr, Bell. ML4 | 111 | CZ41 | Caithness Rd, (E.Kil.) G74 | 123 | CF50 | Caledonian Pl, (Camb.) G72 | 107 | CG40 |
| Cadzow Grn, (E.Kil.) G74 | 135 | BZ51 | Caithness St, G20 | 49 | BP25 | Caledonian Rd, Lark. ML9 | 144 | DC58 |
| Cadzow Ind Est, Ham. ML3 | 140 | CT53 | Caithness St, (Blan.) G72 | 124 | CL47 | Caledonia Rd, G5 | 87 | BR33 |
| Cadzow La, Ham. ML3 | | | Calabar Ct, (Ruther.) G73 | 105 | BY43 | Caledonia Rd, (Baill.) G69 | 92 | CJ34 |
| *off Cadzow St* | | | Cala Sona Ct, Wis. ML2 | 143 | DG52 | Caledonia St, G5 | 88 | BT34 |
| Cadzow St, G2 | 4 | BQ30 | Calcots Path, G34 | | | Caledonia St, Clyde. G81 | 26 | AV18 |
| Cadzow St, Ham. ML3 | 126 | CU49 | *off Auchingill Rd* | 72 | CL28 | Caledonia St, Pais. PA3 | 62 | AT31 |
| Cadzow St, Lark. ML9 | 144 | DC57 | Calcots Pl, G34 | 72 | CL28 | Caledonia Wk, Ham. ML3 | | |
| Cadzow St, Moth. ML1 | 127 | CZ47 | Caldarvan St, G22 | 49 | BR26 | *off Chatelherault Cres* | 140 | CU52 |
| Caerlaverock Pl, (Blan.) G72 | | | Caldeen Rd, Coat. ML5 | 75 | CX32 | Caledonia Way, (Abbots.) | | |
| *off Broompark Rd* | 124 | CL47 | Calder Av, (Barr.) G78 | 99 | AY44 | Pais. PA3 | 62 | AT28 |
| Caird Dr, G11 | 66 | BK27 | Calder Av, Coat. ML5 | 95 | CX33 | Caledonia Way E, (Abbots.) | | |
| Caird Gdns, Ham. ML3 | | | Calderbank Ter, Moth. ML1 | 128 | DB45 | Pais. PA3 | 62 | AU28 |
| *off Caird St* | 126 | CT48 | Calderbank Vw, (Baill.) G69 | 92 | CL34 | Caledonia Way W, (Abbots.) | | |
| Caird Pk, Ham. ML3 | 126 | CT48 | Calderbraes Av, (Udd.) G71 | 93 | CN37 | Pais. PA3 | 62 | AT28 |
| Caird St, Ham. ML3 | 126 | CS48 | Calder Ct, Coat. ML5 | | | Caledon La, G12 | 48 | BL26 |
| Caird Ter, (Bears.) G61 | | | *off Whifflet St* | 95 | CX33 | Caledon St, G12 | 48 | BL26 |
| *off Grampian Way* | 11 | BF14 | Caldercuilt Rd, G20 | 48 | BL21 | Caley Brae, (Udd.) G71 | 109 | CP39 |
| Cairn Av, Renf. PA4 | 64 | BA28 | Caldercuilt Rd, G23 | 30 | BL20 | Calfhill Rd, G53 | 84 | BD34 |
| Cairnban St, G51 | 65 | BF31 | Calder Dr, (Camb.) G72 | 106 | CC40 | Calfmuir Rd, (Kirk.) G66 | 36 | CJ16 |
| Cairnbrook Rd, G34 | 72 | CL29 | Calder Dr, Bell. ML4 | 111 | CY41 | Calfmuir Rd, (Chry.) G69 | 36 | CJ16 |
| Cairn Ct, (E.Kil.) G74 | 122 | CA49 | Calder Gate, (Bishop.) G64 | 32 | BV17 | Calgary Pk, (E.Kil.) G75 | 135 | BZ53 |
| Cairn Ct, Moth. ML1 | 128 | DB48 | Calderglen Av, (Blan.) G72 | 108 | CL42 | Calgary Pl, (E.Kil.) G75 | | |
| Cairncraig St, G31 | 89 | BY33 | Calderglen Rd, (E.Kil.) G74 | 137 | CF51 | *off Calgary Pk* | 135 | BZ53 |
| Cairndow Av, G44 | 103 | BP41 | Calder Gro, Moth. ML1 | 128 | DA45 | Calgary St, G4 | 5 | BS28 |
| Cairndow Av La, G44 | 103 | BP41 | Calderpark Av, (Udd.) G71 | 92 | CK35 | Callaghan Cres, (E.Kil.) G74 | 134 | BT53 |
| Cairndow Ct, G44 | 103 | BP41 | Calderpark Ct, (Udd.) G71 | 92 | CK35 | Callaghan Wynd, (Blan.) G72 | 108 | CL44 |
| Cairn Dr, (Linw.) Pais. PA3 | 60 | AK31 | Calderpark Cres, (Udd.) G71 | 92 | CK35 | Callander Ct, (Cumb.) G68 | | |
| Cairndyke Cres, Air. ML6 | 76 | DC31 | Calderpark Pl, (Udd.) G71 | 92 | CK35 | *off Callander Rd* | 22 | DB9 |
| Cairngorm Ct, Ham. ML3 | 139 | CR54 | Calderpark Rd, (Udd.) G71 | 92 | CK35 | Callander Rd, (Cumb.) G68 | 22 | DB9 |
| Cairngorm Cres, (Bears.) G61 | 28 | BD15 | Calderpark Ter, (Udd.) G71 | 92 | CK35 | Callander Rd, (Chap.) Air. ML6 | 97 | DF36 |
| Cairngorm Cres, (Barr.) G78 | 99 | AY44 | Calder Pl, (Baill.) G69 | 92 | CK33 | Callander St, G20 | 49 | BQ26 |
| Cairngorm Cres, Pais. PA2 | 82 | AU36 | Calder Rd, (Udd.) G71 | 108 | CK40 | Callieburn Rd, (Bishop.) G64 | 33 | BW20 |
| Cairngorm Cres, Wis. ML2 | 129 | DH50 | Calder Rd, Bell. ML4 | 111 | CY42 | Callon St, Air. ML6 | 76 | DC30 |
| Cairngorm Gdns, (Cumb.) | | | Calder Rd, Pais. PA3 | 61 | AQ32 | Cally Av, G15 | 28 | BC18 |
| G68 | 21 | CW12 | Calderside Rd, (Blan.) G72 | 123 | CH49 | Calside, Pais. PA2 | 82 | AU34 |
| Cairngorm Rd, G43 | 102 | BL40 | Calderside Rd, (E.Kil.) G74 | 137 | CG52 | Calside Av, Pais. PA2 | 82 | AT34 |
| Cairnhill Av, Air. ML6 | 76 | DB32 | Calder St, G42 | 87 | BQ35 | Calside Ct, Pais. PA2 | 82 | AU35 |
| Cairnhill Circ, G52 | 84 | BB34 | Calder St, (Blan.) G72 | 124 | CM45 | Calton Entry, G40 | | |
| Cairnhill Ct, (Bears.) G61 | 29 | BG18 | Calder St, (Calder.) Air. ML6 | | | *off Gallowgate* | 5 | BU31 |
| Cairnhill Cres, Coat. ML5 | 95 | CZ34 | *off Main St* | 97 | DE35 | Calvay Cres, G33 | 71 | CF30 |
| Cairnhill Dr, G52 | 84 | BB34 | Calder St, Coat. ML5 | 95 | CX33 | Calvay Pl, G33 | 71 | CG30 |
| Cairnhill Pl, G52 | 84 | BB34 | Calder Twr, (E.Kil.) G74 | 136 | CD54 | Calvay Rd, G33 | 71 | CF30 |
| Cairnhill Rd, (Bears.) G61 | 29 | BH20 | Caldervale St, Air. ML6 | 97 | DG33 | Cambourne Rd, (Chry.) G69 | 37 | CP18 |
| Cairnhill Rd, Air. ML6 | 76 | DB32 | Calder Vw, Ham. ML3 | 139 | CQ53 | Cambridge Av, Clyde. G81 | 27 | AX18 |
| Cairnhill Trd Est, Air. ML6 | 76 | DC31 | Calderview, Moth. ML1 | | | Cambridge Rd, Renf. PA4 | 63 | AY27 |
| Cairnhill Vw, (Bears.) G61 | 29 | BG19 | *off Mill Rd* | 128 | DB46 | Cambridge St, G2 | 4 | BR29 |
| Cairnhope Av, Air. ML6 | 76 | DB32 | Calderview Av, Coat. ML5 | 95 | CZ34 | Cambridge St, G3 | 4 | BR29 |
| Cairnlea Dr, G51 | 66 | BK31 | Calderwood Av, (Baill.) G69 | 92 | CJ34 | Camburn St, G32 | 70 | CB31 |
| Cairnlea Gdns, Bell. ML4 | 111 | CX42 | Calderwood Dr, (Baill.) G69 | 92 | CJ34 | Cambusdoon Rd, G33 | 71 | CE27 |
| Cairnlea Rd, (Miln.) G62 | | | Calderwood Dr, (Blan.) G72 | 124 | CM47 | Cambus Kenneth Gdns, G32 | 71 | CF32 |
| *off Castle Mains Rd* | 11 | BG12 | Calderwood Gdns, (Baill.) G69 | 92 | CJ34 | Cambuskenneth Pl, G33 | 71 | CE27 |
| Cairnmuir Rd, (Camb.) G72 | 122 | CA46 | Calderwood Gdns, (E.Kil.) G74 | 123 | CG49 | Cambuslang Ct, G32 | 90 | CB37 |
| Cairnmuir Rd, (E.Kil.) G74 | 121 | BY48 | Calderwood Rd, G43 | 102 | BM39 | Cambuslang Ind Est, G32 | 90 | CC38 |
| Cairnoch Hill, (Cumb.) G68 | | | Calderwood Rd, (Ruther.) G73 | 89 | BY38 | Cambuslang Investment Pk, G32 | 90 | CD33 |
| *off Dunbrach Rd* | 21 | CY10 | Calderwood Rd, (E.Kil.) G74 | 136 | CD51 | Cambuslang Rd, G32 | 90 | CA37 |
| Cairn Pl, (E.Kil.) G74 | 122 | CA49 | Calderwood Sq, (E.Kil.) G74 | 122 | CD50 | Cambuslang Rd, (Camb.) G72 | 89 | BZ38 |
| Cairnryan, (E.Kil.) G74 | 121 | BZ50 | Caldwell Av, G13 | 46 | BC23 | Cambuslang Rd, (Ruther.) G73 | 89 | BX36 |
| Cairns Av, (Camb.) G72 | 106 | CD40 | Caldwell Gro, (Ruther.) G73 | 105 | BY43 | Cambuslang Way, G32 | 90 | CB37 |
| Cairns Dr, (Miln.) G62 | 12 | BJ11 | Caldwell Gro, Bell. ML4 | 95 | CW37 | Cambusmore Pl, G33 | 71 | CE27 |
| Cairnsmore Dr, (Bears.) G61 | 10 | BD13 | Caldwell Quad, Moth. ML1 | 127 | CY48 | Cambus Pl, G33 | 71 | CE27 |
| Cairnsmore Rd, G15 | 28 | BA19 | Caledonia Av, G5 | 88 | BS34 | Camden Ter, G5 | 88 | BS33 |
| Cairns Rd, (Camb.) G72 | 106 | CD41 | Caledonia Av, (Ruther.) G73 | 89 | BX37 | Camellia Dr, Wis. ML2 | 143 | DG52 |
| Cairns St, Moth. ML1 | 128 | DA47 | Caledonia Ct, Pais. PA3 | | | Camelon Cres, (Blan.) G72 | 124 | CM46 |
| Cairn St, G21 | 50 | BV23 | *off Mossvale St* | 62 | AT31 | Camelon St, G32 | 70 | CB31 |
| Cairnswell Av, (Camb.) G72 | 107 | CE41 | Caledonia Dr, (Baill.) G69 | 92 | CK34 | Cameron Av, Bish. PA7 | 24 | AK17 |
| Cairnswell Pl, (Camb.) G72 | 107 | CE41 | Caledonia Dr, Moth. ML1 | 113 | DG41 | *off Glasgow Rd* | 27 | AY15 |
| Cairntoul Ct, (Cumb.) G68 | 21 | CX11 | Caledonian Av, Bell. ML4 | 110 | CV41 | Cameron Ct, (Ruther.) G73 | 89 | BW38 |
| Cairntoul Dr, G14 | 46 | BC23 | Caledonian Ct, (E.Kil.) G74 | | | Cameron Ct, Air. ML6 | | |
| Cairntoul Pl, G14 | 46 | BC23 | *off East Kilbride Shop Cen* | 136 | CA53 | *off Station Rd* | 77 | DG29 |
| Cairnview, (Kirk.) G66 | 18 | CK14 | | | | | | |

| | | |
|---|---|---|
| Cameron Ct, Clyde. G81 | | |
| off Cameron St | 45 | AY21 |
| Cameron Cres, (Carm.) G76 | 120 | BU46 |
| Cameron Cres, Ham. ML3 | 125 | CR50 |
| Cameron Dr, (Bears.) G61 | 30 | BJ18 |
| Cameron Dr, (Udd.) G71 | 93 | CQ37 |
| Cameron Dr, (Newt. M.) G77 | 117 | BG47 |
| Cameron Pl, Bell. ML4 | 110 | CV42 |
| Cameronian Rbt, Ham. ML3 | 126 | CV49 |
| Cameronian Way, Lark. ML9 | | |
| off Elmbank Dr | 145 | DE60 |
| Cameron Path, Lark. ML9 | | |
| off Stuart Dr | 145 | DE60 |
| Cameron Rd, (Green.) Air. ML6 | 41 | DE19 |
| Cameron Sq, Clyde. G81 | 27 | AY15 |
| Cameron St, G52 | 64 | BA30 |
| Cameron St, Clyde. G81 | 45 | AY21 |
| Cameron St, Coat. ML5 | 75 | CX29 |
| Cameron St, Moth. ML1 | 128 | DA47 |
| Cameron Way, (Blan.) G72 | 124 | CM45 |
| Camlachie St, G31 | 69 | BX32 |
| Campbell Av, (Miln.) G62 | 12 | BJ12 |
| Campbell Av, Bish. PA7 | 24 | AK17 |
| Campbell Cres, (Both.) G71 | 109 | CR41 |
| Campbell Cres, (Newt. M.) G77 | 117 | BG47 |
| Campbell Dr, (Bears.) G61 | 29 | BF16 |
| Campbell Dr, (Barr.) G78 | 99 | AY43 |
| Campbell La, Ham. ML3 | | |
| off Campbell St | 126 | CU49 |
| Campbell Pl, (Torr.) G64 | 15 | BX12 |
| Campbell Pl, (E.Kil.) G75 | 136 | CA54 |
| Campbell St, G20 | 48 | BM22 |
| Campbell St, Bell. ML4 | 111 | CW40 |
| Campbell St, Ham. ML3 | 126 | CU50 |
| Campbell St, John. PA5 | 79 | AH35 |
| Campbell St, Renf. PA4 | 45 | AZ25 |
| Camphill, Pais. PA1 | 82 | AT34 |
| Camphill Av, G41 | 87 | BN38 |
| Camphill Av, (Kirk.) G66 | 17 | CE13 |
| Camphill Ct, Pais. PA2 | 82 | AT34 |
| Camphill Gdns, Bish. PA7 | 24 | AL18 |
| Campion Rd, Moth. ML1 | 127 | CZ45 |
| Camp Rd, (Baill.) G69 | 72 | CK32 |
| Camp Rd, (Ruther.) G73 | 88 | BV35 |
| Camp Rd, Moth. ML1 | 128 | DA49 |
| Camps Cres, Renf. PA4 | 64 | BA27 |
| Campsie Av, (Barr.) G78 | 99 | AY44 |
| Campsie Ct, (Kirk.) G66 | | |
| off Westergreens Av | 35 | CE15 |
| Campsie Ct, Lark. ML9 | 142 | DB56 |
| Campsie Cres, Air. ML6 | 76 | DB29 |
| Campsie Dr, (Bears.) G61 | 11 | BF14 |
| Campsie Dr, (Miln.) G62 | 12 | BK11 |
| Campsie Dr, Pais. PA2 | 82 | AT37 |
| Campsie Dr, (Abbots.) Pais. | | |
| PA3 | 62 | AU28 |
| Campsie Dr, Renf. PA4 | 63 | AW29 |
| Campsie Gdns, (Clark.) G76 | 118 | BL45 |
| Campsie Pl, (Chry.) G69 | 54 | CL21 |
| Campsie Rd, (Torr.) G64 | 15 | BZ11 |
| Campsie Rd, (Kirk.) G66 | 16 | CD12 |
| Campsie Rd, Wis. ML2 | 129 | DG49 |
| Campsie St, G21 | 50 | BV24 |
| Campsie Vw, (Stepps) G33 | 53 | CF25 |
| Campsie Vw, (Kirk.) G66 | 16 | CC13 |
| Campsie Vw, (Cumb.) G67 | 22 | DD10 |
| Campsie Vw, (Baill.) G69 | 73 | CP32 |
| Campsie Vw, (Chry.) G69 | 54 | CL21 |
| Campsie Vw, (Udd.) G71 | 93 | CQ37 |
| Campsie Vw, (Camb.) G72 | 107 | CG42 |
| Campsie Vw, Ham. ML3 | 139 | CP51 |
| Campston Pl, G33 | 70 | CD28 |
| Camp St, Moth. ML1 | 128 | DA48 |
| Camstradden Dr E, (Bears.) | | |
| G61 | 29 | BE17 |
| Camstradden Dr W, (Bears.) | | |
| G61 | 29 | BE17 |
| Camus Pl, G15 | 28 | BB17 |
| Canal Av, John. PA5 | 79 | AH35 |
| Canal Bk La, G22 | 49 | BQ22 |
| Canal Gdns, (Elder.) John. PA5 | | |
| off Canal St | 80 | AM34 |
| Canal La, (Kirk.) G66 | 17 | CF12 |
| Canal La, Renf. PA4 | 45 | AZ25 |
| Canal Rd, John. PA5 | 80 | AJ35 |
| Canal St, G4 | 5 | BS28 |
| Canal St, (Kirk.) G66 | 17 | CF12 |
| Canal St, Clyde. G81 | 27 | AX20 |
| Canal St, John. PA5 | 80 | AJ34 |
| Canal St, (Elder.) John. PA5 | 80 | AM34 |
| Canal St, Pais. PA1 | 82 | AT33 |
| Canal St, Renf. PA4 | 45 | AZ25 |
| Canal Ter, Pais. PA1 | 82 | AT33 |
| Canberra Av, Clyde. G81 | 26 | AT17 |
| Canberra Ct, (Giff.) G46 | 103 | BN42 |
| Canberra Dr, (E.Kil.) G75 | 135 | BY53 |
| Cander Rigg, (Bishop.) G64 | 33 | BW17 |
| Cander St, Lark. ML9 | 144 | DD61 |
| Candleriggs, G1 | 5 | BT31 |
| Candren Rd, Pais. PA3 | 81 | AQ33 |
| Candren Rd, (Linw.) Pais. PA3 | 60 | AM32 |
| Candren Way, Pais. PA3 | | |
| off Ferguslie Pk Av | 61 | AQ32 |
| Candymill La, Ham. ML3 | 126 | CS46 |
| Canmore Pl, G31 | 89 | BZ33 |
| Canmore St, G31 | 89 | BZ33 |
| Cannich Dr, Pais. PA2 | 83 | AX36 |
| Canniesburn Ct, (Bears.) G61 | 29 | BG18 |
| Canniesburn Dr, (Bears.) G61 | 29 | BG19 |
| Canniesburn Quad, (Bears.) G61 | 29 | BG18 |
| Canniesburn Rd, (Bears.) G61 | 29 | BF18 |
| Canniesburn Sq, (Bears.) G61 | | |
| off Switchback Rd | 29 | BH19 |
| Canniesburn Toll, (Bears.) G61 | | |
| off Drymen Rd | 29 | BH19 |
| Canonbie Av, (E.Kil.) G74 | 122 | CB49 |
| Canonbie St, G34 | 72 | CM28 |
| Canon Ct, Moth. ML1 | 113 | DF43 |
| Canongate, (E.Kil.) G74 | | |
| off Ivanhoe | 123 | CF49 |
| Canterbury, (E.Kil.) G75 | 135 | BX54 |
| Cantieslaw Dr, (E.Kil.) G74 | 122 | CC50 |
| Canting Way, G51 | 66 | BL30 |
| Canyon Rd, (Netherton Ind. Est.) | | |
| Wis. ML2 | 143 | DF51 |
| Capel Av, (Newt. M.) G77 | 117 | BH47 |
| Capel Gro, (E.Kil.) G74 | 122 | CD50 |
| Capelrig Dr, (E.Kil.) G74 | 122 | CD50 |
| Capelrig Dr, (Newt. M.) G77 | 117 | BG45 |
| Capelrig La, (Newt. M.) G77 | | |
| off Capelrig Rd | 117 | BF47 |
| Capelrig Rd, (Newt. M.) G77 | 117 | BG45 |
| Capelrig St, (Thornlie.) G46 | 101 | BH41 |
| Caplaw Pl, Wis. ML2 | 143 | DH53 |
| Caplaw Rd, Pais. PA2 | 98 | AS39 |
| Caplethill Rd, (Barr.) G78 | 82 | AV38 |
| Caplethill Rd, Pais. PA2 | 82 | AV38 |
| Caprington Pl, G33 | 70 | CC28 |
| Caprington St, G33 | 70 | CC28 |
| Cara Dr, G51 | | |
| off St. Kenneth Dr | 65 | BG29 |
| Caravelle Way, Renf. PA4 | | |
| off Friendship Way | 63 | AZ28 |
| Carbarns, Wis. ML2 | 143 | DF52 |
| Carbarns E, Wis. ML2 | 143 | DF52 |
| Carbarns Rd, Wis. ML2 | 143 | DF52 |
| Carbarns W, Wis. ML2 | 143 | DF52 |
| Carberry Rd, G41 | 86 | BM35 |
| Carbeth Rd, (Miln.) G62 | 11 | BH12 |
| Carbeth St, G22 | 49 | BR25 |
| Carbisdale St, G22 | 50 | BU24 |
| Carbost St, G23 | 30 | BM20 |
| Carbrain Ind Est, (Cumb.) G67 | 22 | DD12 |
| Carbrook St, G21 | 69 | BW28 |
| Carbrook St, Pais. PA1 | 82 | AS33 |
| Cardarrach St, G21 | 51 | BW24 |
| Cardean Rd, Bell. ML4 | 112 | DA39 |
| Cardell Av, Pais. PA2 | 81 | AQ35 |
| Cardell Cres, (Chap.) Air. ML6 | 97 | DF35 |
| Cardell Dr, Pais. PA2 | 81 | AQ34 |
| Cardell Rd, Pais. PA2 | 81 | AQ34 |
| Cardonald Dr, G52 | 84 | BC33 |
| Cardonald Gdns, G52 | 84 | BC33 |
| Cardonald Pl Rd, G52 | 84 | BD33 |
| Cardowan Dr, (Stepps) G33 | 53 | CG24 |
| Cardowan Dr, (Cumb.) G68 | 20 | CU12 |
| Cardowan Pk, (Udd.) G71 | 93 | CR36 |
| Cardowan Rd, G32 | 70 | CB31 |
| Cardowan Rd, (Stepps) G33 | 53 | CG23 |
| Cardow Rd, G21 | 51 | BY25 |
| Cardrona St, G33 | 52 | CD26 |
| Cardross Ct, G31 | 68 | BV30 |
| Cardross St, G31 | 68 | BV30 |
| Cardwell St, G41 | 87 | BQ33 |
| Cardyke St, G21 | 51 | BW25 |
| Careston Pl, (Bishop.) G64 | 33 | BZ20 |
| Carfin Ind Est, Moth. ML1 | 112 | DD43 |
| Carfin Mill Rd, Moth. ML1 | 113 | DE44 |
| Carfin Rd, Moth. ML1 | 113 | DF42 |
| Carfin Rd, Wis. ML2 | 129 | DE49 |
| Carfin St, G42 | 87 | BR35 |
| Carfin St, Coat. ML5 | 95 | CX33 |
| Carfin St, Moth. ML1 | 112 | DC42 |
| Carfrae St, G3 | 66 | BL29 |
| Cargill Sq, (Bishop.) G64 | 51 | BY21 |
| Carham Cres, G52 | 65 | BE32 |
| Carham Dr, G52 | 65 | BE32 |
| Caribou Grn, (E.Kil.) G75 | | |
| off Winnipeg Dr | 135 | BX53 |
| Carillon Rd, G51 | 66 | BL32 |
| Carisbrooke Cres, (Bishop.) G64 | 33 | BX17 |
| Carlaverock Rd, G43 | 102 | BM39 |
| Carleith Av, Clyde. G81 | 26 | AV15 |
| Carleith Quad, G51 | 65 | BF30 |
| Carleith Ter, Clyde. G81 | 26 | AV15 |
| Carleston St, G21 | 50 | BV25 |
| Carleton Ct, (Giff.) G46 | 102 | BL41 |
| Carleton Dr, (Giff.) G46 | 102 | BL41 |
| Carleton Gate, (Giff.) G46 | 102 | BL41 |
| Carlibar Av, G13 | 46 | BB23 |
| Carlibar Dr, (Barr.) G78 | 99 | AY42 |
| Carlibar Gdns, (Barr.) G78 | 99 | AY42 |
| Carlibar Rd, (Barr.) G78 | 99 | AY42 |
| Carlile Pl, Pais. PA3 | 62 | AU31 |
| Carlisle La, Air. ML6 | 77 | DE30 |
| Carlisle Rd, Air. ML6 | 77 | DE32 |
| Carlisle Rd, Ham. ML3 | 141 | CW51 |
| Carlisle Rd, Lark. ML9 | 144 | CZ53 |
| Carlisle Rd, (Birk.) Lark. ML9 | 144 | DD60 |
| Carlisle St, G21 | 50 | BT25 |
| Carlisle Ter, Pais. PA3 | 62 | AU31 |
| Carlock Wk, G32 | | |
| off Croftspar Pl | 71 | CE31 |
| Carloway Ct, G33 | 70 | CD29 |
| Carlowrie Av, (Blan.) G72 | 108 | CL43 |
| Carlton Ct, G5 | 4 | BR31 |
| Carlton Ct, Ham. ML3 | | |
| off Johnstone Rd | 140 | CU51 |
| Carlton Pl, G5 | 4 | BR31 |

| | | | | | | | | | |
|---|---|---|---|---|---|---|---|---|---|
| Carlyle Av, G52 | 64 | BB29 | Carrick Dr, G32 | 91 | CG34 | Cartside Quad, G42 | 87 | BQ38 |
| Carlyle Dr, (E.Kil.) G74 | 136 | CC51 | Carrick Dr, (Ruther.) G73 | 105 | BW40 | Cartside Rd, (Clark.) G76 | 119 | BP48 |
| Carlyle St, Pais. PA3 | 62 | AU32 | Carrick Dr, Coat. ML5 | 74 | CT31 | Cartside St, G42 | 87 | BP38 |
| Carlyle Ter, (Ruther.) G73 | 89 | BX36 | Carrick Gdns, (Blan.) G72 | 124 | CM47 | Cartside Ter, (Kilb.) John. PA10 | | |
| Carlyle Ter, (E.Kil.) G74 | | | Carrick Gdns, Bell. ML4 | | | *off Kilbarchan Rd* | 79 | AE35 |
| *off Calderwood Rd* | 136 | CD51 | *off Rosegreen Cres* | 95 | CW37 | Cart St, Clyde. G81 | 45 | AX21 |
| Carmaben Rd, G33 | 71 | CG29 | Carrick Gdns, Ham. ML3 | 139 | CN51 | Cartvale La, Pais. PA3 | 62 | AU31 |
| Carment Dr, G41 | 86 | BM37 | Carrick Gro, G32 | 91 | CG33 | Cartvale Rd, G42 | 87 | BP38 |
| Carment La, G41 | 86 | BM37 | Carrick Mans, G32 | | | Cartview Ct, (Clark.) G76 | 119 | BP47 |
| Carmichael Path, (Glenb.) | | | *off Carrick Dr* | 91 | CG34 | Caskie Dr, (Blan.) G72 | 109 | CN44 |
| Coat. ML5 *off The Oval* | 56 | CS23 | Carrick Pl, Bell. ML4 | 95 | CX37 | Cassels Gro, Moth. ML1 | | |
| Carmichael Pl, G42 | 87 | BP38 | Carrick Pl, Coat. ML5 | 74 | CT30 | *off Potts Way* | 111 | CY44 |
| Carmichael St, G51 | 66 | BK31 | Carrick Pl, Lark. ML9 | 144 | DD57 | Cassels St, Moth. ML1 | 128 | DA45 |
| Carmunnock Bypass, G45 | 120 | BS45 | Carrick Rd, (Bishop.) G64 | 33 | BY20 | Cassiltoun Gdns, G45 | | |
| Carmunnock Bypass, G76 | 120 | BS45 | Carrick Rd, (Cumb.) G67 | 22 | DC9 | *off Stravanan Rd* | 104 | BT43 |
| Carmunnock La, G44 | | | Carrick Rd, (Ruther.) G73 | 105 | BW40 | Cassley Av, Renf. PA4 | 64 | BB27 |
| *off Madison Av* | 103 | BR40 | Carrick Rd, (E.Kil.) G74 | 122 | CA50 | Castle Av, (Udd.) G71 | 109 | CN41 |
| Carmunnock Rd, G44 | 87 | BR38 | Carrick Rd, Bish. PA7 | 24 | AL19 | Castle Av, (Elder.) John. PA5 | 80 | AK36 |
| Carmunnock Rd, G45 | 104 | BS40 | Carrickstone Rd, (Cumb.) G68 | 22 | DA9 | Castle Av, Moth. ML1 | 112 | DD39 |
| Carmunnock Rd, (Busby) G76 | 104 | BS44 | Carrickstone Rbt, (Cumb.) G68 | 9 | DA8 | Castlebank Ct, G13 | 47 | BG23 |
| Carmunnock Rd, (Kittochside) | | | Carrickstone Vw, (Cumb.) G68 | 9 | DB8 | Castlebank Cres, G11 | 66 | BJ28 |
| G76 | 121 | BW48 | Carrick St, G2 | 4 | BQ31 | Castlebank Gdns, G13 | 47 | BG23 |
| Carmyle Av, G32 | 90 | CD34 | Carrick St, Lark. ML9 | 145 | DE59 | Castlebank St, G11 | 65 | BH27 |
| Carmyle Gdns, Coat. ML5 | 94 | CU34 | Carrick Vw, (Glenb.) Coat. ML5 | 56 | CU23 | Castlebank Vil, G13 | | |
| Carna Dr, G44 | 104 | BS40 | Carrick Way, (Both.) G71 | 109 | CQ42 | *off Munro Pl* | 47 | BG23 |
| Carnarvon St, G3 | 4 | BP28 | Carriden Pl, G33 | 71 | CG30 | Castlebay Dr, G22 | 32 | BS20 |
| Carnbroe Rd, Bell. ML4 | 95 | CX37 | Carrington St, G4 | 67 | BP27 | Castlebay Pl, G22 | | |
| Carnbroe Rd, Coat. ML5 | 95 | CZ33 | Carroglen Gdns, G32 | 71 | CF32 | *off Castlebay St* | 50 | BS21 |
| Carneddans Rd, (Miln.) G62 | 11 | BE9 | Carroglen Gro, G32 | 71 | CF32 | Castlebay St, G22 | 50 | BS21 |
| Carnegie Hill, (E.Kil.) G75 | 135 | BZ53 | Carroll Cres, (New.) Moth. ML1 | 113 | DF43 | Castlebrae Gdns, G44 | 103 | BR39 |
| Carnegie Pl, (E.Kil.) G75 | 135 | BZ53 | Carron Ct, (Camb.) G72 | 107 | CF40 | Castle Chimmins Av, (Camb.) | | |
| Carnegie Rd, G52 | 64 | BC30 | Carron Ct, Ham. ML3 | 139 | CR52 | G72 | 107 | CF41 |
| Carney Dr, (E.Kil.) G75 | 134 | BT53 | Carron Cres, G22 | 50 | BT24 | Castle Chimmins Rd, (Camb.) | | |
| Carnoch St, G23 | | | Carron Cres, (Bears.) G61 | 29 | BE18 | G72 | 107 | CF42 |
| *off Torrin Rd* | 30 | BM20 | Carron Cres, (Bishop.) G64 | 33 | BX20 | Castle Ct, (Kirk.) G66 | 17 | CF13 |
| Carnock Cres, (Barr.) G78 | 99 | AX43 | Carron Cres, (Lenz.) G66 | 35 | CG17 | Castle Cres, Bish. PA7 | 24 | AK19 |
| Carnock Gdns, (Miln.) G62 | 11 | BG11 | Carron Dr, Bish. PA7 | 24 | AL19 | Castle Cres N Ct, G1 | | |
| Carnock Rd, G53 | 85 | BE37 | Carron La, Pais. PA3 | | | *off Royal Ex Sq* | 5 | BS30 |
| Carnoustie Ct, (Both.) G71 | 109 | CP43 | *off Kilearn Rd* | 63 | AX30 | Castlecroft Gdns, (Udd.) G71 | 109 | CN40 |
| Carnoustie Cres, (Bishop.) G64 | 33 | BY20 | Carron Pl, G22 | 50 | BT24 | Castle Dr, Moth. ML1 | 112 | DD39 |
| Carnoustie Cres, (E.Kil.) G75 | 135 | BW55 | Carron Pl, (E.Kil.) G75 | 136 | CB56 | Castlefern Rd, (Ruther.) G73 | 105 | BX42 |
| Carnoustie Pl, G5 | 67 | BP32 | Carron Pl, Coat. ML5 | 74 | CT28 | Castlefield Ct, G33 | 52 | CD25 |
| Carnoustie Pl, Bell. ML4 | 95 | CW38 | Carron St, G22 | 50 | BU24 | Castlefield Gdns, (E.Kil.) G75 | | |
| Carnoustie St, G5 | 67 | BP32 | Carron Way, (Cumb.) G67 | | | *off Pine Cres* | 135 | BX56 |
| Carnoustie Way, (Cumb.) G68 | 9 | DB7 | *off Cumbernauld Shop Cen* | 22 | DB12 | Castle Gait, Pais. PA1 | 82 | AT34 |
| Carntyne Gdns, G32 | | | Carron Way, Moth. ML1 | | | Castle Gdns, (Chry.) G69 | 37 | CP20 |
| *off Abbeyhill St* | 70 | CA30 | *off Lomond Wk* | 113 | DE41 | Castle Gdns, Pais. PA2 | 81 | AQ34 |
| Carntyne Gro, G32 | 70 | CC30 | Carron Way, Pais. PA3 | | | Castle Gate, (Udd.) G71 | 109 | CN40 |
| Carntynehall Rd, G32 | 70 | CB30 | *off Priory Av* | 63 | AW30 | Castle Gate, (Newt. M.) G77 | 118 | BJ50 |
| Carntyne Ind Est, G32 | 70 | CA31 | Carrour Gdns, (Bishop.) G64 | 32 | BV19 | Castleglen Rd, (E.Kil.) G74 | 120 | BV49 |
| Carntyne Path, G32 | 69 | BZ30 | Carr Quad, Bell. ML4 | 111 | CZ40 | Castle Gro, (Kilsyth) G65 | 7 | CS3 |
| Carntyne Pl, G32 | 69 | BZ30 | Carsaig Dr, G52 | 65 | BG32 | Castlehill Cres, (Chap.) Air. ML6 | 97 | DG36 |
| Carntyne Rd, G31 | 69 | BY31 | Carsaig Ln, (Glenb.) Coat. ML5 | | | Castlehill Cres, Ham. ML3 | 141 | CY52 |
| Carntyne Rd, G32 | 69 | BZ30 | *off Dinyra Pl* | 56 | CS23 | Castlehill Cres, Renf. PA4 | | |
| Carnwadric Rd, (Thornlie.) G46 | 101 | BG41 | Carscallan Rd, Ham. ML3 | 140 | CU56 | *off Ferry Rd* | 45 | AZ25 |
| Carnwath Av, G43 | 103 | BP39 | Carsegreen Av, Pais. PA2 | 81 | AR38 | Castlehill Dr, (Newt. M.) G77 | 117 | BH49 |
| Caroline St, G31 | 70 | CA32 | Carse Vw Dr, (Bears.) G61 | 30 | BJ15 | Castlehill Gdns, Ham. ML3 | 140 | CV51 |
| Carolside Av, (Clark.) G76 | 119 | BN46 | Carstairs St, G40 | 89 | BW35 | Castlehill Grn, (E.Kil.) G74 | 120 | BV49 |
| Carolside Dr, G15 | 28 | BD18 | Carswell Gdns, G41 | 87 | BN36 | Castlehill Rd, (Bears.) G61 | 28 | BD15 |
| Carolside Gdns, (Clark.) G76 | 119 | BN46 | Carswell Rd, (Newt. M.) G77 | 116 | BC48 | Castlehill Rd, Wis. ML2 | 143 | DH53 |
| Carradale Cres, (Cumb.) G68 | 20 | CV13 | Cartbank Gdns, G44 | | | Castlehill Vw, (Kilsyth) G65 | 7 | CS3 |
| Carradale Gdns, (Bishop.) G64 | | | *off Cartbank Rd* | 103 | BQ41 | Castlelaw Gdns, G32 | 70 | CD31 |
| *off Thrums Av* | 33 | BY20 | Cartbank Gro, G44 | | | Castlelaw Pl, G32 | 70 | CD31 |
| Carradale Pl, (Linw.) Pais. PA3 | 60 | AJ31 | *off Cartbank Rd* | 103 | BQ41 | Castlelaw St, G32 | 70 | CD31 |
| Carradale St, Coat. ML5 | | | Cartbank Rd, G44 | 103 | BQ41 | Castle Mains Rd, (Miln.) G62 | 11 | BF11 |
| *off Bowling St* | 74 | CV30 | Cartcraigs Rd, G43 | 102 | BK39 | Castlemilk Arc, G45 | 104 | BU42 |
| Carrbridge Dr, G20 | 48 | BM23 | Cartha Cres, Pais. PA2 | 83 | AW34 | Castlemilk Cres, G44 | 104 | BU40 |
| Carresbrook Av, (Kirk.) G66 | 36 | CK15 | Cartha St, G41 | 86 | BM38 | Castlemilk Dr, G45 | 104 | BU43 |
| Carriagehill Av, Pais. PA2 | 82 | AU35 | Cartsbridge Rd, (Clark.) G76 | 119 | BN47 | Castlemilk Rd, G44 | 88 | BU38 |
| Carriagehill Dr, Pais. PA2 | 82 | AU36 | Cartside Av, John. PA5 | 79 | AF36 | Castlemilk Ter, G45 | | |
| Carrickarden Rd, (Bears.) G61 | 29 | BH18 | Cartside Av, (Inch.) Renf. PA4 | 43 | AR25 | *off Castlemilk Dr* | 104 | BU44 |
| Carrick Ct, (Kirk.) G66 | 18 | CJ11 | Cartside Dr, (Clark.) G76 | 119 | BQ47 | Castlemount Av, (Newt. M.) | | |
| Carrick Cres, (Giff.) G46 | 102 | BL44 | Cartside Pl, (Clark.) G76 | 119 | BP48 | G77 | 117 | BH50 |

Castle Pl, (Udd.) G71 109 CN39
Castle Quad, Air. ML6 77 DF30
Castle Rd, (Newt. M.) G77 117 BE49
Castle Rd, Air. ML6 77 DF29
Castle Rd, (Elder.) John. PA5 80 AL34
Castle Sq, Clyde. G81 26 AU18
Castle St, G4 5 BU29
Castle St, G11 66 BL28
Castle St, (Baill.) G69 92 CJ34
Castle St, (Ruther.) G73 89 BW37
Castle St, (Chap.) Air. ML6 97 DF35
Castle St, Clyde. G81 26 AU18
Castle St, Ham. ML3 126 CV49
Castle St, Pais. PA1 82 AS33
Castleton Av, (Bishop.) G64 50 BU22
Castleton Av, (Newt. M.) G77 117 BH50
Castleton Ct, (Newt. M.) G77
  off Castleton Dr 117 BH50
Castleton Cres, (Newt. M.) G77 117 BH50
Castleton Dr, (Newt. M.) G77 117 BH50
Castleton Gro, (Newt. M.) G77 117 BH50
Castle Vw, Clyde. G81
  off Granville St 27 AX18
Castleview Av, Pais. PA2 81 AQ38
Castleview Dr, Pais. PA2 81 AQ38
Castleview Pl, Pais. PA2
  off Castleview Av 81 AQ38
Castle Way, (Cumb.) G67 23 DE9
Castle Way, (Baill.) G69
  off Dukes Rd 73 CP32
Castle Wynd, (Both.) G71 109 CR43
Cathay St, G22 50 BS21
Cathcart Cres, Pais. PA2 83 AW34
Cathcart Pl, (Ruther.) G73 88 BV38
Cathcart Rd, G42 87 BR37
Cathcart Rd, (Ruther.) G73 88 BU38
Cathedral Sq, G4 5 BU30
Cathedral St, G1 5 BS29
Cathedral St, G4 5 BS29
Catherine Pl, G3
  off Hydepark St 4 BP30
Catherine St, (Kirk.) G66 17 CE13
Catherine St, Moth. ML1 128 DA49
Catherine's Wk, (Blan.) G72
  off Victoria St 124 CM47
Catherine Way, Moth. ML1 112 DB42
Cathkin Av, (Camb.) G72 106 CA39
Cathkin Av, (Ruther.) G73 89 BY38
Cathkin Bypass, (Ruther.) G73 105 BZ42
Cathkin Cres, (Cumb.) G68 22 DA9
Cathkin Dr, (Clark.) G76 118 BL45
Cathkin Gdns, (Udd.) G71
  off Watling St 93 CN36
Cathkin Pl, (Camb.) G72 106 CA39
Cathkin Rd, G42 87 BP38
Cathkin Rd, (Udd.) G71 93 CN36
Cathkin Rd, (Ruther.) G73 105 BY43
Cathkin Rd, (Carm.) G76 120 BU45
Cathkin Vw, G32 90 CD37
Cathkinview Pl, G42 87 BQ38
Cathkinview Rd, G42 87 BR38
Catrine, (E.Kil.) G74 135 BZ51
Catrine Av, Clyde. G81 27 AZ18
Catrine Ct, G53 84 BC37
Catrine Cres, Moth. ML1 128 DC50
Catrine Gdns, G53 84 BC37
Catrine Pl, G53 84 BC37
Catrine Rd, G53 84 BC37
Catrine St, Lark. ML9 145 DE59
Catriona Way, Moth. ML1
  off Shirrel Rd 112 DD41
Catter Gdns, (Miln.) G62 11 BG10
Cauldstream Pl, (Miln.) G62 11 BG12

Caurnie Vw, (Kirk.) G66 36 CL15
Causewayside Cres, G32 90 CC35
Causewayside St, G32 90 CC35
Causeyside St, Pais. PA1 82 AU33
Causeystanes, (Blan.) G72
  off Winton Cres 124 CM46
Cavendish Ct, G5 87 BR33
Cavendish Dr, (Newt. M.) G77 117 BH47
Cavendish Pl, G5 87 BR33
Cavendish St, G5 87 BR33
Cavin Dr, G45 104 BU41
Cavin Rd, G45 104 BU41
Cawder Ct, (Cumb.) G68
  off Cawder Rd 9 DA8
Cawder Pl, (Cumb.) G68
  off Cawder Rd 9 DA8
Cawder Rd, (Cumb.) G68 9 DA8
Cawder Vw, (Cumb.) G68
  off Cawder Rd 9 DA8
Cawder Way, (Cumb.) G68
  off Cawder Rd 9 DA8
Cawdor Cres, Bish. PA7 24 AK19
Cawdor Way, (E.Kil.) G74
  off Dunvegan Pl 121 BZ50
Cayton Gdns, (Baill.) G69 91 CH33
Cecil St, G12 48 BM26
Cecil St, (Clark.) G76 119 BN46
Cecil St, Coat. ML5 75 CW32
Cedar Av, (Udd.) G71
  off Douglas Cres 94 CS37
Cedar Av, Clyde. G81 26 AT17
Cedar Av, John. PA5 79 AH37
Cedar Ct, G20 67 BQ27
Cedar Ct, (Camb.) G72 107 CG41
Cedar Ct, (E.Kil.) G75 135 BY56
Cedar Ct, (Kilb.) John. PA10 78 AC34
Cedar Cres, Ham. ML3 140 CU52
Cedar Dr, (Lenz.) G66 35 CE16
Cedar Dr, (Udd.) G71 94 CS37
Cedar Dr, (E.Kil.) G75 135 BY56
Cedar Gdns, (Ruther.) G73 105 BY41
Cedar Gdns, (New.) Moth. ML1 113 DE41
Cedar La, Air. ML6 77 DE30
Cedar Pl, (Blan.) G72 124 CL45
Cedar Pl, (E.Kil.) G75 135 BY56
Cedar Pl, (Barr.) G78
  off Divernia Way 115 AZ45
Cedar Rd, (Bishop.) G64 51 BX21
Cedar Rd, (Cumb.) G67 23 DF10
Cedar St, G20 67 BQ27
Cedar Wk, (Bishop.) G64 51 BX21
Cedarwood Av, (Newt. M.) G77 117 BH48
Cedric Pl, G13 47 BF22
Cedric Rd, G13 47 BF22
Celtic St, G20 48 BL22
Cemetery Rd, G52 65 BF32
Cemetery Rd, (Blan.) G72 124 CL47
Centenary Av, Air. ML6 75 CZ30
Centenary Ct, (Barr.) G78 99 AX43
Centenary Ct, Clyde. G81 27 AX20
Centenary Gdns, Coat. ML5 75 CW32
Centenary Gdns, Ham. ML3
  off Woodside Wk 140 CU51
Centenary Quad, Moth. ML1 112 DC40
Central Av, G11
  off Broomhill Dr 65 BH27
Central Av, G32 91 CF34
Central Av, (Udd.) G71 110 CS39
Central Av, (Blan.) G72 125 CN48
Central Av, (Camb.) G72 106 CB39
Central Av, Clyde. G81 27 AW19
Central Av, (Holytown)
  Moth. ML1 off Holytown Rd 112 DB40

Central Av, (New Stev.)
  Moth. ML1 112 DC43
Central Cres, (Ashgill)
  Lark. ML9 145 DH61
Central Gro, G32 91 CF33
Central Gro, (Camb.) G72 106 CB39
Central Path, G32 91 CG34
Central Rd, Pais. PA1 62 AU32
Central Sta, G1 4 BR30
Central Way, (Cumb.) G67 22 DA13
Central Way, Pais. PA1
  off Central Rd 62 AU32
Centre, The, (Barr.) G78 99 AX43
Centre Pk Ct, Coat. ML5
  off South Circular Rd 75 CW31
Centre Rbt, The, (E.Kil.) G74 136 CB52
Centre St, G5 67 BQ32
Centre St, (Chap.) Air. ML6 97 DE35
Centre St, (Glenb.) Coat. ML5 56 CS23
Centre Way, (Barr.) G78
  off North Pk Av 99 AX42
Ceres Gdns, (Bishop.) G64 33 BZ20
Cessnock Pl, (Camb.) G72 107 CF40
Cessnock Rd, G33 52 CC24
Cessnock St, G51 66 BL31
Chalmers Ct, G40 5 BU31
Chalmers Cres, (E.Kil.) G75 136 CB54
Chalmers Dr, (E.Kil.) G75 136 CB54
Chalmers Gate, G40
  off Claythorn St 5 BU31
Chalmers Pl, G40
  off Claythorn St 5 BU31
Chalmers St, G40 5 BU31
Chalmers St, Clyde. G81 27 AX20
Chamberlain La, G13 47 BG24
Chamberlain Rd, G13 47 BG23
Chancellor St, G11 66 BK27
Chantinghall Rd, Ham. ML3 125 CR50
Chantinghall Ter, Ham. ML3 125 CR50
Chapel Ct, (Ruther.) G73
  off Western Av 88 BV37
Chapel Cres, Ham. ML3 140 CT55
Chapelcross Av, Air. ML6
  off Chapelside Av 76 DC28
Chapelhall Ind Est, (Chap.)
  Air. ML6 97 DF33
Chapelhill Rd, Pais. PA2 83 AW35
Chapelknowe Rd, Moth. ML1 113 DF44
Chapel Pl, (Neil.) G78 114 AT46
Chapel Rd, Clyde. G81 27 AW15
Chapelside Av, Air. ML6 76 DC29
Chapelside Rd, (E.Kil.) G74 122 CC47
Chapel St, G20 49 BN24
Chapel St, (Ruther.) G73 88 BV37
Chapel St, Air. ML6 76 DC29
Chapel St Ind Est, G20 49 BN23
Chapelton Av, (Bears.) G61 29 BH17
Chapelton Gdns, (Bears.) G61 29 BH17
Chapelton Rd, (Cumb.) G67 39 CY15
Chapelton St, G22 50 BS23
Chaplet Av, G13 47 BE21
Chapman Av, (Glenb.) Coat. ML5 56 CS23
Chapman St, G42
  off Allison St 87 BQ35
Chappell St, (Barr.) G78 99 AX42
Charing Cross, G2 4 BP28
Charing Cross La, G3
  off Granville St 4 BP29
Charles Av, Renf. PA4 45 AZ25
Charles Cres, (Lenz.) G66 35 CF18
Charleson Row, (Kilsyth) G65 20 CV10
Charles Path, (Chap.) Air. ML6
  off Kennelburn Rd 97 DF35

Charles Quad, Moth. ML1 112 DC40
Charles St, G21 5 BU28
Charles St, (Kilsyth) G65 7 CT4
Charles St, Wis. ML2 129 DE49
Charlotte Av, (Torr.) G64 15 BX13
Charlotte La, G1
  off London Rd 5 BT31
Charlotte La S, G1
  off Charlotte St 5 BT31
Charlotte La W, G1
  off London Rd 5 BT31
Charlotte Path, Lark. ML9
  off Margaretvale Dr 144 DC59
Charlotte Pl, Pais. PA2 82 AU35
Charlotte St, G1 5 BT31
Charnwood Av, John. PA5 79 AF37
Chartwell Rd, Bish. PA7 24 AK18
Chassels St, Coat. ML5 75 CW29
Chateau Gro, Ham. ML3 141 CW51
Chatelherault Av, (Camb.) G72 106 CA40
Chatelherault Cres, Ham. ML3 140 CU53
Chatelherault Wk, Ham. ML3
  off Chatelherault Cres 140 CU52
Chatham, (E.Kil.) G75 135 BY54
Chatton St, G23 30 BM20
Chatton Wk, Coat. ML5 95 CY35
Cheapside St, G3 4 BP31
Chelmsford Dr, G12 48 BK24
Cherry Bk, (Kirk.) G66 34 CD16
Cherrybank Rd, G43 103 BP40
Cherrybank Wk, Air. ML6 75 CZ29
Cherry Cres, Clyde. G81 27 AW17
Cherry Gro, (Baill.) G69 73 CR31
Cherryhill Vw, Lark. ML9 144 DB59
Cherry Pl, (Bishop.) G64 51 BX21
Cherry Pl, (Udd.) G71 94 CT37
Cherry Pl, John. PA5 80 AJ36
Cherryridge Dr, (Baill.) G69 73 CQ31
Cherrytree Cres, Lark. ML9 142 DC56
Cherrytree Dr, (Camb.) G72 107 CG41
Cherrytree Wynd, (E.Kil.) G75 136 CA55
Cherry Wk, Moth. ML1 128 DA50
Cherrywood Rd, (Elder.)
  John. PA5 80 AL35
Chesterfield Av, G12 48 BJ24
Chesters Cres, Moth. ML1 127 CY45
Chesters Pl, (Ruther.) G73 88 BV38
Chesters Rd, (Bears.) G61 29 BF16
Chester St, G32 70 CC32
Chestnut Cres, (Udd.) G71 94 CT38
Chestnut Cres, (E.Kil.) G75 135 BY55
Chestnut Cres, Ham. ML3 140 CU51
Chestnut Dr, (Kirk.) G66 34 CD15
Chestnut Dr, Clyde. G81 26 AV16
Chestnut Gro, (Gart.) G69 56 CS23
Chestnut Gro, (Blan.) G72 124 CL45
Chestnut Gro, Lark. ML9 142 DC56
Chestnut Gro, Moth. ML1 127 CZ48
Chestnut La, (Miln.) G62 11 BG12
Chestnut Pl, John. PA5 80 AJ37
Chestnut St, G22 50 BT24
Chestnut Way, (Camb.) G72 107 CG41
Cheviot Av, (Barr.) G78 99 AY43
Cheviot Ct, Air. ML6 76 DD27
Cheviot Cres, Wis. ML2 129 DH49
Cheviot Dr, (Newt. M.) G77 117 BE50
Cheviot Gdns, (Bears.) G61 11 BF14
Cheviot Rd, G43 102 BL40
Cheviot Rd, Ham. ML3 140 CV51
Cheviot Rd, Lark. ML9
  off Burnhead Rd 145 DE59
Cheviot Rd, Pais. PA2 82 AT36
Cheviot St, (Blan.) G72 124 CL46

Chirmorie Cres, G53 84 BC36
Chirmorie Pl, G53 84 BC36
Chirnside Ct, (Blan.) G72
  off Fortingall Rd 125 CP48
Chirnside Pl, G52 64 BC31
Chirnside Rd, G52 64 BC31
Chisholm Av, Bish. PA7 24 AL18
Chisholm Dr, (Newt. M.) G77 117 BG47
Chisholm Pl, Moth. ML1 142 DD51
Chisholm St, G1 5 BT31
Chisholm St, Coat. ML5 75 CX29
Chrighton Grn, (Udd.) G71 93 CQ37
Chriss Av, Ham. ML3 140 CT54
Christchurch Pl, (E.Kil.) G75 135 BX54
Christian St, G43 86 BL38
Christie La, Pais. PA3 62 AU32
Christie Pl, (Camb.) G72 106 CC40
Christie St, Bell. ML4 111 CZ41
Christie St, Pais. PA1 62 AV32
Christopher St, G21 69 BW27
Chryston Business Cen,
  (Chry.) G69 54 CL21
Chryston Rd, (Kirk.) G66 36 CK15
Chryston Rd, (Chry.) G69 54 CM21
Chryston Rd, (Mood.) G69 36 CM16
Church Av, (Stepps) G33 53 CF23
Church Av, (Ruther.) G73 105 BY40
Church Cres, Air. ML6 77 DG28
Church Dr, (Kirk.) G66 35 CE15
Church Hill, Pais. PA1 62 AU32
Churchill Av, (E.Kil.) G74 136 CB52
Churchill Av, John. PA5 79 AE37
Churchill Cres, (Both.) G71 109 CR42
Churchill Dr, G11 48 BJ26
Churchill Dr, Bish. PA7 24 AK18
Churchill Pl, (Kilb.) John. PA10 78 AC34
Churchill Way, (Bishop.) G64 32 BV20
Church La, (Kilsyth) G65
  off Church St 7 CT5
Church La, Coat. ML5 75 CW30
Church Pl, (Old Kil.) G60 25 AQ15
Church Rd, (Giff.) G46 102 BL43
Church Rd, (Muir.) G69 54 CL22
Church Rd, (Clark.) G76 119 BP47
Church St, G11 66 BL27
Church St, (Kilsyth) G65 7 CT5
Church St, (Baill.) G69 92 CK33
Church St, (Udd.) G71 109 CN40
Church St, (Blan.) G72 125 CN46
Church St, Clyde. G81 27 AW18
Church St, Coat. ML5 75 CW30
Church St, Ham. ML3 126 CU49
Church St, John. PA5 79 AH34
Church St, (Kilb.) John. PA10 78 AC34
Church St, Lark. ML9 144 DC58
Church St, Moth. ML1 113 DH41
Church Vw, (Camb.) G72 90 CC38
Church Vw, Coat. ML5 75 CW30
Church Vw Gdns, Bell. ML4 111 CW40
Circus Dr, G31 68 BV30
Circus Pl, G31 68 BV30
Circus Pl La, G31 68 BV29
Citadel Pl, Moth. ML1 127 CY45
Citrus Cres, (Udd.) G71 94 CS37
Cityford Cres, (Ruther.) G73 104 BV39
Cityford Dr, (Ruther.) G73 88 BV38
City Link Cen, G51 66 BJ30
Civic St, G4 67 BR27
Civic Way, (Kirk.) G66 17 CE14
Clachan Dr, G51
  off Skipness Dr 65 BG29
Claddens Pl, G22 49 BR23
Claddens Pl, (Lenz.) G66 35 CG17

Claddens Quad, G22 50 BS23
Claddens St, G22 49 BR23
Claddens Wynd, (Kirk.) G66 35 CG17
Cladence Gro, (E.Kil.) G75 136 CB56
Clairinsh Gdns, Renf. PA4
  off Sandy Rd 63 AY28
Clairmont Gdns, G3 4 BP28
Clair Rd, (Bishop.) G64 33 BZ20
Clamp Rd, Wis. ML2 129 DE49
Clamps Gro, (E.Kil.) G74 136 CC53
Clamps Ter, (E.Kil.) G74 136 CD53
Clamps Wd, (E.Kil.) G74 136 CC53
Clanrye Dr, Coat. ML5 95 CW33
Clapperhow Rd, Moth. ML1 112 DC44
Claremont Av, (Kirk.) G66 16 CD12
Claremont Dr, (Miln.) G62
  off Clober Rd 12 BJ11
Claremont Gdns, (Miln.) G62
  off Clober Rd 12 BJ11
Claremont Pas, G3
  off Claremont Ter 4 BP28
Claremont Pl, G3
  off Claremont Ter 4 BP28
Claremont St, G3 67 BN29
Claremont Ter, G3 4 BP28
Claremont Ter La, G3 67 BN28
Claremount Av, (Giff.) G46 102 BL43
Clarence Dr, G11 48 BJ26
Clarence Dr, G12 48 BJ26
Clarence Dr, Pais. PA1 63 AW32
Clarence Gdns, G11 48 BJ26
Clarence La, G12 48 BK26
Clarence St, Clyde. G81 27 AX18
Clarence St, Pais. PA1 63 AW32
Clarendon La, G20
  off Clarendon St 67 BQ27
Clarendon Pl, G20 67 BQ27
Clarendon Pl, (Stepps) G33 53 CF24
Clarendon Rd, Wis. ML2 143 DG52
Clarendon St, G20 67 BQ27
Clare St, G21 69 BW27
Clarinda Ct, (Kirk.) G66 18 CJ11
Clarinda Pl, Moth. ML1 113 DE42
Clarion Cres, G13 46 BC21
Clarion Rd, G13 46 BC21
Clark Pl, (Torr.) G64 15 BY13
Clark Pl, (Newt. M.) G77 116 BD49
Clarkston Av, G44 103 BP41
Clarkston Dr, Air. ML6 77 DF30
Clarkston Rd, G44 103 BP41
Clarkston Rd, (Clark.) G76 119 BN45
Clarkston Toll, (Clark.) G76 119 BN45
Clark St, Air. ML6 76 DD30
Clark St, Clyde. G81 26 AV17
Clark St, John. PA5 79 AH34
Clark St, Pais. PA3 62 AS31
Clark St, Renf. PA4 45 AX26
Clark Way, (Bellshill Ind. Est.)
  Bell. ML4 94 CV38
Clarkwell Rd, Ham. ML3 139 CN51
Clarkwell Ter, Ham. ML3 125 CP50
Clathic Av, (Bears.) G61 30 BJ17
Claude Av, (Camb.) G72 107 CG42
Claude St, Lark. ML9 144 DC58
Claud Rd, Pais. PA3 63 AW31
Clavens Rd, G52 64 BA31
Claverhouse Pl, Pais. PA2 83 AW34
Claverhouse Rd, G52 64 BB30
Clavering St E, Pais. PA1 62 AS32
Clavering St W, Pais. PA1
  off King St 62 AS32
Clay Ct, Moth. ML1 128 DA49
Clay Cres, Bell. ML4 95 CX38

| | | |
|---|---|---|
| Clayhouse Rd, G33 | 53 | CG25 |
| Claypotts Pl, G33 | 70 | CC28 |
| Claypotts Rd, G33 | 70 | CC28 |
| Clay Rd, Bell. ML4 | 95 | CX38 |
| Clayslaps Rd, G3 | 66 | BM28 |
| Claythorn Av, G40 | 68 | BU32 |
| off Claythorn Av | 5 | BU31 |
| Claythorn Ct, G40 | | |
| off Claythorn Pk | 5 | BU31 |
| Claythorn Pk, G40 | 68 | BU32 |
| Claythorn St, G40 | 5 | BU31 |
| Claythorn Ter, G40 | 5 | BU31 |
| Clayton Path, Bell. ML4 | | |
| off Ashgrove Rd | 95 | CX38 |
| Clayton Ter, G31 | 68 | BV30 |
| Clearfield Av, Ham. ML3 | 125 | CR49 |
| Cleddans Cres, Clyde. G81 | 27 | AY15 |
| Cleddans Rd, (Kirk.) G66 | 17 | CG12 |
| Cleddans Rd, Clyde. G81 | 27 | AX16 |
| Cleddans Vw, (Glenm.) Air. ML6 | 58 | DA25 |
| Cleddans Vw, Clyde. G81 | | |
| off Kirkoswald Dr | 27 | AY18 |
| Cleddens Ct, (Bishop.) G64 | 33 | BW19 |
| Cleddens Ct, Air. ML6 | | |
| off Monkscourt Av | 75 | CZ29 |
| Cleeves Pl, G53 | 100 | BD40 |
| Cleeves Quad, G53 | 100 | BC40 |
| Cleeves Rd, G53 | 100 | BC40 |
| Cleghorn St, G22 | 49 | BR26 |
| Cleish Av, (Bears.) G61 | 11 | BE13 |
| Cleland La, G5 | 68 | BS32 |
| Cleland Pl, (E.Kil.) G74 | 122 | CC50 |
| Cleland Rd, (Cleland) Moth. ML1 | | |
| off Chapelknowe Rd | 113 | DE44 |
| Cleland St, G5 | 68 | BS32 |
| Clelland Av, (Bishop.) G64 | 51 | BW21 |
| Clem Attlee Gdns, Lark. ML9 | | |
| off Machan Rd | 144 | DD59 |
| Clerwood St, G32 | 69 | BZ31 |
| Cleuch Gdns, (Clark.) G76 | 118 | BM45 |
| Cleveden Cres, G12 | 48 | BK24 |
| Cleveden Cres La, G12 | 48 | BK24 |
| Cleveden Dr, G12 | 48 | BK24 |
| Cleveden Dr, (Ruther.) G73 | 105 | BY39 |
| Cleveden Dr La, G12 | | |
| off Mirrlees Dr | 48 | BL25 |
| Cleveden Gdns, G12 | 48 | BL24 |
| Cleveden La, G12 | 48 | BK23 |
| Cleveden Pl, G12 | 48 | BK23 |
| Cleveden Rd, G12 | 48 | BK23 |
| Cleveland La, G3 | 4 | BP29 |
| Cleveland St, G3 | 4 | BP29 |
| Clifford Gdns, G51 | 66 | BK32 |
| Clifford La, G51 | 66 | BL32 |
| Clifford Pl, G51 | | |
| off Clifford St | 66 | BM31 |
| Clifford St, G51 | 66 | BK32 |
| Cliff Rd, G3 | 4 | BP28 |
| Clifton Pl, G3 | | |
| off Clifton St | 67 | BN28 |
| Clifton Pl, Coat. ML5 | 75 | CY31 |
| Clifton Rd, (Giff.) G46 | 102 | BK42 |
| Clifton St, G3 | 67 | BN28 |
| Clifton Ter, (Camb.) G72 | 106 | CA42 |
| Clifton Ter, John. PA5 | 80 | AJ35 |
| Clincarthill Rd, (Ruther.) G73 | 89 | BW38 |
| Clincart Rd, G42 | 87 | BR37 |
| Cloan Av, G15 | 28 | BD19 |
| Cloan Cres, (Bishop.) G64 | 33 | BX18 |
| Clober Fm La, (Miln.) G62 | | |
| off Craigton Rd | 11 | BG10 |
| Cloberfield, (Miln.) G62 | 11 | BH9 |
| Cloberfield Gdns, (Miln.) G62 | 11 | BH10 |
| Cloberhill Rd, G13 | 29 | BE20 |
| Clober Rd, (Miln.) G62 | 11 | BH10 |
| Clochbar Av, (Miln.) G62 | 11 | BH10 |
| Clochbar Gdns, (Miln.) G62 | 11 | BH10 |
| Clochoderick Av, (Kilb.) | | |
| John. PA10 | 78 | AD35 |
| Cloch St, G33 | 70 | CC29 |
| Clockenhill Pl, Moth. ML1 | 113 | DG41 |
| Cloister Av, Air. ML6 | 97 | DE33 |
| Closeburn St, G22 | 50 | BS24 |
| Cloth St, (Barr.) G78 | 99 | AY43 |
| Clouden Rd, (Cumb.) G67 | 22 | DD11 |
| Cloudhowe Ter, (Blan.) G72 | 108 | CL44 |
| Clouston Ct, G20 | | |
| off Fergus Dr | 49 | BN25 |
| Clouston La, G20 | 49 | BN25 |
| Clouston St, G20 | 48 | BM25 |
| Clova Pl, (Udd.) G71 | 109 | CP39 |
| Clova St, (Thornlie.) G46 | 101 | BH41 |
| Clove Mill Wynd, Lark. ML9 | 144 | DA59 |
| Cloverbank Gdns, G21 | 69 | BW28 |
| Cloverbank St, G21 | 69 | BW28 |
| Clovergate, (Bishop.) G64 | 32 | BU20 |
| Cloverhill Pl, (Chry.) G69 | 54 | CL21 |
| Cloverhill Ter, (E.Kil.) G74 | 136 | CA52 |
| Cloverhill Vw, (E.Kil.) G74 | 135 | BZ52 |
| Clunie Pl, Coat. ML5 | 95 | CX34 |
| Clunie Rd, G52 | 85 | BG33 |
| Cluny Av, (Bears.) G61 | 30 | BJ19 |
| Cluny Dr, (Bears.) G61 | 30 | BJ19 |
| Cluny Dr, (Newt. M.) G77 | 116 | BD48 |
| Cluny Dr, Pais. PA3 | 63 | AW31 |
| Cluny Gdns, G14 | 47 | BG25 |
| Cluny Gdns, (Baill.) G69 | 92 | CJ34 |
| Cluny Vil, G14 | | |
| off Westland Dr | 47 | BG25 |
| Clutha Pl, (E.Kil.) G75 | 135 | BW54 |
| Clutha St, G51 | | |
| off Paisley Rd W | 66 | BM31 |
| Clyde Arc, G51 | 67 | BN31 |
| Clyde Av, (Torr.) G64 | 15 | BX13 |
| Clyde Av, (Both.) G71 | 109 | CP44 |
| Clyde Av, (Barr.) G78 | 99 | AZ44 |
| Clyde Av, Ham. ML3 | 141 | CY52 |
| Clydebank Business Pk, | | |
| Clyde. G81 | 27 | AW19 |
| Clydebank Ind Est, Clyde. G81 | 26 | AT19 |
| Clydebrae Dr, (Both.) G71 | 109 | CR44 |
| Clydebrae St, G51 | 66 | BK29 |
| Clyde Ct, Clyde. G81 | 26 | AU16 |
| Clyde Cres, (Blan.) G72 | 124 | CM45 |
| Clyde Dr, Bell. ML4 | 111 | CY41 |
| Clydeford Dr, G32 | 90 | CA34 |
| Clydeford Dr, (Udd.) G71 | 93 | CN38 |
| Clydeford Rd, (Camb.) G72 | 90 | CC37 |
| Clydeholm Rd, G14 | 65 | BF27 |
| Clydeholm Ter, Clyde. G81 | 45 | AZ22 |
| Clyde La, Moth. ML1 | | |
| off Quarry St | 112 | DC41 |
| Clydeneuk Dr, (Udd.) G71 | 92 | CM38 |
| Clyde Pl, G5 | 4 | BQ31 |
| Clyde Pl, (Cumb.) G67 | | |
| off Cumbernauld Shop Cen | 22 | DB11 |
| Clyde Pl, (Camb.) G72 | 107 | CF41 |
| Clyde Pl, John. PA5 | 79 | AE37 |
| Clyde Pl, Moth. ML1 | 112 | DC41 |
| Clyde Rd, Pais. PA3 | 63 | AX30 |
| Clydesdale Av, Ham. ML3 | 140 | CT55 |
| Clydesdale Av, Pais. PA3 | 63 | AW28 |
| Clydesdale Av, Wis. ML2 | 143 | DF52 |
| Clydesdale Pl, Ham. ML3 | | |
| off Clydesdale Av | 140 | CT55 |
| Clydesdale Rd, Bell. ML4 | 111 | CY41 |
| Clydesdale St, Bell. ML4 | 112 | DA41 |
| Clydesdale St, Ham. ML3 | 126 | CS49 |
| Clydesdale St, Lark. ML9 | 144 | DC57 |
| Clydesdale St, Moth. ML1 | 112 | DA41 |
| Clyde Shop Cen, Clyde. G81 | 27 | AY20 |
| Clydeside Expressway, G3 | 66 | BL29 |
| Clydeside Expressway, G14 | 66 | BL29 |
| Clyde Side Ind Est, G14 | 65 | BF27 |
| Clydeside Rd, (Ruther.) G73 | 88 | BV35 |
| Clydesmill Dr, G32 | 90 | CC38 |
| Clydesmill Gro, G32 | 90 | CC38 |
| Clydesmill Ind Est, G32 | 90 | CC37 |
| Clydesmill Pl, G32 | 90 | CC37 |
| Clydesmill Rd, G32 | 90 | CB37 |
| Clyde St, G1 | 4 | BR31 |
| Clyde St, Clyde. G81 | 45 | AY21 |
| Clyde St, Coat. ML5 | 75 | CY30 |
| Clyde St, Renf. PA4 | 45 | AZ24 |
| Clyde Ter, (Both.) G71 | 109 | CQ44 |
| Clyde Ter, Moth. ML1 | 143 | DE51 |
| Clyde Twr, (E.Kil.) G74 | 136 | CD54 |
| Clyde Tunnel, G14 | 65 | BG30 |
| Clyde Tunnel, G51 | 65 | BG28 |
| Clydevale, (Both.) G71 | 109 | CR44 |
| Clyde Valley Av, Moth. ML1 | 128 | DA49 |
| Clydeview, (Both.) G71 | 110 | CS44 |
| Clydeview, (Both.) G71 | 110 | CS44 |
| Clyde Vw, Ham. ML3 | 139 | CR52 |
| Clyde Vw, Pais. PA2 | 83 | AX35 |
| Clydeview La, G11 | | |
| off Broomhill Ter | 65 | BH27 |
| Clydeview Shop Cen, (Blan.) | | |
| G72 | 125 | CN46 |
| Clydeview Ter, G32 | 90 | CD37 |
| Clyde Wk, (Cumb.) G67 | | |
| off Cumbernauld Shop Cen | 22 | DB11 |
| Clyde Way, (Cumb.) G67 | | |
| off Cumbernauld Shop Cen | 22 | DB11 |
| Clyde Way, Pais. PA3 | | |
| off Clyde Rd | 63 | AX30 |
| Clynder St, G51 | 66 | BK31 |
| Clyth Dr, (Giff.) G46 | 102 | BM43 |
| Coach Cl, (Kilsyth) G65 | 8 | CW5 |
| Coach Pl, (Kilsyth) G65 | 7 | CU6 |
| Coach Rd, (Kilsyth) G65 | 8 | CV6 |
| Coalburn Rd, (Both.) G71 | 109 | CR40 |
| Coalburn St, (Green.) Air. ML6 | 41 | DH19 |
| Coalhall Av, Moth. ML1 | 112 | DC44 |
| Coalhill St, G31 | 69 | BX32 |
| Coatbank St, Coat. ML5 | 75 | CX31 |
| Coatbank Way, Coat. ML5 | 75 | CX31 |
| Coatbridge Ind Est, Coat. ML5 | 75 | CW28 |
| Coatbridge Rd, (Baill.) G69 | 73 | CN32 |
| Coatbridge Rd, (Gart.) G69 | 55 | CQ25 |
| Coatbridge Rd, (Glenm.) | | |
| Air. ML6 | 57 | CZ26 |
| Coatbridge Rd, (Glenb.) | | |
| Coat. ML5 | 56 | CV24 |
| Coathill St, Coat. ML5 | 95 | CW33 |
| Coats Cres, (Baill.) G69 | 72 | CJ32 |
| Coats Dr, Pais. PA2 | 81 | AR34 |
| Coatshill Av, (Blan.) G72 | 108 | CL44 |
| Coats St, Coat. ML5 | 75 | CX30 |
| Cobbett Rd, Moth. ML1 | 127 | CX48 |
| Cobblerigg Way, (Udd.) G71 | 109 | CN40 |
| Cobbleton Rd, Moth. ML1 | 112 | DB43 |
| Cobden Rd, G21 | 68 | BV27 |
| Cobington Pl, G33 | 70 | CD28 |
| Cobinshaw St, G32 | 70 | CC31 |
| Coburg St, G5 | 67 | BR32 |
| Cochno St, Clyde. G81 | 45 | AY21 |
| Cochrane Ct, (Miln.) G62 | | |
| off Finlay Ri | 12 | BL13 |

| | | |
|---|---|---|
| Cochranemill Rd, John. PA5 | 79 | AE36 |
| Cochrane Sq, (Linw.) Pais. PA3 | 60 | AK32 |
| Cochrane St, G1 | 5 | BS30 |
| Cochrane St, (Barr.) G78 | 99 | AX43 |
| Cochrane St, Bell. ML4 | 110 | CV39 |
| Cochran St, Pais. PA1 | 82 | AV33 |
| Cockburn Pl, Coat. ML5 | 94 | CV33 |
| Cockels Ln, Renf. PA4 | 63 | AX28 |
| Cockenzie St, G32 | 70 | CC32 |
| Cockhill Way, Bell. ML4 | | |
| off Philip Murray Rd | 110 | CT39 |
| Cockmuir St, G21 | 51 | BW25 |
| Coddington Cres, (Holytown) | | |
| Moth. ML1 | 96 | DB38 |
| Cogan Pl, (Barr.) G78 | | |
| off Cogan St | 99 | AX43 |
| Cogan Rd, G43 | 102 | BL39 |
| Cogan St, G43 | 86 | BL38 |
| Cogan St, (Barr.) G78 | 99 | AX43 |
| Colbert St, G40 | 88 | BV34 |
| Colbreggan Ct, Clyde. G81 | 27 | AY15 |
| Colbreggan Gdns, Clyde. G81 | 27 | AY15 |
| Colbreggan Pl, Clyde. G81 | | |
| off Glasgow Rd | 27 | AY15 |
| Colchester Dr, G12 | 48 | BJ23 |
| Coldingham Av, G14 | 46 | BA23 |
| Coldstream Dr, (Ruther.) | | |
| G73 | 105 | BZ39 |
| Coldstream Dr, Pais. PA2 | 81 | AQ36 |
| Coldstream Pl, G21 | 50 | BS26 |
| Coldstream Rd, Clyde. G81 | 27 | AX20 |
| Coldstream St, (Blan.) G72 | 124 | CM46 |
| Colebrooke La, G12 | | |
| off Colebrooke St | 49 | BN26 |
| Colebrooke Pl, G12 | 49 | BN26 |
| Colebrooke St, G12 | 49 | BN26 |
| Colebrooke Ter, G12 | 49 | BN26 |
| Colebrook St, (Camb.) G72 | 106 | CC39 |
| Coleridge, (E.Kil.) G75 | 135 | BW54 |
| Coleridge Av, (Both.) G71 | 109 | CR42 |
| Colfin St, G34 | 72 | CL28 |
| Colgrain Av, G20 | 49 | BQ23 |
| Colgrain Ter, G20 | 49 | BQ23 |
| Colgrave Cres, G32 | 90 | CB34 |
| Colinbar Circle, (Barr.) G78 | 99 | AX44 |
| Colinslee Av, Pais. PA2 | 82 | AV36 |
| Colinslee Cres, Pais. PA2 | 82 | AV36 |
| Colinslee Dr, Pais. PA2 | 82 | AV36 |
| Colinslie Rd, G53 | 85 | BE37 |
| Colinton Pl, G32 | 70 | CD30 |
| Colintraive Av, G33 | 52 | CB25 |
| Colintraive Cres, G33 | 52 | CA26 |
| Coll, (E.Kil.) G74 | 137 | CE53 |
| Colla Gdns, (Bishop.) G64 | 33 | BZ19 |
| Coll Av, Renf. PA4 | 63 | AZ28 |
| College Gate, (Bears.) G61 | 29 | BE15 |
| College St, G1 | 5 | BT30 |
| College Way, (E.Kil.) G75 | 136 | CC54 |
| Collessie Dr, G33 | 71 | CE27 |
| Collier St, John. PA5 | 79 | AH34 |
| Colliertree Rd, Air. ML6 | 77 | DF29 |
| Collina St, G20 | 48 | BL23 |
| Collins St, G4 | 5 | BU30 |
| Coll Lea, Ham. ML3 | 139 | CP52 |
| Coll Pl, G21 | 69 | BX27 |
| Coll Pl, Air. ML6 | 77 | DE32 |
| Collree Gdns, G34 | | |
| off Easterhouse Rd | 72 | CL30 |
| Coll St, G21 | 69 | BW27 |
| Collylinn Rd, (Bears.) G61 | 29 | BG17 |
| Colmonell Av, G13 | 46 | BB22 |
| Colonsay, (E.Kil.) G74 | 136 | CD54 |
| Colonsay Av, Renf. PA4 | 63 | AY28 |
| Colonsay Cres, Coat. ML5 | 94 | CT33 |
| Colonsay Dr, (Newt. M.) G77 | 116 | BD48 |
| Colonsay Rd, G52 | | |
| off Barfillan Dr | 65 | BG32 |
| Colonsay Rd, Pais. PA2 | 82 | AT38 |
| Colquhoun Av, G52 | 64 | BC30 |
| Colquhoun Dr, (Bears.) G61 | 29 | BF16 |
| Colson Pl, Bell. ML4 | 111 | CY42 |
| Colston Av, (Bishop.) G64 | 50 | BV22 |
| Colston Dr, (Bishop.) G64 | 50 | BV22 |
| Colston Gdns, (Bishop.) G64 | 50 | BU22 |
| Colston Gdns, Air. ML6 | 77 | DE30 |
| Colston Gro, (Bishop.) G64 | 50 | BV22 |
| Colston Path, (Bishop.) G64 | 50 | BU22 |
| Colston Pl, (Bishop.) G64 | 50 | BU22 |
| Colston Pl, Air. ML6 | 77 | DE30 |
| Colston Rd, (Bishop.) G64 | 50 | BU22 |
| Colston Rd, Air. ML6 | 77 | DE30 |
| Colston Ter, Air. ML6 | 77 | DE30 |
| Colt Av, Coat. ML5 | 74 | CU28 |
| Coltmuir Av, (Bishop.) G64 | | |
| off Coltmuir Dr | 50 | BU21 |
| Coltmuir Cres, (Bishop.) G64 | 50 | BU21 |
| Coltmuir Dr, (Bishop.) G64 | 50 | BU21 |
| Coltmuir Gdns, (Bishop.) G64 | 50 | BU21 |
| Coltmuir St, G22 | 49 | BR23 |
| Coltness Dr, Bell. ML4 | 111 | CX41 |
| Coltness La, G33 | 71 | CE30 |
| Coltness St, G33 | 71 | CE29 |
| Coltpark Av, (Bishop.) G64 | 50 | BU21 |
| Coltpark La, (Bishop.) G64 | 50 | BU21 |
| Colt Pl, Coat. ML5 | 75 | CW29 |
| Coltsfoot Dr, G53 | | |
| off Waukglen Dr | 100 | BD42 |
| Coltswood Ct, Coat. ML5 | 75 | CW29 |
| Coltswood Rd, Coat. ML5 | 75 | CW28 |
| Colt Ter, Coat. ML5 | 75 | CW30 |
| Columba, Clyde. G81 | | |
| off Onslow Rd | 27 | AZ19 |
| Columba Cres, Moth. ML1 | 111 | CZ43 |
| Columba Path, (Blan.) G72 | | |
| off Glenfruin Rd | 124 | CL45 |
| Columba St, G51 | 66 | BK30 |
| Columbia Pl, (E.Kil.) G75 | 135 | BX53 |
| Columbia Way, (E.Kil.) G75 | 135 | BX53 |
| Colvend Dr, (Ruther.) G73 | 105 | BX42 |
| Colvend La, G40 | 88 | BV34 |
| Colvend St, G40 | 88 | BV34 |
| Colville Ct, Moth. ML1 | 113 | DE44 |
| Colville Dr, (Ruther.) G73 | 105 | BZ39 |
| Colvilles Pk, (E.Kil.) G75 | 136 | CD55 |
| Colvilles Pl, (E.Kil.) G75 | 136 | CD55 |
| Colvilles Rd, (E.Kil.) G75 | 136 | CC56 |
| Colwood Av, G53 | 100 | BC41 |
| Colwood Gdns, G53 | 100 | BC42 |
| Colwood Path, G53 | | |
| off Parkhouse Rd | 100 | BC41 |
| Colwood Pl, G53 | 100 | BC42 |
| Colwood Sq, G53 | 100 | BC41 |
| Colzium Vw, (Kilsyth) G65 | 7 | CU5 |
| Combe Quad, Bell. ML4 | | |
| off Brandon Pl | 110 | CU42 |
| Comedie Rd, G33 | 53 | CG25 |
| Comely Bk, Ham. ML3 | 125 | CP50 |
| Comelypark Pl, G31 | | |
| off Comelypark St | 69 | BW31 |
| Comelypark St, G31 | 68 | BV31 |
| Commerce St, G5 | 67 | BR32 |
| Commercial Ct, G5 | 68 | BT32 |
| Commercial Rd, G5 | 88 | BS33 |
| Commercial Rd, (Barr.) G78 | 99 | AY42 |
| Common Grn, Ham. ML3 | 126 | CU49 |
| Commonhead Av, Air. ML6 | 76 | DB28 |
| Commonhead La, Air. ML6 | | |
| off Whinhall Av | 76 | DB28 |
| Commonhead Rd, G34 | 72 | CM29 |
| Commonhead St, Air. ML6 | 76 | DB28 |
| Commonside St, Air. ML6 | 76 | DB28 |
| Commore Av, (Barr.) G78 | 99 | AZ44 |
| Commore Dr, G13 | 46 | BC22 |
| Commore Pl, (Neil.) G78 | 114 | AS47 |
| Community Av, Bell. ML4 | | |
| off Community Rd | 111 | CX43 |
| Community Pl, Bell. ML4 | 111 | CX42 |
| Community Rd, Bell. ML4 | 110 | CV42 |
| Compton Ct, (E.Kil.) G74 | 134 | BT53 |
| Comrie Cres, Ham. ML3 | 124 | CM50 |
| Comrie Rd, G33 | 53 | CE24 |
| Comrie St, G32 | 90 | CD34 |
| Conan Ct, (Camb.) G72 | 107 | CF40 |
| Cona St, (Thornlie.) G46 | 101 | BG41 |
| Condor Glen, (Holytown) | | |
| Moth. ML1 | 96 | DA38 |
| Condorrat Ring Rd, (Cumb.) | | |
| G67 | 21 | CX14 |
| Condorrat Rd, G67 | 39 | CX17 |
| Condorrat Rd, (Glenm.) Air. | | |
| ML6 | 57 | CZ22 |
| Congress Rd, G3 | 66 | BM30 |
| Congress Way, G3 | 67 | BN30 |
| Conifer Pl, (Kirk.) G66 | 34 | CD15 |
| Conisborough Cl, G34 | 72 | CJ28 |
| Conisborough Path, G34 | | |
| off Conisborough Rd | 71 | CH27 |
| Conisborough Rd, G34 | 71 | CH27 |
| Coniston, (E.Kil.) G75 | | |
| off Ullswater | 134 | BV56 |
| Coniston Cres, Ham. ML3 | 140 | CS55 |
| Coniston Dr, Bell. ML4 | 111 | CX42 |
| Conistone Cres, (Baill.) G69 | 91 | CH33 |
| Connal St, G40 | 89 | BX34 |
| Connel Cres, (Miln.) G62 | 12 | BL12 |
| Conniston St, G32 | 70 | CA30 |
| Connollys Land, Clyde. G81 | | |
| off Dumbarton Rd | 27 | AW15 |
| Connor Rd, (Barr.) G78 | 99 | AX42 |
| Connor St, Air. ML6 | 77 | DG28 |
| Conon Av, (Bears.) G61 | 29 | BE18 |
| Consett La, G33 | 71 | CE29 |
| Consett St, G33 | 71 | CE29 |
| Constarry Rd, (Kilsyth) G65 | 20 | CU9 |
| Contin Pl, G12 | 48 | BM24 |
| Convair Way, Renf. PA4 | | |
| off Lismore Av | 63 | AZ28 |
| Conval Way, Pais. PA3 | | |
| off Abbotsburn Way | 62 | AT29 |
| Cook St, G5 | 67 | BQ32 |
| Coo La, (Eagle.) G76 | 133 | BN56 |
| Coolgardie Grn, (E.Kil.) G75 | | |
| off Westwood Hill | 135 | BY54 |
| Coolgardie Pl, (E.Kil.) G75 | 135 | BY54 |
| Cooperage Ct, G14 | 45 | AZ23 |
| Cooperage Pl, G3 | 66 | BL29 |
| Coopers Well La, G11 | | |
| off Dumbarton Rd | 66 | BL28 |
| Coopers Well St, G11 | 66 | BL28 |
| Copenhagen Av, (E.Kil.) G75 | 136 | CA55 |
| Copland Pl, G51 | 66 | BK30 |
| Copland Quad, G51 | 66 | BK31 |
| Copland Rd, G51 | 66 | BK31 |
| Coplaw Ct, G42 | 87 | BQ34 |
| Coplaw St, G42 | 87 | BQ34 |
| Copperfield La, (Udd.) G71 | 93 | CQ38 |
| Coppice, The, Ersk. PA8 | | |
| off Newshot Dr | 44 | AT21 |
| Coralmount Gdns, (Kirk.) G66 | 17 | CG14 |

| | | | | | | | | |
|---|---|---|---|---|---|---|---|---|
| Corbett Ct, G32 | 90 | CB34 | Corsford Dr, G53 | 101 | BE39 | Cowell Vw, Clyde. G81 | | |
| Corbett St, G32 | 90 | CB34 | Corsock Av, Ham. ML3 | 139 | CN51 | off Granville St | 27 | AX18 |
| Corbie Pl, (Miln.) G62 | 11 | BF11 | Corsock St, G31 | 69 | BY30 | Cowgate, (Kirk.) G66 | 17 | CE12 |
| Corbiston Way, (Cumb.) G67 | 22 | DD11 | Corston St, G33 | 69 | BZ29 | Cowglen Rd, G53 | 85 | BE38 |
| Cordiner La, G44 | 87 | BR38 | Cortachy Pl, (Bishop.) G64 | 33 | BZ20 | Cowlairs Rd, G21 | 50 | BU25 |
| Cordiner St, G44 | 87 | BR38 | Cortmalaw Av, G33 | 52 | CA22 | Coxdale Av, (Kirk.) G66 | 16 | CD13 |
| Corkerhill Gdns, G52 | 85 | BG33 | Cortmalaw Cl, G33 | 52 | CA22 | Coxhill St, G21 | 50 | BT26 |
| Corkerhill Pl, G52 | 85 | BF35 | Cortmalaw Cres, G33 | 52 | CA22 | Coxton Pl, G33 | 71 | CF28 |
| Corkerhill Rd, G52 | 85 | BF36 | Cortmalaw Gdns, G33 | 52 | CB22 | Coylton Cres, Ham. ML3 | 139 | CN52 |
| Corlaich Av, G42 | 88 | BU38 | Cortmalaw Gate, G33 | 52 | CA22 | Coylton Rd, G43 | 103 | BN40 |
| Corlaich Dr, G42 | 88 | BU38 | Cortmalaw Ln, G33 | 52 | CA22 | Crabb Quad, Moth. ML1 | | |
| Cormack Av, (Torr.) G64 | 15 | BY12 | Cortmalaw Rd, G33 | 52 | CA22 | off Frood St | 111 | CY44 |
| Cornaig Rd, G53 | 84 | BD37 | Coruisk Dr, (Clark.) G76 | 118 | BM45 | Cragdale, (E.Kil.) G74 | 121 | BY50 |
| Cornalee Gdns, G53 | 84 | BC37 | Coruisk Way, Pais. PA2 | | | Craggan Dr, G14 | 46 | BB23 |
| Cornalee Pl, G53 | 84 | BD38 | off Spencer Dr | 81 | AN37 | Crags Av, Pais. PA2 | 82 | AV36 |
| Cornalee Rd, G53 | 84 | BD37 | Corunna St, G3 | 67 | BN29 | Crags Cres, Pais. PA2 | 82 | AV35 |
| Cornelia St, Moth. ML1 | 111 | CX44 | Coshneuk Rd, G33 | 52 | CD24 | Crags Rd, Pais. PA2 | 82 | AV36 |
| Cornfield Ct, (Camb.) G72 | 107 | CG39 | Cosy Neuk, Lark. ML9 | 145 | DE60 | Cragwell Pk, (Clark.) G76 | 120 | BU46 |
| Cornhill Dr, Coat. ML5 | 74 | CV29 | Cottage Homes, (Newt. M.) | | | Craigallian Av, (Miln.) G62 | 12 | BJ10 |
| Cornhill St, G21 | 51 | BW24 | G77 | 117 | BF48 | Craigallian Av, (Camb.) G72 | 107 | CF42 |
| Cornish Ct, Coat. ML5 | | | Cottar St, G20 | 49 | BN22 | Craiganour La, G43 | 102 | BL39 |
| off Gilmour Pl | 74 | CV29 | Cotton Av, (Linw.) Pais. PA3 | 60 | AK32 | Craiganour Pl, G43 | | |
| Cornock Cres, Clyde. G81 | 27 | AX18 | Cotton St, G40 | 88 | BV35 | off Holeburn Rd | 102 | BL39 |
| Cornock St, Clyde. G81 | 27 | AX18 | Cotton St, Pais. PA1 | 82 | AV33 | Craigard Dr, (Ruther.) G73 | 105 | BZ42 |
| Corn St, G4 | 67 | BR27 | Cotton Vale, Moth. ML1 | 113 | DG44 | Craigash Quad, (Miln.) G62 | 11 | BG10 |
| Cornwall Av, (Ruther.) G73 | 105 | BZ40 | Coulin Gdns, G22 | 50 | BT25 | Craigash Rd, (Miln.) G62 | 11 | BG11 |
| Cornwall Ct, (E.Kil.) G74 | | | Coulter Av, Coat. ML5 | 74 | CU29 | Craigbank Cres, (Eagle.) G76 | 133 | BN55 |
| off East Kilbride Shop Cen | 136 | CB52 | Countess Way, (Baill.) G69 | | | Craigbank Dr, G53 | 100 | BC39 |
| Cornwall St, G41 | 66 | BM32 | off Park Rd | 73 | CQ32 | Craigbank Gro, (Eagle.) G76 | 133 | BN55 |
| Cornwall St, (E.Kil.) G74 | 136 | CB52 | Counting Ho, The, Pais. PA1 | | | Craigbank Rd, Lark. ML9 | 144 | DC61 |
| Cornwall St S, G41 | 86 | BM33 | off Turners Av | 81 | AR34 | Craigbank St, Lark. ML9 | 144 | DC60 |
| Cornwall Way, (E.Kil.) G74 | | | County Av, (Camb.) G72 | 89 | BZ38 | Craigbarnet Av, (Torr.) G64 | | |
| off East Kilbride Shop Cen | 136 | CB52 | County Pl, Pais. PA1 | 62 | AU32 | off Allander Dr | 15 | BW13 |
| Coronation Av, Lark. ML9 | 144 | DC61 | County Sq, Pais. PA1 | 62 | AU32 | Craigbarnet Cres, G33 | 52 | CD25 |
| Coronation Cres, Lark. ML9 | 144 | DC61 | Couper Pl, G4 | 5 | BT28 | Craigbarnet Rd, (Miln.) G62 | 11 | BF11 |
| Coronation Pl, (Gart.) G69 | 55 | CN22 | Couper St, G4 | 5 | BT28 | Craigbo Av, G23 | 48 | BM21 |
| Coronation Pl, Lark. ML9 | 144 | DD61 | Coursington Cres, Moth. ML1 | 128 | DC46 | Craigbo Ct, G23 | | |
| Coronation Rd, Bell. ML4 | 112 | DB41 | Coursington Gdns, Moth. ML1 | 128 | DB46 | off Craigbo Rd | 48 | BM21 |
| Coronation Rd, Moth. ML1 | 112 | DB41 | Coursington Pl, Moth. ML1 | | | Craigbo Dr, G23 | | |
| Coronation Rd E, Moth. ML1 | 112 | DB42 | off Albert St | 128 | DB46 | off Craigbo Rd | 48 | BM21 |
| Coronation Way, (Bears.) G61 | 29 | BH19 | Coursington Rd, Moth. ML1 | 128 | DA46 | Craigbog Av, John. PA5 | 79 | AF36 |
| Corpach Pl, G34 | 72 | CM28 | Courthill, (Bears.) G61 | 29 | BF15 | Craigbo Pl, G23 | 48 | BM21 |
| Corra Linn, Ham. ML3 | 125 | CQ50 | Courthill Av, G44 | 103 | BR40 | Craigbo Rd, G23 | 30 | BM20 |
| Corran Av, (Newt. M.) G77 | 117 | BE47 | Courthill Cres, (Kilsyth) G65 | 7 | CU5 | Craigbo St, G23 | | |
| Corran St, G33 | 70 | CB29 | Coustonhill St, G43 | | | off Craigbo Rd | 30 | BM20 |
| Correen Gdns, (Bears.) G61 | 10 | BD14 | off Pleasance St | 86 | BL38 | Craigburn Ct, (Ashgill) | | |
| Corrie Brae, (Kilsyth) G65 | 7 | CS4 | Coustonholm Rd, G43 | 86 | BM37 | Lark. ML9 | 145 | DH60 |
| Corrie Ct, Ham. ML3 | 139 | CP51 | Couther Quad, Air. ML6 | 76 | DB27 | Craigburn St, Ham. ML3 | | |
| Corrie Dr, Moth. ML1 | 127 | CX46 | Covanburn Av, Ham. ML3 | 140 | CV52 | off Tullymet Rd | 140 | CT53 |
| Corrie Dr, Pais. PA1 | 84 | BA33 | Covenant Cres, Lark. ML9 | 144 | DD59 | Craig Cres, (Kirk.) G66 | | |
| Corrie Gro, G44 | 103 | BP41 | Covenant Pl, Wis. ML2 | 143 | DE51 | off Burnbrae Rd | 18 | CK14 |
| Corrie Pl, (Lenz.) G66 | 35 | CG17 | Coventry Dr, G31 | 69 | BX29 | Craigdhu Av, (Miln.) G62 | 11 | BH12 |
| Corrie Rd, (Kilsyth) G65 | 7 | CS4 | Cowal Cres, (Kirk.) G66 | 18 | CK12 | Craigdhu Av, Air. ML6 | 77 | DG30 |
| Corrie Vw, (Cumb.) G68 | 20 | CV13 | Cowal Dr, (Linw.) Pais. PA3 | 60 | AJ32 | Craigdhu Rd, (Bears.) G61 | 11 | BG13 |
| Corrieview Cotts, (Kilsyth) G65 | | | Cowal Rd, G20 | 48 | BL22 | Craigdhu Rd, (Miln.) G62 | 11 | BH12 |
| off Melrose Gdns | 19 | CN9 | Cowal St, G20 | 48 | BL22 | Craigdonald Pl, John. PA5 | 79 | AH34 |
| Corrie Way, Lark. ML9 | 144 | DD59 | Cowan Cl, (Barr.) G78 | 99 | AZ41 | Craigellan Rd, G43 | 102 | BM39 |
| Corrour Rd, G43 | 86 | BM38 | Cowan Cres, (Barr.) G78 | 99 | AZ43 | Craigelvan Av, (Cumb.) G67 | 38 | CV15 |
| Corrour Rd, (Newt. M.) G77 | 117 | BE47 | Cowan La, G12 | | | Craigelvan Ct, (Cumb.) G67 | 38 | CV15 |
| Corsebar Av, Pais. PA2 | 82 | AS35 | off Cowan St | 67 | BN27 | Craigelvan Dr, (Cumb.) G67 | 38 | CV15 |
| Corsebar Cres, Pais. PA2 | 82 | AS36 | Cowan Rd, (Cumb.) G68 | 21 | CX11 | Craigelvan Gdns, (Cumb.) G67 | 38 | CV15 |
| Corsebar Dr, Pais. PA2 | 82 | AS35 | Cowan St, G12 | 67 | BN27 | Craigelvan Gro, (Cumb.) G67 | 38 | CV15 |
| Corsebar La, Pais. PA2 | 81 | AR36 | Cowan Wilson Av, (Blan.) G72 | 124 | CM45 | Craigelvan Pl, (Cumb.) G67 | 38 | CV15 |
| Corsebar Rd, Pais. PA2 | 81 | AR36 | Cowan Wynd, (Udd.) G71 | 93 | CQ37 | Craigelvan Vw, (Cumb.) G67 | 38 | CV15 |
| Corsebar Way, Pais. PA2 | 82 | AS34 | Cowcaddens Rd, G4 | 4 | BR28 | Craigenbay Cres, (Lenz.) G66 | 35 | CG16 |
| Corseford Av, John. PA5 | 79 | AE37 | Cowcaddens St, G2 | | | Craigenbay Rd, (Lenz.) G66 | 35 | CF16 |
| Corsehill Path, G34 | 72 | CL29 | off Renfield St | 4 | BR28 | Craigenbay St, G21 | 51 | BX25 |
| Corsehill Pl, G34 | 72 | CL29 | Cowden Dr, (Bishop.) G64 | 33 | BW18 | Craigencart Ct, Clyde. G81 | | |
| Corsehill St, G34 | 72 | CL29 | Cowdenhill Circ, G13 | 47 | BF21 | off Gentle Row | 26 | AV15 |
| Corselet Rd, G53 | 100 | BD42 | Cowdenhill Pl, G13 | 47 | BF21 | Craigend Circ, G13 | 47 | BG23 |
| Corse Rd, G52 | 64 | BA31 | Cowdenhill Rd, G13 | 47 | BF21 | Craigend Cl, G13 | 47 | BG23 |
| Corsewall Av, G32 | 91 | CG34 | Cowden St, G51 | 65 | BF30 | Craigend Ct, G13 | 47 | BG23 |
| Corsewall St, Coat. ML5 | 74 | CU29 | Cowdray Cres, Renf. PA4 | 45 | AZ26 | Craigend Cres, (Miln.) G62 | 11 | BH11 |

| Street | Page | Grid |
|---|---|---|
| Craigend Dr, Coat. ML5 | 94 | CS33 |
| Craigend Dr W, (Miln.) G62 | 11 | BG11 |
| Craigendmuir Rd, G33 | 53 | CG25 |
| Craigendmuir St, G33 | 69 | BZ27 |
| Craigendon Oval, Pais. PA2 | 98 | AS39 |
| Craigendon Rd, Pais. PA2 | 82 | AS38 |
| Craigend Pl, G13 | 47 | BG23 |
| Craigend Rd, (Cumb.) G67 | 38 | CU16 |
| Craigends Dr, (Kilb.) John. PA10 | 78 | AC34 |
| Craigend St, G13 | 47 | BG23 |
| Craigend Vw, (Cumb.) G67 | 38 | CV16 |
| Craigenfeoch Av, John. PA5 | 79 | AF36 |
| Craigens Rd, Air. ML6 | 77 | DH32 |
| Craigfaulds Av, Pais. PA2 | 81 | AR35 |
| Craigfell Ct, Ham. ML3 | 139 | CN51 |
| Craigflower Gdns, G53 | 100 | BC41 |
| Craigflower Rd, G53 | 100 | BC41 |
| Craig Gdns, (Newt. M.) G77 | 117 | BE49 |
| Craighalbert Rd, (Cumb.) G68 | 21 | CY10 |
| Craighalbert Rbt, (Cumb.) G68 | 21 | CY9 |
| Craighalbert Way, (Cumb.) G68 | 21 | CY9 |
| Craighall Quad, (Neil.) G78 | 114 | AT47 |
| Craighall Rd, G4 | 67 | BR27 |
| Craighead Av, G33 | 51 | BZ26 |
| Craighead Dr, (Miln.) G62 | 11 | BE11 |
| Craighead Pl, G33 | 51 | BZ26 |
| Craighead Rd, Bish. PA7 | 24 | AK19 |
| Craighead St, (Barr.) G78 | 99 | AX43 |
| Craighead St, Air. ML6 | 77 | DG29 |
| Craighead Way, (Barr.) G78 | 99 | AX43 |
| Craig Hill, (E.Kil.) G75 | 135 | BY54 |
| Craighill Dr, (Clark.) G76 | 118 | BM47 |
| Craighill Gro, (Clark.) G76 | 118 | BM47 |
| Craighirst Rd, (Miln.) G62 | 11 | BF11 |
| Craighlaw Av, (Eagle.) G76 | 132 | BM51 |
| Craighlaw Dr, (Eagle.) G76 | 132 | BM51 |
| Craighouse St, G33 | 70 | CC28 |
| Craigiebar Dr, Pais. PA2 | 82 | AS37 |
| Craigieburn Gdns, G20 | 48 | BK21 |
| Craigieburn Rd, (Cumb.) G67 | 22 | DB12 |
| Craigie Dr, (Newt. M.) G77 | 117 | BG50 |
| Craigiehall Av, Ersk. PA8 | 43 | AQ22 |
| Craigiehall Cres, Ersk. PA8 | 43 | AQ22 |
| Craigiehall Pl, G51 | 66 | BM31 |
| Craigiehall St, G51 | | |
| off Craigiehall Pl | 66 | BM31 |
| Craigiehall Way, Ersk. PA8 | 43 | AQ22 |
| Craigie La, Lark. ML9 | | |
| off Duncan Graham St | 144 | DD57 |
| Craigielea Ct, Renf. PA4 | | |
| off Kirklandneuk Rd | 45 | AY25 |
| Craigielea Cres, (Miln.) G62 | 11 | BG11 |
| Craigielea Dr, Pais. PA3 | 61 | AR31 |
| Craigielea Pk, Renf. PA4 | 45 | AY26 |
| Craigielea Rd, Renf. PA4 | 45 | AY26 |
| Craigielea St, G31 | 69 | BW30 |
| Craigie Pk, (Lenz.) G66 | 35 | CG16 |
| Craigie St, G42 | 87 | BQ35 |
| Craigievar Av, G33 | 71 | CF27 |
| Craigievar Ct, G33 | 71 | CG27 |
| Craigievar Cres, G33 | 71 | CG27 |
| Craigievar Pl, (Newt. M.) G77 | 116 | BD48 |
| Craigievar St, G33 | 71 | CG27 |
| Craigknowe Rd, (Blan.) G72 | 108 | CL43 |
| Craiglea Pl, Air. ML6 | 77 | DE29 |
| Craiglea Ter, (Plains) Air. ML6 | 59 | DH26 |
| Craigleith St, G32 | 70 | CA31 |
| Craiglinn, (Cumb.) G68 | 21 | CW11 |
| Craiglinn Gdns, G45 | 104 | BS43 |
| Craiglinn Pk Rd, (Cumb.) G68 | 21 | CW12 |
| Craiglinn Rbt, (Cumb.) G68 | 21 | CW12 |
| Craiglockhart Cres, G33 | 71 | CF27 |
| Craiglockhart Dr, G33 | 71 | CF27 |
| Craiglockhart Pl, G33 | 71 | CF27 |
| Craiglockhart St, G33 | 71 | CF27 |
| Craigmaddie Gdns, (Torr.) G64 | 15 | BW13 |
| Craigmaddie Rd, (Miln.) G62 | 13 | BQ13 |
| Craigmaddie Ter La, G3 | | |
| off Derby St | 67 | BN28 |
| Craigmarloch Av, (Torr.) G64 | 15 | BX13 |
| Craigmillar Av, (Miln.) G62 | 12 | BK10 |
| Craigmillar Rd, G42 | 87 | BQ38 |
| Craigmochan Av, Air. ML6 | 76 | DB27 |
| Craigmont Dr, G20 | 49 | BN24 |
| Craigmont St, G20 | 49 | BN23 |
| Craigmore Pl, Coat. ML5 | | |
| off Haddington Way | 94 | CU34 |
| Craigmore Rd, (Bears.) G61 | 10 | BD14 |
| Craigmore St, G31 | 69 | BY31 |
| Craigmore Wynd, Lark. ML9 | | |
| off Duncan Graham St | 144 | DD57 |
| Craigmount Av, Pais. PA2 | 98 | AS39 |
| Craigmount St, (Kirk.) G66 | 17 | CF14 |
| Craigmuir Ct, G52 | 64 | BB31 |
| Craigmuir Cres, G52 | 64 | BB31 |
| Craigmuir Gdns, (Blan.) G72 | | |
| off Craigmuir Rd | 124 | CK47 |
| Craigmuir Pl, G52 | 64 | BA31 |
| Craigmuir Rd, G52 | 64 | BA31 |
| Craigmuir Rd, (Blan.) G72 | 124 | CK48 |
| Craigneil St, G33 | 71 | CG27 |
| Craigneith Ct, (E.Kil.) G74 | | |
| off Lammermoor | 123 | CG49 |
| Craignethan Gdns, G11 | | |
| off Lawrie St | 66 | BK27 |
| Craignethan Rd, (Giff.) G46 | 118 | BJ46 |
| Craigneuk Av, Air. ML6 | 77 | DE31 |
| Craigneuk St, Moth. ML1 | 128 | DD48 |
| Craigneuk St, Wis. ML2 | 128 | DD48 |
| Craignure Cres, Air. ML6 | 77 | DG30 |
| Craignure Rd, (Ruther.) G73 | 105 | BX42 |
| Craigpark, G31 | 69 | BW30 |
| Craigpark Dr, G31 | 69 | BW30 |
| Craigpark Ter, G31 | | |
| off Craigpark | 69 | BW30 |
| Craigpark Way, (Udd.) G71 | | |
| off Newton Dr | 93 | CQ38 |
| Craig Pl, (Newt. M.) G77 | 116 | BD48 |
| Craig Rd, G44 | 103 | BQ40 |
| Craig Rd, (Neil.) G78 | 114 | AT47 |
| Craigs Av, Clyde. G81 | 27 | AY15 |
| Craigsheen Av, (Carm.) G76 | 120 | BT46 |
| Craigside Ct, (Cumb.) G68 | 20 | CV14 |
| Craigside Pl, (Cumb.) G68 | 20 | CV14 |
| Craigside Rd, (Cumb.) G68 | 20 | CV14 |
| Craigson Pl, Air. ML6 | 77 | DH31 |
| Craigstone Vw, (Kilsyth) G65 | 8 | CV5 |
| Craigston Pl, John. PA5 | 79 | AH35 |
| Craigston Rd, John. PA5 | 79 | AG35 |
| Craig St, (Blan.) G72 | 125 | CN47 |
| Craig St, Air. ML6 | 76 | DB30 |
| Craig St, Coat. ML5 | 94 | CV33 |
| Craigton Av, (Miln.) G62 | 11 | BH11 |
| Craigton Av, (Barr.) G78 | 100 | BA44 |
| Craigton Cres, (Newt. M.) G77 | 116 | BD48 |
| Craigton Dr, G51 | 65 | BH31 |
| Craigton Dr, (Newt. M.) G77 | 117 | BE48 |
| Craigton Dr, (Barr.) G78 | 100 | BA44 |
| Craigton Gdns, (Miln.) G62 | 11 | BG10 |
| Craigton Pl, G51 | 65 | BG31 |
| Craigton Pl, (Blan.) G72 | 108 | CM44 |
| Craigton Rd, G51 | 65 | BH31 |
| Craigton Rd, (Miln.) G62 | 11 | BG10 |
| Craigvale Cres, Air. ML6 | 77 | DG30 |
| Craigvicar Gdns, G32 | 91 | CF33 |
| Craigview Av, John. PA5 | 79 | AF37 |
| Craigview Rd, Moth. ML1 | 128 | DB45 |
| Craigview Ter, John. PA5 | | |
| off Craigview Av | 79 | AF36 |
| Craigwell Av, (Ruther.) G73 | 105 | BZ39 |
| Crail St, G31 | 69 | BZ32 |
| Crammond Av, Coat. ML5 | 94 | CS33 |
| Cramond Av, Renf. PA4 | 64 | BA27 |
| Cramond St, G5 | 88 | BT35 |
| Cramond Ter, G32 | 70 | CD32 |
| Cranborne Rd, G12 | 48 | BJ24 |
| Cranbrooke Dr, G20 | 48 | BM22 |
| Cranston St, G3 | 4 | BP30 |
| Cranworth La, G12 | 48 | BM26 |
| Cranworth St, G12 | 48 | BM26 |
| Crarae Av, (Bears.) G61 | 29 | BG19 |
| Crarae Pl, (Newt. M.) G77 | 116 | BC48 |
| Crathes Ct, G44 | 103 | BN41 |
| Crathie Dr, G11 | 66 | BJ27 |
| Crathie Dr, (Glenm.) Air. ML6 | 58 | DB25 |
| Crathie La, G11 | | |
| off Exeter Dr | 66 | BJ27 |
| Crathie Pl, (Newt. M.) G77 | | |
| off Gleneagles Dr | 118 | BK49 |
| Crawford Av, (Lenz.) G66 | 35 | CG18 |
| Crawford Cres, (Udd.) G71 | 93 | CN38 |
| Crawford Cres, (Blan.) G72 | 108 | CM44 |
| Crawford Dr, G15 | 28 | BB20 |
| Crawford Dr, (E.Kil.) G74 | 136 | CD51 |
| Crawford Gdns, Moth. ML1 | 127 | CY48 |
| Crawford Hill, (E.Kil.) G74 | | |
| off Crawford Dr | 136 | CD51 |
| Crawford La, G11 | | |
| off Crawford St | 66 | BJ27 |
| Crawford Path, G11 | | |
| off Crawford St | 66 | BJ27 |
| Crawford Rd, (Miln.) G62 | 11 | BH9 |
| Crawford St, G11 | 66 | BJ27 |
| Crawford St, Ham. ML3 | | |
| off Greenfield Rd | 125 | CQ48 |
| Crawford St, Moth. ML1 | 127 | CZ47 |
| Crawfurd Dr, Pais. PA3 | 61 | AR31 |
| Crawfurd Gdns, (Ruther.) G73 | 105 | BY41 |
| Crawfurd Rd, (Ruther.) G73 | 105 | BX41 |
| Crawriggs Av, (Kirk.) G66 | 35 | CF15 |
| Craw Rd, Pais. PA2 | 82 | AS34 |
| Crebar Dr, (Barr.) G78 | 99 | AY43 |
| Crebar St, (Thornlie.) G46 | 101 | BG41 |
| Credon Dr, Air. ML6 | 76 | DC32 |
| Credon Gdns, (Ruther.) G73 | 105 | BY41 |
| Cree Av, (Bishop.) G64 | 33 | BZ20 |
| Cree Gdns, G32 | 70 | CB32 |
| Cree Pl, (E.Kil.) G75 | 135 | BX52 |
| Creighton Gro, (E.Kil.) G74 | 136 | CA52 |
| Creran Ct, Ham. ML3 | 139 | CQ52 |
| Creran Dr, Renf. PA4 | 45 | AX25 |
| Crescent, The, (Clark.) G76 | 119 | BQ48 |
| Crescent, The, Clyde. G81 | | |
| off Stewart St | 26 | AU18 |
| Crescent Ct, Clyde. G81 | 26 | AU18 |
| Crescent Rd, G13 | 46 | BD24 |
| Crescent Rd, G14 | 46 | BD24 |
| Cressdale Av, G45 | 104 | BT43 |
| Cressdale Ct, G45 | 104 | BT43 |
| Cressdale Dr, G45 | 104 | BT43 |
| Cressland Dr, G45 | 104 | BT44 |
| Cressland Pl, G45 | 104 | BT44 |
| Cresswell Gro, (Newt. M.) G77 | 117 | BF50 |
| Cresswell La, G12 | 48 | BM26 |
| Cresswell Pl, (Newt. M.) G77 | 131 | BG51 |
| Cresswell St, G12 | 48 | BM26 |
| Cressy St, G51 | 65 | BG29 |
| Crest Av, G13 | 46 | BD21 |
| Crestlea Av, Pais. PA2 | 82 | AU37 |

Creswell Ter, (Udd.) G71
off Kylepark Dr 109 CN39
Crichton Pl, G21
off Crichton St 50 BU25
Crichton St, G21 50 BU25
Crichton St, Coat. ML5 75 CW29
Crieff Av, (Chap.) Air. ML6 97 DF36
Crieff Ct, G3
off North St 4 BP29
Criffel Gdns, G32 91 CF34
Criffell Rd, G32 91 CF33
Criffel Path, Moth. ML1
off Martin Pl 113 DE42
Crighton Wynd, Bell. ML4
off Thomson Dr 110 CT40
Crimea St, G2 4 BQ30
Crimond Pl, (Kilsyth) G65 7 CR4
Crinan Cres, Coat. ML5 74 CT28
Crinan Gdns, (Bishop.) G64 33 BY20
Crinan Pl, Bell. ML4
off Linnet Rd 111 CX41
Crinan Pl, Coat. ML5
off Crinan Cres 74 CT28
Crinan Rd, (Bishop.) G64 33 BY20
Crinan St, G31 69 BX29
Cripps Av, Clyde. G81 27 AZ20
Croft, Lark. ML9 144 DB59
Croftbank Av, (Both.) G71 109 CR44
Croftbank Cres, (Both.) G71 109 CR44
Croftbank Cres, (Udd.) G71 109 CP39
Croftbank Gate, (Both.) G71 109 CR44
Croftbank St, G21 50 BV25
Croftburn Dr, G44 104 BT41
Croftcot Av, Bell. ML4 110 CV42
Croftcroighn Rd, G33 70 CD28
Croftend Av, G44 104 BU39
Croftfoot Cres, G45 105 BW41
Croftfoot Dr, G45 104 BV41
Croftfoot Pl, (Gart.) G69
off Inchnock Av 55 CQ23
Croftfoot Quad, G45 104 BU41
Croftfoot Rd, G44 104 BT41
Croftfoot Rd, G45 104 BT41
Croftfoot St, G45
off Tormusk Rd 105 BW41
Croftfoot Ter, G45 104 BV41
Crofthead Cotts, (Neil.) G78 114 AS46
Crofthead Cres, Bell. ML4 110 CV42
Crofthead Pl, (Newt. M.) G77 117 BG50
Crofthead Pl, Bell. ML4 110 CV42
Crofthead St, (Udd.) G71 109 CP40
Crofthill Av, (Udd.) G71 109 CP39
Crofthill Rd, G44 104 BU40
Crofthouse Dr, G44 104 BU41
Croftmont Av, G44 104 BU41
Croftmoraig Av, (Mood.) G69 37 CQ17
Crofton Av, G44 104 BT41
Croftpark Av, G44 104 BS41
Croftpark Cres, (Blan.) G72 125 CN47
Croftpark St, Bell. ML4 111 CW39
Croft Pl, Lark. ML9 144 DB58
Croft Rd, (Torr.) G64 14 BU13
Croft Rd, (Camb.) G72 106 CD40
Croft Rd, (E.Kil.) G75 136 CA54
Croft Rd, Lark. ML9 144 DB58
Croftside Av, G44 104 BU41
Croftspar Av, G32 71 CE31
Croftspar Ct, G32
off Croftspar Gro 71 CF31
Croftspar Dr, G32 71 CE31
Croftspar Gate, G32
off Croftspar Gro 71 CF31
Croftspar Gro, G32 71 CE31

Croftspar Pl, G32 71 CE31
Croft Way, Renf. PA4 63 AZ28
Croftwood, (Bishop.) G64 33 BW17
Croftwood Av, G44 104 BT41
Croftwood Rd, Ham. ML3 140 CS52
Croft Wynd, (Udd.) G71 109 CQ39
Crogal Cres, (Chap.) Air. ML6 97 DF35
Cromalt Cres, (Bears.) G61 11 BE13
Cromarty Av, G43 103 BP39
Cromarty Av, (Bishop.) G64 33 BZ19
Cromarty Cres, (Bears.) G61 11 BH14
Cromarty Gdns, (Clark.) G76 103 BQ44
Cromarty Pl, (Chry.) G69 36 CM20
Cromarty Pl, (E.Kil.) G74 123 CE50
Cromarty Rd, Air. ML6 96 DB33
Crombie Gdns, (Baill.) G69 91 CH34
Cromdale St, G51 65 BG31
Cromdale Way, (New Stev.)
Moth. ML1 112 DC43
Cromer Gdns, G20 49 BP24
Cromer La, Pais. PA3
off Abbotsburn Way 62 AT29
Cromer Way, Pais. PA3
off Mossland Rd 62 AT30
Crompton Av, G44 103 BR40
Cromptons Gro, Pais. PA1 81 AR34
Cromwell La, G20 67 BQ27
Cromwell St, G20 67 BQ27
Crona Dr, Ham. ML3 125 CN49
Cronberry Quad, G52 84 BB34
Cronberry Ter, G52 84 BB34
Cronin Pl, Bell. ML4 95 CX38
Cronulla Pl, (Kilsyth) G65 8 CV5
Crookedshields Rd, (Camb.)
G72 122 CC46
Crookedshields Rd, (E.Kil.)
G74 122 CC46
Crookfur Rd, (Newt. M.) G77 117 BE47
Crookston Av, G52 84 BC33
Crookston Ct, G52 84 BC33
Crookston Dr, G52 84 BB33
Crookston Dr, Pais. PA1 84 BB33
Crookston Gdns, G52 84 BB33
Crookston Gro, G52 84 BC33
Crookstonhill Path, G52
off Ralston Pl 84 BB33
Crookston Path, G52
off Crookston Quad 84 BB33
Crookston Pl, G52 84 BB33
Crookston Quad, G52 84 BB33
Crookston Rd, G52 84 BB34
Crookston Rd, G53 84 BC37
Crosbie Dr, Pais. PA2 81 AN38
Crosbie La, G20 48 BL21
Crosbie Pl, Pais. PA2 81 AN37
Crosbie St, G20 48 BL21
Crosbie Wd, Pais. PA2 81 AR36
Cross, The, Pais. PA1 62 AU32
Cross Arthurlie St, (Barr.) G78 99 AX42
Crossbank Av, G42 88 BU36
Crossbank Dr, G42 88 BT36
Crossbank Rd, G42 88 BT36
Crossbank Ter, G42 88 BT36
Crossbow Gdns, (Blan.) G72 123 CH47
Crossburn Av, (Miln.) G62 11 BH12
Cross Ct, (Bishop.) G64
off Kenmure Av 32 BV20
Crossdykes, (Kirk.) G66 18 CJ14
Crossflat Cres, Pais. PA1 63 AW32
Crossford Dr, G23
off Broughton Rd 31 BN20
Crossgate, (Kirk.) G66 17 CF12
Cross Gates, Bell. ML4 111 CW41

Crossgates St, Lark. ML9 144 DB57
Crosshill Av, G42 87 BR36
Crosshill Av, (Kirk.) G66 35 CF15
Crosshill Dr, (Ruther.) G73 105 BX39
Crosshill Rd, (Bishop.) G64 33 BY16
Crosshill Rd, (Kirk.) G66 34 CD18
Crosshill Sq, (Baill.) G69
off Bredisholm Rd 92 CL33
Crosshill St, Air. ML6 76 DB30
Cross Hill St, Coat. ML5
off Aitkenhead Av 93 CR33
Crosshill St, Moth. ML1 128 DB47
Crosshouse Rd, (E.Kil.) G75 135 BW56
Crosslees Ct, (Thornlie.) G46
off Crosslees Dr 102 BJ41
Crosslees Dr, (Thornlie.) G46 101 BH42
Crosslees Pk, (Thornlie.) G46 101 BH42
Crosslees Rd, (Thornlie.) G46 101 BH43
Crosslee St, G52 65 BF32
Crossloan Rd, G51 65 BH30
Crossloan Ter, G51 65 BH30
Crossmill Av, (Barr.) G78 99 AZ41
Crossmyloof Gdns, G41 86 BM36
Cross Orchard Way, Bell. ML4
off Main St 111 CW40
Crosspoint Dr, G23
off Invershiel Rd 31 BN20
Cross Rd, Pais. PA2 81 AR35
Cross Stone Pl, Moth. ML1
off Airbles St 128 DB47
Cross St, G32 91 CE36
Cross St, Pais. PA1 82 AS33
Crosstobs Rd, G53 84 BC36
Crossveggate, (Miln.) G62 12 BK12
Crossview Av, (Baill.) G69 72 CM32
Crossview Pl, (Baill.) G69 72 CM32
Crovie Rd, G53 84 BC38
Crow Av, Moth. ML1 112 DD40
Crowflats Rd, (Udd.) G71
off Lady Isle Cres 109 CN39
Crowflats Vw, (Udd.) G71 94 CS36
Crowhall Dr, G32 71 CG31
Crowhill Cres, Air. ML6 76 DB27
Crowhill Rd, (Bishop.) G64 50 BV21
Crowhill St, G22 50 BS23
Crow La, G13 47 BH24
Crowlin Cres, G33 70 CD29
Crown Av, Clyde. G81 27 AW18
Crown Circ, G12 48 BL26
Crown Ct, G1
off Virginia St 5 BS30
Crown Gdns, G12 48 BL26
Crownhall Pl, G32 71 CE32
Crownhall Rd, G32 71 CE32
Crown Mans, G11
off North Gardner St 48 BK26
Crownpoint Rd, G40 68 BV32
Crown Rd N, G12 48 BK26
Crown Rd S, G12 48 BK26
Crown St, G5 68 BS32
Crown St, (Baill.) G69 91 CH34
Crown St, (Calder.) Air. ML6 96 DD34
Crown St, Coat. ML5 75 CY30
Crown Ter, G12 48 BK26
Crow Rd, G11 48 BJ26
Crow Rd, G13 47 BH24
Crowwood Cres, (Calder.)
Air. ML6 96 DD35
Crowwood Dr, Air. ML6 77 DF29
Crow Wd Rd, (Chry.) G69 54 CK22
Crowwood Rd, (Calder.)
Air. ML6 96 DD35
Crowwood Rbt, (Stepps) G33 53 CH22

Crow Wd Ter, (Chry.) G69 54 CK22
Croy, (E.Kil.) G74 121 BZ50
Croy Av, (Newt. M.) G77 118 BJ48
Croy Pl, G21 51 BY24
Croy Rd, G21 51 BY24
Croy Rd, Coat. ML5 94 CU33
Cruachan Av, Pais. PA2 82 AU37
Cruachan Av, Renf. PA4 63 AY28
Cruachan Dr, (Newt. M.) G77 117 BH50
Cruachan Dr, (Barr.) G78 99 AY44
Cruachan Rd, (Bears.) G61 10 BD14
Cruachan Rd, (Ruther.) G73 105 BZ42
Cruachan St, (Thornlie.) G46 101 BH41
Cruachan Way, (Barr.) G78 99 AY44
Cruden St, G51 65 BH31
Crum Av, (Thornlie.) G46 102 BJ42
Crusader Av, G13 29 BF20
Cubie St, G40 68 BV32
Cuckoo Way, Moth. ML1 112 DD40
Cuilhill Rd, (Baill.) G69 73 CP30
Cuillin Pl, (Chap.) Air. ML6 97 DH36
Cuillin Pl, Lark. ML9
off Burnhead Rd 145 DE59
Cuillins, The, (Mood.) G69 37 CQ17
Cuillins, The, (Udd.) G71 93 CN36
Cuillins Rd, (Ruther.) G73 105 BZ42
Cuillin Way, (Barr.) G78 99 AY43
Cuilmuir Ter, (Kilsyth) G65 20 CV9
Cuilmuir Vw, (Kilsyth) G65 8 CV8
Culbin Dr, G13 46 BB21
Cullen, Ersk. PA8 25 AQ18
Cullen La, (E.Kil.) G75
off Cullen Rd 136 CA54
Cullen Pl, (Udd.) G71 93 CQ37
Cullen Rd, (E.Kil.) G75 135 BZ54
Cullen Rd, Moth. ML1 127 CY48
Cullen St, G32 90 CC33
Cullochrig Rd, Air. ML6 58 DB21
Culloch Rd, (Bears.) G61 11 BE13
Culloden Av, Bell. ML4 111 CZ41
Culloden St, G31 69 BX29
Culrain Gdns, G32 70 CC32
Culrain St, G32 70 CC32
Culross Hill, (E.Kil.) G74 135 BZ52
Culross La, G32 91 CE33
Culross Pl, (E.Kil.) G74 135 BZ52
Culross Pl, Coat. ML5 74 CV30
Culross St, G32 91 CE33
Culross Way, (Mood.) G69 37 CQ18
Cult Rd, (Lenz.) G66 35 CG17
Cults St, G51 65 BH31
Culvain Av, (Bears.) G61 10 BD14
Culzean, (Glenm.) Air. ML6 58 DB24
Culzean Av, Coat. ML5 94 CU33
Culzean Cres, (Baill.) G69 92 CJ33
Culzean Cres, (Newt. M.) G77 118 BJ48
Culzean Dr, G32 71 CF32
Culzean Dr, (E.Kil.) G74 121 BZ50
Culzean Dr, (New.) Moth. ML1 113 DE43
Culzean Pl, (E.Kil.) G74 121 BZ50
Cumberland Pl, G5 88 BS33
Cumberland Pl, Coat. ML5 94 CS33
Cumberland St, G5 67 BR32
Cumbernauld Rd, G31 69 BX30
Cumbernauld Rd, G33 69 BZ28
Cumbernauld Rd, (Cumb.) G67 38 CT17
Cumbernauld Rd, (Chry.) G69 54 CJ22
Cumbernauld Shop Cen,
(Cumb.) G67 22 DB11
Cumbrae, (E.Kil.) G74 137 CE52
Cumbrae Ct, Clyde. G81 27 AX19
Cumbrae Cres, Coat. ML5 76 DA32
Cumbrae Dr, Moth. ML1 127 CY45

Cumbrae Pl, Coat. ML5 96 DA33
Cumbrae Rd, Pais. PA2 82 AU38
Cumbrae Rd, Renf. PA4 63 AZ28
Cumbrae St, G33 70 CC29
Cumlodden Dr, G20 48 BL22
Cumming Dr, G42 87 BR37
Cumnock Dr, (Barr.) G78 99 AZ44
Cumnock Dr, Air. ML6
off Maybole Dr 96 DC33
Cumnock Dr, Ham. ML3 138 CM52
Cumnock Rd, G33 52 CA23
Cunard Ct, Clyde. G81 45 AX21
Cunard St, Clyde. G81 45 AX21
Cunningair Dr, Moth. ML1 128 DA49
Cunningham Dr, (Giff.) G46 103 BN42
Cunningham Dr, Clyde. G81 26 AV15
Cunninghame Rd, (E.Kil.) G74 136 CA51
Cunninghame Rd, (Kilb.)
John. PA10 78 AD34
Cunningham Rd, G52 64 BB29
Cunningham Rd, (Ruther.) G73 89 BY36
Cunningham St, Moth. ML1 127 CY47
Cuparhead Av, Coat. ML5 94 CT33
Curfew Rd, G13 29 BF20
Curle St, G14 65 BF27
Curlew Pl, John. PA5 79 AE38
Curling Cres, G44 88 BS38
Curlingmire, (E.Kil.) G75 136 CA55
Curran Av, Wis. ML2 143 DG52
Currie Pl, G20 49 BN23
Currie St, G20 49 BN23
Curtis Av, G44 88 BU38
Curtis Av, (Ruther.) G73 88 BS37
Curzon St, G20 49 BN23
Custom Ho Quay, G1
off Clyde St 5 BS31
Cut, The, (Udd.) G71 109 CP40
Cuthbertson St, G42 87 BQ34
Cuthbert St, (Udd.) G71 93 CR38
Cuthelton Dr, G31 90 CA33
Cuthelton St, G31 89 BZ33
Cuthelton Ter, G31 89 BZ33
Cypress Av, (Udd.) G71 93 CR37
Cypress Av, (Blan.) G72 124 CL45
Cypress Ct, (Kirk.) G66 34 CD15
Cypress Ct, (E.Kil.) G75 135 BY56
Cypress Ct, Ham. ML3 140 CU51
Cypress Cres, (E.Kil.) G75 135 BY56
Cypress La, Ham. ML3 139 CQ53
Cypress Pl, (E.Kil.) G75 135 BY56
Cypress St, G22 50 BT24
Cypress Way, (Camb.) G72 107 CH41
Cyprus Av, (Elder.) John. PA5 80 AK36
Cyprus Gro, (Baill.) G69 73 CR31
Cyril St, Pais. PA1 83 AW33

**D**

Daer Av, Renf. PA4 64 BA28
Daer Wk, Lark. ML9 144 DC61
Daer Way, Ham. ML3 125 CQ50
Daffodil Way, Moth. ML1
off Alyssum Cres 128 DA45
Dairsie Ct, G44
off Clarkston Rd 103 BP41
Dairsie Gdns, (Bishop.) G64 51 BZ21
Dairsie St, G44 103 BP41
Daisy St, G42 87 BR36
Dakota Way, Renf. PA4 63 AZ28
Dalbeattie Braes, (Chap.)
Air. ML6 97 DG35
Dalbeth Pl, G32 90 CB35
Dalbeth Rd, G32 90 CB35

Dalcharn Path, G34
off Kildermorie Rd 72 CJ29
Dalcharn Pl, G34
off Kildermorie Rd 72 CJ29
Dalcraig Cres, (Blan.) G72 108 CL43
Dalcross La, G11
off Byres Rd 66 BL27
Dalcross Pas, G11
off Dalcross St 66 BL27
Dalcross St, G11 66 BL27
Dalcruin Gdns, (Mood.) G69 37 CQ17
Daldowie Av, G32 91 CF34
Daldowie Rd, (Udd.) G71 92 CJ35
Daldowie St, Coat. ML5 94 CU34
Dale Av, (E.Kil.) G75 135 BY54
Dale Ct, Wis. ML2 143 DE51
Dale Dr, Moth. ML1 112 DC41
Dale Path, G40 88 BV33
Dale St, G40 88 BV33
Daleview, G12 48 BK23
Daleview Dr, (Clark.) G76 118 BM47
Daleview Gro, (Clark.) G76 118 BM47
Dale Way, (Ruther.) G73 105 BX41
Dalfoil Ct, Pais. PA1 84 BB33
Dalgarroch Av, Clyde. G81 46 BA21
Dalgleish Av, Clyde. G81 26 AU15
Dalhousie Gdns, (Bishop.) G64 32 BV19
Dalhousie La, G3 4 BQ28
Dalhousie Rd, (Kilb.) John. PA10 78 AD35
Dalhousie St, G3 4 BQ28
Dalilea Dr, G34 72 CM28
Dalilea Pl, G34 72 CM28
Dalintober St, G5 67 BQ32
Dalkeith Av, G41 86 BK33
Dalkeith Av, (Bishop.) G64 33 BX18
Dalkeith Rd, (Bishop.) G64 33 BX17
Dalmacoulter Rd, Air. ML6 58 DD26
Dalmahoy St, G32 70 CA30
Dalmally St, G20 49 BP26
Dalmarnock Br, G40 89 BX35
Dalmarnock Br, (Ruther.) G73 89 BX35
Dalmarnock Ct, G40 89 BX34
Dalmarnock Dr, G40 88 BV33
Dalmarnock Rd, G40 88 BV33
Dalmarnock Rd, (Ruther.) G73 89 BX35
Dalmarnock Rd Trd Est,
(Ruther.) G73 89 BW36
Dalmary Dr, Pais. PA1 63 AX31
Dalmellington Ct, (E.Kil.) G74
off Dalmellington Dr 135 BZ51
Dalmellington Ct, Ham. ML3 138 CM52
Dalmellington Dr, G53 84 BC37
Dalmellington Dr, (E.Kil.) G74 135 BZ51
Dalmellington Rd, G53 84 BC37
Dalmeny Av, (Giff.) G46 102 BL42
Dalmeny Dr, (Barr.) G78 99 AW43
Dalmeny Rd, Ham. ML3
off Edward St 140 CT51
Dalmeny St, G5 88 BU35
Dalmuir Ct, Clyde. G81 26 AU18
Dalnair Pl, (Miln.) G62 11 BF11
Dalnair St, G3 66 BL28
Dalness Pas, G32
off Ochil St 90 CC33
Dalness St, G32 90 CC34
Dalnottar Av, (Old Kil.) G60 25 AR15
Dalnottar Dr, (Old Kil.) G60 25 AR16
Dalnottar Gdns, (Old Kil.) G60 25 AR15
Dalnottar Hill Rd, (Old Kil.) G60 25 AR15
Dalnottar Ter, (Old Kil.) G60 25 AR15
Dalreoch Av, (Baill.) G69 72 CL32
Dalreoch Path, (Baill.) G69
off Dalreoch Av 72 CL31

| | | |
|---|---|---|
| Dalriada Cres, Moth. ML1 | 111 | CZ44 |
| Dalriada Dr, (Torr.) G64 | 15 | BY13 |
| Dalriada St, G40 | 89 | BY33 |
| Dalry Gdns, Ham. ML3 | 138 | CM51 |
| Dalrymple Dr, (E.Kil.) G74 | 122 | CA50 |
| Dalrymple Dr, (Newt. M.) G77 | 118 | BJ49 |
| Dalrymple Dr, Coat. ML5 | 74 | CV32 |
| Dalry Pl, (Chap.) Air. ML6 | 97 | DG36 |
| Dalry Rd, (Udd.) G71 | 93 | CR38 |
| Dalry St, G32 | 90 | CD33 |
| Dalserf Ct, G31 | 69 | BX32 |
| Dalserf Cres, (Giff.) G46 | 102 | BK44 |
| Dalserf Gdns, G31 | 69 | BX32 |
| Dalserf Path, Lark. ML9 | | |
| off Bannockburn Dr | 145 | DE60 |
| Dalserf Pl, G31 | 69 | BX32 |
| Dalserf St, G31 | 69 | BX32 |
| Dalsetter Av, G15 | 28 | BB19 |
| Dalsetter Business Pk, G15 | 28 | BB19 |
| Dalsetter Cres, G15 | 28 | BC19 |
| Dalsetter Dr, G15 | 28 | BB19 |
| Dalsetter Pl, G15 | 28 | BC19 |
| Dalshannon Pl, (Cumb.) G67 | 21 | CW14 |
| Dalshannon Rd, (Cumb.) G67 | 21 | CX14 |
| Dalshannon Vw, (Cumb.) G67 | 21 | CX14 |
| Dalshannon Way, (Cumb.) G67 | 21 | CW14 |
| Dalsholm Av, G20 | 48 | BK21 |
| Dalsholm Ind Est, G20 | 48 | BK21 |
| Dalsholm Pl, G20 | 48 | BK21 |
| Dalsholm Rd, G20 | 48 | BK22 |
| Dalskeith Av, Pais. PA3 | 61 | AQ32 |
| Dalskeith Cres, Pais. PA3 | 61 | AQ32 |
| Dalskeith Rd, Pais. PA3 | 81 | AQ33 |
| Dalswinton Path, G34 | 72 | CL29 |
| Dalswinton Pl, G34 | | |
| off Dalswinton St | 72 | CL29 |
| Dalswinton St, G34 | 72 | CL29 |
| Dalton Av, Clyde. G81 | 28 | BA20 |
| Dalton Ct, G31 | 70 | CA32 |
| Dalton Hill, Ham. ML3 | 138 | CM51 |
| Dalton St, G31 | 70 | CA32 |
| Dalveen Ct, (Barr.) G78 | 99 | AY44 |
| Dalveen Dr, (Udd.) G71 | 93 | CN37 |
| Dalveen Quad, Coat. ML5 | 75 | CZ32 |
| Dalveen St, G32 | 70 | CB32 |
| Dalveen Way, (Ruther.) G73 | 105 | BY42 |
| Dalwhinnie Av, (Blan.) G72 | 108 | CL43 |
| Daly Gdns, (Blan.) G72 | 109 | CN44 |
| Dalzell Av, Moth. ML1 | 128 | DC49 |
| Dalzell Dr, Moth. ML1 | 128 | DC49 |
| Dalziel Dr, G41 | 86 | BL34 |
| Dalziel Quad, G41 | 86 | BL34 |
| Dalziel Rd, G52 | 64 | BB29 |
| Dalziel St, Ham. ML3 | 125 | CR49 |
| Dalziel St, Moth. ML1 | 128 | DB46 |
| Damshot Cres, G53 | 85 | BF36 |
| Damshot Rd, G53 | 85 | BF38 |
| Danby Rd, (Baill.) G69 | 91 | CH33 |
| Danes Av, G14 | 47 | BE25 |
| Danes Cres, G14 | 46 | BD24 |
| Danes Dr, G14 | 46 | BD24 |
| Danes La N, G14 | | |
| off Upland Rd | 47 | BE25 |
| Danes La S, G14 | | |
| off Verona Av | 47 | BE25 |
| Daniel McLaughlin Pl, (Kirk.) | | |
| G66 | 17 | CG12 |
| Dargarvel Av, G41 | 86 | BK33 |
| Dargarvel Path, G41 | | |
| off Dumbreck Av | 86 | BJ34 |
| Dargavel Av, Bish. PA7 | 24 | AK19 |
| Dargavel Rd, Bish. PA7 | 24 | AL20 |
| Dargavel Rd, Ersk. PA8 | 24 | AM20 |
| Darkwood Ct, Pais. PA3 | | |
| off Darkwood Cres | 61 | AR31 |
| Darkwood Cres, Pais. PA3 | 61 | AR31 |
| Darkwood Dr, Pais. PA3 | | |
| off Darkwood Cres | 61 | AR31 |
| Darleith St, G32 | 70 | CB32 |
| Darley Rd, (Cumb.) G68 | 9 | DA8 |
| Darnaway Av, G33 | 71 | CF27 |
| Darnaway Dr, G33 | 71 | CF27 |
| Darnaway St, G33 | 71 | CF27 |
| Darngavel Ct, Air. ML6 | | |
| off Monkscourt Av | 75 | CZ29 |
| Darngavil Rd, Air. ML6 | 59 | DG23 |
| Darnick St, G21 | 51 | BX26 |
| Darnley Cres, (Bishop.) G64 | 32 | BV18 |
| Darnley Gdns, G41 | 87 | BN35 |
| Darnley Ind Est, G53 | 100 | BD41 |
| Darnley Mains Rd, G53 | 101 | BE42 |
| Darnley Path, (Thornlie.) G46 | | |
| off Kennisholm Av | 101 | BG40 |
| Darnley Pl, G41 | | |
| off Darnley Rd | 87 | BN35 |
| Darnley Rd, G41 | 87 | BN35 |
| Darnley Rd, (Barr.) G78 | 99 | AZ42 |
| Darnley St, G41 | 87 | BP35 |
| Darroch Dr, Ersk. PA8 | 25 | AP18 |
| Darroch Way, (Cumb.) G67 | 22 | DC10 |
| Dartford St, G22 | 49 | BR26 |
| Darvel Cres, Pais. PA1 | 63 | AZ32 |
| Darvel Dr, (Newt. M.) G77 | 118 | BJ48 |
| Darwin Pl, Clyde. G81 | 26 | AT17 |
| Darwin Rd, (E.Kil.) G75 | 135 | BY53 |
| Davaar, (E.Kil.) G74 | 137 | CE52 |
| Davaar Dr, Coat. ML5 | 74 | CT30 |
| Davaar Dr, Moth. ML1 | 111 | CY43 |
| Davaar Dr, Pais. PA2 | 82 | AU38 |
| Davaar Pl, (Newt. M.) G77 | 117 | BE47 |
| Davaar Rd, Renf. PA4 | 63 | AZ28 |
| Davaar St, G40 | 89 | BX33 |
| Dava St, G51 | 66 | BJ30 |
| Dave Barrie Av, Lark. ML9 | 142 | DB56 |
| Daventry Dr, G12 | | |
| off Dorchester Pl | 48 | BJ24 |
| David Donnelly Dr, (Kirk.) G66 | | |
| off Catherine St | 17 | CE13 |
| David Gray Dr, (Kirk.) G66 | 18 | CJ12 |
| David Pl, (Baill.) G69 | 91 | CH33 |
| David Pl, Pais. PA3 | 63 | AX30 |
| Davidson Cres, (Kilsyth) G65 | 19 | CP10 |
| Davidson Gdns, G14 | | |
| off Westland Dr | 47 | BG25 |
| Davidson Pl, G32 | 71 | CE31 |
| Davidson St, G40 | 89 | BW35 |
| Davidson St, Air. ML6 | 76 | DB29 |
| Davidson St, Clyde. G81 | 46 | BA21 |
| Davidson St, Coat. ML5 | 95 | CX33 |
| Davidston Pl, (Kirk.) G66 | | |
| off Netherhouse Av | 35 | CH17 |
| David St, G40 | 69 | BW32 |
| David St, Coat. ML5 | 75 | CY30 |
| David Way, Pais. PA3 | 63 | AX30 |
| Davieland Rd, (Giff.) G46 | 102 | BJ44 |
| Davie's Acre, (E.Kil.) G74 | 120 | BV49 |
| Davies Quad, Moth. ML1 | | |
| off Kinloch Dr | 111 | CZ43 |
| Davies Sq, Clyde. G81 | 27 | AW15 |
| Davington Dr, Ham. ML3 | 138 | CM51 |
| Daviot St, G51 | 65 | BF31 |
| Dawson Dr, (E.Kil.) G75 | 135 | BX52 |
| Dawson Pl, G4 | 49 | BR26 |
| Dawson Rd, G4 | 49 | BR26 |
| Deaconsbank Av, (Thornlie.) | | |
| G46 | 101 | BF44 |
| Deaconsbank Cres, (Thornlie.) | | |
| G46 | 101 | BF44 |
| Deaconsbank Gdns, (Thornlie.) | | |
| G46 | 101 | BG44 |
| Deaconsbank Gro, (Thornlie.) | | |
| G46 | 101 | BF44 |
| Deaconsbank Pl, (Thornlie.) | | |
| G46 | 101 | BF44 |
| Deaconsbrook La, (Thornlie.) | | |
| G46 | 101 | BF44 |
| Deaconsbrook Rd, (Thornlie.) | | |
| G46 | 101 | BF44 |
| Deaconsgait Cl, (Thornlie.) G46 | 101 | BF44 |
| Deaconsgait Way, (Thornlie.) | | |
| G46 | 101 | BF44 |
| Deaconsgrange Rd, (Thornlie.) | | |
| G46 | 101 | BF44 |
| Deacons Rd, (Kilsyth) G65 | 7 | CT5 |
| Deaconsview, (Thornlie.) G46 | 101 | BF44 |
| Dealston Rd, (Barr.) G78 | 99 | AX41 |
| Deanbrae St, (Udd.) G71 | 109 | CP39 |
| Dean Cres, (Chry.) G69 | 36 | CM20 |
| Dean Cres, Ham. ML3 | 140 | CS52 |
| Deanfield Quad, G52 | 64 | BB31 |
| Dean Pk Dr, (Camb.) G72 | 107 | CF41 |
| Dean Pk Rd, Renf. PA4 | 64 | BA27 |
| Deans Av, (Camb.) G72 | 107 | CF42 |
| Deanside La, G4 | | |
| off Rottenrow | 5 | BT30 |
| Deanside Rd, G52 | 64 | BC29 |
| Deanston Av, (Barr.) G78 | 99 | AX44 |
| Deanston Dr, G41 | 86 | BM37 |
| Deanston Pl, Coat. ML5 | 95 | CZ34 |
| Deanstone Wk, Coat. ML5 | 95 | CZ35 |
| Deanston Gdns, (Barr.) G78 | 99 | AX44 |
| Deanston Gro, Coat. ML5 | | |
| off Ellismuir St | 94 | CU34 |
| Deanston Pk, (Barr.) G78 | 99 | AX44 |
| Dean St, Bell. ML4 | 111 | CX40 |
| Dean St, Clyde. G81 | 27 | AY20 |
| Deanwood Av, G44 | 103 | BP42 |
| Deanwood Rd, G44 | 103 | BP42 |
| Dechmont, (E.Kil.) G75 | 135 | BZ56 |
| Dechmont Av, (Camb.) G72 | 107 | CF42 |
| Dechmont Av, Moth. ML1 | 127 | CY46 |
| Dechmont Cotts, (Camb.) G72 | 107 | CH42 |
| Dechmont Gdns, (Udd.) G71 | | |
| off Watling St | 93 | CN36 |
| Dechmont Gdns, (Blan.) G72 | 108 | CL44 |
| Dechmont Pl, (Camb.) G72 | 107 | CF42 |
| Dechmont Rd, (Udd.) G71 | | |
| off Watling St | 93 | CN36 |
| Dechmont St, G31 | 69 | BY32 |
| Dechmont St, Ham. ML3 | 140 | CS51 |
| Dechmont Vw, (Udd.) G71 | 93 | CQ38 |
| Dechmont Vw, Bell. ML4 | | |
| off Caledonian Av | 110 | CV42 |
| Dee Av, Pais. PA2 | 81 | AP35 |
| Dee Av, Renf. PA4 | 46 | BA26 |
| Dee Cres, Pais. PA2 | 81 | AP35 |
| Deedes St, Air. ML6 | 75 | CZ31 |
| Dee Dr, Pais. PA2 | 81 | AP36 |
| Dee Path, Lark. ML9 | | |
| off Riverside Rd | 144 | DC61 |
| Dee Path, Moth. ML1 | | |
| off Deveron Rd | 112 | DD40 |
| Deep Dale, (E.Kil.) G74 | 121 | BY50 |
| Deepdene Rd, (Bears.) G61 | 29 | BF18 |
| Deepdene Rd, (Chry.) G69 | 37 | CP19 |
| Dee Pl, (E.Kil.) G75 | 134 | BU54 |
| Dee Pl, John. PA5 | 79 | AE37 |
| Deerdykes Ct N, (Cumb.) G68 | 38 | CU15 |
| Deerdykes Ct S, (Cumb.) G68 | 38 | CU16 |

| | | |
|---|---|---|
| Deerdykes Pl, (Cumb.) G68 | 38 | CU15 |
| Deerdykes Rd, (Cumb.) G68 | 38 | CT16 |
| Deerdykes Vw, (Cumb.) G68 | 38 | CT16 |
| Deer Pk Ct, Ham. ML3 | 140 | CT54 |
| Deer Pk Pl, Ham. ML3 | | |
| off Deer Pk Ct | 140 | CU54 |
| Deeside Pl, Coat. ML5 | | |
| off Paddock St | 95 | CZ33 |
| Dee St, G33 | 69 | BZ28 |
| Dee St, Coat. ML5 | 74 | CT27 |
| Dee Ter, Ham. ML3 | 139 | CR53 |
| Delhi Av, Clyde. G81 | 26 | AS17 |
| Dell, The, (Newt. M.) G77 | 118 | BK48 |
| Dell, The, Bell. ML4 | 111 | CZ42 |
| Dellburn St, Moth. ML1 | 128 | DB48 |
| Delny Pl, G33 | 71 | CG30 |
| Delvin Rd, G44 | 103 | BQ39 |
| Dempsey Rd, Bell. ML4 | 110 | CV42 |
| Den Bak Av, Ham. ML3 | 139 | CQ51 |
| Denbeath Ct, Ham. ML3 | 141 | CY51 |
| Denbeck St, G32 | 70 | CB32 |
| Denbrae St, G32 | 70 | CB32 |
| Dene Wk, (Bishop.) G64 | 51 | BY21 |
| Denewood Av, Pais. PA2 | 82 | AT37 |
| Denham St, G22 | 49 | BR26 |
| Denholm Cres, (E.Kil.) G75 | 136 | CA53 |
| Denholm Dr, (Giff.) G46 | 102 | BL44 |
| Denholm Grn, (E.Kil.) G75 | | |
| off Telford Rd | 136 | CB53 |
| Denholm Ter, Ham. ML3 | 125 | CN50 |
| Denmark St, G22 | 50 | BS25 |
| Denmilne Gdns, G34 | 72 | CL30 |
| Denmilne Path, G34 | 72 | CL30 |
| Denmilne Pl, G34 | 72 | CL30 |
| Denmilne Rd, (Baill.) G69 | 72 | CM30 |
| Denmilne St, G34 | 72 | CL30 |
| Dentdale, (E.Kil.) G74 | 121 | BY50 |
| Deramore Av, (Giff.) G46 | 118 | BJ46 |
| Derby St, G3 | 67 | BN29 |
| Derby Ter La, G3 | 67 | BN29 |
| Derwent Dr, Coat. ML5 | 74 | CS27 |
| Derwent St, G22 | 49 | BR25 |
| Derwentwater, (E.Kil.) G75 | 134 | BV55 |
| Despard Av, G32 | 91 | CF33 |
| Despard Gdns, G32 | 91 | CG33 |
| Deveron Av, (Giff.) G46 | 102 | BM43 |
| Deveron Cres, Ham. ML3 | 124 | CM49 |
| Deveron Rd, (Bears.) G61 | 29 | BE19 |
| Deveron Rd, (E.Kil.) G74 | 136 | CC52 |
| Deveron Rd, Moth. ML1 | 112 | DD39 |
| Deveron St, G33 | 69 | BZ28 |
| Deveron St, Coat. ML5 | 74 | CS28 |
| Devlin Gro, (Blan.) G72 | 125 | CN46 |
| Devol Cres, G53 | 84 | BD37 |
| Devondale Av, (Blan.) G72 | 108 | CM44 |
| Devon Dr, Bish. PA7 | 24 | AL18 |
| Devon Gdns, (Bishop.) G64 | 32 | BV18 |
| Devonhill Av, Ham. ML3 | 140 | CT54 |
| Devon Pl, G41 | 87 | BR33 |
| Devonport Pk, (E.Kil.) G75 | 135 | BW54 |
| Devonshire Gdns, G12 | 48 | BK25 |
| Devonshire Gdns La, G12 | | |
| off Hyndland Rd | 48 | BK25 |
| Devonshire Ter, G12 | 48 | BK25 |
| Devonshire Ter La, G12 | 48 | BK25 |
| Devon St, G5 | 87 | BR33 |
| Devonview Pl, Air. ML6 | 76 | DB31 |
| Devonview St, Air. ML6 | 76 | DB30 |
| Devon Wk, (Cumb.) G68 | 20 | CU13 |
| Devon Way, Moth. ML1 | 127 | CX47 |
| Dewar Cl, (Udd.) G71 | 93 | CQ36 |
| Diamond St, Bell. ML4 | 111 | CW41 |
| Diana Av, G13 | 46 | BD21 |

| | | |
|---|---|---|
| Diana Quad, Moth. ML1 | 112 | DB40 |
| Dickens Av, Clyde. G81 | 26 | AV17 |
| Dickens Gro, (New.) Moth. ML1 | | |
| off Carroll Cres | 113 | DF43 |
| Dickson Path, Bell. ML4 | | |
| off McCallum Gdns | 110 | CV43 |
| Dickson St, Lark. ML9 | 145 | DE60 |
| Dicks Pk, (E.Kil.) G75 | 135 | BZ53 |
| Dick St, G20 | 49 | BP26 |
| Differ Av, (Kilsyth) G65 | 19 | CP11 |
| Dilwara Av, G14 | 65 | BG27 |
| Dimity St, John. PA5 | 79 | AH35 |
| Dinard Dr, (Giff.) G46 | 102 | BL41 |
| Dinart St, G33 | 69 | BZ28 |
| Dinduff St, G34 | 72 | CL28 |
| Dinmont Av, Pais. PA2 | | |
| off Montrose Rd | 81 | AP36 |
| Dinmont Cres, Moth. ML1 | 111 | CY43 |
| Dinmont Pl, G41 | | |
| off Norham St | 87 | BN36 |
| Dinmont Rd, G41 | 86 | BM36 |
| Dinmont Way, Pais. PA2 | | |
| off Ivanhoe Rd | 81 | AP36 |
| Dinwiddie St, G21 | 69 | BZ27 |
| Dinyra Pl, (Glenb.) Coat. ML5 | 56 | CS23 |
| Dipple Pl, G15 | 28 | BD19 |
| Dirleton Dr, G41 | 87 | BN37 |
| Dirleton Dr, Pais. PA2 | | |
| off Tantallon Dr | 81 | AQ36 |
| Dirleton Gate, (Bears.) G61 | 29 | BF18 |
| Dirleton Pl, G41 | 87 | BN37 |
| Disraeli Way, (E.Kil.) G74 | 134 | BT53 |
| Divernia Way, (Barr.) G78 | 115 | AZ45 |
| Dixon Av, G42 | 87 | BQ36 |
| Dixon Pl, (E.Kil.) G74 | 121 | BX50 |
| Dixon Rd, G42 | 87 | BR36 |
| Dixons Blazes Ind Est, G5 | 88 | BS34 |
| Dixon St, G1 | 4 | BR31 |
| Dixon St, Coat. ML5 | 95 | CX33 |
| Dixon St, Ham. ML3 | 126 | CT50 |
| Dixon St, Pais. PA1 | 82 | AV33 |
| Dobbies Ln, G4 | 4 | BR28 |
| Dobbies Ln Pl, G4 | 5 | BT29 |
| Dochart Av, Renf. PA4 | 64 | BA28 |
| Dochart Dr, Coat. ML5 | 74 | CT27 |
| Dochart St, G33 | 70 | CA27 |
| Dock St, Clyde. G81 | 45 | AZ22 |
| Dodhill Pl, G13 | 46 | BD23 |
| Dodside Gdns, G32 | 91 | CE33 |
| Dodside Pl, G32 | 91 | CE33 |
| Dodside Rd, (Newt. M.) G77 | 116 | BD47 |
| Dodside St, G32 | 91 | CE33 |
| Dolan St, (Baill.) G69 | 72 | CK32 |
| Dollar Pk, Moth. ML1 | 128 | DD50 |
| Dollar Ter, G20 | 48 | BL21 |
| Dolphington Av, G5 | 88 | BU34 |
| Dolphin Rd, G41 | 86 | BM35 |
| Dominica Grn, (E.Kil.) G75 | | |
| off Leeward Circle | 135 | BW52 |
| Donaldson Av, (Kilsyth) G65 | 7 | CT6 |
| Donaldson Cres, (Kirk.) G66 | 17 | CE14 |
| Donaldson Dr, Renf. PA4 | | |
| off Ferguson St | 45 | AZ26 |
| Donaldson Grn, (Udd.) G71 | 93 | CR37 |
| Donaldson Pl, (Kirk.) G66 | | |
| off Thistle St | 17 | CF14 |
| Donaldson Rd, Lark. ML9 | 145 | DE60 |
| Donaldson St, (Kirk.) G66 | 17 | CE14 |
| Donaldson St, Ham. ML3 | 125 | CQ48 |
| Donaldswood Pk, Pais. PA2 | 82 | AS37 |
| Donaldswood Rd, Pais. PA2 | 82 | AS37 |
| Donald Ter, Ham. ML3 | | |
| off Dean Cres | 140 | CS52 |

| | | |
|---|---|---|
| Donald Way, (Udd.) G71 | 93 | CQ38 |
| Don Av, Renf. PA4 | 64 | BA27 |
| Doncaster St, G20 | 49 | BQ25 |
| Don Ct, Ham. ML3 | 139 | CQ53 |
| Don Dr, Pais. PA2 | 81 | AP36 |
| Donnies Brae, (Neil.) G78 | 98 | AV44 |
| Donohoe Ct, (Bishop.) G64 | | |
| off Emerson Rd | 33 | BW20 |
| Don Path, Lark. ML9 | 144 | DC61 |
| Don Pl, John. PA5 | 79 | AE37 |
| Don St, G33 | 69 | BZ29 |
| Doon Cres, (Bears.) G61 | 29 | BF18 |
| Doonfoot Ct, (E.Kil.) G74 | 135 | BZ51 |
| Doonfoot Gdns, (E.Kil.) G74 | 135 | BZ51 |
| Doonfoot Rd, G43 | 102 | BM39 |
| Doon Pl, (Kirk.) G66 | 17 | CH11 |
| Doon Rd, (Kirk.) G66 | 17 | CH12 |
| Doon Side, (Cumb.) G67 | 22 | DD11 |
| Doon St, Clyde. G81 | 27 | AZ18 |
| Doon St, Lark. ML9 | 145 | DE59 |
| Doon St, Moth. ML1 | 128 | DC49 |
| Doon Way, (Kirk.) G66 | 18 | CJ12 |
| Dorain Rd, Moth. ML1 | 113 | DF42 |
| Dora St, G40 | 88 | BV34 |
| Dorchester Av, G12 | 48 | BJ23 |
| Dorchester Ct, G12 | 48 | BJ23 |
| Dorchester Pl, G12 | 48 | BJ23 |
| Dorian Dr, (Clark.) G76 | 118 | BK45 |
| Dorlin Rd, G33 | 53 | CG24 |
| Dormanside Ct, G53 | | |
| off Dormanside Rd | 84 | BD34 |
| Dormanside Gate, G53 | | |
| off Dormanside Rd | 84 | BD34 |
| Dormanside Gro, G53 | | |
| off Dormanside Rd | 84 | BD34 |
| Dormanside Pl, G53 | | |
| off Dormanside Rd | 85 | BE35 |
| Dormanside Rd, G53 | 84 | BD34 |
| Dornal Av, G13 | 46 | BA22 |
| Dornford Av, G32 | 91 | CF35 |
| Dornford Rd, G32 | 91 | CF35 |
| Dornie Dr, G32 | 90 | CD37 |
| Dornie Dr, (Thornlie.) G46 | 101 | BG42 |
| Dornoch Av, (Giff.) G46 | 102 | BL44 |
| Dornoch Ct, Bell. ML4 | 111 | CW40 |
| Dornoch Pl, (Bishop.) G64 | 33 | BY19 |
| Dornoch Pl, (Chry.) G69 | 36 | CM20 |
| Dornoch Pl, (E.Kil.) G74 | 135 | BY51 |
| Dornoch Rd, (Bears.) G61 | 29 | BF19 |
| Dornoch Rd, Moth. ML1 | 112 | DD40 |
| Dornoch St, G40 | 68 | BV32 |
| Dornoch Way, (Cumb.) G68 | 9 | DC8 |
| Dornoch Way, Air. ML6 | | |
| off Sutherland Dr | 76 | DB32 |
| Dorset Sq, G3 | | |
| off Dorset St | 4 | BP29 |
| Dorset St, G3 | 4 | BP29 |
| Dosk Av, G13 | 46 | BA21 |
| Dosk Pl, G13 | 46 | BB21 |
| Double Hedges Rd, (Neil.) G78 | 114 | AT47 |
| Dougalston Av, (Miln.) G62 | 12 | BK12 |
| Dougalston Cres, (Miln.) G62 | 12 | BK12 |
| Dougalston Gdns N, (Miln.) G62 | 12 | BK12 |
| Dougalston Gdns S, (Miln.) G62 | 12 | BK12 |
| Dougalston Rd, G23 | 31 | BN20 |
| Douglas Av, G32 | 90 | CD37 |
| Douglas Av, (Giff.) G46 | 102 | BL44 |
| Douglas Av, (Lenz.) G66 | 35 | CF15 |
| Douglas Av, (Ruther.) G73 | 105 | BY40 |
| Douglas Av, (Elder.) John. PA5 | 80 | AK35 |
| Douglas Ct, (Lenz.) G66 | 35 | CF16 |
| Douglas Cres, (Udd.) G71 | 93 | CR37 |
| Douglas Cres, Air. ML6 | 76 | DC31 |

| Name | Page | Grid |
|---|---|---|
| Douglas Cres, Ersk. PA8 | 25 | AP18 |
| Douglas Cres, Ham. ML3 | 140 | CT55 |
| Douglasdale, (E.Kil.) G74 | 135 | BZ51 |
| Douglas Dr, G15 | 28 | BB20 |
| Douglas Dr, (Baill.) G69 | 71 | CH32 |
| Douglas Dr, (Both.) G71 | 109 | CQ44 |
| Douglas Dr, (Camb.) G72 | 106 | CB40 |
| Douglas Dr, (E.Kil.) G75 | 134 | BU54 |
| Douglas Dr, (Newt. M.) G77 | 117 | BG47 |
| Douglas Dr, Bell. ML4 | 111 | CY41 |
| Douglas Dr, (Ashgill) | | |
| Lark. ML9 | 145 | DH61 |
| Douglas Gdns, (Giff.) G46 | 102 | BL44 |
| Douglas Gdns, (Bears.) G61 | 29 | BH17 |
| Douglas Gdns, (Lenz.) G66 | 35 | CF16 |
| Douglas Gdns, (Udd.) G71 | 109 | CP40 |
| Douglas Gate, (Camb.) G72 | 106 | CB40 |
| Douglas La, G2 | 4 | BQ29 |
| Douglas Muir Dr, (Miln.) G62 | 11 | BE10 |
| Douglas Muir Gdns, (Miln.) G62 | 11 | BE10 |
| Douglas Muir Pl, (Miln.) G62 | 11 | BE10 |
| Douglas Pk Cres, (Bears.) G61 | 30 | BJ15 |
| Douglas Pk La, Ham. ML3 | 126 | CS49 |
| Douglas Pl, (Bears.) G61 | 29 | BG16 |
| Douglas Pl, (Kirk.) G66 | 35 | CF16 |
| Douglas Pl, Coat. ML5 | 74 | CV31 |
| Douglas Pl, Ham. ML3 | | |
| off Douglas Cres | 140 | CT55 |
| Douglas Rd, Renf. PA4 | 63 | AW29 |
| Douglas St, G2 | 4 | BQ29 |
| Douglas St, (Miln.) G62 | 12 | BJ12 |
| Douglas St, (Udd.) G71 | 93 | CR38 |
| Douglas St, (Blan.) G72 | 124 | CL47 |
| Douglas St, Air. ML6 | 76 | DC31 |
| Douglas St, Ham. ML3 | 126 | CS48 |
| Douglas St, Lark. ML9 | 144 | DC57 |
| Douglas St, Moth. ML1 | 127 | CZ46 |
| Douglas St, Pais. PA1 | 62 | AS32 |
| Douglas Ter, G41 | | |
| off Glencairn Dr | 87 | BP34 |
| Douglas Ter, Pais. PA3 | | |
| off Abbotsinch Rd | 62 | AU28 |
| Douglas Vw, Coat. ML5 | 94 | CV34 |
| Dougray Pl, (Barr.) G78 | 99 | AY43 |
| Dougrie Cl, G45 | 104 | BT42 |
| Dougrie Dr, G45 | 104 | BT42 |
| Dougrie Dr La, G45 | | |
| off Dougrie Dr | 104 | BT42 |
| Dougrie Gdns, G45 | 104 | BT43 |
| Dougrie Pl, G45 | 104 | BU42 |
| Dougrie Rd, G45 | 104 | BT42 |
| Dougrie St, G45 | 104 | BU42 |
| Dougrie Ter, G45 | 104 | BT42 |
| Doune Cres, (Bishop.) G64 | 33 | BX17 |
| Doune Cres, (Newt. M.) G77 | 117 | BH48 |
| Doune Cres, (Chap.) Air. ML6 | | |
| off Crieff Av | 97 | DF36 |
| Doune Gdns, G20 | 49 | BN26 |
| Doune Gdns La, G20 | 49 | BN26 |
| Doune Pk Way, Coat. ML5 | 94 | CV33 |
| Doune Quad, G20 | 49 | BN26 |
| Doune Ter, Coat. ML5 | 74 | CT28 |
| Dovecot, G43 | 86 | BL37 |
| Dovecote Vw, (Kirk.) G66 | 17 | CH14 |
| Dovecothall St, (Barr.) G78 | 99 | AZ42 |
| Dovecot Wd, (Kilsyth) G65 | 7 | CT4 |
| Dove Pl, (E.Kil.) G75 | 134 | BV55 |
| Dover St, G3 | 67 | BN29 |
| Dover St, Coat. ML5 | 74 | CT27 |
| Dove St, G53 | 100 | BC40 |
| Dove Wynd, (Strathclyde Bus. Pk.) | | |
| Bell. ML4 | 94 | CU38 |
| Dowanfield Rd, (Cumb.) G67 | 21 | CZ12 |
| Dowanhill St, G11 | 66 | BL27 |
| Dowanhill St, G12 | 48 | BL26 |
| Dowan Rd, (Miln.) G62 | 13 | BN11 |
| Dowanside La, G12 | | |
| off Byres Rd | 48 | BM26 |
| Dowanside Rd, G12 | 48 | BL26 |
| Downcraig Dr, G45 | 104 | BT43 |
| Downcraig Gro, G45 | 104 | BS43 |
| Downcraig Rd, G45 | 104 | BS44 |
| Downcraig Ter, G45 | 104 | BT43 |
| Downfield Dr, Ham. ML3 | 139 | CR54 |
| Downfield Gdns, (Both.) G71 | 109 | CP43 |
| Downfield St, G32 | 90 | CA34 |
| Downiebrae Rd, (Ruther.) G73 | 89 | BX35 |
| Downie Cl, (Udd.) G71 | 93 | CR37 |
| Downie St, Ham. ML3 | 140 | CT52 |
| Downs St, G21 | 50 | BV25 |
| Dowrie Cres, G53 | 84 | BD36 |
| Draffen Ct, Moth. ML1 | | |
| off Draffen St | 128 | DB46 |
| Draffen St, Moth. ML1 | 128 | DB46 |
| Drakemire Av, G45 | 104 | BS41 |
| Drakemire Dr, G44 | 104 | BS42 |
| Drakemire Dr, G45 | 104 | BS42 |
| Drake St, G40 | 68 | BU32 |
| Dreghorn St, G31 | 69 | BY30 |
| Drem Pl, G11 | | |
| off Merkland St | 66 | BK27 |
| Drimnin Rd, G33 | 53 | CH24 |
| Drive Rd, G51 | 65 | BG29 |
| Drochil St, G34 | 72 | CJ28 |
| Dromore St, (Kirk.) G66 | 17 | CF14 |
| Drove Hill, (Cumb.) G68 | 21 | CX10 |
| Drumbathie Rd, Air. ML6 | 76 | DD29 |
| Drumbathie Ter, Air. ML6 | 77 | DE29 |
| Drumbeg Dr, G53 | 100 | BC39 |
| Drumbeg Pl, G53 | | |
| off Drumbeg Dr | 100 | BC39 |
| Drumbeg Ter, (Miln.) G62 | 11 | BF11 |
| Drumbottie Rd, G21 | 51 | BW24 |
| Drumbowie Vw, (Cumb.) G68 | 21 | CY10 |
| Drumby Cres, (Clark.) G76 | 118 | BM45 |
| Drumby Dr, (Clark.) G76 | 118 | BM45 |
| Drumcarn Dr, (Miln.) G62 | 11 | BH12 |
| Drumcavel Rd, (Muir.) G69 | 54 | CM22 |
| Drumchapel Gdns, G15 | 28 | BC19 |
| Drumchapel Pl, G15 | 28 | BD19 |
| Drumchapel Rd, G15 | 28 | BD19 |
| Drumchapel Shop Cen, G15 | 28 | BB18 |
| Drumclair Pl, Air. ML6 | 77 | DF30 |
| Drumclog Av, (Miln.) G62 | 12 | BJ9 |
| Drumclog Gdns, G33 | 52 | CB23 |
| Drumcross Pl, G53 | 85 | BE36 |
| Drumcross Rd, G53 | 85 | BE36 |
| Drumcross Rd, Bish. PA7 | 24 | AM18 |
| Drumduff, (E.Kil.) G75 | 135 | BZ56 |
| Drumfearn Dr, G22 | 49 | BR23 |
| Drumfearn Pl, G22 | 49 | BR23 |
| Drumfearn Rd, G22 | 49 | BR23 |
| Drumgelloch St, Air. ML6 | 77 | DF29 |
| Drumglass Vw, (Kilsyth) G65 | 20 | CV9 |
| Drumgray Gdns, (Green.) | | |
| Air. ML6 | 41 | DF20 |
| Drumgray La, (Green.) | | |
| Air. ML6 | 41 | DF20 |
| Drumhead La, G32 | 90 | CB36 |
| Drumhead Pl, G32 | 90 | CB36 |
| Drumhead Rd, G32 | 90 | CB36 |
| Drumhill, (Kirk.) G66 | 18 | CK11 |
| Drumilaw Cres, (Ruther.) G73 | | |
| off Drumilaw Rd | 105 | BW40 |
| Drumilaw Rd, (Ruther.) G73 | 105 | BW40 |
| Drumilaw Way, (Ruther.) G73 | 105 | BW40 |
| Drumlaken Av, G23 | 30 | BL20 |
| Drumlaken Ct, G23 | | |
| off Caldercuilt Rd | 30 | BL20 |
| Drumlaken Ct, G23 | | |
| off Arrochar St | 30 | BL20 |
| Drumlaken Path, G23 | | |
| off Littleton St | 30 | BM20 |
| Drumlaken Pl, G23 | | |
| off Chatton St | 30 | BM20 |
| Drumlaken St, G23 | 30 | BL20 |
| Drumlanrig Av, G34 | 72 | CL28 |
| Drumlanrig Pl, G34 | 72 | CM29 |
| Drumlin Dr, (Miln.) G62 | 11 | BH13 |
| Drumloch Gdns, (E.Kil.) G75 | 136 | CA56 |
| Drumlochy Rd, G33 | 70 | CC28 |
| Drum Mains Pk, (Cumb.) G68 | 20 | CS14 |
| Drummond Av, (Ruther.) G73 | 88 | BV37 |
| Drummond Dr, Pais. PA1 | 83 | AZ33 |
| Drummond Hill, (E.Kil.) G74 | 122 | CD49 |
| Drummond Pl, (E.Kil.) G74 | 122 | CD50 |
| Drummond Way, (Newt. M.) | | |
| G77 | 116 | BC48 |
| Drummore Av, Coat. ML5 | 95 | CZ34 |
| Drummore Rd, G15 | 28 | BD17 |
| Drumnessie Ct, (Cumb.) G68 | 20 | CV13 |
| Drumnessie Rd, (Cumb.) G68 | 20 | CV13 |
| Drumnessie Vw, (Cumb.) G68 | 20 | CV13 |
| Drumore Av, (Chap.) Air. ML6 | | |
| off Callander Rd | 97 | DF36 |
| Drumover Dr, G31 | 90 | CA33 |
| Drumoyne Av, G51 | 65 | BG29 |
| Drumoyne Circ, G51 | 65 | BG31 |
| Drumoyne Dr, G51 | 65 | BG30 |
| Drumoyne Pl, G51 | 65 | BG31 |
| Drumoyne Quad, G51 | 65 | BG31 |
| Drumoyne Rd, G51 | 65 | BG31 |
| Drumoyne Sq, G51 | 65 | BG30 |
| Drumpark St, (Thornlie.) G46 | 101 | BH41 |
| Drumpark St, Coat. ML5 | 93 | CR33 |
| Drumpellier Av, (Cumb.) G67 | 39 | CY15 |
| Drumpellier Av, (Baill.) G69 | 92 | CK34 |
| Drumpellier Av, Coat. ML5 | 74 | CS30 |
| Drumpellier Ct, (Cumb.) G67 | 21 | CY14 |
| Drumpellier Cres, Coat. ML5 | 74 | CT31 |
| Drumpellier Gdns, (Cumb.) G67 | 21 | CY14 |
| Drumpellier Gro, (Cumb.) G67 | 21 | CY14 |
| Drumpellier Pl, (Cumb.) G67 | 21 | CY14 |
| Drumpellier Pl, (Baill.) G69 | 92 | CK33 |
| Drumpellier Rd, (Baill.) G69 | 92 | CJ34 |
| Drumpellier St, G33 | 69 | BZ27 |
| Drumreoch Dr, G42 | 88 | BU37 |
| Drumreoch Pl, G42 | 88 | BU37 |
| Drumry Pl, G15 | 28 | BA18 |
| Drumry Rd, Clyde. G81 | 27 | AY18 |
| Drumry Rd E, G15 | 28 | BA19 |
| Drumsack Av, (Chry.) G69 | 54 | CK21 |
| Drumsargard Rd, (Ruther.) | | |
| G73 | 105 | BZ40 |
| Drums Av, Pais. PA3 | 61 | AR31 |
| Drums Cres, Pais. PA3 | 62 | AS31 |
| Drumshangie Pl, Air. ML6 | 76 | DC27 |
| Drumshangie St, Air. ML6 | 76 | DC27 |
| Drumshaw Dr, G32 | 91 | CE37 |
| Drums Rd, G53 | 84 | BC34 |
| Drumtrocher St, (Kilsyth) G65 | 7 | CT5 |
| Drumvale Dr, (Chry.) G69 | 37 | CN19 |
| Drury La Ct, (E.Kil.) G74 | | |
| off Baillie Dr | 123 | CE49 |
| Drury St, G2 | 4 | BR30 |
| Dryad St, (Thornlie.) G46 | 101 | BG40 |
| Dryburgh Av, (Ruther.) G73 | 89 | BX38 |
| Dryburgh Av, Pais. PA2 | 81 | AQ36 |
| Dryburgh Gdns, G20 | | |
| off Wilton St | 49 | BP26 |

| | | | | | | | | | |
|---|---|---|---|---|---|---|---|---|---|
| Dryburgh Hill, (E.Kil.) G74 | 135 | BZ52 | Dumbreck Pl, G41 | 86 | BJ34 | Duncrub Dr, (Bishop.) G64 | 32 | BU20 |
| Dryburgh La, (E.Kil.) G74 | 135 | BZ52 | Dumbreck Pl, (Kirk.) G66 | 35 | CG17 | Duncruin St, G20 | 48 | BM22 |
| Dryburgh Pl, (Kirk.) G66 | 17 | CH13 | Dumbreck Rd, G41 | 86 | BK34 | Duncryne Av, G32 | 91 | CF33 |
| Dryburgh Pl, Coat. ML5 | 74 | CV30 | Dumbreck Sq, G41 | 86 | BJ33 | Duncryne Gdns, G32 | 91 | CG33 |
| Dryburgh Rd, (Bears.) G61 | 29 | BE15 | Dumbreck Ter, (Kilsyth) G65 | 6 | CP5 | Duncryne Pl, (Bishop.) G64 | 50 | BU21 |
| Dryburgh St, Ham. ML3 | 125 | CR47 | Dumbreck Rd, (Miln.) G62 | 11 | BF11 | Dundaff Hill, (Cumb.) G68 | 21 | CY11 |
| Dryburgh Wk, (Mood.) G69 | 37 | CQ18 | Dumgoyne Av, (Miln.) G62 | 11 | BH12 | Dundas Av, (Torr.) G64 | 15 | BX13 |
| Dryburgh Way, (Blan.) G72 | | | Dumgoyne Dr, (Bears.) G61 | 11 | BF14 | Dundas Ct, (E.Kil.) G74 | 136 | CA51 |
| off Winton Cres | 124 | CM46 | Dumgoyne Gdns, (Miln.) G62 | 11 | BH12 | Dundashill, G4 | 67 | BR27 |
| Dryburn Av, G52 | 64 | BC32 | Dumgoyne Pl, (Clark.) G76 | | | Dundas La, G1 | 5 | BS29 |
| Dryden St, Ham. ML3 | 125 | CR47 | off Lomondside Av | 118 | BL46 | Dundas Pl, (E.Kil.) G74 | 136 | CA51 |
| Drygate, G4 | 5 | BU30 | Dunagoil Gdns, G45 | 104 | BU43 | Dundas St, G1 | 5 | BS29 |
| Drygate St, Lark. ML9 | 144 | DC57 | Dunagoil Pl, G45 | 104 | BU44 | Dundasvale, G4 | | |
| Drygrange Rd, G33 | 71 | CE27 | Dunagoil Rd, G45 | 104 | BT43 | off Maitland St | 4 | BR28 |
| Drymen Pl, (Lenz.) G66 | 35 | CF18 | Dunagoil St, G45 | 104 | BU43 | Dundasvale Rd, G4 | | |
| Drymen Rd, (Bears.) G61 | 29 | BF15 | Dunagoil Ter, G45 | 104 | BU44 | off Maitland St | 4 | BR28 |
| Drymen St, G52 | 65 | BG32 | Dunalistair Dr, G33 | 52 | CD24 | Dundee Dr, G52 | 84 | BD33 |
| Drymen Wynd, (Bears.) G61 | 29 | BH18 | Dunan Pl, G33 | 71 | CG30 | Dundee Path, G52 | 85 | BE34 |
| Drynoch Pl, G22 | 49 | BR22 | Dunard Rd, (Ruther.) G73 | 89 | BX38 | Dundonald Av, John. PA5 | 79 | AF36 |
| Drysdale St, G14 | 46 | BB24 | Dunard St, G20 | 49 | BP25 | Dundonald Cres, (Newt. M.) | | |
| Duart Dr, (E.Kil.) G74 | 121 | BZ50 | Dunard Way, Pais. PA3 | | | G77 | 118 | BJ49 |
| Duart Dr, (Newt. M.) G77 | 118 | BJ48 | off Mosslands Rd | 62 | AT30 | Dundonald Dr, Ham. ML3 | 140 | CT54 |
| Duart Dr, (Elder.) John. PA5 | 80 | AK36 | Dunaskin St, G11 | 66 | BL28 | Dundonald Pl, (Neil.) G78 | 114 | AT46 |
| Duart St, G20 | 48 | BL21 | Dunavon Pl, Coat. ML5 | | | Dundonald Rd, G12 | 48 | BL25 |
| Dubbs Rd, (Barr.) G78 | 100 | BA42 | off Paddock St | 95 | CZ33 | Dundonald Rd, Pais. PA3 | 63 | AW30 |
| Dubton Path, G34 | 72 | CK28 | Dunbar Av, (Ruther.) G73 | 89 | BY38 | Dundonald St, (Blan.) G72 | 124 | CL45 |
| Dubton St, G34 | 72 | CK28 | Dunbar Av, Coat. ML5 | 94 | CT33 | Dundrennan Rd, G42 | 87 | BP38 |
| Duchall Pl, G14 | 46 | BD25 | Dunbar Av, John. PA5 | 79 | AG37 | Dundyvan Gdns, Coat. ML5 | 75 | CW32 |
| Duchess Ct, Ham. ML3 | | | Dunbar Dr, Moth. ML1 | 128 | DC49 | Dundyvan Ind Est, Coat. ML5 | 74 | CV32 |
| off Royal Dr | 141 | CW51 | Dunbar Hill, (E.Kil.) G74 | 135 | BY52 | Dundyvan La, Wis. ML2 | 129 | DH50 |
| Duchess Pl, (Ruther.) G73 | 89 | BY37 | Dunbar La, (New Stev.) | | | Dundyvan Rd, Coat. ML5 | 74 | CV31 |
| Duchess Rd, (Ruther.) G73 | 89 | BY36 | Moth. ML1 | 112 | DC43 | Dundyvan Way, Coat. ML5 | 74 | CV32 |
| Duchess Way, (Baill.) G69 | | | Dunbar Pl, (E.Kil.) G74 | 135 | BY52 | Dunearn Pl, Pais. PA2 | 83 | AW34 |
| off Park Rd | 73 | CP31 | Dunbar Rd, Pais. PA2 | 81 | AQ36 | Dunearn St, G4 | 67 | BP27 |
| Duchray Dr, Pais. PA1 | 84 | BB33 | Dunbar St, Ham. ML3 | 125 | CR48 | Duneaton Wynd, Lark. ML9 | | |
| Duchray La, G33 | 69 | BZ28 | Dunbeath Av, (Newt. M.) G77 | 117 | BH48 | off Carlisle Rd | 144 | DD60 |
| Duchray St, G33 | 69 | BZ28 | Dunbeith Pl, G20 | 48 | BM24 | Dunedin Ct, (E.Kil.) G75 | 135 | BW53 |
| Dudhope St, G33 | 71 | CF27 | Dunbeth Av, Coat. ML5 | 75 | CX30 | Dunedin Dr, (E.Kil.) G75 | 135 | BW52 |
| Dudley Dr, G12 | 48 | BJ26 | Dunbeth Ct, Coat. ML5 | 75 | CX30 | Dunedin Rd, Lark. ML9 | 144 | DD60 |
| Dudley Dr, Coat. ML5 | 74 | CS27 | Dunbeth Rd, Coat. ML5 | 75 | CX29 | Dunedin Ter, Clyde. G81 | 45 | AY21 |
| Dudley La, G12 | 48 | BJ26 | Dunblane Dr, (E.Kil.) G74 | 136 | CB51 | Dunellan Av, (Mood.) G69 | 37 | CQ19 |
| Duffus Pl, G32 | 91 | CE37 | Dunblane Pl, (E.Kil.) G74 | 136 | CB51 | Dunellan Ct, (Mood.) G69 | | |
| Duffus St, G34 | 71 | CH28 | Dunblane Pl, Coat. ML5 | 94 | CV33 | off Dunellan Av | 37 | CQ19 |
| Duffus Ter, G32 | 91 | CE37 | Dunblane St, G4 | 4 | BR28 | Dunellan Cres, (Mood.) G69 | 37 | CQ19 |
| Duich Gdns, G23 | 31 | BN19 | Dunbrach Rd, (Cumb.) G68 | 21 | CX10 | Dunellan Gdns, (Mood.) G69 | | |
| Duisdale Rd, G32 | 91 | CE37 | Duncan Av, G14 | 47 | BE26 | off Dunellan Av | 37 | CQ19 |
| Dukes Gate, (Both.) G71 | 109 | CN41 | Duncan Ct, Moth. ML1 | | | Dunellan Rd, (Miln.) G62 | 11 | BE11 |
| Dukes Pl, Ham. ML3 | 140 | CT55 | off Marmion Cres | 111 | CZ44 | Dunellan St, G52 | 65 | BG32 |
| Dukes Rd, (Baill.) G69 | 73 | CP32 | Duncan Graham St, | | | Dungavel Gdns, Ham. ML3 * | 140 | CU53 |
| Dukes Rd, (Camb.) G72 | 106 | CA39 | Lark. ML9 | 144 | DD57 | Dungeonhill Rd, G34 | 72 | CM29 |
| Dukes Rd, (Ruther.) G73 | 105 | BY40 | Duncan La, G14 | | | Dunglass Av, G14 | 47 | BE25 |
| Duke St, G4 | 5 | BU30 | off Gleneagles La N | 47 | BE26 | Dunglass Av, (E.Kil.) G74 | 122 | CB50 |
| Duke St, G31 | 69 | BW30 | Duncan La N, G14 | | | Dunglass La, G14 | | |
| Duke St, Ham. ML3 | 126 | CU50 | off Duncan Av | 47 | BE25 | off Dunglass Av | 47 | BE25 |
| Duke St, Lark. ML9 | 144 | DC57 | Duncan La S, G14 | | | Dunglass La N, G14 | | |
| Duke St, Moth. ML1 | 128 | DA45 | off Gleneagles La N | 47 | BE25 | off Verona Av | 47 | BE25 |
| Duke St, Pais. PA2 | 82 | AU35 | Dun Cann, Ersk. PA8 | 43 | AR22 | Dunglass La S, G14 | | |
| Duke St, (Linw.) Pais. PA3 | 60 | AL31 | Duncansby Rd, G33 | 71 | CF31 | off Verona Av | 47 | BE25 |
| Dullatur Rd, (Cumb.) G68 | 9 | DA8 | Duncan St, Clyde. G81 | 27 | AX18 | Dunglass Pl, (Miln.) G62 | 11 | BG10 |
| Dullatur Rd, (Dullatur) G68 | 9 | CZ7 | Duncarnock Av, (Neil.) G78 | 114 | AU46 | Dunglass Pl, (Newt. M.) G77 | 116 | BC48 |
| Dullatur Rbt, (Cumb.) G68 | 9 | DB8 | Duncarnock Cres, (Neil.) G78 | 114 | AU46 | Dunglass Rd, Bish. PA7 | 24 | AL19 |
| Dulnain St, (Camb.) G72 | 107 | CF40 | Dunchattan Pl, G31 | 68 | BV31 | Dunglass Sq, (E.Kil.) G74 | | |
| Dulsie Rd, G21 | 51 | BY23 | Dunchattan St, G31 | 68 | BV30 | off Dunglass Av | 122 | CB50 |
| Dumbarton Rd, G11 | 66 | BJ27 | Dunchurch Rd, Pais. PA1 | 63 | AZ32 | Dungoil Av, (Cumb.) G68 | 21 | CX10 |
| Dumbarton Rd, G14 | 65 | BG27 | Dunclutha Dr, (Both.) G71 | 109 | CQ44 | Dungoil Rd, (Lenz.) G66 | 35 | CG17 |
| Dumbarton Rd, G60 | 26 | AT17 | Dunclutha St, G40 | 89 | BX35 | Dungoyne St, G20 | | |
| Dumbarton Rd, Clyde. G81 | 26 | AT17 | Duncolm Pl, (Miln.) G62 | | | off Crosbie St | 48 | BL21 |
| Dumbarton Rd, (Dunt.) | | | off Dunellan Rd | 11 | BF11 | Dunholme Pk, Clyde. G81 | 26 | AT18 |
| Clyde. G81 | 26 | AV15 | Duncombe St, G20 | 48 | BM22 | Dunira St, G32 | 90 | CB34 |
| Dumbreck Av, G41 | 86 | BJ33 | Duncombe Vw, Clyde. G81 | | | Dunivaig St, G33 | 71 | CG29 |
| Dumbreck Ct, G41 | 86 | BJ34 | off Kirkoswald Dr | 27 | AY18 | Dunkeld Av, (Ruther.) G73 | 89 | BX38 |
| Dumbreck Path, G41 | | | Duncraig Cres, John. PA5 | 79 | AE36 | Dunkeld Dr, (Bears.) G61 | 30 | BK17 |
| off Dumbreck Av | 86 | BJ33 | | | | Dunkeld Gdns, (Bishop.) G64 | 33 | BX19 |

Dunkeld La, (Chry.) G69
off Burnbrae Av 37 CQ19
Dunkeld Pl, (Newt. M.) G77 118 BK49
Dunkeld Pl, Coat. ML5 94 CV33
Dunkeld Pl, Ham. ML3 125 CN50
Dunkeld St, G31 89 BY33
Dunkenny Pl, G15 28 BB17
Dunkenny Rd, G15 28 BA18
Dunkenny Sq, G15 28 BB18
Dunlin, G12
off Ascot Av 48 BJ23
Dunlin, (E.Kil.) G74 122 CA50
Dunlin Ct, (Strathclyde Bus. Pk.)
Bell. ML4 94 CU37
Dunlop Ct, Ham. ML3 140 CU54
Dunlop Cres, (Both.) G71 109 CQ44
Dunlop Cres, Renf. PA4
off Fulbar St 45 AZ25
Dunlop Gro, (Udd.) G71 93 CQ36
Dunlop Pl, (Miln.) G62 11 BH10
Dunlop St, G1 5 BS31
Dunlop St, (Camb.) G72 107 CG39
Dunlop St, (Linw.) Pais. PA3 60 AL31
Dunlop St, Renf. PA4
off Fulbar St 45 AZ25
Dunlop Twr, (E.Kil.) G75
off Telford Rd 136 CA53
Dunmore Dr, (Miln.) G62 12 BL13
Dunmore La, G5
off Norfolk St 67 BR32
Dunmore St, Clyde. G81 45 AY21
Dunnachie Dr, Coat. ML5 93 CR33
Dunnachie Pl, Coat. ML5
off Kenmuir St 93 CR33
Dunnet Av, (Glenm.) Air. ML6 58 DB24
Dunnichen Gdns, (Bishop.) G64 33 BZ20
Dunnikier Wk, (Cumb.) G68 20 CU12
Dunnottar Ct, (E.Kil.) G74
off Dunnottar Cres 121 BY50
Dunnottar Cres, (E.Kil.) G74 121 BY50
Dunnottar St, G33 70 CD27
Dunnottar St, (Bishop.) G64 33 BZ19
Dunn St, G40 89 BW33
Dunn St, Clyde. G81 26 AU18
Dunn St, (Dunt.) Clyde. G81 26 AV15
Dunn St, Pais. PA1 63 AW32
Dunolly Dr, (Newt. M.) G77 117 BH48
Dunolly St, G21 69 BW28
Dunottar Av, Coat. ML5 95 CX35
Dunottar Pl, Coat. ML5 95 CX34
Dun Pk, (Kirk.) G66 17 CG13
Dunphail Dr, G34 72 CM29
Dunphail Rd, G34 72 CM29
Dunragit St, G31 69 BY30
Dunrobin Av, (Elder.) John. PA5 80 AK36
Dunrobin Ct, (E.Kil.) G74
off Dunrobin Cres 121 BZ50
Dunrobin Cres, (E.Kil.) G74 121 BZ50
Dunrobin Dr, (E.Kil.) G74 121 BZ50
Dunrobin Gdns, Air. ML6
off Fairhaven Av 77 DG31
Dunrobin Pl, Coat. ML5 74 CV30
Dunrobin Rd, Air. ML6 77 DG30
Dunrobin St, G31 69 BX31
Dunrod Hill, (E.Kil.) G74 122 CB50
Dunrod St, G32 90 CD33
Dunscore Brae, Ham. ML3 139 CN51
Dunside Dr, G53 100 BC39
Dunskaith Pl, G34 72 CM30
Dunskaith St, G34 72 CM29
Dunsmuir St, G51 66 BK30
Duns Path, Coat. ML5 95 CZ34
Dunster Gdns, (Bishop.) G64 33 BX17

Dunswin Av, Clyde. G81 26 AU18
Dunswin Ct, Clyde. G81
off Dunswin Av 26 AU18
Dunsyre Pl, G23 31 BN20
Dunsyre St, G33 70 CA29
Duntarvie Av, G34 72 CL29
Duntarvie Cl, G34 72 CL29
Duntarvie Cres, G34 72 CL29
Duntarvie Dr, G34 72 CK29
Duntarvie Gdns, G34 72 CL29
Duntarvie Gro, G34 72 CL29
Duntarvie Pl, G34 72 CK29
Duntarvie Rd, G34 72 CK29
Dunterlie Av, G13 46 BC23
Dunterlie Ct, (Barr.) G78 99 AY42
Duntiblae Rd, (Kirk.) G66 18 CJ14
Duntiglennan Rd, Clyde. G81 27 AW15
Duntocher Rd, (Bears.) G61 28 BC15
Duntocher Rd, Clyde. G81 26 AV18
Duntocher Rd, (Dunt.)
Clyde. G81 27 AW15
Duntreath Av, G13 46 BA21
Duntreath Av, G15 28 BB20
Duntreath Dr, G15 28 BB20
Duntreath Gdns, G15 28 BB19
Duntreath Gro, G15 28 BB20
Duntreath Ter, (Kilsyth) G65 7 CT5
Duntroon Pl, Bell. ML4 111 CX42
Duntroon St, G31 69 BX29
Dunure Dr, (Ruther.) G73 104 BV40
Dunure Dr, (Newt. M.) G77 118 BJ48
Dunure Dr, Ham. ML3 138 CM51
Dunure Pl, (Newt. M.) G77 118 BJ48
Dunure Pl, Coat. ML5 94 CU34
Dunure St, G20 48 BM22
Dunure St, Coat. ML5 94 CU34
Dunvegan, (Glenm.) Air. ML6 58 DA25
Dunvegan Av, Coat. ML5 74 CT28
Dunvegan Av, (Elder.)
John. PA5 80 AK36
Dunvegan Dr, (Bishop.) G64 33 BW17
Dunvegan Dr, (Newt. M.) G77 118 BJ48
Dunvegan Pl, (Udd.) G71 92 CM37
Dunvegan Pl, (E.Kil.) G74 121 BZ50
Dunvegan Quad, Renf. PA4
off Kirklandneuk Rd 45 AX25
Dunwan Av, G13 46 BB22
Dunwan Pl, G13 46 BB22
Durban Av, Clyde. G81 26 AS17
Durham St, G41 66 BM32
Durisdeer Dr, Ham. ML3 139 CN52
Durness Av, (Bears.) G61 30 BK16
Durno Path, G33 71 CG30
Duror Rd, (Ruther.) G73 105 BZ43
Duror St, G32 70 CC31
Durris Gdns, G32 91 CF34
Durrockstock Cres, Pais. PA2 81 AP38
Durrockstock Rd, Pais. PA2 81 AP38
Durrockstock Way, Pais. PA2
off Durrockstock Cres 81 AP38
Durward, (E.Kil.) G74 123 CG49
Durward Av, G41 86 BM36
Durward Ct, G41 86 BM36
Durward Ct, Moth. ML1
off Marmion Cres 111 CZ43
Durward Cres, Pais. PA2 81 AP36
Durward Way, Pais. PA2
off Durward Cres 81 AP36
Duthie Pk Gdns, G13 47 BF23
Duthie Pk Pl, G13 47 BF22
Duthil St, G51 65 BF31
Dyce Av, Air. ML6 96 DA33
Dyce La, G11 66 BJ27

Dyers Wynd, Pais. PA1
off Gilmour St 62 AU32
Dyfrig St, (Blan.) G72 124 CL45
Dykebar Av, G13 46 BC23
Dykebar Cres, Pais. PA2 83 AX35
Dykehead Cres, Air. ML6 76 DB27
Dykehead La, G33 71 CF30
Dykehead Rd, G65 6 CN5
Dykehead Rd, (Dullatur) G68 8 CY7
Dykehead Rd, (Baill.) G69 73 CP32
Dykehead Rd, Air. ML6 76 DB27
Dykehead Sq, Ham. ML3 125 CP50
Dykehead St, G33 71 CF30
Dykemuir Pl, G21
off Dykemuir St 51 BX25
Dykemuir Quad, G21
off Dykemuir St 51 BW25
Dykemuir St, G21 51 BW25
Dyke Pl, G13 46 BC21
Dyke Rd, G13 46 BC22
Dyke Rd, G14 46 BB23
Dyke St, (Baill.) G69 72 CL32
Dyke St, Coat. ML5 93 CR33
Dysart Ct, (Cumb.) G68 20 CU12

E

Eagle Cres, (Bears.) G61 28 BD15
Eaglesham Ct, G51
off Blackburn St 67 BN31
Eaglesham Path, (Glenb.)
Coat. ML5 off Gayne Dr 56 CS23
Eaglesham Pl, G51 67 BN31
Eaglesham Rd, (E.Kil.) G75 135 BW52
Eaglesham Rd, (Clark.) G76 134 BS54
Eaglesham Rd, (Eagle.) G76 133 BP56
Eaglesham Rd, (Newt. M.) G77 117 BF49
Eagle St, G4 68 BS27
Earlbank Av, G14 47 BE25
Earlbank La N, G14
off Verona Av 47 BE25
Earlbank La S, G14
off Verona Av 47 BE25
Earl Haig Rd, G52 64 BB30
Earl La, G14 47 BE26
Earl Pl, G14 47 BE25
Earlsburn Rd, (Lenz.) G66 35 CG17
Earlscourt, (Mood.) G69 37 CP20
Earls Gate, (Both.) G71 109 CN42
Earls Hill, (Cumb.) G68 21 CX10
Earlspark Av, G43 87 BP38
Earlston Av, G21 68 BV28
Earlston Cres, Coat. ML5 95 CZ34
Earlston Pl, G21 5 BU28
Earl St, G14 47 BE26
Earl Vw, Moth. ML1
off Woodside St 112 DC42
Earlybraes Dr, G32 71 CG31
Earlybraes Gdns, G33 71 CF31
Earn Av, (Bears.) G61 30 BK17
Earn Av, (Righead Ind. Est.)
Bell. ML4 110 CU39
Earn Av, Renf. PA4
off Almond Av 64 BA27
Earn Gdns, Lark. ML9 144 DC61
Earn La, Moth. ML1
off Howden Pl 112 DC40
Earnock Av, Moth. ML1 127 CY47
Earnock Gdns, Ham. ML3 139 CQ51
Earnock Rd, Ham. ML3 139 CN51
Earnock St, G33 51 BZ25
Earnock St, Ham. ML3 125 CQ49
Earn Rd, (Newt. M.) G77 117 BF46

| Name | Page | Grid |
|---|---|---|
| Earnside St, G32 | 70 | CD32 |
| Earn St, G33 | 70 | CA28 |
| Easdale, (E.Kil.) G74 | 136 | CD54 |
| Easdale Dr, G32 | 90 | CC33 |
| Easdale Path, (Carnbroe) Coat. ML5 | | |
| off Bellvue Way | 95 | CZ33 |
| Easdale Path, (Glenb.) Coat. ML5 | | |
| off The Oval | 56 | CS23 |
| Easdale Pl, (Newt. M.) G77 | 116 | BD48 |
| Easdale Ri, Ham. ML3 | 125 | CN50 |
| East Av, (Udd.) G71 | 110 | CS39 |
| East Av, (Blan.) G72 | 125 | CN48 |
| East Av, Moth. ML1 | 112 | DC43 |
| East Av, Renf. PA4 | 45 | AZ26 |
| Eastbank Dr, G32 | 71 | CE32 |
| Eastbank Pl, G32 | 71 | CE32 |
| Eastbank Ri, G32 | 71 | CE32 |
| East Barns St, Clyde. G81 | 45 | AZ21 |
| East Bath La, G2 | | |
| off Sauchiehall St | 5 | BS29 |
| East Buchanan St, Pais. PA1 | 62 | AV32 |
| Eastburn Cres, G21 | 51 | BX23 |
| Eastburn Pl, G21 | | |
| off Eastburn Cres | 51 | BX23 |
| Eastburn Rd, G21 | 51 | BX24 |
| East Burnside St, (Kilsyth) G65 | 7 | CT5 |
| East Campbell St, G1 | 5 | BU31 |
| Eastcote Av, G14 | 47 | BG26 |
| Eastcroft, (Ruther.) G73 | 89 | BX37 |
| Eastcroft Ter, G21 | 51 | BW25 |
| East Dean St, Bell. ML4 | 111 | CX40 |
| East End Av, Moth. ML1 | | |
| off Montalto Av | 112 | DD44 |
| Easter Av, (Udd.) G71 | 109 | CN39 |
| Eastercraigs, G31 | 69 | BX29 |
| Easter Garngaber Rd, (Lenz.) | | |
| G66 | 35 | CG16 |
| Eastergreens Av, (Kirk.) G66 | 17 | CE14 |
| Easterhill Pl, G32 | 90 | CB34 |
| Easterhill St, G32 | 90 | CB34 |
| Easterhouse Pl, G34 | | |
| off Easterhouse Rd | 72 | CL29 |
| Easterhouse Quad, G34 | 72 | CL29 |
| Easterhouse Rd, G34 | 72 | CL29 |
| Easterhouse Rd, (Baill.) G69 | 72 | CK32 |
| Eastermains, (Kirk.) G66 | 18 | CK11 |
| Easter Ms, (Udd.) G71 | 109 | CN39 |
| Easter Queenslie Rd, G33 | 71 | CG29 |
| Easter Rd, (Clark.) G76 | 119 | BQ48 |
| Easterton Av, (Clark.) G76 | 119 | BQ48 |
| Easterwood Cres, (Udd.) G71 | 94 | CT36 |
| Eastfield Av, (Camb.) G72 | 106 | CA39 |
| Eastfield Rd, G21 | 50 | BU25 |
| Eastfield Rd, (Cumb.) G68 | 21 | CX10 |
| Eastfield Ter, Bell. ML4 | 111 | CZ41 |
| Eastgate, (Gart.) G69 | 55 | CQ24 |
| East Gate, (Glenb.) Coat. ML5 | 56 | CT22 |
| East George St, Coat. ML5 | 75 | CX29 |
| East Glebe Ter, Ham. ML3 | 140 | CT51 |
| East Greenlees Av, (Camb.) | | |
| G72 | 107 | CE42 |
| East Greenlees Cres, (Camb.) | | |
| G72 | 106 | CD42 |
| East Greenlees Dr, (Camb.) | | |
| G72 | 107 | CE42 |
| East Greenlees Gro, (Camb.) | | |
| G72 | 106 | CC42 |
| East Greenlees Rd, (Camb.) | | |
| G72 | 106 | CC42 |
| Easthall Pl, G33 | 71 | CH30 |
| East High St, Air. ML6 | 76 | DC29 |
| East Kilbride Rd, (Ruther.) G73 | 105 | BY40 |
| East Kilbride Rd, (Clark.) G76 | 119 | BQ48 |
| East Kilbride Shop Cen, (E.Kil.) | | |
| G74 | 136 | CA52 |
| East La, Pais. PA1 | 83 | AW33 |
| Eastlea Pl, Air. ML6 | 76 | DD31 |
| East Machan St, Lark. ML9 | | |
| off Thistle Cres | 144 | DD60 |
| East Mains Rd, (E.Kil.) G74 | 122 | CB49 |
| East Milton Gro, (E.Kil.) G75 | 135 | BX52 |
| Eastmuir St, G32 | 70 | CD32 |
| East Nerston Ct, (E.Kil.) G74 | 122 | CC47 |
| East Nerston Gro, (E.Kil.) G74 | 122 | CC47 |
| East Nerston Rd, G72 | 123 | CE46 |
| Easton Pl, Coat. ML5 | | |
| off Whifflet St | 75 | CX32 |
| East Queenslie Ind Est, G33 | 71 | CG29 |
| East Rd, (Kilb.) John. PA10 | 78 | AC33 |
| East Rd, Moth. ML1 | 112 | DC41 |
| East Scott Ter, Ham. ML3 | 140 | CT52 |
| Eastside, (Kirk.) G66 | 17 | CE12 |
| Eastside Ind Est, (Kirk.) G66 | 17 | CF12 |
| East Springfield Ter, (Bishop.) | | |
| G64 | 51 | BX21 |
| East Sta Ind Est, Lark. ML9 | 144 | DD57 |
| East Stewart Gdns, Coat. ML5 | | |
| off East Stewart St | 75 | CY30 |
| East Stewart Pl, Coat. ML5 | | |
| off East Stewart St | 75 | CY30 |
| East Stewart St, Coat. ML5 | 75 | CY31 |
| East Thomson St, Clyde. G81 | 27 | AX18 |
| Eastvale Pl, G3 | 66 | BL29 |
| East Wellbrae Cres, Ham. ML3 | 139 | CR52 |
| East Wellington St, G31 | 69 | BZ32 |
| East Whitby St, G31 | 89 | BY33 |
| Eastwood Av, G41 | 86 | BM37 |
| Eastwood Av, (Giff.) G46 | 102 | BL43 |
| Eastwood Ct, (Thornlie.) G46 | | |
| off Crosslees Dr | 102 | BJ41 |
| Eastwood Cres, (Thornlie.) G46 | 101 | BH41 |
| Eastwoodmains Rd, (Giff.) G46 | 102 | BL44 |
| Eastwoodmains Rd, (Clark.) | | |
| G76 | 102 | BL44 |
| Eastwood Pk, (Giff.) G46 | 102 | BJ43 |
| Eastwood Pk, (Thornlie.) G46 | 102 | BJ43 |
| Eastwood Rd, (Mood.) G69 | 37 | CP19 |
| Eastwood Vw, (Camb.) G72 | 107 | CG39 |
| Eastwood Way, Lark. ML9 | | |
| off Roselea St | 144 | DD57 |
| Easwald Bk, (Kilb.) John. PA10 | 78 | AD35 |
| Ebroch Dr, (Kilsyth) G65 | 7 | CU5 |
| Ebroch Pk, (Kilsyth) G65 | 7 | CU5 |
| Eccles St, G22 | | |
| off Carron St | 50 | BU24 |
| Eckford St, G32 | 90 | CC33 |
| Eck Path, Moth. ML1 | | |
| off Howden Pl | 112 | DC40 |
| Eday St, G22 | 50 | BT23 |
| Edderton Pl, G34 | 72 | CJ30 |
| Edderton Way, G34 | 72 | CJ30 |
| Eddington Dr, (Newt. M.) G77 | 117 | BE50 |
| Eddleston Pl, (Camb.) G72 | | |
| off Montgomery St | 107 | CG40 |
| Eddlewood Ct, G33 | 72 | CJ30 |
| Eddlewood Path, G33 | | |
| off Eddlewood Rd | 71 | CH30 |
| Eddlewood Pl, G33 | 71 | CH30 |
| Eddlewood Rd, G33 | 71 | CH30 |
| Edelweiss Ter, G11 | | |
| off Gardner St | 66 | BK27 |
| Eden Dr, (E.Kil.) G75 | 134 | BV55 |
| Eden Gdns, (E.Kil.) G75 | 134 | BV54 |
| Eden Gro, (E.Kil.) G75 | 134 | BV54 |
| Edenhall Ct, (Newt. M.) G77 | 131 | BF51 |
| Edenhall Gro, (Newt. M.) G77 | 131 | BG51 |
| Eden La, G33 | 69 | BZ28 |
| Eden Pk, (Both.) G71 | 109 | CP43 |
| Eden Pl, (Camb.) G72 | 107 | CF40 |
| Eden Pl, Renf. PA4 | 64 | BA27 |
| Eden St, G33 | 69 | BZ28 |
| Edenwood St, G31 | 70 | CA32 |
| Edgam Dr, G52 | 65 | BE32 |
| Edgefauld Av, G21 | 50 | BV26 |
| Edgefauld Dr, G21 | 50 | BV25 |
| Edgefauld Pl, G21 | 50 | BV24 |
| Edgefauld Rd, G21 | 50 | BV25 |
| Edgehill La, G11 | 48 | BJ25 |
| Edgehill Rd, G11 | 47 | BH25 |
| Edgehill Rd, (Bears.) G61 | 29 | BG15 |
| Edgemont Pk, Ham. ML3 | 140 | CS53 |
| Edgemont St, G41 | 87 | BN37 |
| Edinbeg Av, G42 | 88 | BU37 |
| Edinbeg Pl, G42 | 88 | BU37 |
| Edinburgh Rd, G33 | 69 | BZ30 |
| Edinburgh Rd, (Baill.) G69 | 71 | CH31 |
| Edinburgh Rd, Moth. ML1 | 113 | DF39 |
| Edington Gdns, (Mood.) G69 | 37 | CP18 |
| Edington St, G4 | 67 | BR27 |
| Edison St, G52 | 64 | BA29 |
| Edmiston Dr, G51 | 65 | BH31 |
| Edmonstone Ct, Clyde. G81 | | |
| off Hamilton Ter | 45 | AZ22 |
| Edmonstone Dr, (Kilsyth) G65 | 7 | CT6 |
| Edmonton Ter, (E.Kil.) G75 | 135 | BY53 |
| Edmund Kean, (E.Kil.) G74 | 123 | CE48 |
| Edrom Ct, G32 | 70 | CB32 |
| Edrom Path, G32 | | |
| off Edrom St | 70 | CC32 |
| Edrom St, G32 | 70 | CB32 |
| Edward Av, Renf. PA4 | 45 | AZ25 |
| Edward St, (Kilsyth) G65 | 7 | CT4 |
| Edward St, (Baill.) G69 | 73 | CP32 |
| Edward St, Clyde. G81 | 45 | AZ22 |
| Edward St, Ham. ML3 | 140 | CT51 |
| Edward St, Moth. ML1 | 128 | DB48 |
| Edwin St, G51 | 66 | BM32 |
| Edzell Ct, G14 | 65 | BF27 |
| Edzell Dr, (Newt. M.) G77 | 117 | BG49 |
| Edzell Dr, (Elder.) John. PA5 | 80 | AM35 |
| Edzell Gdns, (Bishop.) G64 | 51 | BY21 |
| Edzell Pl, G14 | 47 | BF26 |
| Edzell St, G14 | 65 | BF27 |
| Edzell St, Coat. ML5 | 94 | CT33 |
| Egidia Av, (Giff.) G46 | 102 | BL43 |
| Egilsay Cres, G22 | 50 | BS21 |
| Egilsay Pl, G22 | 50 | BS21 |
| Egilsay St, G22 | 50 | BS21 |
| Egilsay Ter, G22 | 50 | BS21 |
| Eglinton Av, (Udd.) G71 | | |
| off Lady Isle Cres | 109 | CN39 |
| Eglinton Ct, G5 | 67 | BR32 |
| Eglinton Dr, (Giff.) G46 | 102 | BL43 |
| Eglinton St, G5 | 87 | BQ33 |
| Eglinton St, Coat. ML5 | 75 | CX29 |
| Egmont Pk, (E.Kil.) G75 | 135 | BW54 |
| Eider, G12 | | |
| off Ascot Av | 48 | BJ22 |
| Eider Gro, (E.Kil.) G75 | 135 | BW56 |
| Eighth St, (Udd.) G71 | 93 | CN36 |
| Eildon Cres, (Chap.) Air. ML6 | 97 | DH36 |
| Eildon Dr, (Barr.) G78 | 99 | AY44 |
| Eildon Rd, (Kirk.) G66 | 17 | CH13 |
| Eileen Gdns, (Bishop.) G64 | 33 | BX19 |
| Elba La, G31 | | |
| off Gallowgate | 69 | BY32 |
| Elcho St, G40 | 68 | BV31 |
| Elderbank, (Bears.) G61 | 29 | BG18 |
| Elder Cres, (Camb.) G72 | 107 | CG41 |

| | | | | | | | |
|---|---|---|---|---|---|---|---|
| Elder Dr, (Camb.) G72 | 107 | CG41 | Ellismuir Rd, (Baill.) G69 | 92 | CL33 | Elphinstone Pl, G51 | 66 | BL30 |
| Elder Gro, (Udd.) G71 | 93 | CR38 | Ellismuir St, Coat. ML5 | 94 | CT34 | Elphinstone Rd, (Giff.) G46 | 118 | BJ46 |
| Elder Gro Av, G51 | 65 | BF30 | Ellismuir Way, (Udd.) G71 | 93 | CQ36 | Elphin St, G23 |
| Elder Gro Ct, G51 | 65 | BF30 | Ellis St, Coat. ML5 | 75 | CW30 | off Invershiel Rd | 30 | BM20 |
| Elder Gro Pl, G51 | 65 | BF30 | Elliston Av, G53 | 101 | BE40 | Elrig Rd, G44 | 103 | BP40 |
| Elderpark Gdns, G51 | | | Elliston Cres, G53 | 101 | BE40 | Elsinore Path, (E.Kil.) G75 | 136 | CA56 |
| off Elderpark St | 65 | BH30 | Elliston Dr, G53 | 101 | BE40 | Elspeth Gdns, (Bishop.) G64 | 33 | BY19 |
| Elderpark Gro, G51 | 65 | BH30 | Ellis Way, Moth. ML1 | | | Eltham St, G22 |
| Elderpark St, G51 | 65 | BH30 | off Toll St | 128 | DB48 | off Bonhill St | 49 | BR26 |
| Elderslie St, G3 | 4 | BP28 | Ellon Dr, (Linw.) Pais. PA3 | 60 | AJ32 | Elvan Ct, G32 |
| Elder St, G51 | 65 | BH29 | Ellon Gro, Pais. PA3 | | | off Edrom Ct | 70 | CC32 |
| Eldin Pl, (Elder.) John. PA5 | 80 | AK35 | off Ellon Way | 62 | AV30 | Elvan Pl, (E.Kil.) G75 | 134 | BU54 |
| Eldon Ct, G11 | | | Ellon Way, Pais. PA3 | 62 | AV30 | Elvan St, G32 | 70 | CB32 |
| off Caird Dr | 66 | BK27 | Ellrig, (E.Kil.) G75 | 135 | BZ56 | Elvan St, Moth. ML1 | 127 | CZ47 |
| Eldon Gdns, (Bishop.) G64 | 32 | BU20 | Elm Av, (Lenz.) G66 | 35 | CE15 | Embo Dr, G13 | 46 | BD23 |
| Eldon St, G3 | 67 | BN27 | Elm Av, Renf. PA4 | 45 | AY25 | Emerald Ter, Bell. ML4 | 111 | CW41 |
| Elgin Av, (E.Kil.) G74 | 122 | CB50 | Elm Bk, (Bishop.) G64 | 33 | BX20 | Emerson Rd, (Bishop.) G64 | 33 | BW20 |
| Elgin Gdns, (Clark.) G76 | 119 | BP45 | Elm Bk, (Kirk.) G66 | 17 | CF12 | Emerson Rd W, (Bishop.) G64 |
| Elgin Pl, (Kilsyth) G65 | 7 | CT4 | Elmbank Av, (Udd.) G71 | 93 | CR38 | off Crowhill Rd | 33 | BW20 |
| Elgin Pl, (E.Kil.) G74 | 122 | CB50 | Elmbank Cres, G2 | 4 | BQ29 | Emerson St, G20 | 49 | BQ23 |
| Elgin Pl, Air. ML6 | 76 | DA32 | Elmbank Cres, Ham. ML3 | 125 | CQ49 | Emily Dr, Moth. ML1 | 128 | DA49 |
| Elgin Pl, Coat. ML5 | 95 | CX34 | Elmbank Dr, Lark. ML9 | 145 | DE60 | Emma Jay Rd, Bell. ML4 | 111 | CX40 |
| Elgin Rd, (Bears.) G61 | 11 | BH14 | Elmbank La, G3 | | | Empire Way, Moth. ML1 | 111 | CY44 |
| Elgin St, G40 | | | off North St | 4 | BP29 | Endfield Av, G12 | 48 | BK23 |
| off Rowchester St | 69 | BW32 | Elmbank St, G2 | 4 | BQ29 | Endrick Bk, (Bishop.) G64 | 33 | BW17 |
| Elgin Ter, Ham. ML3 | 125 | CN49 | Elmbank St, Bell. ML4 | 111 | CW40 | Endrick Ct, Coat. ML5 |
| Elgin Way, Bell. ML4 | 111 | CW39 | Elmbank St La, G2 | 4 | BQ29 | off Kirk St | 74 | CV31 |
| Elibank St, G33 | 70 | CC28 | Elm Cres, (Udd.) G71 | 94 | CT38 | Endrick Dr, (Bears.) G61 | 29 | BH17 |
| Elie Ct, (Cumb.) G68 | 9 | DB8 | Elm Dr, (Cumb.) G67 | 23 | DH9 | Endrick Dr, Pais. PA1 | 63 | AX31 |
| Elie St, G11 | 66 | BL27 | Elm Dr, (Camb.) G72 | 107 | CE40 | Endrick Gdns, (Miln.) G62 | 11 | BG11 |
| Eliot Cres, Ham. ML3 | 140 | CT52 | Elm Dr, (Chap.) Air. ML6 | 97 | DG34 | Endrick St, G21 | 50 | BT26 |
| Eliot Ter, Ham. ML3 | 140 | CT51 | Elm Dr, John. PA5 | 80 | AJ36 | English Row, (Calder.) Air. ML6 | 97 | DE35 |
| Elison Ct, Moth. ML1 | | | Elmfoot St, G5 | 88 | BT35 | English St, Wis. ML2 | 129 | DF50 |
| off Dunbar Dr | 128 | DD49 | Elm Gdns, (Bears.) G61 | 29 | BG15 | Ennerdale, (E.Kil.) G75 | 134 | BV55 |
| Elizabethan Way, Renf. PA4 | 63 | AY28 | Elmhurst, Moth. ML1 | 127 | CZ49 | Ennisfree Rd, (Blan.) G72 | 124 | CM45 |
| Elizabeth Cres, (Thornlie.) G46 | 102 | BJ42 | Elmira Rd, (Muir.) G69 | 54 | CL22 | Ensay St, G22 | 50 | BT22 |
| Elizabeth Quad, Moth. ML1 | | | Elm La E, G14 | | | Enterkin St, G32 | 90 | CB33 |
| off Sherry Av | 112 | DC40 | off Westland Dr | 47 | BF26 | Eriboll Pl, G22 | 49 | BR22 |
| Elizabeth St, G51 | 66 | BL32 | Elm La W, G14 | | | Eriboll St, G22 | 49 | BR22 |
| Elizabeth Wynd, Ham. ML3 | | | off Westland Dr | 47 | BF26 | Eribol Wk, Moth. ML1 |
| off Bankfield Dr | 140 | CT54 | Elm Lea, John. PA5 | 80 | AK35 | off Loanhead Av | 113 | DF42 |
| Ella Gdns, Bell. ML4 | 111 | CY41 | Elmore Av, G44 | 103 | BR40 | Ericht Rd, G43 | 102 | BL40 |
| Ellangowan Ct, (Bears.) G62 | 12 | BJ11 | Elmore La, G44 | 103 | BR40 | Eriska Av, G14 | 46 | BC24 |
| Ellangowan Rd, G41 | 86 | BL37 | Elm Pl, (E.Kil.) G75 | 135 | BY55 | Eriskay Av, (Newt. M.) G77 | 116 | BD48 |
| Ellangowan Rd, (Miln.) G62 | 12 | BJ11 | Elm Quad, Air. ML6 | 77 | DF31 | Eriskay Av, Ham. ML3 | 139 | CP51 |
| Ellergreen Rd, (Bears.) G61 | 29 | BG17 | Elm Rd, (Ruther.) G73 | 105 | BX41 | Eriskay Cres, (Newt. M.) G77 | 116 | BD48 |
| Ellerslie Rd, G14 | 45 | AZ23 | Elm Rd, Clyde. G81 | 27 | AW16 | Eriskay Dr, (Old Kil.) G60 | 26 | AS15 |
| Ellerslie St, John. PA5 | 80 | AJ34 | Elm Rd, (Holytown) Moth. ML1 | 112 | DD40 | Eriskay Pl, (Old Kil.) G60 | 26 | AS15 |
| Ellesmere St, G22 | 49 | BQ25 | Elm Rd, (New Stev.) Moth. ML1 | 112 | DC43 | Erradale Pl, G22 | 49 | BQ22 |
| Ellinger Ct, Clyde. G81 | | | Elm Rd, Pais. PA2 | 83 | AW36 | Erradale St, G22 | 49 | BQ22 |
| off Scott St | 26 | AU17 | Elmslie Ct, (Baill.) G69 | 92 | CL33 | Errogie St, G34 | 72 | CK29 |
| Elliot Av, (Giff.) G46 | 102 | BL43 | Elm St, G14 | 47 | BF26 | Errol Gdns, G5 | 88 | BS33 |
| Elliot Av, Pais. PA2 | 80 | AM38 | Elm St, (Blan.) G72 | 125 | CN46 | Erskine Av, G41 | 86 | BK33 |
| Elliot Ct, Moth. ML1 | | | Elm St, (Clark.) G76 | 119 | BP47 | Erskine Ct, Air. ML6 |
| off Marmion Cres | 111 | CZ44 | Elm St, Coat. ML5 | 75 | CY32 | off Station Rd | 77 | DG29 |
| Elliot Cres, (E.Kil.) G74 | 136 | CD51 | Elmtree Gdns, G45 | 104 | BV41 | Erskine Cres, Air. ML6 | 76 | DB32 |
| Elliot Dr, (Giff.) G46 | 102 | BL42 | Elmvale Row, G21 | 50 | BU24 | Erskinefauld Rd, (Linw.) |
| Elliot Pl, G3 | | | Elmvale Row E, G21 | | | Pais. PA3 | 60 | AJ31 |
| off Finnieston St | 67 | BN30 | off Elmvale Row | 50 | BU24 | Erskine Ferry Rd, (Old Kil.) G60 | 25 | AQ16 |
| Elliot St, G3 | 67 | BN30 | Elmvale Row W, G21 | | | Erskine Harbour, Ersk. PA8 | 25 | AQ17 |
| Ellisland, (Kirk.) G66 | 18 | CK11 | off Elmvale Row | 50 | BU24 | Erskine Rd, (Giff.) G46 | 118 | BK47 |
| Ellisland, (E.Kil.) G74 | 123 | CF50 | Elmvale St, G21 | 50 | BU24 | Erskine Sq, G52 | 64 | BB30 |
| Ellisland Av, Clyde. G81 | 27 | AY18 | Elm Vw Ct, Bell. ML4 | 111 | CZ41 | Erskine Vw, (Old Kil.) G60 | 25 | AQ15 |
| Ellisland Cres, (Ruther.) G73 | 104 | BV40 | Elm Wk, (Bears.) G61 | 29 | BG15 | Erskine Vw, Clyde. G81 | 27 | AX18 |
| Ellisland Dr, (Kirk.) G66 | 18 | CJ11 | Elm Way, (Camb.) G72 | 107 | CG41 | Ervie St, G34 | 72 | CL30 |
| Ellisland Dr, (Blan.) G72 | 124 | CK47 | Elm Way, Lark. ML9 | 142 | DC56 | Esdaile Ct, Moth. ML1 | 112 | DB42 |
| Ellisland Rd, G43 | 102 | BM39 | Elmwood, Wis. ML2 | 143 | DG52 | Esk Av, Renf. PA4 | 64 | BA27 |
| Ellisland Rd, (Cumb.) G67 | 22 | DD11 | Elmwood Av, G11 | 47 | BH25 | Eskbank St, G32 | 70 | CC31 |
| Ellisland Rd, (Clark.) G76 | 119 | BN48 | Elmwood Av, (Newt. M.) G77 | 117 | BH47 | Eskbank Toll, (Giff.) G46 | 102 | BK44 |
| Ellisland Wynd, Moth. ML1 | 113 | DE42 | Elmwood Ct, (Both.) G71 | 109 | CQ43 | Esk Dale, (E.Kil.) G74 | 121 | BY50 |
| Ellismuir Fm Rd, (Baill.) G69 | | | Elmwood Gdns, (Kirk.) G66 | 34 | CC16 | Eskdale, (Newt. M.) G77 |
| off Bredisholm Ter | 92 | CM33 | Elmwood La, G11 | 47 | BH25 | off Kirkvale Ct | 118 | BK48 |
| Ellismuir Pl, (Baill.) G69 | 92 | CL33 | Elphinstone Cres, (E.Kil.) G75 | 136 | CB54 | Eskdale Dr, (Ruther.) G73 | 89 | BZ38 |

Eskdale Rd, (Bears.) G61 29 BF19
Eskdale St, G42 87 BR36
Esk Dr, Pais. PA2 81 AN36
Esk St, G14 46 BB24
Esk Way, Pais. PA2 81 AN36
Esmond St, G3 66 BL28
Espedair St, Pais. PA2 82 AU34
Espieside Cres, Coat. ML5 74 CT29
Essenside Av, G15 29 BE19
Essex Dr, G14 47 BG25
Essex La, G14 47 BF25
Esslemont Av, G14 46 BD24
Estate Quad, G32 91 CE36
Estate Rd, G32 91 CE36
Etive Av, (Bears.) G61 30 BK17
Etive Av, Ham. ML3 139 CQ52
Etive Ct, (Cumb.) G67 39 CX15
Etive Ct, Clyde. G81 27 AY16
Etive Cres, (Bishop.) G64 33 BX20
Etive Cres, (Cumb.) G67 39 CX15
Etive Dr, (Giff.) G46 102 BM44
Etive Dr, (Cumb.) G67 39 CX15
Etive Dr, Air. ML6 77 DE32
Etive Dr, Bish. PA7 24 AL19
Etive Pl, (Cumb.) G67 39 CY15
Etive Pl, Lark. ML9 142 DB55
Etive St, G32 70 CC32
Etna Ind Est, Wis. ML2 129 DE49
Etna St, Wis. ML2 129 DE49
Eton La, G12 67 BN27
Etterick Wynd, (Blan.) G72
  off Winton Cres 124 CL46
Ettrick Av, Bell. ML4
  off Rockburn Cres 95 CW38
Ettrick Av, Renf. PA4
  off Morriston Cres 64 BB27
Ettrick Ct, (Cumb.) G72
  off Gateside Av 107 CG41
Ettrick Cres, (Ruther.) G73 89 BY38
Ettrick Dr, (Bears.) G61 11 BE14
Ettrick Dr, Bish. PA7 24 AL19
Ettrick Hill, (E.Kil.) G74
  off Cantieslaw Dr 122 CC50
Ettrick Oval, Pais. PA2 81 AN37
Ettrick Pl, G43 86 BM38
Ettrick Sq, (Cumb.) G67
  off Cumbernauld Shop Cen 22 DB12
Ettrick Ter, John. PA5 79 AE37
Ettrick Wk, (Cumb.) G67
  off Cumbernauld Shop Cen 22 DB12
Ettrick Way, (Cumb.) G67
  off Cumbernauld Shop Cen 22 DB12
Ettrick Way, Renf. PA4
  off Morriston Cres 64 BB27
Evan Cres, (Giff.) G46 102 BM43
Evan Dr, (Giff.) G46 102 BM44
Evanton Dr, (Thornlie.) G46 101 BG43
Evanton Pl, (Thornlie.) G46 101 BG42
Everard Ct, G21 50 BU22
Everard Dr, G21 50 BU23
Everard Pl, G21 50 BU22
Everard Quad, G21 50 BU23
Everglades, The, (Chry.) G69 54 CK21
Eversley St, G32 90 CC34
Everton Rd, G53 85 BE35
Ewart Cres, Ham. ML3 139 CQ51
Ewart Ter, Ham. ML3 139 CQ51
Ewing Ct, Ham. ML3 140 CS54
Ewing Pl, G31 69 BY32
Ewing St, (Ruther.) G73 89 BW38
Ewing St, (Kilb.) John. PA10 78 AC34
Ewing Wk, (Miln.) G62 12 BL12
Excelsior St, Wis. ML2 129 DF50

Exchange Pl, G1
  off Buchanan St 5 BS30
Exeter Dr, G11 66 BJ27
Exeter La, G11
  off Exeter Dr 66 BJ27
Exeter St, Coat. ML5 75 CW32
Eynort St, G22 49 BQ22
Eyrepoint Ct, G33
  off Sutherness Dr 70 CC29

**F**

Factory Rd, Moth. ML1 128 DA48
Fagan Ct, (Blan.) G72 109 CN44
Faifley Rd, Clyde. G81 27 AX15
Fairbairn Cres, (Thornlie.) G46 102 BJ43
Fairbairn Path, G40
  off Ruby St 89 BW33
Fairbairn St, G40
  off Dalmarnock Rd 89 BW33
Fairburn St, G32 90 CB33
Fairfax Av, G44 104 BS40
Fairfield Ct, (Clark.) G76 119 BN48
Fairfield Dr, (Clark.) G76 119 BN48
Fairfield Dr, Renf. PA4 63 AZ28
Fairfield Gdns, G51
  off Fairfield St 65 BH29
Fairfield Pl, G51
  off Fairfield St 65 BH29
Fairfield Pl, (Both.) G71 109 CR43
Fairfield Pl, (E.Kil.) G74 135 BY51
Fairfield St, G51 65 BH29
Fairford Dr, (Cumb.) G67 39 CZ15
Fairhaven Av, Air. ML6 77 DG31
Fairhaven Rd, G23 49 BN21
Fairhill Av, Ham. ML3 140 CS52
Fairhill Cres, Ham. ML3 140 CS52
Fairhill Pl, Ham. ML3 139 CR54
Fairholm Av, Ham. ML3 141 CY52
Fairholm St, G32 90 CB33
Fairholm St, Lark. ML9 144 DB57
Fairley St, G51 66 BK31
Fairlie, (E.Kil.) G74 121 BZ50
Fairlie Pk Dr, G11 66 BJ27
Fair Oaks, (Clark.) G76 120 BU45
Fairway, (Bears.) G61 28 BD16
Fairway Av, Pais. PA2 82 AT37
Fairways, Lark. ML9 145 DE58
Fairways Vw, Clyde. G81 27 AZ15
Fairweather Pl, (Newt. M.) G77 117 BE49
Fairyknowe Gdns, (Both.) G71 109 CR43
Falcon Cres, Pais. PA3 61 AR31
Falconer Ter, Ham. ML3
  off Fairhill Av 140 CS52
Falcon Rd, John. PA5 79 AF38
Falcon Ter, G20 48 BL21
Falcon Ter La, G20 48 BL21
Falfield St, G5 87 BQ33
Falkland Av, (Newt. M.) G77 118 BJ47
Falkland Cres, (Bishop.) G64 51 BZ21
Falkland Dr, (E.Kil.) G74 135 BY52
Falkland La, G12 48 BK26
Falkland Pk, (E.Kil.) G74 135 BZ52
Falkland Pl, (E.Kil.) G74 135 BZ52
Falkland Pl, Coat. ML5 95 CX34
Falkland St, G12 48 BK26
Falloch Rd, G42 87 BQ38
Falloch Rd, (Bears.) G61 29 BE19
Falloch Rd, (Miln.) G62 11 BF11
Fallside Av, (Udd.) G71 110 CS39
Fallside Rd, (Both.) G71 109 CQ43
Fallside Rd, Pais. PA2 82 AU36
Fallside Rd, G32 90 CD35

Falside Rd, Pais. PA2 82 AT36
Falstaff, (E.Kil.) G74 123 CE48
Faraday Retail Pk, Coat. ML5 75 CX31
Fara St, G23 49 BP21
Farie St, (Ruther.) G73 88 BV37
Farm Ct, (Both.) G71 109 CR41
Farm Cres, Moth. ML1 113 DH41
Farme Castle Ct, (Ruther.) G73 89 BY36
Farme Castle Est, (Ruther.) G73 89 BY36
Farme Cross, (Ruther.) G73 89 BX36
Farmeloan Ind Est, (Ruther.)
  G73 89 BX36
Farmeloan Rd, (Ruther.) G73 89 BX37
Farmgate Sq, Bell. ML4
  off Crofthead Cres 110 CV41
Farmington Av, G32 71 CF32
Farmington Gdns, G32 71 CF32
Farmington Gate, G32 91 CF33
Farmington Gro, G32 71 CF32
Farm La, (Udd.) G71
  off Myers Cres 109 CQ40
Farm La, Bell. ML4
  off Crofthead Cres 110 CV42
Farm Pk, (Lenz.) G66 35 CF17
Farm Rd, G41 66 BK32
Farm Rd, (Blan.) G72 108 CM44
Farm Rd, Ham. ML3 125 CP49
Farm St, Moth. ML1 127 CZ46
Farm Ter, Ham. ML3 125 CP49
Farndale, (E.Kil.) G74 121 BY50
Farne Dr, G44 103 BR41
Farnell St, G4 67 BR27
Farrier Ct, John. PA5 79 AH34
Faskally Av, (Bishop.) G64 32 BU18
Faskin Cres, G53 84 BB38
Faskine Av, Air. ML6 76 DB31
Faskine Av, (Calder.) Air. ML6 96 DD35
Faskine Cres, Air. ML6 76 DB31
Faskin Pl, G53 84 BB38
Faskin Rd, G53 84 BB38
Fasque Pl, G15 28 BA17
Fastnet St, G33 70 CC29
Fauldhouse Way, G5 88 BT34
Faulds, (Baill.) G69 72 CL32
Faulds Gdns, (Baill.) G69 72 CL32
Fauldshead Rd, Renf. PA4 45 AY26
Faulds La, Coat. ML5
  off Dunblane Pl 94 CV33
Fauldspark Cres, (Baill.) G69 72 CL31
Faulds St, Coat. ML5 94 CU34
Fauldswood Cres, Pais. PA2 81 AR35
Fauldswood Dr, Pais. PA2 81 AR35
Faulkner Gro, Moth. ML1
  off Morris Cres 129 DH45
Fearnach Dr, G20
  off Skaethorn Rd 48 BK22
Fearnmore Rd, G20 48 BM22
Fellsview Av, (Kirk.) G66 17 CH12
Felton Pl, G13 46 BB22
Fendoch St, G32 90 CC33
Fenella St, G32 70 CD32
Fennsbank Av, (Ruther.) G73 105 BZ42
Fenwick Dr, (Barr.) G78 99 AZ44
Fenwick Dr, Ham. ML3 140 CU55
Fenwick Pl, (Giff.) G46 102 BK44
Fenwick Rd, (Giff.) G46 102 BL44
Fereneze Av, (Clark.) G76 118 BL45
Fereneze Av, (Barr.) G78 99 AX42
Fereneze Av, Renf. PA4 63 AW29
Fereneze Cres, G13 46 BC22
Fereneze Cres, Ham. ML3 125 CP50
Fereneze Dr, Pais. PA2 82 AS37

| | | | |
|---|---|---|---|
| Fereneze Gro, (Barr.) G78 | 99 | AX41 | |
| Fereneze Rd, (Neil.) G78 | 114 | AS45 | |
| Fergus Av, Pais. PA3 | 61 | AQ32 | |
| Fergus Ct, G20 | | | |
| off Fergus Dr | 49 | BN25 | |
| Fergus Dr, G20 | 49 | BN25 | |
| Fergus Dr, Pais. PA3 | 61 | AQ32 | |
| Fergus Gdns, Ham. ML3 | 140 | CV51 | |
| Fergus La, G20 | 49 | BP25 | |
| Ferguslie, Pais. PA1 | 81 | AQ33 | |
| Ferguslie Pk Av, Pais. PA3 | 61 | AR31 | |
| Ferguslie Pk Cres, Pais. PA3 | | | |
| off Ferguslie Pk Av | 81 | AQ33 | |
| Ferguslie Wk, Pais. PA1 | 81 | AR33 | |
| Ferguson Av, (Miln.) G62 | 11 | BH11 | |
| Ferguson Dr, Moth. ML1 | 128 | DA50 | |
| Ferguson St, John. PA5 | 79 | AG34 | |
| Ferguson St, Renf. PA4 | 45 | AZ26 | |
| Ferguson Way, Air. ML6 | 76 | DC27 | |
| Fergusson Pl, (E.Kil.) G74 | 123 | CF48 | |
| Fergusson Rd, (Cumb.) G67 | 22 | DB11 | |
| Ferguston Rd, (Bears.) G61 | 29 | BH17 | |
| Fernan St, G32 | 70 | CB32 | |
| Fern Av, (Bishop.) G64 | 51 | BX21 | |
| Fern Av, (Lenz.) G66 | 35 | CE17 | |
| Fern Av, Ersk. PA8 | 43 | AR22 | |
| Fernbank Av, (Camb.) G72 | 107 | CE41 | |
| Fernbank St, G21 | 50 | BU24 | |
| Fernbank St, G22 | 50 | BU24 | |
| Fernbrae Av, (Ruther.) G73 | 105 | BY42 | |
| Fernbrae Way, (Ruther.) G73 | 105 | BX42 | |
| Fern Cotts, G13 | | | |
| off Fern La | 47 | BH24 | |
| Ferncroft Dr, G44 | 104 | BT40 | |
| Ferndale, Lark. ML9 | 144 | DC60 | |
| Ferndale Ct, G23 | 48 | BM21 | |
| Ferndale Dr, G23 | 30 | BM20 | |
| Ferndale Gdns, G23 | 48 | BM21 | |
| Ferndale Pl, G23 | 48 | BM21 | |
| Fern Dr, (Barr.) G78 | 99 | AX41 | |
| Ferness Oval, G21 | 51 | BY22 | |
| Ferness Pl, G21 | 51 | BY22 | |
| Ferness Rd, G21 | 51 | BY23 | |
| Fern Gro, (Gart.) G69 | | | |
| off Inchnock Av | 55 | CQ23 | |
| Ferngrove Av, G12 | 48 | BK23 | |
| Fernhill Gra, (Both.) G71 | 109 | CQ44 | |
| Fernhill Rd, (Ruther.) G73 | 105 | BW41 | |
| Fernie Gdns, G20 | 49 | BN22 | |
| Fern La, G13 | 47 | BH24 | |
| Fernlea, (Bears.) G61 | 29 | BG18 | |
| Fernleigh Pl, (Mood.) G69 | 37 | CP19 | |
| Fernleigh Rd, G43 | 102 | BM40 | |
| Fernside Wk, Ham. ML3 | | | |
| off Chatelherault Cres | 140 | CU52 | |
| Fernslea Av, (Blan.) G72 | 124 | CL45 | |
| Fern St, Moth. ML1 | 128 | DC49 | |
| Ferryden Ct, G14 | | | |
| off Ferryden St | 65 | BG27 | |
| Ferryden St, G14 | 65 | BG28 | |
| Ferry Rd, G3 | 66 | BK28 | |
| Ferry Rd, (Both.) G71 | 109 | CQ43 | |
| Ferry Rd, (Udd.) G71 | 109 | CN39 | |
| Ferry Rd, Renf. PA4 | 45 | AZ25 | |
| Fersit Ct, G43 | 102 | BL39 | |
| Fersit St, G43 | 102 | BL39 | |
| Fetlar Ct, (Camb.) G72 | 106 | CB42 | |
| Fetlar Dr, G44 | 104 | BS40 | |
| Fettercairn Av, G15 | 28 | BA18 | |
| Fettercairn Gdns, (Bishop.) G64 | 33 | BY20 | |
| Fettes St, G33 | 70 | CB29 | |
| Fidra St, G33 | 70 | CB29 | |

| | | | |
|---|---|---|---|
| Fielden Pl, G40 | 69 | BW32 | |
| Fielden St, G40 | 69 | BW32 | |
| Field Gro, (Clark.) G76 | 119 | BP48 | |
| Fieldhead Dr, G43 | 102 | BJ40 | |
| Fieldhead Sq, G43 | 102 | BJ40 | |
| Field Rd, (Clark.) G76 | 119 | BP48 | |
| Field Rd, Lark. ML9 | 144 | DD59 | |
| Field St, Ham. ML3 | 140 | CT52 | |
| Fife Av, Air. ML6 | 76 | DC32 | |
| Fife Av, G52 | 84 | BD33 | |
| Fife Cres, (Both.) G71 | 109 | CQ44 | |
| Fife Dr, Moth. ML1 | 111 | CZ43 | |
| Fife Way, (Bishop.) G64 | 51 | BZ21 | |
| Fifth Av, G12 | 47 | BH24 | |
| Fifth Av, (Stepps) G33 | 52 | CD24 | |
| Fifth Av, (Kirk.) G66 | 35 | CF19 | |
| Fifth Av, Air. ML6 | 77 | DE29 | |
| Fifth Av, Renf. PA4 | 63 | AY27 | |
| Fifth Rd, (Blan.) G72 | 125 | CN48 | |
| Fifty Pitches Pl, G51 | 64 | BD30 | |
| Fifty Pitches Rd, G51 | 64 | BD30 | |
| Fifty Pitches Way, G52 | 64 | BD30 | |
| Finart Dr, Pais. PA2 | 83 | AX36 | |
| Finaven Gdns, (Bears.) G61 | 10 | BD13 | |
| Finch Dr, G13 | 46 | BC21 | |
| Finch Pl, John. PA5 | 79 | AF38 | |
| Findhorn, Ersk. PA8 | 25 | AQ19 | |
| Findhorn Av, Pais. PA2 | 81 | AP36 | |
| Findhorn Av, Renf. PA4 | | | |
| off Dee Av | 46 | BA26 | |
| Findhorn Ct, (E.Kil.) G75 | 134 | BT53 | |
| Findhorn Pl, (E.Kil.) G75 | 134 | BT53 | |
| Findhorn St, G33 | 69 | BZ29 | |
| Findlay Ct, Moth. ML1 | | | |
| off Park Neuk St | 127 | CZ45 | |
| Findlay St, (Kilsyth) G65 | | | |
| off Backbrae St | 7 | CT5 | |
| Findochty, Ersk. PA8 | 25 | AQ18 | |
| Findochty Pl, G33 | 71 | CG27 | |
| Findochty St, G33 | 71 | CF28 | |
| Fingal La, G20 | | | |
| off Fingal St | 48 | BL22 | |
| Fingal St, G20 | 48 | BM22 | |
| Fingalton Rd, (Newt. M.) G77 | 116 | BA48 | |
| Fingask St, G32 | 91 | CE33 | |
| Finglas Av, Pais. PA2 | 83 | AX36 | |
| Finglen Gdns, (Miln.) G62 | 11 | BG11 | |
| Finglen Pl, G53 | 100 | BD41 | |
| Fingleton Av, (Barr.) G78 | 99 | AZ44 | |
| Finhaven St, G32 | 90 | CA34 | |
| Finlarig St, G34 | 72 | CL30 | |
| Finlas St, G22 | 50 | BT25 | |
| Finlay Dr, G31 | 69 | BW30 | |
| Finlay Ri, (Miln.) G62 | 12 | BL12 | |
| Finlayson Dr, Air. ML6 | 77 | DG30 | |
| Finlayson Quad, Air. ML6 | 77 | DG30 | |
| Finlaystone St, Coat. ML5 | 74 | CU30 | |
| Finnart Sq, G40 | 88 | BV34 | |
| Finnart St, G40 | 88 | BV34 | |
| Finnieston Quay, G3 | 67 | BN30 | |
| Finnieston Sq, G3 | | | |
| off Finnieston St | 67 | BN29 | |
| Finnieston St, G3 | 67 | BN30 | |
| Finnie Wynd, Moth. ML1 | | | |
| off Nelson Cres | 128 | DD49 | |
| Finsbay St, G51 | 65 | BF31 | |
| Fintrie Ter, Ham. ML3 | | | |
| off Fleming Way | 125 | CN49 | |
| Fintry Av, Pais. PA2 | 82 | AU37 | |
| Fintry Cres, (Bishop.) G64 | 51 | BY21 | |
| Fintry Cres, (Barr.) G78 | 99 | AY44 | |
| Fintry Dr, G44 | 88 | BS38 | |
| Fintry Gdns, (Bears.) G61 | 11 | BE13 | |

| | | | |
|---|---|---|---|
| Firbank Av, (Torr.) G64 | 15 | BX13 | |
| Fir Bk Av, Lark. ML9 | 144 | DD59 | |
| Firbank Quad, (Chap.) Air. ML6 | 97 | DG34 | |
| Firbank Ter, (Barr.) G78 | 100 | BA44 | |
| Fir Ct, (Camb.) G72 | 107 | CG41 | |
| Fir Ct, Coat. ML5 | | | |
| off Ailsa Rd | 94 | CV33 | |
| Firdon Cres, G15 | 28 | BC20 | |
| Fir Dr, (E.Kil.) G75 | 135 | BX56 | |
| Fir Gro, (Udd.) G71 | 93 | CR38 | |
| Fir Gro, (New Stev.) Moth. ML1 | 112 | DC43 | |
| Firhill Av, Air. ML6 | 76 | DB31 | |
| Firhill Rd, G20 | 49 | BQ25 | |
| Firhill St, G20 | 49 | BQ25 | |
| Firlee, (E.Kil.) G75 | 134 | BV53 | |
| Firpark Pl, G31 | | | |
| off Firpark St | 68 | BV29 | |
| Firpark Rd, (Bishop.) G64 | 51 | BX21 | |
| Firpark St, G31 | 68 | BV29 | |
| Fir Pk St, Moth. ML1 | 128 | DB49 | |
| Firpark Ter, G31 | 68 | BV30 | |
| Fir Pl, (Baill.) G69 | 92 | CJ34 | |
| Fir Pl, (Camb.) G72 | 107 | CE39 | |
| Fir Pl, John. PA5 | 80 | AJ35 | |
| First Av, (Millerston) G33 | 52 | CD24 | |
| First Av, G44 | 103 | BP43 | |
| First Av, (Bears.) G61 | 30 | BJ18 | |
| First Av, (Kirk.) G66 | 35 | CF20 | |
| First Av, (Udd.) G71 | 93 | CN37 | |
| First Av, Renf. PA4 | 63 | AY27 | |
| First Gdns, G41 | 86 | BJ33 | |
| First Rd, (Blan.) G72 | 125 | CN48 | |
| First St, (Udd.) G71 | 93 | CP37 | |
| First Ter, Clyde. G81 | 27 | AW18 | |
| Fir Vw, (Calder.) Air. ML6 | 96 | DD35 | |
| Firwood Cts, (Newt. M.) G77 | 117 | BG49 | |
| Firwood Dr, G44 | 104 | BS39 | |
| Firwood Rd, (Newt. M.) G77 | 117 | BG48 | |
| Fischer Gdns, Pais. PA1 | 81 | AP33 | |
| Fisher Av, (Kilsyth) G65 | 7 | CT5 | |
| Fisher Av, Pais. PA1 | 81 | AP33 | |
| Fisher Ct, G31 | 68 | BV30 | |
| Fisher Cres, Clyde. G81 | 27 | AX15 | |
| Fisher Dr, Pais. PA1 | 81 | AP33 | |
| Fishers Rd, Renf. PA4 | 45 | AY23 | |
| Fisher St, Lark. ML9 | 144 | DD60 | |
| Fisher Way, Pais. PA1 | 81 | AP33 | |
| Fishescoates Av, (Ruther.) G73 | 105 | BY40 | |
| Fishescoates Gdns, (Ruther.) G73 | 105 | BY40 | |
| Fitzalan Dr, Pais. PA3 | 63 | AW31 | |
| Fitzalan Rd, Renf. PA4 | 63 | AW28 | |
| Fitzroy Gro, (E.Kil.) G74 | 134 | BT53 | |
| Fitzroy La, G3 | 67 | BN29 | |
| Fitzroy Pl, G3 | | | |
| off Royal Ter | 67 | BN28 | |
| Flakefield, (E.Kil.) G74 | 135 | BX51 | |
| Flaxfield Gro, Moth. ML1 | 111 | CZ43 | |
| Flaxmill Av, Wis. ML2 | 129 | DF49 | |
| Flax Rd, (Udd.) G71 | 109 | CQ40 | |
| Fleet Av, Renf. PA4 | 64 | BA28 | |
| Fleet St, G32 | 90 | CD33 | |
| Fleming Av, (Chry.) G69 | 54 | CL22 | |
| Fleming Av, Clyde. G81 | 27 | AZ20 | |
| Fleming Ct, Ham. ML3 | 125 | CN49 | |
| Fleming Ct, Moth. ML1 | 128 | DC49 | |
| Fleming Pl, (E.Kil.) G75 | 135 | BZ53 | |
| Fleming Rd, (Cumb.) G67 | 22 | DB11 | |
| Fleming Rd, Bell. ML4 | 111 | CX39 | |
| Fleming Rd, Bish. PA7 | 24 | AK18 | |
| Fleming St, G31 | 69 | BX31 | |
| Fleming St, Pais. PA3 | 62 | AU30 | |

| | | |
|---|---|---|
| Flemington Rd, (Camb.) G72 | 107 | CH44 |
| Flemington St, G21 | 50 | BV26 |
| Fleming Way, Ham. ML3 | 124 | CM49 |
| Fleming Way, Lark. ML9 | | |
| off Bannockburn Dr | 145 | DE59 |
| Flenders Av, (Clark.) G76 | 118 | BL47 |
| Flenders Rd, (Clark.) G76 | 118 | BL47 |
| Fleurs Av, G41 | 86 | BK33 |
| Fleurs Rd, G41 | 86 | BK33 |
| Flinders Pl, (E.Kil.) G75 | 135 | BX53 |
| Flloyd St, Coat. ML5 | 74 | CV30 |
| Floorsburn Cres, John. PA5 | 79 | AG35 |
| Floors Rd, (Eagle.) G76 | 132 | BL52 |
| Floors St, John. PA5 | 79 | AH35 |
| Floors St Ind Est, John. PA5 | 79 | AG35 |
| Flora Gdns, (Bishop.) G64 | 33 | BY19 |
| Florence Dr, (Giff.) G46 | 102 | BL43 |
| Florence Gdns, (Ruther.) G73 | 105 | BY41 |
| Florence St, G5 | 68 | BS32 |
| Florida Av, G42 | 87 | BR37 |
| Florida Cres, G42 | 87 | BR37 |
| Florida Dr, G42 | 87 | BQ37 |
| Florida Gdns, (Baill.) G69 | 72 | CJ32 |
| Florida Sq, G42 | 87 | BR37 |
| Florida St, G42 | 87 | BR37 |
| Florish Rd, Ersk. PA8 | 44 | AT21 |
| Flowerdale Pl, G53 | | |
| off Waukglen Rd | 100 | BD42 |
| Flowerhill Ind Est, Air. ML6 | 76 | DD29 |
| Flowerhill St, Air. ML6 | 76 | DD29 |
| Flures Av, Ersk. PA8 | 44 | AU21 |
| Flures Cres, Ersk. PA8 | 44 | AU21 |
| Flures Dr, Ersk. PA8 | 44 | AU21 |
| Flures Pl, Ersk. PA8 | 44 | AU21 |
| Fochabers Dr, G52 | 65 | BE31 |
| Fogo Pl, G20 | 48 | BM23 |
| Foinaven Dr, (Thornlie.) G46 | 101 | BH40 |
| Foinaven Gdns, (Thornlie.) G46 | 101 | BH39 |
| Foinaven Way, (Thornlie.) G46 | 102 | BJ40 |
| Footfield Rd, Bell. ML4 | 110 | CV41 |
| Forbes Dr, G40 | 68 | BV32 |
| Forbes Dr, Moth. ML1 | 111 | CX43 |
| Forbes Pl, Pais. PA1 | 82 | AU33 |
| Forbes St, G40 | 68 | BV31 |
| Fordneuk St, G40 | 69 | BW32 |
| Fordoun St, G34 | 72 | CM29 |
| Ford Rd, G12 | 48 | BM25 |
| Ford Rd, (Newt. M.) G77 | 117 | BF50 |
| Fordyce Ct, (Newt. M.) G77 | | |
| off Capelrig Rd | 117 | BF49 |
| Fordyce St, G11 | 66 | BK27 |
| Forehouse Rd, (Kilb.) John. PA10 | 78 | AA34 |
| Foremount Ter La, G12 | 48 | BK26 |
| Fore Row, Ham. ML3 | | |
| off Muir St | 126 | CU49 |
| Forest Dr, (Both.) G71 | 109 | CQ42 |
| Forest Dr, Bell. ML4 | 111 | CY42 |
| Forest Gdns, (Kirk.) G66 | 34 | CC17 |
| Forest Gate, Ham. ML3 | 139 | CR52 |
| Foresthall Cres, G21 | 51 | BW26 |
| Foresthall Dr, G21 | 51 | BW26 |
| Forest La, Ham. ML3 | 140 | CT55 |
| Forest Pl, (Kirk.) G66 | 34 | CC17 |
| Forest Pl, Pais. PA2 | 82 | AU35 |
| Fore St, G14 | 47 | BE26 |
| Forest Rd, (Cumb.) G67 | 23 | DE12 |
| Forest Rd, Lark. ML9 | 144 | DD59 |
| Forest Vw, (Cumb.) G67 | 23 | DE10 |
| Forfar Av, G52 | 84 | BD33 |
| Forfar Cres, (Bishop.) G64 | 51 | BY21 |
| Forgan Gdns, (Bishop.) G64 | 51 | BZ21 |
| Forge, The, (Giff.) G46 | | |
| off Braidpark Dr | 102 | BM42 |

| | | |
|---|---|---|
| Forge Dr, Coat. ML5 | 74 | CV30 |
| Forge Pl, G21 | 69 | BX27 |
| Forge Retail Pk, G31 | 69 | BX31 |
| Forge Rd, Air. ML6 | 77 | DH31 |
| Forge Row, (Calder.) Air. ML6 | 97 | DE35 |
| Forge Shop Cen, The, G31 | 69 | BY32 |
| Forge St, G21 | 69 | BX27 |
| Forgewood Path, Air. ML6 | | |
| off Forge Rd | 77 | DH31 |
| Forgewood Rd, Moth. ML1 | 111 | CY43 |
| Forglen St, G34 | 72 | CK28 |
| Formby Dr, G23 | 30 | BM20 |
| Forres Av, (Giff.) G46 | 102 | BL42 |
| Forres Cres, Bell. ML4 | 111 | CW39 |
| Forres Gate, (Giff.) G46 | 102 | BM43 |
| Forres St, G23 | | |
| off Tolsta St | 31 | BN20 |
| Forres St, (Blan.) G72 | 124 | CL47 |
| Forrest Av, Ham. ML3 | 140 | CT55 |
| Forrest Burn Ct, Air. ML6 | | |
| off Monkscourt Av | 75 | CZ29 |
| Forrest Dr, (Bears.) G61 | 10 | BD12 |
| Forrester Ct, (Bishop.) G64 | | |
| off Crowhill Rd | 50 | BV21 |
| Forrestfield Cres, (Newt. M.) | | |
| G77 | 117 | BF48 |
| Forrestfield Gdns, (Newt. M.) | | |
| G77 off Forrestfield Cres | 117 | BG48 |
| Forrestfield St, G21 | 69 | BW28 |
| Forrest Gate, (Udd.) G71 | 93 | CR36 |
| Forrest St, G40 | 69 | BW32 |
| Forrest St, (Blan.) G72 | 125 | CP46 |
| Forrest St, Air. ML6 | 77 | DF29 |
| Forsyth St, Air. ML6 | 76 | DD29 |
| Forteviot Av, (Baill.) G69 | 72 | CL32 |
| Forteviot Pl, (Baill.) G69 | 72 | CL32 |
| Forth Av, Pais. PA2 | 81 | AN36 |
| Forth Ct, (E.Kil.) G75 | 134 | BU54 |
| Forth Cres, (E.Kil.) G75 | 134 | BU53 |
| Forth Gro, (E.Kil.) G75 | 134 | BU54 |
| Forth Pl, John. PA5 | 79 | AE37 |
| Forth Pl, Lark. ML9 | | |
| off Glengonnar St | 144 | DD61 |
| Forth Rd, (Bears.) G61 | 29 | BF19 |
| Forth Rd, (Torr.) G64 | 15 | BX13 |
| Forth St, G41 | 87 | BP34 |
| Forth St, Clyde. G81 | 27 | AY20 |
| Forth Ter, Ham. ML3 | 139 | CR53 |
| Forth Wk, (Cumb.) G67 | | |
| off Cumbernauld Shop Cen | 22 | DB11 |
| Forties Ct, (Thornlie.) G46 | 101 | BH40 |
| Forties Cres, (Thornlie.) G46 | 102 | BJ40 |
| Forties Gdns, (Thornlie.) G46 | 102 | BJ40 |
| Forties Way, (Thornlie.) G46 | 102 | BJ40 |
| Fortieth Av, (E.Kil.) G75 | 136 | CB56 |
| Fortingall Av, G12 | 48 | BL23 |
| Fortingall Pl, G12 | 48 | BL23 |
| Fortingall Rd, (Blan.) G72 | 125 | CP48 |
| Fortrose St, G11 | 66 | BK27 |
| Fort St, Moth. ML1 | 127 | CY45 |
| Forum Pl, Moth. ML1 | 111 | CY44 |
| Fossil Gro, (Kirk.) G66 | 18 | CJ12 |
| Foswell Dr, G15 | 28 | BB16 |
| Foswell Pl, G15 | 28 | BB16 |
| Fotheringay La, G41 | 86 | BM35 |
| Fotheringay Rd, G41 | 86 | BM35 |
| Foulis La, G13 | 47 | BH23 |
| Foulis St, G13 | | |
| off Crow Rd | 47 | BH23 |
| Foundry La, (Barr.) G78 | 99 | AY42 |
| Foundry St, G21 | 50 | BV25 |
| Fountain Av, (Inch.) Renf. PA4 | 43 | AR25 |
| Fountain Cres, (Inch.) Renf. PA4 | 43 | AR24 |

| | | |
|---|---|---|
| Fountain Dr, (Inch.) Renf. PA4 | 44 | AS24 |
| Fountainwell Av, G21 | 50 | BT26 |
| Fountainwell Dr, G21 | 68 | BT27 |
| Fountainwell Pl, G21 | 68 | BT27 |
| Fountainwell Rd, G21 | 68 | BT27 |
| Fountainwell Sq, G21 | 68 | BU27 |
| Fountainwell Ter, G21 | 68 | BU27 |
| Fourth Av, G33 | 52 | CD24 |
| Fourth Av, (Kirk.) G66 | 35 | CF20 |
| Fourth Av, Renf. PA4 | 63 | AY27 |
| Fourth Gdns, G41 | 86 | BJ33 |
| Fourth Rd, (Blan.) G72 | 125 | CN48 |
| Fourth St, (Udd.) G71 | 93 | CP36 |
| Fowlis Dr, (Newt. M.) G77 | 117 | BE47 |
| Foxbar Cres, Pais. PA2 | 81 | AN38 |
| Foxbar Dr, G13 | 46 | BD23 |
| Foxbar Dr, Pais. PA2 | 81 | AN38 |
| Foxbar Rd, (Elder.) John. PA5 | 80 | AM38 |
| Foxbar Rd, Pais. PA2 | 81 | AP38 |
| Foxes Gro, (Lenz.) G66 | 35 | CG16 |
| Foxglove Pl, G53 | 100 | BD42 |
| Fox Gro, Moth. ML1 | 127 | CX46 |
| Foxhills Pl, G23 | 31 | BN20 |
| Foxley St, G32 | 91 | CE36 |
| Fox St, G1 | 4 | BR31 |
| Foyers Ter, G21 | 51 | BW25 |
| Francis St, G5 | 87 | BQ33 |
| Frankfield Rd, G33 | 53 | CG24 |
| Frankfield St, G33 | 69 | BZ27 |
| Frankfort St, G41 | 87 | BN36 |
| Franklin Pl, (E.Kil.) G75 | 135 | BX52 |
| Franklin St, G40 | 88 | BV34 |
| Fraser Av, (Ruther.) G73 | 89 | BY38 |
| Fraser Av, (Newt. M.) G77 | 117 | BG47 |
| Fraser Av, Bish. PA7 | 24 | AK17 |
| Fraser Av, John. PA5 | 80 | AJ35 |
| Fraser Ct, Air. ML6 | | |
| off Station Rd | 77 | DG29 |
| Fraser Cres, Ham. ML3 | 139 | CR51 |
| Fraser Gdns, (Kirk.) G66 | 16 | CD13 |
| Fraser River Twr, (E.Kil.) G75 | 135 | BZ52 |
| Fraser St, (Camb.) G72 | 106 | CA39 |
| Frazer St, G40 | 69 | BW32 |
| Frederick St, Coat. ML5 | 74 | CU29 |
| Freeland Ct, G53 | 101 | BE39 |
| Freeland Cres, G53 | 100 | BD39 |
| Freeland Dr, G53 | 100 | BD39 |
| Freeland Dr, (Inch.) Renf. PA4 | 44 | AS23 |
| Freeland La, (E.Kil.) G75 | | |
| off Bell Grn E | 136 | CB53 |
| Freeland Pl, (Kirk.) G66 | 17 | CF13 |
| Freelands Ct, (Old Kil.) G60 | | |
| off Freelands Rd | 26 | AS16 |
| Freelands Cres, (Old Kil.) G60 | 26 | AS16 |
| Freelands Pl, (Old Kil.) G60 | | |
| off Freelands Rd | 26 | AS17 |
| Freelands Rd, (Old Kil.) G60 | 26 | AS16 |
| Freesia Ct, Moth. ML1 | 128 | DA48 |
| French St, G40 | 88 | BV34 |
| French St, Clyde. G81 | 26 | AU18 |
| French St, Renf. PA4 | 63 | AX27 |
| Freuchie St, G34 | 72 | CK30 |
| Frew St, Air. ML6 | 76 | DC29 |
| Friar Av, (Bishop.) G64 | 33 | BX17 |
| Friarscourt Av, G13 | 47 | BF21 |
| Friarscourt Rd, (Chry.) G69 | 36 | CK20 |
| Friars Cft, (Kirk.) G66 | 17 | CG13 |
| Friars Pl, G13 | | |
| off Knightswood Rd | 47 | BF21 |
| Friars Way, Air. ML6 | 97 | DE33 |
| Friarton Rd, G43 | 103 | BP39 |
| Friendship Way, Renf. PA4 | 63 | AZ28 |
| Frood St, Moth. ML1 | 111 | CY44 |

| Name | Page | Grid |
|---|---|---|
| Fruin Av, (Newt. M.) G77 | 117 | BG47 |
| Fruin Pl, G22 | 50 | BS25 |
| Fruin Ri, Ham. ML3 | 139 | CN51 |
| Fruin Rd, G15 | 28 | BB20 |
| Fruin St, G22 | 50 | BS25 |
| Fulbar Av, Renf. PA4 | 45 | AY25 |
| Fulbar Ct, Renf. PA4 | | |
| *off Fulbar Av* | 45 | AZ25 |
| Fulbar Cres, Pais. PA2 | 81 | AP35 |
| Fulbar Gdns, Pais. PA2 | 81 | AP35 |
| Fulbar La, Renf. PA4 | 45 | AZ25 |
| Fulbar Rd, G51 | 65 | BE30 |
| Fulbar Rd, Pais. PA2 | 81 | AP34 |
| Fulbar St, Renf. PA4 | 45 | AZ25 |
| Fullarton Av, G32 | 90 | CC35 |
| Fullarton Dr, G32 | 90 | CC36 |
| Fullarton La, G32 | 90 | CC35 |
| Fullarton Pl, Coat. ML5 | 94 | CT34 |
| Fullarton Rd, G32 | 90 | CB37 |
| Fullarton Rd, (Cumb.) G68 | 9 | DA8 |
| Fullarton St, Coat. ML5 | 94 | CU34 |
| Fullerton St, Pais. PA3 | 62 | AT30 |
| Fullerton Ter, Pais. PA3 | 62 | AU30 |
| Fulmar Ct, (Bishop.) G64 | 50 | BV21 |
| Fulmar Pk, (E.Kil.) G74 | 121 | BZ50 |
| Fulmar Pl, John. PA5 | 79 | AE38 |
| Fulton Cres, (Kilb.) John. PA10 | 78 | AC34 |
| Fulton St, G13 | 47 | BF22 |
| Fulwood Av, G13 | 46 | BC22 |
| Fulwood Av, (Linw.) Pais. PA3 | 60 | AK31 |
| Fulwood Pl, G13 | 46 | BB22 |
| Furlongs, The, Ham. ML3 | 126 | CU48 |
| Fyne Av, (Righead Ind. Est.) Bell. ML4 | 94 | CU38 |
| Fyne Ct, Ham. ML3 | 139 | CQ52 |
| Fyne Cres, Lark. ML9 | 142 | DB56 |
| Fyne Way, Moth. ML1 | | |
| *off Howden Pl* | 112 | DC40 |
| Fyvie Av, G43 | 102 | BK40 |
| Fyvie Cres, Air. ML6 | | |
| *off Grantown Av* | 77 | DH30 |

## G

| Name | Page | Grid |
|---|---|---|
| Gadie Av, Renf. PA4 | 64 | BA27 |
| Gadie St, G33 | 69 | BZ29 |
| Gadloch Av, (Kirk.) G66 | 35 | CF19 |
| Gadloch Gdns, (Kirk.) G66 | 35 | CF18 |
| Gadloch St, G22 | 50 | BS23 |
| Gadloch Vw, (Kirk.) G66 | 35 | CF19 |
| Gadsburn Ct, G21 | 51 | BY23 |
| Gadshill St, G21 | 68 | BV28 |
| Gailes Pk, (Both.) G71 | 109 | CP43 |
| Gailes Rd, (Cumb.) G68 | 9 | DB8 |
| Gailes St, G40 | 89 | BX33 |
| Gain & Shankburn Rd, G67 | 39 | CX20 |
| Gainburn Ct, (Cumb.) G67 | 38 | CV15 |
| Gainburn Cres, (Cumb.) G67 | 38 | CV16 |
| Gainburn Gdns, (Cumb.) G67 | 38 | CV16 |
| Gainburn Pl, (Cumb.) G67 | 38 | CV15 |
| Gainburn Vw, (Cumb.) G67 | 39 | CW15 |
| Gain Rd, G67 | 39 | CW20 |
| Gain St, Coat. ML5 | 39 | CW20 |
| Gainside Rd, (Glenb.) Coat. ML5 | 56 | CS23 |
| Gairbraid Av, G20 | 48 | BL23 |
| Gairbraid Ct, G20 | 48 | BL23 |
| Gairbraid Pl, G20 | 48 | BM23 |
| Gairbraid Ter, (Baill.) G69 | 73 | CQ32 |
| Gairloch Gdns, (Kirk.) G66 | 18 | CK12 |
| Gala Av, Renf. PA4 | 64 | BA27 |
| Gala St, G33 | 70 | CA27 |
| Galbraith Av, G51 | | |
| *off Burghead Dr* | 65 | BG29 |

| Name | Page | Grid |
|---|---|---|
| Galbraith Dr, G51 | | |
| *off Skipness Dr* | 65 | BF29 |
| Galbraith Dr, (Miln.) G62 | 11 | BH13 |
| Galbraith St, G51 | | |
| *off Moss Rd* | 65 | BF29 |
| Galdenoch St, G33 | 70 | CD27 |
| Gallacher Av, Pais. PA2 | 81 | AQ36 |
| Gallacher Ct, Moth. ML1 | 128 | DD50 |
| Gallan Av, G23 | 31 | BN20 |
| Galloway Av, Ham. ML3 | 140 | CS54 |
| Galloway Dr, (Ruther.) G73 | 105 | BX42 |
| Galloway Rd, (E.Kil.) G74 | 123 | CE50 |
| Galloway Rd, Air. ML6 | 76 | DB32 |
| Galloway St, G21 | 50 | BV23 |
| Gallowflat St, (Ruther.) G73 | 89 | BX37 |
| Gallowgate, G1 | 5 | BT31 |
| Gallowgate, G4 | 5 | BU31 |
| Gallowgate, G31 | 69 | BW31 |
| Gallowgate, G40 | 5 | BU31 |
| Gallow Grn Rd, Pais. PA1 | 82 | AS33 |
| Gallowhill, Lark. ML9 | 144 | DC59 |
| Gallowhill Av, (Lenz.) G66 | 35 | CE15 |
| Gallowhill Ct, Pais. PA3 | | |
| *off Montgomery Rd* | 63 | AW29 |
| Gallowhill Gro, (Kirk.) G66 | 17 | CE14 |
| Gallowhill Rd, (Kirk.) G66 | 35 | CE15 |
| Gallowhill Rd, (Carm.) G76 | 120 | BT45 |
| Gallowhill Rd, Pais. PA3 | 63 | AW31 |
| Galston Av, (Newt. M.) G77 | 118 | BJ48 |
| Galston Ct, Ham. ML3 | 140 | CU54 |
| Galston St, G53 | 100 | BB39 |
| Galt Pl, (E.Kil.) G75 | 135 | BZ54 |
| Gamrie Dr, G53 | 84 | BC38 |
| Gamrie Gdns, G53 | 84 | BC38 |
| Gamrie Rd, G53 | 84 | BC37 |
| Gannochy Dr, (Bishop.) G64 | 33 | BY20 |
| Gantock Cres, G33 | 70 | CD29 |
| Gardenhall, (E.Kil.) G75 | 134 | BT53 |
| Gardenhall Ct, (E.Kil.) G75 | 134 | BT53 |
| Gardenside Av, G32 | 90 | CD37 |
| Gardenside Av, (Udd.) G71 | 109 | CN39 |
| Gardenside Cres, G32 | 90 | CD37 |
| Gardenside Gro, G32 | 90 | CD37 |
| Gardenside Pl, G32 | 90 | CD37 |
| Gardenside St, (Udd.) G71 | 109 | CN39 |
| Gardensquare Wk, Air. ML6 | 75 | CZ29 |
| Gardner Gro, (Udd.) G71 | 93 | CQ37 |
| Gardner St, G11 | 66 | BK27 |
| Gardyne St, G34 | | |
| *off Conisborough Rd* | 72 | CJ28 |
| Gareloch Av, Air. ML6 | 76 | DB27 |
| Garelock Av, Pais. PA2 | 81 | AQ35 |
| Garfield Av, Bell. ML4 | 111 | CY40 |
| Garfield Dr, Bell. ML4 | 111 | CX41 |
| Garfield St, G31 | 69 | BW31 |
| Garforth Rd, (Baill.) G69 | 91 | CH33 |
| Gargrave Av, (Baill.) G69 | 91 | CH33 |
| Garion Dr, G13 | 46 | BD23 |
| Garlieston Rd, G33 | 71 | CH31 |
| Garmouth Ct, G51 | 66 | BJ29 |
| Garmouth Gdns, G51 | | |
| *off Garmouth St* | 66 | BJ29 |
| Garmouth St, G51 | 65 | BH29 |
| Garnet Ct, G4 | | |
| *off New City Rd* | 4 | BQ28 |
| Garnethill St, G3 | 4 | BQ28 |
| Garnet St, G3 | 4 | BQ28 |
| Garngaber Av, (Lenz.) G66 | 35 | CF16 |
| Garngaber Ct, (Kirk.) G66 | 35 | CG16 |
| Garnie Av, Ersk. PA8 | 26 | AT20 |
| Garnie Cres, Ersk. PA8 | 26 | AT20 |
| Garnieland Rd, Ersk. PA8 | 26 | AT20 |
| Garnie La, Ersk. PA8 | 44 | AT21 |

| Name | Page | Grid |
|---|---|---|
| Garnie Oval, Ersk. PA8 | 26 | AT20 |
| Garnie Pl, Ersk. PA8 | 26 | AT20 |
| Garnkirk La, G33 | 53 | CG24 |
| Garnock Pk, (E.Kil.) G74 | 136 | CD52 |
| Garnock St, G21 | 68 | BV27 |
| Garrell Av, (Kilsyth) G65 | 7 | CT4 |
| Garrell Gro, (Kilsyth) G65 | 7 | CT3 |
| Garrell Pl, G65 | 7 | CS5 |
| Garrell Rd, (Kilsyth) G65 | 7 | CS5 |
| Garrell Way, G65 | 7 | CS5 |
| Garrell Way, (Cumb.) G67 | 22 | DA11 |
| Garrick Av, (Newt. M.) G77 | 131 | BF51 |
| Garrick Ct, (Newt. M.) G77 | | |
| *off Garrick Av* | 131 | BF51 |
| Garrioch Cres, G20 | 48 | BM24 |
| Garrioch Dr, G20 | 48 | BM24 |
| Garrioch Gate, G20 | | |
| *off Garrioch Rd* | 48 | BM24 |
| Garriochmill Rd, G20 | 49 | BN25 |
| Garriochmill Way, G20 | | |
| *off South Woodside Rd* | 49 | BP26 |
| Garrioch Quad, G20 | 48 | BM24 |
| Garrioch Rd, G20 | 48 | BM25 |
| Garrion Pl, (Ashgill) Lark. ML9 | 145 | DH60 |
| Garrowhill Dr, (Baill.) G69 | 91 | CH33 |
| Garry Av, (Bears.) G61 | 30 | BJ18 |
| Garry Dr, Pais. PA2 | 81 | AQ35 |
| Garry St, G44 | 87 | BQ38 |
| Garscadden Rd, G15 | 28 | BC20 |
| Garscadden Rd S, G13 | 46 | BC21 |
| Garscadden Vw, Clyde. G81 | | |
| *off Kirkoswald Dr* | 27 | AZ18 |
| Garscube Cross, G4 | 67 | BR27 |
| Garscube Rd, G4 | 49 | BQ26 |
| Garscube Rd, G20 | 49 | BQ26 |
| Gartartan Rd, Pais. PA1 | 64 | BB32 |
| Gartcarron Hill, (Cumb.) G68 | 21 | CY10 |
| Gartcloss Rd, Coat. ML5 | 74 | CS27 |
| Gartconnell Dr, (Bears.) G61 | 29 | BG15 |
| Gartconnell Gdns, (Bears.) G61 | 29 | BG15 |
| Gartconnell Rd, (Bears.) G61 | 29 | BG15 |
| Gartconner Av, (Kirk.) G66 | 18 | CK13 |
| Gartcosh Rd, (Gart.) G69 | 73 | CQ29 |
| Gartcosh Wk, Bell. ML4 | 110 | CV40 |
| Gartcraig Path, G33 | | |
| *off Gartcraig Pl* | 70 | CC28 |
| Gartcraig Pl, G33 | 70 | CB28 |
| Gartcraig Rd, G33 | 70 | CA29 |
| Gartferry Av, (Chry.) G69 | 37 | CP19 |
| Gartferry Rd, (Mood.) G69 | 37 | CN19 |
| Gartferry St, G21 | 50 | BV25 |
| Gartfield St, Air. ML6 | 76 | DD31 |
| Gartgill Rd, Coat. ML5 | 74 | CU27 |
| Garth Dr, Clyde. G81 | 45 | AX22 |
| Garthland Dr, G31 | 69 | BW30 |
| Garthland La, Pais. PA1 | 62 | AV32 |
| Garth St, G1 | | |
| *off Glassford St* | 5 | BS30 |
| Gartlea Av, Air. ML6 | 76 | DC30 |
| Gartlea Gdns, Air. ML6 | | |
| *off South Nimmo St* | 76 | DD30 |
| Gartleahill, Air. ML6 | 76 | DD31 |
| Gartlea Rd, Air. ML6 | 76 | DC30 |
| Gartliston Rd, Coat. ML5 | 56 | CV26 |
| Gartliston Ter, (Baill.) G69 | 73 | CQ32 |
| Gartloch Av, (Gart.) G69 | 54 | CL26 |
| Gartloch Cotts, (Gart.) G69 | 55 | CN26 |
| Gartloch Cotts, (Muir.) G69 | 54 | CK24 |
| Gartloch Ct, (Gart.) G69 | 54 | CL26 |
| Gartloch Rd, G33 | 70 | CB27 |
| Gartloch Rd, G34 | 71 | CE28 |
| Gartloch Rd, (Gart.) G69 | 54 | CL26 |
| Gartloch Way, (Gart.) G69 | 54 | CL26 |

| | | |
|---|---|---|
| Gartly St, G44 | | |
| off Clarkston Rd | 103 | BP41 |
| Gartmore Gdns, (Udd.) G71 | 93 | CN37 |
| Gartmore La, (Mood.) G69 | 37 | CQ19 |
| Gartmore Rd, Pais. PA1 | 83 | AX33 |
| Gartmore Ter, (Camb.) G72 | 106 | CA42 |
| Gartness Dr, Air. ML6 | 77 | DG32 |
| Gartness St, G31 | 69 | BX31 |
| Gartocher Dr, G32 | 71 | CE32 |
| Gartocher Rd, G32 | 71 | CE32 |
| Gartocher Ter, G32 | 71 | CE32 |
| Gartons Rd, G21 | 51 | BY24 |
| Gartsherrie Av, (Glenb.) | | |
| Coat. ML5 | 56 | CV24 |
| Gartsherrie Ind Est, Coat. ML5 | 74 | CV28 |
| Gartsherrie Rd, Coat. ML5 | 74 | CU29 |
| Gartshore Cres, (Kilsyth) G65 | 19 | CP11 |
| Gartshore Gdns, (Cumb.) G68 | 20 | CU12 |
| Gartshore Rd, (Kirk.) G66 | 37 | CQ15 |
| Gartshore Rd, (Cumb.) G68 | 37 | CQ15 |
| Garturk St, G42 | 87 | BR36 |
| Garturk St, Coat. ML5 | 95 | CX33 |
| Garvald Ct, G40 | | |
| off Baltic St | 89 | BW35 |
| Garvald St, G40 | 89 | BX34 |
| Garve Av, G44 | 103 | BQ41 |
| Garvel Cres, G33 | 71 | CG31 |
| Garvel Pl, (Miln.) G62 | 11 | BF11 |
| Garvel Rd, G33 | 71 | CG31 |
| Garvel Rd, (Miln.) G62 | 11 | BG11 |
| Garvin Lea, Bell. ML4 | 95 | CW37 |
| Garvock Dr, G43 | 102 | BJ40 |
| Garwhitter Dr, (Miln.) G62 | 12 | BK11 |
| Gascoyne, (E.Kil.) G75 | 135 | BY54 |
| Gaskin Path, G33 | 53 | CG24 |
| Gask Pl, G13 | 46 | BB21 |
| Gas St, John. PA5 | 80 | AJ34 |
| Gatehouse St, G32 | 70 | CD32 |
| Gateside Av, (Kilsyth) G65 | 7 | CR5 |
| Gateside Av, (Camb.) G72 | 107 | CF40 |
| Gateside Cres, (Barr.) G78 | 99 | AW44 |
| Gateside Cres, Air. ML6 | 76 | DC29 |
| Gateside Gdns, (Barr.) G78 | 98 | AV43 |
| Gateside Pk, (Kilsyth) G65 | 7 | CR5 |
| Gateside Pl, (Kilb.) John. PA10 | 78 | AC34 |
| Gateside Rd, (Barr.) G78 | 98 | AV44 |
| Gateside Rd, Wis. ML2 | 129 | DG49 |
| Gateside St, G31 | 69 | BX31 |
| Gateside St, Ham. ML3 | 140 | CU51 |
| Gateway, The, (E.Kil.) G74 | 122 | CC49 |
| Gaughan Quad, Moth. ML1 | | |
| off Thomson Dr | 127 | CZ48 |
| Gauldry Av, G52 | 85 | BE34 |
| Gauze St, Pais. PA1 | 62 | AU32 |
| Gavell Rd, (Kilsyth) G65 | 6 | CQ6 |
| Gavins Mill Rd, (Miln.) G62 | 12 | BJ12 |
| Gavins Rd, Clyde. G81 | 27 | AX16 |
| Gavin St, Moth. ML1 | 128 | DA48 |
| Gavinton St, G44 | 103 | BP40 |
| Gayne Dr, (Glenb.) Coat. ML5 | 56 | CS23 |
| Gean Ct, (Cumb.) G67 | 23 | DH9 |
| Gear Ter, G40 | 89 | BX35 |
| Geary St, G23 | | |
| off Torrin Rd | 30 | BM20 |
| Geddes Hill, (E.Kil.) G74 | 122 | CD49 |
| Geddes Rd, G21 | 51 | BY22 |
| Gelston St, G32 | 90 | CD33 |
| Gemini Gro, Moth. ML1 | | |
| off Glen Dr | 112 | DD40 |
| Gemmel Pl, (Newt. M.) G77 | 116 | BD49 |
| Generals Gate, (Udd.) G71 | 109 | CN39 |
| General Terminus Quay, G51 | 4 | BP31 |
| Gentle Row, Clyde. G81 | 26 | AV15 |
| George Av, Clyde. G81 | 27 | AY18 |
| George Ct, Ham. ML3 | | |
| off George St | 125 | CQ48 |
| George Ct, Pais. PA1 | | |
| off George St | 82 | AT33 |
| George Cres, Clyde. G81 | 27 | AY18 |
| George Gray St, (Ruther.) G73 | 89 | BY37 |
| George La, Pais. PA1 | 82 | AU33 |
| George Mann Ter, (Ruther.) | | |
| G73 | 105 | BW40 |
| George Pl, Pais. PA1 | 82 | AU33 |
| George Reith Av, G12 | 47 | AF38 |
| George Sq, G2 | 5 | BS30 |
| George St, G1 | 5 | BS30 |
| George St, (Baill.) G69 | 92 | CK33 |
| George St, (Barr.) G78 | 99 | AX42 |
| George St, Air. ML6 | 76 | DA30 |
| George St, (Chap.) Air. ML6 | 97 | DF34 |
| George St, Ham. ML3 | 125 | CQ48 |
| George St, John. PA5 | 79 | AH34 |
| George St, Moth. ML1 | 128 | DA49 |
| George St, (New Stev.) | | |
| Moth. ML1 | 112 | DD41 |
| George St, Pais. PA1 | 82 | AT33 |
| George Way, Lark. ML9 | | |
| off Muirshot Rd | 144 | DD57 |
| Gerard Pl, Bell. ML4 | | |
| off Mosshill Rd | 95 | CW38 |
| Gertrude Pl, (Barr.) G78 | 99 | AW43 |
| Ghillies La, Moth. ML1 | 111 | CY44 |
| Gibbon Cres, (E.Kil.) G74 | 123 | CE50 |
| Gibb St, (Chap.) Air. ML6 | 97 | DF34 |
| Gibson Cres, John. PA5 | 79 | AG35 |
| Gibson Quad, Moth. ML1 | | |
| off Frood St | 111 | CY44 |
| Gibson Rd, Renf. PA4 | 63 | AX29 |
| Gibson St, G12 | 67 | BN27 |
| Gibson St, G40 | 5 | BU31 |
| Giffnock Pk Av, (Giff.) G46 | 102 | BL41 |
| Gifford Dr, G52 | 64 | BC32 |
| Gifford Wynd, Pais. PA2 | 81 | AP35 |
| Gigha Quad, Wis. ML2 | | |
| off Montgomery Cres | 143 | DG52 |
| Gilbertfield Path, G33 | | |
| off Gilbertfield St | 70 | CD27 |
| Gilbertfield Pl, G33 | 70 | CD27 |
| Gilbertfield Rd, (Camb.) G72 | 107 | CE42 |
| Gilbertfield St, G33 | 70 | CD27 |
| Gilbert St, G3 | 66 | BL29 |
| Gilchrist St, Coat. ML5 | 75 | CX29 |
| Gilderdale, (E.Kil.) G74 | 135 | BY51 |
| Gilfillan Way, Pais. PA2 | | |
| off Spencer Dr | 81 | AN37 |
| Gilhill St, G20 | 48 | BM22 |
| Gilia St, (Camb.) G72 | 106 | CA39 |
| Gillbank La, Lark. ML9 | | |
| off Carrick St | 145 | DE59 |
| Gillies Cres, (E.Kil.) G74 | 123 | CF48 |
| Gillies La, (Baill.) G69 | 92 | CL33 |
| Gilmerton St, G32 | 90 | CC33 |
| Gilmour Av, (Thornton.) G74 | 133 | BR51 |
| Gilmour Av, Clyde. G81 | 27 | AX16 |
| Gilmour Cres, (Ruther.) G73 | 88 | BV37 |
| Gilmour Cres, (Eagle.) G76 | 133 | BN56 |
| Gilmour Dr, Ham. ML3 | 139 | CP51 |
| Gilmour Pl, G5 | 88 | BS33 |
| Gilmour Pl, Bell. ML4 | 110 | CV40 |
| Gilmour Pl, Coat. ML5 | 74 | CU29 |
| Gilmour St, (Eagle.) G76 | 133 | BN56 |
| Gilmour St, Clyde. G81 | 27 | AY17 |
| Gilmour St, Pais. PA1 | 62 | AU32 |
| Gilmourton Cres, (Newt. M.) | | |
| G77 | 117 | BF49 |
| Gimmerscroft Cres, Air. ML6 | | |
| off Ream Av | 77 | DH31 |
| Girdons Way, (Udd.) G71 | 109 | CN39 |
| Girdwood Ln, G5 | 88 | BT33 |
| Girthon St, G32 | 91 | CE33 |
| Girvan Cres, (Chap.) Air. ML6 | 97 | DF36 |
| Girvan St, G33 | 69 | BZ28 |
| Glade, The, Lark. ML9 | 144 | DD59 |
| Gladney Av, G13 | 46 | BA21 |
| Gladsmuir Rd, G52 | 64 | BD31 |
| Gladstone Av, (Barr.) G78 | 99 | AX43 |
| Gladstone Av, John. PA5 | 79 | AF38 |
| Gladstone Ct, Ham. ML3 | 125 | CQ48 |
| Gladstone Dr, (E.Kil.) G74 | 134 | BT53 |
| Gladstone St, G4 | 67 | BQ27 |
| Gladstone St, Bell. ML4 | 111 | CX40 |
| Gladstone St, Clyde. G81 | 26 | AV19 |
| Glaive Rd, G13 | 29 | BF20 |
| Glamis Av, (Newt. M.) G77 | 117 | BH48 |
| Glamis Av, (Elder.) John. PA5 | 80 | AK36 |
| Glamis Ct, (New.) Moth. ML1 | 113 | DE43 |
| Glamis Dr, (E.Kil.) G74 | 122 | CB50 |
| Glamis Gdns, (Bishop.) G64 | 33 | BX17 |
| Glamis Rd, G31 | 89 | BZ33 |
| Glanderston Av, (Newt. M.) | | |
| G77 | 116 | BD47 |
| Glanderston Av, (Barr.) G78 | | |
| off Aurs Rd | 100 | BA43 |
| Glanderston Ct, G13 | 46 | BC21 |
| Glanderston Dr, G13 | 46 | BC22 |
| Glanderston Gate, (Newt. M.) | | |
| G77 | 116 | BD47 |
| Glanderston Rd, (Newt. M.) | | |
| G77 | 115 | AZ48 |
| Glasgow Airport, (Abbots.) | | |
| Pais. PA3 | 62 | AT27 |
| Glasgow & Edinburgh Rd, (Baill.) | | |
| G69 | 93 | CP33 |
| Glasgow & Edinburgh Rd, | | |
| Moth. ML1 | 97 | DG37 |
| Glasgow Br, G1 | 4 | BR31 |
| Glasgow Br, G5 | 4 | BR31 |
| Glasgow Br, (Bishop.) G64 | 16 | CB14 |
| Glasgow Business Pk, (Baill.) | | |
| G69 | 72 | CK30 |
| Glasgow Cross, G1 | 5 | BT31 |
| Glasgow E Investment Pk, G32 | 90 | CB36 |
| Glasgow Fort, G34 | 71 | CG28 |
| Glasgow Grn, G1 | 68 | BT32 |
| Glasgow Grn, G40 | 68 | BT32 |
| Glasgow N Retail Pk, G33 | 52 | CA23 |
| Glasgow Rd, G53 | 99 | AZ41 |
| Glasgow Rd, (Miln.) G62 | 12 | BK12 |
| Glasgow Rd, (Kilsyth) G65 | 7 | CR5 |
| Glasgow Rd, (Kirk.) G66 | 16 | CC13 |
| Glasgow Rd, (Cumb.) G67 | 21 | CY14 |
| Glasgow Rd, (Cumb.V.) G67 | 22 | DD9 |
| Glasgow Rd, (Baill.) G69 | 91 | CH33 |
| Glasgow Rd, (Udd.) G71 | 93 | CN38 |
| Glasgow Rd, (Blan.) G72 | 108 | CL44 |
| Glasgow Rd, (Camb.) G72 | 106 | CA39 |
| Glasgow Rd, (Turnlaw) G72 | 106 | CB44 |
| Glasgow Rd, (Ruther.) G73 | 88 | BV35 |
| Glasgow Rd, (E.Kil.) G74 | 122 | CC46 |
| Glasgow Rd, (Eagle.) G76 | 118 | BM50 |
| Glasgow Rd, (Barr.) G78 | 99 | AZ41 |
| Glasgow Rd, Clyde. G81 | 45 | AX21 |
| Glasgow Rd, (Hardgate) | | |
| Clyde. G81 | 27 | AY15 |
| Glasgow Rd, Coat. ML5 | 74 | CS32 |
| Glasgow Rd, Ham. ML3 | 125 | CP47 |
| Glasgow Rd, Pais. PA1 | 63 | AW32 |
| Glasgow Rd, Renf. PA4 | 46 | BA26 |

| | | |
|---|---|---|
| Glasgow Rd, Wis. ML2 | 129 | DG50 |
| Glasgow St, G12 | 49 | BN26 |
| Glassel Rd, G34 | 72 | CM28 |
| Glasserton Pl, G43 | 103 | BP40 |
| Glasserton Rd, G43 | 103 | BP40 |
| Glassford St, G1 | 5 | BS30 |
| Glassford St, (Miln.) G62 | 12 | BK11 |
| Glassford St, Moth. ML1 | 128 | DC49 |
| Glaudhall Av, (Gart.) G69 | 55 | CN22 |
| Glebe, The, (Both.) G71 | 109 | CR43 |
| Glebe Av, (Both.) G71 | 109 | CR43 |
| Glebe Av, (Carm.) G76 | 120 | BT46 |
| Glebe Av, Coat. ML5 | 94 | CT34 |
| Glebe Ct, G4 | 5 | BT29 |
| Glebe Cres, (E.Kil.) G74 | 136 | CB52 |
| Glebe Cres, Air. ML6 | 77 | DF29 |
| Glebe Cres, Ham. ML3 | | |
| *off Glebe St* | 140 | CS51 |
| Glebe Hollow, (Both.) G71 | 109 | CR43 |
| Glebe La, (Newt. M.) G77 | 117 | BF49 |
| Glebe Pl, (Camb.) G72 | 106 | CD40 |
| Glebe Pl, (Ruther.) G73 | 88 | BV37 |
| Glebe Rd, (Newt. M.) G77 | 117 | BF49 |
| Glebe St, G4 | 5 | BT28 |
| Glebe St, (E.Kil.) G74 | 136 | CB52 |
| Glebe St, Bell. ML4 | 110 | CV40 |
| Glebe St, Ham. ML3 | 140 | CS51 |
| Glebe St, Renf. PA4 | 45 | AZ26 |
| Glebe Wynd, (Both.) G71 | 109 | CR43 |
| Gleddoch Cl, G52 | 64 | BA31 |
| Gleddoch Ct, G52 | 64 | BA31 |
| Gleddoch Gate, G52 | 64 | BB31 |
| Gleddoch Rd, G52 | 64 | BA31 |
| Gledstane Rd, Bish. PA7 | 24 | AK19 |
| Glenacre Cres, (Udd.) G71 | 93 | CN37 |
| Glenacre Dr, G45 | 104 | BT42 |
| Glenacre Dr, Air. ML6 | 77 | DF31 |
| Glenacre Gdns, G51 | 104 | BT41 |
| Glenacre Gro, G45 | 104 | BU41 |
| Glenacre Rd, (Cumb.) G67 | 22 | DB13 |
| Glenacre St, G45 | 104 | BT42 |
| Glenacre Ter, G45 | 104 | BT42 |
| Glen Affric, (E.Kil.) G74 | 136 | CD52 |
| Glen Affric Av, G53 | 101 | BE41 |
| Glen Affric Way, (Chap.) Air. ML6 | | |
| *off Glenavon Dr* | 97 | DF36 |
| Glenafton Vw, Ham. ML3 | 139 | CR53 |
| Glenallan Ter, Moth. ML1 | | |
| *off Marmion Cres* | 111 | CZ44 |
| Glenallan Way, Pais. PA2 | 80 | AM38 |
| Glen Almond, (E.Kil.) G74 | 137 | CF51 |
| Glenalmond Rd, (Ruther.) G73 | | |
| *off Fennsbank Av* | 105 | BZ42 |
| Glenalmond St, G32 | 90 | CC33 |
| Glenalva Ct, (Kilsyth) G65 | 7 | CT4 |
| Glenapp Av, Pais. PA2 | 83 | AX36 |
| Glenapp Pl, (Mood.) G69 | | |
| *off Whithorn Cres* | 37 | CP18 |
| Glenapp Rd, Pais. PA2 | 83 | AX36 |
| Glenapp St, G41 | 87 | BP34 |
| Glenarklet Cres, Pais. PA2 | 83 | AW37 |
| Glenarklet Dr, Pais. PA2 | 83 | AW36 |
| Glen Arroch, (E.Kil.) G74 | 136 | CD52 |
| Glenartney Rd, (Chry.) G69 | 36 | CL20 |
| Glenashdale Way, Pais. PA2 | 83 | AW36 |
| Glen Av, G32 | 70 | CD31 |
| Glen Av, (Chry.) G69 | 37 | CP19 |
| Glen Av, (Neil.) G78 | 114 | AU46 |
| Glen Av, Lark. ML9 | 144 | DB60 |
| Glenavon Ct, Ham. ML3 | | |
| *off Swisscot Av* | 139 | CR52 |
| Glenavon Dr, Air. ML6 | 97 | DF36 |
| Glenavon Rd, G20 | 48 | BM22 |
| Glenbank Av, (Lenz.) G66 | 35 | CE17 |
| Glenbank Ct, (Thornlie.) G46 | | |
| *off Glenbank Dr* | 101 | BH43 |
| Glenbank Dr, (Thornlie.) G46 | 101 | BH43 |
| Glenbank Rd, (Lenz.) G66 | 35 | CF17 |
| Glenbarr St, G21 | 68 | BV28 |
| Glen Bervie, (E.Kil.) G74 | 136 | CD51 |
| Glenbervie Cres, (Cumb.) G68 | | |
| *off Lansdowne Dr* | 22 | DB9 |
| Glenbervie Pl, G23 | | |
| *off Hollinwell Rd* | 31 | BN20 |
| Glenbervie Pl, (Newt. M.) G77 | 116 | BC48 |
| Glenboig Fm Rd, (Glenb.) | | |
| Coat. ML5 | 56 | CU23 |
| Glenboig Rd, (Gart.) G69 | 55 | CR21 |
| Glenboig Rd, Coat. ML5 | 56 | CS23 |
| Glenbrittle Dr, Pais. PA2 | 83 | AW36 |
| Glenbrittle Way, Pais. PA2 | 83 | AW36 |
| Glenbuck Av, G33 | 52 | CB23 |
| Glenbuck Dr, G33 | 52 | CB23 |
| Glenburn Av, (Baill.) G69 | 72 | CL32 |
| Glenburn Av, (Chry.) G69 | 37 | CP19 |
| Glenburn Av, (Camb.) G72 | 105 | BZ40 |
| Glenburn Av, Moth. ML1 | 113 | DE41 |
| Glenburn Ct, (Kirk.) G66 | 17 | CF13 |
| Glenburn Cres, (Udd.) G71 | 94 | CS36 |
| Glenburn Cres, Pais. PA2 | 82 | AT37 |
| Glenburn Gdns, (Bishop.) G64 | 32 | BV19 |
| Glenburn Gdns, (Glenb.) | | |
| Coat. ML5 | 56 | CS23 |
| Glenburnie Pl, G34 | 71 | CH30 |
| Glenburn La, G20 | | |
| *off Thornton St* | 49 | BN22 |
| Glenburn Rd, (Giff.) G46 | 102 | BK44 |
| Glenburn Rd, (Bears.) G61 | 29 | BG16 |
| Glenburn Rd, (E.Kil.) G74 | 121 | BW50 |
| Glenburn Rd, Ham. ML3 | 125 | CR50 |
| Glenburn Rd, Pais. PA2 | 81 | AR37 |
| Glenburn St, G20 | 49 | BN22 |
| Glenburn Ter, Moth. ML1 | 112 | DD44 |
| Glenburn Wk, (Baill.) G69 | | |
| *off Glenburn Av* | 72 | CL32 |
| Glenburn Way, (E.Kil.) G74 | 120 | BV50 |
| Glenburn Wynd, Lark. ML9 | | |
| *off Muirshot Rd* | 144 | DD57 |
| Glencairn Av, Wis. ML2 | 129 | DF49 |
| Glencairn Ct, Pais. PA3 | | |
| *off Montgomery Rd* | 63 | AX29 |
| Glencairn Dr, G41 | 86 | BM35 |
| Glencairn Dr, (Chry.) G69 | 37 | CN19 |
| Glencairn Dr, (Ruther.) G73 | 88 | BV37 |
| Glencairn Gdns, G41 | 87 | BN35 |
| Glencairn Gdns, (Camb.) G72 | 107 | CF40 |
| Glencairn La, G41 | 87 | BP35 |
| Glencairn Path, G32 | | |
| *off Hallhill Rd* | 71 | CE31 |
| Glencairn Rd, (Cumb.) G67 | 23 | DE11 |
| Glencairn Rd, Pais. PA3 | 63 | AW29 |
| Glencairn St, (Kirk.) G66 | 17 | CF14 |
| Glencairn St, Moth. ML1 | 128 | DA48 |
| Glencalder Cres, Bell. ML4 | 111 | CX42 |
| Glen Cally, (E.Kil.) G74 | 136 | CD51 |
| Glencally Av, Pais. PA2 | 83 | AX36 |
| Glen Cannich, (E.Kil.) G74 | 136 | CD52 |
| Glen Carron, (E.Kil.) G74 | 136 | CD52 |
| Glencart Gro, (Kilb.) John. PA10 | | |
| *off Milliken Pk Rd* | 79 | AE36 |
| Glencleland Rd, Wis. ML2 | 129 | DF49 |
| Glenclora Dr, Pais. PA2 | 83 | AW36 |
| Glen Clova, (E.Kil.) G74 | 136 | CD51 |
| Glen Clova Dr, (Cumb.) G68 | 21 | CY9 |
| Glenclou St, G20 | 48 | BL22 |
| Glen Clunie, (E.Kil.) G74 | 137 | CF51 |
| Glen Clunie Dr, G53 | 101 | BE41 |
| Glen Clunie Pl, G53 | 101 | BE41 |
| Glencoats Dr, Pais. PA3 | 61 | AQ32 |
| Glencoe Dr, Moth. ML1 | 112 | DC40 |
| Glencoe Pl, G13 | 47 | BG22 |
| Glencoe Pl, Ham. ML3 | 139 | CR53 |
| Glencoe Rd, (Ruther.) G73 | 105 | BZ42 |
| Glencoe St, G13 | 47 | BH22 |
| Glen Cona Dr, G53 | 101 | BE40 |
| Glenconner Way, (Kirk.) G66 | 18 | CJ12 |
| Glencorse Rd, Pais. PA2 | 82 | AS35 |
| Glencorse St, G32 | 70 | CA30 |
| Glen Ct, Coat. ML5 | 74 | CT32 |
| Glen Ct, Moth. ML1 | | |
| *off Range Rd* | 128 | DD49 |
| Glencraig St, Air. ML6 | 76 | DA30 |
| Glen Creran Cres, (Neil.) G78 | 114 | AS47 |
| Glen Cres, G13 | 46 | BA22 |
| Glencroft Av, (Udd.) G71 | 93 | CN37 |
| Glencroft Rd, G44 | 104 | BT40 |
| Glencryan Rd, (Cumb.) G67 | 22 | DD12 |
| Glendale Av, Air. ML6 | 77 | DF31 |
| Glendale Cres, (Bishop.) G64 | 51 | BY21 |
| Glendale Dr, (Bishop.) G64 | 51 | BY21 |
| Glendale Gro, Coat. ML5 | | |
| *off Haddington Way* | 94 | CU34 |
| Glendale Pl, G31 | 69 | BX31 |
| Glendale Pl, (Bishop.) G64 | 51 | BY22 |
| Glendale St, G31 | 69 | BX31 |
| Glendaruel Av, (Bears.) G61 | 30 | BK17 |
| Glendaruel Rd, (Ruther.) G73 | 106 | CA43 |
| Glendarvel Gdns, G22 | 50 | BT25 |
| Glendee Gdns, Renf. PA4 | 63 | AZ27 |
| Glendee Rd, Renf. PA4 | 63 | AZ27 |
| Glen Dene Way, G53 | 101 | BE41 |
| Glen Derry, (E.Kil.) G74 | 137 | CF51 |
| Glen Dessary, (E.Kil.) G74 | 136 | CD53 |
| Glendeveron Way, (Carfin) | | |
| Moth. ML1 | 112 | DC43 |
| Glen Devon, (E.Kil.) G74 | 137 | CF52 |
| Glendevon Pl, Clyde. G81 | 26 | AV18 |
| Glendevon Pl, Ham. ML3 | | |
| *off Swisscot Av* | 139 | CR53 |
| Glendevon Sq, G33 | 70 | CD27 |
| Glen Dewar Pl, G53 | 101 | BE41 |
| Glendinning Rd, G13 | 29 | BG20 |
| Glendoick Pl, (Newt. M.) G77 | 116 | BC48 |
| Glen Doll, (E.Kil.) G74 | 136 | CD52 |
| Glendore St, G14 | 65 | BG27 |
| Glen Douglas Dr, (Cumb.) G68 | 21 | CY9 |
| Glendoune Rd, (Clark.) G76 | 119 | BN48 |
| Glendower Way, Pais. PA2 | 81 | AN37 |
| Glen Dr, Moth. ML1 | 112 | DD40 |
| Glenduffhill Rd, (Baill.) G69 | 71 | CH32 |
| Glen Dye, (E.Kil.) G74 | 136 | CD51 |
| Glen Eagles, (E.Kil.) G74 | 137 | CE52 |
| Gleneagles Av, (Cumb.) G68 | 9 | DC8 |
| Gleneagles Dr, (Bishop.) G64 | 33 | BW18 |
| Gleneagles Dr, (Newt. M.) G77 | 118 | BK49 |
| Gleneagles Gdns, (Bishop.) | | |
| G64 | 32 | BV18 |
| Gleneagles Gate, (Newt. M.) | | |
| G77 | 118 | BK49 |
| Gleneagles La N, G14 | 47 | BE25 |
| Gleneagles La S, G14 | 47 | BE25 |
| Gleneagles Pk, (Both.) G71 | 109 | CP43 |
| Glenelg Cres, (Kirk.) G66 | 18 | CJ12 |
| Glenelg Path, (Glenb.) Coat. ML5 | | |
| *off Glenboig Rd* | 56 | CS23 |
| Glenelg Quad, G34 | 72 | CM28 |
| Glenelm Pl, Bell. ML4 | 111 | CW39 |
| Glen Esk, (E.Kil.) G74 | 137 | CE51 |
| Glen Esk Cres, G53 | 101 | BE41 |

| | | |
|---|---|---|
| Glen Esk Dr, G53 | 101 | BE41 |
| Glen Esk Pl, G53 | | |
| *off Kennishead Rd* | 101 | BE41 |
| Glen Etive Pl, (Ruther.) G73 | 106 | CA43 |
| Glen Falloch, (E.Kil.) G74 | 137 | CE52 |
| Glen Falloch Cres, (Neil.) G78 | 114 | AS48 |
| Glen Farg, (E.Kil.) G74 | 137 | CF52 |
| Glenfarg Ct, Ham. ML3 | 139 | CR53 |
| Glenfarg Cres, (Bears.) G61 | 30 | BK17 |
| Glenfarg Rd, (Ruther.) G73 | 105 | BX41 |
| Glenfarg St, G20 | 67 | BQ27 |
| Glenfarm Rd, Moth. ML1 | 113 | DG41 |
| Glen Farrar, (E.Kil.) G74 | 136 | CD52 |
| Glen Feshie, (E.Kil.) G74 | 136 | CD52 |
| Glenfield Av, Pais. PA2 | 82 | AT38 |
| Glenfield Cres, Pais. PA2 | 98 | AT39 |
| Glenfield Gdns, Pais. PA2 | 98 | AT39 |
| Glenfield Gra, Pais. PA2 | 98 | AU39 |
| Glenfield Gro, Pais. PA2 | 98 | AT39 |
| Glenfield Rd, (E.Kil.) G75 | 136 | CC55 |
| Glenfield Rd, Pais. PA2 | 82 | AS38 |
| Glenfinnan Dr, G20 | 48 | BM23 |
| Glenfinnan Dr, (Bears.) G61 | 30 | BK18 |
| Glenfinnan Gro, Bell. ML4 | 111 | CZ41 |
| Glenfinnan Pl, G20 | | |
| *off Glenfinnan Rd* | 48 | BM23 |
| Glenfinnan Rd, G20 | 48 | BM23 |
| Glenfruin Cres, Pais. PA2 | 83 | AX36 |
| Glen Fruin Dr, Lark. ML9 | 145 | DE60 |
| Glen Fruin Pl, (Chap.) Air. ML6 | | |
| *off Glen Rannoch Dr* | 97 | DF36 |
| Glenfruin Rd, (Blan.) G72 | 124 | CL46 |
| Glen Fyne Rd, (Cumb.) G68 | 21 | CX9 |
| Glen Gairn, (E.Kil.) G74 | 137 | CF51 |
| Glen Gairn Cres, (Neil.) G78 | 114 | AS47 |
| Glen Gdns, (Elder.) John. PA5 | 80 | AL34 |
| Glen Garrel Pl, (Kilsyth) G65 | 7 | CR4 |
| Glengarriff Rd, Bell. ML4 | 95 | CX37 |
| Glen Garry, (E.Kil.) G74 | 136 | CD53 |
| Glengarry Dr, G52 | 65 | BE32 |
| Glengavel Cres, G33 | 52 | CB23 |
| Glen Gavin Way, Pais. PA2 | 83 | AW36 |
| Glengonnar St, Lark. ML9 | 144 | DC61 |
| Glen Gro, (Kilsyth) G65 | 7 | CT3 |
| Glen Gro, (E.Kil.) G75 | 135 | BZ54 |
| Glengyre Pl, G34 | 72 | CM29 |
| Glengyre St, G34 | 72 | CL29 |
| Glenhead Cres, G22 | 50 | BS23 |
| Glenhead Dr, Moth. ML1 | 128 | DA49 |
| Glenhead Rd, (Lenz.) G66 | 35 | CE17 |
| Glenhead Rd, Clyde. G81 | 26 | AV16 |
| Glenhead St, G22 | 50 | BS23 |
| Glenholme Av, Pais. PA2 | | |
| *off Corsebar Rd* | 81 | AR36 |
| Glenhove Rd, (Cumb.) G67 | 22 | DC11 |
| Gleniffer Av, G13 | 46 | BC23 |
| Gleniffer Ct, Pais. PA2 | 81 | AR38 |
| Gleniffer Cres, (Elder.) John. PA5 | 80 | AL36 |
| Gleniffer Dr, (Barr.) G78 | 99 | AW40 |
| Gleniffer Rd, Pais. PA2 | 81 | AR38 |
| Gleniffer Rd, Renf. PA4 | 63 | AX29 |
| Gleniffer Vw, (Neil.) G78 | 114 | AT45 |
| Gleniffer Vw, Clyde. G81 | | |
| *off Kirkoswald Dr* | 27 | AZ18 |
| Glen Isla, (E.Kil.) G74 | 137 | CE51 |
| Glenisla Av, (Mood.) G69 | 37 | CQ17 |
| Glen Isla Av, (Neil.) G78 | 114 | AS48 |
| Glenisla St, G31 | 89 | BZ34 |
| Glenkirk Dr, G15 | 28 | BD19 |
| Glen Kyle Dr, G53 | 101 | BE41 |
| Glen La, Pais. PA3 | 62 | AU32 |
| Glen Lednock Dr, (Cumb.) G68 | 21 | CX9 |
| Glen Lee, (E.Kil.) G74 | 137 | CE51 |
| Glenlee Cres, G52 | 84 | BB34 |
| Glenlee St, Ham. ML3 | 125 | CP48 |
| Glen Lethnot, (E.Kil.) G74 | 137 | CE51 |
| Glen Livet Pl, G53 | | |
| *off Glen Moriston Rd* | 101 | BE41 |
| Glen Livet Rd, (Neil.) G78 | 114 | AS47 |
| Glen Lochay Gdns, (Cumb.) G68 | 21 | CX9 |
| Glenlora Dr, G53 | 84 | BC38 |
| Glenlora Ter, G53 | 84 | BD38 |
| Glen Loy Pl, G53 | 101 | BE41 |
| Glenluce Dr, G32 | 91 | CF34 |
| Glenluce Gdns, (Mood.) G69 | | |
| *off Brady Cres* | 37 | CQ18 |
| Glenluce Ter, (E.Kil.) G74 | 135 | BY51 |
| Glenluggie Rd, (Kirk.) G66 | 18 | CJ14 |
| Glenlui Av, (Ruther.) G73 | 105 | BX40 |
| Glen Luss Gdns, (Cumb.) G68 | 21 | CX9 |
| Glen Luss Pl, G53 | 101 | BE41 |
| Glen Luss Pl, Coat. ML5 | | |
| *off Strathmore Wk* | 75 | CZ32 |
| Glen Lyon, (E.Kil.) G74 | 137 | CE52 |
| Glen Lyon Ct, (Cumb.) G68 | 21 | CX9 |
| Glenlyon Ct, Ham. ML3 | 139 | CR53 |
| Glenlyon Pl, (Ruther.) G73 | 105 | BY43 |
| Glen Lyon Rd, (Neil.) G78 | 114 | AS47 |
| Glen Mallie, (E.Kil.) G74 | 137 | CE52 |
| Glenmalloch Pl, (Elder.) | | |
| John. PA5 | 80 | AL34 |
| Glenmanor Av, (Mood.) G69 | 37 | CN19 |
| Glenmanor Rd, (Chry.) G69 | 37 | CN19 |
| Glenmare Av, (Kirk.) G66 | 18 | CJ14 |
| Glen Mark, (E.Kil.) G74 | 137 | CE51 |
| Glen Mark Rd, (Neil.) G78 | 114 | AS47 |
| Glenmavis Rd, Air. ML6 | 58 | DA26 |
| Glenmavis St, G4 | 4 | BR28 |
| Glen More, (E.Kil.) G74 | 136 | CC52 |
| Glenmore Av, G42 | 88 | BU37 |
| Glenmore Av, Bell. ML4 | 111 | CX42 |
| Glenmore Rd, Moth. ML1 | 113 | DE42 |
| Glen Moriston, (E.Kil.) G74 | 136 | CD52 |
| Glen Moriston Rd, G53 | 101 | BE41 |
| Glen Moriston Rd, (Cumb.) G68 | 21 | CX9 |
| Glenmoss Av, Ersk. PA8 | 25 | AP20 |
| Glen Moy, (E.Kil.) G74 | 136 | CD52 |
| Glenmuir Av, G53 | 101 | BE40 |
| Glenmuir Ct, G53 | 101 | BF40 |
| Glenmuir Cres, G53 | 101 | BE40 |
| Glenmuir Dr, G53 | 100 | BD40 |
| Glen Muir Rd, (Neil.) G78 | 114 | AS47 |
| Glen Nevis, (E.Kil.) G74 | 136 | CD53 |
| Glen Nevis Pl, (Ruther.) G73 | 105 | BY43 |
| Glen Ochil Rd, (Chap.) Air. ML6 | 97 | DF36 |
| Glen Ogilvie, (E.Kil.) G74 | 137 | CE51 |
| Glen Ogle St, G32 | 91 | CF33 |
| Glenoran La, Lark. ML9 | | |
| *off Station Rd* | 144 | DD57 |
| Glenorchard Rd, (Torr.) G64 | 14 | BU13 |
| Glen Orchy Ct, (Cumb.) G68 | 8 | CX8 |
| Glen Orchy Dr, G53 | 101 | BF41 |
| Glen Orchy Dr, (Cumb.) G68 | 21 | CX9 |
| Glen Orchy Gro, G53 | 101 | BE41 |
| Glen Orchy Pl, G53 | | |
| *off Glen Orchy Dr* | 101 | BF41 |
| Glen Orchy Pl, (Cumb.) G68 | 8 | CX8 |
| Glen Orchy Pl, (Chap.) Air. ML6 | | |
| *off Glen Rannoch Dr* | 97 | DF36 |
| Glen Orchy Way, G53 | 101 | BE41 |
| Glen Orrin Way, (Neil.) G78 | 114 | AS47 |
| Glen Pk, Air. ML6 | 77 | DG31 |
| Glenpark Av, (Thornlie.) G46 | 101 | BH43 |
| Glenpark Gdns, (Camb.) G72 | | |
| *off Glenpark Ter* | 90 | CA38 |
| Glenpark Rd, G31 | 69 | BX31 |
| Glenpark St, G31 | 69 | BX31 |
| Glenpark Ter, (Camb.) G72 | 90 | CA38 |
| Glenpatrick Bldgs, (Elder.) | | |
| John. PA5 | 80 | AL36 |
| Glenpatrick Rd, (Elder.) | | |
| John. PA5 | 80 | AM35 |
| Glen Pl, (Clark.) G76 | 119 | BN46 |
| Glen Prosen, (E.Kil.) G74 | 137 | CE51 |
| Glen Quoich, (E.Kil.) G74 | 123 | CF50 |
| Glenraith Path, G33 | | |
| *off Glenraith Rd* | 52 | CD26 |
| Glenraith Rd, G33 | 52 | CD26 |
| Glenraith Sq, G33 | 52 | CD26 |
| Glenraith Wk, G33 | 52 | CD26 |
| Glen Rannoch Dr, (Chap.) | | |
| Air. ML6 | 97 | DF36 |
| Glen Rinnes Dr, (Neil.) G78 | 114 | AT47 |
| Glen Rd, G32 | 70 | CD30 |
| Glen Rd, (Old Kil.) G60 | 25 | AR15 |
| Glen Rd, (Dullatur) G68 | 9 | CZ6 |
| Glen Rd, (E.Kil.) G74 | 120 | BV49 |
| Glen Rd, Air. ML6 | 77 | DG31 |
| Glen Rosa Gdns, (Cumb.) G68 | 21 | CX9 |
| Glen Roy Dr, (Neil.) G78 | 114 | AS47 |
| Glen Sannox Dr, (Cumb.) G68 | 21 | CX9 |
| Glen Sannox Gro, (Cumb.) G68 | 21 | CY9 |
| Glen Sannox Ln, (Cumb.) G68 | 21 | CY9 |
| Glen Sannox Vw, (Cumb.) G68 | 21 | CX9 |
| Glen Sannox Way, (Cumb.) G68 | 21 | CY9 |
| Glen Sannox Wynd, (Cumb.) G68 | 21 | CY9 |
| Glen Sax Dr, Renf. PA4 | 64 | BA28 |
| Glen Shee, (E.Kil.) G74 | 137 | CE51 |
| Glen Shee Av, (Neil.) G78 | 114 | AS47 |
| Glenshee Ct, G31 | 89 | BZ34 |
| Glen Shee Cres, Air. ML6 | | |
| *off Glenavon Dr* | 97 | DF36 |
| Glenshee Gdns, G31 | 90 | CA34 |
| Glenshee St, G31 | 89 | BZ33 |
| Glenshee Ter, Ham. ML3 | 139 | CR53 |
| Glenshiel Av, Pais. PA2 | 83 | AW36 |
| Glenshira Av, Pais. PA2 | 83 | AW36 |
| Glen Shirva Rd, (Kilsyth) G65 | 19 | CP9 |
| Glenside Av, G53 | 84 | BD35 |
| Glenside Dr, (Ruther.) G73 | 105 | BZ42 |
| Glenspean Pl, G43 | | |
| *off Glenspean St* | 86 | BM38 |
| Glenspean Pl, Coat. ML5 | | |
| *off Strathmore Wk* | 75 | CZ32 |
| Glenspean St, G43 | 102 | BL39 |
| Glen St, (Camb.) G72 | 107 | CF41 |
| Glen St, (Barr.) G78 | 99 | AY42 |
| Glen St, Moth. ML1 | 112 | DA44 |
| Glen St, (New.) Moth. ML1 | 113 | DF41 |
| Glen St, Pais. PA3 | 62 | AT32 |
| Glentanar Dr, (Mood.) G69 | 37 | CQ19 |
| Glentanar Pl, G22 | 49 | BR22 |
| Glentanar Rd, G22 | 49 | BR21 |
| Glen Tanner, (E.Kil.) G74 | 123 | CF50 |
| Glen Tarbert Dr, (Neil.) G78 | 114 | AS47 |
| Glentarbert Rd, (Ruther.) G73 | 105 | BZ42 |
| Glen Tennet, (E.Kil.) G74 | 137 | CE51 |
| Glentore Quad, Air. ML6 | 76 | DC27 |
| Glentrool Gdns, G22 | 50 | BS25 |
| Glentrool Gdns, (Mood.) G69 | 37 | CQ18 |
| Glen Turret, (E.Kil.) G74 | 137 | CE51 |
| Glenturret St, G32 | 90 | CC33 |
| Glentyan Av, (Kilb.) John. PA10 | 78 | AC33 |
| Glentyan Dr, G53 | 84 | BC38 |
| Glentyan Pl, G53 | 84 | BC38 |
| Glen Urquhart, (E.Kil.) G74 | 136 | CD52 |
| Glenview, (Kirk.) G66 | 17 | CF13 |
| Glen Vw, (Cumb.) G67 | 23 | DE10 |

| Entry | | |
|---|---|---|
| Glenview, Air. ML6 | | |
| *off North Calder Dr* | 77 | DF31 |
| Glen Vw, Ham. ML3 | 140 | CT54 |
| Glenview, Lark. ML9 | 144 | DB57 |
| Glenview Cres, (Mood.) G69 | 37 | CP18 |
| Glenview Pl, (Blan.) G72 | 108 | CM44 |
| Glenview St, (Glenm.) Air. ML6 | 58 | DA25 |
| Glenvilla Circle, Pais. PA2 | 98 | AT39 |
| Glenvilla Cres, Pais. PA2 | 98 | AT39 |
| Glenvilla Pl, Pais. PA2 | 98 | AT39 |
| Glenvilla Rd, Pais. PA2 | 98 | AT39 |
| Glenvilla Wynd, Pais. PA2 | 98 | AT39 |
| Glenville Av, (Giff.) G46 | 102 | BK42 |
| Glenville Gate, (Clark.) G76 | 119 | BQ48 |
| Glenville Ter, (Clark.) G76 | | |
| *off The Paddock* | 119 | BQ48 |
| Glenwell St, (Glenm.) Air. ML6 | 58 | DA26 |
| Glenwood Av, Air. ML6 | 97 | DE33 |
| Glenwood Business Pk, G45 | 104 | BU42 |
| Glenwood Ct, (Kirk.) G66 | 34 | CC16 |
| Glenwood Dr, (Thornlie.) G46 | 101 | BH43 |
| Glenwood Gdns, (Kirk.) G66 | 34 | CC16 |
| Glenwood Path, G45 | 104 | BU42 |
| Glenwood Pl, G45 | 104 | BU42 |
| Glenwood Pl, (Kirk.) G66 | 34 | CC16 |
| Glenwood Rd, (Kirk.) G66 | 34 | CC16 |
| Globe Ct, (E.Kil.) G74 | | |
| *off Bosworth Rd* | 123 | CF48 |
| Gloucester Av, (Ruther.) G73 | 105 | BZ40 |
| Gloucester Av, (Clark.) G76 | 118 | BM46 |
| Gloucester St, G5 | 67 | BQ32 |
| Gockston Rd, Pais. PA3 | 62 | AT30 |
| Gogar Pl, G33 | 70 | CA29 |
| Gogar St, G33 | 70 | CA29 |
| Goil Av, (Righead Ind. Est.) | | |
| Bell. ML4 | 110 | CT39 |
| Goil Way, Moth. ML1 | | |
| *off Howden Pl* | 112 | DC40 |
| Goldberry Av, G14 | 46 | BD24 |
| Goldenacre Pl, (Plains) Air. ML6 | 59 | DH26 |
| Goldie Rd, (Udd.) G71 | 109 | CQ41 |
| Golf Av, Bell. ML4 | 111 | CX42 |
| Golf Course Rd, (Torr.) G64 | 14 | BU13 |
| Golf Ct, G44 | 103 | BN43 |
| Golf Dr, G15 | 28 | BB20 |
| Golf Dr, Pais. PA1 | 83 | AY33 |
| Golf Gdns, Lark. ML9 | 145 | DE59 |
| Golfhill Dr, G31 | 69 | BW29 |
| Golfhill Quad, Air. ML6 | 76 | DC27 |
| Golfhill Rd, Wis. ML2 | 129 | DF49 |
| Golfhill Ter, G31 | | |
| *off Firpark St* | 68 | BV29 |
| Golf Pl, Bell. ML4 | 111 | CX42 |
| Golf Rd, (Ruther.) G73 | 105 | BX41 |
| Golf Rd, (Clark.) G76 | 118 | BM46 |
| Golf Vw, (Bears.) G61 | 28 | BD16 |
| Golf Vw, Clyde. G81 | 26 | AV17 |
| Golfview Dr, Coat. ML5 | 74 | CS30 |
| Golfview Pl, Coat. ML5 | 74 | CS31 |
| Golspie Av, Air. ML6 | 96 | DA33 |
| Golspie St, G51 | 66 | BJ29 |
| Goodview Gdns, Lark. ML9 | 145 | DE59 |
| Goosedubbs, G1 | 5 | BS31 |
| Gopher Av, (Udd.) G71 | 93 | CR37 |
| Gorbals Cross, G5 | 68 | BS32 |
| Gorbals La, G5 | | |
| *off Oxford St* | 4 | BR31 |
| Gorbals St, G5 | 67 | BR32 |
| Gordon Av, G44 | 103 | BN43 |
| Gordon Av, G52 | 64 | BA29 |
| Gordon Av, (Baill.) G69 | 71 | CH32 |
| Gordon Ct, Air. ML6 | | |
| *off Katherine St* | 77 | DG29 |
| Gordon Cres, (Newt. M.) G77 | 117 | BG47 |
| Gordon Dr, G44 | 103 | BN42 |
| Gordon Dr, (E.Kil.) G74 | 122 | CD50 |
| Gordon La, G1 | | |
| *off Mitchell St* | 4 | BR30 |
| Gordon McMaster Gdns, John. | | |
| PA5 *off Laighcartside St* | 80 | AJ34 |
| Gordon Pl, Bell. ML4 | 110 | CV42 |
| Gordon Rd, G44 | 103 | BN43 |
| Gordon Rd, Ham. ML3 | 125 | CP49 |
| Gordon St, G1 | 4 | BR30 |
| Gordon St, Pais. PA1 | 82 | AU33 |
| Gordon Ter, (Blan.) G72 | 108 | CL43 |
| Gordon Ter, Ham. ML3 | 125 | CP50 |
| Gorebridge St, G32 | 70 | CA30 |
| Gorget Av, G13 | 29 | BE20 |
| Gorget Pl, G13 | 29 | BE20 |
| Gorget Quad, G13 | 28 | BD20 |
| Gorse Dr, (Barr.) G78 | 99 | AX41 |
| Gorse Pl, (Udd.) G71 | 93 | CR37 |
| Gorsewood, (Bishop.) G64 | 32 | BU20 |
| Gorstan Pl, G20 | | |
| *off Wyndford Rd* | 48 | BL24 |
| Gorstan St, G23 | 48 | BM21 |
| Gosford La, G14 | 46 | BC25 |
| Gough St, G33 | 69 | BZ29 |
| Gourlay, (E.Kil.) G74 | 123 | CF48 |
| Gourlay Path, G21 | | |
| *off Endrick St* | 50 | BT26 |
| Gourlay St, G21 | 50 | BT26 |
| Gourock St, G5 | 87 | BQ33 |
| Govan Cross, G51 | | |
| *off Govan Rd* | 66 | BJ29 |
| Govan Cross Shop Cen, G51 | 66 | BJ29 |
| Govanhill St, G42 | 87 | BR35 |
| Govan Rd, G51 | 66 | BL31 |
| Gowanbank Gdns, John. PA5 | | |
| *off Floors St* | 79 | AG35 |
| Gowan Brae, (Kirk.) G66 | | |
| *off Marguerite Av* | 35 | CE15 |
| Gowanlea Av, G15 | 28 | BC20 |
| Gowanlea Dr, (Giff.) G46 | 102 | BM41 |
| Gowanlea Ter, (Udd.) G71 | 93 | CR38 |
| Gower La, G51 | | |
| *off North Gower St* | 66 | BM32 |
| Gower St, G41 | 86 | BL33 |
| Gower St, G51 | 86 | BL33 |
| Gower Ter, G41 | 66 | BL32 |
| Gowkhall Av, Moth. ML1 | 113 | DH42 |
| Goyle Av, G15 | 29 | BE18 |
| Grace Av, (Baill.) G69 | 73 | CP32 |
| Grace St, G3 | 4 | BP30 |
| Graeme Ct, Moth. ML1 | | |
| *off Marmion Cres* | 111 | CZ43 |
| Graffham Av, (Giff.) G46 | 102 | BM42 |
| Grafton Pl, G1 | 5 | BS29 |
| Graham Av, (Camb.) G72 | 107 | CF40 |
| Graham Av, (E.Kil.) G74 | 136 | CA51 |
| Graham Av, Clyde. G81 | 27 | AX18 |
| Graham Av, Ham. ML3 | 140 | CT53 |
| Graham Dr, (Miln.) G62 | 11 | BG11 |
| Graham Pl, (Kilsyth) G65 | 7 | CS3 |
| Graham Pl, (Ashgill) Lark. ML9 | 145 | DH60 |
| Grahamsdyke Rd, (Kirk.) G66 | 17 | CG12 |
| Grahamshill Av, Air. ML6 | 77 | DF29 |
| Grahamshill St, Air. ML6 | 77 | DE29 |
| Graham Sq, G31 | 68 | BV31 |
| Grahamston Ct, Pais. PA2 | 83 | AY37 |
| Grahamston Cres, Pais. PA2 | 83 | AY37 |
| Grahamston Pk, (Barr.) G78 | 99 | AX40 |
| Grahamston Pl, Pais. PA2 | 83 | AY37 |
| Grahamston Rd, (Barr.) G78 | 99 | AX39 |
| Grahamston Rd, Pais. PA2 | 99 | AX39 |
| Graham St, (Barr.) G78 | 99 | AX42 |
| Graham St, Air. ML6 | 76 | DC30 |
| Graham St, Ham. ML3 | 126 | CU50 |
| Graham St, John. PA5 | 79 | AG35 |
| Graham St, Moth. ML1 | 112 | DC40 |
| Graham Ter, (Bishop.) G64 | 51 | BX22 |
| Graignestock Pl, G40 | | |
| *off London Rd* | 68 | BU32 |
| Graignestock St, G40 | 68 | BU32 |
| Grainger Rd, (Bishop.) G64 | 33 | BZ20 |
| Grammar Sch Sq, Ham. ML3 | | |
| *off Church St* | 126 | CU49 |
| Grampian Av, Pais. PA2 | 82 | AT37 |
| Grampian Ct, (Bears.) G61 | 11 | BE13 |
| Grampian Cres, G32 | 90 | CD33 |
| Grampian Cres, (Chap.) | | |
| Air. ML6 | 97 | DH36 |
| Grampian Pl, G32 | 90 | CD33 |
| Grampian Rd, Wis. ML2 | 129 | DH49 |
| Grampian St, G32 | 90 | CD33 |
| Grampian Way, (Bears.) G61 | 10 | BD13 |
| Grampian Way, (Cumb.) G68 | 21 | CW11 |
| Grampian Way, (Barr.) G78 | 99 | AY44 |
| Granby La, G12 | 48 | BM26 |
| Grandtully Dr, G12 | 48 | BL23 |
| Grange Av, (Miln.) G62 | 12 | BK11 |
| Grange Av, Wis. ML2 | 143 | DG52 |
| Grange Gdns, (Both.) G71 | | |
| *off Blairston Av* | 109 | CR44 |
| Grangeneuk Gdns, (Cumb.) | | |
| G68 | 21 | CY12 |
| Grange Rd, G42 | 87 | BQ37 |
| Grange Rd, (Bears.) G61 | 29 | BH16 |
| Grange St, Moth. ML1 | 128 | DC49 |
| Grannoch Pl, Coat. ML5 | 95 | CZ35 |
| Gran St, Clyde. G81 | 46 | BA21 |
| Grant Ct, Air. ML6 | 77 | DG29 |
| Grant Ct, Ham. ML3 | 140 | CS55 |
| Grantholm Av, Moth. ML1 | 112 | DD39 |
| Grantlea Gro, G32 | 91 | CF33 |
| Grantlea Ter, G32 | 91 | CF33 |
| Grantley Gdns, G41 | 86 | BM37 |
| Grantley St, G41 | 86 | BM37 |
| Grantoften Path, (E.Kil.) G75 | 135 | BZ55 |
| Granton St, G5 | 88 | BU35 |
| Grantown Av, Air. ML6 | 77 | DG31 |
| Grantown Gdns, (Glenm.) | | |
| Air. ML6 | 58 | DB24 |
| Grants Av, Pais. PA2 | 82 | AS36 |
| Grants Cres, Pais. PA2 | 82 | AT37 |
| Grants Pl, Pais. PA2 | 82 | AS37 |
| Grant St, G3 | 4 | BP28 |
| Grants Way, Pais. PA2 | 82 | AS36 |
| Granville St, G3 | 4 | BP29 |
| Granville St, Clyde. G81 | 27 | AX18 |
| Grasmere, (E.Kil.) G75 | 134 | BV56 |
| Grasmere Ct, Ham. ML3 | | |
| *off Ambleside Ri* | 140 | CT55 |
| Grathellen Ct, Moth. ML1 | 128 | DC45 |
| Gray Dr, (Bears.) G61 | 29 | BH18 |
| Grayshill Rd, (Cumb.) G68 | 38 | CU15 |
| Gray's Rd, (Udd.) G71 | 109 | CR40 |
| Gray St, G3 | 67 | BN28 |
| Gray St, (Kirk.) G66 | 18 | CK14 |
| Gray St, Lark. ML9 | 144 | DC57 |
| Great Dovehill, G1 | 5 | BT31 |
| Great George St, G12 | 48 | BM26 |
| Great Hamilton St, Pais. PA2 | 82 | AU35 |
| Great Kelvin La, G12 | | |
| *off Glasgow St* | 67 | BN27 |
| Great Western Business Pk, G15 | 28 | BA19 |
| Great Western Retail Pk, G15 | 28 | BA20 |

Great Western Rd, G4 — 49 BN26
Great Western Rd, G12 — 48 BK25
Great Western Rd, G13 — 28 BB20
Great Western Rd, G15 — 28 BB20
Great Western Ter, G12 — 48 BL25
Great Western Ter La, G12 — 48 BL25
Green, The, G40 — 68 BU32
Greenacres, Moth. ML1 — 127 CY48
Greenacres Ct, G53 — 101 BE41
Greenacres Dr, G53 — 101 BE41
Greenacres Vw, Moth. ML1
  off Greenacres — 127 CY48
Greenacres Way, G53 — 101 BE41
Greenan Av, G42 — 88 BU38
Greenbank, (Blan.) G72
  off Moorfield Rd — 124 CL46
Greenbank Av, (Giff.) G46 — 118 BJ46
Greenbank Dr, Pais. PA2 — 82 AT38
Greenbank Rd, (Cumb.) G68 — 21 CY11
Greenbank St, (Ruther.) G73 — 89 BW37
Greendyke St, G1 — 5 BT31
Greenend Av, John. PA5 — 79 AF36
Greenend Pl, G32 — 71 CE30
Greenend Vw, Bell. ML4 — 110 CV41
Greenfarm Rd, (Newt. M.) G77 — 116 BD47
Greenfarm Rd, (Linw.) Pais. PA3 — 60 AK31
Greenfaulds Cres, (Cumb.) G67 — 22 DC13
Greenfaulds Rd, (Cumb.) G67 — 22 DA14
Greenfield Av, G32 — 70 CD31
Greenfield Pl, G32 — 70 CD31
Greenfield Quad, Moth. ML1
  off Mossbank Cres — 113 DH41
Greenfield Rd, G32 — 71 CE30
Greenfield Rd, (Clark.) G76 — 119 BN47
Greenfield Rd, Ham. ML3 — 125 CQ47
Greenfield St, G51 — 65 BH30
Greengairs Av, G51 — 65 BF29
Greengairs Rd, (Green.)
  Air. ML6 — 58 DD21
Greenhall Pl, (Blan.) G72 — 124 CL47
Greenhead Rd, (Bears.) G61 — 29 BH17
Greenhead Rd, (Inch.)
  Renf. PA4 — 44 AS22
Greenhead St, G40 — 88 BU33
Greenhill, (Bishop.) G64 — 51 BY21
Greenhill Av, (Giff.) G46 — 102 BK44
Greenhill Av, (Gart.) G69 — 55 CN22
Greenhill Business Pk, Pais. PA3 — 62 AS31
Greenhill Ct, (Ruther.) G73 — 89 BW37
Greenhill Cres, (Elder.)
  John. PA5 — 80 AM35
Greenhill Cres, (Linw.) Pais. PA3 — 60 AK31
Greenhill Dr, (Linw.) Pais. PA3 — 60 AL31
Greenhill Rd, (Ruther.) G73 — 89 BW37
Greenhill Rd, Pais. PA3 — 62 AS31
Greenhills Cres, (E.Kil.) G75 — 135 BX56
Greenhills Rd, (E.Kil.) G75 — 134 BU53
Greenhills Sq, (E.Kil.) G75
  off Greenhills Cres — 135 BX56
Greenhill St, (Ruther.) G73 — 89 BW38
Greenholm Av, (Udd.) G71 — 93 CN38
Greenholm Av, (Clark.) G76 — 119 BN46
Greenholme St, G44 — 103 BQ39
Greenknowe Rd, G43 — 102 BK39
Greenlaw Av, Pais. PA1 — 63 AW32
Greenlaw Ct, G14 — 45 AZ23
Greenlaw Cres, Pais. PA1 — 63 AW31
Greenlaw Dr, (Newt. M.) G77 — 117 BE48
Greenlaw Dr, Pais. PA1 — 63 AW32
Greenlaw Gdns, Pais. PA1 — 63 AW31
Greenlaw Rd, G14 — 45 AZ23
Greenlaw Rd, (Newt. M.) G77 — 117 BE48
Greenlea Rd, (Chry.) G69 — 54 CK21

Greenlea St, G13 — 47 BG23
Greenlees Gdns, (Camb.) G72 — 106 CB42
Greenlees Pk, (Camb.) G72 — 106 CC42
Greenlees Rd, (Camb.) G72 — 106 CC40
Greenless Gro, Coat. ML5
  off Laxford Pl — 75 CZ32
Green Ln, Moth. ML1
  off Woodside St — 112 DC42
Greenloan Av, G51 — 65 BF29
Greenloan Vw, Lark. ML9
  off Keir Hardie Rd — 144 DD60
Greenlodge Ter, G40
  off Greenhead St — 88 BU33
Greenmoss Pl, Bell. ML4 — 111 CX40
Greenmount, G22 — 49 BQ22
Greenoakhill Av, (Udd.) G71 — 92 CK35
Greenoakhill Cres, (Udd.) G71 — 92 CJ35
Greenoakhill Pl, (Udd.) G71 — 92 CJ35
Greenoakhill Rd, (Udd.) G71 — 92 CJ35
Greenock Av, G44 — 103 BR40
Greenock Rd, Pais. PA3 — 62 AS29
Greenock Rd, (Inch.) Renf. PA4 — 43 AR23
Green Pl, (Both.) G71 — 109 CR43
Green Pl, (Calder.) Air. ML6
  off Faskine Av — 96 DD35
Greenrig, (Udd.) G71 — 109 CP39
Greenrigg Rd, (Cumb.) G67 — 22 DC12
Greenrig St, G33 — 51 BZ26
Greenrig St, (Udd.) G71 — 109 CP39
Green Rd, (Ruther.) G73 — 89 BW37
Green Rd, Pais. PA2 — 81 AP34
Greens Av, (Kirk.) G66 — 17 CE14
Greens Cres, (Kirk.) G66 — 17 CE14
Greenshields Rd, (Baill.) G69 — 72 CK32
Greenside Cres, G33 — 52 CA26
Greenside Pl, (Bears.) G61
  off Moorfoot Way — 11 BE13
Greenside Rd, (Clark.) G76 — 120 BT45
Greenside Rd, Moth. ML1 — 97 DE38
Greenside St, G33 — 52 CA26
Greenside St, Coat. ML5 — 75 CX28
Greenside St, Moth. ML1
  off Manse Vw — 113 DH41
Greens Rd, (Cumb.) G67 — 40 DB15
Green St, G40 — 68 BU32
Green St, (Both.) G71 — 109 CR43
Green St, Clyde. G81 — 27 AW18
Greentree Dr, (Baill.) G69 — 91 CH34
Greenview St, G43 — 86 BL37
Greenway La, (Blan.) G72
  off Hunthill Rd — 124 CL47
Greenways Av, Pais. PA2 — 81 AQ35
Greenways Ct, Pais. PA2 — 81 AQ35
Greenwood Av, (Chry.) G69 — 37 CP19
Greenwood Av, (Camb.) G72 — 107 CF39
Greenwood Ct, (Clark.) G76 — 119 BN47
Greenwood Cres, Coat. ML5 — 75 CY32
Greenwood Dr, (Bears.) G61 — 30 BJ17
Greenwood Dr, John. PA5 — 79 AF37
Greenwood Quad, Clyde. G81 — 27 AZ20
Greenwood Rd, (Clark.) G76 — 118 BM46
Greer Quad, Clyde. G81 — 27 AX17
Grenada Pl, (E.Kil.) G75 — 135 BW52
Grenadier Gdns, Moth. ML1 — 127 CZ50
Grenville Dr, (Camb.) G72 — 106 CB41
Gresham Vw, Moth. ML1 — 142 DD51
Gretna St, G40 — 89 BX33
Greyfriars Rd, (Udd.) G71 — 92 CL37
Greyfriars St, G32 — 70 CB30
Greystone Av, (Ruther.) G73 — 105 BY39
Greywood St, G13 — 47 BG22
Grier Path, G31
  off Crail St — 69 BZ32

Grier Pl, Lark. ML9 — 144 DB59
Grierson La, G33
Grierson St, G33
  off Lomax St — 69 BZ29
Grierson St, G33 — 69 BZ29
Grieve Cft, (Both.) G71 — 109 CP44
Grieve Rd, (Cumb.) G67 — 22 DC10
Griffin Av, Pais. PA1 — 61 AN32
Griffin Pl, Bell. ML4
  off Garvin Lea — 95 CW37
Griqua Ter, (Both.) G71 — 109 CR43
Grogarry Rd, G15 — 28 BC17
Grosvenor Cres, G12 — 48 BM26
Grosvenor Cres La, G12
  off Byres Rd — 48 BM26
Grosvenor La, G12 — 48 BM26
Grosvenor Ter, G12 — 48 BM26
Grove, The, (Giff.) G46 — 118 BK45
Grove, The, (Neil.) G78 — 114 AS47
Grove, The, (Kilb.) John. PA10 — 78 AC33
Groveburn Av, (Thornlie.) G46 — 102 BJ41
Grove Cres, Lark. ML9 — 145 DE59
Grove Pk, (Lenz.) G66 — 35 CF17
Grovepark Ct, G20 — 67 BQ27
Grovepark Gdns, G20 — 67 BQ27
Grovepark Pl, G20 — 49 BQ26
Grovepark St, G20 — 49 BQ26
Groves, The, (Bishop.) G64
  off Woodhill Gro — 51 BY22
Grove Way, Bell. ML4
  off Caledonian Av — 110 CV41
Grove Wd, (Udd.) G71 — 94 CT36
Grovewood Business Pk,
  Bell. ML4 — 94 CU37
Grove Wynd, Moth. ML1
  off Moore St — 112 DC42
Grudie St, G34 — 72 CJ29
Gryffe Av, Renf. PA4 — 45 AX24
Gryffe Cres, Pais. PA2 — 81 AP35
Gryffe St, G44 — 103 BQ39
Guildford St, G33 — 71 CE28
Gullane Ct, Ham. ML3
  off Loch Grn — 139 CR53
Gullane Cres, (Cumb.) G68 — 9 DB7
Gullane St, G11 — 66 BK28
Gunn Quad, Bell. ML4 — 110 CU42
Guthrie Ct, Moth. ML1
  off Malcolm St — 127 CY47
Guthrie Dr, (Udd.) G71 — 93 CQ36
Guthrie Pl, (Torr.) G64 — 15 BY13
Guthrie Pl, (E.Kil.) G74 — 136 CB51
Guthrie St, G20 — 48 BM23
Guthrie St, Ham. ML3 — 126 CT49

## H

Haberlea Av, G53 — 101 BE42
Haberlea Gdns, G53
  off Haberlea Av — 101 BE42
Haddington Way, Coat. ML5 — 94 CU34
Haddow Gro, (Udd.) G71 — 93 CQ37
Haddow St, Ham. ML3 — 126 CU50
Hadrian Ter, Moth. ML1 — 127 CY45
Hagen Dr, Moth. ML1 — 113 DG44
Hagg Cres, John. PA5 — 79 AG34
Hagg Pl, John. PA5 — 79 AG34
Hagg Rd, John. PA5 — 79 AG35
Haggs Rd, G41 — 86 BL36
Haggswood Av, G41 — 86 BL35
Haghill Rd, G31 — 69 BY31
Hagmill Cres, Coat. ML5 — 95 CY35
Hagmill Rd, Coat. ML5 — 95 CX35
Haig Dr, (Baill.) G69 — 91 CH33
Haig St, G21 — 50 BV25

| | | | | | | | | |
|---|---|---|---|---|---|---|---|---|
| Hailes Av, G32 | 71 | CF32 | Hamilton Int Tech Pk, (Blan.) | | | Hareleeshill Rd, Lark. ML9 | 145 | DE59 |
| Haining, The, Renf. PA4 | 63 | AZ27 | G72 | 124 | CL48 | Harestanes Gdns, (Kirk.) G66 | 18 | CJ12 |
| Haining Rd, Renf. PA4 | 45 | AZ26 | Hamilton Pk Av, G12 | 49 | BN26 | Harfield Dr, G32 | 71 | CG31 |
| Hairmyres Dr, (E.Kil.) G75 | 134 | BU53 | Hamilton Pk N, Ham. ML3 | 126 | CT47 | Harfield Gdns, G32 | 71 | CG31 |
| Hairmyres Pk, (E.Kil.) G75 | 134 | BV53 | Hamilton Pk S, Ham. ML3 | 126 | CT47 | Harhill St, G51 | 65 | BH30 |
| Hairmyres Rbt, (E.Kil.) G75 | 134 | BV52 | Hamilton Pl, (E.Kil.) G75 | 136 | CA54 | Harkins Av, (Blan.) G72 | 124 | CL46 |
| Hairst St, Renf. PA4 | 45 | AZ25 | Hamilton Pl, (Neil.) G78 | 114 | AV46 | Harland Cotts, G14 | | |
| Halbeath Av, G15 | 28 | BB18 | Hamilton Pl, Ham. ML3 | 140 | CT55 | off South St | 47 | BE26 |
| Halbert St, G41 | 87 | BN36 | Hamilton Pl, (Holytown) | | | Harland St, G14 | 47 | BE26 |
| Haldane La, G14 | | | Moth. ML1 | 112 | DD41 | Harlaw Gdns, (Bishop.) G64 | 33 | BZ19 |
| off Victoria Pk St | 47 | BF26 | Hamilton Pl, (New.) Moth. ML1 | 113 | DE41 | Harlequin Ct, Ham. ML3 | 139 | CP54 |
| Haldane Pl, (E.Kil.) G75 | 136 | CB54 | Hamilton Rd, G32 | 91 | CF35 | Harley St, G51 | 66 | BL32 |
| Haldane St, G14 | 47 | BF26 | Hamilton Rd, (Both.) G71 | 109 | CR44 | Harmetray St, G22 | 50 | BT23 |
| Halfmerk N, (E.Kil.) G74 | 136 | CC51 | Hamilton Rd, (Udd.) G71 | 92 | CJ35 | Harmony Ct, G52 | 66 | BJ30 |
| Halfmerk S, (E.Kil.) G74 | 136 | CC51 | Hamilton Rd, (Blan.) G72 | 124 | CJ47 | Harmony Pl, G51 | 66 | BJ30 |
| Halgreen Av, G15 | 28 | BA19 | Hamilton Rd, (Camb.) G72 | 106 | CD40 | Harmony Row, G51 | 66 | BJ30 |
| Halifax Way, Renf. PA4 | | | Hamilton Rd, (Ruther.) G73 | 89 | BX37 | Harmony Sq, G51 | | |
| off Britannia Way | 63 | AY28 | Hamilton Rd, (E.Kil.) G74 | 123 | CF48 | off Harmony Row | 66 | BJ30 |
| Hallbrae St, G33 | 70 | CA27 | Hamilton Rd, Bell. ML4 | 110 | CU42 | Harmsworth St, G11 | 65 | BG27 |
| Hallcraig St, Air. ML6 | 76 | DC29 | Hamilton Rd, Lark. ML9 | 142 | DB56 | Harport St, (Thornlie.) G46 | 101 | BG40 |
| Halley Dr, G13 | 46 | BA22 | Hamilton Rd, Moth. ML1 | 127 | CX48 | Harriet Pl, G43 | 102 | BK39 |
| Halley Pl, G13 | 46 | BA23 | Hamilton St, G42 | 88 | BS36 | Harriet St, (Ruther.) G73 | 89 | BW37 |
| Halley Sq, G13 | 46 | BA23 | Hamilton St, Clyde. G81 | 45 | AZ22 | Harrington Rd, (E.Kil.) G74 | 136 | CA52 |
| Halley St, G13 | 46 | BA22 | Hamilton St, Lark. ML9 | 144 | DC57 | Harris Cl, (Newt. M.) G77 | 116 | BD47 |
| Hallforest St, G33 | | | Hamilton St, Pais. PA3 | 62 | AV31 | Harris Cres, (Old Kil.) G60 | 25 | AR16 |
| off Gartloch Rd | 70 | CD27 | Hamilton Ter, Clyde. G81 | 45 | AZ22 | Harris Dr, (Old Kil.) G60 | 25 | AR16 |
| Hallhill Cres, G33 | 71 | CG33 | Hamilton Vw, (Udd.) G71 | 93 | CQ38 | Harris Gdns, (Old Kil.) G60 | 26 | AS16 |
| Hallhill Rd, G32 | 71 | CE31 | Hamlet, (E.Kil.) G74 | 122 | CD49 | Harrison Dr, G51 | | |
| Hallhill Rd, G33 | 71 | CG31 | Hampden Dr, G42 | 87 | BR38 | off Copland Rd | 66 | BK31 |
| Hallhill Rd, John. PA5 | 79 | AE38 | Hampden La, G42 | 87 | BR37 | Harris Rd, G23 | 30 | BM20 |
| Halliburton Cres, G34 | | | Hampden Pk, G42 | 88 | BS38 | Harris Rd, (Old Kil.) G60 | 25 | AR16 |
| off Ware Rd | 72 | CJ30 | Hampden Ter, G42 | 87 | BR37 | Harrow Ct, G15 | | |
| Halliburton Rd, G34 | 71 | CH30 | Hampden Way, Renf. PA4 | | | off Linkwood Dr | 28 | BB18 |
| Halliburton Ter, G34 | 72 | CJ30 | off Lewis Av | 63 | AZ28 | Harrow Pl, G15 | 28 | BB18 |
| Hallidale Cres, Renf. PA4 | 64 | BB27 | Handel Pl, G5 | 88 | BS33 | Hartfield Cres, (Neil.) G78 | 114 | AU46 |
| Hallinan Gdns, Wis. ML2 | 143 | DH51 | Hangingshaw Pl, G42 | 88 | BS37 | Hartfield Ter, Pais. PA2 | 82 | AV35 |
| Hall Pl, (Stepps) G33 | 53 | CH24 | Hannover Ct, G1 | 5 | BS29 | Hartlaw Cres, G52 | 64 | BC31 |
| Hallrule Dr, G52 | 65 | BE32 | Hanover Cl, G42 | | | Hartree Av, G13 | 46 | BA21 |
| Hallside Av, (Camb.) G72 | 107 | CG40 | off Battlefield Gdns | 87 | BQ37 | Hartstone Pl, G53 | 84 | BD38 |
| Hallside Boul, (Camb.) G72 | 107 | CH42 | Hanover Ct, Pais. PA1 | | | Hartstone Rd, G53 | 84 | BD38 |
| Hallside Cres, (Camb.) G72 | 107 | CG40 | off Kelburne Gdns | 63 | AW32 | Hartstone Ter, G53 | 84 | BD38 |
| Hallside Dr, (Camb.) G72 | 107 | CG40 | Hanover Gdns, Pais. PA1 | 82 | AS33 | Hart St, G31 | 70 | CA32 |
| Hallside Pl, G5 | 88 | BS33 | Hanover St, G1 | 5 | BS29 | Hart St, (Linw.) Pais. PA3 | 60 | AK32 |
| Hallside Rd, (Camb.) G72 | 107 | CH41 | Hanson Pk, G31 | 68 | BV29 | Hartwood Gdns, (Newt. M.) | | |
| Hall St, Clyde. G81 | 27 | AW20 | Hanson St, G31 | 68 | BV29 | G77 | 131 | BF51 |
| Hall St, Ham. ML3 | 140 | CT52 | Hapland Av, G53 | 85 | BE35 | Harvest Dr, Moth. ML1 | 127 | CZ49 |
| Hall St, Moth. ML1 | 112 | DC41 | Hapland Rd, G53 | 85 | BE35 | Harvey St, G4 | 68 | BS27 |
| Hallydown Dr, G13 | 47 | BE24 | Harbour La, Pais. PA3 | 62 | AU32 | Harvey Way, Bell. ML4 | 95 | CY38 |
| Halpin Cl, Bell. ML4 | 110 | CT40 | Harbour Rd, Pais. PA3 | 62 | AU31 | Harvie Av, (Newt. M.) G77 | 117 | BE47 |
| Halton Gdns, (Baill.) G69 | 91 | CH33 | Harburn Pl, G23 | 31 | BN19 | Harvie St, G51 | 66 | BM31 |
| Hamersley Pl, (E.Kil.) G75 | 135 | BX54 | Harbury Pl, G14 | 46 | BB23 | Harwood Gdns, (Mood.) G69 | | |
| Hamilcomb Rd, Bell. ML4 | 111 | CW42 | Harcourt Dr, G31 | 69 | BX29 | off Dryburgh Wk | 37 | CQ18 |
| Hamill Dr, (Kilsyth) G65 | 8 | CV5 | Hardgate Dr, G51 | 65 | BE29 | Harwood St, G32 | 70 | CA30 |
| Hamilton Av, G41 | 86 | BK34 | Hardgate Gdns, G51 | 65 | BE29 | Hastie St, G3 | 66 | BM28 |
| Hamilton Business Pk, | | | Hardgate Path, G51 | | | Hastings, (E.Kil.) G75 | 135 | BW54 |
| Ham. ML3 | 126 | CT48 | off Hardgate Dr | 65 | BE29 | Hatfield Dr, G12 | 47 | BH24 |
| Hamilton Ct, Pais. PA2 | 82 | AU35 | Hardgate Pl, G51 | | | Hathaway Dr, (Giff.) G46 | 102 | BK43 |
| Hamilton Cres, (Bears.) G61 | 11 | BG14 | off Hardgate Dr | 65 | BE29 | Hathaway La, G20 | 49 | BN24 |
| Hamilton Cres, (Camb.) G72 | 107 | CE41 | Hardgate Rd, G51 | 65 | BE29 | Hathaway St, G20 | 49 | BN24 |
| Hamilton Cres, Coat. ML5 | 75 | CW32 | Hardie Av, (Ruther.) G73 | 89 | BY37 | Hathersage Av, (Baill.) G69 | 72 | CK32 |
| Hamilton Cres, Renf. PA4 | 45 | AZ24 | Hardie St, (Blan.) G72 | 124 | CM46 | Hathersage Dr, (Baill.) G69 | 72 | CK32 |
| Hamilton Dr, G12 | 49 | BN26 | Hardie St, Ham. ML3 | 139 | CR51 | Hathersage Gdns, (Baill.) G69 | 72 | CK32 |
| Hamilton Dr, (Giff.) G46 | 102 | BM43 | Hardie St, Moth. ML1 | 128 | DA45 | Hatton Dr, G52 | 84 | BC33 |
| Hamilton Dr, (Both.) G71 | 109 | CR44 | Hardmuir Gdns, (Kirk.) G66 | 17 | CG12 | Hatton Gdns, G52 | 84 | BC33 |
| Hamilton Dr, (Blan.) G72 | 124 | CM46 | Hardmuir Rd, (Kirk.) G66 | 17 | CG12 | Hatton Hill, Moth. ML1 | 113 | DE43 |
| Hamilton Dr, (Camb.) G72 | 106 | CB40 | Hardridge Av, G52 | 85 | BF35 | Hatton Path, G52 | 84 | BC33 |
| Hamilton Dr, Air. ML6 | 76 | DD28 | Hardridge Pl, G52 | 85 | BG35 | Hatton Pl, Moth. ML1 | 113 | DE43 |
| Hamilton Dr, Ersk. PA8 | 25 | AP18 | Hardridge Rd, G52 | 85 | BF35 | Hattonrigg Rd, Bell. ML4 | 111 | CW39 |
| Hamilton Dr, Moth. ML1 | 128 | DB49 | Harefield Dr, G14 | 46 | BD24 | Hatton Ter, Moth. ML1 | 113 | DE43 |
| Hamiltonhill Cres, G22 | | | Harelaw Av, G44 | 103 | BN41 | Haughburn Pl, G53 | 84 | BD38 |
| off Hamiltonhill Rd | 49 | BR25 | Harelaw Av, (Barr.) G78 | 99 | AZ44 | Haughburn Rd, G53 | 84 | BD38 |
| Hamiltonhill Gdns, G22 | 49 | BR25 | Harelaw Av, (Neil.) G78 | 114 | AT47 | Haughburn Ter, G53 | | |
| Hamiltonhill Rd, G22 | 49 | BR26 | Harelaw Cres, Pais. PA2 | 82 | AS38 | off Haughburn Rd | 85 | BE38 |

| | | | | | | | | |
|---|---|---|---|---|---|---|---|---|
| Haugh Rd, G3 | 66 | BM29 | Hayston Rd, (Cumb.) G68 | 22 | DA9 | Heath Rd, Lark. ML9 | 144 | DD58 |
| Haugh Rd, (Kilsyth) G65 | 7 | CS5 | Hayston St, G22 | 49 | BR24 | Heathside Rd, (Giff.) G46 | 102 | BM42 |
| Haughton Av, (Kilsyth) G65 | 7 | CU5 | Haywood St, G22 | 49 | BR23 | Heathwood Dr, (Thornlie.) G46 | 102 | BJ42 |
| Haughview Rd, Moth. ML1 | | | Hazel Av, G44 | 103 | BP41 | Hecla Av, G15 | 28 | BB18 |
| off Strathclyde Rd | 127 | CX47 | Hazel Av, (Bears.) G61 | 11 | BH14 | Hecla Pl, G15 | 28 | BB18 |
| Haughview Ter, G5 | 88 | BT34 | Hazel Av, (Lenz.) G66 | 35 | CF15 | Hecla Sq, G15 | 28 | BB19 |
| Havelock La, G11 | 66 | BL27 | Hazel Av, John. PA5 | 80 | AJ36 | Hector Rd, G41 | 86 | BM37 |
| Havelock Pk, (E.Kil.) G75 | 135 | BW52 | Hazel Av La, G44 | | | Heddle Pl, G2 | | |
| Havelock St, G11 | 66 | BL27 | off Hazel Av | 103 | BP41 | off Cadogan St | 4 | BQ30 |
| Haven Pk, (E.Kil.) G75 | 134 | BV55 | Hazel Bk, (M. of Cam.) G66 | 16 | CD9 | Helena Pl, (Clark.) G76 | | |
| Hawbank Rd, (E.Kil.) G74 | 121 | BW50 | Hazelbank, (Plains) Air. ML6 | | | off Busby Rd | 119 | BN45 |
| Hawick Av, Pais. PA2 | 81 | AR36 | off Arondale Rd | 59 | DH26 | Helena Ter, Clyde. G81 | | |
| Hawick Cres, Lark. ML9 | 144 | DC59 | Hazelbank, Moth. ML1 | | | off Chapel Rd | 27 | AW15 |
| Hawick Dr, Coat. ML5 | 95 | CZ34 | off Myrtle Dr | 112 | DD40 | Helensburgh Dr, G13 | 47 | BF23 |
| Hawick St, G13 | 46 | BA22 | Hazelbank Wk, Air. ML6 | 75 | CZ29 | Helenslea, (Camb.) G72 | 107 | CF41 |
| Hawkhead Av, Pais. PA2 | 83 | AX35 | Hazel Dene, (Bishop.) G64 | 33 | BX20 | Helenslea Pl, Bell. ML4 | 110 | CV41 |
| Hawkhead Rd, Air. ML6 | | | Hazeldene La, Lark. ML9 | | | Helen St, G51 | 66 | BJ30 |
| off Raebog Rd | 58 | DB25 | off Dickson St | 145 | DE60 | Helen St, G52 | 65 | BH32 |
| Hawkhead Rd, Pais. PA1 | 83 | AX33 | Hazelden Gdns, G44 | 103 | BN41 | Helenvale Ct, G31 | 89 | BZ33 |
| Hawkhead Rd, Pais. PA2 | 83 | AY36 | Hazelden Pk, G44 | 103 | BN41 | Helenvale St, G31 | 89 | BY33 |
| Hawksland Wk, Ham. ML3 | | | Hazelden Rd, (Newt. M.) G77 | 131 | BE53 | Helen Wynd, Lark. ML9 | 144 | DC59 |
| off Silvertonhill Av | 140 | CU52 | Hazelfield Gro, (Chap.) | | | Helmsdale Av, (Blan.) G72 | 108 | CL42 |
| Hawkwood, (E.Kil.) G75 | 135 | BZ56 | Air. ML6 | 97 | DG36 | Helmsdale Ct, (Camb.) G72 | 107 | CF40 |
| Hawthorn Av, (Bears.) G61 | 12 | BJ14 | Hazel Gdns, Moth. ML1 | 127 | CZ50 | Helmsdale Dr, Pais. PA2 | 81 | AP35 |
| Hawthorn Av, (Bishop.) G64 | 51 | BX21 | Hazel Gro, (Kirk.) G66 | 35 | CF15 | Hemlock St, G13 | 47 | BG22 |
| Hawthorn Av, (Lenz.) G66 | 35 | CE16 | Hazelhead, (E.Kil.) G74 | 136 | CD51 | Henderland Dr, (Bears.) G61 | 29 | BG19 |
| Hawthorn Av, Ersk. PA8 | 44 | AU21 | Hazellea Dr, (Giff.) G46 | 102 | BM41 | Henderland Rd, (Bears.) G61 | 29 | BG19 |
| Hawthorn Av, John. PA5 | 80 | AJ36 | Hazel Pk, Ham. ML3 | 140 | CU51 | Henderson Av, (Camb.) G72 | 107 | CF39 |
| Hawthorn Ct, (Clark.) G76 | | | Hazel Rd, (Cumb.) G67 | 23 | DF10 | Henderson St, G20 | 49 | BP26 |
| off Hawthorn Rd | 119 | BN47 | Hazel Ter, (Udd.) G71 | 93 | CR38 | Henderson St, Air. ML6 | 76 | DD29 |
| Hawthorn Cres, Ersk. PA8 | 44 | AU21 | Hazelton, Moth. ML1 | 127 | CZ48 | Henderson St, Clyde. G81 | 46 | BA21 |
| Hawthornden Gdns, G23 | 31 | BN19 | Hazelwood Av, (Newt. M.) G77 | 117 | BG49 | Henderson St, Coat. ML5 | 74 | CV31 |
| Hawthorn Dr, (Barr.) G78 | 115 | AZ45 | Hazelwood Av, Pais. PA2 | 81 | AN38 | Henderson St, Pais. PA1 | 62 | AT32 |
| Hawthorn Dr, Air. ML6 | 77 | DF30 | Hazelwood Dr, (Blan.) G72 | 124 | CL45 | Henrietta St, G14 | 47 | BE26 |
| Hawthorn Dr, Coat. ML5 | | | Hazelwood Gdns, (Ruther.) G73 | 105 | BY41 | Henry Bell Grn, (E.Kil.) G75 | | |
| off Southfield Cres | 75 | CZ32 | Hazelwood Rd, G41 | 86 | BL33 | off Bell Grn E | 136 | CB53 |
| Hawthorn Dr, Moth. ML1 | 112 | DD42 | Hazlitt Gdns, G20 | | | Henry St, (Barr.) G78 | 99 | AX42 |
| Hawthorn Gdns, (Camb.) G72 | 107 | CG41 | off Bilsland Dr | 49 | BQ23 | Hepburn Hill, Ham. ML3 | 139 | CR53 |
| Hawthorn Gdns, (Clark.) G76 | 119 | BN47 | Hazlitt Pl, G20 | | | Hepburn Rd, G52 | 64 | BD30 |
| Hawthorn Gdns, Bell. ML4 | 111 | CY41 | off Hazlitt St | 49 | BR23 | Herald Av, G13 | 29 | BF20 |
| Hawthorn Gdns, Lark. ML9 | 145 | DE59 | Hazlitt St, G20 | 49 | BR23 | Herald Gro, Moth. ML1 | 127 | CZ49 |
| Hawthorn Hill, Ham. ML3 | 140 | CU52 | Headhouse Ct, (E.Kil.) G75 | 135 | BZ53 | Herald Way, Renf. PA4 | | |
| Hawthorn Pl, (Blan.) G72 | 125 | CN46 | Headhouse Grn, (E.Kil.) G75 | | | off Viscount Av | 63 | AY28 |
| Hawthorn Quad, G22 | 50 | BS24 | off Mid Pk | 136 | CA53 | Herbertson Gro, (Blan.) G72 | 108 | CL44 |
| Hawthorn Rd, (Cumb.) G67 | 23 | DH9 | Heath Av, (Bishop.) G64 | 51 | BX21 | Herbertson St, G5 | 67 | BR32 |
| Hawthorn Rd, (Clark.) G76 | 119 | BN47 | Heath Av, (Lenz.) G66 | 35 | CE17 | Herbert St, G20 | 49 | BP26 |
| Hawthorn Rd, Ersk. PA8 | 44 | AU21 | Heathcliff Av, (Blan.) G72 | 108 | CL44 | Herbison Ct, Lark. ML9 | 144 | DD57 |
| Hawthorn St, G22 | 50 | BS24 | Heathcot Av, G15 | 28 | BA19 | Hercules Way, Renf. PA4 | 63 | AZ28 |
| Hawthorn St, (Torr.) G64 | 15 | BY12 | Heathcot Pl, G15 | | | Heriot Av, Pais. PA2 | 81 | AN37 |
| Hawthorn St, Clyde. G81 | 27 | AW17 | off Heathcot Av | 27 | AZ19 | Heriot Ct, Pais. PA2 | | |
| Hawthorn Ter, (Udd.) G71 | 93 | CR38 | Heather Av, (Bears.) G61 | 11 | BG13 | off Heriot Av | 81 | AP37 |
| Hawthorn Ter, (E.Kil.) G75 | 135 | BX55 | Heather Av, (Barr.) G78 | 99 | AW40 | Heriot Cres, (Bishop.) G64 | 33 | BW18 |
| Hawthorn Wk, (Camb.) G72 | 105 | BZ40 | Heather Av, Moth. ML1 | 112 | DC40 | Heriot Rd, (Lenz.) G66 | 35 | CE18 |
| Hawthorn Way, Ersk. PA8 | 44 | AU21 | Heatherbank Av, (Gart.) G69 | 54 | CK26 | Heriot Way, Pais. PA2 | | |
| Hay Av, Bish. PA7 | 24 | AL18 | Heatherbank Dr, (Gart.) G69 | 54 | CK26 | off Heriot Av | 81 | AN37 |
| Hayburn Ct, G11 | | | Heatherbank Gro, (Gart.) G69 | 54 | CL26 | Heritage Ct, (Newt. M.) G77 | 117 | BG48 |
| off Hayburn St | 66 | BK27 | Heatherbank Wk, Air. ML6 | 75 | CZ29 | Heritage Vw, Coat. ML5 | 74 | CV29 |
| Hayburn Cres, G11 | 48 | BJ26 | Heatherbrae, (Bishop.) G64 | 32 | BU20 | Heritage Way, Coat. ML5 | 74 | CV30 |
| Hayburn Gate, G11 | 66 | BK27 | Heather Dr, (Kirk.) G66 | 34 | CC16 | Herma St, G23 | 49 | BN21 |
| Hayburn La, G11 | 48 | BJ26 | Heather Gdns, (Kirk.) G66 | 34 | CC17 | Hermes Way, Bell. ML4 | 112 | DB40 |
| Hayburn Pl, G11 | | | Heather Gro, (E.Kil.) G75 | | | Hermiston Av, G32 | 70 | CD31 |
| off Hayburn St | 66 | BK27 | off Strathcona La | 136 | CA54 | Hermiston Pl, G32 | 71 | CE31 |
| Hayburn St, G11 | 66 | BK28 | Heather Pl, (Kirk.) G66 | 34 | CC16 | Hermiston Pl, Moth. ML1 | | |
| Hayfield Ct, G5 | 88 | BT33 | Heather Pl, John. PA5 | 80 | AJ35 | off Windsor Rd | 112 | DC40 |
| Hayfield St, G5 | 88 | BT33 | Heather Way, Moth. ML1 | | | Hermiston Rd, G32 | 70 | CD30 |
| Hayhill Rd, (Thornton.) G74 | 133 | BR54 | off Thistle Rd | 112 | DC41 | Hermitage Av, G13 | 47 | BE22 |
| Hayle Gdns, (Chry.) G69 | 37 | CP18 | Heathery Knowe, (E.Kil.) G75 | 136 | CA54 | Hermitage Cres, Coat. ML5 | 95 | CX34 |
| Haylynn St, G14 | 65 | BG27 | Heatheryknowe Rd, (Baill.) G69 | 73 | CN29 | Herndon Ct, (Newt. M.) G77 | 118 | BJ47 |
| Haymarket St, G32 | 70 | CA30 | Heathery Lea Av, Coat. ML5 | 95 | CZ34 | Heron Ct, Clyde. G81 | 27 | AX16 |
| Haystack Pl, (Lenz.) G66 | 35 | CF17 | Heathery Rd, Wis. ML2 | 129 | DH50 | Heron Pl, John. PA5 | 79 | AF38 |
| Hayston Ct, (Kirk.) G66 | 16 | CC13 | Heathfield Av, (Mood.) G69 | 37 | CQ19 | Heron St, G40 | 88 | BV33 |
| Hayston Cres, G22 | 49 | BR24 | Heathfield Dr, (Miln.) G62 | 12 | BK10 | Heron Way, Renf. PA4 | | |
| Hayston Rd, (Kirk.) G66 | 16 | CC13 | Heathfield St, G33 | 71 | CE29 | off Britannia Way | 63 | AY28 |

| | | |
|---|---|---|
| Herries Rd, G41 | 86 | BL35 |
| Herriet St, G41 | 87 | BP34 |
| Herriot St, Coat. ML5 | 74 | CU29 |
| Hertford Av, G12 | 48 | BK23 |
| Hexham Gdns, G41 | 86 | BM36 |
| Heys St, (Barr.) G78 | 99 | AY43 |
| Hickman St, G42 | 87 | BR36 |
| Hickman Ter, G42 | 88 | BS35 |
| Hickory Cres, (Udd.) G71 | 94 | CS36 |
| Hickory St, G22 | 50 | BU24 |
| High Av, St, Lark. ML9 | 144 | DB57 |
| High Barholm, (Kilb.) John. PA10 | 78 | AC34 |
| High Barrwood Rd, (Kilsyth) G65 | 7 | CU5 |
| High Beeches, (Carm.) G76 | 120 | BU45 |
| High Blantyre Rd, Ham. ML3 | 125 | CP48 |
| Highburgh Dr, (Ruther.) G73 | 105 | BX40 |
| Highburgh Rd, G12 | 48 | BL26 |
| High Burnside Av, Coat. ML5 | 74 | CU32 |
| High Calside, Pais. PA2 | 82 | AT34 |
| Highcoats, Coat. ML5 | 75 | CX30 |
| High Common Rd, (E.Kil.) G74 | 137 | CE52 |
| Highcraig Av, John. PA5 | 79 | AF36 |
| High Craigends, (Kilsyth) G65 | 7 | CU5 |
| High Craighall Rd, G4 | 67 | BR27 |
| Highcroft Av, G44 | 104 | BT40 |
| Highcross Av, Coat. ML5 | 94 | CT33 |
| Higher Ness Way, Coat. ML5 | 94 | CT34 |
| Highfield Av, (Kirk.) G66 | 17 | CG13 |
| Highfield Av, Pais. PA2 | 82 | AS38 |
| Highfield Ct, (Kirk.) G66 | 17 | CH13 |
| Highfield Cres, Moth. ML1 | 128 | DC45 |
| Highfield Cres, Pais. PA2 | 82 | AT38 |
| Highfield Dr, G12 | 48 | BK23 |
| Highfield Dr, (Ruther.) G73 | 105 | BY42 |
| Highfield Dr, (Clark.) G76 | 118 | BM46 |
| Highfield Gro, (Kirk.) G66 | | |
| *off Highfield Rd* | 17 | CG12 |
| Highfield Pl, G12 | 48 | BK23 |
| Highfield Pl, (E.Kil.) G74 | 122 | CB50 |
| Highfield Rd, (Kirk.) G66 | 17 | CG12 |
| Highfield Rd, Lark. ML9 | 144 | DD58 |
| High Flenders Rd, (Clark.) G76 | 118 | BM48 |
| Highkirk Vw, John. PA5 | 79 | AH35 |
| Highland Av, (Blan.) G72 | 124 | CL45 |
| Highland La, G51 | 66 | BL29 |
| Highland Pk, (Kilsyth) G65 | 7 | CS4 |
| Highland Pl, (Kilsyth) G65 | 7 | CS3 |
| Highland Rd, (Miln.) G62 | 12 | BJ11 |
| High Mair, Renf. PA4 | 63 | AY27 |
| High Parksail, Ersk. PA8 | 44 | AS21 |
| High Parks Cres, Ham. ML3 | 140 | CT55 |
| High Patrick St, Ham. ML3 | 140 | CU51 |
| High Pleasance, Lark. ML9 | 144 | DC58 |
| High Rd, Moth. ML1 | 127 | CZ46 |
| High Rd, (Castlehead) Pais. PA2 | 82 | AS34 |
| High Row, (Bishop.) G64 | 33 | BX16 |
| Highstonehall Rd, Ham. ML3 | 139 | CP53 |
| High St, G1 | 5 | BT31 |
| High St, G4 | 5 | BT31 |
| High St, (Kirk.) G66 | 17 | CE12 |
| High St, (Ruther.) G73 | 89 | BW37 |
| High St, (Neil.) G78 | 114 | AT46 |
| High St, Air. ML6 | 76 | DB29 |
| High St, John. PA5 | 79 | AH34 |
| High St, Moth. ML1 | 113 | DG41 |
| High St, Pais. PA1 | 82 | AT33 |
| High St, Renf. PA4 | 45 | AZ25 |
| High Whitehills Rd, (E.Kil.) G75 | 135 | BZ56 |
| High Wd Gdns, Bell. ML4 | 110 | CU40 |
| Hilary Dr, (Baill.) G69 | 71 | CH32 |
| Hilda Cres, G33 | 52 | CA25 |
| Hillary Av, (Ruther.) G73 | 105 | BZ39 |
| Hill Av, (Newt. M.) G77 | 117 | BE49 |
| Hillbrae St, G51 | 65 | BF31 |
| Hill Cres, (Clark.) G76 | 119 | BN47 |
| Hillcrest, (Chry.) G69 | 54 | CM21 |
| Hillcrest, (Carm.) G76 | 120 | BT45 |
| Hillcrest Av, G32 | 90 | CD37 |
| Hillcrest Av, G44 | 103 | BN41 |
| Hillcrest Av, (Cumb.) G67 | | |
| *off North Carbrain Rd* | 22 | DB12 |
| Hillcrest Av, Coat. ML5 | 75 | CY31 |
| Hillcrest Av, Pais. PA2 | 98 | AS39 |
| Hillcrest Av, Wis. ML2 | 129 | DG50 |
| Hillcrest Ct, (Cumb.) G67 | 22 | DB12 |
| Hillcrest Dr, (Newt. M.) G77 | 118 | BJ48 |
| Hillcrest Rd, G32 | 91 | CE37 |
| Hillcrest Rd, (Bears.) G61 | 29 | BH17 |
| Hillcrest Rd, (Kilsyth) G65 | 6 | CN5 |
| Hillcrest Rd, (Udd.) G71 | 93 | CQ38 |
| Hillcrest St, (Miln.) G62 | 12 | BJ11 |
| Hillcrest Ter, (Both.) G71 | 109 | CR42 |
| Hillcrest Vw, Lark. ML9 | 144 | DD58 |
| Hillcroft Ter, (Bishop.) G64 | 50 | BV21 |
| Hillend Cres, (Clark.) G76 | 118 | BL47 |
| Hillend Cres, Clyde. G81 | 26 | AV15 |
| Hillend Rd, G22 | 49 | BQ22 |
| Hillend Rd, (Ruther.) G73 | 105 | BX40 |
| Hillend Rd, (Clark.) G76 | 118 | BL47 |
| Hillfoot Av, (Bears.) G61 | 29 | BH16 |
| Hillfoot Av, (Ruther.) G73 | 89 | BW38 |
| Hillfoot Dr, (Bears.) G61 | 29 | BH16 |
| Hillfoot Dr, Coat. ML5 | 74 | CT31 |
| Hillfoot Gdns, (Udd.) G71 | 93 | CN37 |
| Hillfoot Rd, Air. ML6 | 76 | DD31 |
| Hillfoot St, G31 | 69 | BW30 |
| Hillhead Av, (Chry.) G69 | 37 | CP19 |
| Hillhead Av, (Ruther.) G73 | 105 | BX41 |
| Hillhead Av, Moth. ML1 | 112 | DC43 |
| Hillhead Cres, Ham. ML3 | 125 | CN50 |
| Hillhead Cres, Moth. ML1 | 112 | DC43 |
| Hillhead Dr, Air. ML6 | 76 | DC31 |
| Hillhead Dr, Moth. ML1 | 112 | DC44 |
| Hillhead Pl, G12 | | |
| *off Bank St* | 67 | BN27 |
| Hillhead Rd, (Ruther.) G73 | 105 | BX41 |
| Hillhead Rd, G21 | 51 | BZ22 |
| Hillhead Rd, (Kirk.) G66 | 17 | CF12 |
| Hillhead St, G12 | 66 | BM27 |
| Hillhead St, (Miln.) G62 | 12 | BJ11 |
| Hillhead Ter, Ham. ML3 | 125 | CN50 |
| Hillhouse Cres, Ham. ML3 | 125 | CP50 |
| Hillhouse Pk Ind Est, Ham. ML3 | 125 | CQ49 |
| Hillhouse Rd, (Blan.) G72 | 124 | CL48 |
| Hillhouse Rd, Ham. ML3 | 125 | CN49 |
| Hillhouse St, G21 | 51 | BW25 |
| Hillhouse Ter, Ham. ML3 | 125 | CP50 |
| Hillington Gdns, G52 | 85 | BE33 |
| Hillington Ind Est, G52 | 64 | BB29 |
| Hillington Pk Circ, G52 | 65 | BE32 |
| Hillington Quad, G52 | 64 | BC32 |
| Hillington Rd, G52 | 64 | BB27 |
| Hillington Rd S, G52 | 64 | BC32 |
| Hillington Shop Cen, (Hillington Ind. Est.) G52 | 64 | BB29 |
| Hillington Ter, G52 | 64 | BC32 |
| Hillkirk Pl, G21 | | |
| *off Hillkirk St* | 50 | BU25 |
| Hillkirk St, G21 | 50 | BU25 |
| Hillkirk St La, G21 | | |
| *off Hillkirk St* | 50 | BV25 |
| Hillman Cres, Pais. PA3 | 81 | AN33 |
| Hillman Rd, Pais. PA3 | 81 | AN33 |
| Hillneuk Av, (Bears.) G61 | 29 | BH16 |
| Hillneuk Dr, (Bears.) G61 | 30 | BJ16 |
| Hillpark Av, Pais. PA2 | 82 | AT36 |
| Hillpark Dr, G43 | 102 | BL39 |
| Hill Path, G52 | 64 | BC32 |
| Hill Pl, G52 | 64 | BC32 |
| Hill Pl, Bell. ML4 | 110 | CV42 |
| Hill Pl, Moth. ML1 | 113 | DE43 |
| Hillrigg, (Green.) Air. ML6 | 41 | DF20 |
| Hillrigg Av, Air. ML6 | 77 | DE29 |
| Hill Rd, (Kilsyth) G65 | 7 | CT3 |
| Hill Rd, (Cumb.) G67 | 22 | DA11 |
| Hillsborough Rd, (Baill.) G69 | 71 | CH32 |
| Hillsborough Ter, G12 | | |
| *off Bower St* | 49 | BN26 |
| Hillside, (Kilsyth) G65 | 8 | CV8 |
| Hillside Av, (Bears.) G61 | 29 | BH16 |
| Hillside Av, (Clark.) G76 | 118 | BM46 |
| Hillside Cotts, (Glenb.) Coat. ML5 | 56 | CU23 |
| Hillside Ct, (Thornlie.) G46 | 101 | BH42 |
| Hillside Ct, (Camb.) G72 | 107 | CG42 |
| Hillside Cres, (Neil.) G78 | 114 | AT46 |
| Hillside Cres, Coat. ML5 | 94 | CV33 |
| Hillside Cres, Ham. ML3 | 140 | CT51 |
| Hillside Cres, Moth. ML1 | 113 | DF41 |
| Hillside Dr, (Bears.) G61 | 30 | BJ16 |
| Hillside Dr, (Bishop.) G64 | 33 | BW19 |
| Hillside Dr, (Barr.) G78 | 99 | AW42 |
| Hillside Gdns La, G11 | | |
| *off North Gardner St* | 48 | BK26 |
| Hillside Gro, (Barr.) G78 | 99 | AW42 |
| Hillside La, Ham. ML3 | 140 | CS51 |
| Hillside Pk, Clyde. G81 | 27 | AX15 |
| Hillside Pl, Moth. ML1 | 113 | DF42 |
| Hillside Quad, G43 | 102 | BK40 |
| Hillside Rd, G43 | 102 | BK40 |
| Hillside Rd, (Barr.) G78 | 99 | AW42 |
| Hillside Rd, (Neil.) G78 | 114 | AT46 |
| Hillside Rd, Pais. PA2 | 83 | AW35 |
| Hillside Ter, (Old Kil.) G60 | | |
| *off Dalnottar Av* | 25 | AR15 |
| Hillside Ter, Ham. ML3 | 140 | CS51 |
| Hill St, G3 | 4 | BQ28 |
| Hill St, G14 | 46 | BC24 |
| Hill St, (Chap.) Air. ML6 | 97 | DF35 |
| Hill St, Ham. ML3 | 125 | CP50 |
| Hill St, Lark. ML9 | 144 | DC59 |
| Hillsview, (Chry.) G69 | 54 | CK21 |
| Hillswick Cres, G22 | 49 | BR21 |
| Hill Ter, Moth. ML1 | 113 | DE43 |
| Hilltop Av, Bell. ML4 | 95 | CW38 |
| Hilltop Rd, (Mood.) G69 | 37 | CP19 |
| Hill Vw, (E.Kil.) G75 | 136 | CA53 |
| Hillview, (Green.) Air. ML6 | 41 | DH19 |
| Hillview Av, (Kilsyth) G65 | 7 | CT6 |
| Hillview Cres, (Udd.) G71 | 93 | CN37 |
| Hillview Cres, Bell. ML4 | 95 | CW37 |
| Hillview Cres, Lark. ML9 | 144 | DD60 |
| Hillview Dr, (Blan.) G72 | 108 | CM43 |
| Hillview Dr, (Clark.) G76 | 118 | BM46 |
| Hillview Gdns, (Bishop.) G64 | 51 | BZ21 |
| Hillview Pl, (Clark.) G76 | 119 | BN46 |
| Hillview Rd, (Elder.) John. PA5 | 80 | AL35 |
| Hillview St, G32 | 70 | CB32 |
| Hillview Ter, (Old Kil.) G60 | | |
| *off Station Rd* | 25 | AR15 |
| Hiltonbank St, Ham. ML3 | 125 | CR49 |
| Hilton Ct, Ham. ML3 | | |
| *off Johnstone Rd* | 140 | CU51 |
| Hilton Gdns, G13 | 47 | BH22 |
| Hilton Gdns La, G13 | | |
| *off Fulton St* | 47 | BG22 |

| | | |
|---|---|---|
| Hilton Pk, (Bishop.) G64 | 32 | BV17 |
| Hilton Rd, (Miln.) G62 | 11 | BG11 |
| Hilton Rd, (Bishop.) G64 | 32 | BV18 |
| Hilton Ter, G13 | 47 | BG22 |
| Hilton Ter, (Bishop.) G64 | 32 | BV17 |
| Hilton Ter, (Camb.) G72 | 106 | CA42 |
| Hindsland Rd, Lark. ML9 | 144 | DD60 |
| Hinshaw St, G20 | 49 | BQ26 |
| Hinshelwood Dr, G51 | 66 | BJ31 |
| Hirsel Pl, (Both.) G71 | 109 | CR42 |
| Hobart Cres, Clyde. G81 | 26 | AT16 |
| Hobart Rd, (E.Kil.) G75 | 135 | BY54 |
| Hobart St, G22 | 49 | BR25 |
| Hobden St, G21 | 51 | BW26 |
| Hoddam Av, G45 | 104 | BW42 |
| Hoddam Ter, G45 | 105 | BW42 |
| Hogan Ct, Clyde. G81 | 26 | AV15 |
| Hogan Way, Moth. ML1 | | |
|   off Morris Cres | 129 | DG45 |
| Hogarth Av, G32 | 69 | BZ30 |
| Hogarth Cres, G32 | 69 | BZ30 |
| Hogarth Dr, G32 | 69 | BZ30 |
| Hogarth Gdns, G32 | 69 | BZ30 |
| Hogganfield Ct, G33 | 69 | BZ27 |
| Hogganfield St, G33 | 69 | BZ27 |
| Hogg Av, John. PA5 | 79 | AG36 |
| Hogg Rd, Air. ML6 | | |
|   off Moncrieffe Rd | 97 | DF33 |
| Hogg St, Air. ML6 | 76 | DC30 |
| Holeburn La, G43 | 102 | BL39 |
| Holeburn Rd, G43 | 102 | BL39 |
| Holehills Dr, Air. ML6 | 76 | DD27 |
| Holehills Pl, Air. ML6 | 76 | DD27 |
| Holehouse Brae, (Neil.) G78 | 114 | AS46 |
| Holehouse Dr, G13 | 46 | BC23 |
| Holehouse Rd, (E.Kil.) G74 | 133 | BQ54 |
| Holehouse Rd, (Eagle.) G76 | 133 | BN56 |
| Holehouse Ter, (Neil.) G78 | 114 | AS46 |
| Hollandbush Gro, Ham. ML3 | | |
|   off Meikle Earnock Rd | 140 | CS53 |
| Hollandhurst Rd, Coat. ML5 | 74 | CV28 |
| Holland St, G2 | 4 | BQ29 |
| Hollinwell Rd, G23 | 48 | BM21 |
| Hollowglen Rd, G32 | 70 | CD31 |
| Hollows, The, (Giff.) G46 | | |
|   off Ayr Rd | 102 | BK44 |
| Hollows Av, Pais. PA2 | 81 | AP38 |
| Hollows Cres, Pais. PA2 | 81 | AP38 |
| Hollybank Pl, (Camb.) G72 | 106 | CA42 |
| Hollybank St, G21 | 69 | BW28 |
| Hollybrook Pl, G42 | | |
|   off Hollybrook St | 88 | BS35 |
| Hollybrook St, G42 | 87 | BR35 |
| Hollybush Av, Pais. PA2 | 81 | AR38 |
| Hollybush Rd, G52 | 64 | BB32 |
| Holly Dr, G21 | 51 | BW26 |
| Holly Gro, Bell. ML4 | 112 | DB40 |
| Hollymount, (Bears.) G61 | 29 | BH19 |
| Holly Pl, John. PA5 | 80 | AJ37 |
| Holly St, Air. ML6 | 77 | DE30 |
| Holly St, Clyde. G81 | 27 | AW17 |
| Holm Av, (Udd.) G71 | 109 | CN39 |
| Holm Av, Pais. PA2 | 82 | AV35 |
| Holmbank Av, G41 | 86 | BM38 |
| Holmbrae Av, (Udd.) G71 | 93 | CP38 |
| Holmbrae Rd, (Udd.) G71 | 93 | CP38 |
| Holmbyre Ct, G45 | 103 | BR43 |
| Holmbyre Rd, G45 | 104 | BS44 |
| Holmbyre Ter, G45 | 104 | BS43 |
| Holmes Av, Renf. PA4 | 63 | AY28 |
| Holmes Quad, Bell. ML4 | | |
|   off Sapphire Rd | 111 | CX41 |
| Holmfauldhead Dr, G51 | 65 | BG29 |

| | | |
|---|---|---|
| Holmfauldhead Pl, G51 | | |
|   off Govan Rd | 65 | BG28 |
| Holmfauld Rd, G51 | 65 | BG28 |
| Holmfield, (Kirk.) G66 | 17 | CG14 |
| Holm Gdns, Bell. ML4 | 111 | CY41 |
| Holmhead Cres, G44 | 103 | BQ39 |
| Holmhead Pl, G44 | 103 | BQ39 |
| Holmhead Rd, G44 | 103 | BQ40 |
| Holmhill Av, (Camb.) G72 | 106 | CC41 |
| Holmhills Dr, (Camb.) G72 | 106 | CB42 |
| Holmhills Gdns, (Camb.) G72 | 106 | CB41 |
| Holmhills Gro, (Camb.) G72 | 106 | CB41 |
| Holmhills Pl, (Camb.) G72 | 106 | CB41 |
| Holmhills Rd, (Camb.) G72 | 106 | CB41 |
| Holmhills Ter, (Camb.) G72 | 106 | CB41 |
| Holm La, (E.Kil.) G74 | 136 | CA52 |
| Holmlea Rd, G44 | 87 | BQ38 |
| Holm Pl, Lark. ML9 | | |
|   off Clove Mill Wynd | 144 | DA59 |
| Holm Pl, (Linw.) Pais. PA3 | 60 | AK30 |
| Holms Cres, Ersk. PA8 | 25 | AP19 |
| Holms Pl, (Gart.) G69 | 55 | CN22 |
| Holm St, G2 | 4 | BQ30 |
| Holm St, Moth. ML1 | 112 | DC42 |
| Holmswood Av, (Blan.) G72 | 124 | CM45 |
| Holmwood Av, (Udd.) G71 | 93 | CP38 |
| Holmwood Gdns, (Udd.) G71 | 109 | CP39 |
| Holmwood Gro, G44 | 103 | BQ41 |
| Holyrood Cres, G20 | 67 | BP27 |
| Holyrood Quad, G20 | 67 | BP27 |
| Holyrood St, Ham. ML3 | 125 | CQ48 |
| Holytown Rd, Bell. ML4 | 112 | DA40 |
| Holytown Rd, Moth. ML1 | 112 | DA40 |
| Holywell St, G31 | 69 | BX32 |
| Homer Pl, Bell. ML4 | 112 | DA40 |
| Homeston Av, (Both.) G71 | 109 | CQ42 |
| Honeybog Rd, G52 | 64 | BA30 |
| Honeywell Av, G33 | 54 | CJ25 |
| Honeywell Ct, G33 | 53 | CH25 |
| Honeywell Cres, (Chap.) | | |
|   Air. ML6 | 97 | DG36 |
| Honeywell Dr, G33 | 54 | CJ25 |
| Honeywell Gro, G33 | 54 | CJ24 |
| Honeywell Pl, G33 | 54 | CJ25 |
| Hood St, Clyde. G81 | 27 | AY19 |
| Hope Cres, Lark. ML9 | 144 | DD58 |
| Hopefield Av, G12 | 48 | BL24 |
| Hopehill Gdns, G20 | 49 | BQ26 |
| Hopehill Rd, G20 | 49 | BQ26 |
| Hopeman, Ersk. PA8 | 25 | AQ18 |
| Hopeman Av, (Thornlie.) G46 | 101 | BG41 |
| Hopeman Dr, (Thornlie.) G46 | 101 | BG41 |
| Hopeman Path, (Thornlie.) G46 | | |
|   off Kennishead Pl | 101 | BG40 |
| Hopeman Rd, (Thornlie.) G46 | 101 | BG41 |
| Hopeman St, (Thornlie.) G46 | 101 | BG41 |
| Hope St, G2 | 4 | BR30 |
| Hope St, Bell. ML4 | 111 | CY40 |
| Hope St, Ham. ML3 | 126 | CU50 |
| Hope St, Moth. ML1 | 128 | DA46 |
| Hopetoun Pl, G23 | | |
|   off Broughton Rd | 31 | BN19 |
| Hopetoun Ter, G21 | 51 | BW26 |
| Hopkins Brae, (Kirk.) G66 | | |
|   off Hillhead Rd | 17 | CF12 |
| Horatius St, Moth. ML1 | 111 | CX44 |
| Hornal Rd, (Udd.) G71 | 109 | CP41 |
| Hornbeam Dr, Clyde. G81 | 26 | AV17 |
| Hornbeam Rd, (Udd.) G71 | 93 | CR37 |
| Horndean Ct, (Bishop.) G64 | 33 | BW17 |
| Horndean Cres, G33 | 71 | CF29 |
| Horne St, G22 | | |
|   off Hawthorn St | 50 | BU24 |

| | | |
|---|---|---|
| Hornock Cotts, Coat. ML5 | | |
|   off Gartsherrie Rd | 74 | CV29 |
| Hornock Rd, Coat. ML5 | 74 | CV28 |
| Hornshill Fm Rd, (Stepps) G33 | 53 | CG22 |
| Hornshill St, G21 | 51 | BW25 |
| Horsbrugh Av, (Kilsyth) G65 | 7 | CT4 |
| Horsburgh St, G33 | | |
|   off Dudhope St | 71 | CF27 |
| Horselethill Rd, G12 | 48 | BL25 |
| Horseshoe La, (Bears.) G61 | 29 | BG17 |
| Horseshoe Rd, (Bears.) G61 | 29 | BG16 |
| Hospital St, G5 | 68 | BS32 |
| Hospital St, Coat. ML5 | 95 | CW33 |
| Hotspur St, G20 | 49 | BN24 |
| Houldsworth La, G3 | | |
|   off Finnieston St | 67 | BN29 |
| Houldsworth St, G3 | 67 | BN29 |
| Househillmuir Cres, G53 | 101 | BE39 |
| Househillmuir La, G53 | | |
|   off Househillmuir Rd | 85 | BE38 |
| Househillmuir Pl, G53 | 85 | BE38 |
| Househillmuir Rd, G53 | 100 | BD39 |
| Househillwood Cres, G53 | 84 | BD38 |
| Househillwood Rd, G53 | 100 | BD39 |
| Housel Av, G13 | 46 | BD23 |
| Houston Pl, G5 | 4 | BP31 |
| Houston Pl, (Elder.) John. PA5 | 80 | AL35 |
| Houston Rd, (Inch.) Renf. PA4 | 43 | AP25 |
| Houston St, G5 | 67 | BP32 |
| Houston St, Ham. ML3 | 140 | CT52 |
| Houston St, Renf. PA4 | 45 | AZ25 |
| Houston Ter, (E.Kil.) G74 | 135 | BZ51 |
| Houstoun Ct, John. PA5 | | |
|   off William St | 79 | AH34 |
| Houstoun Sq, John. PA5 | 79 | AH34 |
| Howard Av, (E.Kil.) G74 | 122 | CC48 |
| Howard Ct, (E.Kil.) G74 | 122 | CC48 |
| Howard St, G1 | 4 | BR31 |
| Howard St, Lark. ML9 | 145 | DE60 |
| Howard St, Pais. PA1 | 63 | AW32 |
| Howat St, G51 | 66 | BJ29 |
| Howcraigs Ct, Clyde. G81 | | |
|   off Mill Rd | 45 | AZ22 |
| Howden Av, Moth. ML1 | 97 | DF37 |
| Howden Dr, (Linw.) Pais. PA3 | 60 | AJ32 |
| Howden Pl, Moth. ML1 | 112 | DC40 |
| Howe Gdns, (Udd.) G71 | 93 | CQ38 |
| Howe Rd, (Kilsyth) G65 | 7 | CT6 |
| Howes St, Coat. ML5 | 95 | CX33 |
| Howford Rd, G52 | 84 | BD33 |
| Howgate Av, G15 | 28 | BB18 |
| Howgate Rd, Ham. ML3 | 139 | CR53 |
| Howie Bldgs, (Clark.) G76 | | |
|   off Busby Rd | 119 | BN45 |
| Howieshill Av, (Camb.) G72 | 106 | CD40 |
| Howieshill Rd, (Camb.) G72 | 107 | CE40 |
| Howie St, Lark. ML9 | 144 | DD60 |
| Howletnest Rd, Air. ML6 | 77 | DF31 |
| Howson Lea, Moth. ML1 | | |
|   off Nelson Cres | 128 | DD49 |
| Howson Vw, Moth. ML1 | 127 | CX46 |
| Howth Dr, G13 | 47 | BH21 |
| Howth Ter, G13 | 47 | BH21 |
| Hoxley Pl, G20 | 49 | BP23 |
| Hoylake Pk, (Both.) G71 | 109 | CP43 |
| Hoylake Pl, G23 | 31 | BN20 |
| Hozier Cres, (Udd.) G71 | 93 | CP37 |
| Hozier Ln, Lark. ML9 | | |
|   off Muirshot Rd | 144 | DD57 |
| Hozier Pl, (Both.) G71 | 109 | CR43 |
| Hozier St, Coat. ML5 | 95 | CW33 |
| Hudson Ter, (E.Kil.) G75 | 135 | BX53 |
| Hudson Way, (E.Kil.) G75 | 135 | BY53 |

Hughenden Dr, G12 48 BK25
Hughenden Gdns, G12 48 BJ25
Hughenden La, G12 48 BK25
Hughenden Rd, G12 48 BK25
Hughenden Ter, G12
 off Hughenden Rd 48 BK25
Hugh Murray Gro, (Camb.)
 G72 107 CE40
Hugo St, G20 49 BP24
Hulks Rd, (Green.) Air. ML6 40 DD18
Humbie Ct, (Newt. M.) G77 131 BG51
Humbie Gate, (Newt. M.) G77 131 BG51
Humbie Gro, (Newt. M.) G77 117 BG50
Humbie Lawns, (Newt. M.) G77 131 BG51
Humbie Rd, (Eagle.) G76 132 BJ52
Humbie Rd, (Newt. M.) G77 131 BG51
Hume Dr, (Both.) G71 109 CQ42
Hume Dr, (Udd.) G71 93 CN38
Hume Pl, (E.Kil.) G75 135 BZ53
Hume Rd, (Cumb.) G67 22 DC10
Hume St, Clyde. G81 27 AX20
Hunter Dr, (Newt. M.) G77 116 BD49
Hunterfield Dr, (Camb.) G72 106 CA40
Hunterhill Av, Pais. PA2 82 AV34
Hunterhill Rd, Pais. PA2 82 AV34
Hunter Pl, (Miln.) G62 11 BG12
Hunter Pl, (Kilb.) John. PA10 78 AC35
Hunter Rd, (Miln.) G62 11 BG11
Hunter Rd, (Ruther.) G73 89 BY36
Hunter Rd, Ham. ML3 125 CR47
Huntersfield Rd, John. PA5 79 AE36
Hunters Hill Ct, G21
 off Belmont Rd 50 BV23
Huntershill Rd, (Bishop.) G64 51 BW21
Huntershill St, G21
 off Springburn Rd 50 BV23
Huntershill Way, (Bishop.) G64 50 BV22
Hunter St, G4 5 BU31
Hunter St, (E.Kil.) G74 136 CB51
Hunter St, Air. ML6 76 DB28
Hunter St, Bell. ML4
 off Motherwell Rd 111 CW40
Hunter St, Pais. PA1 62 AU32
Hunthill La, (Blan.) G72 124 CK47
Hunthill Pl, (Clark.) G76 119 BQ48
Hunt Hill Rd, (Cumb.) G68 20 CS12
Hunthill Rd, (Blan.) G72 124 CK46
Huntingdon Rd, G21 68 BU27
Huntingdon Sq, G21 68 BU27
Hunting Lo Gdns, Ham. ML3 141 CW51
Huntingtower Rd, (Baill.) G69 91 CH33
Huntley Rd, G52 64 BB29
Huntly Av, (Giff.) G46 102 BM43
Huntly Av, Bell. ML4 111 CW39
Huntly Ct, (Bishop.) G64 51 BW21
Huntly Dr, (Bears.) G61
 off Montrose Dr 11 BG14
Huntly Dr, (Camb.) G72 106 CD41
Huntly Dr, Coat. ML5 94 CT33
Huntly Gdns, G12 48 BL26
Huntly Path, (Chry.) G69
 off Burnbrae Av 37 CP19
Huntly Rd, G12 48 BL26
Huntly Ter, Pais. PA2 83 AW36
Hurlethill Ct, G53 84 BB38
Hurlet Rd, G53 83 AY37
Hurlet Rd, Pais. PA2 83 AY37
Hurlford Av, G13 46 BB22
Hurly Hawkin, (Bishop.) G64 51 BW21
Hutcheson Rd, (Thornlie.) G46 102 BJ43
Hutcheson St, G1 5 BS30
Hutchinson Pl, (Camb.) G72 107 CG42
Hutchinsontown Ct, G5 88 BS33

Hutchison Ct, (Giff.) G46
 off Berryhill Rd 102 BL44
Hutchison Dr, (Bears.) G61 30 BJ19
Hutchison Pl, Coat. ML5 74 CV31
Hutchison St, Ham. ML3 140 CT53
Hutton, G12
 off Ascot Av 48 BJ23
Hutton Dr, G51 65 BG29
Hutton Dr, (E.Kil.) G74 122 CB49
Hydepark St, G3 4 BP30
Hyndal Av, G53 84 BD36
Hyndland Av, G11 66 BK27
Hyndland Rd, G12 48 BK25
Hyndland St, G11 66 BL27
Hyndlee Dr, G52 65 BE32
Hyslop Pl, Clyde. G81 27 AW18
Hyslop St, Air. ML6 76 DA29

# I

Iain Dr, (Bears.) G61 29 BE15
Iain Rd, (Bears.) G61 29 BE15
Ian Smith Ct, Clyde. G81 45 AZ21
Ibroxholm Av, G51 66 BK32
Ibroxholm Oval, G51 66 BK32
Ibroxholm Pl, G51
 off Paisley Rd W 66 BK32
Ibrox Ind Est, G51 66 BK31
Ibrox St, G51 66 BL31
Ibrox Ter, G51 66 BK31
Ibrox Ter La, G51 66 BK31
Ida Quad, Bell. ML4
 off St. Marys Rd 110 CV40
Iddesleigh Av, (Miln.) G62 12 BJ11
Ilay Av, (Bears.) G61 47 BH21
Ilay Ct, (Bears.) G61 48 BJ21
Ilay Rd, (Bears.) G61 48 BJ21
Imlach Pl, Moth. ML1 127 CZ48
Imperial Dr, Air. ML6 76 DB32
Inchbrae Rd, G52 85 BE33
Inchcolm Gdns, (Mood.) G69
 off Culross Way 37 CQ18
Inchcolm Pl, (E.Kil.) G74 135 BY51
Inchcruin Pl, G15 28 BA17
Inchfad Cres, G15 28 BA18
Inchfad Dr, G15 28 BA18
Inchfad Pl, G15 28 BA18
Inch Garvie, (E.Kil.) G74 137 CF52
Inchholm La, G11
 off Byron St 65 BG27
Inchholm St, G11 65 BG27
Inchinnan Business Pk, (Inch.)
 Renf. PA4 43 AR25
Inchinnan Dr, (Inch.) Renf. PA4 44 AT23
Inchinnan Ind Est, (Inch.)
 Renf. PA4 43 AR24
Inchinnan Rd, Bell. ML4 94 CV38
Inchinnan Rd, Pais. PA3 62 AU30
Inchinnan Rd, Renf. PA4 45 AX25
Inchkeith, (E.Kil.) G74 137 CF52
Inchkeith Pl, G32 70 CD30
Inchlaggan Pl, G15 28 BA17
Inchlee St, G14 65 BG27
Inch Marnock, (E.Kil.) G74 137 CE53
Inch Meadow, Ersk. PA8
 off Newshot Dr 44 AT21
Inchmoan Pl, G15 28 BB17
Inch Murrin, (E.Kil.) G74 137 CF52
Inchmurrin Av, (Kirk.) G66
 off Iona Way 18 CK13
Inchmurrin Dr, (Ruther.) G73 105 BZ43
Inchmurrin Gdns, (Ruther.)
 G73 105 BZ43

Inchmurrin Pl, (Ruther.) G73 105 BZ43
Inchneuk Rd, (Glenb.)
 Coat. ML5 56 CU23
Inchnock Av, (Gart.) G69 55 CP23
Inchoch Gro, G33 71 CG27
Inchoch St, G33 71 CG27
Inchrory Pl, G15 28 BA17
Inchwood Ct, (Cumb.) G68 21 CW14
Inchwood Pl, (Cumb.) G68 20 CV14
Inchwood Rd, (Cumb.) G68 20 CV14
Incle St, Pais. PA1 62 AV32
India Dr, (Inch.) Renf. PA4 44 AS23
India St, G2 4 BQ29
Industry St, (Kirk.) G66 17 CF14
Inga St, G20 49 BN22
Ingerbreck Av, (Ruther.) G73 105 BZ41
Ingleby Dr, G31 69 BW30
Ingleby Pl, (Neil.) G78 114 AU46
Inglefield St, Air. ML6 76 DC30
Inglefield St, G42 87 BR35
Ingleneuk Av, G33 52 CD24
Ingleside, (Lenz.) G66 35 CE15
Inglestone Av, (Thornlie.) G46 102 BJ43
Inglewood Cres, (E.Kil.) G75 135 BW53
Inglewood Cres, Pais. PA2 81 AN35
Inglis Pl, (E.Kil.) G75 136 CA54
Inglis St, G31 69 BW31
Inglis St, Wis. ML2 143 DF51
Ingram St, G1 5 BS30
Inishail Rd, G33 71 CE28
Inkerman Rd, G52 64 BB32
Innellan Gdns, G20 48 BK22
Innellan Pl, G20 48 BK22
Innermanse Quad, Moth. ML1
 off Manse Vw 113 DH40
Innerwick Dr, G52 64 BD32
Innes Ct, (E.Kil.) G74 122 CA49
Innes Ct, Air. ML6 77 DG29
Innspark, (Kilsyth) G65 7 CT4
International Av, (Blan.) G72 124 CM49
Inveraray Dr, (Bishop.) G64 33 BX17
Inveraray Gdns, (New.)
 Moth. ML1 113 DE42
Inveravon Dr, Moth. ML1 127 CX48
Inverbervie, Ersk. PA8 25 AQ19
Invercanny Dr, G15 28 BB17
Invercanny Pl, G15 28 BC17
Invercargill, (E.Kil.) G75 135 BW54
Inverclyde Gdns, (Ruther.) G73 105 BZ42
Invercree Wk, (Glenb.) Coat. ML5
 off Dinyra Pl 56 CS23
Inveresk Pl, Coat. ML5 75 CW29
Inveresk Quad, G32 70 CC31
Inveresk St, G32 70 CC31
Inverewe Av, (Thornlie.) G46 101 BF42
Inverewe Dr, (Thornlie.) G46 101 BF43
Inverewe Gdns, (Thornlie.) G46 101 BF43
Inverewe Pl, (Thornlie.) G46 101 BF42
Inverewe Way, (Newt. M.) G77 116 BC48
Invergarry Av, (Thornlie.) G46 101 BF44
Invergarry Ct, (Thornlie.) G46 101 BG44
Invergarry Dr, (Thornlie.) G46 101 BF43
Invergarry Gdns, (Thornlie.)
 G46 101 BF44
Invergarry Gro, (Thornlie.) G46 101 BF43
Invergarry Pl, (Thornlie.) G46
 off Invergarry Dr 101 BG43
Invergarry Quad, (Thornlie.)
 G46 101 BG43
Invergarry Vw, (Thornlie.) G46 101 BG43
Inverglas Av, Renf. PA4
 off Morriston Cres 64 BB28
Invergordon Av, G43 87 BP38

| | | |
|---|---|---|
| Invergyle Dr, G52 | 64 | BD32 |
| Inverkar Dr, Pais. PA2 | 81 | AQ35 |
| Inverlair Av, G43 | 103 | BP39 |
| Inverlair Av, G44 | 103 | BP39 |
| Inverleith St, G32 | 69 | BZ31 |
| Inverlochy St, G33 | 71 | CF28 |
| Inverness St, G51 | 65 | BF31 |
| Inveroran Dr, (Bears.) G61 | 30 | BK17 |
| Inver Rd, G33 | 71 | CG30 |
| Invershiel Rd, G23 | 30 | BM20 |
| Invershin Dr, G20 | 48 | BM24 |
| Inverurie St, G21 | 50 | BT26 |
| Invervale Av, Air. ML6 | 77 | DH31 |
| Inzievar Ter, G32 | 90 | CD36 |
| Iona, Air. ML6 | 77 | DF32 |
| Iona Av, (E.Kil.) G74 | 122 | CC49 |
| Iona Cres, (Old Kil.) G60 | 26 | AS16 |
| Iona Dr, (Old Kil.) G60 | 26 | AS16 |
| Iona Dr, Pais. PA2 | 82 | AT38 |
| Iona Gdns, (Old Kil.) G60 | 26 | AS16 |
| Iona La, (Mood.) G69 | 37 | CQ19 |
| Iona Path, (Blan.) G72 | 124 | CL46 |
| Iona Pl, (Old Kil.) G60 | 26 | AS16 |
| Iona Pl, Coat. ML5 | 74 | CT28 |
| Iona Ridge, Ham. ML3 | 139 | CP52 |
| Iona Rd, (Ruther.) G73 | 106 | CA42 |
| Iona Rd, Renf. PA4 | 63 | AY28 |
| Iona St, G51 | 66 | BK30 |
| Iona St, Moth. ML1 | 111 | CZ44 |
| Iona Wk, Coat. ML5 | | |
| *off Tarbert Way* | 94 | CU33 |
| Iona Way, (Stepps) G33 | 53 | CG25 |
| Iona Way, (Kirk.) G66 | 18 | CJ13 |
| Iris Av, G45 | 105 | BW42 |
| Irongray St, G31 | 69 | BY30 |
| Irvine Cres, Coat. ML5 | 75 | CY30 |
| Irvine Pl, (Kilsyth) G65 | 7 | CR4 |
| Irvine St, G40 | 89 | BX34 |
| Irvine St, (Glenm.) Air. ML6 | 58 | DB25 |
| Irvine Ter, Ham. ML3 | 140 | CT53 |
| Irving Av, Clyde. G81 | 27 | AX16 |
| Irving Ct, Clyde. G81 | | |
| *off Stewart Dr* | 27 | AX15 |
| Irving Quad, Clyde. G81 | 27 | AX15 |
| Isabella Gdns, Ham. ML3 | 141 | CX52 |
| Iser La, G41 | 87 | BP37 |
| Island Rd, (Cumb.) G67 | 21 | CZ13 |
| Islay, Air. ML6 | 77 | DG31 |
| Islay Av, (Ruther.) G73 | 106 | CA42 |
| Islay Ct, Ham. ML3 | | |
| *off Wellhall Rd* | 139 | CP51 |
| Islay Cres, (Old Kil.) G60 | 26 | AS16 |
| Islay Cres, Pais. PA2 | 82 | AT38 |
| Islay Dr, (Old Kil.) G60 | 26 | AS16 |
| Islay Dr, (Newt. M.) G77 | 116 | BD48 |
| Islay Gdns, Lark. ML9 | 144 | DD58 |
| Islay Quad, Wis. ML2 | 143 | DG52 |
| Islay Rd, (Kirk.) G66 | 18 | CJ13 |
| Islay Way, Coat. ML5 | 94 | CT33 |
| Ivanhoe, (E.Kil.) G74 | 123 | CF49 |
| Ivanhoe Dr, (Kirk.) G66 | 17 | CG13 |
| Ivanhoe Pl, Moth. ML1 | | |
| *off Rowantree Ter* | 112 | DD40 |
| Ivanhoe Rd, G13 | 47 | BF21 |
| Ivanhoe Rd, (Cumb.) G67 | 22 | DA13 |
| Ivanhoe Rd, Pais. PA2 | 81 | AP36 |
| Ivanhoe Way, Pais. PA2 | | |
| *off Ivanhoe Rd* | 81 | AP36 |
| Ivybank Av, (Camb.) G72 | 107 | CE41 |
| Ivy Gro, Coat. ML5 | 75 | CX31 |
| Ivy Pl, (Blan.) G72 | 124 | CL45 |
| Ivy Pl, Moth. ML1 | 112 | DC42 |
| Ivy Rd, (Udd.) G71 | 94 | CS37 |

| | | |
|---|---|---|
| Ivy Ter, Moth. ML1 | 112 | DC40 |
| Ivy Way, (Chap.) Air. ML6 | 97 | DG34 |

**J**

| | | |
|---|---|---|
| Jackson Ct, Coat. ML5 | 75 | CX31 |
| Jackson Dr, G33 | 53 | CH24 |
| Jackson Pl, (Bears.) G61 | 29 | BG18 |
| Jackson St, Coat. ML5 | 75 | CX30 |
| Jacks Rd, (Udd.) G71 | 109 | CQ41 |
| Jack St, Ham. ML3 | 140 | CT53 |
| Jack St, Moth. ML1 | 128 | DD49 |
| Jackton Rd, (E.Kil.) G75 | 134 | BS55 |
| Jacobite Pl, Bell. ML4 | 111 | CZ41 |
| Jade Ter, Bell. ML4 | | |
| *off Ruby Ter* | 111 | CW41 |
| Jagger Gdns, (Baill.) G69 | 91 | CH33 |
| Jamaica Dr, (E.Kil.) G75 | 135 | BW52 |
| Jamaica St, G1 | 4 | BR31 |
| James Dempsey Ct, Coat. ML5 | 74 | CV31 |
| James Dempsey Gdns, Coat. | | |
| ML5 *off James Dempsey Ct* | 74 | CV31 |
| James Dunlop Gdns, (Bishop.) | | |
| G64 | 51 | BX22 |
| James Gray St, G41 | 87 | BN36 |
| James Hamilton Dr, Bell. ML4 | 111 | CX40 |
| James Healy Dr, Ham. ML3 | 140 | CS54 |
| James Morrison St, G1 | 5 | BT31 |
| James Murdie Gdns, | | |
| Ham. ML3 | 125 | CQ47 |
| James Nisbet St, G21 | 5 | BU29 |
| James St, G40 | 88 | BU33 |
| James St, (Righead Ind. Est.) | | |
| Bell. ML4 | 110 | CU39 |
| James St, Moth. ML1 | 127 | CZ46 |
| James Vw, Moth. ML1 | 112 | DB42 |
| James Watt Av, (E.Kil.) G75 | 136 | CB53 |
| James Watt La, G2 | | |
| *off James Watt St* | 4 | BQ30 |
| James Watt Pl, (E.Kil.) G74 | 121 | BX50 |
| James Watt Rd, (Miln.) G62 | 11 | BH10 |
| James Watt St, G2 | 4 | BQ30 |
| Jamieson Ct, G42 | 87 | BR35 |
| Jamieson Dr, (E.Kil.) G74 | 136 | CC51 |
| Jamieson Path, G42 | | |
| *off Jamieson St* | 87 | BR35 |
| Jamieson St, G42 | 87 | BR35 |
| Janebank Av, (Camb.) G72 | 107 | CE41 |
| Jane Ct, Lark. ML9 | | |
| *off Margaretvale Dr* | 144 | DC59 |
| Janefield Av, John. PA5 | 79 | AG35 |
| Janefield Pl, (Blan.) G72 | 124 | CL47 |
| Janefield St, G31 | 69 | BX32 |
| Jane Pl, G5 | 88 | BS33 |
| Jane Rae Gdns, Clyde. G81 | 45 | AZ21 |
| Jane's Brae, (Cumb.) G67 | 22 | DB13 |
| Janesmith St, Wis. ML2 | 129 | DE49 |
| Janetta St, Clyde. G81 | 27 | AW17 |
| Jardine St, G20 | | |
| *off Tillie St* | 49 | BP26 |
| Jardine Ter, (Gart.) G69 | 55 | CP24 |
| Jarvie Cres, (Kilsyth) G65 | 7 | CT6 |
| Jarvie Way, Pais. PA2 | 81 | AN37 |
| Jasmine Pl, (Cumb.) G67 | 21 | CX14 |
| Java St, Moth. ML1 | 111 | CY44 |
| Jean Armour Dr, Clyde. G81 | 27 | AY18 |
| Jeanette Av, Ham. ML3 | 140 | CT54 |
| Jean Maclean Pl, (Bishop.) G64 | 33 | BX17 |
| Jedburgh Av, (Ruther.) G73 | 89 | BX38 |
| Jedburgh Dr, Pais. PA2 | 81 | AQ36 |
| Jedburgh Gdns, G20 | | |
| *off Wilton St* | 49 | BP26 |
| Jedburgh Pl, (E.Kil.) G74 | 136 | CB51 |

| | | |
|---|---|---|
| Jedburgh Pl, Coat. ML5 | 94 | CV34 |
| Jedburgh St, (Blan.) G72 | 124 | CM46 |
| Jedworth Av, G15 | 28 | BD18 |
| Jedworth Pl, G15 | | |
| *off Tallant Rd* | 29 | BE18 |
| Jedworth Rd, G15 | 28 | BD18 |
| Jeffrey Pl, (Kilsyth) G65 | 7 | CS4 |
| Jellicoe St, Clyde. G81 | 26 | AU18 |
| Jenny Lind Ct, G46 | 101 | BF43 |
| Jenny's Well Ct, Pais. PA2 | 83 | AY35 |
| Jenny's Well Rd, Pais. PA2 | 83 | AX35 |
| Jervis Ter, (E.Kil.) G75 | 135 | BX54 |
| Jerviston Ct, Moth. ML1 | | |
| *off Jerviston Rd* | 112 | DC44 |
| Jerviston Rd, G33 | 71 | CE27 |
| Jerviston Rd, Moth. ML1 | 112 | DC43 |
| Jerviston St, Moth. ML1 | 128 | DB45 |
| Jerviston St, (Holytown) | | |
| Moth. ML1 | 112 | DC41 |
| Jerviston St, (New Stev.) | | |
| Moth. ML1 | 112 | DC43 |
| Jerviswood, Moth. ML1 | 112 | DC44 |
| Jessie St, G42 | 88 | BT35 |
| Jessiman Sq, Renf. PA4 | 63 | AX28 |
| Jimmy Sneddon Way, Moth. ML1 | | |
| *off Columba Cres* | 111 | CZ43 |
| Joanna Ter, (Blan.) G72 | 124 | CM45 |
| Jocelyn Sq, G1 | 5 | BS31 |
| John Bowman Gdns, Bell. ML4 | 111 | CW39 |
| John Brannan Way, Bell. ML4 | 110 | CT39 |
| John Brown Pl, (Chry.) G69 | 54 | CL21 |
| John Ewing Gdns, Lark. ML9 | 144 | DC57 |
| John Hendry Rd, (Udd.) G71 | 109 | CQ41 |
| John Jarvie Sq, (Kilsyth) G65 | | |
| *off Main St* | 7 | CT4 |
| John Knox La, G4 | | |
| *off Drygate* | 5 | BU30 |
| John Knox La, Ham. ML3 | | |
| *off Brankholm Brae* | 124 | CM49 |
| John Knox St, G4 | 5 | BU30 |
| John Knox St, Clyde. G81 | 45 | AY21 |
| John Lang St, John. PA5 | 80 | AJ34 |
| John Marshall Dr, (Bishop.) G64 | 50 | BU22 |
| John McEwan Way, (Torr.) G64 | 15 | BX13 |
| John Murray Ct, Moth. ML1 | 128 | DA50 |
| John Neilson Av, Pais. PA1 | 81 | AQ33 |
| Johnsburn Dr, G53 | 100 | BD39 |
| Johnsburn Rd, G53 | 100 | BD39 |
| Johnshaven, Ersk. PA8 | | |
| *off North Barr Av* | 25 | AQ19 |
| Johnshaven St, G43 | | |
| *off Bengal St* | 86 | BL38 |
| John Smith Ct, Air. ML6 | 76 | DB29 |
| John Smith Gdns, Coat. ML5 | 75 | CZ32 |
| John Smith Gate, (Barr.) G78 | 99 | AY41 |
| Johnson Dr, (Camb.) G72 | 106 | CC40 |
| Johnston Av, (Kilsyth) G65 | 7 | CT6 |
| Johnston Av, Clyde. G81 | 45 | AZ21 |
| Johnstone Av, G52 | 64 | BD31 |
| Johnstone Dr, (Ruther.) G73 | 89 | BW38 |
| Johnstone Rd, Ham. ML3 | 140 | CU51 |
| Johnstone St, Bell. ML4 | 111 | CY40 |
| Johnstone Ter, (Kilsyth) G65 | 19 | CP10 |
| Johnston Rd, (Gart.) G69 | 55 | CQ23 |
| Johnston St, Air. ML6 | 76 | DD29 |
| Johnston St, Pais. PA1 | 82 | AU33 |
| John St, G1 | 5 | BS30 |
| John St, (Kirk.) G66 | 17 | CF12 |
| John St, (Blan.) G72 | 125 | CN46 |
| John St, (Barr.) G78 | 99 | AX42 |
| John St, Bell. ML4 | 111 | CW40 |
| John St, Ham. ML3 | 126 | CU50 |
| John St, Lark. ML9 | 144 | DC59 |

| | | |
|---|---|---|
| John St, Pais. PA1 | | |
| off Broomlands St | 82 | AS33 |
| John St, Wis. ML2 | 129 | DE49 |
| John Wilson Dr, (Kilsyth) G65 | 7 | CR4 |
| Jones Wynd, Moth. ML1 | | |
| off Morris Cres | 113 | DG44 |
| Joppa St, G33 | 70 | CA30 |
| Jordanhill Cres, G13 | 47 | BF24 |
| Jordanhill Dr, G13 | 47 | BE24 |
| Jordanhill La, G13 | 47 | BG24 |
| Jordan St, G14 | 65 | BF27 |
| Jordanvale Av, G14 | 65 | BF27 |
| Jowitt Av, Clyde. G81 | 27 | AZ20 |
| Jubilee Bk, (Kirk.) G66 | | |
| off Heriot Rd | 35 | CE18 |
| Jubilee Ct, G52 | 64 | BB30 |
| Jubilee Gdns, (Bears.) G61 | 29 | BH17 |
| Jubilee Path, (Bears.) G61 | | |
| off Jubilee Gdns | 29 | BH17 |
| Jubilee Ter, John. PA5 | 79 | AF35 |
| Julian Av, G12 | 48 | BL25 |
| Julian La, G12 | 48 | BL25 |
| Juniper Av, (E.Kil.) G75 | 135 | BZ55 |
| Juniper Ct, (Kirk.) G66 | 34 | CD16 |
| Juniper Dr, (M. of Cam.) G66 | 16 | CD9 |
| Juniper Dr, Ham. ML3 | 139 | CP54 |
| Juniper Gro, Ham. ML3 | 140 | CV51 |
| Juniper Pl, G32 | 91 | CH33 |
| Juniper Pl, (Udd.) G71 | | |
| off Juniper Rd | 94 | CT37 |
| Juniper Pl, John. PA5 | 80 | AJ37 |
| Juniper Rd, (Udd.) G71 | 94 | CT37 |
| Juniper Ter, G32 | 91 | CG33 |
| Juniper Wynd, Moth. ML1 | | |
| off Willow Gro | 112 | DD40 |
| Juno St, Moth. ML1 | 111 | CZ44 |
| Jupiter St, Moth. ML1 | 111 | CZ44 |
| Jura, (E.Kil.) G74 | 136 | CD54 |
| Jura Av, Renf. PA4 | 63 | AZ28 |
| Jura Ct, G52 | 65 | BG32 |
| Jura Dr, (Old Kil.) G60 | 26 | AS16 |
| Jura Dr, (Kirk.) G66 | 18 | CJ13 |
| Jura Dr, (Blan.) G72 | 108 | CL42 |
| Jura Dr, (Newt. M.) G77 | 116 | BD47 |
| Jura Gdns, (Old Kil.) G60 | 26 | AS16 |
| Jura Gdns, Ham. ML3 | 139 | CQ51 |
| Jura Gdns, Lark. ML9 | 145 | DE58 |
| Jura Pl, (Old Kil.) G60 | 26 | AS16 |
| Jura Quad, Wis. ML2 | | |
| off Montgomery Cres | 143 | DG52 |
| Jura Rd, (Old Kil.) G60 | 26 | AS16 |
| Jura Rd, Pais. PA2 | 82 | AT38 |
| Jura St, G52 | 65 | BH32 |
| Jura Wynd, (Glenb.) Coat. ML5 | 56 | CS23 |

**K**

| | | |
|---|---|---|
| Kaim Dr, G53 | 101 | BE39 |
| Karadale Gdns, Lark. ML9 | 144 | DC59 |
| Karol Path, G4 | | |
| off St. Peters St | 67 | BQ27 |
| Kashmir Av, (Linw.) Pais. PA3 | 60 | AK32 |
| Katewell Av, G15 | 28 | BA17 |
| Katewell Pl, G15 | 28 | BA17 |
| Katherine St, Air. ML6 | 77 | DG29 |
| Katrine Av, (Bishop.) G64 | 33 | BX20 |
| Katrine Av, (Righead Ind. Est.) | | |
| Bell. ML4 | 110 | CT39 |
| Katrine Cres, Air. ML6 | | |
| off Ballochney St | 76 | DB28 |
| Katrine Dr, (Newt. M.) G77 | 118 | BK49 |
| Katrine Dr, Pais. PA2 | 81 | AP35 |
| Katrine Pl, (Camb.) G72 | 106 | CC39 |

| | | |
|---|---|---|
| Katrine Pl, Coat. ML5 | 74 | CT27 |
| Katrine Way, (Both.) G71 | | |
| off Belstane Pl | 109 | CQ42 |
| Katrine Wynd, Moth. ML1 | | |
| off Howden Pl | 112 | DC40 |
| Katriona Path, Lark. ML9 | | |
| off Stuart Dr | 145 | DE60 |
| Kay Gdns, Moth. ML1 | 127 | CX47 |
| Kaystone Rd, G15 | 28 | BC20 |
| Kay St, G21 | 50 | BV25 |
| Keal Av, G15 | 46 | BC21 |
| Keal Cres, G15 | 46 | BC21 |
| Keal Dr, G15 | 46 | BC21 |
| Keal Pl, G15 | 46 | BC21 |
| Keane Path, Moth. ML1 | 128 | DD50 |
| Kearn Av, G15 | 28 | BD20 |
| Kearn Pl, G15 | 28 | BD20 |
| Keats Pk, (Both.) G71 | 109 | CR42 |
| Keir Dr, (Bishop.) G64 | 32 | BV19 |
| Keir Hardie Av, Moth. ML1 | 112 | DD40 |
| Keir Hardie Ct, (Bishop.) G64 | 33 | BW20 |
| Keir Hardie Dr, (Kilsyth) G65 | | |
| off Murray Av | 7 | CT5 |
| Keir Hardie Dr, Bell. ML4 | 110 | CV41 |
| Keir Hardie Pl, Bell. ML4 | 110 | CV41 |
| Keir Hardie Rd, Lark. ML9 | 145 | DE60 |
| Keir St, G41 | 87 | BP34 |
| Keirs Wk, (Camb.) G72 | 106 | CC39 |
| Keith Av, (Giff.) G46 | 102 | BM42 |
| Keith Ct, G11 | 66 | BL28 |
| Keith St, G11 | 66 | BL27 |
| Keith St, Bell. ML4 | 111 | CW39 |
| Keith St, Ham. ML3 | 126 | CV50 |
| Kelbourne Cres, Bell. ML4 | | |
| off Cochrane St | 110 | CV40 |
| Kelbourne St, G20 | 49 | BN25 |
| Kelburne Dr, Pais. PA1 | 63 | AX32 |
| Kelburne Gdns, (Baill.) G69 | 92 | CJ34 |
| Kelburne Gdns, Pais. PA1 | 63 | AW32 |
| Kelburne Oval, Pais. PA1 | 63 | AW32 |
| Kelburn St, (Barr.) G78 | 99 | AW44 |
| Kelhead Av, G52 | 64 | BB32 |
| Kelhead Dr, G52 | 64 | BB32 |
| Kelhead Path, G52 | 64 | BB32 |
| Kelhead Pl, G52 | 64 | BB32 |
| Kellas St, G51 | 66 | BJ30 |
| Kellie Gro, (E.Kil.) G74 | 121 | BZ50 |
| Kellock Cres, Coat. ML5 | 94 | CT33 |
| Kells Pl, G15 | 28 | BA17 |
| Kelso Av, (Ruther.) G73 | 89 | BX38 |
| Kelso Av, Pais. PA2 | 81 | AQ36 |
| Kelso Dr, (E.Kil.) G74 | 122 | CC50 |
| Kelso Gdns, (Mood.) G69 | | |
| off Whithorn Cres | 37 | CP18 |
| Kelso Pl, G14 | 46 | BA23 |
| Kelso Quad, Coat. ML5 | 74 | CV29 |
| Kelso St, G13 | 46 | BB21 |
| Kelso St, G14 | 46 | BA23 |
| Kelton St, G32 | 90 | CD33 |
| Kelty Pl, G5 | | |
| off Bedford St | 67 | BR32 |
| Kelvin Av, G52 | 64 | BB29 |
| Kelvinbridge Rbt, (Torr.) G64 | 15 | BX13 |
| Kelvin Ct, G12 | 47 | BH23 |
| Kelvin Ct, (E.Kil.) G75 | 136 | CC54 |
| Kelvin Cres, (Bears.) G61 | 29 | BH19 |
| Kelvin Cres, (E.Kil.) G75 | 136 | CC54 |
| Kelvindale, (Torr.) G64 | 15 | BY12 |
| Kelvindale Bldgs, G12 | | |
| off Kelvindale Rd | 48 | BL24 |
| Kelvindale Gdns, G20 | 48 | BL23 |
| Kelvindale Pl, G20 | | |
| off Kelvindale Rd | 48 | BM23 |

| | | |
|---|---|---|
| Kelvindale Rd, G12 | 48 | BK23 |
| Kelvindale Rd, G20 | 48 | BM23 |
| Kelvin Dr, G20 | 48 | BM25 |
| Kelvin Dr, (Bishop.) G64 | 33 | BW19 |
| Kelvin Dr, (Kirk.) G66 | 16 | CC13 |
| Kelvin Dr, (Chry.) G69 | 37 | CN19 |
| Kelvin Dr, (E.Kil.) G75 | 136 | CB54 |
| Kelvin Dr, (Barr.) G78 | 99 | AZ44 |
| Kelvin Dr, Air. ML6 | 76 | DD28 |
| Kelvin Gdns, (Kilsyth) G65 | 7 | CT6 |
| Kelvin Gdns, Ham. ML3 | 125 | CN49 |
| Kelvingrove St, G3 | 67 | BN29 |
| Kelvinhaugh Gate, G3 | 66 | BM29 |
| Kelvinhaugh Pl, G3 | 66 | BM29 |
| Kelvinhaugh St, G3 | 66 | BL29 |
| Kelvinhead Rd, (Kilsyth) G65 | 9 | DA3 |
| Kelvin Ind Est, (E.Kil.) G75 | 136 | CB55 |
| Kelvin Pl, (E.Kil.) G75 | 136 | CC54 |
| Kelvin Rd, (Miln.) G62 | 11 | BG10 |
| Kelvin Rd, (Cumb.) G67 | 22 | DC13 |
| Kelvin Rd, (Udd.) G71 | 93 | CN38 |
| Kelvin Rd, (E.Kil.) G75 | 136 | CB54 |
| Kelvin Rd, Bell. ML4 | 95 | CX38 |
| Kelvin Rd N, (Cumb.) G67 | 22 | DC13 |
| Kelvinside Av, G20 | 49 | BN25 |
| Kelvinside Dr, G20 | 49 | BP25 |
| Kelvinside Gdns, G20 | 49 | BN25 |
| Kelvinside Gdns E, G20 | 49 | BP26 |
| Kelvinside Gdns La, G20 | 49 | BN25 |
| Kelvinside Ter S, G20 | 49 | BN26 |
| Kelvinside Ter W, G20 | | |
| off Kelvinside Ter S | 49 | BN26 |
| Kelvin St, Coat. ML5 | 75 | CY32 |
| Kelvin Ter, (Kilsyth) G65 | | |
| off Differ Av | 19 | CP11 |
| Kelvinvale, (Kirk.) G66 | 17 | CF12 |
| Kelvin Vw, (Torr.) G64 | 15 | BY13 |
| Kelvin Vw, (Kilsyth) G65 | 19 | CP11 |
| Kelvin Way, G3 | 66 | BM28 |
| Kelvin Way, (Kilsyth) G65 | 7 | CS4 |
| Kelvin Way, (Kirk.) G66 | 16 | CC13 |
| Kelvin Way, (Both.) G71 | 109 | CQ42 |
| Kemp Av, Pais. PA3 | 63 | AW28 |
| Kemp Ct, Ham. ML3 | 126 | CU50 |
| Kempock St, G40 | 89 | BY33 |
| Kempsthorn Cres, G53 | 84 | BC36 |
| Kempsthorn Path, G53 | | |
| off Kempsthorn Rd | 84 | BD36 |
| Kempsthorn Pl, G53 | 84 | BD36 |
| Kempsthorn Rd, G53 | 84 | BC36 |
| Kemp St, G21 | 50 | BU25 |
| Kemp St, Ham. ML3 | 126 | CT50 |
| Kendal Av, G12 | | |
| off Ripon Dr | 48 | BJ23 |
| Kendal Av, (Giff.) G46 | 102 | BL42 |
| Kendal Dr, G12 | 48 | BJ23 |
| Kendal Rd, (E.Kil.) G75 | 134 | BV55 |
| Kendoon Av, G15 | 28 | BA18 |
| Kenilburn Av, Air. ML6 | 76 | DD27 |
| Kenilburn Cres, Air. ML6 | 76 | DD27 |
| Kenilworth, (E.Kil.) G74 | 123 | CF49 |
| Kenilworth Av, G41 | 86 | BM37 |
| Kenilworth Av, Pais. PA2 | 81 | AP37 |
| Kenilworth Ct, (Cumb.) G67 | 22 | DA13 |
| Kenilworth Ct, Moth. ML1 | | |
| off Ivy Ter | 112 | DD40 |
| Kenilworth Cres, (Bears.) G61 | 29 | BE15 |
| Kenilworth Cres, Bell. ML4 | 111 | CW39 |
| Kenilworth Cres, Ham. ML3 | 125 | CP49 |
| Kenilworth Dr, Air. ML6 | 77 | DE29 |
| Kenilworth Rd, (Kirk.) G66 | 17 | CG13 |
| Kenilworth Way, Pais. PA2 | | |
| off Kenilworth Av | 81 | AP37 |

Kenley Rd, Renf. PA4 46 BB26
Kenmar Gdns, (Udd.) G71 93 CN37
Kenmar Rd, Ham. ML3 125 CR48
Kenmar Ter, Ham. ML3 125 CR48
Kenmore Gdns, (Bears.) G61
  *off Methven Av* 30 BK16
Kenmore Rd, (Cumb.) G67 22 DD11
Kenmore St, G32 70 CC32
Kenmuiraid Pl, Bell. ML4 110 CV42
Kenmuir Av, G32 91 CG34
Kenmuirhill Gdns, G32 91 CF35
Kenmuirhill Gate, G32 91 CF35
Kenmuirhill Rd, G32 91 CF35
Kenmuir Rd, G32 91 CE37
Kenmuir St, Coat. ML5 93 CR33
Kenmure Av, (Bishop.) G64 32 BU20
Kenmure Cres, (Bishop.) G64 32 BV20
Kenmure Dr, (Bishop.) G64 32 BV20
Kenmure Gdns, (Bishop.) G64 32 BU20
Kenmure La, (Bishop.) G64 32 BV20
Kenmure Rd, (Giff.) G46 118 BK47
Kenmure Row, G22
  *off Castlebay St* 31 BR20
Kenmure St, G41 87 BP35
Kenmure Way, (Ruther.) G73 105 BX42
Kennedar Dr, G51 65 BG29
Kennedy Av, (Kilsyth) G65 19 CP10
Kennedy Ct, (Giff.) G46 102 BL41
Kennedy Dr, Air. ML6 76 DA30
Kennedy Path, G4 5 BT29
Kennedy St, G4 5 BT28
Kennelburn Rd, (Chap.)
  Air. ML6 97 DF36
Kenneth Rd, Moth. ML1 127 CY48
Kennet St, G21 69 BW28
Kennihill, Air. ML6 76 DC28
Kennihill Quad, Air. ML6 76 DC28
Kennishead Av, (Thornlie.) G46 101 BG40
Kennishead Path, (Thornlie.)
  G46 *off Kennishead Pl* 101 BG40
Kennishead Pl, (Thornlie.) G46 101 BG40
Kennishead Rd, G43 101 BH40
Kennishead Rd, (Thornlie.) G46 101 BG40
Kennishead Rd, G53 100 BD41
Kennisholm Av, (Thornlie.) G46 101 BG40
Kennisholm Path, (Thornlie.)
  G46 *off Kennisholm Av* 101 BG40
Kennisholm Pl, (Thornlie.) G46 101 BG40
Kennoway Cres, Ham. ML3 141 CY52
Kennoway Dr, G11 65 BH27
Kennyhill Sq, G31 69 BX29
Kenshaw Av, Lark. ML9 144 DC61
Kenshaw Pl, Lark. ML9 144 DC61
Kensington Dr, (Giff.) G46 102 BM44
Kensington Gate, G12 48 BL25
Kensington Gate La, G12 48 BL25
Kensington Rd, G12 48 BL25
Kensington Sq, (Bears.) G61 30 BK18
Kentallen Rd, G33 71 CG31
Kent Dr, (Ruther.) G73 105 BZ34
Kentigern Ter, (Bishop.) G64 51 BW21
Kentmere Cl, (E.Kil.) G75 135 BW55
Kentmere Dr, (E.Kil.) G75 135 BW55
Kentmere Pl, (E.Kil.) G75 134 BV55
Kent Pl, (E.Kil.) G75 134 BV55
Kent Rd, G3 67 BN29
Kent St, G40 5 BU31
Keppel Dr, G44 88 BU38
Keppochhill Dr, G21 50 BT26
Keppochhill Pl, G21 68 BT27
Keppochhill Rd, G21 50 BT26
Keppochhill Rd, G22 50 BS26
Keppochhill Way, G21 68 BT27

Keppoch St, G21 50 BT26
Kerfield La, G15 28 BA17
Kerfield Pl, G15 28 BA17
Kerr Cres, Ham. ML3 140 CS52
Kerr Dr, G40 68 BV32
Kerrera Pl, G33 71 CF31
Kerrera Rd, G33 71 CF31
Kerr Gdns, (Udd.) G71 93 CQ37
Kerr Pl, G40 68 BV32
Kerr Rd, (Miln.) G62
  *off Craigton Gdns* 11 BG10
Kerr St, G40 68 BV32
Kerr St, (Kirk.) G66 17 CE13
Kerr St, (Blan.) G72 125 CN45
Kerr St, (Barr.) G78 99 AW43
Kerr St, Pais. PA3 62 AT32
Kerrycroy Av, G42 88 BT38
Kerrycroy Pl, G42
  *off Kerrycroy Av* 88 BT37
Kerrycroy St, G42 88 BT37
Kerrydale St, G40 89 BX33
Kerrylamont Av, G42 88 BU38
Kerry Pl, G15 28 BA18
Kersland Dr, (Miln.) G62 12 BK11
Kersland La, G12 48 BM26
Kersland St, G12 48 BM26
Kessington Dr, (Bears.) G61 30 BJ17
Kessington Rd, (Bears.) G61 30 BJ18
Kessock Dr, G22 49 BR26
Kessock Pl, G22 49 BR26
Kestrel Ct, Clyde. G81 27 AW16
Kestrel Pl, John. PA5 79 AF38
Kestrel Rd, G13 47 BE23
Kestrel Vw, (Strathclyde Bus. Pk.)
  Bell. ML4 94 CU36
Keswick Dr, Ham. ML3 140 CS55
Keswick Rd, (E.Kil.) G75 134 BV55
Kethers La, Moth. ML1 127 CX47
Kethers St, Moth. ML1 127 CY46
Kew Gdns, G12
  *off Ruthven St* 48 BM26
Kew Gdns, (Udd.) G71 93 CR38
Kew La, G12 48 BM26
Kew Ter, G12 48 BM26
Keynes Sq, Bell. ML4
  *off Clydesdale Rd* 111 CZ41
Keystone Av, (Miln.) G62 12 BJ12
Keystone Quad, (Miln.) G62 11 BH13
Keystone Rd, (Miln.) G62 12 BJ13
Kibbleston Rd, (Kilb.)
  John. PA10 78 AC34
Kidston Pl, G5 88 BS33
Kidston Ter, G5 88 BS33
Kierhill Rd, (Cumb.) G68 21 CY11
Kilbarchan Rd, John. PA5 79 AF35
Kilbarchan Rd, (Kilb.)
  John. PA10 79 AF35
Kilbarchan St, G5
  *off Bedford St* 67 BR32
Kilbeg Ter, (Thornlie.) G46 101 BF42
Kilberry St, G21 69 BW28
Kilbirnie Pl, G5 87 BQ33
Kilbirnie St, G5 87 BQ33
Kilbowie Ct, Clyde. G81
  *off Crown Av* 27 AX18
Kilbowie Pl, Air. ML6 77 DF32
Kilbowie Retail Pk, Clyde. G81 27 AY19
Kilbowie Rd, (Cumb.) G67 22 DC13
Kilbowie Rd, Clyde. G81 27 AX15
Kilbowie Rbt, Clyde. G81 27 AX16
Kilbreck Gdns, (Bears.) G61 11 BE13
Kilbreck La, Moth. ML1
  *off Glenburn Av* 113 DE41

Kilbrennan Dr, Moth. ML1 127 CW46
Kilbrennan Rd, (Linw.) Pais. PA3 60 AK31
Kilbride St, G5 88 BT35
Kilbride Ter, G5 88 BT34
Kilbride Vw, (Udd.) G71 93 CQ38
Kilburn Gro, (Blan.) G72 108 CM44
Kilburn Pl, G13 46 BD23
Kilchattan Dr, G44 88 BS38
Kilchoan Rd, G33 71 CE27
Kilcloy Av, G15 28 BC17
Kildale Way, (Ruther.) G73 88 BV37
Kildary Av, G44 103 BQ40
Kildary Rd, G44 103 BQ40
Kildermorie Path, G34
  *off Kildermorie Rd* 72 CJ29
Kildermorie Rd, G34 71 CH29
Kildonan Dr, G11 66 BJ27
Kildonan Pl, Moth. ML1 127 CY46
Kildonan St, Coat. ML5 75 CX30
Kildrostan St, G41 87 BP35
Kildrummy Pl, (E.Kil.) G74 121 BZ50
Kildrum Rd, (Cumb.) G67 22 DD10
Kilearn Rd, Pais. PA3 63 AX30
Kilearn Sq, Pais. PA3
  *off Kilearn Rd* 63 AX30
Kilearn Way, Pais. PA3 63 AX30
Kilfinan St, G22 49 BR22
Kilgarth St, Coat. ML5 93 CR33
Kilkerran Ct, (Newt. M.) G77 116 BD49
Kilkerran Dr, G33 52 CB23
Kilkerran Way, (Newt. M.) G77 116 BD49
Killearn Dr, Pais. PA1 84 BB33
Killearn St, G22 49 BR25
Killermont Av, (Bears.) G61 30 BJ19
Killermont Ct, (Bears.) G61 30 BK18
Killermont Meadows, (Both.)
  G71 109 CN43
Killermont Rd, (Bears.) G61 30 BJ18
Killermont St, G2 5 BS29
Killermont Vw, G20 30 BJ19
Killiegrew Rd, G41 86 BM35
Killin St, G32 90 CD34
Killoch Av, Pais. PA3 61 AQ32
Killoch Dr, G13 46 BC22
Killoch Dr, (Barr.) G78 99 AZ44
Killoch La, Pais. PA3
  *off Killoch Av* 61 AQ32
Killoch Rd, Pais. PA3 61 AQ32
Killoch Way, Pais. PA3
  *off Killoch Av* 61 AQ32
Kilmailing Rd, G44 103 BR40
Kilmair Pl, G20 48 BM24
Kilmaluag Ter, (Thornlie.) G46
  *off Kyleakin Rd* 101 BG42
Kilmannan Gdns, (Miln.) G62
  *off Achray Pl* 11 BF10
Kilmany Dr, G32 70 CB32
Kilmany Gdns, G32 70 CB32
Kilmardinny Av, (Bears.) G61 29 BH15
Kilmardinny Cres, (Bears.) G61 29 BH15
Kilmardinny Dr, (Bears.) G61 29 BH15
Kilmardinny Gate, (Bears.) G61
  *off Kilmardinny Av* 29 BH15
Kilmardinny Gro, (Bears.) G61 29 BH15
Kilmari Gdns, G15 28 BA17
Kilmarnock Rd, G41 102 BM39
Kilmarnock Rd, G43 102 BM39
Kilmartin Pl, (Thornlie.) G46 101 BG41
Kilmartin Pl, (Udd.) G71 93 CQ36
Kilmartin Pl, Air. ML6 77 DF31
Kilmaurs Dr, (Giff.) G46 103 BN42
Kilmaurs St, G51 65 BH31
Kilmore Cres, G15 28 BA17

| | | |
|---|---|---|
| Kilmorie Dr, (Ruther.) G73 | 88 | BU38 |
| Kilmory Av, (Udd.) G71 | 93 | CQ38 |
| Kilmory Dr, (Newt. M.) G77 | 117 | BG48 |
| Kilmuir Cres, (Thornlie.) G46 | 101 | BF41 |
| Kilmuir Dr, (Thornlie.) G46 | 101 | BG41 |
| Kilmuir Rd, (Thornlie.) G46 | 101 | BG41 |
| Kilmuir Rd, (Udd.) G71 | 93 | CP36 |
| Kilmun St, G20 | 48 | BM22 |
| Kilnburn Rd, Moth. ML1 | 127 | CY46 |
| Kilncroft La, Pais. PA2 | 82 | AU35 |
| Kilnside Rd, Pais. PA1 | 62 | AV32 |
| Kilnwell Quad, Moth. ML1 | 127 | CZ46 |
| Kiloran Gro, (Newt. M.) G77 | 116 | BC49 |
| Kiloran Pl, (Newt. M.) G77 | 116 | BC48 |
| Kiloran St, (Thornlie.) G46 | 101 | BH41 |
| Kilpatrick Av, Pais. PA2 | 81 | AR35 |
| Kilpatrick Ct, (Old Kil.) G60 | 25 | AQ15 |
| Kilpatrick Cres, Pais. PA2 | 82 | AT36 |
| Kilpatrick Dr, G33 | 53 | CG24 |
| Kilpatrick Dr, (Bears.) G61 | 11 | BE13 |
| Kilpatrick Dr, Ersk. PA8 | 25 | AR18 |
| Kilpatrick Dr, Renf. PA4 | 63 | AX29 |
| Kilpatrick Gdns, (Clark.) G76 | 118 | BL45 |
| Kilpatrick Way, (Udd.) G71 | 93 | CQ37 |
| Kilsyth Rd, (Kilsyth) G65 | 6 | CN6 |
| Kilsyth Rd, (Kirk.) G66 | 17 | CF12 |
| Kiltarie Cres, Air. ML6 | 77 | DH30 |
| Kiltearn Rd, G33 | 71 | CH30 |
| Kiltongue Cotts, Air. ML6 | 75 | CZ29 |
| Kilvaxter Dr, (Thornlie.) G46 | 101 | BG41 |
| Kilwinning Cres, Ham. ML3 | | |
| off Durisdeer Dr | 139 | CN52 |
| Kilwynet Way, Pais. PA3 | 63 | AW30 |
| Kimberley Gdns, (E.Kil.) G75 | 135 | BY53 |
| Kimberley St, Clyde. G81 | 26 | AT16 |
| Kimberley St, Wis. ML2 | 129 | DE49 |
| Kinalty Rd, G44 | 103 | BQ40 |
| Kinarvie Cres, G53 | 84 | BB38 |
| Kinarvie Gdns, G53 | 84 | BB38 |
| Kinarvie Pl, G53 | 84 | BB38 |
| Kinarvie Rd, G53 | 84 | BB38 |
| Kinarvie Ter, G53 | 84 | BB38 |
| Kinbuck St, G22 | 50 | BT25 |
| Kincaid Gdns, (Camb.) G72 | 90 | CC38 |
| Kincardine Dr, (Bishop.) G64 | 51 | BX21 |
| Kincardine Pl, (Bishop.) G64 | | |
| off Kincardine Dr | 51 | BY22 |
| Kincardine Pl, (E.Kil.) G74 | 123 | CE50 |
| Kincardine Sq, G33 | 71 | CF27 |
| Kincath Av, (Ruther.) G73 | 105 | BZ42 |
| Kinclaven Av, G15 | 28 | BC18 |
| Kincraig St, G51 | 65 | BF31 |
| Kinellan Rd, (Bears.) G61 | 29 | BH20 |
| Kinellar Dr, G14 | 46 | BC23 |
| Kinfauns Dr, G15 | 28 | BB18 |
| Kinfauns Dr, (Newt. M.) G77 | 117 | BH48 |
| Kingarth La, G42 | 87 | BQ35 |
| Kingarth St, G42 | 87 | BQ35 |
| Kingarth St, Ham. ML3 | 140 | CT53 |
| King Edward La, G13 | | |
| off King Edward Rd | 47 | BG24 |
| King Edward Rd, G13 | 47 | BH24 |
| Kingfisher Dr, G13 | 46 | BB22 |
| Kingfisher Gdns, G13 | 46 | BC22 |
| King George Ct, Renf. PA4 | | |
| off King George Pk Av | 64 | BA28 |
| King George V Br, G1 | 4 | BR31 |
| King George V Br, G5 | 4 | BR31 |
| King George V Dock, G51 | 64 | BD27 |
| King George Gdns, Renf. PA4 | 64 | BA27 |
| King George Pk Av, Renf. PA4 | 64 | BA28 |
| King George Pl, Renf. PA4 | | |
| off King George Pk Av | 64 | BA28 |
| King George Way, Renf. PA4 | | |
| off King George Pk Av | 64 | BA28 |
| Kinghorn Dr, G44 | 104 | BS39 |
| Kinglass Rd, (Bears.) G61 | 29 | BE19 |
| King Pl, (Baill.) G69 | 73 | CQ32 |
| Kingsacre Rd, G44 | 88 | BT38 |
| Kingsacre Rd, (Ruther.) G73 | 88 | BU38 |
| Kingsbarns Dr, G44 | 87 | BR38 |
| Kingsborough Gdns, G12 | 48 | BK26 |
| Kingsborough Gate, G12 | | |
| off Prince Albert Rd | 48 | BK26 |
| Kingsborough La, G12 | 48 | BK26 |
| Kingsborough La E, G12 | 48 | BK26 |
| Kingsbrae Av, G44 | 88 | BS38 |
| King's Br, G5 | 88 | BT33 |
| King's Br, G40 | 88 | BT33 |
| Kingsbridge Cres, G44 | 104 | BT39 |
| Kingsbridge Dr, G44 | 104 | BT39 |
| Kingsbridge Dr, (Ruther.) G73 | 104 | BU39 |
| Kingsbridge Pk Gdns, G44 | 104 | BT39 |
| Kingsburgh Dr, Pais. PA1 | 63 | AX31 |
| Kingsburn Dr, (Ruther.) G73 | 105 | BW39 |
| Kingsburn Gro, (Ruther.) G73 | 105 | BW39 |
| Kingscliffe Av, G44 | 104 | BS39 |
| Kingscourt Av, G44 | 88 | BT38 |
| Kings Cres, (Camb.) G72 | 106 | CD40 |
| Kings Cres, (Elder.) John. PA5 | 80 | AL34 |
| Kings Cross, G31 | 68 | BV30 |
| Kingsdale Av, G44 | 88 | BS38 |
| King's Dr, G40 | 88 | BU33 |
| King's Dr, (Cumb.) G68 | 9 | DB7 |
| Kings Dr, (Newt. M.) G77 | 117 | BH49 |
| Kings Dr, Moth. ML1 | 112 | DB42 |
| Kingsdyke Av, G44 | 88 | BS38 |
| Kingsford Av, G44 | 103 | BN41 |
| Kingsford Ct, (Newt. M.) G77 | | |
| off Greenfarm Rd | 116 | BD47 |
| Kings Gdns, (Newt. M.) G77 | 118 | BJ50 |
| Kingsgate Retail Pk, (E.Kil.) G74 | 122 | CB47 |
| Kingsheath Av, (Ruther.) G73 | 104 | BU39 |
| Kingshill Av, (Cumb.) G68 | 20 | CU12 |
| Kingshill Dr, G44 | 104 | BS39 |
| Kingshouse Av, G44 | 88 | BS38 |
| Kingshurst Av, G44 | 88 | BS38 |
| Kings Inch Dr, G51 | 64 | BD28 |
| Kings Inch Pl, Renf. PA4 | 64 | BB27 |
| Kings Inch Rd, G51 | 46 | BA25 |
| Kings Inch Rd, Renf. PA4 | 46 | BA25 |
| Kings Inch Way, Renf. PA4 | 46 | BB25 |
| Kingsknowe Dr, (Ruther.) G73 | 104 | BU39 |
| Kingsland Cres, G52 | 64 | BD31 |
| Kingsland Dr, G52 | 64 | BD31 |
| Kingsland La, G52 | | |
| off Berryknowes Rd | 65 | BE32 |
| Kings La W, Renf. PA4 | | |
| off Bell St | 45 | AZ25 |
| Kingsley Av, G42 | 87 | BR36 |
| Kingsley Ct, (Udd.) G71 | 93 | CQ38 |
| Kingslynn Dr, G44 | 104 | BT39 |
| Kingslynn La, G44 | | |
| off Kingslynn Dr | 104 | BT39 |
| Kingsmuir Dr, (Ruther.) G73 | | |
| off King's Pk Av | 104 | BU39 |
| Kings Pk, (Torr.) G64 | 15 | BY12 |
| King's Pk Av, G44 | 104 | BS39 |
| King's Pk Av, (Ruther.) G73 | 104 | BU39 |
| Kings Pk Rd, G44 | 87 | BR38 |
| Kings Pl, G22 | 49 | BR22 |
| Kings Rd, John. PA5 | 80 | AK35 |
| Kingston Av, (Udd.) G71 | 93 | CQ37 |
| Kingston Av, (Neil.) G78 | 114 | AT47 |
| Kingston Av, Air. ML6 | | |
| off Forrest St | 77 | DE30 |
| Kingston Br, G3 | 4 | BQ31 |
| Kingston Br, G5 | 4 | BQ31 |
| Kingston Flats, (Kilsyth) G65 | 7 | CT4 |
| Kingston Gro, Bish. PA7 | 24 | AK18 |
| Kingston Ind Est, G5 | 67 | BP32 |
| Kingston Pl, Clyde. G81 | 26 | AT17 |
| Kingston Rd, (Kilsyth) G65 | 7 | CT4 |
| Kingston Rd, (Neil.) G78 | 114 | AT48 |
| Kingston Rd, Bish. PA7 | 24 | AK19 |
| Kingston St, G5 | 4 | BQ31 |
| King St, G1 | 5 | BS31 |
| King St, (Kilsyth) G65 | 7 | CT5 |
| King St, (Ruther.) G73 | 89 | BX37 |
| King St, Clyde. G81 | 45 | AZ21 |
| King St, Coat. ML5 | 74 | CU31 |
| King St, Ham. ML3 | 125 | CP49 |
| King St, Lark. ML9 | 144 | DC58 |
| King St, Pais. PA1 | 62 | AS32 |
| King's Vw, (Cumb.) G68 | 9 | DB7 |
| King's Vw, (Ruther.) G73 | 88 | BV38 |
| Kingsway, G14 | 46 | BC24 |
| Kingsway, (Kilsyth) G65 | 7 | CT4 |
| Kingsway, (Kirk.) G66 | 18 | CK11 |
| Kingsway, (E.Kil.) G74 | 122 | CC48 |
| Kingsway Ct, G14 | 46 | BD24 |
| Kingswood Dr, G44 | 104 | BS39 |
| Kingussie Dr, G44 | 104 | BS39 |
| Kiniver Dr, G15 | 28 | BC20 |
| Kinkell Gdns, (Kirk.) G66 | 18 | CK12 |
| Kinloch Av, (Camb.) G72 | 106 | CD41 |
| Kinloch Av, (Linw.) Pais. PA3 | 60 | AJ31 |
| Kinloch Dr, Moth. ML1 | 111 | CZ43 |
| Kinloch Rd, (Newt. M.) G77 | 117 | BE47 |
| Kinloch Rd, Renf. PA4 | 63 | AX28 |
| Kinloch St, G40 | 89 | BY33 |
| Kinloss Pl, (E.Kil.) G74 | 136 | CB51 |
| Kinmount Av, G44 | 87 | BR38 |
| Kinnaird Av, (Newt. M.) G77 | 118 | BJ48 |
| Kinnaird Cres, (Bears.) G61 | 30 | BK17 |
| Kinnaird Dr, (Linw.) Pais. PA3 | 60 | AK30 |
| Kinnaird Pl, (Bishop.) G64 | 51 | BX21 |
| Kinnear Rd, G40 | 89 | BX34 |
| Kinneil Pl, Ham. ML3 | 139 | CP51 |
| Kinnell Av, G52 | 85 | BE34 |
| Kinnell Cres, G52 | 85 | BE34 |
| Kinnell Path, G52 | | |
| off Kinnell Cres | 85 | BE34 |
| Kinnell Pl, G52 | | |
| off Mosspark Dr | 85 | BF34 |
| Kinnell Sq, G52 | 85 | BE34 |
| Kinning Pk Ind Est, G5 | 67 | BP32 |
| Kinning St, G5 | 67 | BQ32 |
| Kinnoul Gdns, (Bears.) G61 | 11 | BE14 |
| Kinnoul La, G12 | | |
| off Dowanside Rd | 48 | BL26 |
| Kinnoull Pl, (Blan.) G72 | 124 | CM46 |
| Kinpurnie Rd, Pais. PA1 | 63 | AZ32 |
| Kinross Av, G52 | 84 | BD33 |
| Kinross Pk, (E.Kil.) G74 | 123 | CF50 |
| Kinsail Dr, G52 | 64 | BB31 |
| Kinstone Av, G14 | 46 | BC24 |
| Kintail Gdns, (Kirk.) G66 | 18 | CK12 |
| Kintessack Pl, (Bishop.) G64 | 33 | BZ19 |
| Kintillo Dr, G13 | 46 | BD23 |
| Kintore Pk, Ham. ML3 | 139 | CR54 |
| Kintore Rd, G43 | 103 | BP39 |
| Kintra St, G51 | 66 | BK31 |
| Kintyre Av, (Linw.) Pais. PA3 | 60 | AJ32 |
| Kintyre Cres, (Newt. M.) G77 | 117 | BE47 |
| Kintyre Cres, (Plains) Air. ML6 | 59 | DH26 |
| Kintyre Gdns, (Kirk.) G66 | 18 | CK11 |

| Name | Page | Grid |
|---|---|---|
| Kintyre Rd, (Blan.) G72 | | |
| off Glenfruin Rd | 124 | CK45 |
| Kintyre St, G21 | 69 | BW28 |
| Kipland Wk, Coat. ML5 | 75 | CZ32 |
| Kippen Dr, (Clark.) G76 | 119 | BQ48 |
| Kippen St, G22 | 50 | BT23 |
| Kippen St, Air. ML6 | 75 | CZ31 |
| Kippford Pl, (Chap.) Air. ML6 | 97 | DG36 |
| Kippford St, G32 | 91 | CE33 |
| Kipps Av, Air. ML6 | 76 | DA29 |
| Kippsbyre Ct, Air. ML6 | | |
| off Monkscourt Av | 75 | CZ30 |
| Kirkaig Av, Renf. PA4 | 64 | BB27 |
| Kirkandrews Pl, Air. ML6 | 97 | DH35 |
| Kirkbean Av, (Ruther.) G73 | 105 | BW41 |
| Kirkburn Av, (Camb.) G72 | 106 | CC41 |
| Kirkcaldy Rd, G41 | 86 | BM35 |
| Kirkconnel Av, G13 | 46 | BB22 |
| Kirkconnel Av, (Cumb.) G68 | 20 | CU12 |
| Kirkconnel Dr, (Ruther.) G73 | 104 | BV40 |
| Kirkcudbright Pl, (E.Kil.) G74 | 123 | CF50 |
| Kirkdale Dr, G52 | 85 | BG33 |
| Kirkdene Av, (Newt. M.) G77 | 118 | BK48 |
| Kirkdene Bk, (Newt. M.) G77 | 118 | BK48 |
| Kirkdene Cres, (Newt. M.) G77 | 118 | BK48 |
| Kirkdene Gro, (Newt. M.) G77 | 118 | BK48 |
| Kirkdene Pl, (Newt. M.) G77 | 118 | BK48 |
| Kirkfieldbank Way, Ham. ML3 | | |
| off Beattock Wynd | 125 | CQ50 |
| Kirkfield Rd, (Both.) G71 | 109 | CQ42 |
| Kirkford Rd, (Chry.) G69 | | |
| off Bridgeburn Dr | 37 | CN19 |
| Kirk Glebe, (Neil.) G78 | 114 | AU46 |
| Kirkhall Rd, Moth. ML1 | 113 | DF41 |
| Kirkhill Av, (Camb.) G72 | 106 | CC42 |
| Kirkhill Cres, (Neil.) G78 | 114 | AU45 |
| Kirkhill Dr, G20 | 48 | BM24 |
| Kirkhill Gdns, (Camb.) G72 | 106 | CC42 |
| Kirkhill Gate, (Newt. M.) G77 | 118 | BK49 |
| Kirkhill Gro, (Camb.) G72 | 106 | CC42 |
| Kirkhill Pl, G20 | | |
| off Kirkhill Dr | 48 | BM24 |
| Kirkhill Pl, Wis. ML2 | 143 | DE51 |
| Kirkhill Rd, (Gart.) G69 | 55 | CP24 |
| Kirkhill Rd, (Udd.) G71 | 93 | CN37 |
| Kirkhill Rd, (Newt. M.) G77 | 118 | BK48 |
| Kirkhill Rd, Wis. ML2 | 143 | DE52 |
| Kirkhill St, Wis. ML2 | | |
| off Clydesdale Av | 143 | DF52 |
| Kirkhill Ter, (Camb.) G72 | 106 | CC42 |
| Kirkhope Dr, G15 | 28 | BD19 |
| Kirkinner Rd, G32 | 91 | CF34 |
| Kirkintilloch Rd, (Bishop.) G64 | 50 | BV21 |
| Kirkintilloch Rd, (Kirk.) G66 | 35 | CE16 |
| Kirkland Gro, John. PA5 | 79 | AH34 |
| Kirklandneuk Cres, Renf. PA4 | | |
| off Kirklandneuk Rd | 45 | AW25 |
| Kirklandneuk Rd, Renf. PA4 | 45 | AX25 |
| Kirklands Cres, (Kilsyth) G65 | 7 | CT6 |
| Kirklands Cres, (Both.) G71 | 109 | CQ42 |
| Kirklands Dr, (Newt. M.) G77 | 131 | BF51 |
| Kirklands Pl, (Newt. M.) G77 | 131 | BF51 |
| Kirklands Rd, (Newt. M.) G77 | 131 | BF51 |
| Kirkland St, G20 | 49 | BP26 |
| Kirkland St, Moth. ML1 | 127 | CZ46 |
| Kirk La, G43 | | |
| off Riverbank St | 86 | BL38 |
| Kirk La, (Bears.) G61 | 29 | BG16 |
| Kirklea Av, Pais. PA3 | | |
| off Blackstone Rd | 61 | AQ31 |
| Kirklea Gdns, Pais. PA3 | 61 | AQ32 |
| Kirkle Dr, (Newt. M.) G77 | 118 | BK48 |
| Kirklee Circ, G12 | 48 | BL25 |
| Kirklee Gdns, G12 | 48 | BL24 |
| Kirklee Gdns La, G12 | 48 | BM25 |
| Kirklee Gate, G12 | 48 | BM25 |
| Kirklee Pl, G12 | 48 | BM25 |
| Kirklee Quad, G12 | 48 | BM25 |
| Kirklee Quad La, G12 | | |
| off Kirklee Quad | 48 | BM25 |
| Kirklee Rd, G12 | 48 | BL25 |
| Kirklee Rd, Bell. ML4 | 112 | DA43 |
| Kirklee Ter, G12 | 48 | BL25 |
| Kirklee Ter La, G12 | 48 | BL25 |
| Kirkliston St, G32 | 70 | CB31 |
| Kirk Ms, (Camb.) G72 | 106 | CC40 |
| Kirkmichael Av, G11 | | |
| off Blairatholl Av | 48 | BJ26 |
| Kirkmichael Gdns, G11 | | |
| off Blairatholl Av | 48 | BJ26 |
| Kirkmuir Dr, (Ruther.) G73 | 105 | BX42 |
| Kirkness St, Air. ML6 | 76 | DC29 |
| Kirknethan, Wis. ML2 | 143 | DE52 |
| Kirknewton St, G32 | 70 | CC31 |
| Kirkoswald, (E.Kil.) G74 | 123 | CF50 |
| Kirkoswald Dr, Clyde. G81 | 27 | AY18 |
| Kirkoswald Rd, G43 | 102 | BM39 |
| Kirkoswald Rd, Moth. ML1 | 113 | DG41 |
| Kirkpatrick St, G40 | 69 | BW32 |
| Kirk Pl, (Bears.) G61 | 29 | BG16 |
| Kirk Pl, (Cumb.) G67 | 21 | CW14 |
| Kirk Pl, (Udd.) G71 | 109 | CN40 |
| Kirkriggs Av, (Ruther.) G73 | 105 | BX40 |
| Kirkriggs Gdns, (Ruther.) G73 | 105 | BX40 |
| Kirkriggs Vw, (Ruther.) G73 | | |
| off Kirkriggs Av | 105 | BX40 |
| Kirkriggs Way, (Ruther.) G73 | | |
| off Kirkriggs Gdns | 105 | BX40 |
| Kirk Rd, (Bears.) G61 | 29 | BG16 |
| Kirk Rd, (Carm.) G76 | 120 | BT46 |
| Kirk Rd, Moth. ML1 | 97 | DF38 |
| Kirkshaws Av, Coat. ML5 | 94 | CU34 |
| Kirkshaws Pl, Coat. ML5 | | |
| off Kirkshaws Av | 94 | CV34 |
| Kirkshaws Rd, Coat. ML5 | 94 | CV35 |
| Kirkstall Gdns, (Bishop.) G64 | 33 | BX17 |
| Kirkstone, (Newt. M.) G77 | | |
| off Kirkvale Ct | 118 | BK48 |
| Kirkstone Cl, (E.Kil.) G75 | 134 | BV55 |
| Kirk St, (Miln.) G62 | 11 | BG11 |
| Kirk St, Coat. ML5 | 74 | CV31 |
| Kirk St, Moth. ML1 | 128 | DA46 |
| Kirkstyle Cotts, Coat. ML5 | 94 | CT34 |
| Kirkstyle Cres, (Neil.) G78 | 114 | AT46 |
| Kirkstyle Cres, Air. ML6 | 76 | DB27 |
| Kirkstyle La, (Neil.) G78 | | |
| off Main St | 114 | AU46 |
| Kirkstyle Pl, (Glenm.) Air. ML6 | 57 | CZ25 |
| Kirksyde Av, (Kirk.) G66 | 17 | CF14 |
| Kirkton, Ersk. PA8 | 25 | AQ18 |
| Kirkton Av, G13 | 46 | BC23 |
| Kirkton Av, (Blan.) G72 | 124 | CM48 |
| Kirkton Av, (Barr.) G78 | 99 | AX43 |
| Kirkton Cres, G13 | 46 | BC23 |
| Kirkton Cres, Coat. ML5 | 95 | CZ33 |
| Kirkton Dr, (Eagle.) G76 | 133 | BN56 |
| Kirktonfield Dr, (Neil.) G78 | 114 | AV46 |
| Kirktonfield Pl, (Neil.) G78 | 114 | AV46 |
| Kirktonfield Rd, (Neil.) G78 | 114 | AU46 |
| Kirkton Gate, (E.Kil.) G74 | 136 | CA51 |
| Kirktonholme Cres, (E.Kil.) G74 | 135 | BZ51 |
| Kirktonholme Rd, (E.Kil.) G74 | 135 | BX51 |
| Kirkton Moor Rd, (Eagle.) G76 | 131 | BH56 |
| Kirkton Pk, (E.Kil.) G74 | 136 | CB52 |
| Kirkton Pl, (Blan.) G72 | | |
| off Kirkton Av | 124 | CM47 |
| Kirkton Pl, (E.Kil.) G74 | 136 | CB51 |
| Kirkton Pl, Coat. ML5 | 95 | CZ33 |
| Kirkton Rd, (Camb.) G72 | 106 | CD40 |
| Kirkton Rd, (Neil.) G78 | 114 | AU47 |
| Kirktonside, (Barr.) G78 | 99 | AX44 |
| Kirkvale Ct, (Newt. M.) G77 | 118 | BK48 |
| Kirkvale Cres, (Newt. M.) G77 | 118 | BK48 |
| Kirkvale Dr, (Newt. M.) G77 | 118 | BK48 |
| Kirkview, (Cumb.) G67 | 39 | CW15 |
| Kirkview Ct, (Cumb.) G67 | 39 | CW15 |
| Kirkview Cres, (Newt. M.) G77 | 117 | BG50 |
| Kirkview Gdns, (Udd.) G71 | 93 | CN37 |
| Kirkville Pl, G15 | 28 | BD20 |
| Kirkwall, (Cumb.) G67 | 9 | DC8 |
| Kirkwall Av, (Blan.) G72 | 108 | CL43 |
| Kirkwell Rd, G44 | 103 | BR40 |
| Kirkwood Av, (Stepps) G33 | 53 | CH24 |
| Kirkwood Av, Clyde. G81 | 27 | AZ20 |
| Kirkwood Pl, Coat. ML5 | 94 | CU33 |
| Kirkwood Quad, Clyde. G81 | | |
| off Kirkwood Av | 27 | AZ20 |
| Kirkwood Rd, (Udd.) G71 | 93 | CQ37 |
| Kirkwood St, G51 | 66 | BL32 |
| Kirkwood St, (Ruther.) G73 | 89 | BW37 |
| Kirkwood St, Coat. ML5 | 74 | CU32 |
| Kirn St, G20 | 48 | BL21 |
| Kirriemuir, (E.Kil.) G74 | 123 | CF48 |
| Kirriemuir Av, G52 | 85 | BE34 |
| Kirriemuir Gdns, (Bishop.) G64 | 33 | BY19 |
| Kirriemuir Pl, G52 | 85 | BE33 |
| Kirriemuir Rd, (Bishop.) G64 | 33 | BY20 |
| Kirtle Dr, Renf. PA4 | 64 | BA27 |
| Kirtle Pl, (E.Kil.) G75 | 134 | BU54 |
| Kishorn Pl, G33 | 71 | CE28 |
| Kittoch Pl, (E.Kil.) G74 | | |
| off Kittoch St | 136 | CB51 |
| Kittochside Rd, (Clark.) G76 | 120 | BV47 |
| Kittoch St, (E.Kil.) G74 | 136 | CA51 |
| Klondike Ct, (New Stev.) | | |
| Moth. ML1 | 112 | DD42 |
| Knapdale St, G22 | 49 | BQ22 |
| Knightsbridge St, G13 | 47 | BF22 |
| Knightscliffe Av, G13 | 47 | BF21 |
| Knights Gate, (Both.) G71 | 109 | CN40 |
| Knightswood Ct, G13 | | |
| off Knightswood Rd | 47 | BF23 |
| Knightswood Cross, G13 | 47 | BF22 |
| Knightswood Rd, G13 | 29 | BE20 |
| Knightswood Ter, (Blan.) G72 | 109 | CN44 |
| Knivysbridge Pl, Bell. ML4 | 110 | CV42 |
| Knockburnie Rd, (Both.) G71 | 109 | CQ41 |
| Knockhall St, G33 | 71 | CF27 |
| Knockhill Dr, G44 | 87 | BR38 |
| Knockhill Rd, Renf. PA4 | 63 | AW28 |
| Knockside Av, Pais. PA2 | 82 | AT38 |
| Knock Way, Pais. PA3 | 63 | AW30 |
| Knollpark Dr, (Clark.) G76 | 118 | BM46 |
| Knowe Cres, Moth. ML1 | 113 | DF41 |
| Knowehead Dr, (Udd.) G71 | 109 | CN39 |
| Knowehead Gdns, G41 | 87 | BN34 |
| Knowehead Gdns, (Udd.) G71 | 109 | CN39 |
| Knowehead Ter, G41 | 87 | BN34 |
| Knowe Rd, (Chry.) G69 | 54 | CL21 |
| Knowe Rd, Pais. PA3 | 63 | AX30 |
| Knowes Av, (Newt. M.) G77 | 117 | BG48 |
| Knowes Rd, (Newt. M.) G77 | 117 | BH48 |
| Knowe St, (Miln.) G62 | 11 | BH11 |
| Knowetap St, G20 | 49 | BN22 |
| Knowetop Av, Moth. ML1 | 128 | DB48 |
| Knox Pl, (Newt. M.) G77 | 116 | BD49 |
| Knox St, Air. ML6 | 76 | DD29 |
| Knox St, Pais. PA1 | 81 | AR33 |
| Kronborg Way, (E.Kil.) G75 | 135 | BZ56 |

Kyleakin Dr, (Blan.) G72
*off Dalcraig Cres* 108 CK43
Kyleakin Rd, (Thornlie.) G46 101 BF42
Kyleakin Ter, (Thornlie.) G46 101 BF42
Kyle Ct, (Camb.) G72 106 CC39
Kyle Dr, (Giff.) G46 103 BN42
Kylemore Cres, Moth. ML1 111 CZ43
Kylepark Av, (Udd.) G71 108 CM39
Kylepark Cres, (Udd.) G71 92 CM38
Kylepark Dr, (Udd.) G71 92 CM38
Kyle Quad, Moth. ML1
*off Lintie Rd* 113 DE41
Kyle Quad, Wis. ML2 143 DG52
Kylerhea Rd, (Thornlie.) G46 101 BF42
Kyle Rd, (Cumb.) G67 22 DD11
Kyle Sq, (Ruther.) G73 104 BV40
Kyle St, G4 5 BS28
Kyle St, Moth. ML1 127 CX46

**L**

La Belle Allee, G3 67 BN28
La Belle Pl, G3 67 BN28
Laberge Gdns, (New Stev.)
Moth. ML1 112 DD42
Laburnum Av, (Camb.) G72 107 CG42
Laburnum Av, (E.Kil.) G75 135 BY55
Laburnum Ct, (E.Kil.) G75 135 BY55
Laburnum Gdns, (Kirk.) G66
*off Laburnum Gro* 34 CD16
Laburnum Gro, (Kirk.) G66 34 CD16
Laburnum Gro, Coat. ML5 75 CX31
Laburnum Lea, Ham. ML3 140 CU51
Laburnum Pl, John. PA5 80 AJ37
Laburnum Rd, G41 86 BL33
Laburnum Rd, (Cumb.) G67 23 DF11
Laburnum Rd, (Udd.) G71 94 CT38
Lachlan Cres, Ersk. PA8 24 AN20
La Crosse Ter, G12 49 BN26
Lacy St, Pais. PA1 63 AW32
Ladeside Cl, (Newt. M.) G77 117 BE47
Ladeside Dr, (Kilsyth) G65 7 CU4
Ladeside Dr, John. PA5 79 AF35
Lade Ter, G52 84 BC33
Ladhope Pl, G13 46 BA21
Ladyacres, (Inch.) Renf. PA4 44 AT23
Ladyacres Way, (Inch.) Renf. PA4 44 AT23
Lady Anne Cres, Air. ML6 77 DE31
Lady Anne St, G14
*off Speirshall Cl* 46 BB23
Ladybank, (Cumb.) G68 9 DB7
Ladybank Ct, (E.Kil.) G74
*off West Mains Rd* 136 CA51
Ladybank Dr, G52 85 BG33
Ladybank Gdns, (E.Kil.) G74 136 CA51
Ladybank Pl, (E.Kil.) G74
*off Parkhall St* 136 CB51
Ladyburn St, Pais. PA1 83 AW33
Ladyhill Dr, (Baill.) G69 92 CJ33
Lady Isle Cres, (Udd.) G71 109 CN39
Lady Jane Gate, (Both.) G71 109 CN41
Ladykirk Cres, G52 64 BD31
Ladykirk Cres, Pais. PA2 82 AV34
Ladykirk Dr, G52 64 BD31
Lady La, Pais. PA1 82 AT33
Ladyloan Av, G15 28 BA17
Ladyloan Ct, G15 28 BB17
Ladyloan Gdns, G15 28 BB17
Ladyloan Gro, G15 28 BB17
Ladyloan Pl, G15 28 BA17
Lady Mary Wk, Ham. ML3
*off Silvertonhill Av* 140 CU52

Ladymuir Circle, Ersk. PA8 25 AP20
Ladymuir Cres, G53 85 BE35
Ladysmith Av, (Kilb.)
John. PA10 78 AD35
Ladysmith St, Wis. ML2 129 DE50
Lady Watson Gdns, Ham. ML3 139 CQ51
Ladywell Rd, Moth. ML1 127 CY47
Ladywell St, G4 5 BU30
Lady Wilson St, Air. ML6 76 DD31
Ladywood Est, (Miln.) G62
*off Moor Rd* 12 BK11
Laggan Quad, Air. ML6 76 DA28
Laggan Rd, G43 103 BN40
Laggan Rd, (Bishop.) G64 33 BX20
Laggan Rd, (Newt. M.) G77 117 BF46
Laggan Rd, Air. ML6 76 DB28
Laggan Ter, Renf. PA4 45 AX25
Lagos La, (Ruther.) G73 105 BY43
Laidlaw Av, Moth. ML1
*off Catherine Way* 112 DB42
Laidlaw Gdns, (Udd.) G71 93 CP36
Laidlaw St, G5 67 BQ32
Laidon Rd, Air. ML6
*off Laggan Rd* 76 DB28
Laighcartside St, John. PA5 80 AJ34
Laighlands Rd, (Both.) G71 109 CR43
Laighmuir St, (Udd.) G71 109 CP40
Laighpark Av, Bish. PA7 24 AK18
Laighpark Harbour, Pais. PA3 62 AU30
Laighpark Vw, Pais. PA3 62 AU30
Laigh Rd, (Newt. M.) G77 118 BK48
Laighstonehall Rd, Ham. ML3 139 CR51
Laightoun Ct, (Cumb.) G67 39 CW15
Laightoun Dr, (Cumb.) G67 39 CW15
Laightoun Gdns, (Cumb.) G67 39 CW15
Lainshaw Dr, G45 103 BQ43
Laird Gro, (Udd.) G71 93 CQ37
Laird Pl, G40 88 BV33
Lairds Gate, (Udd.) G71 108 CM40
Lairds Hill, (Cumb.) G67 22 DA11
Lairds Hill Ct, (Kilsyth) G65 6 CQ5
Lairds Hill Pl, (Kilsyth) G65 6 CQ5
Laird St, Coat. ML5 75 CX30
Lairg Dr, (Blan.) G72 108 CL43
Lairhills Rd, (E.Kil.) G75 136 CB54
Lamberton Dr, G52 64 BD31
Lambhill Quad, G41 67 BN32
Lambhill St, G41 66 BM32
Lambie Cres, (Newt. M.) G77 117 BE48
Lamb St, G22 49 BR23
Lamb St, Ham. ML3 126 CU50
Lamerton Rd, (Cumb.) G67 22 DA14
Lamington Rd, G52 84 BD33
Lamlash Cres, G33 70 CD29
Lamlash Pl, G33
*off Lamlash Cres* 70 CD29
Lamlash Pl, Moth. ML1 127 CY46
Lamlash Sq, G33 71 CE29
Lammermoor, (E.Kil.) G74 123 CG49
Lammermoor Av, G52 85 BE33
Lammermoor Cres, (Kirk.) G66 17 CH13
Lammermoor Dr, (Cumb.) G67 22 DA14
Lammermoor Gdns, (Kirk.) G66 17 CH13
Lammermoor Rd, (Kirk.) G66 17 CH13
Lammermuir Ct, Pais. PA2 82 AU37
Lammermuir Dr, Pais. PA2 82 AT37
Lammermuir Gdns, (Bears.)
G61 11 BE14
Lammermuir Pl, Moth. ML1
*off Dornoch Rd* 112 DD41
Lammermuir Way, (Chap.)
Air. ML6 97 DH36
Lammermuir Wynd, Lark. ML9 142 DB56

Lammer Wynd, Lark. ML9
*off Elmbank Dr* 145 DE60
Lamont Av, Bish. PA7 24 AL18
Lamont Rd, G21 51 BX23
Lanark Av, Air. ML6 96 DB33
Lanark Rd, Lark. ML9 142 DB54
Lanark Rd End, Lark. ML9 142 DA54
Lanark St, G1 5 BT31
Lancaster Av, (Chap.) Air. ML6 97 DG37
Lancaster Cres, G12 48 BL25
Lancaster Cres La, G12 48 BL25
Lancaster Rd, (Bishop.) G64 33 BX17
Lancaster Ter, G12 48 BL25
Lancaster Ter La, G12
*off Westbourne Gdns W* 48 BL25
Lancaster Way, Renf. PA4
*off Tiree Av* 63 AY28
Lancefield Quay, G3 67 BN30
Lancefield St, G3 4 BP30
Landemer Dr, (Ruther.) G73 104 BV39
Landressy Pl, G40 88 BU33
Landressy St, G40 88 BV33
Landsdowne Rd, Lark. ML9 145 DE59
Lane, The, (Dullatur) G68 9 CZ7
Lane Gdns, G11
*off North Gardner St* 48 BK26
Lanfine Rd, Pais. PA1 63 AX32
Langa St, G20 49 BN22
Lang Av, Bish. PA7 24 AL18
Lang Av, Renf. PA4 63 AY28
Langbank St, G5
*off Eglinton St* 67 BR32
Langbar Cres, G33 71 CG30
Langbar Gdns, G33 71 CH30
Langbar Path, G33
*off Bartiebeith Rd* 71 CF30
Langcraigs Dr, Pais. PA2 98 AS39
Langcraigs Ter, Pais. PA2 98 AS39
Langcroft Dr, (Camb.) G72 107 CE41
Langcroft Pl, G51 65 BE30
Langcroft Rd, G51 65 BF30
Langcroft Ter, G51
*off Langcroft Rd* 65 BF30
Langdale, (E.Kil.) G74 121 BY50
Langdale, (Newt. M.) G77
*off Kirkvale Ct* 118 BK48
Langdale Av, G33 52 CA26
Langdale Rd, (Chry.) G69 37 CP19
Langdale's Av, (Cumb.) G68 21 CY11
Langdale St, G33 52 CA26
Langford Dr, G53 100 BC42
Langford Pl, G53 100 BD42
Langhaul Pl, G53 84 BB36
Langhaul Rd, G53 84 BB36
Langhill Dr, (Cumb.) G68 21 CZ10
Langholm, (E.Kil.) G75 134 BV55
Langholm Ct, (Chry.) G69
*off Heathfield Av* 37 CP19
Langholm Dr, (Linw.) Pais. PA3 60 AL32
Langholm Path, (Blan.) G72
*off Broompark Rd* 124 CL46
Langlands Av, G51 65 BF29
Langlands Ct, G51
*off Langlands Rd* 65 BH29
Langlands Dr, G51 65 BF30
Langlands Rd, G51 65 BF30
Langlands-Seafar Interchange,
(Cumb.) G67 22 DA13
Langlea Av, (Camb.) G72 105 BZ41
Langlea Ct, (Camb.) G72 106 CA41
Langlea Dr, (Camb.) G72 106 CA40
Langlea Gdns, (Camb.) G72 106 CA40
Langlea Gro, (Camb.) G72 106 CA41

| Name | Page | Ref | Name | Page | Ref | Name | Page | Ref |
|---|---|---|---|---|---|---|---|---|
| Langlea Rd, (Camb.) G72 | 106 | CA41 | Larch Gro, (Cumb.) G67 | 23 | DG9 | Laurel Pl, G11 | 48 | BJ26 |
| Langlea Way, (Camb.) G72 | 106 | CA40 | Larch Gro, Ham. ML3 | 140 | CU51 | Laurel Pl, (E.Kil.) G75 | 135 | BZ56 |
| Langlees Av, (Newt. M.) G77 | 118 | BK48 | Larch Gro, Moth. ML1 | | | Laurel St, G11 | 66 | BJ27 |
| Langley Av, G13 | 46 | BD21 | *off Elm Rd* | 112 | DD40 | Laurels, The, (Newt. M.) G77 | 117 | BF48 |
| Langloan Cres, Coat. ML5 | 74 | CU31 | Larchgrove Av, G32 | 71 | CE31 | Laurels, The, (Carfin) | | |
| Langloan Pl, Coat. ML5 | 74 | CU31 | Larchgrove Pl, G32 | | | Moth. ML1 | 112 | DD43 |
| Langloan St, Coat. ML5 | 74 | CU32 | *off Larchgrove Rd* | 71 | CE30 | Laurel St, G11 | 66 | BJ27 |
| Langlook Rd, G53 | 84 | BB36 | Larchgrove Rd, G32 | 71 | CE30 | Laurel Wk, (Ruther.) G73 | 105 | BY42 |
| Langmuir Av, (Kirk.) G66 | 17 | CG12 | Larch Pl, (Udd.) G71 | 94 | CT37 | Laurel Way, (Barr.) G78 | 99 | AX42 |
| Langmuirhead Rd, (Kirk.) G66 | 52 | CC21 | Larch Pl, (Camb.) G72 | 107 | CG42 | Laurel Wynd, (Camb.) G72 | 107 | CH42 |
| Langmuir Rd, (Kirk.) G66 | 17 | CH12 | Larch Pl, (E.Kil.) G75 | 135 | BX56 | Laurence Ct, G15 | 28 | BA18 |
| Langmuir Rd, (Baill.) G69 | 73 | CQ32 | Larch Pl, John. PA5 | 79 | AH37 | Laurence Dr, G15 | 28 | BA18 |
| Langmuir Way, (Baill.) G69 | 73 | CQ32 | Larch Rd, G41 | 86 | BK33 | Laurence Dr, (Bears.) G61 | 29 | BF15 |
| Langness Rd, G33 | 70 | CD29 | Larch Rd, (Cumb.) G67 | 23 | DF9 | Laurence Gdns, G15 | | |
| Langoreth Av, Ham. ML3 | 139 | CP51 | Larch Sq, (Camb.) G72 | 107 | CG42 | *off Laurence Dr* | 28 | BA18 |
| Lang Pl, John. PA5 | 79 | AG34 | Larchwood Ter, (Barr.) G78 | | | Laurenstone Ter, (E.Kil.) G74 | 122 | CD50 |
| Langrig Rd, G21 | 51 | BW25 | *off Newton Av* | 99 | AZ44 | Lauren Way, Pais. PA2 | 81 | AP36 |
| Langshot St, G51 | 66 | BM32 | Largie Rd, G43 | 103 | BP40 | Laurie Ct, (Udd.) G71 | 93 | CQ38 |
| Langside Av, G41 | 87 | BN36 | Largo Pl, G51 | 65 | BG30 | Laurieston Cres, (Chap.) | | |
| Langside Av, (Udd.) G71 | 110 | CS39 | Largs St, G31 | 69 | BX30 | Air. ML6 | 97 | DF36 |
| Langside Ct, (Both.) G71 | 109 | CR44 | Larkfield Ct, (Blan.) G72 | | | Laurieston Rd, G5 | 87 | BR33 |
| Langside Dr, G43 | 103 | BN40 | *off Larkfield Dr* | 124 | CL47 | Laurieston Way, (Ruther.) G73 | 105 | BX41 |
| Langside Dr, (Kilb.) John. PA10 | 78 | AC35 | Larkfield Dr, (Blan.) G72 | 124 | CM47 | Lauriston Gro, (Newt. M.) G77 | 116 | BD48 |
| Langside Gdns, G42 | 87 | BQ38 | Larkfield Rd, (Lenz.) G66 | 35 | CG16 | Lavelle Dr, Coat. ML5 | 75 | CY30 |
| Langside La, G42 | 87 | BQ36 | Larkhill Ind Est, Lark. ML9 | 144 | DD60 | Lavender Dr, (E.Kil.) G75 | 135 | BZ56 |
| Langside Pk, (Kilb.) John. PA10 | 78 | AC35 | Larkin Gdns, Pais. PA3 | 62 | AT30 | Laverock Av, Ham. ML3 | 141 | CW51 |
| Langside Pl, G41 | 87 | BP37 | Larkin Way, Bell. ML4 | 94 | CV38 | Laverockhall St, G21 | 50 | BV26 |
| Langside Rd, G42 | 87 | BQ36 | Larkspur Dr, (E.Kil.) G74 | 121 | BY49 | Laverock Rd, Air. ML6 | 76 | DD27 |
| Langside Rd, (Both.) G71 | 109 | CR44 | Lark Way, (Strathclyde Bus. Pk.) | | | Laverock Ter, (Chry.) G69 | 37 | CP20 |
| Langside St, Clyde. G81 | 28 | BA15 | Bell. ML4 | 94 | CV37 | Law Dr, Moth. ML1 | 113 | DE41 |
| Langstile Pl, G52 | 64 | BB32 | Lasswade St, G14 | 46 | BA23 | Lawers Dr, (Bears.) G61 | 29 | BE15 |
| Langstile Rd, G52 | 64 | BB32 | Latherton Dr, G20 | 48 | BM24 | Lawers La, Moth. ML1 | | |
| Lang St, Pais. PA1 | 83 | AW33 | Latherton Pl, G20 | | | *off Hamilton Pl* | 113 | DE41 |
| Langton Cres, G53 | 85 | BE36 | *off Latherton Dr* | 48 | BM24 | Lawers Rd, G43 | 102 | BK40 |
| Langton Cres, (Barr.) G78 | 99 | AZ44 | Latimer Gdns, G52 | 84 | BC33 | Lawers Rd, Renf. PA4 | 63 | AX28 |
| Langton Gdns, (Baill.) G69 | 91 | CH33 | Latimer Path, G52 | | | Lawfield Av, (Newt. M.) G77 | 118 | BK48 |
| Langton Gate, (Newt. M.) G77 | 117 | BE48 | *off Paisley Rd W* | 84 | BC33 | Lawhill Av, G44 | | |
| Langton Pl, (Newt. M.) G77 | 117 | BE48 | Lauchlin Pl, (Kirk.) G66 | 18 | CK14 | *off Croftfoot Rd* | 104 | BT41 |
| Langton Rd, G53 | 85 | BE37 | Lauchope Rd, Moth. ML1 | 97 | DF38 | Lawhope Mill Rd, Air. ML6 | 97 | DH34 |
| Langtree Av, (Giff.) G46 | 102 | BJ44 | Lauchope St, (Chap.) Air. ML6 | 97 | DG35 | Lawmoor Av, G5 | 88 | BS34 |
| Lanrig Pl, (Chry.) G69 | 54 | CK21 | Laudedale La, G12 | 48 | BK26 | Lawmoor Pl, G5 | 88 | BS35 |
| Lanrig Rd, (Chry.) G69 | 54 | CL21 | Lauderdale Dr, (Newt. M.) G77 | 117 | BE50 | Lawmoor Rd, G5 | 88 | BS34 |
| Lanrig Rd, (Newt. M.) G77 | 117 | BE50 | Lauderdale Gdns, G12 | 48 | BK26 | Lawmoor St, G5 | 88 | BS34 |
| Lansbury Gdns, Pais. PA3 | 62 | AT30 | Lauder Dr, (Ruther.) G73 | 105 | BZ39 | Lawmuir Cres, Clyde. G81 | 10 | BA14 |
| Lansbury Ter, Lark. ML9 | 145 | DE60 | Lauder Dr, (Linw.) Pais. PA3 | 60 | AK32 | Lawmuir Pl, Bell. ML4 | 111 | CW43 |
| Lansdowne Cres, G20 | 67 | BP27 | Lauder Gdns, (Blan.) G72 | 108 | CL43 | Lawmuir Rd, Bell. ML4 | 111 | CW42 |
| Lansdowne Cres La, G20 | 67 | BP27 | Lauder Gdns, Coat. ML5 | 95 | CZ34 | Lawn Pk, (Miln.) G62 | 12 | BL12 |
| Lansdowne Dr, (Cumb.) G68 | 9 | DB8 | Lauder Grn, (E.Kil.) G74 | 122 | CD49 | Lawn St, Pais. PA1 | 62 | AV32 |
| Lansdowne Gdns, Ham. ML3 | 126 | CV50 | Lauder La, Ham. ML3 | | | Law Pl, (E.Kil.) G74 | 122 | CA49 |
| Lantana Gro, Moth. ML1 | | | *off Clarkwell Rd* | 125 | CN50 | Lawrence Av, (Giff.) G46 | 102 | BL44 |
| *off Alyssum Cres* | 127 | CZ45 | Lauder St, G5 | 87 | BQ33 | Lawrence St, G11 | 66 | BL27 |
| Lanton Dr, G52 | 64 | BD32 | Laughland Dr, Moth. ML1 | 113 | DF42 | Lawrie St, G11 | 66 | BK27 |
| Lanton Rd, G43 | 103 | BN40 | Laundry La, G33 | 53 | CE24 | Lawrie Way, Lark. ML9 | | |
| Lappin St, Clyde. G81 | 45 | AZ21 | Lauranne Pl, Bell. ML4 | 110 | CU40 | *off Stuart Dr* | 145 | DE60 |
| Larbert St, G4 | 4 | BR28 | Laurel Av, (Lenz.) G66 | 35 | CF15 | Lawson Av, Moth. ML1 | 128 | DA50 |
| Larch Av, (Bishop.) G64 | 51 | BX21 | Laurel Av, Clyde. G81 | 26 | AT17 | Law St, G40 | 69 | BW32 |
| Larch Av, (Lenz.) G66 | 35 | CE15 | Laurelbank, Coat. ML5 | 75 | CW29 | Laxford Av, G44 | 103 | BQ41 |
| Larch Cl, (Camb.) G72 | 107 | CG42 | Laurel Bk, Ham. ML3 | 140 | CS53 | Laxford Pl, Coat. ML5 | 75 | CZ32 |
| Larch Ct, (Cumb.) G67 | 23 | DG9 | Laurelbank Rd, (Chry.) G69 | 54 | CK22 | Laxford Rd, Ersk. PA8 | 24 | AN20 |
| Larch Ct, (Blan.) G72 | 124 | CL45 | Laurel Ct, (Camb.) G72 | 107 | CG41 | Laxford Way, Moth. ML1 | | |
| Larch Ct, (Camb.) G72 | 107 | CH42 | Laurel Ct, (E.Kil.) G75 | 135 | BZ56 | *off Hamilton Pl* | 113 | DE41 |
| Larch Ct, (E.Kil.) G75 | 135 | BX56 | Laurel Dr, (E.Kil.) G75 | 135 | BZ56 | Laxton Dr, (Lenz.) G66 | 35 | CG17 |
| Larch Cres, (Kirk.) G66 | 35 | CE15 | Laurel Dr, Lark. ML9 | 145 | DE59 | Laymoor Av, Renf. PA4 | 46 | BB26 |
| Larch Dr, (E.Kil.) G75 | 135 | BX56 | Laurel Dr, Wis. ML2 | 129 | DF49 | Laymoor Wk, Renf. PA4 | 46 | BB26 |
| Larches, The, (Mood.) G69 | 37 | CQ17 | Laurel Gait, (Camb.) G72 | 107 | CG42 | Lea Av, (Neil.) G78 | 114 | AT46 |
| Larchfield Av, G14 | 46 | BD25 | Laurel Gdns, (Udd.) G71 | 93 | CP37 | Leabank Av, Pais. PA2 | 82 | AU37 |
| Larchfield Av, (Newt. M.) G77 | 117 | BG49 | Laurel Gdns, (Chap.) Air. ML6 | 97 | DG35 | Leadburn Rd, G21 | 51 | BY25 |
| Larchfield Ct, (Newt. M.) G77 | 117 | BF49 | Laurel Gro, (Green.) Air. ML6 | 41 | DH19 | Leadburn St, G32 | 70 | CA30 |
| Larchfield Dr, (Ruther.) G73 | 105 | BY41 | Laurel La, (Camb.) G72 | 107 | CG42 | Leader St, G33 | 69 | BZ28 |
| Larchfield Pl, G14 | 46 | BD25 | Laurel La, Lark. ML9 | | | Leaend Rd, Air. ML6 | 76 | DA28 |
| Larchfield Rd, (Bears.) G61 | 29 | BH20 | *off Dickson St* | 145 | DE60 | Leander Cres, Bell. ML4 | 112 | DA40 |
| Larchfield Rd, (Mood.) G69 | 37 | CP19 | Laurel Pk Cl, G13 | 47 | BE24 | Leander Cres, Renf. PA4 | 64 | BA27 |
| Larch Gait, (Camb.) G72 | 107 | CH42 | Laurel Pk Gdns, G13 | 47 | BE24 | Learmont Pl, (Miln.) G62 | 11 | BH11 |

| | | |
|---|---|---|
| Leathem Pl, Wis. ML2 | 143 | DE52 |
| Leathen Pl, Ersk. PA8 | 24 | AN20 |
| Leckethill Av, (Cumb.) G68 | 20 | CV14 |
| Leckethill Ct, (Cumb.) G68 | 20 | CV14 |
| Leckethill Pl, (Cumb.) G68 | 20 | CU14 |
| Leckethill Vw, (Cumb.) G68 | 20 | CV14 |
| Leckie Dr, Ham. ML3 | 126 | CS49 |
| Leckie St, G43 | 86 | BL37 |
| Ledaig Pl, G31 | 69 | BY30 |
| Ledaig St, G31 | 69 | BY30 |
| Ledard Rd, G42 | 87 | BP37 |
| Ledcameroch Cres, (Bears.) G61 | 29 | BF17 |
| Ledcameroch Pk, (Bears.) G61 | 29 | BF17 |
| Ledcameroch Rd, (Bears.) G61 | 29 | BF17 |
| Ledgate, (Kirk.) G66 | 17 | CF12 |
| Ledgowan Pl, G20 | 48 | BM21 |
| Ledi Dr, (Bears.) G61 | 10 | BD14 |
| Ledi Path, Moth. ML1 | | |
| _off Martin Pl_ | 113 | DE41 |
| Ledi Rd, G43 | 102 | BL40 |
| Ledmore Dr, G15 | 28 | BB17 |
| Lednock Rd, (Stepps) G33 | 53 | CE24 |
| Lednock Rd, G52 | 64 | BC32 |
| Lee Av, G33 | 70 | CA28 |
| Leebank Dr, G44 | 103 | BP44 |
| Leechlee Rd, Ham. ML3 | 126 | CU50 |
| Lee Cres, (Bishop.) G64 | 51 | BW21 |
| Leefield Dr, G44 | 103 | BP43 |
| Leehill Rd, G21 | 50 | BU22 |
| Lee Pl, Bell. ML4 | 111 | CZ41 |
| Lee's Burn Ct, (E.Kil.) G74 | 122 | CC48 |
| Leesburn Pl, (E.Kil.) G74 | 122 | CB49 |
| Lees Ct, Coat. ML5 | 75 | CW32 |
| Leeside Rd, G21 | 50 | BU22 |
| Leesland, (Udd.) G71 | 93 | CQ37 |
| Leeward Circle, (E.Kil.) G75 | 135 | BW52 |
| Leewood Dr, G44 | 103 | BQ43 |
| Le Froy Gdns, (E.Kil.) G75 | 135 | BY53 |
| Le Froy La, (E.Kil.) G75 | 135 | BY53 |
| Lefroy St, Coat. ML5 | 74 | CU30 |
| Legbrannock Cres, Moth. ML1 | 113 | DF41 |
| Legbrannock Rd, Moth. ML1 | 113 | DG39 |
| Leggatston Dr, G53 | 101 | BE42 |
| Leggatston Rd, G53 | 101 | BE43 |
| Leglen Wd Cres, G21 | 51 | BZ23 |
| Leglen Wd Dr, G21 | 51 | BZ23 |
| Leglen Wd Pl, G21 | 51 | BZ23 |
| Leglen Wd Rd, G21 | 51 | BZ23 |
| Leicester Av, G12 | 48 | BK24 |
| Leighton St, G20 | 49 | BN23 |
| Leisure Way, Lark. ML9 | | |
| _off Broomhill Dr_ | 144 | DC59 |
| Leitchland Rd, (Elder.) | | |
| John. PA5 | 80 | AM37 |
| Leitchland Rd, Pais. PA2 | 80 | AM37 |
| Leithland Av, G53 | 84 | BD36 |
| Leithland Rd, G53 | 84 | BD36 |
| Leith St, G33 | 69 | BZ29 |
| Lembert Dr, (Clark.) G76 | 118 | BM45 |
| Lendale La, (Bishop.) G64 | 33 | BW18 |
| Lendalfoot Gdns, Ham. ML3 | 138 | CM51 |
| Lendal Pl, (E.Kil.) G75 | 134 | BU55 |
| Lendel Pl, G51 | | |
| _off Paisley Rd W_ | 66 | BM32 |
| Lenihall Dr, G45 | 104 | BU43 |
| Lenihall Ter, G45 | 104 | BU43 |
| Lennox Av, G14 | 47 | BE26 |
| Lennox Av, (Miln.) G62 | 12 | BJ12 |
| Lennox Av, Bish. PA7 | 24 | AK18 |
| Lennox Av, Coat. ML5 | 74 | CU30 |
| Lennox Ct, (Bears.) G61 | | |
| _off Montrose Dr_ | 11 | BG14 |
| Lennox Cres, (Bishop.) G64 | 50 | BV21 |

| | | |
|---|---|---|
| Lennox Dr, (Bears.) G61 | 29 | BH15 |
| Lennox Dr, (Newt. M.) G77 | 131 | BG51 |
| Lennox Gdns, G14 | 47 | BF25 |
| Lennox La E, G14 | 47 | BF26 |
| Lennox La W, G14 | | |
| _off Lennox Av_ | 47 | BF25 |
| Lennox Pl, G14 | | |
| _off Scotstoun St_ | 47 | BE26 |
| Lennox Pl, Clyde. G81 | 26 | AU18 |
| Lennox Rd, (Cumb.) G67 | 22 | DB11 |
| Lennox St, G20 | | |
| _off Maryhill Rd_ | 48 | BL22 |
| Lennox Ter, Pais. PA3 | 63 | AW29 |
| Lennox Vw, Clyde. G81 | | |
| _off Granville St_ | 27 | AX18 |
| Lentran St, G34 | 72 | CM30 |
| Leny St, G20 | 49 | BP25 |
| Lenziemill Ind Est, (Cumb.) G67 | 22 | DC13 |
| Lenziemill Rd, (Cumb.) G67 | 22 | DD13 |
| Lenzie Pl, G21 | 50 | BV23 |
| Lenzie Rd, (Stepps) G33 | 53 | CF23 |
| Lenzie Rd, (Kirk.) G66 | 35 | CF15 |
| Lenzie St, G21 | 50 | BV24 |
| Lenzie Ter, G21 | 50 | BV24 |
| Lenzie Way, G21 | 50 | BV23 |
| Lesley Quad, Bell. ML4 | | |
| _off McLean Dr_ | 110 | CV43 |
| Leslie Av, (Newt. M.) G77 | 117 | BG46 |
| Leslie Av, Bish. PA7 | 24 | AK18 |
| Leslie Rd, G41 | 87 | BN34 |
| Leslie St, G41 | 87 | BP34 |
| Leslie St, Moth. ML1 | 128 | DB46 |
| Lesmuir Dr, G14 | 46 | BB24 |
| Lesmuir Pl, G14 | 46 | BB23 |
| Letham Ct, G43 | 103 | BN40 |
| Letham Dr, G43 | 103 | BN40 |
| Letham Dr, (Bishop.) G64 | 51 | BY21 |
| Letham Gra, (Cumb.) G68 | 22 | DB9 |
| Lethamhill Cres, G33 | 70 | CB28 |
| Lethamhill Pl, G33 | 70 | CA28 |
| Lethamhill Rd, G33 | 70 | CA28 |
| Letham Oval, (Bishop.) G64 | 51 | BZ21 |
| Lethbridge Pl, (E.Kil.) G75 | | |
| _off Edmonton Ter_ | 135 | BY53 |
| Letherby Dr, G42 | 87 | BR38 |
| Letherby Dr, G44 | 87 | BR38 |
| Lethington Av, G41 | 87 | BN37 |
| Lethington Pl, G41 | 87 | BN37 |
| Lethington Rd, (Giff.) G46 | 118 | BJ46 |
| Letterfearn Dr, G23 | 31 | BN20 |
| Letterickhills Cres, (Camb.) | | |
| G72 | 107 | CG42 |
| Lettoch St, G51 | 66 | BJ30 |
| Leven Av, (Bishop.) G64 | 33 | BX20 |
| Leven Ct, (Barr.) G78 | | |
| _off Linnhe Dr_ | 99 | AX40 |
| Leven Dr, (Bears.) G61 | 29 | BH17 |
| Leven Path, Moth. ML1 | | |
| _off Graham St_ | 112 | DC40 |
| Leven Pl, Ersk. PA8 | 24 | AN20 |
| Leven Quad, Air. ML6 | 76 | DB27 |
| Leven Rd, Coat. ML5 | 74 | CT28 |
| Leven Sq, Renf. PA4 | 45 | AX25 |
| Leven St, G41 | 87 | BP34 |
| Leven St, Moth. ML1 | 128 | DA49 |
| Leven Ter, Moth. ML1 | 113 | DE43 |
| Leven Vw, Clyde. G81 | | |
| _off Crown Av_ | 27 | AX18 |
| Leven Way, (Cumb.) G67 | | |
| _off Cumbernauld Shop Cen_ | 22 | DB12 |
| Leven Way, (E.Kil.) G75 | 134 | BV55 |
| Leven Way, Pais. PA2 | 81 | AN36 |
| Levern Br Ct, G53 | 84 | BB38 |

| | | |
|---|---|---|
| Levern Br Gro, G53 | 84 | BB38 |
| Levern Br Pl, G53 | 100 | BB39 |
| Levern Br Rd, G53 | 100 | BB39 |
| Levern Br Way, G53 | 100 | BB39 |
| Levern Cres, (Barr.) G78 | 99 | AX44 |
| Leverndale Ct, G53 | 84 | BB36 |
| Leverndale Ind Cen, G53 | 84 | BB37 |
| Leverndale Rd, G53 | 84 | BB36 |
| Levern Gdns, (Barr.) G78 | 99 | AX42 |
| Levernside Av, G53 | | |
| _off Levernside Cres_ | 85 | BE37 |
| Levernside Av, (Barr.) G78 | 99 | AW43 |
| Levernside Cres, G53 | 84 | BD36 |
| Levernside Rd, G53 | 85 | BE36 |
| Lewis Av, Renf. PA4 | 63 | AZ28 |
| Lewis Cres, (Old Kil.) G60 | 25 | AR16 |
| Lewis Cres, (Kilb.) John. PA10 | 79 | AE35 |
| Lewis Dr, (Old Kil.) G60 | 25 | AR16 |
| Lewis Gdns, (Old Kil.) G60 | 26 | AS16 |
| Lewis Gdns, (Bears.) G61 | 28 | BD15 |
| Lewis Gro, (Old Kil.) G60 | 26 | AS16 |
| Lewis Pl, (Old Kil.) G60 | 26 | AS16 |
| Lewis Pl, (Newt. M.) G77 | | |
| _off Tiree Pl_ | 116 | BD47 |
| Lewis Pl, Air. ML6 | 77 | DF31 |
| Lewiston Dr, G23 | | |
| _off Lewiston Rd_ | 30 | BM20 |
| Lewiston Pl, G23 | | |
| _off Lewiston Rd_ | 30 | BM20 |
| Lewiston Rd, G23 | 30 | BM20 |
| Lexwell Av, (Elder.) John. PA5 | 80 | AM34 |
| Leyden Ct, G20 | 49 | BN24 |
| Leyden Gdns, G20 | 49 | BN24 |
| Leyden St, G20 | 49 | BN24 |
| Leyland Av, Ham. ML3 | 139 | CQ53 |
| Leyland Wynd, Ham. ML3 | 139 | CQ54 |
| Leys, The, (Bishop.) G64 | 33 | BW20 |
| Leys Pk, Ham. ML3 | 125 | CQ49 |
| Libberton Way, Ham. ML3 | 125 | CQ50 |
| Liberton St, G33 | 69 | BZ29 |
| Liberty Av, (Baill.) G69 | 73 | CQ32 |
| Liberty Path, (Blan.) G72 | | |
| _off Burnbrae Rd_ | 124 | CM46 |
| Liberty Rd, Bell. ML4 | 111 | CW41 |
| Libo Av, G53 | 85 | BF36 |
| Libo Pl, Ersk. PA8 | 24 | AN19 |
| Library Gdns, (Camb.) G72 | 106 | CB39 |
| Library La, (Thornlie.) G46 | 101 | BH42 |
| Lickprivick Rd, (E.Kil.) G75 | 135 | BX55 |
| Liddell Gro, (E.Kil.) G75 | 135 | BZ54 |
| Liddells Ct, (Bishop.) G64 | 51 | BW21 |
| Liddell St, G32 | 91 | CE36 |
| Liddel Rd, (Cumb.) G67 | 22 | DA12 |
| Liddesdale Av, Pais. PA2 | 80 | AM38 |
| Liddesdale Pl, G22 | | |
| _off Torogay St_ | 50 | BU22 |
| Liddesdale Rd, G22 | 50 | BS22 |
| Liddesdale Sq, G22 | 50 | BT22 |
| Liddesdale Ter, G22 | 50 | BU22 |
| Liddoch Way, (Ruther.) G73 | 88 | BV37 |
| Liff Gdns, (Bishop.) G64 | 51 | BZ21 |
| Liff Pl, G34 | 72 | CL28 |
| Lightburn Pl, G32 | 70 | CD30 |
| Lightburn Rd, G31 | 69 | BY31 |
| Lightburn Rd, (Camb.) G72 | 107 | CF41 |
| Lilac Av, Clyde. G81 | 26 | AT16 |
| Lilac Cres, (Udd.) G71 | 93 | CR37 |
| Lilac Gdns, (Bishop.) G64 | 51 | BX21 |
| Lilac Hill, Ham. ML3 | 140 | CV51 |
| Lilac Pl, John. PA5 | | |
| _off Spruce Av_ | 80 | AJ36 |
| Lilac Way, Moth. ML1 | | |
| _off Myrtle Dr_ | 112 | DD40 |

| | | | |
|---|---|---|---|
| Lilac Wynd, (Camb.) G72 | 107 | CG41 | |
| Lillyburn Pl, G15 | 28 | BA16 | |
| Lilybank Av, (Muir.) G69 | 54 | CL22 | |
| Lilybank Av, (Camb.) G72 | 107 | CE41 | |
| Lilybank Av, Air. ML6 | 76 | DD27 | |
| Lilybank Gdns, G12 | 66 | BM27 | |
| Lilybank Gdns La, G12 | 66 | BM27 | |
| Lilybank La, G12 | | | |
| off Lilybank Gdns | 66 | BM27 | |
| Lilybank St, Ham. ML3 | 126 | CS49 | |
| Lilybank Ter, G12 | | | |
| off Great George St | 66 | BM27 | |
| Lily St, G40 | 89 | BX34 | |
| Limecraigs Av, Pais. PA2 | 82 | AS38 | |
| Limecraigs Cres, Pais. PA2 | 82 | AS38 | |
| Limecraigs Rd, Pais. PA2 | 81 | AR38 | |
| Lime Cres, (Cumb.) G67 | 23 | DG10 | |
| Lime Cres, Air. ML6 | 77 | DE30 | |
| Lime Gro, (Lenz.) G66 | 35 | CF16 | |
| Lime Gro, (Blan.) G72 | 108 | CL44 | |
| Lime Gro, Moth. ML1 | | | |
| off Ferguson Dr | 128 | DA49 | |
| Limegrove St, Bell. ML4 | | | |
| off Primrose Av | 95 | CW38 | |
| Limekilns Rd, (Cumb.) G67 | 40 | DB15 | |
| Lime La, G14 | | | |
| off Westland Dr | 47 | BF26 | |
| Lime Ln, Moth. ML1 | 112 | DD41 | |
| Limeside Av, (Ruther.) G73 | 89 | BX38 | |
| Limeside Gdns, (Ruther.) G73 | 89 | BY38 | |
| Lime St, G14 | 47 | BF26 | |
| Limetree Av, (Udd.) G71 | 93 | CR37 | |
| Limetree Ct, Ham. ML3 | 125 | CQ48 | |
| Limetree Cres, (Newt. M.) G77 | 117 | BF49 | |
| Limetree Dr, Clyde. G81 | 27 | AW17 | |
| Limetree Quad, (Udd.) G71 | 94 | CS37 | |
| Limetree Wk, (M. of Cam.) G66 | 16 | CD9 | |
| Limeview Av, Pais. PA2 | 81 | AR38 | |
| Limeview Cres, Pais. PA2 | 81 | AR38 | |
| Limeview Rd, Pais. PA2 | 81 | AR38 | |
| Limeview Way, Pais. PA2 | | | |
| off Limeview Av | 81 | AR38 | |
| Linacre Dr, G32 | 71 | CE32 | |
| Linacre Gdns, G32 | 71 | CF32 | |
| Linburn Pl, G52 | 64 | BC31 | |
| Linburn Rd, G52 | 64 | BA30 | |
| Linburn Rd, Ersk. PA8 | 24 | AN20 | |
| Linclive Interchange, (Linw.) | | | |
| Pais. PA3 | 60 | AM32 | |
| Linclive Link Rd, (Linw.) | | | |
| Pais. PA3 | 61 | AN31 | |
| Linclive Ter, (Linw.) Pais. PA3 | | | |
| off Candren Rd | 60 | AM32 | |
| Lincuden Path, G41 | | | |
| off McCulloch St | 87 | BP33 | |
| Lincoln Av, G13 | 47 | BE22 | |
| Lincoln Av, (Udd.) G71 | 93 | CP36 | |
| Lincuan Av, (Giff.) G46 | 102 | BL44 | |
| Lindams, (Udd.) G71 | 109 | CP40 | |
| Linden Ct, Clyde. G81 | | | |
| off Linden Dr | 27 | AW15 | |
| Linden Dr, Clyde. G81 | 27 | AW15 | |
| Linden Lea, Ham. ML3 | 125 | CR49 | |
| Linden Pl, G13 | 47 | BH22 | |
| Linden St, G13 | 47 | BH22 | |
| Linden Way, G13 | | | |
| off Sutcliffe Rd | 47 | BH22 | |
| Lindores Av, (Ruther.) G73 | 89 | BX38 | |
| Lindores Dr, (E.Kil.) G74 | 135 | BY52 | |
| Lindores Pl, (E.Kil.) G74 | | | |
| off Lindores Dr | 135 | BY52 | |
| Lindores St, G42 | | | |
| off Somerville Dr | 87 | BR37 | |

| | | | |
|---|---|---|---|
| Lindrick Dr, G23 | 31 | BN20 | |
| Lindsaybeg Ct, (Chry.) G69 | 54 | CL21 | |
| Lindsaybeg Rd, (Lenz.) G66 | 35 | CH17 | |
| Lindsaybeg Rd, (Chry.) G69 | 36 | CK19 | |
| Lindsay Dr, G12 | 48 | BK23 | |
| Lindsay Gro, (E.Kil.) G74 | 136 | CB51 | |
| Lindsay Pl, G12 | 48 | BK23 | |
| Lindsay Pl, (Lenz.) G66 | 35 | CF18 | |
| Lindsay Pl, (E.Kil.) G74 | 136 | CC52 | |
| Lindsay Pl, John. PA5 | | | |
| off Thorn Brae | 80 | AJ34 | |
| Lindsay Rd, (E.Kil.) G74 | 136 | CB52 | |
| Lindum Cres, Moth. ML1 | 127 | CX45 | |
| Lindum St, Moth. ML1 | 127 | CX45 | |
| Linfern Rd, G12 | 48 | BL26 | |
| Lingley Av, Air. ML6 | 76 | DC31 | |
| Linhope Pl, (E.Kil.) G75 | 134 | BU54 | |
| Links Rd, G32 | 91 | CF34 | |
| Links Rd, G44 | 104 | BS41 | |
| Links Vw, Lark. ML9 | 145 | DE59 | |
| Linksview Rd, Moth. ML1 | 112 | DD44 | |
| Linkwood Av, G15 | 28 | BB18 | |
| Linkwood Cres, G15 | 28 | BC18 | |
| Linkwood Dr, G15 | 28 | BB18 | |
| Linkwood Gdns, G15 | 28 | BD18 | |
| Linkwood Gro, G15 | 28 | BD18 | |
| Linkwood Pl, G15 | 28 | BB18 | |
| Linlithgow Gdns, G32 | 71 | CF32 | |
| Linn Brae, John. PA5 | 79 | AH35 | |
| Linn Cres, Pais. PA2 | 82 | AS38 | |
| Linndale Dr, G51 | 104 | BS44 | |
| Linndale Gdns, G51 | 104 | BS44 | |
| Linndale Gro, G51 | 104 | BS44 | |
| Linndale Oval, G45 | 104 | BS43 | |
| Linndale Rd, G51 | 104 | BS44 | |
| Linndale Way, G45 | 104 | BS43 | |
| Linn Dr, G44 | 103 | BP42 | |
| Linnet Av, John. PA5 | 79 | AE38 | |
| Linnet Pl, G13 | 46 | BB22 | |
| Linnet Rd, Bell. ML4 | 111 | CX41 | |
| Linnet Way, (Strathclyde Bus. Pk.) | | | |
| Bell. ML4 | 94 | CV37 | |
| Linn Gdns, (Cumb.) G68 | 20 | CV11 | |
| Linnhead Dr, G53 | 100 | BD39 | |
| Linnhead Pl, G14 | 46 | BD25 | |
| Linnhe Av, G44 | 103 | BQ41 | |
| Linnhe Av, (Bishop.) G64 | 33 | BX20 | |
| Linnhe Av, Ham. ML3 | 139 | CQ52 | |
| Linnhe Ct, Lark. ML9 | 142 | DB56 | |
| Linnhe Dr, (Barr.) G78 | 99 | AX40 | |
| Linnhe Pl, (Blan.) G72 | 108 | CL43 | |
| Linnhe Pl, Ersk. PA8 | 24 | AN20 | |
| Linn Pk, G44 | 103 | BR42 | |
| Linnpark Av, G44 | 103 | BP43 | |
| Linnpark Ct, G44 | 103 | BP43 | |
| Linn Pk Gdns, John. PA5 | 79 | AH35 | |
| Linn Pk Ind Est, G45 | 103 | BR43 | |
| Linnvale Way, (Dullatur) G68 | 8 | CY7 | |
| Linn Valley Vw, G45 | 104 | BT42 | |
| Linnwell Cres, Pais. PA2 | 82 | AT37 | |
| Linnwood Ct, G44 | 103 | BQ40 | |
| Linside Av, Pais. PA1 | 83 | AW33 | |
| Lint Butts, (Blan.) G72 | | | |
| off Stewart Av | 124 | CL46 | |
| Lintfield Ln, (Udd.) G71 | | | |
| off Myers Cres | 109 | CQ40 | |
| Linthaugh Rd, G53 | 84 | BC35 | |
| Linthaugh Ter, G53 | | | |
| off Linthaugh Rd | 85 | BF36 | |
| Linthouse Bldgs, G51 | 65 | BG29 | |
| Linthouse Rd, G51 | 65 | BG28 | |
| Lintie Rd, Moth. ML1 | 113 | DE41 | |
| Lintlaw, (Blan.) G72 | 108 | CM44 | |

| | | | |
|---|---|---|---|
| Lintlaw Dr, G52 | 64 | BD31 | |
| Lintmill Ter, (Neil.) G78 | 114 | AS47 | |
| Linton Pl, Coat. ML5 | | | |
| off Ellismuir St | 94 | CU34 | |
| Linton St, G33 | 70 | CA29 | |
| Linwood Av, (E.Kil.) G74 | 134 | BV51 | |
| Linwood Av, (Clark.) G76 | 119 | BP46 | |
| Linwood Ind Est, (Linw.) | | | |
| Pais. PA3 | 80 | AL33 | |
| Linwood Rd, Pais. PA1 | 60 | AM32 | |
| Linwood Rd, (Linw.) Pais. PA3 | 60 | AL32 | |
| Linwood Ter, Ham. ML3 | 125 | CR49 | |
| Lion Bk, (Kirk.) G66 | 17 | CF12 | |
| Lismore, (E.Kil.) G74 | 137 | CE53 | |
| Lismore Av, Moth. ML1 | 127 | CX45 | |
| Lismore Av, Renf. PA4 | 63 | AZ28 | |
| Lismore Dr, Coat. ML5 | 94 | CT33 | |
| Lismore Dr, Pais. PA2 | 82 | AT38 | |
| Lismore Gdns, (Kilb.) | | | |
| John. PA10 | 79 | AE35 | |
| Lismore Hill, Ham. ML3 | 124 | CM50 | |
| Lismore Pl, (Mood.) G69 | | | |
| off Altnacreag Gdns | 37 | CQ18 | |
| Lismore Pl, (Newt. M.) G77 | 116 | BD48 | |
| Lismore Rd, G12 | 48 | BK24 | |
| Lister Gdns, (Clark.) G76 | 119 | BQ48 | |
| Lister Pl, G52 | | | |
| off Lister Rd | 64 | BC30 | |
| Lister Rd, G52 | 64 | BC30 | |
| Lister St, G4 | 5 | BT28 | |
| Lister Twr, (E.Kil.) G75 | 136 | CB53 | |
| Lister Wk, Bell. ML4 | | | |
| off Harvey Way | 95 | CY38 | |
| Lister Way, (Blan.) G72 | 124 | CL48 | |
| Lithgow Av, (Kirk.) G66 | 17 | CF14 | |
| Lithgow Cres, Pais. PA2 | 83 | AW35 | |
| Lithgow Pl, (E.Kil.) G74 | 135 | BX51 | |
| Little Dovehill, G1 | 5 | BT31 | |
| Little Drum Rd, (Cumb.) G68 | 19 | CR13 | |
| Littleholm Pl, Clyde. G81 | 26 | AU17 | |
| Littlemill Av, (Cumb.) G68 | 20 | CU12 | |
| Littlemill Cres, G53 | 84 | BC37 | |
| Littlemill Dr, G53 | 84 | BC37 | |
| Littlemill Gdns, G53 | 84 | BC37 | |
| Littlemill Way, (Carfin) | | | |
| Moth. ML1 | 112 | DD44 | |
| Littleston Gdns, Ersk. PA8 | 25 | AP20 | |
| Little St, G3 | | | |
| off McIntyre St | 4 | BP30 | |
| Littleton Dr, G23 | | | |
| off Littleton St | 30 | BL20 | |
| Littleton St, G23 | 30 | BM20 | |
| Lively Pl, (Blan.) G72 | | | |
| off Burnbrae Rd | 124 | CL46 | |
| Livingstone Av, G52 | 64 | BC29 | |
| Livingstone Boul, (Blan.) G72 | 124 | CL48 | |
| Livingstone Cres, (Blan.) G72 | 108 | CM44 | |
| Livingstone Cres, (E.Kil.) G75 | | | |
| off Livingstone Dr | 135 | BZ54 | |
| Livingstone Dr, (E.Kil.) G75 | 135 | BZ53 | |
| Livingstone Gdns, Lark. ML9 | 144 | DD58 | |
| Livingstone La, (Both.) G71 | | | |
| off Appledore Cres | 109 | CQ42 | |
| Livingstone Pk, (Kilsyth) G65 | 7 | CR3 | |
| Livingstone St, Clyde. G81 | 27 | AY20 | |
| Livingstone St, Ham. ML3 | 125 | CP49 | |
| Livingston Pl, Air. ML6 | 76 | DD31 | |
| Lloyd Av, G32 | 90 | CC35 | |
| Lloyd Ct, (Ruther.) G73 | 89 | BX36 | |
| Lloyd Dr, Moth. ML1 | 112 | DC44 | |
| Lloyds St, Coat. ML5 | 75 | CW32 | |
| Lloyd St, G31 | 69 | BW29 | |
| Lloyd St, (Ruther.) G73 | 89 | BX36 | |

| Name | Page | Grid |
|---|---|---|
| Lloyd St, Moth. ML1 · | 112 | DC44 |
| Loan, The, (Miln.) G62 | 11 | BE9 |
| Loanbank Quad, G51 | 65 | BH30 |
| Loancroft Av, (Baill.) G69 | 92 | CL34 |
| Loancroft Gdns, (Udd.) G71 | 109 | CN40 |
| Loancroft Gate, (Udd.) G71 | 109 | CN40 |
| Loancroft Pl, (Baill.) G69 | 92 | CK34 |
| Loanend Cotts, (Camb.) G72 | 107 | CH44 |
| Loanfoot Av, G13 | 46 | BC22 |
| Loanfoot Av, (Neil.) G78 | 114 | AT47 |
| Loanfoot Rd, (Blan.) G72 | | |
| off Kirkton Av | 124 | CM47 |
| Loanhead Av, Moth. ML1 | 113 | DF42 |
| Loanhead Av, (Linw.) Pais. PA3 | 60 | AJ31 |
| Loanhead Av, Renf. PA4 | 45 | AZ26 |
| Loanhead Cres, Moth. ML1 | 113 | DF42 |
| Loanhead La, (Linw.) Pais. PA3 | 60 | AJ31 |
| Loanhead Rd, Moth. ML1 | 113 | DE42 |
| Loanhead Rd, (Linw.) Pais. PA3 | 60 | AJ31 |
| Loanhead St, G32 | 70 | CB30 |
| Loanhead St, Coat. ML5 | 94 | CU34 |
| Loaning, Lark. ML9 | | |
| off Shawrigg Rd | 145 | DE59 |
| Loaning, The, (Giff.) G46 | 118 | BJ45 |
| Loaning, The, (Bears.) G61 | | |
| off Manse Rd | 29 | BG16 |
| Loaning, The, (Kirk.) G66 | 17 | CE14 |
| Loaning, The, Moth. ML1 | 127 | CY46 |
| Loan Lea Cres, Lark. ML9 | 144 | DD60 |
| Lobnitz Av, Renf. PA4 | 45 | AZ26 |
| Lochaber Dr, (Ruther.) G73 | 105 | BZ41 |
| Lochaber Path, (Blan.) G72 | | |
| off Burnbrae Rd | 124 | CM46 |
| Lochaber Pl, (E.Kil.) G74 | 122 | CB50 |
| Lochaber Rd, (Bears.) G61 | 30 | BJ19 |
| Loch Achray Gdns, G32 | 91 | CE33 |
| Loch Achray St, G32 | 91 | CE33 |
| Lochaline Av, Pais. PA2 | 81 | AQ35 |
| Lochaline Dr, G44 | 103 | BQ41 |
| Lochalsh Dr, Pais. PA2 | 81 | AP35 |
| Lochalsh Pl, (Blan.) G72 | 108 | CK43 |
| Lochar Cres, G53 | 85 | BF35 |
| Lochard Dr, Pais. PA2 | 81 | AQ36 |
| Lochar Pl, (E.Kil.) G75 | 134 | BU54 |
| Loch Assynt, (E.Kil.) G74 | 136 | CD53 |
| Loch Awe, (E.Kil.) G74 | 136 | CC53 |
| Loch Awe Pl, Coat. ML5 | | |
| off Loch Brora Cres | 74 | CV31 |
| Lochay St, G32 | 91 | CE33 |
| Lochbrae Dr, (Ruther.) G73 | 105 | BZ41 |
| Lochbridge Rd, G34 | 72 | CJ30 |
| Lochbroom Ct, (Newt. M.) G77 | | |
| off Lochbroom Dr | 117 | BH47 |
| Lochbroom Dr, (Newt. M.) G77 | 118 | BJ47 |
| Lochbroom Rd, Pais. PA2 | 81 | AQ35 |
| Loch Brora Cres, Coat. ML5 | 74 | CU31 |
| Lochbuie La, (Glenm.) Air. ML6 | 58 | DA25 |
| Lochburn Cres, G20 | 49 | BN22 |
| Lochburn Gdns, G20 | 49 | BN22 |
| Lochburn Gate, G20 | 49 | BN22 |
| Lochburn Gro, G20 | | |
| off Cadder Rd | 49 | BN22 |
| Lochburn Pas, G20 | 49 | BN22 |
| Lochburn Rd, G20 | 48 | BM23 |
| Lochdochart Path, G34 | | |
| off Lochdochart Rd | 72 | CL30 |
| Lochdochart Rd, G34 | 72 | CL30 |
| Lochearn Cres, Air. ML6 | 76 | DB27 |
| Lochearn Cres, Pais. PA2 | 81 | AQ35 |
| Lochearnhead Rd, G33 | 52 | CD24 |
| Lochend Av, (Gart.) G69 | 55 | CN23 |
| Lochend Cres, (Bears.) G61 | 29 | BF18 |
| Lochend Dr, (Bears.) G61 | 29 | BF18 |
| Lochend Path, G34 | | |
| off Dubton St | 72 | CK28 |
| Lochend Rd, G34 | 72 | CK28 |
| Lochend Rd, (Bears.) G61 | 29 | BG18 |
| Lochend Rd, G69 | 73 | CN27 |
| Lochend Rd, (Gart.) G69 | 55 | CP24 |
| Lochend Rd, Coat. ML5 | 73 | CN27 |
| Lochend St, Moth. ML1 | 128 | DB47 |
| Lochfauld Rd, G23 | 31 | BQ19 |
| Lochfield Cres, Pais. PA2 | 82 | AV36 |
| Lochfield Dr, Pais. PA2 | 83 | AW36 |
| Lochfield Gdns, G34 | 72 | CL28 |
| Lochfield Rd, Pais. PA2 | 82 | AV36 |
| Lochgarry Way, Coat. ML5 | | |
| off Newton St | 94 | CU33 |
| Lochgilp St, G20 | 48 | BL22 |
| Loch Goil, (E.Kil.) G74 | 136 | CC52 |
| Lochgoin Av, G15 | 28 | BA17 |
| Lochgoin Gdns, G15 | 28 | BA17 |
| Loch Grn, Ham. ML3 | 139 | CR53 |
| Lochgreen Pl, Coat. ML5 | 74 | CS27 |
| Lochgreen St, G33 | 51 | BZ26 |
| Lochhead Av, (Linw.) Pais. PA3 | 60 | AK32 |
| Lochiel Ct, Air. ML6 | | |
| off Monkscourt Av | 75 | CZ30 |
| Lochiel La, (Ruther.) G73 | 105 | BZ41 |
| Lochiel Rd, (Thornlie.) G46 | 101 | BH41 |
| Lochinch Pl, (Newt. M.) G77 | 116 | BC48 |
| Lochinvar Rd, (Cumb.) G67 | 21 | CZ14 |
| Lochinver Cres, Pais. PA2 | 81 | AQ35 |
| Lochinver Dr, G44 | 103 | BQ41 |
| Lochinver Gro, (Camb.) G72 | | |
| off Andrew Sillars Av | 106 | CD40 |
| Loch Katrine St, G32 | 91 | CE33 |
| Loch Laidon St, G32 | 91 | CF33 |
| Loch Laxford, (E.Kil.) G74 | 136 | CD53 |
| Loch Lea, (Kirk.) G66 | 17 | CH11 |
| Lochlea, (E.Kil.) G74 | 123 | CF49 |
| Lochlea Av, Clyde. G81 | 27 | AY18 |
| Lochlea Ln, Lark. ML9 | | |
| off Shawrigg Rd | 145 | DE59 |
| Lochlea Rd, G43 | 102 | BM39 |
| Lochlea Rd, (Cumb.) G67 | 22 | DD10 |
| Lochlea Rd, (Ruther.) G73 | 104 | BV40 |
| Lochlea Rd, (Clark.) G76 | 119 | BN48 |
| Lochlea Way, Moth. ML1 | 113 | DG41 |
| Lochleven La, G42 | 87 | BQ38 |
| Lochleven Rd, G42 | 87 | BQ38 |
| Lochlibo Av, G13 | 46 | BB23 |
| Lochlibo Cres, (Barr.) G78 | 99 | AW44 |
| Lochlibo Rd, (Barr.) G78 | 114 | AU45 |
| Lochlibo Ter, (Barr.) G78 | 99 | AW44 |
| Loch Long, (E.Kil.) G74 | 136 | CC53 |
| Loch Loyal, (E.Kil.) G74 | 136 | CD53 |
| Lochmaben Rd, G52 | 84 | BB33 |
| Lochmaddy Av, G44 | 103 | BQ40 |
| Loch Maree, (E.Kil.) G74 | 136 | CD53 |
| Loch Meadie, (E.Kil.) G74 | 136 | CD53 |
| Lochnagar Dr, (Bears.) G61 | 10 | BD14 |
| Lochnagar Way, Lark. ML9 | | |
| off Bannockburn Dr | 145 | DE60 |
| Loch Naver, (E.Kil.) G74 | | |
| off Loch Loyal | 136 | CD53 |
| Lochore Av, Pais. PA3 | 62 | AV30 |
| Loch Pk Pl, Lark. ML9 | 144 | DC60 |
| Lochranza Ct, (Carfin) | | |
| Moth. ML1 | 112 | DD43 |
| Loch Rd, (Stepps) G33 | 53 | CF24 |
| Loch Rd, (Miln.) G62 | 12 | BK16 |
| Loch Rd, (Kirk.) G66 | 17 | CG14 |
| Loch Rd, (Chap.) Air. ML6 | 97 | DF35 |
| Loch Shin, (E.Kil.) G74 | 136 | CD53 |
| Lochside, (Bears.) G61 | 29 | BH18 |
| Lochside, (Gart.) G69 | 55 | CP23 |
| Lochside St, G41 | | |
| off Minard Rd | 87 | BN36 |
| Lochsloy Ct, G22 | 50 | BT25 |
| Loch St, (Calder.) Air. ML6 | 96 | DD35 |
| Loch Striven, (E.Kil.) G74 | 136 | CC52 |
| Loch Torridon, (E.Kil.) G74 | 136 | CD53 |
| Loch Vw, (Calder.) Air. ML6 | 96 | DD35 |
| Lochview Cotts, (Gart.) G69 | 55 | CN26 |
| Lochview Cres, G33 | 52 | CB26 |
| Lochview Dr, G33 | 52 | CB26 |
| Lochview Gdns, G33 | 52 | CB26 |
| Lochview Gate, G33 | 52 | CB26 |
| Lochview Pl, G33 | 52 | CB26 |
| Lochview Quad, Bell. ML4 | | |
| off Dempsey Rd | 110 | CV42 |
| Lochview Rd, (Bears.) G61 | 29 | BG18 |
| Lochview Rd, Coat. ML5 | 74 | CS28 |
| Lochview Ter, (Gart.) G69 | 55 | CP24 |
| Loch Voil St, G32 | 91 | CF33 |
| Lochwood Ln, (Mood.) G69 | 37 | CQ18 |
| Lochwood St, G33 | 70 | CA27 |
| Lochy Av, Renf. PA4 | 64 | BB28 |
| Lochy Gdns, (Bishop.) G64 | 33 | BX20 |
| Lochy Pl, Ersk. PA8 | 24 | AN20 |
| Locke Gro, Moth. ML1 | 113 | DH44 |
| Lockerbie Av, G43 | 103 | BP39 |
| Locket Yett Vw, Bell. ML4 | 110 | CU40 |
| Lockhart Av, (Camb.) G72 | 107 | CF39 |
| Lockhart Ct, (Newt. M.) G77 | 131 | BF51 |
| Lockhart Dr, (Camb.) G72 | 107 | CF39 |
| Lockhart Dr, (Newt. M.) G77 | 131 | BF51 |
| Lockhart St, G21 | 69 | BX27 |
| Lockhart St, Ham. ML3 | 140 | CS55 |
| Lockhart Ter, (E.Kil.) G74 | 136 | CD51 |
| Locksley Av, G13 | 47 | BE21 |
| Locksley Av, (Cumb.) G67 | 40 | DA15 |
| Locksley Ct, (Cumb.) G67 | 40 | DA15 |
| Locksley Cres, (Cumb.) G67 | 40 | DA15 |
| Locksley Pl, (Cumb.) G67 | 40 | DA15 |
| Locksley Rd, (Cumb.) G67 | 40 | DA15 |
| Locksley Rd, Pais. PA2 | 81 | AP36 |
| Locksley Way, Pais. PA2 | | |
| off Locksley Rd | 81 | AP36 |
| Locks St, Coat. ML5 | 75 | CZ31 |
| Logan Dr, (Newt. M.) G77 | 117 | BE47 |
| Logan Dr, (Cumb.) G68 | 21 | CZ10 |
| Logan Dr, Pais. PA3 | 62 | AS31 |
| Loganlea Dr, Moth. ML1 | 112 | DC44 |
| Logans Rd, Moth. ML1 | 127 | CX46 |
| Logan St, G5 | 88 | BT34 |
| Logan St, (Blan.) G72 | 125 | CN46 |
| Loganswell Dr, (Thornlie.) G46 | 101 | BG43 |
| Loganswell Gdns, (Thornlie.) | | |
| G46 | 101 | BG43 |
| Loganswell Pl, (Thornlie.) G46 | 101 | BG43 |
| Loganswell Rd, (Thornlie.) G46 | 101 | BG43 |
| Logan Twr, (Camb.) G72 | | |
| off Claude Av | 107 | CG41 |
| Logie Pk, (E.Kil.) G74 | 122 | CC50 |
| Logie Sq, (E.Kil.) G74 | 122 | CC50 |
| Lomax St, G33 | 69 | BZ29 |
| Lomond Av, Renf. PA4 | 63 | AX28 |
| Lomond Ct, (Cumb.) G67 | 21 | CY14 |
| Lomond Ct, (Barr.) G78 | | |
| off Eildon Dr | 99 | AY43 |
| Lomond Cres, (Cumb.) G67 | 21 | CY14 |
| Lomond Cres, Pais. PA2 | 82 | AT37 |
| Lomond Dr, (Bishop.) G64 | 32 | BV18 |
| Lomond Dr, (Cumb.) G67 | 21 | CX14 |
| Lomond Dr, (Both.) G71 | 109 | CR42 |
| Lomond Dr, (Newt. M.) G77 | 117 | BF46 |
| Lomond Dr, (Barr.) G78 | 99 | AX41 |

Lomond Dr, Air. ML6 76 DA28
Lomond Gdns, (Elder.) John. PA5 80 AL35
Lomond Gro, (Cumb.) G67 21 CY14
Lomond Pl, (Stepps) G33 53 CG25
Lomond Pl, (Cumb.) G67 21 CX14
Lomond Pl, Coat. ML5 74 CU28
Lomond Pl, Ersk. PA8 24 AN20
Lomond Rd, (Bears.) G61 29 BG19
Lomond Rd, (Lenz.) G66 35 CF16
Lomond Rd, (Udd.) G71 93 CP36
Lomond Rd, Coat. ML5 74 CT27
Lomondside Av, (Clark.) G76 118 BL45
Lomond St, G22 49 BR24
Lomond Vw, (Cumb.) G67 21 CY14
Lomond Vw, Clyde. G81
    off Granville St 27 AX18
Lomond Vw, Ham. ML3 139 CP51
Lomond Wk, Lark. ML9
    off Muirshot Rd 144 DD57
Lomond Wk, Moth. ML1 113 DE41
Lomond Way, Moth. ML1
    off Graham St 112 DC40
London Arc, G1
    off London Rd 5 BT31
London La, G1
    off London Rd 5 BT31
London Rd, G1 5 BT31
London Rd, G31 89 BX33
London Rd, G32 90 CA35
London Rd, G40 68 BU32
London St, Lark. ML9 144 DC57
London St, Renf. PA4 45 AZ24
London Way, G1 5 BT31
Lonend, Pais. PA1 82 AV33
Longay Pl, G22 50 BS21
Longay St, G22 50 BS21
Longcroft Dr, Renf. PA4 45 AY25
Longden St, Clyde. G81 45 AZ21
Longford St, G33 69 BZ29
Longlee, (Baill.) G69 92 CK33
Longmeadow, John. PA5 79 AE36
Long Row, (Kirk.) G66
    off Burnbrae Rd 18 CK14
Long Row, (Baill.) G69 72 CL31
Longstone Pl, G33
    off Longstone Rd 70 CD29
Longstone Rd, G33 70 CD29
Longwill Ter, (Cumb.) G67 22 DD9
Lonmay Dr, G33 71 CF29
Lonmay Pl, G33 71 CF29
Lonmay Rd, G33 71 CF29
Lonsdale Av, (Giff.) G46 102 BL42
Loom Wk, (Kilb.) John. PA10 78 AC34
Lora Dr, G52 85 BG33
Lord Way, (Baill.) G69
    off Dukes Rd 73 CP32
Loretto Pl, G33 70 CB29
Loretto St, G33 70 CB29
Lorimer Cres, (E.Kil.) G75 135 BZ54
Lorn Av, (Chry.) G69 54 CM21
Lorne Cres, (Bishop.) G64 33 BZ19
Lorne Dr, Moth. ML1 111 CZ43
Lorne Dr, (Linw.) Pais. PA3 60 AJ32
Lorne Pl, Coat. ML5 75 CZ32
Lorne Rd, G52 64 BB29
Lorne St, G51 66 BM31
Lorne St, Ham. ML3 126 CS49
Lorne Ter, (Camb.) G72 106 CB42
Lorn Pl, (Kirk.) G66 18 CL12
Lorraine Gdns, G12
    off Kensington Rd 48 BL25
Lorraine Gdns La, G12
    off Westbourne Gdns La 48 BL25

Lorraine Rd, G12
    off Kensington Rd 48 BL25
Loskin Dr, G22 49 BR22
Lossie Cres, Renf. PA4 64 BB27
Lossie St, G33 69 BZ28
Lothian Cres, Pais. PA2 82 AT36
Lothian Dr, (Clark.) G76 118 BM45
Lothian Gdns, G20
    off Wilton St 49 BN26
Lothian St, G52 64 BA29
Lothian Way, (E.Kil.) G74 123 CE50
Louden Hill Dr, G33
    off Louden Hill Rd 52 CA23
Louden Hill Gdns, G33
    off Louden Hill Rd 52 CA23
Louden Hill Pl, G33
    off Louden Hill Rd 52 CA23
Louden Hill Rd, G33 52 CA23
Louden Hill Way, G33
    off Louden Hill Rd 52 CA23
Loudon, (E.Kil.) G75 136 CA56
Loudon Gdns, John. PA5 80 AJ34
Loudonhill Av, Ham. ML3 140 CT53
Loudon Rd, G33 52 CD24
Loudon St, Air. ML6 76 DC30
Loudon Ter, G12
    off Observatory Rd 48 BM26
Loudon Ter, (Bears.) G61 11 BF13
Louise Gdns, (Holytown)
    Moth. ML1 112 DB40
Lounsdale Av, Pais. PA2 81 AR34
Lounsdale Cres, Pais. PA2 81 AQ35
Lounsdale Dr, Pais. PA2 81 AR35
Lounsdale Gro, Pais. PA2 81 AR34
Lounsdale Ho, Pais. PA2 81 AQ36
Lounsdale Pl, G14 46 BD25
Lounsdale Rd, Pais. PA2 81 AR35
Lounsdale Way, Pais. PA2 81 AR34
Lourdes Av, G52 85 BF33
Lourdes Ct, G52 85 BF33
Lovat Av, (Bears.) G61 11 BG14
Lovat Dr, (Kirk.) G66 16 CD13
Lovat Path, Lark. ML9
    off Shawrigg Rd 145 DE59
Lovat Pl, G52 64 BA30
Lovat Pl, (Ruther.) G73 105 BZ41
Lovat St, G4
    off Borron St 68 BS27
Love St, Pais. PA3 62 AU30
Low Barholm, (Kilb.) John. PA10 78 AD35
Low Broadlie Rd, (Neil.) G78 114 AT45
Low Craigends, (Kilsyth) G65 7 CU5
Low Cres, Clyde. G81 45 AZ21
Lower Auchingramont Rd, Ham.
    ML3 off Muir St 126 CU49
Lower Bourtree Dr, (Ruther.)
    G73 105 BY41
Lower Millgate, (Udd.) G71 109 CP39
Lower Mill Rd, (Clark.) G76 119 BP47
Low Flenders Rd, (Clark.) G76 118 BM48
Low Moss Ind Est, (Bishop.) G64 33 BX17
Lowndes St, (Barr.) G78 99 AY43
Low Parksail, Ersk. PA8 44 AS21
Low Patrick St, Ham. ML3 126 CV50
Low Pleasance, Lark. ML9 144 DC58
Low Quarry Gdns, Ham. ML3 140 CT51
Low Rd, (Castlehead) Pais. PA2 82 AS34
Lowther Av, (Bears.) G61 11 BE14
Lowther Ter, G12
    off Redlands La 48 BL25
Low Waters Rd, Ham. ML3 140 CT53
Low Wd Interchange, (Cumb.)
    G67 21 CX13

Loyal Av, Ersk. PA8 25 AP20
Loyal Gdns, (Bears.) G61 10 BD13
Loyal Pl, Ersk. PA8 25 AP20
Loyne Dr, Renf. PA4 64 BB27
Luath St, G51 66 BJ29
Lubas Av, G42 88 BT38
Lubas Pl, G42 88 BT38
Lubnaig Dr, Ersk. PA8 25 AP20
Lubnaig Gdns, (Bears.) G61 11 BE14
Lubnaig Pl, Air. ML6 76 DA27
Lubnaig Rd, G43 103 BN39
Lubnaig Wk, Moth. ML1
    off Graham St 112 DC40
Luckiesfauld, (Neil.) G78 114 AT46
Luckingsford Av, (Inch.)
    Renf. PA4 44 AT22
Luckingsford Dr, (Inch.)
    Renf. PA4 44 AS22
Luckingsford Rd, (Inch.)
    Renf. PA4 44 AS22
Lucy Brae, (Udd.) G71 93 CN37
Ludovic Sq, John. PA5 79 AH34
Luffness Gdns, G32 90 CD35
Lugar Dr, G52 85 BG33
Lugar Pl, G44 104 BU40
Lugar St, Coat. ML5 75 CX29
Luggiebank Pl, (Baill.) G69 93 CQ33
Luggiebank Rd, (Kirk.) G66 17 CF13
Luggie Gro, (Kirk.) G66 18 CJ14
Luggie Vw, (Cumb.) G67 39 CW15
Luing, Air. ML6 77 DG31
Luing Rd, G52 65 BG32
Luma Gdns, G51 65 BE30
Lumloch St, G21 51 BW25
Lumsden St, G3 66 BM29
Lunan Dr, (Bishop.) G64 51 BY21
Lunan Pl, G51 65 BG30
Lunar Path, (Chap.) Air. ML6
    off Michael Ter 97 DF36
Luncarty Pl, G32 90 CC33
Luncarty St, G32 90 CC34
Lunderston Cl, G53 100 BD39
Lunderston Dr, G53 84 BC38
Lunderston Gdns, G53 100 BD39
Lundie Gdns, (Bishop.) G64 51 BZ21
Lundie St, G32 90 CA34
Luss Brae, Ham. ML3 139 CN51
Lusset Glen, (Old Kil.) G60 25 AR15
Lusset Rd, (Old Kil.) G60 25 AR15
Lusset Vw, Clyde. G81
    off Granville St 27 AX18
Lusshill Ter, (Udd.) G71 92 CK35
Luss Rd, G51 65 BH30
Lybster Cres, (Ruther.) G73 105 BZ42
Lye Brae, (Cumb.) G67 22 DD11
Lyell Ct, (E.Kil.) G74 122 CA50
Lyell Gro, (E.Kil.) G74 122 CA50
Lyle Pl, Pais. PA2 82 AV35
Lyle Rd, Air. ML6 77 DH30
Lylesland Ct, Pais. PA2 82 AU35
Lyle Sq, (Miln.) G62 11 BG11
Lymburn St, G3 66 BM28
Lymekilns Rd, (E.Kil.) G74 135 BZ51
Lyndale Pl, G20 48 BM21
Lyndale Rd, G20 48 BM21
Lyndhurst Gdns, G20 49 BP26
Lyndhurst Gdns La, G20 49 BN25
Lynebank Gro, (Newt. M.) G77 131 BF51
Lynebank Pl, (Newt. M.) G77 131 BF51
Lyne Cft, (Bishop.) G64 33 BW17
Lynedoch Cres, G3 4 BP28
Lynedoch Cres La, G3 4 BP28
Lynedoch Pl, G3 4 BP28

|  | | |
|---|---|---|
| Lynedoch St, G3 | 4 | BP28 |
| Lynedoch Ter, G3 | 4 | BP28 |
| Lyne Dr, G23 | 31 | BN20 |
| Lynnburn Av, Bell. ML4 | 111 | CW40 |
| Lynn Ct, Lark. ML9 | 144 | DC59 |
| Lynn Dr, (Miln.) G62 | 12 | BL12 |
| Lynn Dr, (Eagle.) G76 | 133 | BN55 |
| Lynnhurst, (Udd.) G71 | 93 | CP38 |
| Lynn Wk, (Udd.) G71 | | |
| *off Flax Rd* | 109 | CQ40 |
| Lynton Av, (Giff.) G46 | 102 | BJ44 |
| Lyoncross Av, (Barr.) G78 | 99 | AZ43 |
| Lyoncross Cres, (Barr.) G78 | | |
| *off Lyoncross Av* | 99 | AZ42 |
| Lyoncross Rd, G53 | 84 | BD35 |
| Lyon Rd, Ersk. PA8 | 24 | AN20 |
| Lyon Rd, Pais. PA2 | 81 | AP36 |
| Lyon Rd, (Linw.) Pais. PA3 | 80 | AK33 |
| Lyons Quad, Wis. ML2 | | |
| *off Charles St* | 129 | DF49 |
| Lysander Way, Renf. PA4 | | |
| *off Lewis Av* | 63 | AZ28 |
| Lysa Vale Pl, Bell. ML4 | 110 | CU40 |
| Lytham Dr, G23 | 31 | BN20 |
| Lytham Meadows, (Both.) G71 | 109 | CN43 |
| Lyttleton, (E.Kil.) G75 | 135 | BX55 |

**M**

| | | |
|---|---|---|
| Mabel St, Moth. ML1 | 128 | DA48 |
| Macadam Gdns, Bell. ML4 | 111 | CW39 |
| Macadam Pl, (E.Kil.) G75 | 136 | CA53 |
| McAllister Av, Air. ML6 | 77 | DF29 |
| McAlpine St, G2 | 4 | BQ31 |
| McArdle Av, Moth. ML1 | 127 | CX46 |
| McArthur Av, (Glenm.) Air. ML6 | 57 | CZ26 |
| Macarthur Ct, (E.Kil.) G74 | 121 | BY50 |
| Macarthur Cres, (E.Kil.) G74 | 121 | BY50 |
| Macarthur Dr, (E.Kil.) G74 | 121 | BY50 |
| Macarthur Gdns, (E.Kil.) G74 | 121 | BY50 |
| McArthur Pk, (Kirk.) G66 | 17 | CE14 |
| McArthur St, G43 | | |
| *off Pleasance St* | 86 | BL37 |
| Macarthur Wynd, (Camb.) G72 | 107 | CE40 |
| McAslin Ct, G4 | 5 | BT29 |
| McAslin St, G4 | 5 | BU29 |
| Macbeth, (E.Kil.) G74 | | |
| *off Bosworth Rd* | 122 | CD48 |
| Macbeth Pl, G31 | 89 | BZ33 |
| Macbeth St, G31 | 89 | BZ33 |
| McBride Av, (Kirk.) G66 | 17 | CE14 |
| McBride Path, (Stepps) G33 | 53 | CG24 |
| McCallum Av, (Ruther.) G73 | 89 | BX38 |
| McCallum Ct, (E.Kil.) G74 | 121 | BX49 |
| Maccallum Dr, (Camb.) G72 | 107 | CE40 |
| McCallum Gdns, Bell. ML4 | 110 | CV43 |
| McCallum Gro, (E.Kil.) G74 | 121 | BW49 |
| McCallum Pl, (E.Kil.) G74 | 121 | BX49 |
| McCallum Rd, Lark. ML9 | 144 | DD60 |
| McCash Pl, (Kirk.) G66 | | |
| *off Greens Av* | 17 | CE14 |
| McCloy Gdns, G53 | 100 | BB40 |
| McClue Av, Renf. PA4 | 45 | AX25 |
| McClue Rd, Renf. PA4 | 45 | AY25 |
| McClurg Ct, Moth. ML1 | | |
| *off Albion St* | 128 | DA48 |
| McCourt Gdns, Bell. ML4 | | |
| *off Unitas Rd* | 111 | CY40 |
| McCracken Av, Renf. PA4 | 63 | AX27 |
| McCracken Dr, (Udd.) G71 | 94 | CS37 |
| McCreery St, Clyde. G81 | 45 | AZ21 |
| Maccrimmon Pk, (E.Kil.) G74 | 121 | BX49 |
| McCrorie Pl, (Kilb.) John. PA10 | 78 | AC34 |
| McCulloch Av, (Udd.) G71 | 110 | CS39 |
| McCulloch St, G41 | 87 | BP33 |
| McCulloch Way, (Stepps) G33 | 53 | CG24 |
| McCulloch Way, (Neil.) G78 | 114 | AT46 |
| Macdairmid Dr, Ham. ML3 | 139 | CR54 |
| McDonald Av, John. PA5 | 79 | AG36 |
| Macdonald Cres, (Kilsyth) G65 | 19 | CP10 |
| McDonald Cres, Clyde. G81 | 45 | AZ21 |
| Macdonald Gro, Bell. ML4 | 110 | CV42 |
| McDonald Pl, (Neil.) G78 | 114 | AU46 |
| McDonald Pl, Moth. ML1 | | |
| *off Graham St* | 112 | DC40 |
| Macdonald St, (Ruther.) G73 | | |
| *off Greenhill Rd* | 89 | BW38 |
| McDonald St, Moth. ML1 | 128 | DB48 |
| Macdougall Dr, (Camb.) G72 | 107 | CE40 |
| Macdougall Quad, Bell. ML4 | | |
| *off McCallum Gdns* | 110 | CV43 |
| Macdougall St, G43 | 86 | BL38 |
| Macdowall St, John. PA5 | 79 | AH34 |
| Macdowall St, Pais. PA3 | 62 | AT31 |
| Macduff, Ersk. PA8 | 25 | AQ19 |
| Macduff Pl, G31 | 89 | BZ33 |
| Macduff St, G31 | 89 | BZ33 |
| Macedonian Gro, (New.) | | |
| Moth. ML1 | 113 | DE41 |
| Mace Rd, G13 | 29 | BE20 |
| McEwan Gdns, (E.Kil.) G74 | 121 | BW49 |
| Macfarlane Cres, (Camb.) G72 | 107 | CE40 |
| Macfarlane Rd, (Bears.) G61 | 29 | BH18 |
| McFarlane St, G4 | 5 | BU31 |
| McFarlane St, Pais. PA3 | 62 | AS30 |
| Macfie Pl, (E.Kil.) G74 | 121 | BX49 |
| McGhee St, Clyde. G81 | 27 | AX17 |
| McGoldrick Pl, (Stepps) G33 | 53 | CH24 |
| McGowan Pl, Ham. ML3 | 125 | CQ48 |
| McGown St, Pais. PA3 | 62 | AT31 |
| Macgregor Av, Air. ML6 | 77 | DF29 |
| McGregor Av, Renf. PA4 | 63 | AX27 |
| Macgregor Ct, (Camb.) G72 | | |
| *off Macarthur Wynd* | 107 | CE40 |
| McGregor Path, (Glenb.) Coat. | | |
| ML5 *off Gayne Dr* | 56 | CS23 |
| McGregor Rd, (Cumb.) G67 | 22 | DA12 |
| McGregor St, G51 | 65 | BH31 |
| McGregor St, Clyde. G81 | 45 | AZ21 |
| McGregor St, Wis. ML2 | | |
| *off Ladysmith St* | 129 | DF49 |
| McGrigor Rd, (Miln.) G62 | 11 | BH10 |
| Machan Av, Lark. ML9 | 144 | DC58 |
| Machanhill, Lark. ML9 | 144 | DD59 |
| Machanhill Vw, Lark. ML9 | 144 | DD59 |
| Machan Rd, Lark. ML9 | 144 | DC59 |
| Machrie Dr, G45 | 104 | BV41 |
| Machrie Dr, (Newt. M.) G77 | 117 | BG47 |
| Machrie Rd, G45 | 104 | BV41 |
| Machrie St, G45 | 104 | BV41 |
| Machrie St, Moth. ML1 | 127 | CX46 |
| McIntosh Ct, G31 | 68 | BV30 |
| McIntosh Quad, Bell. ML4 | | |
| *off McCallum Gdns* | 110 | CV43 |
| McIntosh St, G31 | 68 | BV30 |
| McIntosh Way, Moth. ML1 | 127 | CY48 |
| McIntyre Pl, Pais. PA2 | 82 | AU35 |
| McIntyre St, G3 | 4 | BP30 |
| McIntyre Ter, (Camb.) G72 | | |
| *off Keirs Wk* | 106 | CC39 |
| McIver St, (Camb.) G72 | 107 | CG39 |
| Macivor Cres, (E.Kil.) G74 | 121 | BW49 |
| McKay Cres, John. PA5 | 80 | AJ35 |
| McKay Gro, Bell. ML4 | 110 | CV40 |
| McKay Pl, (E.Kil.) G74 | 121 | BW49 |
| McKay Pl, (Newt. M.) G77 | 117 | BE49 |
| Mackean St, Pais. PA3 | 62 | AS31 |
| McKechnie St, G51 | 66 | BJ29 |
| Mackeith St, G40 | 88 | BV33 |
| McKenna Dr, Air. ML6 | 76 | DA30 |
| McKenzie Av, Clyde. G81 | 27 | AX17 |
| Mackenzie Dr, (Kilb.) | | |
| John. PA10 | 78 | AD36 |
| Mackenzie Gdns, (E.Kil.) G74 | 121 | BW49 |
| McKenzie Gate, (Camb.) G72 | 107 | CG39 |
| McKenzie St, Pais. PA3 | 62 | AS32 |
| Mackenzie Ter, Bell. ML4 | 111 | CW39 |
| McKeown Gdns, Bell. ML4 | 111 | CZ41 |
| McKerrell St, Pais. PA1 | 63 | AW32 |
| Mackiesmill Rd, (Elder.) | | |
| John. PA5 | 80 | AM37 |
| Mackie St, G4 | | |
| *off Borron St* | 68 | BS27 |
| McKinlay Pl, (Newt. M.) G77 | | |
| *off School Rd* | 117 | BF49 |
| Mackinlay St, G5 | 87 | BR33 |
| Mackintosh Pl, (E.Kil.) G75 | 135 | BY54 |
| Mack St, Air. ML6 | 76 | DC29 |
| McLaren Av, Renf. PA4 | 63 | AY28 |
| McLaren Ct, (Giff.) G46 | | |
| *off Fenwick Pl* | 102 | BK44 |
| McLaren Cres, G20 | 49 | BN22 |
| McLaren Dr, Bell. ML4 | 111 | CZ41 |
| McLaren Gdns, G20 | 49 | BN22 |
| McLaren Gro, (E.Kil.) G74 | 121 | BW49 |
| Maclaren Pl, G44 | | |
| *off Clarkston Rd* | 103 | BP43 |
| McLaurin Cres, John. PA5 | 79 | AF36 |
| Maclay Av, (Kilb.) John. PA10 | 78 | AC35 |
| Maclean Ct, (E.Kil.) G74 | 121 | BX49 |
| McLean Dr, Bell. ML4 | 110 | CV43 |
| Maclean Gro, (E.Kil.) G74 | 121 | BX49 |
| Maclean Pl, (E.Kil.) G74 | 121 | BX49 |
| McLean Pl, Pais. PA3 | | |
| *off Gockston Rd* | 62 | AT30 |
| Maclean Sq, G51 | 66 | BM31 |
| Maclean St, G51 | 66 | BM31 |
| Maclean St, Clyde. G81 | 46 | BA21 |
| McLees La, Moth. ML1 | 127 | CX46 |
| Maclehose Rd, (Cumb.) G67 | 23 | DE10 |
| Maclellan Rd, (Neil.) G78 | 114 | AU47 |
| Maclellan St, G41 | 66 | BL32 |
| McLennan St, G42 | 87 | BQ37 |
| Macleod Pl, (E.Kil.) G74 | 122 | CD50 |
| Macleod St, G4 | 5 | BU29 |
| Macleod Way, (Camb.) G72 | 107 | CE40 |
| McMahon Gro, Bell. ML4 | 111 | CX39 |
| Macmillan Gdns, (Udd.) G71 | 93 | CQ37 |
| McMillan Rd, (Netherton Ind. Est.) | | |
| Wis. ML2 | 143 | DF51 |
| Macmillan St, Lark. ML9 | 144 | DB59 |
| McNair St, G32 | 70 | CC32 |
| McNeil Dr, (Holytown) | | |
| Moth. ML1 | 96 | DB37 |
| McNeil Gdns, G5 | 88 | BT33 |
| McNeil Gate, Lark. ML9 | 144 | DC58 |
| McNeil La, Lark. ML9 | 144 | DC58 |
| Macneill Dr, (E.Kil.) G74 | 121 | BX49 |
| Macneill Gdns, (E.Kil.) G74 | 121 | BW49 |
| McNeil St, G5 | 88 | BT33 |
| McNeil St, Lark. ML9 | 144 | DB58 |
| Macneish Way, (E.Kil.) G74 | 121 | BY49 |
| Macnicol Ct, (E.Kil.) G74 | 121 | BW49 |
| Macnicol Pk, (E.Kil.) G74 | 121 | BW49 |
| Macnicol Pl, (E.Kil.) G74 | 121 | BW49 |
| McPhail Av, (New.) Moth. ML1 | 113 | DH40 |
| McPhail St, G40 | 88 | BU33 |

| | | |
|---|---|---|
| McPhater St, G4 | 4 | BR28 |
| McPherson Cres, (Chap.) | | |
| Air. ML6 | 97 | DG36 |
| McPherson Dr, (Both.) G71 | 109 | CR42 |
| Macpherson Pk, (E.Kil.) G74 | 121 | BY50 |
| McPherson St, Bell. ML4 | 111 | CZ40 |
| Macrae Gdns, (E.Kil.) G74 | 121 | BY50 |
| Macrimmon Pl, (E.Kil.) G75 | 136 | CA53 |
| McShannon Gro, Bell. ML4 | | |
| off Sapphire Rd | 111 | CW42 |
| McSparran Rd, (Kilsyth) G65 | 20 | CV9 |
| Mactaggart Rd, (Cumb.) G67 | 22 | DA13 |
| Madison Av, G44 | 103 | BR40 |
| Madison Path, (Blan.) G72 | | |
| off Burnbrae Rd | 124 | CM46 |
| Madras Pl, G40 | 88 | BU34 |
| Madras Pl, (Neil.) G78 | 114 | AU46 |
| Madras St, G40 | 88 | BU34 |
| Mafeking St, G51 | 66 | BK31 |
| Mafeking St, Wis. ML2 | 129 | DF49 |
| Mafeking Ter, (Neil.) G78 | 114 | AS46 |
| Magdalen Way, Pais. PA2 | 80 | AM38 |
| Magna St, Moth. ML1 | 127 | CX45 |
| Magnolia Dr, (Camb.) G72 | 107 | CH42 |
| Magnolia Gdns, Moth. ML1 | 113 | DE42 |
| Magnolia Pl, (Udd.) G71 | 94 | CS37 |
| Magnus Cres, G44 | 103 | BR41 |
| Mahon Ct, (Mood.) G69 | 37 | CP20 |
| Maidens, (E.Kil.) G74 | 121 | BZ50 |
| Maidens Av, (Newt. M.) G77 | 118 | BJ48 |
| Maidland Rd, G53 | 85 | BE37 |
| Mailerbeg Gdns, (Mood.) G69 | 37 | CP18 |
| Mailie Wk, Moth. ML1 | | |
| off Clarinda Pl | | |
| Mailing Av, (Bishop.) G64 | 33 | BY19 |
| Mainhill Av, (Baill.) G69 | 72 | CM32 |
| Mainhill Dr, (Baill.) G69 | 72 | CL32 |
| Mainhill Pl, (Baill.) G69 | 72 | CL32 |
| Mainhill Rd, (Baill.) G69 | 73 | CP32 |
| Main Rd, (Cumb.) G67 | 39 | CW15 |
| Main Rd, (Elder.) John. PA5 | 80 | AL34 |
| Main Rd, (Millarston) Pais. PA1 | 81 | AN34 |
| Main Rd, (Castlehead) Pais. PA2 | 82 | AT33 |
| Mains Av, (Giff.) G46 | 102 | BK44 |
| Mainscroft, Ersk. PA8 | 26 | AS20 |
| Mains Dr, Ersk. PA8 | 26 | AS20 |
| Mains Hill, Ersk. PA8 | 25 | AR20 |
| Mainshill Av, Ersk. PA8 | 25 | AR20 |
| Mainshill Gdns, Ersk. PA8 | 25 | AR20 |
| Mains Pl, Bell. ML4 | 111 | CW42 |
| Mains River, Ersk. PA8 | 26 | AS20 |
| Mains Rd, (E.Kil.) G74 | 122 | CA48 |
| Main St, G40 | 88 | BV34 |
| Main St, (Thornlie.) G46 | 101 | BH42 |
| Main St, (Miln.) G62 | 12 | BJ12 |
| Main St, (Torr.) G64 | 15 | BX13 |
| Main St, (Kilsyth) G65 | 7 | CT5 |
| Main St, (Twechar) G65 | 19 | CQ9 |
| Main St, (Baill.) G69 | 92 | CL33 |
| Main St, (Chry.) G69 | 54 | CL21 |
| Main St, (Both.) G71 | 109 | CQ43 |
| Main St, (Udd.) G71 | 109 | CQ39 |
| Main St, (Blan.) G72 | 124 | CM47 |
| Main St, (Camb.) G72 | 106 | CC39 |
| Main St, (Ruther.) G73 | 89 | BW37 |
| Main St, (E.Kil.) G74 | 136 | CB51 |
| Main St, (Clark.) G76 | 119 | BP47 |
| Main St, (Barr.) G78 | 99 | AX43 |
| Main St, (Neil.) G78 | 114 | AT46 |
| Main St, (Calder.) Air. ML6 | 97 | DE35 |
| Main St, (Chap.) Air. ML6 | 97 | DG34 |
| Main St, Bell. ML4 | 110 | CV40 |
| Main St, Coat. ML5 | 75 | CW30 |

| | | |
|---|---|---|
| Main St, (Glenb.) Coat. ML5 | 56 | CU23 |
| Main St, (Holytown) | | |
| Moth. ML1 | 112 | DC39 |
| Mains Wd, Ersk. PA8 | 26 | AT20 |
| Mair St, G51 | 67 | BN31 |
| Maitland Bk, Lark. ML9 | 145 | DE58 |
| Maitland Dr, (Torr.) G64 | 15 | BX12 |
| Maitland Pl, Renf. PA4 | 63 | AX27 |
| Maitland St, G4 | 4 | BR28 |
| Malcolm Gdns, (E.Kil.) G74 | 135 | BY51 |
| Malcolm St, Moth. ML1 | 127 | CY47 |
| Maleny Gro, (Newt. M.) G77 | 116 | BD50 |
| Malin Pl, G33 | 70 | CB29 |
| Mallaig Path, G51 | | |
| off Moss Rd | 65 | BF30 |
| Mallaig Pl, G51 | | |
| off Mallaig Rd | 65 | BF30 |
| Mallaig Rd, G51 | 65 | BF30 |
| Mallard Cres, (E.Kil.) G75 | 135 | BW56 |
| Mallard La, (Both.) G71 | | |
| off Fallside Rd | 109 | CR42 |
| Mallard Pl, (E.Kil.) G75 | 135 | BW56 |
| Mallard Rd, Clyde. G81 | 27 | AX16 |
| Mallard Ter, (E.Kil.) G75 | 135 | BW56 |
| Mallard Way, (Strathclyde | | |
| Bus. Pk.) Bell. ML4 | 94 | CV36 |
| Malleable Gdns, Moth. ML1 | 111 | CY43 |
| Malletsheugh Rd, (Newt. M.) | | |
| G77 | 116 | BD50 |
| Malloch Cres, (Elder.) | | |
| John. PA5 | 80 | AK35 |
| Malloch Pl, (E.Kil.) G74 | | |
| off Angus Av | 136 | CD51 |
| Malloch St, G20 | 49 | BN24 |
| Mallots Vw, (Newt. M.) G77 | 116 | BD50 |
| Malov Ct, (E.Kil.) G75 | 136 | CA56 |
| Malta Ter, G5 | 87 | BR33 |
| Maltbarns St, G20 | 49 | BQ26 |
| Malvaig La, (Blan.) G72 | | |
| off Moorfield Rd | 124 | CL47 |
| Malvern Ct, G31 | 69 | BW31 |
| Malvern Way, Pais. PA3 | 62 | AT29 |
| Mambeg Dr, G51 | | |
| off St. Kenneth Dr | 65 | BG29 |
| Mamore Pl, G43 | 102 | BL39 |
| Mamore St, G43 | 102 | BL39 |
| Manchester Dr, G12 | 48 | BJ23 |
| Manitoba Cres, (E.Kil.) G75 | 135 | BX52 |
| Mannering, (E.Kil.) G74 | 123 | CF49 |
| Mannering Ct, G41 | 86 | BL37 |
| Mannering Rd, G41 | 86 | BL37 |
| Mannering Rd, Pais. PA2 | 81 | AN37 |
| Mannering Way, Pais. PA2 | | |
| off Brediland Rd | 81 | AN37 |
| Mannoch Pl, Coat. ML5 | 95 | CZ34 |
| Mannofield, (Bears.) G61 | 29 | BE17 |
| Manor Dr, Air. ML6 | 76 | DA29 |
| Manor Gate, (Newt. M.) G77 | 117 | BH50 |
| Manor Pk Av, Pais. PA2 | 81 | AR36 |
| Manor Rd, G14 | 47 | BG25 |
| Manor Rd, G15 | 28 | BB20 |
| Manor Rd, (Gart.) G69 | 55 | CP24 |
| Manor Rd, Pais. PA2 | 81 | AP36 |
| Manor Vw, (Calder.) Air. ML6 | 96 | DD35 |
| Manor Vw, Lark. ML9 | 145 | DE59 |
| Manor Way, (Ruther.) G73 | 105 | BY41 |
| Manresa Pl, G4 | 67 | BR27 |
| Manse Av, (Bears.) G61 | 29 | BH16 |
| Manse Av, (Both.) G71 | 109 | CQ43 |
| Manse Av, Coat. ML5 | 94 | CT33 |
| Manse Brae, G44 | 103 | BR39 |
| Manse Brae, (Camb.) G72 | 108 | CJ40 |
| Manse Ct, (Kilsyth) G65 | 7 | CT6 |

| | | |
|---|---|---|
| Manse Ct, (Barr.) G78 | 99 | AZ42 |
| Mansefield Av, (Camb.) G72 | 106 | CC41 |
| Mansefield Cres, (Clark.) G76 | 118 | BM47 |
| Mansefield Rd, (Clark.) G76 | 118 | BM47 |
| Mansefield Rd, Ham. ML3 | 140 | CT54 |
| Manse Gdns, G32 | 91 | CF33 |
| Manse La, (E.Kil.) G74 | 122 | CB50 |
| Mansel St, G21 | 50 | BV24 |
| Manse Pl, Air. ML6 | 76 | DC30 |
| Manse Rd, G32 | 91 | CF33 |
| Manse Rd, (Bears.) G61 | 29 | BG16 |
| Manse Rd, (Kilsyth) G65 | 7 | CT6 |
| Manse Rd, (Baill.) G69 | 73 | CN31 |
| Manse Rd, (Clark.) G76 | 120 | BT46 |
| Manse Rd, Moth. ML1 | 114 | AT46 |
| Manse Rd, Moth. ML1 | 128 | DB49 |
| Manse Rd Gdns, (Bears.) G61 | 29 | BG16 |
| Manse St, Coat. ML5 | 74 | CV31 |
| Manse St, Renf. PA4 | 45 | AZ25 |
| Manse Vw, Lark. ML9 | 144 | DD59 |
| Manse Vw, Moth. ML1 | 113 | DH41 |
| Manseview Ter, (Eagle.) G76 | | |
| off Pollock Av | 133 | BN56 |
| Mansewood Rd, G43 | 102 | BK39 |
| Mansfield Dr, (Udd.) G71 | 109 | CP39 |
| Mansfield Rd, G52 | 64 | BB30 |
| Mansfield Rd, Bell. ML4 | 110 | CV42 |
| Mansfield St, G11 | 66 | BL27 |
| Mansion Ct, (Camb.) G72 | 106 | CC39 |
| Mansionhouse Av, G32 | 91 | CE37 |
| Mansionhouse Dr, G32 | 71 | CE31 |
| Mansionhouse Gdns, G41 | 87 | BN38 |
| Mansionhouse Gro, G32 | 91 | CG34 |
| Mansionhouse Rd, G32 | 91 | CG33 |
| Mansionhouse Rd, G41 | 87 | BN38 |
| Mansionhouse Rd, Pais. PA1 | 63 | AW32 |
| Mansion St, G22 | 50 | BS24 |
| Mansion St, (Camb.) G72 | 106 | CC39 |
| Manson Pl, (E.Kil.) G75 | 136 | CC56 |
| Manus Duddy Ct, (Blan.) G72 | 124 | CM45 |
| Maple Av, (Newt. M.) G77 | 117 | BF49 |
| Maple Bk, Ham. ML3 | 140 | CV51 |
| Maple Ct, Coat. ML5 | | |
| off Ailsa Rd | 94 | CV33 |
| Maple Cres, (Camb.) G72 | 107 | CH42 |
| Maple Dr, (Kirk.) G66 | 34 | CC16 |
| Maple Dr, (Barr.) G78 | | |
| off Oakbank Dr | 115 | AZ45 |
| Maple Dr, Clyde. G81 | 26 | AV16 |
| Maple Dr, John. PA5 | 79 | AH37 |
| Maple Dr, Lark. ML9 | 142 | DC56 |
| Maple Gro, (E.Kil.) G75 | 135 | BX55 |
| Maple Pl, (Udd.) G71 | 94 | CT37 |
| Maple Pl, (E.Kil.) G75 | 135 | BX55 |
| Maple Quad, Air. ML6 | 77 | DF31 |
| Maple Rd, G41 | 86 | BK33 |
| Maple Rd, Moth. ML1 | 112 | DD40 |
| Maple Ter, (E.Kil.) G75 | 135 | BX55 |
| Maple Way, (Blan.) G72 | | |
| off Moorfield Rd | 124 | CL46 |
| Maplewood, Wis. ML2 | 143 | DF52 |
| Mar Av, Bish. PA7 | 24 | AK18 |
| Marchbank Gdns, Pais. PA1 | 83 | AZ33 |
| Marchburn Dr, (Abbots.) | | |
| Pais. PA3 | 62 | AT29 |
| Marchfield, (Bishop.) G64 | 32 | BU18 |
| Marchfield Av, Pais. PA3 | 62 | AT29 |
| Marchglen Pl, G51 | | |
| off Mallaig Rd | 65 | BF30 |
| March La, G41 | | |
| off Nithsdale Dr | 87 | BP35 |
| Marchmont Gdns, (Bishop.) | | |
| G64 | 32 | BV18 |

Marchmont Ter, G12
  *off Observatory Rd* 48 BL26
March St, G41 87 BP35
Mardale, (E.Kil.) G74 121 BY50
Mar Dr, (Bears.) G61 11 BH14
Maree Dr, G52 85 BG33
Maree Dr, (Cumb.) G67 21 CX14
Maree Gdns, (Bishop.) G64 33 BX20
Maree Rd, Pais. PA2 81 AQ35
Maree Way, (Blan.) G72
  *off Clyde Cres* 124 CM45
Marfield St, G32 70 CA30
Mar Gdns, (Ruther.) G73 105 BZ41
Margaret Gdns, Ham. ML3 125 CR47
Margaret Pl, Bell. ML4 110 CU40
Margaret Rd, Ham. ML3 125 CR47
Margaret's Pl, Lark. ML9 144 DC58
Margaret St, Coat. ML5 95 CW33
Margaretta Bldgs, G44
  *off Clarkston Rd* 103 BQ39
Margaretvale Dr, Lark. ML9 144 DC59
Marguerite Av, (Lenz.) G66 35 CE15
Marguerite Dr, (Kirk.) G66 35 CE15
Marguerite Gdns, (Kirk.) G66 35 CE15
Marguerite Gdns, (Both.) G71 109 CR43
Marguerite Gro, (Kirk.) G66 35 CE15
Marian Dr, Moth. ML1 113 DE43
Marigold Av, Moth. ML1 128 DA45
Marina Ct, Bell. ML4
  *off Hamilton Rd* 110 CV42
Marine Cres, G51 67 BN31
Marine Gdns, G51 4 BP31
Marion St, Bell. ML4 111 CZ40
Mariscat Rd, G41 87 BN35
Marjory Dr, Pais. PA3 63 AW30
Marjory Rd, Renf. PA4 63 AW28
Markdow Av, G53 84 BC36
Market Cl, (Kilsyth) G65
  *off Main St* 7 CT5
Market Ct, (Kilsyth) G65
  *off Market St* 7 CT5
Markethill Rd, (E.Kil.) G74 121 BZ47
Markethill Rbt, (E.Kil.) G74 122 CA50
Market Pl, (Kilsyth) G65
  *off Market St* 7 CT5
Market Pl, (Udd.) G71
  *off Market St* 94 CS38
Market Rd, (Kirk.) G66 18 CJ14
Market Rd, (Udd.) G71 94 CS38
Market Sq, (Kilsyth) G65
  *off Market St* 7 CT5
Market St, (Kilsyth) G65 7 CT5
Market St, (Udd.) G71 94 CS38
Marlach Pl, G53 84 BC36
Marlborough Av, G11 47 BH26
Marlborough La N, G11 47 BH26
Marlborough La S, G11 47 BH26
Marlborough Pk, (E.Kil.) G75 135 BW54
Marldon La, G11 47 BH26
Marlfield Gdns, Bell. ML4
  *off Merlin Av* 95 CW38
Marlow St, G41 87 BN33
Marmion Ct, Pais. PA2
  *off Heriot Av* 81 AP37
Marmion Cres, Moth. ML1 111 CZ43
Marmion Dr, (Kirk.) G66 17 CH13
Marmion Pl, (Cumb.) G67 22 DA14
Marmion Rd, (Cumb.) G67 22 DA14
Marmion Rd, Pais. PA2 81 AN37
Marne St, G31 69 BX30
Marnoch Dr, (Glenb.) Coat. ML5 56 CT23
Marnoch Way, (Mood.) G69
  *off Braeside Av* 37 CP19

Marnock Ter, Pais. PA2 83 AW34
Marquis Av, Ham. ML3 125 CQ47
Marquis Gate, (Udd.) G71 109 CN40
Marrswood Grn, Ham. ML3 125 CQ49
Marshall Gro, Ham. ML3 125 CR50
Marshall St, Lark. ML9 144 DC58
Marshall St, Wis. ML2 143 DH51
Martha Pl, Lark. ML9 144 DD59
Martha St, G1 5 BS29
Martin Ct, Ham. ML3
  *off Bent Rd* 126 CS50
Martin Cres, (Baill.) G69 72 CL32
Martin Pl, Moth. ML1 113 DE42
Martinside, (E.Kil.) G75 136 CA56
Martin St, G40 88 BV34
Martin St, Coat. ML5 75 CZ30
Martlet Dr, John. PA5 79 AE38
Mart St, G1 5 BS31
Martyn St, Air. ML6 76 DA30
Martyrs Pl, (Bishop.) G64 51 BW21
Marwick St, G31 69 BX30
Mary Dr, Bell. ML4 110 CU42
Maryhill Rd, G20 49 BP26
Maryhill Rd, (Bears.) G61 30 BJ19
Maryhill Shop Cen, G20 48 BM24
Maryknowe Rd, Moth. ML1 113 DE44
Maryland Dr, G52 85 BG33
Maryland Gdns, G52 65 BG32
Mary Rae Rd, Bell. ML4 110 CU42
Mary Slessor Wynd, (Ruther.)
  G73 105 BY43
Mary Sq, (Baill.) G69 73 CP32
Maryston Pl, G33 69 BZ27
Maryston St, G33 69 BZ27
Mary St, G4 67 BR27
Mary St, Ham. ML3 140 CS51
Mary St, John. PA5 80 AJ34
Mary St, Pais. PA2 82 AU35
Maryville Av, (Giff.) G46 102 BL43
Maryville Gdns, (Giff.) G46 102 BL43
Maryville Vw, (Udd.) G71 92 CM36
Marywood Sq, G41 87 BP35
Mary Young Pl, (Clark.) G76
  *off Riverside Ter* 119 BP47
Masonfield Av, (Cumb.) G68 21 CZ11
Mason La, Moth. ML1 128 DA47
Mason St, Lark. ML9 145 DE60
Mason St, Moth. ML1 128 DA47
Masterton St, G21 50 BS26
Masterton Way, (Udd.) G71 93 CR36
Matherton Av, (Newt. M.) G77 118 BK48
Mathew McWhirter Pl,
  Lark. ML9 144 DD57
Mathieson Cres, (Stepps) G33 53 CH24
Mathieson Rd, (Ruther.) G73 89 BY36
Mathieson St, Pais. PA1 63 AX32
Mathieson Ter, G5 88 BT33
Matilda Rd, G41 87 BN34
Mauchline, (E.Kil.) G74
  *off Alloway Rd* 123 CF50
Mauchline Av, (Kirk.) G66 18 CJ11
Mauchline Ct, (Kirk.) G66 18 CJ11
Mauchline Ct, Ham. ML3 138 CM51
Mauchline St, G5 87 BQ33
Maukinfauld Ct, G32 89 BZ34
Maukinfauld Gdns, G31 90 CA33
Maukinfauld Rd, G32 90 CA34
Mauldslie Pl, (Ashgill)
  Lark. ML9 145 DH61
Mauldslie St, G40 89 BX33
Mauldslie St, Bell. ML4
  *off Cross Gates* 111 CW41

Mauldslie St, Coat. ML5 75 CW32
Maule Dr, G11 66 BJ27
Mavis Bk, (Bishop.) G64 50 BV21
Mavis Bk, (Blan.) G72
  *off Moorfield Rd* 124 CL46
Mavisbank Gdns, G51 67 BN31
Mavisbank Gdns, Bell. ML4 111 CW39
Mavisbank St, Air. ML6 76 DB29
Mavisbank Ter, John. PA5
  *off Campbell St* 79 AH35
Mavisbank Ter, Pais. PA1 82 AV34
Mavor Av, (E.Kil.) G74 122 CC48
Mavor Rbt, (E.Kil.) G74 122 CB50
Maxton Av, (Barr.) G78 99 AW42
Maxton Gro, (Barr.) G78 99 AW43
Maxton Ter, (Camb.) G72 106 CB42
Maxwell Av, G41 87 BN33
Maxwell Av, (Bears.) G61 29 BG18
Maxwell Av, (Baill.) G69 92 CJ33
Maxwell Ct, G41
  *off St. John's Rd* 87 BN33
Maxwell Cres, (Blan.) G72 124 CM47
Maxwell Dr, G41 86 BL33
Maxwell Dr, (Baill.) G69 72 CJ32
Maxwell Dr, (E.Kil.) G74 136 CB51
Maxwell Dr, Ersk. PA8 25 AP18
Maxwell Gdns, G41 86 BM33
Maxwell Gro, G41 86 BM33
Maxwell La, G41
  *off Maxwell Dr* 87 BN33
Maxwell Oval, G41 87 BP33
Maxwell Path, Lark. ML9
  *off Wallace Dr* 145 DE59
Maxwell Pl, G41 87 BQ34
Maxwell Pl, (Kilsyth) G65
  *off Charles St* 7 CT4
Maxwell Pl, (Udd.) G71
  *off North British Rd* 109 CQ39
Maxwell Pl, Coat. ML5 74 CV31
Maxwell Rd, G41 87 BP33
Maxwell Rd, Bish. PA7 24 AK18
Maxwell St, G1 5 BS31
Maxwell St, (Baill.) G69 92 CK33
Maxwell St, Clyde. G81 26 AV17
Maxwell St, Pais. PA3 62 AU32
Maxwell Ter, G41 87 BN33
Maxwellton Av, (E.Kil.) G74 136 CC51
Maxwellton Ct, Pais. PA1 82 AS33
Maxwellton Pl, (E.Kil.) G74 122 CD50
Maxwellton Rd, (E.Kil.) G74 122 CD49
Maxwellton Rd, Pais. PA1 81 AR33
Maxwellton St, Pais. PA1 82 AS34
Maxwelton Rd, G33 69 BZ27
Maybank La, G42 87 BQ36
Maybank St, G42
  *off Albert Av* 87 BQ36
Mayberry Cres, G32 71 CF32
Mayberry Gdns, G32 71 CF32
Mayberry Gro, G32 71 CF32
Mayberry Pl, (Blan.) G72 124 CM45
Maybole Cres, (Newt. M.) G77 118 BJ49
Maybole Dr, Air. ML6 96 DC33
Maybole Gdns, Ham. ML3
  *off Barnhill Dr* 138 CM51
Maybole Gro, (Newt. M.) G77 118 BJ49
Maybole Pl, Coat. ML5 95 CZ34
Maybole St, G53 100 BB39
Mayfield Av, (Clark.) G76 119 BN46
Mayfield Pl, Coat. ML5 95 CW34
Mayfield Rd, Ham. ML3 125 CP49
Mayfield St, G20 49 BP23
May Gdns, Ham. ML3 126 CS48
May Rd, Pais. PA2 82 AU38

| | | |
|---|---|---|
| May St, Ham. ML3 | 126 | CT48 |
| May Ter, G42 | 87 | BR37 |
| May Ter, (Giff.) G46 | 102 | BL42 |
| Meadow Av, (Blan.) G72 | 124 | CM47 |
| Meadowbank La, (Udd.) G71 | 109 | CN39 |
| Meadowbank Pl, (Newt. M.) G77 | 117 | BF48 |
| Meadowburn, (Bishop.) G64 | 32 | BV17 |
| Meadowburn Av, (Lenz.) G66 | 35 | CG16 |
| Meadowburn Av, (Newt. M.) G77 | 117 | BF48 |
| Meadowhead Av, (Chry.) G69 | 37 | CP19 |
| Meadowhead Rd, (Plains) Air. ML6 | 59 | DH26 |
| Meadowhead Rd, Wis. ML2 | 129 | DE49 |
| Meadowhill, (Newt. M.) G77 | 117 | BF48 |
| Meadowhill St, Lark. ML9 | 144 | DD58 |
| Meadow La, (Both.) G71 | 109 | CR43 |
| Meadow La, Renf. PA4 | 45 | AZ24 |
| Meadowpark St, G31 | 69 | BX30 |
| Meadow Path, (Chap.) Air. ML6 off Timmons Ter | 97 | DF36 |
| Meadow Ri, (Newt. M.) G77 | 117 | BE48 |
| Meadow Rd, G11 | 66 | BJ27 |
| Meadow Rd, Moth. ML1 | 128 | DC48 |
| Meadows Av, Ersk. PA8 | 26 | AS20 |
| Meadows Av, Lark. ML9 | 144 | DD58 |
| Meadows Dr, Ersk. PA8 | 26 | AS20 |
| Meadowside, Ham. ML3 off Parks Vw | 140 | CT55 |
| Meadowside Av, (Elder.) John. PA5 | 80 | AL35 |
| Meadowside Gdns, Air. ML6 off Castle Quad | 77 | DF30 |
| Meadowside Ind Est, Renf. PA4 | 45 | AZ23 |
| Meadowside Pl, Air. ML6 | 77 | DF30 |
| Meadowside Quay, G11 | 65 | BG28 |
| Meadowside Rd, (Kilsyth) G65 | 6 | CN5 |
| Meadowside St, G11 | 66 | BJ28 |
| Meadowside St, Renf. PA4 | 45 | AZ24 |
| Meadow St, Coat. ML5 | 95 | CX33 |
| Meadow Vw, (Cumb.) G67 | 23 | DE10 |
| Meadow Wk, Coat. ML5 | 75 | CX31 |
| Meadow Way, (Newt. M.) G77 | 117 | BF48 |
| Meadowwell St, G32 | 70 | CD32 |
| Meadside Av, (Kilb.) John. PA10 | 78 | AC33 |
| Meadside Rd, (Kilb.) John. PA10 | 78 | AC33 |
| Mearns Ct, Ham. ML3 | 140 | CU54 |
| Mearnscroft Gdns, (Newt. M.) G77 | 117 | BH50 |
| Mearnscroft Rd, (Newt. M.) G77 | 117 | BH50 |
| Mearnskirk Ho, (Newt. M.) G77 off Mearnskirk Rd | 131 | BF52 |
| Mearnskirk Rd, (Newt. M.) G77 | 131 | BF51 |
| Mearns Rd, (Clark.) G76 | 118 | BL46 |
| Mearns Rd, (Newt. M.) G77 | 131 | BG51 |
| Mearns Rd, Moth. ML1 | 127 | CY45 |
| Mearns Way, (Bishop.) G64 | 33 | BZ19 |
| Medlar Ct, (Camb.) G72 off Maple Cres | 107 | CH42 |
| Medlar Rd, (Cumb.) G67 | 23 | DF10 |
| Medrox Gdns, (Cumb.) G67 | 38 | CV16 |
| Medwin Ct, (E.Kil.) G75 | 134 | BU54 |
| Medwin Gdns, (E.Kil.) G75 | 134 | BU54 |
| Medwin St, (Camb.) G72 | 107 | CF40 |
| Medwyn St, G14 | 47 | BF26 |
| Meek Pl, (Camb.) G72 | 106 | CD40 |
| Meetinghouse La, Pais. PA1 off Moss St | 62 | AU32 |
| Megan Gate, G40 off Megan St | 88 | BV33 |
| Megan St, G40 | 88 | BV33 |
| Meigle Rd, Air. ML6 | 96 | DB33 |
| Meikle Av, Renf. PA4 | 63 | AY27 |
| Meikle Cres, (Green.) Air. ML6 | 59 | DF21 |
| Meikle Cres, Ham. ML3 | 140 | CS54 |
| Meikle Drumgray Rd, (Green.) Air. ML6 | 59 | DF21 |
| Meikle Earnock Rd, Ham. ML3 | 139 | CQ55 |
| Meiklehill Ct, (Kirk.) G66 | 17 | CG12 |
| Meiklehill Rd, (Kirk.) G66 | 17 | CG12 |
| Meiklem St, Bell. ML4 | 111 | CY40 |
| Meiklerig Cres, G53 | 85 | BE35 |
| Meikleriggs Dr, Pais. PA2 | 81 | AQ36 |
| Meikle Rd, G53 | 85 | BE37 |
| Meiklewood Rd, G51 | 65 | BF31 |
| Melbourne Av, (E.Kil.) G75 | 135 | BY54 |
| Melbourne Av, Clyde. G81 | 26 | AT16 |
| Melbourne Ct, (Giff.) G46 | 102 | BM42 |
| Melbourne Grn, (E.Kil.) G75 | 135 | BY53 |
| Melbourne St, G31 | 68 | BV31 |
| Meldon Pl, G51 off Mallaig Rd | 65 | BG30 |
| Meldrum Gdns, G41 | 86 | BM35 |
| Meldrum Mains, (Glenm.) Air. ML6 | 58 | DA25 |
| Meldrum St, Clyde. G81 | 45 | AZ21 |
| Melford Av, (Giff.) G46 | 102 | BM43 |
| Melford Av, (Kirk.) G66 | 16 | CD13 |
| Melford Rd, (Righead Ind. Est.) Bell. ML4 | 110 | CU39 |
| Melford Way, Pais. PA3 off Knock Way | 63 | AW30 |
| Melfort Av, G41 | 86 | BK33 |
| Melfort Av, Clyde. G81 | 27 | AX18 |
| Melfort Ct, Clyde. G81 | 27 | AY19 |
| Melfort Gdns, (Kilb.) John. PA10 off Milliken Pk Rd | 79 | AE36 |
| Melfort Quad, Moth. ML1 off Glenmore Av | 113 | DF42 |
| Melfort Rd, Ham. ML3 | 125 | CN50 |
| Mellerstain Dr, G14 | 46 | BA23 |
| Mellerstain Gro, G14 off Mellerstain Dr | 46 | BB23 |
| Melness Pl, G51 off Mallaig Rd | 65 | BF30 |
| Melrose Av, (Baill.) G69 off Roslyn Dr | 73 | CP32 |
| Melrose Av, (Ruther.) G73 | 89 | BX38 |
| Melrose Av, (Chap.) Air. ML6 | 97 | DF35 |
| Melrose Av, Moth. ML1 | 112 | DD39 |
| Melrose Av, Pais. PA2 | 81 | AQ36 |
| Melrose Av, (Linw.) Pais. PA3 | 60 | AK32 |
| Melrose Ct, (Ruther.) G73 | 89 | BX37 |
| Melrose Gdns, G20 | 49 | BP26 |
| Melrose Gdns, (Kilsyth) G65 | 19 | CN9 |
| Melrose Gdns, (Udd.) G71 | 93 | CP36 |
| Melrose Pl, (Blan.) G72 | 108 | CL44 |
| Melrose Pl, Coat. ML5 | 74 | CV30 |
| Melrose Pl, Lark. ML9 | 144 | DC60 |
| Melrose Rd, (Cumb.) G67 | 22 | DA14 |
| Melrose St, G4 off Queens Cres | 67 | BP27 |
| Melrose St, Ham. ML3 | 125 | CR48 |
| Melrose Ter, (E.Kil.) G74 | 136 | CB51 |
| Melrose Ter, Ham. ML3 | 125 | CR47 |
| Melvaig Pl, G20 | 48 | BM24 |
| Melvick Pl, G51 off Mallaig Rd | 65 | BF30 |
| Melville Ct, G1 off Brunswick St | 5 | BT31 |
| Melville Dr, Moth. ML1 | 128 | DB47 |
| Melville Gdns, (Bishop.) G64 | 33 | BW19 |
| Melville Pk, (E.Kil.) G74 | 122 | CD50 |
| Melville St, G41 | 87 | BP34 |
| Memel St, G21 | 50 | BU24 |
| Memus Av, G52 | 85 | BE33 |
| Mennock Ct, Ham. ML3 | 139 | CN51 |
| Mennock Dr, (Bishop.) G64 | 33 | BW17 |
| Menock Rd, G44 | 103 | BR39 |
| Menteith Av, (Bishop.) G64 | 33 | BX20 |
| Menteith Ct, Moth. ML1 off Melville Dr | 128 | DA47 |
| Menteith Dr, (Ruther.) G73 | 105 | BZ43 |
| Menteith Gdns, (Bears.) G61 | 11 | BE13 |
| Menteith Ln, Moth. ML1 off Windsor Rd | 112 | DC40 |
| Menteith Pl, (Ruther.) G73 | 105 | BZ43 |
| Menteith Rd, Moth. ML1 | 128 | DA46 |
| Menzies Dr, G21 | 51 | BW24 |
| Menzies Pl, G21 | 51 | BW24 |
| Menzies Rd, G21 | 51 | BW24 |
| Merchant La, G1 | 5 | BS31 |
| Merchants Cl, (Kilb.) John. PA10 | 78 | AC34 |
| Merchiston St, G32 | 70 | CA30 |
| Merkland Ct, G11 off Vine St | 66 | BK28 |
| Merkland Ct, (Kirk.) G66 | 17 | CH12 |
| Merkland Dr, (Kirk.) G66 | 18 | CJ12 |
| Merkland Pl, (Kirk.) G66 | 17 | CH12 |
| Merkland Rd, Coat. ML5 | 74 | CS27 |
| Merkland St, G11 | 66 | BK27 |
| Merksworth Way, Pais. PA3 off Mosslands Rd | 62 | AU30 |
| Merlewood Av, (Both.) G71 | 109 | CR41 |
| Merlin Av, Bell. ML4 | 95 | CW37 |
| Merlinford Av, Renf. PA4 | 46 | BA26 |
| Merlinford Cres, Renf. PA4 | 46 | BA26 |
| Merlinford Dr, Renf. PA4 | 46 | BA26 |
| Merlinford Way, Renf. PA4 | 46 | BA26 |
| Merlin Way, Pais. PA3 | 63 | AX30 |
| Merrick Av, Air. ML6 | 76 | DD27 |
| Merrick Ct, Air. ML6 | 76 | DD27 |
| Merrick Gdns, G51 | 66 | BK32 |
| Merrick Gdns, (Bears.) G61 | 11 | BE13 |
| Merrick Path, G51 off Merrick Gdns | 66 | BK32 |
| Merrick Ter, (Udd.) G71 | 93 | CR38 |
| Merrick Way, (Ruther.) G73 | 105 | BX42 |
| Merryburn Av, (Giff.) G46 | 102 | BM40 |
| Merrycrest Av, (Giff.) G46 | 102 | BM41 |
| Merrycroft Av, (Giff.) G46 | 102 | BM41 |
| Merryflats, (Kilsyth) G65 | 19 | CP9 |
| Merryland Pl, G51 | 66 | BK30 |
| Merryland St, G51 | 66 | BK30 |
| Merrylee Cres, (Giff.) G46 | 102 | BL40 |
| Merrylee Pk Av, (Giff.) G46 | 102 | BM41 |
| Merrylee Pk La, (Giff.) G46 | 102 | BL41 |
| Merrylee Pk Ms, (Giff.) G46 | 102 | BM40 |
| Merrylee Rd, G43 | 102 | BM40 |
| Merrylee Rd, G44 | 103 | BN40 |
| Merrylees Rd, (Blan.) G72 | 124 | CL46 |
| Merryston Ct, Coat. ML5 | 74 | CU31 |
| Merry St, Moth. ML1 | 128 | DA46 |
| Merryton Av, G15 | 28 | BD18 |
| Merryton Av, (Giff.) G46 | 102 | BL41 |
| Merryton Pl, G15 | 28 | BD18 |
| Merryton Rd, Lark. ML9 | 142 | DB55 |
| Merryton Rd, Moth. ML1 | 142 | DD51 |
| Merryton St, Lark. ML9 | 142 | DB56 |
| Merryvale Av, (Giff.) G46 | 102 | BM41 |
| Merryvale Pl, (Giff.) G46 | 102 | BL40 |
| Merton Dr, G52 | 64 | BC32 |
| Meryon Gdns, G32 | 91 | CF35 |
| Meryon Rd, G32 off Dornford Av | 91 | CF34 |
| Methil St, G14 | 47 | BE26 |
| Methlick Av, Air. ML6 | 96 | DA33 |
| Methuen Rd, Pais. PA3 | 62 | AV28 |

| | | | | | | | | |
|---|---|---|---|---|---|---|---|---|
| Methven Av, (Bears.) G61 | 30 | BK16 | Millbrae Ct, Coat. ML5 | 74 | CT32 | Mill Gro, Ham. ML3 | 140 | CS51 |
| Methven Pl, (E.Kil.) G74 | 135 | BY51 | Millbrae Cres, G42 | 87 | BN38 | Millheugh, Lark. ML9 | 144 | DA59 |
| Methven Rd, (Giff.) G46 | 118 | BJ47 | Millbrae Cres, Clyde. G81 | 45 | AZ22 | Millheugh Brae, Lark. ML9 | 144 | DA59 |
| Methven St, G31 | 89 | BZ34 | Millbrae Gdns, G42 | 87 | BP38 | Millheugh Pl, (Blan.) G72 | 124 | CL47 |
| Methven St, Clyde. G81 | 26 | AV17 | Millbrae Rd, G42 | 87 | BN38 | Millholm Rd, G44 | 103 | BR41 |
| Metropole La, G1 | | | Millbrix Av, G14 | 46 | BC24 | Millhouse Cres, G20 | 48 | BL22 |
| off Clyde St | 5 | BS31 | Millbrook, (E.Kil.) G74 | 135 | BX52 | Millhouse Dr, G20 | 48 | BK22 |
| Mews La, Pais. PA3 | 62 | AV30 | Millburn Av, (Ruther.) G73 | 105 | BW39 | Millichen Rd, G23 | 30 | BM16 |
| Mey Ct, (Newt. M.) G77 | 116 | BC49 | Millburn Av, Clyde. G81 | 46 | BA21 | Milliken Dr, (Kilb.) John. PA10 | 79 | AE35 |
| Mey Pl, (Newt. M.) G77 | 116 | BC49 | Millburn Av, Renf. PA4 | 45 | AZ26 | Milliken Pk Rd, (Kilb.) | | |
| Michael McParland Dr, (Torr.) | | | Millburn Ct, (E.Kil.) G75 | 134 | BU54 | John. PA10 | 79 | AE36 |
| G64 | 15 | BX12 | Millburn Dr, Renf. PA4 | 46 | BA26 | Milliken Rd, (Kilb.) John. PA10 | 79 | AE35 |
| Michael Ter, (Chap.) Air. ML6 | 97 | DF36 | Millburn Gdns, (E.Kil.) G75 | 134 | BU54 | Mill Pk, Ham. ML3 | | |
| Micklehouse Oval, (Baill.) G69 | 72 | CK31 | Millburn La, Lark. ML9 | | | off Mill Ct | 140 | CS51 |
| Micklehouse Pl, (Baill.) G69 | 72 | CK31 | off Afton St | 145 | DE59 | Mill Pl, (Linw.) Pais. PA3 | 60 | AJ31 |
| Micklehouse Rd, (Baill.) G69 | 72 | CK31 | Millburn Pl, Lark. ML9 | 144 | DD61 | Millport Av, G44 | 88 | BS38 |
| Micklehouse Wynd, (Baill.) G69 | 72 | CK31 | Millburn Rd, Renf. PA4 | 45 | AZ26 | Mill Rig, (E.Kil.) G75 | 135 | BZ56 |
| Midas Pl, Bell. ML4 | 112 | DA40 | Millburn St, G21 | 68 | BV28 | Mill Ri, (Lenz.) G66 | 35 | CF17 |
| Mid Barwood Rd, (Kilsyth) G65 | 8 | CV5 | Millburn St, Moth. ML1 | 128 | DA46 | Mill Rd, (Queenzieburn) G65 | 6 | CN6 |
| Mid Carbarns, Wis. ML2 | | | Millburn Way, (E.Kil.) G75 | 134 | BU54 | Mill Rd, (Both.) G71 | 109 | CQ44 |
| off Carbarns | 143 | DF52 | Millburn Way, Renf. PA4 | 46 | BA26 | Mill Rd, (Camb.) G72 | 107 | CF40 |
| Mid Cotts, (Gart.) G69 | 54 | CL26 | Mill Ct, (Ruther.) G73 | 89 | BW37 | Mill Rd, Air. ML6 | 76 | DC28 |
| Midcroft, (Bishop.) G64 | 32 | BU18 | Mill Ct, Ham. ML3 | 140 | CS51 | Mill Rd, (Riggend) Air. ML6 | 40 | DC20 |
| Midcroft Av, G44 | 104 | BT40 | Mill Cres, G40 | 88 | BV34 | Mill Rd, Clyde. G81 | 45 | AZ22 |
| Middlefield, (E.Kil.) G75 | 136 | CA56 | Mill Cres, (Torr.) G64 | 15 | BY12 | Mill Rd, Ham. ML3 | 140 | CS52 |
| Middlemuir Av, (Kirk.) G66 | 35 | CF15 | Millcroft Rd, (Cumb.) G67 | 22 | DD12 | Mill Rd, Moth. ML1 | 128 | DB46 |
| Middlemuir Rd, (Lenz.) G66 | 35 | CF15 | Millcroft Rd, (Ruther.) G73 | 88 | BV35 | Millroad Dr, G40 | 5 | BU31 |
| Middle Pk, Pais. PA2 | 82 | AT35 | Millcroft Rd, Air. ML6 | 40 | DC17 | Millroad Gdns, G40 | 68 | BV31 |
| Middlerigg Rd, (Cumb.) G68 | 21 | CZ11 | Millennium Ct, G34 | 72 | CL29 | Millroad St, G40 | 5 | BU31 |
| Middlesex Gdns, G41 | 67 | BN31 | Millennium Gdns, G34 | 72 | CL30 | Millstream Ct, Pais. PA1 | 82 | AV33 |
| Middlesex St, G41 | 67 | BN32 | Miller Cl, (Bishop.) G64 | 51 | BZ21 | Mill St, G40 | 88 | BV34 |
| Middleton Av, (Strutherhill | | | Miller Dr, (Bishop.) G64 | 51 | BZ21 | Mill St, (Ruther.) G73 | 89 | BW37 |
| Ind. Est.) Lark. ML9 | 144 | DD61 | Millerfield Pl, G40 | 89 | BX34 | Mill St, Pais. PA1 | 82 | AV33 |
| Middleton Cres, Pais. PA3 | 61 | AR31 | Millerfield Rd, Ham. ML3 | | | Mill Vennel, Renf. PA4 | 45 | AZ26 |
| Middleton Dr, (Miln.) G62 | 12 | BK11 | off Miller St | 126 | CV50 | Millview, (Barr.) G78 | 99 | AZ42 |
| Middleton Rd, Pais. PA3 | 61 | AR30 | Millerfield Rd, G40 | 89 | BX34 | Millview Meadows, (Neil.) | | |
| Middleton Rd, (Linw.) Pais. PA3 | 60 | AM30 | Miller Gdns, (Bishop.) G64 | 51 | BZ21 | G78 | 114 | AS46 |
| Middleton St, G51 | 66 | BL31 | Miller La, Clyde. G81 | 27 | AX20 | Millview Pl, G53 | 100 | BD41 |
| Midfaulds Av, Renf. PA4 | | | Miller Pl, (Bishop.) G64 | 51 | BZ21 | Millview Ter, (Neil.) G78 | 114 | AS46 |
| off King George Pk Av | 64 | BA27 | Millersneuk Av, (Lenz.) G66 | 35 | CF18 | Mill Way, (Kirk.) G66 | 18 | CJ14 |
| Midhope Dr, G5 | 88 | BT34 | Millersneuk Cres, G33 | 52 | CC24 | Millwood St, G41 | 87 | BN37 |
| Midland St, G1 | 4 | BR30 | Millersneuk Dr, (Lenz.) G66 | 35 | CF17 | Milnbank St, G31 | 69 | BW29 |
| Midlem Dr, G52 | 65 | BE32 | Millersneuk Rd, (Kirk.) G66 | 35 | CF17 | Milncroft Pl, G33 | 70 | CC28 |
| Midlem Oval, G52 | 65 | BE32 | Millers Pl, (Lenz.) G66 | 35 | CF17 | Milncroft Rd, G33 | 70 | CC28 |
| Midlock St, G51 | 66 | BL32 | Millers Pl, Air. ML6 | 76 | DD30 | Milner La, G13 | 47 | BG24 |
| Midlothian Dr, G41 | 86 | BM36 | Millerston St, G31 | 69 | BW31 | Milner Rd, G13 | 47 | BG24 |
| Mid Pk, (E.Kil.) G75 | 136 | CA53 | Miller St, G1 | 5 | BS30 | Milngavie Rd, (Bears.) G61 | 29 | BH18 |
| Mid Rd, (Cumb.) G67 | 40 | DB15 | Miller St, (Baill.) G69 | 92 | CK33 | Milnpark Gdns, G41 | 66 | BM32 |
| Midton Cotts, (Mood.) G69 | 37 | CQ20 | Miller St, Clyde. G81 | 27 | AX20 | Milnpark St, G41 | 67 | BN32 |
| Midton St, G21 | 50 | BV26 | Miller St, Coat. ML5 | 75 | CX32 | Milnwood Dr, Bell. ML4 | 111 | CY41 |
| Midwharf St, G4 | 68 | BS27 | Miller St, Ham. ML3 | 126 | CV50 | Milnwood Dr, Moth. ML1 | 111 | CY43 |
| Migvie Pl, G20 | | | Miller St, John. PA5 | 80 | AK34 | Milovaig Av, G23 | 30 | BM19 |
| off Wyndford Rd | 48 | BM24 | Miller St, Lark. ML9 | 144 | DD58 | Milovaig St, G23 | 30 | BM20 |
| Milan St, G41 | 87 | BQ34 | Miller Wk, (Bishop.) G64 | 51 | BZ21 | Milrig Rd, (Ruther.) G73 | 88 | BV38 |
| Milford, (E.Kil.) G75 | 135 | BX54 | Millfield Av, Ersk. PA8 | 25 | AP20 | Milroy Gdns, Bell. ML4 | | |
| Milford Ct, G33 | 70 | CC29 | Millfield Av, Moth. ML1 | 128 | DB45 | off Caldwell Gro | 95 | CW37 |
| Milford St, G33 | 70 | CC29 | Millfield Cres, Ersk. PA8 | 25 | AQ20 | Milton Av, (Camb.) G72 | 106 | CA40 |
| Millands Av, (Blan.) G72 | 108 | CL44 | Millfield Dr, Ersk. PA8 | 43 | AQ21 | Milton Ct, Air. ML6 | | |
| Millarbank St, G21 | 50 | BU25 | Millfield Gdns, Ersk. PA8 | 25 | AQ20 | off Milton St | 76 | DC29 |
| Millar Gro, Ham. ML3 | 125 | CR49 | Millfield Hill, Ersk. PA8 | 25 | AP20 | Milton Douglas Rd, Clyde. G81 | 27 | AW15 |
| Millarston Av, Pais. PA1 | 81 | AQ33 | Millfield La, Ersk. PA8 | 25 | AP20 | Milton Dr, (Bishop.) G64 | 50 | BU22 |
| Millarston Ct, Pais. PA1 | 81 | AR33 | Millfield Meadows, Ersk. PA8 | 25 | AP20 | Milton Gdns, (Udd.) G71 | 93 | CN37 |
| Millarston Dr, Pais. PA1 | 81 | AQ33 | Millfield Pl, Ersk. PA8 | 25 | AP20 | Milton Mains Rd, Clyde. G81 | 27 | AW16 |
| Millarston Ind Est, Pais. PA1 | 81 | AQ34 | Millfield Vw, Ersk. PA8 | 25 | AP20 | Milton Rd, (Kirk.) G66 | 17 | CE11 |
| Millar St, Pais. PA1 | | | Millfield Wk, Ersk. PA8 | 43 | AQ21 | Milton Rd, (E.Kil.) G74 | 135 | BW51 |
| off Christie St | 62 | AV32 | Millfield Wynd, Ersk. PA8 | 25 | AP20 | Milton St, G4 | 5 | BS28 |
| Millar Ter, (Ruther.) G73 | 89 | BX36 | Millford Dr, (Linw.) Pais. PA3 | 60 | AK32 | Milton St, Air. ML6 | 76 | DC29 |
| Millbank Av, Bell. ML4 | 111 | CX42 | Millgate, (Udd.) G71 | 93 | CP37 | Milton St, Ham. ML3 | 125 | CQ49 |
| Millbank Rd, Wis. ML2 | 143 | DH51 | Millgate Av, (Udd.) G71 | 93 | CP37 | Milton St, Moth. ML1 | 128 | DA46 |
| Millbeg Cres, G33 | 71 | CH31 | Millgate Ct, (Udd.) G71 | 93 | CP38 | Milton Ter, Ham. ML3 | 125 | CQ48 |
| Millbeg Pl, G33 | 71 | CG32 | Millgate Rd, Ham. ML3 | 140 | CS52 | Milverton Av, (Bears.) G61 | 29 | BE15 |
| Millbrae Av, (Chry.) G69 | 54 | CM21 | Millgate Ter, Ham. ML3 | | | Milverton Rd, (Giff.) G46 | 102 | BJ44 |
| Millbrae Ct, G42 | 87 | BP38 | off Millgate Rd | 140 | CS51 | Minard Rd, G41 | 87 | BN36 |

| Entry | Page | Grid |
|---|---|---|
| Minard Way, (Udd.) G71 | | |
| *off Newton Dr* | 93 | CQ38 |
| Mincher Cres, Moth. ML1 | 128 | DA49 |
| Minch Way, Air. ML6 | 77 | DF32 |
| Minella Gdns, Bell. ML4 | 95 | CW37 |
| Minerva St, G3 | 67 | BN29 |
| Minerva Way, G3 | 67 | BN29 |
| Mingarry La, G20 | | |
| *off Clouston St* | 49 | BN25 |
| Mingarry St, G20 | 49 | BN25 |
| Mingulay Cres, G22 | 50 | BT21 |
| Mingulay Pl, G22 | 50 | BU21 |
| Mingulay St, G22 | 50 | BT21 |
| Minister Wk, (Baill.) G69 | | |
| *off Dukes Rd* | 73 | CP32 |
| Minmoir Rd, G53 | 84 | BB38 |
| Minsters Pk, (E.Kil.) G74 | 120 | BV49 |
| Minstrel Rd, G13 | 29 | BF20 |
| Minto Av, (Ruther.) G73 | 105 | BZ41 |
| Minto Cres, G52 | 65 | BH32 |
| Minto St, G52 | 65 | BH32 |
| Mireton St, G20 | 49 | BR24 |
| Mirrlees Dr, G12 | 48 | BL25 |
| Mirrlees La, G12 | 48 | BL25 |
| Mitchell Arc, (Ruther.) G73 | | |
| *off Stonelaw Rd* | 89 | BX37 |
| Mitchell Av, (Camb.) G72 | 107 | CG39 |
| Mitchell Av, Renf. PA4 | 63 | AX27 |
| Mitchell Ct, (E.Kil.) G74 | 135 | BY51 |
| Mitchell Dr, (Miln.) G62 | 12 | BL12 |
| Mitchell Dr, (Ruther.) G73 | 105 | BX39 |
| Mitchell Gro, (E.Kil.) G74 | 135 | BV51 |
| Mitchellhill Rd, G45 | 104 | BV43 |
| Mitchell La, G1 | 4 | BR30 |
| Mitchell Rd, (Cumb.) G67 | 22 | DB11 |
| Mitchell St, G1 | 4 | BR30 |
| Mitchell St, Air. ML6 | 76 | DB29 |
| Mitchell St, Coat. ML5 | 73 | CR32 |
| Mitchison Rd, (Cumb.) G67 | 22 | DC10 |
| Mitre Ct, G11 | 47 | BH25 |
| Mitre Gate, G11 | 47 | BH25 |
| Mitre La, G14 | 47 | BF25 |
| Mitre La W, G14 | 47 | BF25 |
| Mitre Rd, G11 | 47 | BH25 |
| Mitre Rd, G14 | 47 | BG25 |
| Moat Av, G13 | 47 | BE22 |
| Mochrum Rd, G43 | 103 | BN39 |
| Moffat Ct, (E.Kil.) G75 | 134 | BU54 |
| Moffat Gdns, (E.Kil.) G75 | 134 | BU54 |
| Moffathill, Air. ML6 | 77 | DG32 |
| Moffat Pl, (Blan.) G72 | 108 | CM44 |
| Moffat Pl, (E.Kil.) G75 | 134 | BT54 |
| Moffat Pl, Air. ML6 | 77 | DH29 |
| Moffat Pl, Coat. ML5 | 95 | CZ33 |
| Moffat Rd, Air. ML6 | 77 | DH30 |
| Moffat St, G5 | 88 | BT33 |
| Mogarth Av, Pais. PA2 | 81 | AP37 |
| Moidart Av, Renf. PA4 | 45 | AX25 |
| Moidart Ct, (Barr.) G78 | 99 | AX40 |
| Moidart Cres, G52 | 65 | BG32 |
| Moidart Gdns, (Kirk.) G66 | 18 | CK12 |
| Moidart Gdns, (Newt. M.) G77 | 117 | BG47 |
| Moidart Pl, G52 | 65 | BG32 |
| Moidart Rd, G52 | 65 | BG32 |
| Moir St, G1 | 5 | BT31 |
| Molendinar Cl, G33 | 70 | CA27 |
| Molendinar Gdns, G33 | 69 | BZ27 |
| Molendinar St, G1 | 5 | BT31 |
| Molendinar Ter, (Neil.) G78 | 114 | AS46 |
| Mollinsburn Rd, (Glenm.) | | |
| Air. ML6 | 57 | CX22 |
| Mollinsburn Rd, (Glenb.) | | |
| Coat. ML5 | 38 | CU18 |
| Mollinsburn St, G21 | 50 | BU26 |
| Mollins Ct, (Cumb.) G68 | 38 | CT16 |
| Mollins Rd, G68 | 20 | CS14 |
| Monach Rd, G33 | 71 | CE29 |
| Monar Dr, G22 | | |
| *off Monar St* | 49 | BR26 |
| Monar Pl, G22 | | |
| *off Monar St* | 49 | BR26 |
| Monar St, G22 | 49 | BR26 |
| Monart Pl, G20 | 49 | BP24 |
| Moncrieff Av, (Lenz.) G66 | 35 | CE16 |
| Moncrieffe Rd, Air. ML6 | 97 | DF33 |
| Moncrieff Gdns, (Kirk.) G66 | | |
| *off Moncrieff Av* | 35 | CF16 |
| Moncrieff St, Pais. PA3 | | |
| *off Back Sneddon St* | 62 | AU32 |
| Moncur St, G40 | 5 | BU31 |
| Moness Dr, G52 | 85 | BG33 |
| Money Gro, Moth. ML1 | 128 | DD49 |
| Monieburgh Cres, (Kilsyth) G65 | 7 | CU4 |
| Monieburgh Rd, (Kilsyth) G65 | 7 | CU4 |
| Monifieth Av, G52 | 85 | BF34 |
| Monikie Gdns, (Bishop.) G64 | 33 | BZ20 |
| Monkcastle Dr, (Camb.) G72 | 106 | CC39 |
| Monkland Av, (Kirk.) G66 | 17 | CF14 |
| Monkland La, Coat. ML5 | 94 | CU33 |
| Monkland St, Air. ML6 | 76 | DD30 |
| Monkland Ter, (Glenb.) | | |
| Coat. ML5 | 56 | CT23 |
| Monkland Vw, (Udd.) G71 | | |
| *off Lincoln Av* | 93 | CQ36 |
| Monkland Vw, (Calder.) Air. ML6 | | |
| *off Woodhall Av* | 96 | DD35 |
| Monkland Vw Cres, (Baill.) G69 | 93 | CP33 |
| Monksbridge Av, G13 | 29 | BE20 |
| Monkscourt Av, Air. ML6 | 76 | DA29 |
| Monkscroft Av, G11 | 48 | BJ26 |
| Monkscroft Ct, G11 | | |
| *off Crow Rd* | 66 | BJ27 |
| Monkscroft Gdns, G11 | | |
| *off Monkscroft Av* | 48 | BJ26 |
| Monks Rd, Air. ML6 | 97 | DE33 |
| Monkton Dr, G15 | 28 | BD19 |
| Monkton Gdns, (Newt. M.) G77 | | |
| *off Maybole Cres* | 118 | BJ47 |
| Monmouth Av, G12 | 48 | BJ23 |
| Monreith Av, (Bears.) G61 | 29 | BF19 |
| Monreith Rd, G43 | 103 | BN39 |
| Monreith Rd E, G44 | 103 | BQ40 |
| Monroe Dr, (Udd.) G71 | 93 | CP36 |
| Monroe Pl, (Udd.) G71 | 93 | CP36 |
| Montague La, G12 | 48 | BK25 |
| Montague St, G4 | 67 | BP27 |
| Montalto Av, Moth. ML1 | 112 | DC44 |
| Montclair Pl, (Linw.) Pais. PA3 | 60 | AJ31 |
| Montego Grn, (E.Kil.) G75 | | |
| *off Leeward Circle* | 135 | BW52 |
| Monteith Dr, (Clark.) G76 | 119 | BP45 |
| Monteith Gdns, (Clark.) G76 | 119 | BP45 |
| Monteith Pl, G40 | 68 | BU32 |
| Monteith Pl, (Blan.) G72 | 125 | CN45 |
| Monteith Row, G40 | 68 | BU32 |
| Monteith Row La, G40 | | |
| *off Monteith Pl* | 68 | BU32 |
| Montford Av, G44 | 88 | BT38 |
| Montford Av, (Ruther.) G73 | 88 | BU38 |
| Montfort Gate, (Barr.) G78 | 100 | BA42 |
| Montgarrie St, G51 | 65 | BF31 |
| Montgomery Av, Coat. ML5 | 74 | CV29 |
| Montgomery Av, Pais. PA3 | 63 | AX29 |
| Montgomery Ct, Pais. PA3 | | |
| *off Montgomery Av* | 63 | AX30 |
| Montgomery Cres, Wis. ML2 | 143 | DG52 |
| Montgomery Dr, (Giff.) G46 | 102 | BL44 |
| Montgomery Dr, (Kilb.) John. | | |
| PA10 *off Meadside Av* | 78 | AC33 |
| Montgomery Pl, (E.Kil.) G74 | 136 | CB51 |
| Montgomery Pl, Lark. ML9 | | |
| *off John St* | 144 | DD59 |
| Montgomery Rd, Pais. PA3 | 63 | AW29 |
| Montgomery St, G40 | 89 | BW33 |
| Montgomery St, (Camb.) G72 | 107 | CG40 |
| Montgomery St, (E.Kil.) G74 | 136 | CB51 |
| Montgomery St, Lark. ML9 | 144 | DC58 |
| Montraive St, (Ruther.) G73 | 89 | BY36 |
| Montrave Path, G52 | | |
| *off Montrave St* | 85 | BF33 |
| Montrave St, G52 | 65 | BF32 |
| Montreal Ho, Clyde. G81 | | |
| *off Perth Cres* | 26 | AT15 |
| Montreal Pk, (E.Kil.) G75 | 135 | BY52 |
| Montrose Av, G32 | 91 | CE36 |
| Montrose Av, G52 | 64 | BB29 |
| Montrose Ct, Pais. PA2 | | |
| *off Montrose Rd* | 81 | AP37 |
| Montrose Cres, Ham. ML3 | 126 | CT49 |
| Montrose Dr, (Bears.) G61 | 11 | BG14 |
| Montrose Gdns, (Miln.) G62 | 12 | BJ10 |
| Montrose Gdns, (Kilsyth) G65 | 7 | CS4 |
| Montrose Gdns, (Blan.) G72 | 108 | CL43 |
| Montrose Pl, (Linw.) Pais. PA3 | 60 | AJ31 |
| Montrose Rd, Pais. PA2 | 81 | AP37 |
| Montrose St, G1 | 5 | BT30 |
| Montrose St, G4 | 5 | BT29 |
| Montrose St, Clyde. G81 | 27 | AX19 |
| Montrose St, Moth. ML1 | 111 | CZ44 |
| Montrose Ter, (Bishop.) G64 | 51 | BY22 |
| Monument Dr, G33 | 52 | CA24 |
| Monymusk Gdns, (Bishop.) G64 | 33 | BZ19 |
| Monymusk Pl, G15 | 28 | BA16 |
| Moodiesburn St, G33 | 69 | BZ27 |
| Moorburn Av, (Giff.) G46 | 102 | BK42 |
| Moorcroft Dr, Air. ML6 | 77 | DG30 |
| Moore Dr, (Bears.) G61 | 29 | BH18 |
| Moore Gdns, Ham. ML3 | 140 | CU54 |
| Moore St, G31 | | |
| *off Gallowgate* | 68 | BV31 |
| Moore St, Moth. ML1 | 112 | DC42 |
| Moorfield Cres, Air. ML6 | 77 | DH30 |
| Moorfield Rd, (Blan.) G72 | 124 | CL47 |
| Moorfoot, (Bishop.) G64 | 33 | BY19 |
| Moorfoot Av, (Thornlie.) G46 | 102 | BJ42 |
| Moorfoot Av, Pais. PA2 | 82 | AT36 |
| Moorfoot Dr, Wis. ML2 | 129 | DH50 |
| Moorfoot Path, Pais. PA2 | | |
| *off Moorfoot Av* | 82 | AT37 |
| Moorfoot St, G32 | 70 | CA31 |
| Moorfoot Way, (Bears.) G61 | 11 | BE13 |
| Moorhill Cres, (Newt. M.) G77 | 117 | BE50 |
| Moorhill Rd, (Newt. M.) G77 | 117 | BE49 |
| Moorhouse Av, G13 | 46 | BB23 |
| Moorhouse Av, Pais. PA2 | 81 | AR35 |
| Moorhouse St, (Barr.) G78 | 99 | AY43 |
| Moorings, The, Pais. PA2 | 81 | AR34 |
| Moorland Dr, Air. ML6 | 77 | DG30 |
| Moorpark Av, G52 | 64 | BB31 |
| Moorpark Av, (Muir.) G69 | 54 | CL22 |
| Moorpark Av, Air. ML6 | | |
| *off Moorcroft Dr* | 77 | DG30 |
| Moorpark Dr, G52 | 64 | BC31 |
| Moorpark Pl, G52 | 64 | BB31 |
| Moorpark Sq, Renf. PA4 | 63 | AX27 |
| Moor Rd, (Miln.) G62 | 12 | BK11 |
| Morag Av, (Blan.) G72 | 108 | CL44 |
| Moraine Av, G15 | 28 | BD20 |

| | | |
|---|---|---|
| Moraine Circ, G15 | 28 | BC20 |
| Moraine Dr, G15 | 28 | BC20 |
| Moraine Dr, (Clark.) G76 | 118 | BL45 |
| Moraine Pl, G15 | | |
| *off Moraine Av* | 28 | BD20 |
| Morar Av, Clyde. G81 | 27 | AX17 |
| Morar Ct, (Cumb.) G67 | 21 | CX13 |
| Morar Ct, Clyde. G81 | 27 | AX17 |
| Morar Ct, Ham. ML3 | 139 | CQ52 |
| Morar Ct, Lark. ML9 | | |
| *off Etive Pl* | 142 | DB56 |
| Morar Cres, (Bishop.) G64 | 32 | BV19 |
| Morar Cres, Air. ML6 | 76 | DA28 |
| Morar Cres, Bish. PA7 | 24 | AL19 |
| Morar Cres, Clyde. G81 | 27 | AX17 |
| Morar Cres, Coat. ML5 | 74 | CT28 |
| Morar Dr, (Bears.) G61 | 30 | BK18 |
| Morar Dr, (Cumb.) G67 | 21 | CX14 |
| Morar Dr, (Ruther.) G73 | 105 | BX42 |
| Morar Dr, Clyde. G81 | 27 | AX17 |
| Morar Dr, Pais. PA2 | 81 | AP35 |
| Morar Dr, (Linw.) Pais. PA3 | 60 | AJ32 |
| Morar Pl, (E.Kil.) G74 | 122 | CB50 |
| Morar Pl, (Newt. M.) G77 | 117 | BF46 |
| Morar Pl, Clyde. G81 | 27 | AX17 |
| Morar Pl, Renf. PA4 | 45 | AX25 |
| Morar Rd, G52 | 65 | BG32 |
| Morar Rd, Clyde. G81 | 27 | AX17 |
| Morar Ter, (Udd.) G71 | 93 | CR38 |
| Morar Ter, (Ruther.) G73 | 105 | BZ42 |
| Morar Way, Moth. ML1 | | |
| *off Clarinda Pl* | 113 | DE42 |
| Moravia Av, (Both.) G71 | 109 | CQ42 |
| Moray Av, Air. ML6 | 76 | DC32 |
| Moray Ct, (Ruther.) G73 | 89 | BW37 |
| Moray Dr, (Torr.) G64 | 15 | BX12 |
| Moray Dr, (Clark.) G76 | 119 | BP46 |
| Moray Gdns, (Cumb.) G68 | 9 | DB8 |
| Moray Gdns, (Udd.) G71 | 93 | CP37 |
| Moray Gdns, (Clark.) G76 | 119 | BP45 |
| Moray Gate, (Both.) G71 | 109 | CN41 |
| Moray Pl, G41 | 87 | BN35 |
| Moray Pl, (Bishop.) G64 | 33 | BY20 |
| Moray Pl, (Kirk.) G66 | 18 | CJ12 |
| Moray Pl, (Chry.) G69 | 54 | CM21 |
| Moray Pl, (Blan.) G72 | 124 | CL47 |
| Moray Pl, (Linw.) Pais. PA3 | 60 | AJ31 |
| Moray Quad, Bell. ML4 | 111 | CW40 |
| Moray Way, Moth. ML1 | | |
| *off Ivy Ter* | 112 | DC40 |
| Mordaunt St, G40 | 89 | BW34 |
| Moredun Cres, G32 | 71 | CE30 |
| Moredun Dr, Pais. PA2 | 81 | AR36 |
| Moredun Rd, Pais. PA2 | 81 | AR36 |
| Moredun St, G32 | 71 | CE30 |
| Morefield Rd, G51 | 65 | BF30 |
| Morgan Ms, G42 | 87 | BR34 |
| Morgan St, Ham. ML3 | 140 | CT51 |
| Morgan St, Lark. ML9 | 144 | DB58 |
| Morina Gdns, G53 | | |
| *off Waukglen Cres* | 101 | BE42 |
| Morion Rd, G13 | 47 | BF21 |
| Morland, (E.Kil.) G74 | 123 | CF48 |
| Morley St, G42 | 87 | BQ38 |
| Morna Pl, G14 | | |
| *off Victoria Pk Dr S* | 65 | BG27 |
| Morningside St, G33 | 69 | BZ29 |
| Morrin Path, G21 | | |
| *off Crichton St* | 50 | BU25 |
| Morrin Sq, G21 | | |
| *off Collins St* | 5 | BU29 |
| Morrin St, G21 | 50 | BU25 |
| Morris Cres, (Blan.) G72 | 124 | CM46 |
| Morris Cres, Moth. ML1 | 113 | DG44 |
| Morrishall Rd, (E.Kil.) G74 | 123 | CE49 |
| Morrison Ct, G2 | 4 | BR30 |
| Morrison Gdns, (Torr.) G64 | 15 | BY13 |
| Morrison Quad, Clyde. G81 | 28 | BA19 |
| Morrison St, G5 | 4 | BQ31 |
| Morrison St, Clyde. G81 | 26 | AV15 |
| Morris St, Ham. ML3 | 140 | CT52 |
| Morris St, Lark. ML9 | 145 | DE60 |
| Morriston Cres, Renf. PA4 | 64 | BB28 |
| Morriston Pk Dr, (Camb.) G72 | 106 | CC39 |
| Morriston St, (Camb.) G72 | 106 | CC39 |
| Morton Gdns, G41 | 86 | BL36 |
| Morton St, Moth. ML1 | 128 | DA45 |
| Morven Av, (Bishop.) G64 | 33 | BY20 |
| Morven Av, (Blan.) G72 | 108 | CL44 |
| Morven Av, Pais. PA2 | 82 | AT37 |
| Morven Dr, (Clark.) G76 | 118 | BM45 |
| Morven Dr, (Linw.) Pais. PA3 | 60 | AJ32 |
| Morven Gait, Ersk. PA8 | 44 | AU21 |
| Morven Gdns, (Udd.) G71 | 93 | CP37 |
| Morven La, (Blan.) G72 | 108 | CL44 |
| Morven Rd, (Bears.) G61 | 29 | BG15 |
| Morven Rd, (Camb.) G72 | 106 | CB42 |
| Morven St, G52 | 65 | BG32 |
| Morven St, Coat. ML5 | 75 | CW29 |
| Morven Way, (Kirk.) G66 | | |
| *off Gartconner Av* | 18 | CK13 |
| Morven Way, (Both.) G71 | 109 | CR42 |
| Mosesfield St, G21 | 50 | BV24 |
| Mosque Av, G5 | 68 | BS32 |
| Moss Av, (Linw.) Pais. PA3 | 60 | AK31 |
| Mossbank, (Blan.) G72 | 124 | CM47 |
| Mossbank, (E.Kil.) G75 | 134 | BV53 |
| Mossbank Av, G33 | 52 | CB25 |
| Mossbank Cres, Moth. ML1 | 113 | DH40 |
| Mossbank Dr, G33 | 52 | CB25 |
| Mossbell Rd, (Bellshill Ind. Est.) | | |
| Bell. ML4 | 110 | CU39 |
| Mossblown St, Lark. ML9 | 144 | DB58 |
| Mosscastle Rd, G33 | | |
| *off Mossvale Rd* | 71 | CE27 |
| Mossdale, (E.Kil.) G74 | 121 | BY50 |
| Mossdale Ct, Bell. ML4 | | |
| *off Christie St* | 111 | CZ40 |
| Mossdale Gdns, Ham. ML3 | 139 | CN51 |
| Moss Dr, (Barr.) G78 | 99 | AW40 |
| Moss Dr, Ersk. PA8 | 43 | AR22 |
| Mossedge Ind Est, (Linw.) | | |
| Pais. PA3 | 60 | AL31 |
| Mossend La, G33 | 71 | CF29 |
| Mossend St, G33 | 71 | CF30 |
| Mossgiel Av, Lark. ML9 | | |
| *off Lansbury Ter* | 145 | DE60 |
| Mossgiel, (E.Kil.) G75 | 135 | BX54 |
| Mossgiel Av, (Ruther.) G73 | 105 | BW40 |
| Mossgiel Cres, (Clark.) G76 | 119 | BP48 |
| Mossgiel Dr, Clyde. G81 | 27 | AY18 |
| Mossgiel Gdns, (Kirk.) G66 | 17 | CH12 |
| Mossgiel Gdns, (Udd.) G71 | 93 | CN37 |
| Mossgiel Pl, (Ruther.) G73 | 105 | BW40 |
| Mossgiel Rd, G43 | 86 | BM38 |
| Mossgiel Rd, (Cumb.) G67 | 22 | DD10 |
| Mossgiel Ter, (Blan.) G72 | 108 | CL43 |
| Mossgiel Way, Moth. ML1 | 113 | DE41 |
| Mosshall Gro, Moth. ML1 | 113 | DH41 |
| Mosshall Rd, Moth. ML1 | 97 | DF38 |
| Mosshall St, Moth. ML1 | 113 | DH41 |
| Mosshead Rd, (Bears.) G61 | 11 | BH14 |
| Moss Hts Av, G52 | 65 | BF32 |
| Mosshill Rd, Bell. ML4 | 95 | CX38 |
| Moss Knowe, (Cumb.) G67 | 23 | DE11 |
| Mossland Rd, G52 | 64 | BA29 |
| Mosslands Rd, Pais. PA3 | 62 | AT29 |
| Mosslingal, (E.Kil.) G75 | 136 | CA56 |
| Mossmulloch, (E.Kil.) G75 | 136 | CA56 |
| Mossneuk Av, (E.Kil.) G75 | 134 | BU53 |
| Mossneuk Dr, (E.Kil.) G75 | 134 | BV54 |
| Mossneuk Dr, Pais. PA2 | 82 | AS37 |
| Mossneuk Rd, (E.Kil.) G75 | 134 | BV53 |
| Mossneuk St, Coat. ML5 | 94 | CV34 |
| Mosspark Av, G52 | 85 | BH34 |
| Mosspark Av, (Miln.) G62 | 12 | BJ10 |
| Mosspark Boul, G52 | 85 | BG33 |
| Mosspark Dr, G52 | 85 | BE33 |
| Mosspark La, G52 | | |
| *off Mosspark Dr* | 85 | BG34 |
| Mosspark Oval, G52 | 85 | BG34 |
| Mosspark Rd, (Miln.) G62 | 12 | BJ10 |
| Mosspark Rd, Coat. ML5 | 74 | CT29 |
| Mosspark Sq, G52 | 85 | BG34 |
| Moss Path, (Baill.) G69 | 91 | CH34 |
| Moss Rd, G51 | 65 | BE31 |
| Moss Rd, (Kirk.) G66 | 34 | CD15 |
| Moss Rd, (Cumb.) G67 | 23 | DG10 |
| Moss Rd, (Muir.) G69 | 54 | CL22 |
| Moss Rd, Air. ML6 | 76 | DC31 |
| Moss Rd, (Hous.) John. PA6 | 60 | AK27 |
| Moss Rd, (Linw.) Pais. PA3 | 60 | AL29 |
| Moss Side Av, Air. ML6 | 76 | DA29 |
| Moss-Side Rd, G41 | 86 | BM36 |
| Moss St, Pais. PA1 | 62 | AU32 |
| Mossvale Cres, G33 | 71 | CE27 |
| Mossvale La, Pais. PA3 | 62 | AT31 |
| Mossvale Path, G33 | 53 | CE26 |
| Mossvale Rd, G33 | 52 | CD26 |
| Mossvale Sq, G33 | 52 | CD26 |
| Mossvale Sq, Pais. PA3 | 62 | AT31 |
| Mossvale St, Pais. PA3 | 62 | AT30 |
| Mossvale Ter, (Chry.) G69 | 37 | CQ18 |
| Mossvale Wk, G33 | 71 | CE27 |
| Mossvale Way, G33 | | |
| *off Mossvale Rd* | 53 | CE26 |
| Mossview Cres, Air. ML6 | 76 | DC31 |
| Mossview Quad, G52 | 65 | BE32 |
| Mossview Rd, G33 | 53 | CG24 |
| Mosswell Rd, (Miln.) G62 | 12 | BK10 |
| Mossywood Ct, (Cumb.) G68 | 20 | CV14 |
| Mossywood Pl, (Cumb.) G68 | 20 | CV14 |
| Mossywood Rd, (Cumb.) G68 | 20 | CU14 |
| Mote Hill, Ham. ML3 | 126 | CU48 |
| Mote Hill Ct, Ham. ML3 | 126 | CU48 |
| Mote Hill Gro, Ham. ML3 | 126 | CU48 |
| Mote Hill Rd, Pais. PA3 | 63 | AW31 |
| Motherwell Rd, Bell. ML4 | 111 | CX41 |
| Motherwell Rd, Ham. ML3 | 113 | DE44 |
| Motherwell Rbt, Ham. ML3 | 126 | CV50 |
| Motherwell St, Air. ML6 | 77 | DE28 |
| Moulin Circ, G52 | 84 | BC33 |
| Moulin Pl, G52 | 84 | BC33 |
| Moulin Rd, G52 | 84 | BC33 |
| Moulin Ter, G52 | 84 | BC33 |
| Mount, The, Moth. ML1 | 127 | CZ47 |
| Mountainblue St, G31 | 69 | BW32 |
| Mount Annan Dr, G44 | 87 | BR38 |
| Mountblow Ho, Clyde. G81 | | |
| *off Melbourne Av* | 26 | AT16 |
| Mountblow Rd, Clyde. G81 | 26 | AU15 |
| Mount Cameron Dr N, (E.Kil.) | | |
| G74 | 136 | CC53 |
| Mount Cameron Dr S, (E.Kil.) | | |
| G74 | 136 | CC53 |
| Mountgarrie Path, G51 | | |
| *off Mountgarrie Rd* | 65 | BF30 |
| Mountgarrie Rd, G51 | 65 | BF30 |

Mount Harriet Av, (Stepps) G33 53 CG23
Mount Harriet Dr, (Stepps) G33 53 CF23
Mountherrick, (E.Kil.) G75 136 CA56
Mount Lockhart, (Udd.) G71 92 CK35
Mount Lockhart Gdns, (Udd.) G71
  off Mount Lockhart 92 CK35
Mount Lockhart Pl, (Udd.) G71
  off Mount Lockhart 92 CK35
Mount Pleasant Pl, (Old Kil.) G60
  off Station Rd 25 AR15
Mount St, G20 49 BP26
Mount Stuart St, G41 87 BN37
Mount Vernon Av, G32 91 CG34
Mount Vernon Av, Coat. ML5 74 CU30
Mournian Way, Ham. ML3 140 CT52
Mousa Pk, (Camb.) G72 106 CB42
Mowbray, (E.Kil.) G74 123 CE49
Mowbray Av, (Gart.) G69 55 CP24
Moyne Rd, G53 84 BC35
Moy St, G11
  off Church St 66 BL27
Muckcroft Rd, (Mood.) G69 36 CK17
Mugdock Rd, (Miln.) G62 12 BJ11
Muirbank Av, (Ruther.) G73 88 BV38
Muirbank Gdns, (Ruther.) G73 88 BV38
Muirbrae Rd, (Ruther.) G73 105 BX41
Muirbrae Way, (Ruther.) G73
  off Muirbrae Rd 105 BX41
Muirburn Av, G44 103 BN41
Muir Ct, G44
  off Strathdon Av 103 BP43
Muirdrum Av, G52 85 BF34
Muirdykes Rd, Coat. ML5 74 CT29
Muirdyke Rd, (Glenb.)
  Coat. ML5 56 CV25
Muirdykes Av, G52 64 BC32
Muirdykes Cres, Pais. PA3 61 AR31
Muirdykes Rd, G52 64 BC32
Muirdykes Rd, Pais. PA3 61 AR31
Muiredge Ct, (Udd.) G71 109 CP39
Muiredge Ter, (Baill.) G69 92 CK33
Muirend Av, G44 103 BP40
Muirend Rd, G44 103 BN41
Muirfield Ct, G44
  off Muirend Rd 103 BN41
Muirfield Cres, G23 31 BN20
Muirfield Meadows, (Both.)
  G71 109 CN43
Muirfield Rd, (Cumb.) G68 9 DC8
Muirhead-Braehead Rbt,
  (Cumb.) G67 22 DD10
Muirhead Cotts, (Kirk.) G66 18 CK14
Muirhead Ct, (Baill.) G69 92 CL33
Muirhead Dr, Moth. ML1 113 DH41
Muirhead Dr, (Linw.) Pais. PA3 60 AJ32
Muirhead Gdns, (Baill.) G69 92 CL33
Muirhead Gate, (Udd.) G71 93 CQ37
Muirhead Gro, (Baill.) G69 92 CL33
Muirhead Rd, (Baill.) G69 92 CK34
Muirhead St, G11
  off Purdon St 66 BK27
Muirhead St, (Kirk.) G66 17 CE14
Muirhead Ter, Moth. ML1 128 DA48
Muirhead Way, (Bishop.) G64 33 BZ20
Muirhill Av, G44 103 BN41
Muirhill Cres, G13 46 BC22
Muirhouse Av, Moth. ML1 128 DD50
Muirhouse Dr, Moth. ML1 143 DE51
Muirhouse La, (E.Kil.) G75
  off Bell Grn W 136 CA53
Muirhouse Pk, (Bears.) G61 11 BF13
Muirhouse Rd, Moth. ML1 142 DD51

Muirkirk Dr, G13 47 BH22
Muirkirk Dr, Ham. ML3 138 CM51
Muirlees Cres, (Miln.) G62 11 BG11
Muirmadkin Rd, Bell. ML4 111 CX40
Muirpark Av, Renf. PA4 63 AY27
Muirpark Dr, (Bishop.) G64 51 BW21
Muirpark St, G11 66 BK27
Muir Pk Ter, (Bishop.) G64 50 BV21
Muirshiel Av, G53 101 BE39
Muirshiel Cres, G53 101 BE39
Muirshot Rd, Lark. ML9 144 DD57
Muirside Av, G32 91 CG34
Muirside Av, (Kirk.) G66 18 CJ13
Muirside Rd, (Baill.) G69 92 CK33
Muirside Rd, Pais. PA3 61 AR30
Muirside St, (Baill.) G69 92 CK33
Muirskeith Cres, G43 103 BP39
Muirskeith Pl, G43 103 BP39
Muirskeith Rd, G43 103 BP39
Muir St, (Bishop.) G64 33 BW20
Muir St, (Blan.) G72 124 CM47
Muir St, Coat. ML5 74 CU30
Muir St, Ham. ML3 126 CU49
Muir St, Lark. ML9 144 DC58
Muir St, Moth. ML1 127 CZ45
Muir St, Renf. PA4 45 AZ25
Muir Ter, Pais. PA3 63 AW30
Muirton Dr, (Bishop.) G64 32 BV18
Muiryfauld Dr, G31 90 CA33
Muiryhall St, Coat. ML5 75 CW30
Muiryhall St E, Coat. ML5 75 CY30
Mulben Cres, G53 84 BB38
Mulben Pl, G53 84 BB38
Mulben Ter, G53 84 BB38
Mulberry Cres, (Chap.)
  Air. ML6 97 DG34
Mulberry Dr, (E.Kil.) G75 135 BY56
Mulberry Rd, G43 102 BM40
Mulberry Rd, (Udd.) G71 94 CS36
Mulberry Way, (E.Kil.) G75 135 BY56
Mulberry Wynd, (Camb.) G72 107 CH42
Mull, (E.Kil.) G74 137 CE53
Mull, Air. ML6 77 DF32
Mullardoch St, G23 30 BM20
Mull Av, Pais. PA2 82 AT38
Mull Av, Renf. PA4 63 AY28
Mull Ct, Ham. ML3 139 CP52
Mullen Ct, (Stepps) G33 53 CH24
Mull St, G21 69 BX27
Mulvey Cres, Air. ML6 76 DA30
Mungo Pk, (E.Kil.) G75 135 BZ53
Mungo Pl, (Udd.) G71
  off Lincoln Av 93 CQ36
Munlochy Rd, G51 65 BF30
Munro Ct, Clyde. G81 26 AV15
Munro La, G13 47 BG24
Munro La E, G13 47 BG24
Munro Pl, G13 47 BG22
Munro Pl, (E.Kil.) G74 122 CD50
Munro Rd, G13 47 BG24
Murano Pl, G20 49 BP25
Murano St, G20 49 BP25
Murchison, G12
  off Ascot Av 47 BH23
Murchison Dr, (E.Kil.) G75 135 BX53
Murdoch Dr, (Miln.) G62
  off Finlay Ri 12 BL13
Murdoch Pl, Moth. ML1 112 DB42
Murdoch Rd, (E.Kil.) G75 136 CA53
Murdoch St, G21
  off Lenzie St 50 BV24
Murdock Sq, Bell. ML4 95 CY38
Muriel St, (Barr.) G78 99 AY42

Muriel St Ind Est, (Barr.) G78 99 AY41
Murray Av, (Kilsyth) G65 7 CT6
Murray Business Area,
  Pais. PA3 62 AT31
Murrayfield, (Bishop.) G64 33 BW18
Murrayfield Dr, (Bears.) G61 29 BG20
Murrayfield St, G32 70 CA30
Murray Gro, (Bears.) G61 10 BD13
Murrayhill, (E.Kil.) G75 135 BZ53
Murray Path, (Udd.) G71 109 CN39
Murray Pl, (Barr.) G78 99 AZ41
Murray Pl, (Righead Ind. Est.)
  Bell. ML4 94 CU38
Murray Rd, (Both.) G71 109 CQ42
Murray Rd, The, (E.Kil.) G75 136 CA54
Murray Rbt, The, (E.Kil.) G75 136 CB53
Murray Sq, The, (E.Kil.) G75
  off The Murray Rd 136 CA54
Murray St, Pais. PA3 62 AS31
Murray St, Renf. PA4 45 AY26
Murray Ter, Moth. ML1 127 CX46
Murrin Av, (Bishop.) G64 33 BZ20
Murroes Rd, G51 65 BF30
Musgrove Pl, (E.Kil.) G75 135 BY53
Muslin St, G40 88 BV33
Muttonhole Rd, Ham. ML3 138 CM54
Mybster Pl, G51
  off Mallaig Rd 65 BF30
Myers Cres, (Udd.) G71 109 CQ40
Myreside Pl, G32 69 BZ31
Myreside St, G32 69 BZ31
Myres Rd, G53 85 BF37
Myrie Gdns, (Bishop.) G64 33 BX19
Myroch Pl, G34 72 CL28
Myrtle Av, (Lenz.) G66 35 CE16
Myrtle Dr, Moth. ML1 112 DD40
Myrtle Dr, Wis. ML2 129 DF49
Myrtle Hill La, G42 88 BS37
Myrtle La, Lark. ML9 144 DD60
Myrtle Pk, G42 87 BR36
Myrtle Pl, G42 88 BS37
Myrtle Rd, (Udd.) G71 93 CR37
Myrtle Rd, Clyde. G81 26 AT17
Myrtle Sq, (Bishop.) G64 51 BW21
Myrtle St, (Blan.) G72 108 CM44
Myrtle Vw Rd, G42 88 BS37
Myrtle Wk, (Camb.) G72 106 CB39
Myvot Av, (Cumb.) G67 39 CX15
Myvot Rd, (Cumb.) G67 39 CW17

**N**

Naburn Gate, G5 88 BS33
Nagle Gdns, Moth. ML1 129 DH45
Nairn Av, (Blan.) G72 108 CL43
Nairn Av, Bell. ML4 111 CW39
Nairn Cres, Air. ML6 76 DC32
Nairn Pl, (E.Kil.) G74 123 CE50
Nairn Pl, Clyde. G81 26 AV18
Nairnside Rd, G21 51 BY22
Nairn St, G3 66 BM28
Nairn St, (Blan.) G72 124 CL47
Nairn St, Clyde. G81 26 AV18
Nairn St, Lark. ML9 144 DB59
Nairn Way, (Cumb.) G68 9 DC8
Naismith St, G32 91 CE36
Naismith Wk, Bell. ML4 95 CY38
Nansen St, G20 49 BQ26
Napier Ct, (Old Kil.) G60
  off Freelands Rd 26 AS16
Napier Dr, G51 66 BK29
Napier Gdns, (Linw.) Pais. PA3 60 AL31
Napier Hill, (E.Kil.) G75 136 CA53

| | | | | | | | | |
|---|---|---|---|---|---|---|---|---|
| Napier La, (E.Kil.) G75 | 136 | CA53 | Ness Dr, (Blan.) G72 | 109 | CN44 | Netherton Fm La, (Bears.) G61 | 47 | BH21 |
| Napier Pl, G51 | 66 | BK29 | Ness Dr, (E.Kil.) G74 | 136 | CD52 | Netherton Ind Est, Wis. ML2 | 143 | DG51 |
| Napier Pl, (Old Kil.) G60 | 26 | AS16 | Ness Gdns, (Bishop.) G64 | | | Netherton Rd, G13 | 47 | BG21 |
| Napier Rd, G51 | 66 | BK29 | *off Wester Cleddens Rd* | 33 | BX20 | Netherton Rd, (E.Kil.) G75 | 135 | BY55 |
| Napier Rd, G52 | 64 | BB28 | Ness Gdns, Lark. ML9 | 144 | DC60 | Netherton Rd, (Newt. M.) G77 | 117 | BH47 |
| Napiershall La, G20 | 67 | BP27 | Ness Rd, Renf. PA4 | 45 | AX25 | Netherton Rd, Wis. ML2 | 143 | DE51 |
| Napiershall Pl, G20 | | | Ness St, G33 | 70 | CA28 | Netherton St, G13 | 47 | BH22 |
| *off Napiershall St* | 67 | BP27 | Ness Ter, Ham. ML3 | 139 | CQ52 | Netherton St, Wis. ML2 | 143 | DH51 |
| Napiershall St, G20 | 67 | BP27 | Ness Way, Moth. ML1 | | | Nethervale Av, G44 | 103 | BP44 |
| Napier Sq, Bell. ML4 | 95 | CX38 | *off Graham St* | 112 | DC40 | Netherview Rd, G44 | 103 | BQ44 |
| Napier St, Clyde. G81 | 45 | AY22 | Nethan Av, Wis. ML2 | 143 | DE51 | Netherway, G44 | 103 | BP44 |
| Napier St, John. PA5 | 79 | AG34 | Nethan Gate, Ham. ML3 | 126 | CS50 | Netherwood Av, (Cumb.) G68 | 20 | CV13 |
| Napier St, (Linw.) Pais. PA3 | 60 | AL31 | Nethan Path, Lark. ML9 | | | Netherwood Ct, (Cumb.) G68 | 21 | CW13 |
| Napier Ter, G51 | 66 | BK29 | *off Riverside Rd* | 144 | DC61 | Netherwood Ct, Moth. ML1 | 142 | DD51 |
| Naproch Pl, (Newt. M.) G77 | 118 | BL48 | Nethan Pl, Ham. ML3 | 140 | CT55 | Netherwood Gro, (Cumb.) G68 | 21 | CW13 |
| Naseby Av, G11 | 47 | BH26 | Nethan St, G51 | 66 | BJ29 | Netherwood Pl, (Cumb.) G68 | 20 | CV13 |
| Naseby La, G11 | 47 | BH26 | Nethan St, Moth. ML1 | 111 | CY43 | Netherwood Rd, (Cumb.) G68 | 20 | CV13 |
| Nasmyth Av, (Bears.) G61 | 10 | BD13 | Nether Auldhouse Rd, G43 | 86 | BK38 | Netherwood Rd, Moth. ML1 | 128 | DD50 |
| Nasmyth Av, (E.Kil.) G75 | 136 | CB54 | Netherbank Rd, (Netherton | | | Netherwood Way, (Cumb.) G68 | 21 | CW13 |
| Nasmyth Pl, G52 | 64 | BC30 | Ind. Est.) Wis. ML2 | 143 | DF51 | Nethy Way, Renf. PA4 | | |
| Nasmyth Pl, (E.Kil.) G75 | | | Netherburn Av, G44 | 103 | BP43 | *off Teith Av* | 64 | BB28 |
| *off Nasmyth Av* | 136 | CB54 | Netherby Dr, G41 | 86 | BM33 | Neuk, The, Wis. ML2 | 129 | DG50 |
| Nasmyth Rd, G52 | 64 | BC30 | Nethercairn Pl, (Newt. M.) G77 | 118 | BL48 | Neuk Av, (Muir.) G69 | 54 | CL22 |
| Nasmyth Rd N, G52 | 64 | BC30 | Nethercairn Rd, G43 | 102 | BL41 | Neuk Way, G32 | 91 | CE37 |
| Nasmyth Rd S, G52 | 64 | BC30 | Nethercliffe Av, G44 | 103 | BP43 | Neville, (E.Kil.) G74 | 123 | CE48 |
| Nassau Pl, (E.Kil.) G75 | 135 | BW52 | Nethercommon Harbour, | | | Nevis Av, Ham. ML3 | 139 | CQ51 |
| Navar Pl, Pais. PA2 | 83 | AW35 | Pais. PA3 | 62 | AU30 | Nevis Ct, (Barr.) G78 | 99 | AY44 |
| Naver St, G33 | 70 | CA28 | Nethercraigs Ct, Pais. PA2 | 81 | AR38 | Nevis Ct, Moth. ML1 | | |
| Naylor La, Air. ML6 | 76 | DD29 | Nethercraigs Dr, Pais. PA2 | 82 | AS37 | *off Glenhead Dr* | 128 | DA49 |
| Naysmyth Bk, (E.Kil.) G75 | 136 | CB54 | Nethercraigs Rd, Pais. PA2 | 81 | AR38 | Nevis Dr, (Torr.) G64 | 15 | BX12 |
| Neidpath, (Baill.) G69 | 92 | CJ33 | Nethercroy Rd, (Kilsyth) G65 | 7 | CU8 | Nevison St, Lark. ML9 | 144 | DD59 |
| Neidpath Av, Coat. ML5 | 95 | CX34 | Netherdale, (Newt. M.) G77 | | | Nevis Rd, G43 | 102 | BK40 |
| Neidpath E, (E.Kil.) G74 | | | *off Kirkvale Ct* | 118 | BK48 | Nevis Rd, (Bears.) G61 | 10 | BD14 |
| *off Kirktonholme Rd* | 135 | BZ52 | Netherdale Cres, Wis. ML2 | 143 | DE51 | Nevis Rd, Renf. PA4 | 63 | AX28 |
| Neidpath Pl, Coat. ML5 | 95 | CW34 | Netherdale Dr, Pais. PA1 | 84 | BB34 | Nevis Way, (Abbots.) Pais. PA3 | 62 | AU28 |
| Neidpath Rd E, (Giff.) G46 | 118 | BJ47 | Netherdale Rd, (Netherton | | | Newark Dr, G41 | 86 | BM34 |
| Neidpath Rd W, (Giff.) G46 | 118 | BJ46 | Ind. Est.) Wis. ML2 | 143 | DG51 | Newark Dr, Pais. PA2 | 82 | AS37 |
| Neidpath W, (E.Kil.) G74 | | | Netherfield St, G31 | 69 | BY31 | Newarthill Rd, Moth. ML1 | 113 | DE43 |
| *off Kirktonholme Rd* | 135 | BZ52 | Nethergreen Cres, Renf. PA4 | 45 | AX26 | New Ashtree St, Wis. ML2 | 129 | DF50 |
| Neilsland Dr, Ham. ML3 | 139 | CR54 | Nethergreen Rd, Renf. PA4 | 45 | AX26 | Newbank Ct, G31 | 90 | CA33 |
| Neilsland Dr, Moth. ML1 | 127 | CX47 | Nethergreen Wynd, Renf. PA4 | 45 | AX26 | Newbank Gdns, G31 | 89 | BZ33 |
| Neilsland Oval, G53 | 85 | BF37 | Netherhall Rd, (Netherton | | | Newbank Rd, G31 | 90 | CA33 |
| Neilsland Rd, Ham. ML3 | 139 | CR54 | Ind. Est.) Wis. ML2 | 143 | DF51 | Newbattle Av, (Calder.) | | |
| Neilsland Sq, G53 | 85 | BF36 | Netherhill Av, G44 | 103 | BP44 | Air. ML6 | 96 | DD35 |
| Neilsland Sq, Ham. ML3 | | | Netherhill Cotts, Pais. PA3 | | | Newbattle Ct, G32 | 90 | CD35 |
| *off Neilsland Rd* | 140 | CS52 | *off Netherhill* | 63 | AX30 | Newbattle Gdns, G32 | 90 | CD35 |
| Neilsland St, Ham. ML3 | 140 | CS52 | Netherhill Cres, Pais. PA3 | 63 | AW31 | Newbattle Pl, G32 | 90 | CC35 |
| Neilson Ct, Ham. ML3 | | | Netherhill Rd, (Mood.) G69 | 37 | CP20 | Newbattle Rd, G32 | 90 | CC36 |
| *off Portland Pl* | 140 | CU51 | Netherhill Rd, Pais. PA3 | 62 | AV31 | Newbold Av, G21 | 50 | BU22 |
| Neilson St, Bell. ML4 | 111 | CW40 | Netherhill Way, Pais. PA3 | 63 | AX30 | Newburgh, Ersk. PA8 | 25 | AQ18 |
| Neilston Av, G53 | 101 | BE40 | Netherhouse Av, (Lenz.) G66 | 35 | CG17 | Newburgh St, G43 | 86 | BM38 |
| Neilston Ct, G53 | 101 | BE40 | Netherhouse Av, Coat. ML5 | 94 | CV34 | Newcastleton Dr, G23 | | |
| Neilston Pl, (Kilsyth) G65 | 7 | CR4 | Netherhouse Pl, G34 | 73 | CN29 | *off Broughton Rd* | 31 | BN20 |
| Neilston Rd, (Barr.) G78 | 114 | AV45 | Netherhouse Rd, (Baill.) G69 | 72 | CM30 | New City Rd, G4 | 4 | BR28 |
| Neilston Rd, Pais. PA2 | 82 | AU34 | Nether Kirkton Av, (Neil.) G78 | 114 | AU45 | Newcraigs Dr, (Clark.) G76 | 120 | BT46 |
| Neilston Wk, (Kilsyth) G65 | | | Nether Kirkton Vw, (Neil.) G78 | 114 | AU45 | Newcroft Dr, G44 | 104 | BT40 |
| *off Balmalloch Rd* | 7 | CR4 | Nether Kirkton Way, (Neil.) | | | Newdyke Av, (Kirk.) G66 | 17 | CG13 |
| Neil St, Pais. PA1 | 82 | AS33 | G78 | 114 | AV45 | Newdyke Rd, (Kirk.) G66 | 17 | CG13 |
| Neil St, Renf. PA4 | 45 | AZ24 | Nether Kirkton Wynd, (Neil.) | | | New Edinburgh Rd, (Udd.) G71 | 93 | CP38 |
| Neilvaig Dr, (Ruther.) G73 | 105 | BY42 | G78 | 114 | AU45 | New Edinburgh Rd, Bell. ML4 | 93 | CP38 |
| Neistpoint Dr, G33 | 70 | CC29 | Netherlee Pl, G44 | 103 | BQ41 | Newfield Cres, Ham. ML3 | 125 | CR49 |
| Nelson Av, Coat. ML5 | 94 | CU33 | Netherlee Rd, G44 | 103 | BP42 | Newfield La, (Both.) G71 | 109 | CR42 |
| Nelson Cres, Moth. ML1 | 128 | DD50 | Nethermains Rd, (Miln.) G62 | 12 | BJ13 | Newfield Pl, (Thornlie.) G46 | 101 | BH43 |
| Nelson Mandela Pl, G2 | 5 | BS29 | Netherpark Av, G44 | 103 | BP44 | Newfield Pl, (Ruther.) G73 | 88 | BU38 |
| Nelson Pl, (Baill.) G69 | 92 | CK33 | Netherplace Cres, G53 | 84 | BD37 | Newfield Sq, G53 | 100 | BC39 |
| Nelson St, G5 | 4 | BQ31 | Netherplace Cres, (Newt. M.) | | | Newford Gro, (Clark.) G76 | 119 | BN48 |
| Nelson St, (Baill.) G69 | 92 | CK33 | G77 | 117 | BE49 | Newgrove Gdns, (Camb.) G72 | 106 | CC39 |
| Nelson Ter, (E.Kil.) G74 | 136 | CC53 | Netherplace Rd, G53 | 84 | BD37 | Newhall St, G40 | 88 | BV34 |
| Neptune St, G51 | 66 | BK30 | Netherplace Rd, (Newt. M.) | | | Newhaven Rd, G33 | 70 | CD29 |
| Neptune Way, Bell. ML4 | 112 | DA40 | G77 | 116 | BD50 | Newhaven St, G32 | 70 | CC30 |
| Nerston Ind Est, (E.Kil.) G74 | 122 | CB49 | Netherton Av, G13 | 47 | BG21 | Newhills Rd, G33 | 71 | CG30 |
| Nerston Rd, (E.Kil.) G74 | 122 | CB47 | Netherton Ct, (Newt. M.) G77 | 118 | BJ46 | Newhouse Ind Est, Moth. ML1 | 97 | DE38 |
| Ness Av, John. PA5 | 79 | AE37 | Netherton Dr, (Barr.) G78 | 99 | AZ43 | Newhousemill Rd, (E.Kil.) G74 | 137 | CF54 |

New Inchinnan Rd, Pais. PA3   62   AU30
Newington St, G32   70   CB31
New Kirk Pl, (Bears.) G61
   *off New Kirk Rd*   29   BG16
New Kirk Rd, (Bears.) G61   29   BG16
New Lairdsland Rd, (Kirk.) G66   17   CE12
Newlandscraigs Av, John. PA5   80   AM35
Newlandscraigs Dr, John. PA5   80   AM35
Newlands Dr, Ham. ML3   140   CT53
Newlands Gdns, (Elder.)
   John. PA5   80   AL35
Newlandsmuir Rd, (E.Kil.) G75   135   BW55
Newlands Pl, (E.Kil.) G74   136   CA52
Newlands Rd, G43   103   BN39
Newlands Rd, G44   103   BQ39
Newlands Rd, (Udd.) G71   93   CP37
Newlands Rd, (E.Kil.) G75   134   BU56
Newlands St, Coat. ML5   95   CW33
New La, (Calder.) Air. ML6   96   DD35
Newliston Dr, G5   88   BT34
New Luce Dr, G32   91   CF34
Newmains Av, (Inch.) Renf. PA4   43   AQ24
Newmains Rd, Renf. PA4   63   AX27
Newmill Rd, G21   51   BY24
Newmilns St, G53   100   BB40
Newnham Rd, Pais. PA1   83   AZ33
Newpark Cres, (Camb.) G72
   *off Morriston Pk Dr*   90   CC38
New Pk St, Ham. ML3   126   CS48
New Plymouth, (E.Kil.) G75   135   BW54
New Rd, (Camb.) G72   107   CG41
New Rd, (Glenb.) Coat. ML5   56   CV23
Newrose Av, Bell. ML4   95   CX38
Newshot Ct, Clyde. G81
   *off Clydeholm Ter*   45   AZ22
Newshot Dr, Ersk. PA8   26   AS20
New Sneddon St, Pais. PA3   62   AU32
Newstead Gdns, G23   31   BN20
New Stevenston Rd,
   Moth. ML1   112   DD43
New St, (Blan.) G72   124   CL46
New St, Clyde. G81   27   AW15
New St, (Kilb.) John. PA10   78   AC34
New St, Pais. PA1   82   AU33
Newton Av, (Camb.) G72   107   CF39
Newton Av, (Barr.) G78   99   AY44
Newton Av, (Elder.) John. PA5   81   AN34
Newton Brae, (Camb.) G72   107   CG39
Newton Ct, (Newt. M.) G77   117   BF50
Newton Dr, (Udd.) G71   93   CQ38
Newton Dr, (Elder.) John. PA5   81   AN34
Newton Fm Rd, (Camb.) G72   91   CH38
Newtongrange Av, G32   90   CD34
Newtongrange Gdns, G32   90   CD35
Newton Gro, (Newt. M.) G77   117   BF50
Newtonlea Av, (Newt. M.) G77   117   BG49
Newton Pl, G3   4   BP28
Newton Pl, (Newt. M.) G77   117   BG50
Newton Rd, (Lenz.) G66   35   CG18
Newton Sta Rd, (Camb.) G72   107   CG41
Newton St, G3
   *off Argyle St*   4   BQ29
Newton St, Coat. ML5   94   CU33
Newton St, Pais. PA1   82   AS33
Newton Ter, G3
   *off Sauchiehall St*   4   BP29
Newton Ter, Pais. PA1   81   AP34
Newton Ter La, G3   4   BP29
Newton Way, Pais. PA3
   *off Merlin Way*   63   AX30
Newtown St, (Kilsyth) G65   7   CT5
Newtyle Dr, G53   84   BB36

Newtyle Pl, G53   84   BB36
Newtyle Pl, (Bishop.) G64   33   BZ20
Newtyle Rd, Pais. PA1   83   AX33
New Vw Cres, Bell. ML4
   *off New Vw Dr*   111   CW42
New Vw Dr, Bell. ML4   111   CW42
New Vw Pl, Bell. ML4   111   CW42
New Wynd, G1   5   BS31
Niamh Ct, (Inch.) Renf. PA4   44   AS22
Nicholas St, G1   5   BT30
Nicholson La, G5
   *off Nicholson St*   4   BR31
Nicholson St, G5   67   BR32
Nicolson Ct, (Stepps) G33   53   CG24
Nicol St, Air. ML6   77   DE28
Niddrie Rd, G42   87   BP35
Niddrie Sq, G42   87   BP36
Niddry St, Pais. PA3   62   AV32
Nigel Gdns, G41   86   BM36
Nigel St, Moth. ML1   127   CZ47
Nigg Pl, G34   72   CJ29
Nimmo Dr, G51   65   BG30
Ninian Rd, Air. ML6   77   DE32
Ninians Ri, (Kirk.) G66   17   CH14
Nisbet St, G31   69   BZ32
Nisbett Pl, (Chap.) Air. ML6   97   DG34
Nisbett St, (Chap.) Air. ML6   97   DG35
Nissen Pl, G53   84   BB36
Nith Av, Pais. PA2
   *off Don Dr*   81   AP35
Nith Dr, Renf. PA4   64   BA27
Nith Pl, John. PA5   79   AE37
Nith Quad, Moth. ML1   113   DE42
Nithsdale, (E.Kil.) G74   123   CF50
Nithsdale Cres, (Bears.) G61   29   BE15
Nithsdale Dr, G41   87   BP35
Nithsdale Pl, G41
   *off Nithsdale Rd*   87   BP34
Nithsdale Rd, G41   87   BP35
Nithsdale St, G41   87   BP35
Nith St, G33   69   BZ28
Nitshill Rd, (Thornlie.) G46   101   BF42
Nitshill Rd, G53   100   BB39
Niven St, G20   48   BL23
Noble Rd, Bell. ML4   111   CW40
Nobles Pl, Bell. ML4   110   CV41
Nobles Vw, Bell. ML4   110   CV41
Noldrum Av, G32   91   CE37
Noldrum Gdns, G32
   *off Park Rd*   91   CE37
Norbreck Dr, (Giff.) G46   102   BL41
Norby Rd, G11   47   BH26
Noremac Way, (Bellshill Ind. Est.)
   Bell. ML4   94   CV38
Norfield Dr, G44   87   BR38
Norfolk Ct, G5   67   BR32
Norfolk Cres, (Bishop.) G64   32   BU18
Norfolk Ho, (E.Kil.) G74
   *off East Kilbride Shop Cen*   136   CA52
Norfolk La, G5
   *off Norfolk St*   67   BR32
Norfolk St, G5   67   BR32
Norham St, G41   87   BN36
Norman St, G40   88   BV34
Norse La N, G14
   *off Verona Av*   47   BE25
Norse La S, G14
   *off Verona Av*   47   BE25
Norse Pl, G14   47   BE25
Norse Rd, G14   47   BE25
Northall Quad, Moth. ML1
   *off Clapperhow Rd*   112   DD44
Northampton Dr, G12   48   BK23

Northampton La, G12   48   BK23
North Av, (Camb.) G72   106   CB39
North Av, Clyde. G81   27   AW19
North Av, Moth. ML1   112   DC43
Northbank Av, (Kirk.) G66   17   CE13
Northbank Av, (Camb.) G72   107   CF39
North Bk Pl, Clyde. G81   45   AY21
Northbank Rd, (Kirk.) G66   17   CE13
Northbank St, (Camb.) G72
   *off Westburn Rd*   107   CF39
North Bk St, Clyde. G81   45   AY21
North Barr Av, Ersk. PA8   25   AQ18
North Berwick Av, (Cumb.) G68   9   DB8
North Berwick Cres, (E.Kil.) G75   135   BW55
North Berwick Gdns, (Cumb.)
   G68   9   DB8
North Biggar Rd, Air. ML6   76   DD29
North Brae Pl, G13   46   BD22
North Br St, Air. ML6   76   DB29
North British Rd, (Udd.) G71   109   CP39
Northburn Av, Air. ML6   76   DD28
Northburn Pl, Air. ML6   76   DD27
Northburn Rd, Coat. ML5   75   CY28
North Bute St, Coat. ML5   95   CX33
North Caldeen Rd, Coat. ML5   75   CY32
North Calder Dr, Air. ML6   77   DF31
North Calder Gro, (Udd.) G71   92   CK35
North Calder Pl, (Udd.) G71   92   CK35
North Calder Rd, (Udd.) G71   94   CS36
North Campbell Av, (Miln.)
   G62   11   BH12
North Canal Bk, G4   68   BS27
North Canal Bk St, G4   68   BS27
North Carbrain Rd, (Cumb.) G67   22   DB13
North Claremont St, G3
   *off Royal Ter*   67   BN28
North Corsebar Rd, Pais. PA2   82   AS35
North Ct, G1
   *off St. Vincent Pl*   5   BS30
North Ct La, G1   5   BS30
Northcroft Rd, G21   50   BV25
Northcroft Rd, (Chry.) G69   37   CN19
North Cft St, Pais. PA3   62   AV32
North Dean Pk Av, (Both.) G71   109   CQ42
North Douglas St, Clyde. G81   45   AY21
North Dr, G1   4   BR30
North Dr, (Linw.) Pais. PA3   60   AK31
North Dumgoyne Av, (Miln.)
   G62   11   BH11
North Elgin Pl, Clyde. G81   45   AY22
North Elgin St, Clyde. G81   45   AY22
North Erskine Pk, (Bears.) G61   29   BF16
Northfield, (E.Kil.) G75   134   BV54
Northfield Rd, (Kilsyth) G65   7   CR4
Northfield St, Moth. ML1   128   DA45
North Frederick St, G1   5   BS30
North Gardner St, G11   66   BK27
Northgate Quad, G21   51   BY23
Northgate Rd, G21   51   BY22
North Gower St, G51   66   BL32
North Gra Rd, (Bears.) G61   29   BG15
North Hanover Pl, G4
   *off North Hanover St*   5   BS29
North Hanover St, G1   5   BS29
North Hillhead Rd, (Newt. M.)
   G77   130   BC52
Northinch Ct, G14   65   BF27
Northinch St, G14   65   BF27
North Iverton Pk Rd, John. PA5   80   AJ34
Northland Av, G14   47   BE24
Northland Dr, G14   47   BE24
Northland Gdns, G14
   *off Northland Dr*   47   BE24

Northland La, G14
*off Northland Dr*   47   BE25
North La, (Linw.) Pais. PA3   60   AL31
North Lo Av, Moth. ML1   128   DA49
North Lo Rd, Renf. PA4   45   AY25
North Moraine La, G15
*off Moraine Av*   29   BE19
Northmuir Rd, G15   28   BD17
North Orchard St, Moth. ML1   127   CZ46
North Pk Av, (Thornlie.) G46   101   BH41
North Pk Av, (Barr.) G78   99   AX42
Northpark St, G20   49   BP25
North Pk Vil, (Thornlie.) G46
*off North Pk Av*   101   BH41
North Pl, G3
*off North St*   4   BP29
North Portland St, G1   5   BT30
North Rd, (Cumb.) G68   21   CW13
North Rd, Bell. ML4   111   CW39
North Rd, John. PA5   79   AG35
North Sq, Coat. ML5   74   CU29
North St, G3   4   BP29
North St, Lark. ML9   144   DC57
North St, Moth. ML1   128   DB45
North St, Pais. PA3   62   AU31
Northumberland St, G20   49   BN25
North Vw, (Bears.) G61   29   BF19
North Wallace St, G4   5   BT28
Northway, (Blan.) G72   108   CL44
North Woodside Rd, G20   49   BP26
Norval St, G11   66   BJ27
Norwich Dr, G12   48   BK24
Norwood Av, (Kirk.) G66   16   CD12
Norwood Dr, (Giff.) G46   102   BJ44
Norwood Pk, (Bears.) G61   29   BH18
Norwood Ter, (Udd.) G71   93   CQ38
Nottingham Av, G12
*off Northampton Dr*   48   BJ23
Nottingham La, G12
*off Northampton Dr*   48   BK23
Novar Dr, G12   48   BJ25
Novar Gdns, (Bishop.) G64   32   BU19
Novar St, Ham. ML3   140   CT51
Nova Tech Pk, G33   52   CA24
Nuneaton St, G40   89   BW34
Nuneaton St Ind Est, G40   89   BW34
Nurseries Rd, (Baill.) G69   71   CH31
Nursery Av, (Erskine Hosp.)
Bish. PA7   24   AN17
Nursery La, G41   87   BP35
Nursery Pl, (Blan.) G72   124   CM47
Nursery St, G41
*off Pollokshaws Rd*   87   BQ34
Nutberry Ct, G42   87   BR36

**O**

Oak Av, (Bears.) G61   11   BH14
Oak Av, (E.Kil.) G75   135   BX55
Oakbank Av, Wis. ML2   143   DG52
Oakbank Dr, (Barr.) G78   115   AZ45
Oakbank Ind Est, G20   49   BQ26
Oakbank St, Air. ML6   77   DF30
Oakburn Av, (Miln.) G62   11   BH12
Oakburn Cres, (Miln.) G62   11   BH12
Oak Cres, (Baill.) G69   92   CJ33
Oakdene Av, (Udd.) G71   93   CR38
Oakdene Av, Bell. ML4   95   CW38
Oakdene Cres, (New.)
Moth. ML1   113   DE42
Oak Dr, (Kirk.) G66   34   CD16
Oak Dr, (Camb.) G72   107   CE41
Oak Fern Dr, (E.Kil.) G74   121   BZ49

Oak Fern Gro, (E.Kil.) G74   121   BZ49
Oakfield Av, G12   67   BN27
Oakfield Dr, Moth. ML1
*off Brandon St*   128   DB47
Oakfield La, G12   67   BN27
Oakfield Rd, Moth. ML1   128   DA47
Oak Gro, (Chap.) Air. ML6   97   DG34
Oakhill Av, (Baill.) G69   91   CH34
Oak Lea, Ham. ML3   140   CV51
Oaklea Cres, (Blan.) G72   124   CL45
Oakley Dr, G44   103   BP42
Oakley Ter, G31   68   BV30
Oak Pk, (Bishop.) G64   33   BX20
Oak Pk, Moth. ML1   127   CZ48
Oak Path, Moth. ML1
*off Myrtle Dr*   112   DD40
Oak Pl, (Udd.) G71   94   CS38
Oak Pl, (E.Kil.) G75   135   BX55
Oak Pl, Coat. ML5   75   CY32
Oakridge Cres, Pais. PA3   61   AR32
Oakridge Rd, (Baill.) G69   73   CQ31
Oak Rd, (Cumb.) G67   23   DG9
Oak Rd, Clyde. G81   26   AV16
Oak Rd, Pais. PA2   83   AW36
Oaks, The, John. PA5   79   AG35
Oakshaw Brae, Pais. PA1   62   AT32
Oakshawhead, Pais. PA1   62   AT32
Oakshaw St E, Pais. PA1   62   AT32
Oakshaw St W, Pais. PA1   62   AT32
Oakside Pl, Ham. ML3
*off Chriss Av*   140   CT54
Oak St, G2   4   BQ30
Oaktree Gdns, G45   104   BW41
Oakwood Av, Pais. PA2   81   AR36
Oakwood Cres, G34   72   CM28
Oakwood Dr, G34   72   CM28
Oakwood Dr, (Newt. M.) G77   117   BH49
Oakwood Dr, Coat. ML5
*off Rowanwood Cres*   74   CT32
Oak Wynd, (Camb.) G72   107   CH42
Oates Gdns, Moth. ML1   128   DD49
Oatfield St, G21   51   BX25
Oatlands Sq, G5   88   BT34
Oban Ct, G20
*off Kelvinside Gdns*   49   BN25
Oban Dr, G20   49   BN25
Oban La, G20   49   BN25
Observatory La, G12
*off Observatory Rd*   48   BM26
Observatory Rd, G12   48   BL26
Ochel Path, (Chap.) Air. ML6   97   DH36
Ochil Dr, (Barr.) G78   99   AX44
Ochil Dr, Pais. PA2   82   AU37
Ochil Pl, G32   90   CC33
Ochil Rd, (Bears.) G61   10   BD14
Ochil Rd, (Bishop.) G64   33   BY20
Ochil Rd, Renf. PA4   63   AX28
Ochil St, G32   90   CC33
Ochil St, Wis. ML2   129   DH49
Ochiltree Av, G13   47   BH22
Ochiltree Dr, Ham. ML3   139   CN52
Ochil Vw, (Udd.) G71   93   CQ37
Odense Ct, (E.Kil.) G75   136   CA55
Ogilvie Ct, Air. ML6
*off Station Rd*   77   DG29
Ogilvie Pl, G31   89   BZ33
Ogilvie St, G31   89   BZ33
Old Aisle Rd, G66   17   CG14
Old Avon Rd, Ham. ML3   141   CW51
Old Balmore Rd, G64   14   BU14
Old Biggar Rd, (Chap.) Air. ML6   97   DH37
Old Biggar Rd, (Riggend)
Air. ML6   40   DD20

Old Bore Rd, Air. ML6   77   DF29
Old Bothwell Rd, (Both.) G71   109   CR44
Old Castle Gdns, G44   103   BR39
Old Castle Rd, G44   103   BR39
Old Ch Gdns, (Baill.) G69   73   CQ32
Old Coach Rd, (E.Kil.) G74   122   CB50
Old Cotts, Pais. PA2
*off Grahamston Rd*   83   AY37
Old Dalmarnock Rd, G40   88   BV33
Old Dalnottar Rd, (Old Kil.) G60   25   AR16
Old Dullatur Rd, (Dullatur) G68   9   CZ7
Old Dumbarton Rd, G3   66   BL28
Old Edinburgh Rd, (Udd.) G71   93   CN36
Old Edinburgh Rd, Bell. ML4   93   CQ38
Old Fm La, (Bears.) G61   47   BH21
Old Fm Rd, Pais. PA2   83   AZ36
Old Ferry Rd, Ersk. PA8   25   AQ17
Old Gartloch Rd, (Gart.) G69   55   CP25
Old Glasgow Rd, (Udd.) G71   92   CM37
Old Govan Rd, Renf. PA4   46   BB26
Old Greenock Rd, Bish. PA7   24   AK18
Old Greenock Rd, Ersk. PA8   24   AN20
Old Greenock Rd, (Inch.)
Renf. PA4   44   AT22
Oldhall Rd, Pais. PA1   63   AY32
Old Humbie Rd, (Newt. M.)
G77   131   BG51
Old Manse Rd, G32   91   CF33
Old Manse Rd, Wis. ML2   143   DG53
Old Mill Ct, (Dunt.) Clyde. G81   27   AW16
Old Mill Pk Ind Est, (Kirk.) G66   17   CE12
Old Mill Rd, (Both.) G71   109   CQ44
Old Mill Rd, (Udd.) G71   109   CP40
Old Mill Rd, (Camb.) G72   107   CF39
Old Mill Rd, (E.Kil.) G74   136   CB51
Old Mill Rd, Clyde. G81   27   AW15
Old Mill Rd, Pais. PA2   81   AR34
Old Mill Vw, (Kilsyth) G65   20   CV9
Old Monkland Rd, Coat. ML5   94   CT34
Old Playfield Rd, (Carm.) G76   120   BT45
Old Quarry Rd, (Cumb.) G68   38   CT16
Old Rd, (Elder.) John. PA5   80   AL34
Old Rutherglen Rd, G5   88   BS33
Old Sch Ct, Coat. ML5   95   CW33
Old Shettleston Rd, G32   70   CC32
Old Sneddon St, Pais. PA3   62   AU32
Old Stable Row, Coat. ML5   75   CX30
Old Sta Ct, (Both.) G71   109   CQ43
Old St, Clyde. G81   26   AV15
Old Union St, Air. ML6   76   DD30
Old Vic Ct, (E.Kil.) G74   122   CD49
Old Wd Rd, (Baill.) G69   92   CJ34
Old Wynd, G1   5   BS31
Olifard Av, (Both.) G71   109   CR42
Oliphant Ct, Pais. PA2
*off Heriot Av*   81   AP37
Oliphant Cres, (Clark.) G76   119   BN48
Oliphant Cres, Pais. PA2   81   AN37
Oliphant Oval, Pais. PA2
*off Bothwell Pl*   81   AN37
Olive Bk, (Udd.) G71   94   CS36
Olive Ct, Moth. ML1
*off Poplar Pl*   112   DD40
Olive St, G33   51   BZ25
Olympia, (E.Kil.) G74
*off East Kilbride Shop Cen*   136   CB53
Olympia Arc, (E.Kil.) G74
*off East Kilbride Shop Cen*   136   CB53
Olympia Ct, (E.Kil.) G74
*off East Kilbride Shop Cen*   136   CB53
Olympia St, G40   68   BV32
Olympia Way, (E.Kil.) G74
*off East Kilbride Shop Cen*   136   CB53

O'Neill Av, (Bishop.) G64 — 51 BX21
Onslow, (E.Kil.) G75 — 135 BY54
Onslow Dr, G31 — 69 BW30
Onslow Rd, Clyde. G81 — 27 AY19
Onslow Sq, G31 — 69 BW30
Ontario Pk, (E.Kil.) G75 — 135 BX52
Ontario Pl, (E.Kil.) G75 — 135 BX52
Onyx St, Bell. ML4 — 111 CW41
Oran Gdns, G20 — 49 BN24
Oran Gate, G20 — 49 BN24
Oran Pl, G20 — 49 BN25
Oran St, G20 — 49 BN24
Orbiston Ct, Moth. ML1
  off Orbiston St — 128 DC48
Orbiston Dr, Bell. ML4 — 111 CX41
Orbiston Gdns, G32 — 70 CC32
Orbiston Rd, Bell. ML4 — 110 CV41
Orbiston Sq, Bell. ML4
  off Busby Rd — 110 CV42
Orbiston St, Moth. ML1 — 128 DC48
Orcades Dr, G44 — 103 BR41
Orchard Av, (Both.) G71 — 109 CR44
Orchard Brae, (Lenz.) G66
  off Lindsaybeg Rd — 35 CG17
Orchard Ct, G32 — 90 CD37
Orchard Ct, (Thornlie.) G46 — 102 BJ42
Orchard Ct, Renf. PA4 — 45 AZ25
Orchard Dr, (Giff.) G46 — 102 BK42
Orchard Dr, (Blan.) G72 — 124 CL45
Orchard Dr, (Ruther.) G73 — 88 BV37
Orchardfield, (Lenz.) G66 — 35 CG17
Orchard Gate, Lark. ML9 — 144 DC59
Orchard Grn, (E.Kil.) G74 — 122 CD49
Orchard Gro, (Giff.) G46 — 102 BK41
Orchard Gro, Coat. ML5 — 75 CX31
Orchard Pk, (Giff.) G46 — 102 BL42
Orchard Pk Av, (Giff.) G46 — 102 BJ41
Orchard Pl, (Kirk.) G66 — 18 CJ14
Orchard Pl, Bell. ML4 — 110 CV42
Orchard Pl, Ham. ML3 — 126 CT50
Orchard St, (Baill.) G69 — 91 CH34
Orchard St, Ham. ML3 — 126 CT50
Orchard St, Moth. ML1 — 127 CZ46
Orchard St, Pais. PA1 — 82 AU33
Orchard St, Renf. PA4 — 45 AZ25
Orchardton Rd, (Cumb.)
  G68 — 20 CT14
Orchardton Wds Ind Pk, (Cumb.)
  G68 — 20 CS13
Orchy Av, (Clark.) G76
  off The Oval — 103 BP44
Orchy Ct, Clyde. G81 — 27 AY16
Orchy Cres, (Bears.) G61 — 29 BF19
Orchy Cres, Air. ML6 — 77 DE32
Orchy Cres, Pais. PA2 — 81 AP36
Orchy Dr, (Clark.) G76 — 103 BP44
Orchy Gdns, (Clark.) G76 — 103 BP44
Orchy St, G44 — 103 BQ39
Orchy Ter, (E.Kil.) G74 — 136 CC52
Orefield Pl, (E.Kil.) G74 — 122 CA50
Oregon Pl, G5 — 88 BS33
Orion Pl, Bell. ML4 — 112 DA40
Orion Way, (Camb.) G72 — 106 CC39
Orkney Pl, G51
  off Orkney St — 66 BK30
Orkney St, G51 — 66 BK30
Orlando, (E.Kil.) G74 — 123 CE48
Orleans Av, G14 — 47 BG26
Orleans La, G14 — 47 BG26
Orlington Ct, Coat. ML5
  off Gilmour Pl — 74 CV29
Ormiston Av, G14 — 47 BE25
Ormiston Dr, Ham. ML3 — 140 CS53

Ormiston La, G14
  off Ormiston Av — 47 BE25
Ormiston La N, G14
  off Ormiston Av — 47 BE25
Ormiston La S, G14
  off Ormiston Av — 47 BE25
Ormonde Av, G44 — 103 BP42
Ormonde Ct, G44 — 103 BN42
Ormonde Cres, G44 — 103 BP42
Ormonde Dr, G44 — 103 BP42
Ornsay St, G22 — 50 BT22
Oronsay Ct, (Old Kil.) G60 — 26 AS15
Oronsay Cres, (Old Kil.) G60 — 26 AS15
Oronsay Cres, (Bears.) G61 — 30 BK18
Oronsay Gdns, (Old Kil.) G60 — 26 AS15
Oronsay Pl, (Old Kil.) G60 — 26 AS15
Oronsay Sq, (Old Kil.) G60 — 26 AS15
Orr Sq, Pais. PA1 — 62 AU32
Orr St, G40 — 68 BV32
Orr St, Pais. PA1 — 62 AT32
Orr St, Pais. PA2 — 82 AU34
Orr Ter, (Neil.) G78 — 114 AS47
Orton Pl, G51 — 66 BJ31
Osborne Cres, (Thornton.) G74 — 119 BR50
Osborne St, G1 — 5 BS31
Osborne St, Clyde. G81 — 27 AW18
Osborne Vil, G44
  off Holmhead Rd — 103 BQ40
Osprey Cres, Pais. PA3 — 62 AT29
Osprey Dr, (Udd.) G71 — 93 CQ38
Osprey Rd, Pais. PA3 — 62 AT29
Osprey Vw, Pais. PA3 — 62 AT29
Ossian Av, Pais. PA1 — 64 BB32
Ossian Rd, G43 — 103 BN39
Ossian Way, Clyde. G81 — 45 AX21
Oswald St, G1 — 4 BR31
Oswald Wk, (Miln.) G62 — 12 BL13
Otago La, G12 — 67 BN27
Otago La N, G12
  off Otago St — 67 BN27
Otago Pk, (E.Kil.) G75 — 135 BW52
Otago St, G12 — 67 BN27
Othello, (E.Kil.) G74 — 122 CD48
Ottawa Cres, Clyde. G81 — 26 AT17
Otterburn Dr, (Giff.) G46 — 102 BL43
Otterswick Pl, G33 — 71 CE27
Oval, The, (Clark.) G76 — 103 BP44
Oval, The, (Glenb.) Coat. ML5 — 56 CS23
Overbrae Gdns, G15 — 28 BB16
Overbrae Pl, G15 — 28 BB16
Overdale Av, G42 — 87 BP37
Overdale Gdns, G42 — 87 BP37
Overdale St, G42 — 87 BP37
Overdale Vil, G42
  off Overdale St — 87 BP37
Overjohnstone Dr, Wis. ML2 — 129 DE49
Overlea Av, (Ruther.) G73 — 105 BZ39
Overlee Rd, (Clark.) G76 — 119 BN46
Overnewton Pl, G3 — 66 BM29
Overnewton Sq, G3
  off Blackie St — 66 BM28
Overnewton St, G3 — 66 BM28
Overton Cres, John. PA5 — 80 AK35
Overton Gro, (Camb.) G72
  off Hallside Rd — 107 CG41
Overton Rd, (Camb.) G72 — 107 CF41
Overton Rd, John. PA5 — 80 AJ35
Overton St, (Camb.) G72 — 107 CF41
Overtoun Ct, Clyde. G81
  off Dunswin Av — 26 AU18
Overtoun Dr, (Ruther.) G73 — 89 BW38
Overtoun Dr, Clyde. G81 — 26 AV17
Overtoun Rd, Clyde. G81 — 26 AU17

Overtown Av, G53 — 100 BC39
Overtown Pl, G31 — 69 BW32
Overtown St, G31 — 69 BW32
Overwood Dr, G44 — 104 BS39
Owen Av, (E.Kil.) G75 — 135 BZ54
Owendale Av, Bell. ML4 — 95 CX38
Owen Pk, (E.Kil.) G75 — 135 BY54
Owen St, Moth. ML1 — 128 DA45
O'Wood Av, Moth. ML1 — 112 DD39
Oxford Dr, (Linw.) Pais. PA3 — 60 AK31
Oxford La, G5 — 67 BR32
Oxford La, Renf. PA4 — 45 AY26
Oxford Rd, Renf. PA4 — 45 AY26
Oxford St, G5 — 4 BR31
Oxford St, (Kirk.) G66 — 17 CE13
Oxford St, Coat. ML5 — 74 CV31
Oxgang Pl, (Kirk.) G66 — 17 CG14
Oxton Dr, G52 — 64 BD32

**P**

Pacific Dr, G51 — 66 BL31
Pacific Quay, G51 — 66 BM30
Paddock, The, (Clark.) G76 — 119 BQ48
Paddock, The, Ham. ML3 — 126 CT47
Paddock St, Coat. ML5 — 95 CZ33
Paidmyre Cres, (Newt. M.)
  G77 — 117 BF50
Paidmyre Gdns, (Newt. M.)
  G77 — 117 BF50
Paidmyre Rd, (Newt. M.) G77 — 117 BE50
Paisley Rd, G5 — 4 BQ31
Paisley Rd, (Barr.) G78 — 99 AX40
Paisley Rd, Renf. PA4 — 63 AX28
Paisley Rd W, G51 — 66 BL32
Paisley Rd W, G52 — 66 BJ32
Palacecraig St, Coat. ML5 — 95 CW34
Palace Grds Rd, Ham. ML3 — 126 CV49
Paladin Av, G13 — 46 BD21
Palermo St, G21
  off Atlas Rd — 50 BU25
Palladium Pl, G14
  off Dumbarton Rd — 47 BF26
Palmer Av, G13 — 29 BF20
Palmerston, (E.Kil.) G75 — 135 BW54
Palmerston Pl, G3
  off Kelvinhaugh St — 66 BM29
Palmerston Pl, John. PA5 — 79 AE38
Palm Pl, (Udd.) G71 — 93 CR36
Pandora Way, (Udd.) G71 — 93 CQ38
Pankhurst Pl, (E.Kil.) G74 — 136 CB51
Panmure Cl, G22 — 49 BQ25
Panmure St, G20 — 49 BQ25
Parcville Way, G53 — 100 BB41
Park Av, G3 — 67 BP27
Park Av, (Miln.) G62 — 12 BJ12
Park Av, (Bishop.) G64 — 33 BW18
Park Av, (Kilsyth) G65 — 19 CN9
Park Av, (Kirk.) G66 — 17 CE13
Park Av, (Barr.) G78 — 99 AX44
Park Av, (Elder.) John. PA5 — 80 AL35
Park Av, Moth. ML1 — 112 DC40
Park Av, Pais. PA2 — 82 AS36
Park Bk, Ersk. PA8 — 25 AR20
Park Brae, Ersk. PA8 — 44 AS21
Parkbrae Gdns, G20 — 49 BQ23
Parkbrae Pl, G20 — 49 BQ23
Parkburn Av, (Kirk.) G66 — 16 CD14
Parkburn Ct, Ham. ML3 — 125 CP47
Parkburn Ind Est, Ham. ML3 — 125 CP47
Parkburn Rd, (Kilsyth) G65 — 7 CT4
Park Circ, G3 — 67 BN28
Park Circ La, G3 — 67 BN28

Park Circ Pl, G3 4 BP28
Park Ct, (Giff.) G46 102 BL43
Park Ct, (Bishop.) G64 33 BX18
Park Ct, Clyde. G81 26 AU17
Park Cres, (Bears.) G61 28 BD16
Park Cres, (Bishop.) G64 33 BW18
Park Cres, (Torr.) G66 15 BY12
Park Cres, (Blan.) G72 124 CL47
Park Cres, (Eagle.) G76 133 BN56
Park Cres, Air. ML6 76 DA29
Park Cres, (Inch.) Renf. PA4 44 AS22
Parkdale Gro, G53 100 BC42
Parkdale Way, G53 100 BC42
Park Dr, G3 67 BN28
Park Dr, (Ruther.) G73 89 BW38
Park Dr, (Thornton.) G74 120 BS50
Park Dr, Bell. ML4 111 CW41
Park Dr, Ersk. PA8 44 AS21
Park Dr, Ham. ML3 141 CY52
Parker Pl, (Kilsyth) G65 7 CT5
Parker Pl, Lark. ML9 144 DD57
Parker St, G14
*off Dumbarton Rd* 65 BG27
Parkfield, (E.Kil.) G75 136 CA56
Parkfoot St, (Kilsyth) G65 7 CT4
Park Gdns, G3 67 BN28
Park Gdns, (Kilb.) John. PA10 78 AD33
Park Gdns La, G3 67 BN28
Park Gate, G3 67 BN28
Park Gate, Ersk. PA8 43 AR21
Park Gate Pl, Bell. ML4 110 CV40
Park Glade, Ersk. PA8 43 AR21
Park Grn, Ersk. PA8 43 AR21
Park Gro, Ersk. PA8 44 AS21
Parkgrove Av, (Giff.) G46 102 BM42
Parkgrove Ct, (Giff.) G46 102 BM42
Parkgrove Ter, G3 67 BN28
Parkgrove Ter La, G3
*off Derby St* 67 BN28
Parkhall Rd, Clyde. G81 26 AV17
Parkhall St, (E.Kil.) G74 136 CB51
Parkhall Ter, Clyde. G81 26 AV16
Parkhead Cross, G31 69 BZ32
Parkhead La, Air. ML6
*off Parkhead St* 76 DC29
Parkhead St, Air. ML6 76 DC29
Parkhead St, Moth. ML1 128 DB48
Parkhill, Ersk. PA8 25 AR20
Parkhill Dr, (Ruther.) G73 89 BW38
Parkhill Rd, G43 86 BL37
Park Holdings, Ersk. PA8 43 AR22
Parkholm Av, G53 100 BB42
Parkholm Dr, G53 100 BB41
Park Holme Ct, Ham. ML3 126 CT48
Parkholm Gdns, G53 100 BC42
Parkholm Quad, G53 100 BC42
Parkhouse Path, G53
*off Whitehaugh Rd* 100 BD41
Parkhouse Rd, G53 100 BB41
Parkhouse Rd, (Barr.) G78 100 BB41
Parkinch, Ersk. PA8 44 AS21
Parklands Oval, G53 84 BB35
Parklands Rd, G44 103 BP42
Parklands Vw, G53 84 BB35
Park La, (Kilsyth) G65 7 CT5
Park La, (Blan.) G72 124 CM45
Parklea, (Bishop.) G64
*off Westfields* 32 BU18
Parklee Dr, (Carm.) G76 120 BU46
Parkmanor Av, G53 100 BB42
Parkmanor Grn, G53 100 BC42
Parkmeadow Av, G53 100 BC42
Parkmeadow Way, G53 100 BC42

Park Moor, Ersk. PA8 43 AR21
Parkneuk Rd, G43 102 BL41
Parkneuk Rd, (Blan.) G72 138 CJ51
Park Neuk St, Moth. ML1 128 DA45
Parknook Way, Lark. ML9
*off Muirshot Rd* 144 DD57
Park Pl, (Thornton.) G74 120 BS50
Park Pl, Bell. ML4 110 CU42
Park Pl, Coat. ML5
*off Kirkton Cres* 95 CZ33
Park Pl, John. PA5
*off Park Rd* 79 AH35
Park Quad, G3 67 BN28
Park Quad, Wis. ML2
*off Montgomery Cres* 143 DG52
Park Ridge, Ersk. PA8 25 AR20
Park Rd, G4 67 BN27
Park Rd, G32 91 CE37
Park Rd, (Giff.) G46 102 BL43
Park Rd, (Miln.) G62 12 BJ12
Park Rd, (Bishop.) G64 33 BW19
Park Rd, (Baill.) G69 73 CP32
Park Rd, (Muir.) G69 54 CL21
Park Rd, (Calder.) Air. ML6 96 DD35
Park Rd, Bell. ML4 111 CW41
Park Rd, Clyde. G81 26 AV17
Park Rd, Ham. ML3 126 CT50
Park Rd, John. PA5 79 AH35
Park Rd, Moth. ML1 112 DD43
Park Rd, Pais. PA2 82 AT36
Park Rd, (Inch.) Renf. PA4 44 AT22
Parksail, Ersk. PA8 44 AS22
Parksail Dr, Ersk. PA8 44 AS21
Parkside Gdns, G20 49 BQ23
Parkside Pl, G20 49 BQ23
Parkside Rd, Moth. ML1 127 CX47
Park St, (Kirk.) G66 18 CK14
Park St, Air. ML6 76 DA29
Park St, Coat. ML5 75 CX29
Park St, Moth. ML1 128 DA46
Park St, (New Stev.) Moth. ML1 112 DB42
Park St S, G3 67 BN28
Parks Vw, Ham. ML3 140 CT55
Park Ter, G3 67 BN28
Park Ter, (Giff.) G46 102 BL43
Park Ter, (E.Kil.) G74 136 CA52
Park Ter E La, G3 67 BN28
Park Ter La, G3 67 BN28
Park Top, Ersk. PA8 26 AS20
Parkvale Av, Ersk. PA8 26 AT20
Parkvale Cres, Ersk. PA8 44 AT21
Parkvale Dr, Ersk. PA8 44 AT21
Parkvale Gdns, Ersk. PA8 26 AT20
Parkvale Pl, Ersk. PA8 26 AT20
Parkvale Way, Ersk. PA8 44 AT21
Park Vw, (Kilb.) John. PA10 78 AC33
Park Vw, Lark. ML9 144 DD59
Park Vw, Pais. PA2 82 AT35
Parkview Av, (Kirk.) G66 17 CF14
Parkview Ct, (Kirk.) G66 17 CF14
Parkview Dr, (Stepps) G33 53 CG23
Parkview Dr, Coat. ML5 74 CU30
Parkville Dr, (Blan.) G72 125 CN47
Parkville Rd, Bell. ML4
*off Rosebank Rd* 95 CY38
Park Way, G32
*off Park Rd* 91 CE37
Park Way, (Cumb.) G67 22 DD9
Parkway Pl, Coat. ML5 74 CU32
Park Winding, Ersk. PA8 44 AS21
Park Wd, Ersk. PA8 26 AS20
Parkwood Lea, Ham. ML3 125 CQ47
Parkwood Ter, Ham. ML3 125 CQ47

Parnell St, Air. ML6 76 DB32
Parnie St, G1 5 BS31
Parry Ter, (E.Kil.) G75 135 BX52
Parsonage Row, G1 5 BT30
Parsonage Sq, G4 5 BT31
Parson St, G4 5 BU29
Partick Br St, G11 66 BL27
Partickhill Av, G11 66 BK27
Partickhill Ct, G11 48 BK26
Partickhill Rd, G11 48 BK26
Patchy Pk, Lark. ML9 144 DC61
Paterson Pl, (Bears.) G61 11 BE13
Paterson's Laun, (Torr.) G64 14 BU14
Paterson St, G5 67 BQ32
Paterson St, Moth. ML1 128 DA46
Paterson Ter, (E.Kil.) G75 135 BZ54
Pathhead Gdns, G33 52 CB23
Pathhead Rd, (Carm.) G76 120 BT46
Patna Ct, Ham. ML3
*off Ochiltree Dr* 139 CN52
Patna St, G40 89 BX34
Paton Ct, Wis. ML2
*off Shaw Cres* 143 DF52
Paton St, G31 69 BX30
Patrickbank Cres, John. PA5 80 AL36
Patrickbank Gdns, John. PA5 80 AL36
Patrickbank Vw, John. PA5 80 AL36
Patrickbank Wynd, John. PA5 80 AM36
Patrick St, Pais. PA2 82 AV34
Patterton Dr, (Barr.) G78 99 AZ43
Pattison St, Clyde. G81 26 AU18
Paxton Ct, (E.Kil.) G74
*off Canonbie Av* 122 CB49
Paxton Cres, (E.Kil.) G74
*off Canonbie Av* 122 CB49
Payne St, G4 68 BS27
Peacock Av, Pais. PA2 81 AP35
Peacock Cross Ind Pk,
Ham. ML3 126 CS49
Peacock Dr, Ham. ML3 126 CS49
Peacock Dr, Pais. PA2 81 AP34
Pearce La, G51
*off Pearce St* 66 BJ29
Pearce St, G51 66 BJ29
Pearl Rd, Bell. ML4
*off Sapphire Rd* 111 CX42
Pearson Dr, Renf. PA4 63 AZ27
Pearson Pl, (Linw.) Pais. PA3 60 AK32
Peathill Av, (Chry.) G69 36 CK20
Peathill St, G21 50 BS26
Peat Pl, G53
*off Peat Rd* 100 BC40
Peat Rd, G53 100 BD39
Pedmyre La, (Carm.) G76 120 BS46
Peebles Dr, (Ruther.) G73 89 BZ38
Peebles Path, Coat. ML5 95 CZ34
Peel Av, Moth. ML1 128 DA49
Peel Glen Gdns, G15 28 BC16
Peel Glen Rd, G15 28 BC17
Peel Glen Rd, (Bears.) G61 28 BC15
Peel La, G11 66 BK27
Peel Pk Pl, (E.Kil.) G74 134 BV51
Peel Pl, (Both.) G71 109 CQ42
Peel Pl, Coat. ML5 74 CT32
Peel Rd, (Thornton.) G74 133 BR51
Peel St, G11 66 BK27
Peel Vw, Clyde. G81
*off Kirkoswald Dr* 27 AZ18
Pegasus Rd, Bell. ML4 112 DA40
Pegasus Rd, Pais. PA1 60 AM32
Peinchorran, Ersk. PA8 44 AS22
Peiter Pl, (Blan.) G72
*off Burnbrae Rd* 124 CL46

| Name | Page | Grid |
|---|---|---|
| Pelham Ct, (E.Kil.) G74 | 134 | BT53 |
| Pembroke, (E.Kil.) G74 | 123 | CF49 |
| Pembroke St, G3 | 4 | BP29 |
| Pembury Cres, Ham. ML3 | 139 | CP54 |
| Pencaitland Dr, G32 | 90 | CC34 |
| Pencaitland Gro, G32 | 90 | CC35 |
| Pencaitland Pl, G23 | 31 | BN20 |
| Pendale Ri, G45 | 104 | BT42 |
| Pendeen Cres, G33 | 71 | CG32 |
| Pendeen Pl, G33 | 71 | CH31 |
| Pendeen Rd, G33 | 71 | CG32 |
| Pendicle Cres, (Bears.) G61 | 29 | BF18 |
| Pendicle Rd, (Bears.) G61 | 29 | BF18 |
| Pendle Ct, (Gart.) G69 | 55 | CP23 |
| Penfold Cres, (E.Kil.) G75 | 135 | BZ53 |
| Penicuik St, G32 | 69 | BZ31 |
| Penilee Rd, G52 | 63 | AZ29 |
| Penilee Rd, Pais. PA1 | 64 | BA32 |
| Penilee Ter, G52 | 64 | BA31 |
| Peninver Dr, G51 | 65 | BF29 |
| Penman Av, (Ruther.) G73 | 88 | BV37 |
| Pennan, Ersk. PA8 | 25 | AQ19 |
| Pennan Pl, G14 | 46 | BC24 |
| Penneld Rd, G52 | 64 | BB32 |
| Pennine Gro, (Chap.) Air. ML6 | 97 | DH36 |
| Pennyroyal Ct, (E.Kil.) G74 | 121 | BZ50 |
| Penrith Av, (Giff.) G46 | 102 | BL42 |
| Penrith Dr, G12 | 48 | BJ23 |
| Penrith Pl, (E.Kil.) G75 | 134 | BV55 |
| Penryn Gdns, G32 | 91 | CF34 |
| Penston Rd, G33 | 71 | CF29 |
| Pentland Av, (Linw.) Pais. PA3 | 60 | AJ31 |
| Pentland Ct, (Barr.) G78 | | |
|   off Pentland Dr | 99 | AX44 |
| Pentland Ct, Air. ML6 | 76 | DD21 |
| Pentland Cres, Lark. ML9 | 142 | DB56 |
| Pentland Cres, Pais. PA2 | 82 | AT37 |
| Pentland Dr, (Bishop.) G64 | 33 | BZ19 |
| Pentland Dr, (Barr.) G78 | 99 | AX44 |
| Pentland Dr, Renf. PA4 | 63 | AX29 |
| Pentland Pl, (Bears.) G61 | 10 | BD14 |
| Pentland Rd, G43 | 102 | BL40 |
| Pentland Rd, (Chry.) G69 | 36 | CM20 |
| Pentland Rd, Wis. ML2 | 129 | DG49 |
| Pentland Way, Ham. ML3 | 139 | CR54 |
| Penzance Way, (Chry.) G69 | 37 | CN18 |
| Peockland Gdns, John. PA5 | 80 | AJ34 |
| Peockland Pl, John. PA5 | | |
|   off Thorn Brae | 80 | AJ34 |
| Peploe Dr, (E.Kil.) G74 | 123 | CF48 |
| Percy Dr, (Giff.) G46 | 102 | BL44 |
| Percy Rd, Renf. PA4 | 63 | AW29 |
| Percy St, G51 | | |
|   off Clifford St | 66 | BM31 |
| Percy St, Lark. ML9 | 144 | DC57 |
| Perran Gdns, (Chry.) G69 | 37 | CN19 |
| Perth Av, Air. ML6 | 76 | DC32 |
| Perth Cres, Clyde. G81 | 26 | AT16 |
| Perth St, G3 | | |
|   off Argyle St | 4 | BP30 |
| Peter D Stirling Rd, (Kirk.) G66 | 17 | CF12 |
| Petersburn Pl, Air. ML6 | | |
|   off Petersburn Rd | 77 | DF31 |
| Petersburn Rd, Air. ML6 | 77 | DE31 |
| Petershill Ct, G21 | 51 | BY25 |
| Petershill Dr, G21 | 51 | BX25 |
| Petershill Pl, G21 | 51 | BX25 |
| Petershill Rd, G21 | 50 | BV26 |
| Peterson Dr, G13 | 46 | BA21 |
| Peterson Gdns, G13 | 46 | BA21 |
| Petition Pl, (Udd.) G71 | 109 | CQ40 |
| Pettigrew St, G32 | 70 | CC32 |
| Petty Ct, (E.Kil.) G74 | 134 | BT53 |
| Peveril Av, G41 | 86 | BM36 |
| Peveril Av, (Ruther.) G73 | 105 | BY40 |
| Peveril Ct, (Ruther.) G73 | 105 | BY40 |
| Pharonhill St, G31 | | |
| Philip Murray Rd, Bell. ML4 | 110 | CT39 |
| Philipshill Gate, (E.Kil.) G74 | 120 | BU50 |
| Philipshill Rd, (Clark.) G76 | 120 | BU50 |
| Phoenix Business Pk, Pais. PA1 | 61 | AN32 |
| Phoenix Ct, (E.Kil.) G74 | | |
|   off Bosworth Rd | 123 | CE48 |
| Phoenix Cres, (Strathclyde | | |
|   Bus. Pk.) Bell. ML4 | 94 | CU37 |
| Phoenix Ind Est, Pais. PA3 | 62 | AU29 |
| Phoenix Pk Ter, G4 | | |
|   off Corn St | 67 | BR27 |
| Phoenix Pl, (Elder.) John. PA5 | 80 | AM34 |
| Phoenix Pl, Moth. ML1 | 112 | DC42 |
| Phoenix Retail Pk, The, | | |
|   Pais. PA1 | 81 | AN33 |
| Phoenix Rd, G4 | | |
|   off Great Western Rd | 4 | BQ28 |
| Phoenix Rd, Bell. ML4 | 112 | DA40 |
| Piccadilly St, G3 | 4 | BP30 |
| Pickerstonhill, Moth. ML1 | 113 | DG41 |
| Picketlaw Dr, (Carm.) G76 | 120 | BT46 |
| Picketlaw Fm Rd, (Carm.) G76 | 120 | BS46 |
| Piershill St, G32 | 70 | CB30 |
| Pikeman Rd, G13 | 47 | BE23 |
| Pillans Ct, Ham. ML3 | 125 | CQ47 |
| Pilmuir Av, G44 | 103 | BP41 |
| Pilmuir Rd, (Newt. M.) G77 | 130 | BC51 |
| Pilrig St, G32 | 70 | CA30 |
| Pilton Rd, G15 | 28 | BC17 |
| Pine Av, (Camb.) G72 | 107 | CH42 |
| Pine Cl, (Cumb.) G67 | 23 | DG9 |
| Pine Ct, (Cumb.) G67 | 23 | DG9 |
| Pine Ct, (E.Kil.) G75 | 135 | BX56 |
| Pine Ct, Coat. ML5 | | |
|   off Ailsa Rd | 94 | CV33 |
| Pine Cres, (Cumb.) G67 | 23 | DG9 |
| Pine Cres, (E.Kil.) G75 | 135 | BX56 |
| Pine Cres, Ham. ML3 | 139 | CQ54 |
| Pine Cres, John. PA5 | 80 | AJ36 |
| Pine Gro, (Cumb.) G67 | 23 | DG9 |
| Pine Gro, (Baill.) G69 | 73 | CQ31 |
| Pine Gro, (Udd.) G71 | 93 | CR37 |
| Pinegrove, (Calder.) Air. ML6 | 96 | DD35 |
| Pinelands, (Bishop.) G64 | 33 | BW17 |
| Pine Pk, Ham. ML3 | 140 | CU52 |
| Pine Pl, G5 | 88 | BS33 |
| Pine Pl, (Cumb.) G67 | 23 | DG9 |
| Pine Quad, (Chap.) Air. ML6 | 97 | DG34 |
| Pine Rd, (Cumb.) G67 | 23 | DG9 |
| Pine Rd, Clyde. G81 | 26 | AT17 |
| Pine St, Air. ML6 | 77 | DF30 |
| Pine St, Pais. PA2 | 83 | AW35 |
| Pineview Ct, G15 | 28 | BD18 |
| Pinewood Av, (Kirk.) G66 | 34 | CC16 |
| Pinewood Ct, (Kirk.) G66 | 34 | CC16 |
| Pinewood Pl, (Kirk.) G66 | 34 | CC16 |
| Pinewood Sq, G15 | 28 | BD17 |
| Pinkerton Av, (Ruther.) G73 | 88 | BU37 |
| Pinkerton La, Renf. PA4 | 63 | AZ28 |
| Pinkston Dr, G21 | 68 | BU27 |
| Pinkston Rd, G4 | 50 | BT26 |
| Pinkston Rd, G21 | 50 | BT26 |
| Pinmore Path, G53 | | |
|   off Seamill St | 100 | BB40 |
| Pinmore Pl, G53 | 100 | BB39 |
| Pinmore St, G53 | 100 | BB39 |
| Pinwherry Dr, G33 | 52 | CB23 |
| Pinwherry Pl, (Both.) G71 | 109 | CQ42 |
| Piper Rd, Air. ML6 | 77 | DE32 |
| Pirnie Pl, (Kilsyth) G65 | 7 | CT5 |
| Pirnmill Av, Moth. ML1 | 127 | CX46 |
| Pitcairn Cres, (E.Kil.) G75 | 134 | BV53 |
| Pitcairn Gro, (E.Kil.) G75 | 135 | BW53 |
| Pitcairn Pl, (E.Kil.) G75 | 134 | BV53 |
| Pitcairn St, G31 | 90 | CA33 |
| Pitcairn Ter, Ham. ML3 | 125 | CQ49 |
| Pitcaple Dr, G43 | 102 | BK39 |
| Pitlochry Dr, G52 | 84 | BD33 |
| Pitlochry Dr, Lark. ML9 | 145 | DE60 |
| Pitmedden Rd, (Bishop.) G64 | 33 | BZ19 |
| Pitmilly Rd, G15 | 29 | BE17 |
| Pitreavie Ct, Ham. ML3 | 139 | CR53 |
| Pitreavie Pl, G33 | 71 | CE27 |
| Pit Rd, (Kirk.) G66 | 18 | CK14 |
| Pit Rd, (Bellshill Ind. Est.) | | |
|   Bell. ML4 | 110 | CV39 |
| Pitt St, G2 | 4 | BQ30 |
| Pladda Rd, Renf. PA4 | 63 | AZ28 |
| Pladda St, Moth. ML1 | 127 | CX45 |
| Plaintrees Ct, Pais. PA2 | 82 | AU35 |
| Plane Pl, (Udd.) G71 | 93 | CR36 |
| Planetree Pl, John. PA5 | 80 | AJ36 |
| Planetree Rd, Clyde. G81 | 27 | AW17 |
| Plantation Av, Moth. ML1 | 112 | DD39 |
| Plantation Pk Gdns, G51 | | |
|   off Clifford La | 66 | BM32 |
| Plantation Sq, G51 | 67 | BN31 |
| Plant St, G31 | 69 | BY31 |
| Platthorn Ct, (E.Kil.) G74 | 136 | CB52 |
| Platthorn Dr, (E.Kil.) G74 | 136 | CB52 |
| Platthorn Rd, (E.Kil.) G74 | | |
|   off Avondale Av | 136 | CB52 |
| Playfair St, G40 | 89 | BW34 |
| Pleaknowe Cres, (Chry.) G69 | 37 | CN19 |
| Pleamuir Pl, (Cumb.) G68 | 21 | CY12 |
| Plean St, G14 | 46 | BC24 |
| Pleasance La, G43 | | |
|   off Pleasance St | 86 | BL38 |
| Pleasance St, G43 | 86 | BL37 |
| Pleasance Way, G43 | 86 | BM38 |
| Plover Dr, (E.Kil.) G75 | 135 | BW56 |
| Plover Pl, John. PA5 | 79 | AE38 |
| Pochard Way, (Strathclyde | | |
|   Bus. Pk.) Bell. ML4 | 94 | CV37 |
| Poets Vw, (Kirk.) G66 | 17 | CH14 |
| Pointhouse Rd, G3 | 67 | BN30 |
| Polbae Cres, (Eagle.) G76 | 132 | BM56 |
| Pollock Av, (Eagle.) G76 | 133 | BN56 |
| Pollock Av, (Hillhouse Ind. Est.) | | |
|   Ham. ML3 | 125 | CQ49 |
| Pollock Rd, (Bears.) G61 | 30 | BJ18 |
| Pollock Rd, (Newt. M.) G77 | 117 | BE49 |
| Pollock St, Moth. ML1 | 128 | DA46 |
| Pollok Av, G43 | 86 | BK37 |
| Pollok Castle Est, (Newt. M.) | | |
|   G77 | 116 | BC47 |
| Pollok Dr, (Bishop.) G64 | 32 | BU20 |
| Pollok La, (E.Kil.) G74 | 122 | CD50 |
| Pollok Pl, (E.Kil.) G74 | 122 | CD50 |
| Pollokshaws Rd, G41 | 87 | BQ35 |
| Pollokshaws Rd, G43 | 86 | BK38 |
| Pollokshields Sq, G41 | | |
|   off Glencairn Dr | 87 | BP35 |
| Polmadie Av, G5 | 88 | BT35 |
| Polmadie Ind Est, G5 | 88 | BU35 |
| Polmadie Rd, G5 | 88 | BT35 |
| Polmadie Rd, G42 | 88 | BT35 |
| Polmadie St, G42 | 88 | BS36 |
| Polnoon Av, G13 | 46 | BC23 |
| Polnoon Dr, (Eagle.) G76 | 133 | BN56 |
| Polquhap Ct, G53 | 84 | BC37 |

| | | |
|---|---|---|
| Polquhap Gdns, G53 | 84 | BC37 |
| Polquhap Pl, G53 | 84 | BC37 |
| Polquhap Rd, G53 | 84 | BC37 |
| Polson Dr, John. PA5 | 79 | AG35 |
| Polsons Cres, Pais. PA2 | 82 | AT35 |
| Polwarth La, G12 | 48 | BK25 |
| Polwarth St, G12 | 48 | BK26 |
| Pomona Pl, Ham. ML3 | | |
| off Gilmour Dr | 139 | CP51 |
| Poplar Av, G11 | | |
| off Crow Rd | 47 | BH25 |
| Poplar Av, (Newt. M.) G77 | 117 | BG50 |
| Poplar Av, Bish. PA7 | 24 | AK19 |
| Poplar Av, John. PA5 | 79 | AH36 |
| Poplar Ct, Coat. ML5 | | |
| off Ailsa Rd | 94 | CV33 |
| Poplar Cres, Bish. PA7 | 24 | AK19 |
| Poplar Dr, (Kirk.) G66 | 34 | CC16 |
| Poplar Dr, Clyde. G81 | 26 | AV16 |
| Poplar Gdns, (E.Kil.) G75 | 135 | BY56 |
| Poplar Pl, (Udd.) G71 | | |
| off Laburnum Rd | 94 | CT37 |
| Poplar Pl, (Blan.) G72 | 108 | CL44 |
| Poplar Pl, (Holytown) Moth. ML1 | 112 | DD41 |
| Poplar Rd, G41 | | |
| off Urrdale Rd | 66 | BK32 |
| Poplars, The, (Bears.) G61 | 11 | BF13 |
| Poplar St, Air. ML6 | 77 | DF30 |
| Poplar Way, (Camb.) G72 | 107 | CH42 |
| Poplin St, G40 | 88 | BV34 |
| Porchester St, G33 | 71 | CF27 |
| Portal Rd, G13 | 47 | BE21 |
| Port Dundas Ind Est, G4 | 68 | BS27 |
| Port Dundas Pl, G2 | 5 | BS29 |
| Port Dundas Rd, G4 | 4 | BR28 |
| Port Dundas Trd Centres, G4 | 68 | BS27 |
| Porterfield Rd, Renf. PA4 | 45 | AX26 |
| Porters La, (Chap.) Air. ML6 | | |
| off Aitkenhead Rd | 97 | DF35 |
| Porter St, G51 | 66 | BL32 |
| Porters Well, (Udd.) G71 | 109 | CN40 |
| Portessie, Ersk. PA8 | 25 | AQ19 |
| Portland Pk, Ham. ML3 | 140 | CU51 |
| Portland Pl, Ham. ML3 | 140 | CU51 |
| Portland Rd, (Cumb.) G68 | 9 | DB8 |
| Portland Sq, Ham. ML3 | | |
| off Portland Pl | 140 | CU51 |
| Portland St, Coat. ML5 | 75 | CX29 |
| Portland St, Pais. PA2 | 83 | AX34 |
| Portland Wynd, Lark. ML9 | | |
| off Muirshot Rd | 144 | DD57 |
| Portlethen, Ersk. PA8 | 25 | AQ19 |
| Portman Pl, G12 | | |
| off Cowan St | 67 | BN27 |
| Portman St, G41 | 67 | BN32 |
| Portmarnock Dr, G23 | | |
| off Fairhaven Rd | 49 | BN21 |
| Portreath Rd, (Chry.) G69 | 37 | CP18 |
| Portree Av, Coat. ML5 | 94 | CU33 |
| Portree Pl, G15 | 28 | BA17 |
| Portsoy, Ersk. PA8 | 25 | AQ19 |
| Portsoy Av, G13 | | |
| off Wyvis Av | 46 | BB21 |
| Portsoy Pl, G13 | 46 | BA21 |
| Port St, G3 | 4 | BP29 |
| Portugal La, G5 | | |
| off Bedford St | 67 | BR32 |
| Portugal St, G5 | 67 | BR32 |
| Portwell, Ham. ML3 | | |
| off Church St | 126 | CU49 |
| Possil Cross, G22 | 50 | BS26 |
| Possil Rd, G4 | 67 | BR27 |

| | | |
|---|---|---|
| Postgate, Ham. ML3 | 126 | CU49 |
| Potassels Rd, (Muir.) G69 | 54 | CL22 |
| Potrail Pl, Ham. ML3 | 125 | CQ50 |
| Potter Cl, G32 | 90 | CA34 |
| Potter Gro, G32 | 90 | CA34 |
| Potterhill Av, Pais. PA2 | 82 | AU37 |
| Potterhill Rd, G53 | 84 | BD35 |
| Potter Path, G32 | | |
| off Rattray St | 90 | CA34 |
| Potter Pl, G32 | 90 | CA34 |
| Potter St, G32 | 90 | CA34 |
| Potts Way, Moth. ML1 | 111 | CY44 |
| Powbrone, (E.Kil.) G75 | 136 | CA56 |
| Powburn Cres, (Udd.) G71 | 92 | CM38 |
| Powfoot St, G31 | 69 | BZ32 |
| Powforth Cl, Lark. ML9 | 144 | DA58 |
| Powrie St, G33 | 53 | CE26 |
| Prentice La, (Udd.) G71 | 93 | CQ37 |
| Prentice Rd, Moth. ML1 | 127 | CX48 |
| Prestonfield, (Miln.) G62 | 11 | BG12 |
| Preston Pl, G42 | 87 | BR35 |
| Preston St, G42 | 87 | BR35 |
| Prestwick Ct, (Cumb.) G68 | 22 | DB9 |
| Prestwick Pl, (Newt. M.) G77 | 118 | BJ49 |
| Prestwick St, G53 | 100 | BC39 |
| Priestfield Ind Est, (Blan.) G72 | 124 | CM48 |
| Priestfield St, (Blan.) G72 | 124 | CL47 |
| Priesthill Av, G53 | 101 | BE39 |
| Priesthill Cres, G53 | 101 | BE39 |
| Priesthill Gdns, G53 | 101 | BE39 |
| Priesthill Rd, G53 | 100 | BD39 |
| Priestley Way, (Camb.) G72 | 90 | CA37 |
| Primrose Av, Bell. ML4 | 95 | CW38 |
| Primrose Av, Lark. ML9 | 144 | DC60 |
| Primrose Ct, G14 | | |
| off Dumbarton Rd | 47 | BF26 |
| Primrose Cres, Moth. ML1 | | |
| off Gavin St | 128 | DA48 |
| Primrose Pl, (Cumb.) G67 | 21 | CX14 |
| Primrose Pl, (Udd.) G71 | 94 | CS37 |
| Primrose St, G14 | 47 | BE26 |
| Prince Albert Rd, G12 | 48 | BK26 |
| Prince Edward St, G42 | 87 | BQ35 |
| Prince of Wales Gdns, G20 | | |
| off Crosbie St | 48 | BL21 |
| Prince's Dock, G51 | 66 | BL30 |
| Princes Gdns, G12 | 48 | BK26 |
| Princes Gate, (Both.) G71 | 109 | CN41 |
| Princes Gate, (Ruther.) G73 | 89 | BW37 |
| Princes Gate, Ham. ML3 | 125 | CP47 |
| Princes Mall, (E.Kil.) G74 | | |
| off East Kilbride Shop Cen | 136 | CB52 |
| Princes Pl, G12 | 48 | BL26 |
| Princess Anne Quad, Moth. ML1 off Woodhall Av | 112 | DB40 |
| Princess Cres, Pais. PA1 | 63 | AX32 |
| Princess Dr, (Baill.) G69 | 73 | CQ32 |
| Princess Pk, (Erskine Hosp.) Bish. PA7 | 24 | AN17 |
| Princes Sq, G1 | | |
| off Buchanan St | 5 | BS30 |
| Princes Sq, (E.Kil.) G74 | | |
| off East Kilbride Shop Cen | 136 | CA52 |
| Princes Sq, (Barr.) G78 | 99 | AZ42 |
| Princess Rd, Moth. ML1 | 112 | DB41 |
| Princes St, (Ruther.) G73 | 89 | BW37 |
| Princes St, Moth. ML1 | 128 | DA45 |
| Princes Ter, G12 | 48 | BL26 |
| Printers Land, (Clark.) G76 | | |
| off Main St | 119 | BQ47 |
| Priorwood Ct, G13 | 47 | BF23 |
| Priorwood Gdns, G13 | 47 | BE23 |
| Priorwood Gate, (Newt. M.) G77 | 116 | BC49 |

| | | |
|---|---|---|
| Priorwood Pl, G13 | 47 | BF23 |
| Priorwood Rd, (Newt. M.) G77 | 116 | BC49 |
| Priorwood Way, (Newt. M.) G77 | 116 | BC49 |
| Priory Av, Pais. PA3 | 63 | AW30 |
| Priory Dr, (Udd.) G71 | 92 | CM38 |
| Priory Pl, G13 | 47 | BF22 |
| Priory Pl, (Cumb.) G68 | 20 | CU12 |
| Priory Rd, G13 | 47 | BF22 |
| Priory St, (Blan.) G72 | 124 | CM46 |
| Priory Ter, Wis. ML2 | 143 | DE51 |
| Professors Sq, G12 | 66 | BM27 |
| Prosen St, G32 | 90 | CB34 |
| Prospect Av, (Udd.) G71 | 109 | CN39 |
| Prospect Av, (Camb.) G72 | 106 | CB39 |
| Prospect Ct, (Blan.) G72 | 124 | CM48 |
| Prospect Dr, (Ashgill) Lark. ML9 | 145 | DH61 |
| Prospecthill Circ, G42 | 88 | BT36 |
| Prospecthill Cres, G42 | 88 | BU37 |
| Prospecthill Dr, G42 | 88 | BS37 |
| Prospecthill Gro, G42 | 87 | BQ37 |
| Prospecthill Pl, G42 | 88 | BU37 |
| Prospecthill Rd, G42 | 87 | BQ37 |
| Prospecthill Sq, G42 | 88 | BT37 |
| Prospecthill Way, G42 | | |
| off Prospecthill Gro | 87 | BQ37 |
| Prospect Rd, G43 | 86 | BM37 |
| Prospect Rd, (Dullatur) G68 | 8 | CY7 |
| Provand Hall Cres, (Baill.) G69 | 92 | CK34 |
| Provanhill St, G21 | 68 | BV28 |
| Provanmill Pl, G33 | | |
| off Provanmill Rd | 51 | BZ26 |
| Provanmill Rd, G33 | 51 | BZ26 |
| Provan Rd, G33 | 69 | BY28 |
| Provan Wk, G34 | 71 | CG28 |
| Provost Cl, John. PA5 | | |
| off High St | 79 | AH34 |
| Provost Driver Ct, Renf. PA4 | 63 | AZ27 |
| Provost Gate, Lark. ML9 | 144 | DC58 |
| Provost Way, G5 | 88 | BU34 |
| Purdie, (E.Kil.) G74 | 123 | CF48 |
| Purdie St, Ham. ML3 | 125 | CQ48 |
| Purdon St, G11 | 66 | BK27 |
| Pyatshaw Rd, Lark. ML9 | 144 | DD60 |

## Q

| | | |
|---|---|---|
| Quadrant, The, (Clark.) G76 | 119 | BP45 |
| Quadrant Rd, G43 | 103 | BN40 |
| Quadrant Shop Cen, Coat. ML5 | 8 | CW30 |
| Quarrelton Rd, John. PA5 | 79 | AG35 |
| Quarry Av, (Camb.) G72 | 107 | CG42 |
| Quarrybank, (Kilb.) John. PA10 | 79 | AE35 |
| Quarrybrae Av, (Clark.) G76 | 118 | BM46 |
| Quarrybrae Gdns, (Udd.) G71 | | |
| off Roman Way | 110 | CS39 |
| Quarrybrae St, G31 | 70 | CA34 |
| Quarry Dr, (Kirk.) G66 | 17 | CH13 |
| Quarryknowe, (Ruther.) G73 | 88 | BV38 |
| Quarryknowe Pl, Bell. ML4 | 110 | CV42 |
| Quarryknowe St, G31 | 70 | CA32 |
| Quarryknowe St, Clyde. G81 | 10 | BA14 |
| Quarry Pk, (E.Kil.) G75 | 136 | CA53 |
| Quarry Pl, (Camb.) G72 | 106 | CA39 |
| Quarry Pl, Ham. ML3 | | |
| off Quarry St | 126 | CU50 |
| Quarry Rd, (E.Kil.) G75 | 135 | BZ56 |
| Quarry Rd, (Barr.) G78 | 99 | AX41 |
| Quarry Rd, Air. ML6 | 76 | DC28 |
| Quarry Rd, Lark. ML9 | 144 | DC59 |
| Quarry Rd, Pais. PA2 | 82 | AV36 |
| Quarryside St, (Glenm.) Air. ML6 | 57 | CZ25 |
| Quarry St, Coat. ML5 | 75 | CZ30 |
| Quarry St, Ham. ML3 | 126 | CU50 |

| | | |
|---|---|---|
| Quarry St, John. PA5 | 79 | AH34 |
| Quarry St, Lark. ML9 | 144 | DD60 |
| Quarry St, Moth. ML1 | 112 | DC41 |
| Quarrywood Av, G21 | 51 | BY25 |
| Quarrywood Rd, G21 | 51 | BZ25 |
| Quay Rd, (Ruther.) G73 | 89 | BW36 |
| Quay Rd N, (Ruther.) G73 | 89 | BW36 |
| Quebec Dr, (E.Kil.) G75 | 135 | BY52 |
| Quebec Grn, (E.Kil.) G75 | 135 | BY52 |
| Quebec Ho, Clyde. G81 | | |
| off Perth Cres | 26 | AT15 |
| Quebec Wynd, G32 | 91 | CE37 |
| Queen Elizabeth Av, G52 | 64 | BA30 |
| Queen Elizabeth Ct, Clyde. G81 | 27 | AW18 |
| Queen Elizabeth Ct, Moth. ML1 | | |
| off Ladywell Rd | 127 | CZ46 |
| Queen Elizabeth Gdns, G5 | 88 | BS33 |
| Queen Elizabeth Sq, G5 | 88 | BT33 |
| Queen Margaret Ct, G20 | | |
| off Fergus Dr | 49 | BN25 |
| Queen Margaret Dr, G12 | 48 | BM26 |
| Queen Margaret Dr, G20 | 48 | BM26 |
| Queen Margaret Rd, G20 | 49 | BN25 |
| Queen Mary Av, G42 | 87 | BQ36 |
| Queen Mary Av, Clyde. G81 | 27 | AZ19 |
| Queen Mary Gdns, Clyde. G81 | 27 | AW18 |
| Queen Mary St, G40 | 88 | BV33 |
| Queens Av, (Camb.) G72 | 106 | CD39 |
| Queensbank Av, (Gart.) G69 | 55 | CN22 |
| Queensberry Av, (Bears.) G61 | 11 | BG14 |
| Queensberry Av, (Clark.) G76 | 119 | BN46 |
| Queensborough Gdns, G12 | 48 | BJ25 |
| Queensbury Av, G52 | 64 | BB30 |
| Queensby Av, (Baill.) G69 | 72 | CK32 |
| Queensby Dr, (Baill.) G69 | 72 | CK31 |
| Queensby Pl, (Baill.) G69 | 72 | CL31 |
| Queensby Rd, (Baill.) G69 | 72 | CK31 |
| Queens Ct, (Miln.) G62 | 12 | BJ13 |
| Queens Cres, G4 | 67 | BP27 |
| Queen's Cres, (Baill.) G69 | 73 | CP32 |
| Queens Cres, (Chap.) Air. ML6 | 97 | DF34 |
| Queens Cres, Bell. ML4 | | |
| off Hamilton Rd | 110 | CV41 |
| Queens Cres, Moth. ML1 | 112 | DB41 |
| Queens Cross, G20 | 49 | BP25 |
| Queensdale Av, Lark. ML9 | 144 | DD61 |
| Queensdale Rd, Lark. ML9 | 144 | DD61 |
| Queens Dr, G42 | 87 | BP35 |
| Queens Dr, (Cumb.) G68 | 9 | DB7 |
| Queens Dr, Bish. PA7 | 24 | AK17 |
| Queens Dr, Ham. ML3 | 140 | CT55 |
| Queens Dr La, G42 | 87 | BQ36 |
| Queensferry St, G5 | 88 | BU35 |
| Queens Gdns, G12 | | |
| off Victoria Cres Rd | 48 | BL26 |
| Queens Gate, (Clark.) G76 | 119 | BN45 |
| Queens Gate La, G12 | | |
| off Victoria Cres Rd | 48 | BL26 |
| Queens Gro, (Lenz.) G66 | 35 | CE17 |
| Queenside Cres, Ersk. PA8 | 25 | AP20 |
| Queensland Ct, G52 | 65 | BE31 |
| Queensland Dr, G52 | 65 | BE31 |
| Queensland Gdns, G52 | 65 | BE31 |
| Queensland La E, G52 | 65 | BE31 |
| Queensland La W, G52 | 65 | BE31 |
| Queenslie Ind Est, G33 | 71 | CE29 |
| Queenslie St, G33 | 69 | BZ27 |
| Queens Pk Av, G42 | 87 | BQ36 |
| Queens Pl, G12 | 48 | BL26 |
| Queen Sq, G41 | 87 | BP35 |
| Queens Rd, (Elder.) John. PA5 | 80 | AL35 |
| Queens St, Ham. ML3 | 125 | CQ48 |
| Queen St, G1 | 5 | BS30 |

| | | |
|---|---|---|
| Queen St, (Kirk.) G66 | 17 | CE13 |
| Queen St, (Ruther.) G73 | 89 | BW37 |
| Queen St, Ham. ML3 | 125 | CQ48 |
| Queen St, Moth. ML1 | 128 | DA46 |
| Queen St, Pais. PA1 | 82 | AS33 |
| Queen St, Renf. PA4 | 45 | AZ26 |
| Queen's Vw, (Torr.) G64 | 15 | BX13 |
| Queensway, (E.Kil.) G74 | 135 | BY52 |
| Queensway, (E.Kil.) G75 | 136 | CA53 |
| Queen Victoria Ct, G14 | | |
| off Queen Victoria Dr | 47 | BE25 |
| Queen Victoria Dr, G13 | 47 | BE24 |
| Queen Victoria Dr, G14 | 47 | BE25 |
| Queen Victoria Gate, G13 | 47 | BE24 |
| Queen Victoria St, Air. ML6 | 76 | DB30 |
| Queenzieburn Ind Est, (Kilsyth) | | |
| G65 | 6 | CP6 |
| Quendale Dr, G32 | 90 | CB34 |
| Quentin St, G41 | 87 | BN36 |
| Quinton Gdns, (Baill.) G69 | 72 | CJ32 |

### R

| | | |
|---|---|---|
| Raasay Cres, Air. ML6 | 77 | DG31 |
| Raasay Dr, Pais. PA2 | 82 | AT38 |
| Raasay Gdns, (Newt. M.) G77 | 116 | BD48 |
| Raasay Pl, G22 | 50 | BS21 |
| Raasay St, G22 | 50 | BS21 |
| Radnor St, G3 | 66 | BM28 |
| Radnor St, Clyde. G81 | 27 | AW18 |
| Raeberry St, G20 | 49 | BP26 |
| Raebog Cres, Air. ML6 | 76 | DB27 |
| Raebog Rd, (Glenm.) Air. ML6 | 58 | DA25 |
| Raeburn Av, (E.Kil.) G74 | 122 | CD49 |
| Raeburn Av, Pais. PA1 | 82 | AV33 |
| Raeburn Cres, Ham. ML3 | 125 | CN50 |
| Raeburn Pl, (E.Kil.) G74 | 122 | CD49 |
| Raeburn Wk, Bell. ML4 | | |
| off Hattonrigg Rd | 95 | CW38 |
| Raeside Av, (Newt. M.) G77 | 117 | BF50 |
| Raeswood Dr, G53 | 84 | BB37 |
| Raeswood Gdns, G53 | 84 | BB37 |
| Raeswood Pl, G53 | 84 | BC37 |
| Raeswood Rd, G53 | 84 | BB37 |
| Raewell Cres, Bell. ML4 | 110 | CV42 |
| Rafford St, G51 | 66 | BJ30 |
| Raglan St, G4 | 67 | BQ27 |
| Railway Rd, Air. ML6 | 75 | CZ30 |
| Raith Av, G44 | | |
| off Croftfoot Rd | 104 | BT41 |
| Raithburn Av, G45 | 104 | BS42 |
| Raithburn Rd, G45 | 104 | BS42 |
| Raith Dr, (Cumb.) G68 | 20 | CT12 |
| Raith Dr, Bell. ML4 | 111 | CX41 |
| Ralston Av, G52 | 84 | BB33 |
| Ralston Av, Pais. PA1 | 84 | BB34 |
| Ralston Ct, G52 | 84 | BB33 |
| Ralston Dr, G52 | 84 | BB33 |
| Ralston Path, G52 | 84 | BB33 |
| Ralston Pl, G52 | 84 | BB33 |
| Ralston Rd, (Bears.) G61 | 29 | BG16 |
| Ralston Rd, (Barr.) G78 | 99 | AY43 |
| Ralston St, Air. ML6 | 76 | DA30 |
| Ralston St, Pais. PA1 | 83 | AW33 |
| Ramillies Ct, Clyde. G81 | 27 | AY19 |
| Rampart Av, G13 | 46 | BC21 |
| Ramsay Av, John. PA5 | 79 | AG36 |
| Ramsay Ct, (Newt. M.) G77 | 117 | BG50 |
| Ramsay Cres, (Kilb.) John. PA10 | 78 | AD35 |
| Ramsay Hill, (E.Kil.) G74 | 122 | CC50 |
| Ramsay Ind Est, G66 | 16 | CD12 |
| Ramsay Pl, Coat. ML5 | 74 | CS32 |
| Ramsay Pl, John. PA5 | 79 | AG36 |

| | | |
|---|---|---|
| Ramsay St, Clyde. G81 | 26 | AV18 |
| Ramsey Wynd, Bell. ML4 | | |
| off Kelvin Rd | 95 | CX38 |
| Ram St, G32 | 70 | CB32 |
| Ranald Gdns, (Ruther.) G73 | 105 | BZ42 |
| Randolph Av, (Clark.) G76 | 103 | BP44 |
| Randolph Dr, (Clark.) G76 | 103 | BP44 |
| Randolph Gdns, (Clark.) G76 | 103 | BP44 |
| Randolph Gate, G11 | 47 | BH25 |
| Randolph La, G11 | 47 | BH26 |
| Randolph Rd, G11 | 47 | BH25 |
| Ranfurly Dr, (Cumb.) G68 | 22 | DA9 |
| Ranfurly Rd, G52 | 64 | BB32 |
| Rangerhouse Rd, (E.Kil.) G75 | 136 | CB56 |
| Range Rd, Moth. ML1 | 128 | DD49 |
| Range Rd Ind Est, Moth. ML1 | 129 | DE50 |
| Range St, Moth. ML1 | 128 | DD49 |
| Rankin Cres, (Green.) Air. ML6 | 41 | DH19 |
| Rankin Dr, (Newt. M.) G77 | 117 | BE47 |
| Rankine Av, (E.Kil.) G75 | 136 | CC54 |
| Rankine La, John. PA5 | 79 | AH34 |
| Rankine Pl, (E.Kil.) G75 | | |
| off Rankine Av | 136 | CC54 |
| Rankine Pl, John. PA5 | 79 | AH34 |
| Rankines La, Renf. PA4 | | |
| off Manse St | 45 | AZ25 |
| Rankine St, John. PA5 | 79 | AH34 |
| Rankin Way, (Barr.) G78 | 99 | AZ42 |
| Rannoch Av, (Bishop.) G64 | 33 | BX20 |
| Rannoch Av, (Newt. M.) G77 | 117 | BF46 |
| Rannoch Av, Coat. ML5 | 74 | CT28 |
| Rannoch Av, Ham. ML3 | 139 | CQ52 |
| Rannoch Ct, (Cumb.) G67 | 39 | CX15 |
| Rannoch Ct, (Blan.) G72 | | |
| off Fortingall Rd | 125 | CP48 |
| Rannoch Dr, (Bears.) G61 | 30 | BJ19 |
| Rannoch Dr, (Kirk.) G66 | 18 | CK12 |
| Rannoch Dr, (Cumb.) G67 | 39 | CX15 |
| Rannoch Dr, Renf. PA4 | 45 | AY25 |
| Rannoch Gdns, (Bishop.) G64 | 33 | BY19 |
| Rannoch Grn, (E.Kil.) G74 | 122 | CB50 |
| Rannoch La, (Chry.) G69 | | |
| off Heathfield Av | 37 | CQ19 |
| Rannoch Pl, Pais. PA2 | 83 | AW34 |
| Rannoch Rd, (Udd.) G71 | 93 | CN36 |
| Rannoch Rd, Air. ML6 | 76 | DB28 |
| Rannoch Rd, John. PA5 | 79 | AH36 |
| Rannoch St, G44 | 103 | BQ39 |
| Rannoch Ter, Lark. ML9 | 145 | DE60 |
| Rannoch Way, (Both.) G71 | | |
| off Appledore Cres | 109 | CQ42 |
| Raploch Av, G14 | 46 | BD25 |
| Raploch La, G14 | 46 | BD25 |
| Raploch Rd, Lark. ML9 | 144 | DB59 |
| Raploch St, Lark. ML9 | 144 | DB58 |
| Rashieburn, Ersk. PA8 | 25 | AQ19 |
| Rashieglen, Ersk. PA8 | 25 | AQ19 |
| Rashiehill, Ersk. PA8 | 25 | AQ19 |
| Rashielee Av, Ersk. PA8 | 25 | AR19 |
| Rashielee Dr, Ersk. PA8 | 25 | AR19 |
| Rashielee Rd, Ersk. PA8 | 25 | AQ19 |
| Rashiewood, Ersk. PA8 | 25 | AR19 |
| Rathlin St, G51 | 66 | BJ29 |
| Ratho Dr, G21 | 50 | BU24 |
| Ratho Dr, (Cumb.) G68 | 9 | DA8 |
| Ratho Pk, Ham. ML3 | 139 | CR54 |
| Rattray, Ersk. PA8 | 25 | AQ18 |
| Rattray St, G32 | 90 | CA34 |
| Ravel Row, G31 | 69 | BZ32 |
| Ravelston Rd, (Bears.) G61 | 29 | BG19 |
| Ravelston St, G32 | 69 | BZ31 |
| Ravel Wynd, (Udd.) G71 | 93 | CQ37 |
| Ravenscliffe Dr, (Giff.) G46 | 102 | BK42 |

Ravens Ct, (Bishop.) G64
off Lennox Cres 50 BV21
Ravenscourt, (Thornton.) G74 120 BS50
Ravenscraig Av, Pais. PA2 82 AS35
Ravenscraig Ct, Bell. ML4 111 CX40
Ravenscraig Dr, G53 100 BD39
Ravenscraig Ter, G53
off Ravenscraig Dr 101 BE40
Ravenshall Rd, G41 86 BL37
Ravenstone Dr, (Giff.) G46 102 BL40
Ravenswood Av, Pais. PA2 81 AN38
Ravenswood Dr, G41 86 BM36
Ravenswood Rd, (Baill.) G69 92 CL33
Rawyards Av, Air. ML6 76 DD27
Raymond Pl, (E.Kil.) G75 135 BY52
Rayne Pl, G15 28 BD17
Ream Av, Air. ML6 77 DH31
Reay Av, (E.Kil.) G74 135 BX51
Reay Gdns, (E.Kil.) G74
off Reay Av 135 BX51
Redan St, G40 68 BV32
Redbrae Pl, (Kirk.) G66 17 CF12
Redbrae Rd, (Kirk.) G66 17 CG13
Redburn Av, (Giff.) G46 118 BK45
Redcastle Sq, G33 71 CF28
Redcliffe Dr, (E.Kil.) G75 135 BX53
Red Deer Rd, (E.Kil.) G75
off Westwood Rd 135 BY53
Rederech Cres, Ham. ML3 139 CP51
Redford St, G33 69 BU29
Redgate Pl, G14 46 BD25
Redgrave, (E.Kil.) G74 123 CE48
Redhill Rd, (Cumb.) G68 21 CZ10
Redholm Path, Lark. ML9
off Fisher St 144 DD60
Redhurst Cres, Pais. PA2 81 AR38
Redhurst La, Pais. PA2 81 AR38
Redhurst Way, Pais. PA2 81 AR38
Redlands La, G12 48 BL25
Redlands Rd, G12 48 BL25
Redlands Ter, G12
off Julian Av 48 BL25
Redlands Ter La, G12 48 BL25
Redlawood Pl, (Camb.) G72 108 CJ39
Redlawood Rd, (Camb.) G72 108 CJ39
Redmoss Rd, Clyde. G81 26 AV15
Redmoss St, G22 49 BR24
Rednock St, G22 50 BS25
Redpath Dr, G52 65 BE32
Red Rd, G21 51 BX25
Red Rd Ct, G21 51 BX26
Redwood Av, (E.Kil.) G74 134 BU52
Redwood Cl, Ham. ML3 139 CP54
Redwood Ct, (E.Kil.) G74 134 BU52
Redwood Cres, (Udd.) G71 94 CS37
Redwood Cres, (Camb.) G72 107 CH41
Redwood Cres, (E.Kil.) G74 134 BU51
Redwood Cres, Bish. PA7 24 AL18
Redwood Cres, Ham. ML3 139 CP54
Redwood Dr, G21 51 BW26
Redwood Dr, (Thornton.) G74 134 BU51
Redwood Dr, Ham. ML3 139 CQ54
Redwood Gro, Coat. ML5 75 CX31
Redwood La, Ham. ML3 139 CQ53
Redwood Pl, (Kirk.) G66
off Almond Dr 34 CD16
Redwood Pl, (Udd.) G71
off Redwood Cres 94 CS37
Redwood Pl, (E.Kil.) G74 134 BU51
Redwood Rd, (Cumb.) G67 23 DF11
Redwood Rd, Moth. ML1 112 DD40
Redwood Way, (Camb.) G72 107 CH42

Reelick Av, G13 46 BA21
Reelick Quad, G13 46 BA21
Reema Rd, Bell. ML4 111 CX39
Reen Pl, (Both.) G71 109 CR41
Regency Ct, Ham. ML3 141 CW51
Regency Shop Cen,
Ham. ML3 126 CV50
Regency Way, Moth. ML1
off Princess Rd 112 DB41
Regent Dr, (Ruther.) G73
off King St 89 BW37
Regent Moray St, G3 66 BM28
Regent Pk Sq, G41 87 BP35
Regent Pl, Clyde. G81 26 AU17
Regents Gate, (Both.) G71 108 CM41
Regent Sq, (Lenz.) G66 35 CE17
Regent St, (Kirk.) G66 17 CE13
Regent St, Clyde. G81 26 AU17
Regent St, Pais. PA1 63 AX32
Regent Way, Ham. ML3 126 CV50
Register Av, Bell. ML4 111 CW42
Register Rd, (Kilsyth) G65 7 CU5
Regwood St, G41 86 BM37
Reid Av, (Bears.) G61 30 BJ15
Reid Av, (Linw.) Pais. PA3 60 AK32
Reid Ct, (Ruther.) G73 89 BX37
Reid Gro, Moth. ML1 128 DD49
Reidhouse St, G21 50 BV25
Reid Pl, G40 88 BV33
Reid St, G40 88 BV34
Reid St, (Ruther.) G73 89 BX37
Reid St, Air. ML6 76 DD28
Reid St, Coat. ML5 75 CX29
Reid St, Ham. ML3 125 CP48
Reidvale St, G31 68 BV31
Reith Dr, (E.Kil.) G75 135 BZ54
Remus Pl, Bell. ML4 112 DA40
Renfield La, G2 4 BR30
Renfield St, G2 4 BR30
Renfield St, Renf. PA4 45 AZ25
Renfrew Ct, G2 5 BS29
Renfrew La, G2 4 BR29
Renfrew Rd, G51 64 BD29
Renfrew Rd, Pais. PA3 62 AV32
Renfrew Rd, Renf. PA4 64 BC28
Renfrew St, G2 4 BR29
Renfrew St, G3 4 BQ28
Renfrew St, Coat. ML5 94 CS33
Rennie Pl, (E.Kil.) G74 121 BW50
Rennie Rd, (Kilsyth) G65 6 CQ4
Rennies Rd, (Inch.) Renf. PA4 44 AS22
Renshaw Dr, G52 64 BD31
Renshaw Rd, Bish. PA7 24 AK18
Renshaw Rd, (Elder.) John. PA5 80 AL35
Renton St, G4 5 BS28
Resipol Rd, (Stepps) G33 53 CG24
Reston Dr, G52 64 BD31
Reuther Av, (Ruther.) G73 89 BX38
Revoch Dr, G13 46 BC22
Reynolds Av, (E.Kil.) G75 136 CC54
Reynolds Dr, (Stepps) G33 53 CH24
Rhannan Rd, G44 103 BQ40
Rhannan Ter, G44 103 BQ40
Rhindhouse Pl, (Baill.) G69 72 CM32
Rhindhouse Rd, (Baill.) G69 72 CM32
Rhindmuir Av, (Baill.) G69 72 CL32
Rhindmuir Ct, (Baill.) G69 72 CL31
Rhindmuir Cres, (Baill.) G69 72 CM31
Rhindmuir Dr, (Baill.) G69 72 CL31
Rhindmuir Gdns, (Baill.) G69 72 CL31
Rhindmuir Gate, (Baill.) G69 72 CM31
Rhindmuir Gro, (Baill.) G69 72 CM31
Rhindmuir Path, (Baill.) G69 72 CM31

Rhindmuir Pl, (Baill.) G69 72 CL31
Rhindmuir Rd, (Baill.) G69 72 CL31
Rhindmuir Vw, (Baill.) G69 72 CM31
Rhindmuir Wynd, (Baill.) G69 72 CM31
Rhinds St, Coat. ML5 93 CR33
Rhinsdale Cres, (Baill.) G69 72 CL32
Rhumhor Gdns, (Kilb.) John. PA10
off Ladysmith Av 78 AD35
Rhymer St, G21 5 BU28
Rhymie Rd, G32 91 CF34
Rhynie Dr, G51 66 BK32
Riach Gdns, Moth. ML1 111 CY44
Ribblesdale, (E.Kil.) G74 121 BY50
Riccarton, (E.Kil.) G75 135 BX54
Riccarton St, G42 88 BS35
Riccartsbar Av, Pais. PA2 82 AS34
Rice Way, Moth. ML1 128 DD49
Richard St, G2
off Cadzow St 4 BQ30
Richard St, Renf. PA4 45 AZ25
Richmond Av, (Clark.) G76 119 BN46
Richmond Ct, (Ruther.) G73 89 BY37
Richmond Dr, (Bishop.) G64 33 BX17
Richmond Dr, (Camb.) G72 106 CA40
Richmond Dr, (Ruther.) G73 89 BY38
Richmond Dr, (Linw.) Pais. PA3 60 AJ30
Richmond Gdns, (Chry.) G69 36 CK20
Richmond Gro, (Ruther.) G73 89 BY38
Richmond Pk Gdns, G5 88 BU34
Richmond Pl, (Ruther.) G73 89 BY37
Richmond St, G1 5 BT30
Richmond St, Clyde. G81 27 AY20
Riddell St, Clyde. G81 27 AY18
Riddell St, Coat. ML5 75 CY30
Riddon Av, G13 46 BA21
Riddon Av, Clyde. G81 46 BA21
Riddon Pl, G13 46 BA21
Riddrie Cres, G33 70 CA29
Riddrie Knowes, G33 70 CA29
Riddrievale Ct, G33 70 CA28
Riddrievale St, G33 70 CA28
Rigby St, G32 70 CA31
Rigg Pl, G33 71 CG30
Riggs, The, (Miln.) G62 12 BJ10
Riggside Rd, G33 71 CE27
Righead Gate, (E.Kil.) G74
off East Kilbride Shop Cen 136 CA52
Righead Ind Est, Bell. ML4 94 CT38
Righead Rbt, (E.Kil.) G75 135 BZ53
Riglands Gate, Renf. PA4 45 AY25
Riglands Way, Renf. PA4 45 AY25
Riglaw Pl, G13 46 BC22
Rigmuir Rd, G51 65 BE30
Rimsdale St, G40 69 BW32
Ringford St, G21 50 BV26
Ripon Dr, G12 48 BJ23
Risk St, Clyde. G81 26 AV17
Ristol Rd, G13
off Anniesland Rd 46 BD24
Ritchie Cres, (Elder.) John. PA5 80 AL34
Ritchie Pk, John. PA5 80 AK34
Ritchie Pl, (Newt. M.) G77 117 BE49
Ritchie St, G5 87 BQ33
Ritchie St, Wis. ML2 129 DF50
Ritz Pl, G5 88 BT34
Riverbank Dr, Bell. ML4 111 CY42
Riverbank St, G43 86 BL38
River Cart Wk, Pais. PA1
off Marshall's La 82 AU33
River Dr, (Inch.) Renf. PA4 44 AS24
Riverford Rd, G43 86 BL38
Riverford Rd, (Ruther.) G73 89 BY36
River Rd, G32 91 CE37

River Rd, G41
off Mansionhouse Rd 87 BP37
Riversdale La, G14 46 BC25
Riverside, (Miln.) G62 12 BJ11
Riverside Ct, G44 103 BP43
Riverside Gdns, (Clark.) G76 119 BP48
Riverside Ind Est, Clyde. G81 27 AW20
Riverside Pk, G44 103 BQ43
Riverside Pl, (Camb.) G72 107 CG39
Riverside Rd, G43 87 BN38
Riverside Rd, (Eagle.) G76 133 BN53
Riverside Rd, Lark. ML9 144 DC61
Riverside Ter, (Clark.) G76 119 BP48
Riverside Way, Ersk. PA8 25 AQ16
Riverton Dr, (E.Kil.) G75 135 BX53
Riverview Dr, G5 4 BQ31
Riverview Gdns, G5 4 BQ31
Riverview Pl, G5 4 BQ31
Roaden Av, Pais. PA2 81 AP38
Roaden Rd, Pais. PA2 81 AP38
Roadside Pl, (Green.) Air. ML6 59 DF21
Robb Ter, (Kirk.) G66 36 CJ15
Robert Burns Av, Clyde. G81 27 AY18
Robert Burns Av, Moth. ML1 113 DG41
Robert Burns Quad, Bell. ML4 110 CV40
Robert Dr, G51 66 BJ29
Robert Gilson Gdns, Coat. ML5 75 CX32
Roberton Av, G41 86 BL35
Roberton St, (Chap.) Air. ML6 97 DG34
Robert Smillie Cres, Lark. ML9 144 DC61
Robertson Av, Renf. PA4 45 AX26
Robertson Cl, Renf. PA4 45 AY26
Robertson Cres, (Neil.) G78 114 AT45
Robertson Dr, (E.Kil.) G74 136 CD51
Robertson Dr, Bell. ML4
off Motherwell Rd 111 CW41
Robertson Dr, Renf. PA4 45 AX26
Robertson La, G2 4 BQ30
Robertson's Gait, Pais. PA2 82 AU34
Robertson St, G2 4 BR30
Robertson St, (Barr.) G78 99 AX42
Robertson St, Air. ML6 76 DA29
Robertson St, Ham. ML3 125 CP48
Robertson Ter, (Baill.) G69
off Edinburgh Rd 72 CL32
Roberts Quad, Bell. ML4
off Sapphire Rd 111 CX42
Roberts St, Clyde. G81 26 AU18
Robert St, G51 66 BJ29
Robert Templeton Dr, (Camb.)
G72 106 CD40
Robinson La, (E.Kil.) G74 134 BT52
Robin Way, G32 91 CE37
Robroyston Av, G33 52 CA26
Robroyston Dr, G33 52 CA25
Robroyston Oval, G33 52 CA24
Robroyston Rd, G33 52 CA23
Robroyston Rd, (Bishop.) G64 34 CB20
Robroyston Way, G33 52 CA24
Robshill Ct, (Newt. M.) G77
off Capelrig Rd 117 BF49
Robslee Cres, (Giff.) G46 102 BJ42
Robslee Dr, (Giff.) G46 102 BK42
Robslee Rd, (Thornlie.) G46 102 BJ43
Robson Gro, G42 87 BR35
Rocep Dr, Renf. PA4 64 BB27
Rochdale Pl, (Kirk.) G66
off New Lairdsland Rd 17 CE12
Rochsoles Cres, Air. ML6
off Rochsoles Dr
Rochsoles Dr, Air. ML6 76 DC27
Rochsolloch Fm Cotts, Air. ML6
off Victoria Pl 76 DA30

Rochsolloch Rd, Air. ML6 75 CZ31
Rockall Dr, G44 104 BS41
Rockbank Pl, G40 69 BW32
Rockbank Pl, Clyde. G81
off Glasgow Rd 27 AX15
Rockbank St, G40 69 BW32
Rockburn Cres, Bell. ML4 95 CW38
Rockburn Dr, (Clark.) G76 118 BL45
Rockcliffe Path, (Chap.) Air. ML6 97 DG37
Rockcliffe St, G40 88 BV34
Rock Dr, (Kilb.) John. PA10 78 AD35
Rockfield Pl, G21 51 BY24
Rockfield Rd, G21 51 BY24
Rockhampton Av, (E.Kil.) G75 135 BX54
Rockmount Av, (Thornlie.) G46 102 BJ41
Rockmount Av, (Barr.) G78 99 AZ44
Rock St, G4 49 BR26
Rockwell Av, Pais. PA2 82 AS37
Roddinghead Rd, (Giff.) G46 118 BJ47
Rodger Av, (Newt. M.) G77 117 BE48
Rodger Dr, (Ruther.) G73 105 BW39
Rodger Pl, (Ruther.) G73 105 BW39
Rodil Av, G44 104 BS41
Rodney St, G4 67 BR27
Roebank Dr, (Barr.) G78 99 AY44
Roebank St, G31 69 BX29
Roffey Pk Rd, Pais. PA1 63 AZ32
Rogart St, G40 68 BV32
Rogerfield Rd, (Baill.) G69 72 CL30
Roland Cres, (Newt. M.) G77 117 BH50
Roman Av, G15 28 BC20
Roman Av, (Bears.) G61 29 BH16
Roman Ct, (Bears.) G61 29 BH16
Roman Dr, (Bears.) G61 29 BH16
Roman Dr, Bell. ML4 111 CX41
Roman Gdns, (Bears.) G61 29 BH16
Roman Pl, Bell. ML4 110 CU42
Roman Rd, (Bears.) G61 29 BG16
Roman Rd, (Kirk.) G66 16 CD13
Roman Rd, Clyde. G81 27 AW15
Roman Rd, Moth. ML1 128 DA46
Roman Way, (Udd.) G71 110 CS39
Romney Av, G44 104 BS40
Romulus Ct, Moth. ML1 111 CV44
Ronaldsay Dr, (Bishop.) G64 33 BZ19
Ronaldsay Pas, G22
off Scalpay St 50 BT22
Ronaldsay Pl, (Cumb.) G67 21 CZ13
Ronaldsay St, G22 50 BS22
Ronald St, Coat. ML5
off Stewart St 75 CW29
Rona St, G21 69 BX27
Rona Ter, (Camb.) G72 106 CB42
Ronay St, G22 50 BT21
Rooksdell Av, Pais. PA2 82 AS36
Ropework La, G1 5 BS31
Rorison Pl, (Ashgill) Lark. ML9 145 DH60
Rosaburn Cres, (E.Kil.) G75 135 BX56
Rosebank Av, (Kirk.) G66 17 CG13
Rosebank Av, (Blan.) G72 109 CN44
Rosebank Dr, (Udd.) G71 94 CS38
Rosebank Dr, (Camb.) G72 107 CE41
Rosebank Gdns, (Udd.) G71 92 CK35
Rosebank Gdns, John. PA5 80 AJ35
Rosebank La, (Both.) G71
off Lomond Dr 109 CR42
Rosebank Pl, (Dullatur) G68 8 CY7
Rosebank Pl, (Udd.) G71 92 CK35
Rosebank Rd, Bell. ML4 95 CX37
Rosebank St, Air. ML6 77 DF29
Rosebank Ter, (Baill.) G69 93 CP33
Roseberry La, Air. ML6 97 DG34

Roseberry Pl, Ham. ML3 125 CQ49
Roseberry Rd, Air. ML6 97 DF33
Roseberry St, G5 88 BU34
Rose Cres, Ham. ML3 125 CP49
Rosedale, (Bishop.) G64
off Woodfield Av 51 BX21
Rosedale, (E.Kil.) G74 121 BY50
Rosedale Av, Pais. PA2 80 AM38
Rosedale Dr, (Baill.) G69 92 CJ33
Rosedale Gdns, G20 48 BL21
Rosedene Ter, Bell. ML4
off Airlie Dr 111 CW39
Rosefield Gdns, (Udd.) G71 93 CN38
Rosegreen Cres, Bell. ML4 95 CW37
Rosehall Av, Coat. ML5 95 CX33
Rosehall Ind Est, Coat. ML5 95 CW34
Rosehall Rd, (Bellshill Ind. Est.)
Bell. ML4 110 CV39
Rosehall Ter, Wis. ML2 143 DG52
Rosehill Cres, G53 100 BC39
Rosehill Dr, G53 100 BC39
Rosehill Dr, (Cumb.) G67 21 CW14
Rosehill Rd, (Torr.) G64 15 BY13
Rose Knowe Rd, G42 88 BT36
Roseland Brae, Ersk. PA8
off Newshot Dr 44 AT21
Roselea Dr, (Miln.) G62 12 BK10
Roselea Gdns, G13 47 BH22
Roselea Pl, (Blan.) G72 108 CL44
Roselea St, Lark. ML9 144 DD57
Rosemary Cres, (E.Kil.) G74 121 BZ49
Rosemary Pl, (E.Kil.) G74 121 BZ49
Rosemount, (Cumb.) G68 9 DB8
Rosemount Av, (Newt. M.) G77 131 BF51
Rosemount Ct, (Newt. M.) G77 131 BF52
Rose Mt Ct, Air. ML6 77 DE29
Rosemount Cres, G21 68 BV29
Rosemount La, Lark. ML9
off Dickson St 145 DE60
Rosemount Meadows, (Both.)
G71 109 CP43
Rosemount St, G21 68 BV28
Rosendale Way, (Blan.) G72 125 CN46
Roseneath Gate, (E.Kil.) G74 135 BY51
Roseness Pl, G33 70 CC29
Rosepark Av, (Udd.) G71 110 CS39
Rose Pk Cotts, Coat. ML5 94 CV34
Rose Pl, (E.Kil.) G74 123 CE50
Rose St, G3 4 BR29
Rose St, (Kirk.) G66 17 CF13
Rose St, (Cumb.) G67 39 CX15
Rose St, Moth. ML1 128 DC48
Rosevale Cres, Bell. ML4 111 CY41
Rosevale Cres, Ham. ML3 139 CR51
Rosevale Rd, (Bears.) G61 29 BG17
Rosevale St, G11 66 BJ27
Rosewood Av, Bell. ML4 95 CX38
Rosewood Av, Pais. PA2 81 AR36
Rosewood Path, Bell. ML4 110 CU40
Rosewood St, G13 47 BG22
Roslea Dr, G31 69 BW30
Roslin Twr, (Camb.) G72 106 CA42
Roslyn Dr, (Baill.) G69 73 CP32
Rosneath St, G51 66 BJ29
Ross Av, (Kirk.) G66 17 CH13
Ross Av, Renf. PA4 63 AW28
Ross Cres, Moth. ML1 127 CY48
Ross Dr, (Udd.) G71 94 CS36
Ross Dr, Air. ML6 96 DA33
Ross Dr, Moth. ML1 127 CY48
Rossendale Ct, G43 86 BL37
Rossendale Rd, G41 86 BL37
Rossendale Rd, G43 86 BL37

Ross Gdns, Moth. ML1 127 CY48
Rosshall Av, Pais. PA1 83 AY33
Ross Hall Pl, Renf. PA4 45 AZ26
Rosshill Av, G52 64 BB32
Rosshill Rd, G52 64 BB32
Rossie Cres, (Bishop.) G64 51 BY21
Rossie Gro, (Newt. M.) G77 116 BD48
Rosslea Dr, (Giff.) G46 102 BL43
Rosslyn Av, (Ruther.) G73 89 BY38
Rosslyn Av, (E.Kil.) G74 122 CB50
Rosslyn Ct, Ham. ML3 125 CQ49
Rosslyn Rd, (Bears.) G61 28 BD15
Rosslyn Rd, (Ashgill) Lark. ML9 145 DH61
Rosslyn Ter, G12 48 BL25
Ross Pl, (Ruther.) G73 105 BZ41
Ross St, G40 5 BT31
Ross St, Coat. ML5 75 CW30
Ross St, Pais. PA1 82 AV34
Ross Ter, Ham. ML3 141 CY52
Rostan Rd, G43 102 BL40
Rosyth Rd, G5 88 BU35
Rosyth St, G5 88 BU35
Rotherwick Dr, Pais. PA1 84 BA33
Rotherwood Av, G13 29 BE20
Rotherwood Av, Pais. PA2 81 AP37
Rotherwood La, G13 29 BE19
Rotherwood Pl, G13 47 BG21
Rotherwood Way, Pais. PA2
  off Rotherwood Av 81 AP37
Rothesay Cres, Coat. ML5 95 CX33
Rothesay Pl, Coat. ML5
  off Rothesay Cres 95 CX33
Rothesay St, (E.Kil.) G74 136 CA53
Rothes Dr, G23 30 BM20
Rothes Pl, G23
  off Rothes Dr 30 BL20
Rottenrow, G4 5 BT29
Rottenrow E, G4 5 BT30
Roughcraig St, Air. ML6 76 DC27
Roukenburn St, (Thornlie.) G46 101 BG41
Rouken Glen Pk, (Thornlie.)
  G46 101 BH44
Rouken Glen Rd, (Thornlie.)
  G46 101 BH43
Roundhill Dr, (Elder.) John. PA5 81 AN34
Roundknowe Rd, (Udd.) G71 92 CL36
Rowallan Gdns, G11 48 BJ26
Rowallan La, G11 47 BH26
Rowallan La, (Clark.) G76 119 BN46
Rowallan La E, G11 48 BJ26
Rowallan Rd, (Thornlie.) G46 101 BH43
Rowallan Ter, G33 52 CD25
Rowan Av, Moth. ML1 97 DF38
Rowan Av, Renf. PA4 45 AY25
Rowanbank Pl, Air. ML6 75 CY30
Rowan Ct, (Camb.) G72 107 CH41
Rowan Ct, Pais. PA2 82 AU35
Rowan Ct, Wis. ML2
  off Netherton Rd 143 DF51
Rowan Cres, (Lenz.) G66 35 CE16
Rowan Cres, (Chap.) Air. ML6 97 DG34
Rowandale Av, (Baill.) G69 92 CJ33
Rowand Av, (Giff.) G46 102 BL43
Rowanden Av, Bell. ML4 111 CW39
Rowan Dr, (Bears.) G61 11 BH14
Rowan Dr, Clyde. G81 26 AV17
Rowan Gdns, G41 86 BK33
Rowan Gate, Pais. PA2 82 AV35
Rowan La, Moth. ML1 112 DC43
Rowanlea, (Plains) Air. ML6
  off Silverdale Ter 59 DH26
Rowanlea Av, Pais. PA2 80 AM38
Rowanlea Dr, (Giff.) G46 102 BM41

Rowanpark Dr, (Barr.) G78 99 AW40
Rowan Pl, (Blan.) G72 124 CM45
Rowan Pl, (Camb.) G72 107 CE39
Rowan Pl, Coat. ML5
  off Old Monkland Rd 94 CU33
Rowan Rd, G41 86 BK33
Rowan Rd, (Cumb.) G67 23 DF10
Rowans, The, (Bishop.) G64 32 BV19
Rowans Gdns, (Both.) G71 109 CR41
Rowan St, Pais. PA2 82 AU35
Rowantree Av, (Udd.) G71 94 CS38
Rowantree Av, (Ruther.) G73 105 BX40
Rowantree Gdns, (Ruther.) G73 105 BX40
Rowantree Pl, John. PA5
  off Rowantree Rd 79 AH36
Rowantree Pl, Lark. ML9 145 DF59
Rowantree Rd, John. PA5 79 AH36
Rowantree Ter, Moth. ML1 112 DD40
Rowanwood Cres, Coat. ML5 74 CT32
Rowchester St, G40 69 BW32
Rowena Av, G13 29 BF20
Roxburgh Dr, (Bears.) G61 11 BG14
Roxburgh Dr, Coat. ML5 95 CZ33
Roxburgh La, G12
  off Saltoun St 48 BM26
Roxburgh Pk, (E.Kil.) G74 136 CB52
Roxburgh Pl, (Blan.) G72
  off Coldstream St 124 CM46
Roxburgh Rd, Pais. PA2 80 AM38
Roxburgh St, G12 48 BM26
Royal Bk Pl, G1
  off Buchanan St 5 BS30
Royal Cres, G3 67 BN29
Royal Cres, G42
  off Queens Dr 87 BQ36
Royal Dr, Ham. ML3 141 CW51
Royal Ex Bldgs, G1
  off Royal Sq 5 BS30
Royal Ex Ct, G1 5 BS30
Royal Ex Sq, G1 5 BS30
Royal Gdns, (Both.) G71 109 CN43
Royal Inch Cres, Renf. PA4
  off Campbell St 45 AZ24
Royal Ter, G3 67 BN28
Royal Ter La, G3 67 BN28
Royellen Av, Ham. ML3 139 CP51
Roystonhill, G21 68 BV28
Roystonhill Pl, G21 68 BV28
Royston Rd, G21 5 BU28
Royston Rd, G33 52 CA26
Royston Sq, G21 5 BU28
Roy St, G21 50 BT26
Rozelle Av, G15 28 BD18
Rozelle Av, (Newt. M.) G77 116 BD49
Rozelle Dr, (Newt. M.) G77 116 BD49
Rozelle Pl, (Newt. M.) G77 116 BD49
Rubislaw Dr, (Bears.) G61 29 BG17
Ruby St, G40 89 BW33
Ruby Ter, Bell. ML4 111 CW41
Ruchazie Pl, G33 70 CB29
Ruchazie Rd, G32 70 CB30
Ruchazie Rd, G33 70 CB30
Ruchill Pl, G20
  off Ruchill St 49 BP24
Ruchill St, G20 49 BN24
Ruel St, G44 87 BQ38
Rufflees Av, (Barr.) G78 99 AZ41
Rugby Av, G13 46 BD21
Rullion Pl, G33 70 CB29
Rumford St, G40 88 BV34
Runciman Pl, (E.Kil.) G74 122 CD49
Rupert St, G4 67 BP27
Rushyhill St, G21 51 BW25

Ruskin La, G12 49 BN26
Ruskin Pl, G12 49 BN26
Ruskin Pl, (Kilsyth) G65
  off Murray Av 7 CT5
Ruskin Sq, (Bishop.) G64 33 BW20
Ruskin Ter, G12 49 BN26
Ruskin Ter, (Ruther.) G73 89 BX37
Russellcolt St, Coat. ML5 75 CW29
Russell Cres, (Baill.) G69 92 CM33
Russell Dr, (Bears.) G61 29 BG15
Russell Gdns, (Udd.) G71
  off Kingston Av 93 CQ37
Russell Gdns, (Newt. M.) G77 117 BE49
Russell Pl, (E.Kil.) G75 135 BY54
Russell Pl, (Clark.) G76 119 BQ48
Russell St, G11
  off Vine St 66 BK27
Russell St, (Chap.) Air. ML6 97 DG35
Russell St, Bell. ML4 111 CZ40
Russell St, Ham. ML3 125 CP48
Russell St, John. PA5 80 AJ34
Russell St, Pais. PA3 62 AT30
Rutherford Av, (Bears.) G61 10 BD13
Rutherford Av, (Kirk.) G66 36 CK15
Rutherford Gra, (Kirk.) G66 35 CE15
Rutherford La, (E.Kil.) G75
  off Murdoch Rd 136 CB53
Rutherford Sq, (E.Kil.) G75 136 CA53
Rutherglen Br, G40 88 BV34
Rutherglen Br, G42 88 BV34
Rutherglen Ind Est, (Ruther.)
  G73 88 BV36
Rutherglen Rd, G5 88 BT34
Rutherglen Rd, (Ruther.) G73 88 BT34
Ruthven Av, (Giff.) G46 102 BM44
Ruthven La, G12 48 BM26
Ruthven La, (Glenb.) Coat. ML5
  off Chapman Av 56 CS23
Ruthven Pl, (Bishop.) G64 51 BY21
Ruthven St, G12 48 BM26
Rutland Ct, G51
  off Govan Rd 67 BN31
Rutland Cres, G51 67 BN31
Rutland Pl, G51 67 BN31
Ryan Rd, (Bishop.) G64 33 BX20
Ryan Way, (Ruther.) G73 105 BY42
Ryat Dr, (Newt. M.) G77 117 BE47
Ryat Grn, (Newt. M.) G77 117 BE48
Ryat Linn, Ersk. PA8 25 AP20
Rydal Gro, (E.Kil.) G75 134 BV55
Rydal Pl, (E.Kil.) G75 134 BV55
Ryden Mains Rd, (Glenm.)
  Air. ML6 57 CZ25
Ryebank Rd, G21 51 BY24
Rye Cres, G21 51 BX24
Ryecroft Dr, (Baill.) G69 72 CK32
Ryedale Pl, G15 28 BC17
Ryefield Av, Coat. ML5 74 CT30
Ryefield Av, John. PA5 79 AF36
Ryefield Pl, John. PA5 79 AF36
Ryefield Rd, G21 51 BX24
Ryehill Pl, G21 51 BY24
Ryehill Rd, G21 51 BY24
Ryemount Rd, G21 51 BY24
Rye Rd, G21 51 BX24
Ryeside Rd, G21 51 BX24
Rye Way, Pais. PA2 81 AN36
Ryewraes Rd, (Linw.) Pais. PA3 60 AK32
Rylands Dr, G32 91 CF33
Rylands Gdns, G32 91 CG33
Rylees Cres, G52 64 BA31
Rylees Pl, G52 64 BA31
Rylees Rd, G52 64 BA31

| | | |
|---|---|---|
| Rysland Av, (Newt. M.) G77 | 117 | BG48 |
| Rysland Cres, (Newt. M.) G77 | 117 | BG48 |
| Ryvra Rd, G13 | 47 | BF23 |

**S**

| | | |
|---|---|---|
| Sachelcourt Av, Bish. PA7 | 24 | AK19 |
| Sackville Av, G13 | 47 | BH24 |
| Sackville La, G13 | 47 | BH23 |
| Saddell Rd, G15 | 28 | BD17 |
| Sadlers Wells Ct, (E.Kil.) G74 | 122 | CD49 |
| Saffron Cres, Wis. ML2 | 143 | DF52 |
| Saffronhall Cres, Ham. ML3 | 126 | CT49 |
| off Almada St | | |
| Saffronhall Gdns, Ham. ML3 | 126 | CT49 |
| Saffronhall La, Ham. ML3 | 126 | CT49 |
| off Montrose Cres | | |
| St. Abbs Dr, Pais. PA2 | 81 | AQ36 |
| St. Andrews Av, (Bishop.) G64 | 32 | BU19 |
| St. Andrew's Av, (Both.) G71 | 109 | CQ44 |
| St. Andrew's Av, Pais. PA3 | 62 | AS28 |
| St. Andrews Cl, G41 | 87 | BP33 |
| St. Andrews Ct, (E.Kil.) G75 | 135 | BY55 |
| St. Andrews Cres, G41 | 87 | BN33 |
| St. Andrews Cres, Pais. PA3 | 62 | AS28 |
| St. Andrews Cross, G41 | 87 | BQ34 |
| St. Andrews Dr, G41 | 87 | BN33 |
| St. Andrews Dr, (Bears.) G61 | 11 | BF14 |
| St. Andrews Dr, Coat. ML5 | 74 | CU31 |
| St. Andrews Dr, Ham. ML3 | 124 | CM49 |
| St. Andrews Dr, (Abbots.) Pais. PA3 | 62 | AT29 |
| St. Andrews Dr W, (Abbots.) Pais. PA3 | 62 | AS28 |
| St. Andrews Gate, Bell. ML4 | | |
| off Cochrane St | 110 | CV40 |
| St. Andrews La, G1 | 5 | BT31 |
| off Gallowgate | | |
| St. Andrew's Oval, Pais. PA3 | 62 | AS29 |
| St. Andrew's Parkway, Pais. PA3 | 62 | AS29 |
| St. Andrews Path, Lark. ML9 | | |
| off Glen Fruin Dr | 145 | DE60 |
| St. Andrews Pl, (Kilsyth) G65 | 7 | CS4 |
| St. Andrews Rd, G41 | 87 | BP33 |
| St. Andrews Rd, Renf. PA4 | 45 | AY26 |
| St. Andrews Sq, G1 | 5 | BT31 |
| St. Andrews St, G1 | 5 | BT31 |
| St. Andrews St, Moth. ML1 | 112 | DC40 |
| St. Andrew's Way, Pais. PA3 | 62 | AS29 |
| St. Annes Av, Ersk. PA8 | | |
| off St. Annes Wynd | 44 | AT21 |
| St. Annes Wynd, Ersk. PA8 | 44 | AS21 |
| St. Anns Dr, (Giff.) G46 | 102 | BL43 |
| St. Barchan's Rd, (Kilb.) John. PA10 off Easwald Bk | 78 | AD35 |
| St. Blanes Dr, (Ruther.) G73 | 104 | BU39 |
| St. Boswell's Cres, Pais. PA2 | 81 | AQ36 |
| St. Boswells Dr, Coat. ML5 | 95 | CZ33 |
| St. Brides Av, (Udd.) G71 | 94 | CS38 |
| St. Brides Rd, G43 | 102 | BM39 |
| St. Brides Way, (Both.) G71 | 109 | CQ42 |
| St. Bryde St, (E.Kil.) G74 | 136 | CB51 |
| St. Catherines Rd, (Giff.) G46 | 102 | BL43 |
| St. Clair Av, (Giff.) G46 | 102 | BL42 |
| St. Clair St, G20 | | |
| off North Woodside Rd | 67 | BP27 |
| St. Columba Dr, (Kirk.) G66 | 17 | CG14 |
| St. Cyrus Gdns, (Bishop.) G64 | 33 | BY20 |
| St. Cyrus Rd, (Bishop.) G64 | 33 | BY20 |
| St. Davids Dr, Air. ML6 | 97 | DE33 |
| St. Davids Pl, Lark. ML9 | 144 | DC58 |
| St. Denis Way, Coat. ML5 | | |
| off Heritage Vw | 74 | CV29 |

| | | |
|---|---|---|
| St. Edmunds Gro, (Miln.) G62 | 12 | BJ10 |
| St. Edmunds La, (Miln.) G62 | 12 | BJ10 |
| St. Enoch Av, (Udd.) G71 | 94 | CS37 |
| St. Enoch Shop Cen, G1 | 5 | BS31 |
| St. Enoch Sq, G1 | 4 | BR31 |
| St. Fillans Rd, G33 | 53 | CE24 |
| St. Francis Rigg, G5 | 88 | BS33 |
| St. Georges Pl, G20 | | |
| off St. Georges Rd | 67 | BQ27 |
| St. Georges Rd, G3 | 67 | BQ27 |
| St. Germains, (Bears.) G61 | 29 | BG17 |
| St. Giles Pk, Ham. ML3 | 139 | CR51 |
| St. Giles Way, Ham. ML3 | 125 | CR50 |
| St. Helena Cres, Clyde. G81 | 27 | AY15 |
| St. Helens Gdns, G41 | 87 | BN37 |
| St. Ives Rd, (Mood.) G69 | 37 | CP18 |
| St. James Av, (E.Kil.) G74 | 134 | BU52 |
| St. James Av, Pais. PA3 | 61 | AR30 |
| St. James Business Cen, (Linw.) Pais. PA3 | 81 | AN33 |
| St. James Ct, (E.Kil.) G74 | 134 | BU52 |
| St. James Ct, Coat. ML5 | 94 | CU34 |
| St. James Rd, G4 | 5 | BT29 |
| St. James St, Pais. PA3 | 62 | AU32 |
| St. James Way, Coat. ML5 | 94 | CU34 |
| St. John's Ct, G41 | 87 | BN33 |
| St. John's Quad, G41 | 87 | BN33 |
| St. John's Rd, G41 | 87 | BN34 |
| St. John St, Coat. ML5 | 75 | CW30 |
| St. Joseph's Ct, G21 | 68 | BV28 |
| St. Joseph's Pl, G21 | 68 | BV28 |
| St. Joseph's Vw, G21 | 68 | BV28 |
| St. Kenneth Dr, G51 | 65 | BF29 |
| St. Kilda Dr, G14 | 47 | BG25 |
| St. Lawrence Pk, (E.Kil.) G75 | 135 | BY52 |
| St. Leonards Dr, (Giff.) G46 | 102 | BL42 |
| St. Leonards Rd, (E.Kil.) G74 | 137 | CE51 |
| St. Leonards Sq, (E.Kil.) G74 | | |
| off Blacklaw Dr | 137 | CE52 |
| St. Leonards Wk, Coat. ML5 | 95 | CY34 |
| St. Luke's Pl, G5 | 68 | BS32 |
| St. Luke's Ter, G5 | 68 | BS32 |
| St. Margaret's Av, Pais. PA3 | 62 | AV30 |
| St. Margaret's Ct, Bell. ML4 | 111 | CX40 |
| St. Margaret's Ct, Pais. PA3 | 62 | AV30 |
| St. Margaret's Dr, Wis. ML2 | 143 | DG52 |
| St. Margarets Pl, G1 | | |
| off Bridgegate | 5 | BS31 |
| St. Mark Gdns, G32 | 70 | CB32 |
| St. Mark St, G32 | 70 | CA32 |
| St. Marnock St, G40 | 69 | BW32 |
| St. Martins Gate, Coat. ML5 | 95 | CW33 |
| St. Mary's Cres, (Barr.) G78 | 99 | AY43 |
| St. Mary's Gdns, (Barr.) G78 | 99 | AY43 |
| St. Marys La, G2 | 4 | BR30 |
| St. Marys Rd, (Bishop.) G64 | 32 | BU19 |
| St. Marys Rd, Bell. ML4 | 110 | CU40 |
| St. Maurice's Rbt, (Cumb.) G68 | 20 | CV12 |
| St. Michael Rd, Wis. ML2 | 143 | DE52 |
| St. Michael's Ct, G31 | | |
| off St. Michael's La | 69 | BY32 |
| St. Michael's La, G31 | 69 | BY32 |
| St. Mirrens Rd, (Kilsyth) G65 | 7 | CU5 |
| St. Mirren St, Pais. PA1 | 62 | AU32 |
| St. Monance St, G21 | 50 | BV24 |
| St. Monica's Way, Coat. ML5 | 94 | CT33 |
| St. Mungo Av, G4 | 5 | BS29 |
| St. Mungo Pl, G4 | 5 | BT29 |
| St. Mungo Pl, Ham. ML3 | | |
| off Fleming Way | 124 | CM49 |
| St. Mungos Ct, Moth. ML1 | 112 | DD44 |
| St. Mungo's Rd, (Cumb.) G67 | 22 | DB11 |
| St. Mungo St, (Bishop.) G64 | 50 | BV21 |

| | | |
|---|---|---|
| St. Mungos Wk, (Cumb.) G67 | | |
| off Cumbernauld Shop Cen | 22 | DB12 |
| St. Ninians Cres, Pais. PA2 | 82 | AV35 |
| St. Ninian's Pl, Ham. ML3 | | |
| off St. Ninian's Rd | 125 | CP50 |
| St. Ninian's Rd, Ham. ML3 | 125 | CN50 |
| St. Ninians Rd, Pais. PA2 | 82 | AV35 |
| St. Ninian Ter, G5 | | |
| off Ballater St | 68 | BS32 |
| St. Oswald's Glebe, G44 | 104 | BU39 |
| St. Peters La, G2 | 4 | BQ30 |
| St. Peter's Path, G4 | | |
| off Braid St | 67 | BQ27 |
| St. Peters St, G4 | 67 | BQ27 |
| St. Roberts Gdns, G53 | 101 | BE40 |
| St. Rollox Brae, G21 | 68 | BU27 |
| St. Ronans Dr, G41 | 86 | BM36 |
| St. Ronans Dr, (Ruther.) G73 | 105 | BY39 |
| St. Ronan's Dr, Ham. ML3 | 140 | CS53 |
| St. Stephens Av, (Ruther.) G73 | 105 | BZ42 |
| St. Stephens Cres, (Ruther.) G73 | 106 | CA42 |
| St. Valentine Ter, G5 | 88 | BT33 |
| St. Vigeans Av, (Newt. M.) G77 | 116 | BD49 |
| St. Vigeans Pl, (Newt. M.) G77 | 117 | BE50 |
| St. Vincent Cres, G3 | 66 | BM29 |
| St. Vincent Cres La, G3 | 66 | BM29 |
| St. Vincent La, G2 | 4 | BQ29 |
| St. Vincent Pl, G1 | 5 | BS30 |
| St. Vincent Pl, (E.Kil.) G75 | 135 | BW52 |
| St. Vincent Pl, Moth. ML1 | | |
| off Milton St | 128 | DA46 |
| St. Vincent St, G2 | 4 | BQ29 |
| St. Vincent St, G3 | 4 | BP29 |
| St. Vincent Ter, G3 | 4 | BP29 |
| Salamanca St, G31 | 69 | BZ32 |
| Salasaig Ct, G33 | | |
| off Sutherness Dr | 70 | CC30 |
| Salen St, G52 | 65 | BH32 |
| Salford Pl, (Kirk.) G66 | | |
| off West High St | 17 | CE12 |
| Saline St, Air. ML6 | 75 | CZ31 |
| Salisbury, (E.Kil.) G74 | 123 | CF49 |
| Salisbury Pl, G5 | 87 | BR33 |
| Salisbury Pl, Clyde. G81 | 26 | AT16 |
| Salisbury St, G5 | 87 | BR33 |
| Salkeld St, G5 | 87 | BR33 |
| Salmona St, G22 | 49 | BR25 |
| Saltaire Av, (Udd.) G71 | 109 | CQ40 |
| Salterland Rd, G53 | 100 | BA40 |
| Salterland Rd, (Barr.) G78 | 100 | BA40 |
| Saltire Cres, Lark. ML9 | 145 | DE58 |
| Saltmarket, G1 | 5 | BS31 |
| Saltmarket Pl, G1 | | |
| off Bridgegate | 5 | BS31 |
| Saltoun Gdns, G12 | | |
| off Roxburgh St | 48 | BM26 |
| Saltoun La, G12 | 48 | BM26 |
| Saltoun St, G12 | 48 | BL26 |
| Salvia St, (Camb.) G72 | 106 | CB39 |
| Sandaig Rd, G33 | 71 | CG31 |
| Sandale Path, (Blan.) G72 | | |
| off Moorfield Rd | 124 | CL47 |
| Sandalwood Av, (E.Kil.) G74 | 121 | BZ49 |
| Sandalwood Ct, (E.Kil.) G74 | 121 | BZ49 |
| Sanda St, G20 | 49 | BN25 |
| Sandbank Av, G20 | 48 | BM22 |
| Sandbank Cres, G20 | 48 | BM23 |
| Sandbank Dr, G20 | 48 | BM22 |
| Sandbank St, G20 | 48 | BM23 |
| Sandbank Ter, G20 | 48 | BM22 |
| Sandend, Ersk. PA8 | 25 | AQ18 |
| Sandend Rd, G53 | 84 | BC38 |

| | | |
|---|---|---|
| Sanderling Parkway, Pais. PA3 | 62 | AS29 |
| Sanderling Pl, (E.Kil.) G75 | 135 | BW56 |
| Sanderling Rd, Pais. PA3 | 62 | AT29 |
| Sanderson Av, (Udd.) G71 | 110 | CT39 |
| Sandfield Av, (Miln.) G62 | 12 | BJ10 |
| Sandfield St, G20 | 49 | BN24 |
| Sandford Gdns, (Baill.) G69 | | |
| off Scott St | 72 | CK32 |
| Sandgate Av, G32 | 91 | CF34 |
| Sandhaven Pl, G53 | | |
| off Sandhaven Rd | 84 | BC38 |
| Sandhaven Rd, G53 | 84 | BC38 |
| Sandhead Cres, (Chap.) Air. ML6 | | |
| off Honeywell Cres | 97 | DG36 |
| Sandholes St, Pais. PA1 | 82 | AS33 |
| Sandholm Pl, G14 | 46 | BB24 |
| Sandholm Ter, G14 | 46 | BB24 |
| Sandiefield Rd, G5 | 88 | BS33 |
| Sandielands Av, Ersk. PA8 | 44 | AT22 |
| Sandilands Cres, Moth. ML1 | 127 | CX48 |
| Sandilands St, G32 | 70 | CD32 |
| Sandmill St, G21 | 69 | BW28 |
| Sandpiper Dr, (E.Kil.) G75 | 135 | BW56 |
| Sandpiper Pl, (E.Kil.) G75 | 135 | BW56 |
| Sandpiper Way, (Strathclyde Bus. Pk.) Bell. ML4 | 94 | CU37 |
| Sandra Rd, (Bishop.) G64 | 33 | BY19 |
| Sandringham Av, (Newt. M.) G77 | 118 | BJ47 |
| Sandringham Ct, (Newt. M.) G77 off Duart Dr | 118 | BJ48 |
| Sandringham Dr, (Elder.) John. PA5 off Glamis Av | 80 | AK36 |
| Sandringham La, G12 off Kersland St | 48 | BM26 |
| Sandwood Cres, G52 | 64 | BC32 |
| Sandwood Path, G52 off Hillington Rd S | 64 | BC32 |
| Sandwood Rd, G52 | 84 | BC33 |
| Sandyford Av, Moth. ML1 | 97 | DF37 |
| Sandyford Pl, G3 | 4 | BP29 |
| off Sauchiehall St | | |
| Sandyford Pl La, G3 | 67 | BN29 |
| Sandyford Pl, Moth. ML1 | 97 | DF38 |
| Sandyford Rd, Pais. PA3 | 62 | AV29 |
| Sandyford St, G3 | 66 | BL29 |
| Sandyhills Cres, G32 | 90 | CD34 |
| Sandyhills Dr, G32 | 90 | CD34 |
| Sandyhills Gro, G32 | 91 | CE35 |
| Sandyhills Pl, G32 | 90 | CD34 |
| Sandyhills Rd, G32 | 90 | CD34 |
| Sandyknowes Rd, (Cumb.) G67 | 22 | DB13 |
| Sandy La, G11 off Crawford St | 66 | BJ27 |
| Sandy Rd, G11 | 66 | BJ28 |
| Sandy Rd, Renf. PA4 | 63 | AY28 |
| Sannox Dr, Moth. ML1 | 127 | CX46 |
| Sannox Gdns, G31 | 69 | BX29 |
| Sanquhar Dr, G53 | 84 | BC37 |
| Sanquhar Gdns, G53 | 84 | BC37 |
| Sanquhar Gdns, (Blan.) G72 | 108 | CK43 |
| Sanquhar Pl, G53 | 84 | BC37 |
| Sanquhar Rd, G53 | 84 | BC37 |
| Sapphire Rd, Bell. ML4 | 111 | CW42 |
| Saracen Head La, G1 off Gallowgate | 5 | BU31 |
| Saracen Head Rd, G1 | 5 | BU31 |
| Saracen St, G22 | 50 | BS26 |
| Sarazen Ct, Moth. ML1 off Morris Cres | 129 | DG45 |
| Sardinia La, G12 | 48 | BM26 |
| Sardinia Ter, G12 off Cecil St | 48 | BM26 |
| Saskatoon Pl, (E.Kil.) G75 | 135 | BX52 |
| Saturn Av, Pais. PA1 | 81 | AN33 |
| Saucel Cres, Pais. PA1 | 82 | AU33 |
| Saucelhill Ter, Pais. PA2 | 82 | AV34 |
| Saucel St, Pais. PA1 | 82 | AU33 |
| Sauchenhall Rd, (Kirk.) G66 | 37 | CN16 |
| Sauchiehall La, G2 | 4 | BQ29 |
| Sauchiehall St, G2 | 4 | BQ29 |
| Sauchiehall St, G3 | 66 | BM28 |
| Saughs Av, G33 | 52 | CB23 |
| Saughs Dr, G33 | 52 | CB23 |
| Saughs Gate, G33 | 52 | CB23 |
| Saughs Pl, G33 | 52 | CB23 |
| Saughs Rd, G33 | 52 | CA24 |
| Saughton St, G32 | 70 | CA30 |
| Saunders Ct, (Barr.) G78 off John St | 99 | AX42 |
| Savoy St, G40 | 88 | BV33 |
| Sawmillfield St, G4 | 67 | BR27 |
| Sawmill Rd, G11 off South St | 65 | BH27 |
| Saxon Rd, G13 | 47 | BF22 |
| Scadlock Rd, Pais. PA3 | 61 | AR31 |
| Scalloway La, (Camb.) G72 | 106 | CB42 |
| Scalloway Rd, (Camb.) G72 | 106 | CA42 |
| Scalpay, (E.Kil.) G74 | 137 | CE52 |
| Scalpay Pas, G22 | 50 | BT22 |
| Scalpay Pl, G22 | 50 | BT22 |
| Scalpay St, G22 | 50 | BS22 |
| Scapa St, G23 | 49 | BN21 |
| Scaraway Dr, G22 | 50 | BT21 |
| Scaraway Pl, G22 | 50 | BT21 |
| Scaraway St, G22 | 50 | BS21 |
| Scaraway Ter, G22 | 50 | BT21 |
| Scarba Dr, G43 | 102 | BK40 |
| Scarba Quad, Wis. ML2 | 143 | DG52 |
| Scarhill Av, Air. ML6 | 76 | DB32 |
| Scarhill La, Air. ML6 off Scarhill Av | 76 | DC32 |
| Scarhill St, Coat. ML5 | 94 | CV34 |
| Scarrel Dr, G45 | 105 | BW41 |
| Scarrel Gdns, G45 | 105 | BW41 |
| Scarrel Rd, G45 | 105 | BW41 |
| Scarrel Ter, G45 | 105 | BW41 |
| Scavaig Cres, G15 | 28 | BA17 |
| Schaw Ct, (Bears.) G61 | 29 | BF15 |
| Schaw Dr, (Bears.) G61 | 29 | BG15 |
| Schaw Rd, Pais. PA3 | 63 | AW31 |
| Schipka Pas, G1 off Gallowgate | 5 | BT31 |
| Scholar's Gate, (E.Kil.) G75 | 135 | BZ55 |
| Schoolhouse La, (Blan.) G72 | 124 | CL47 |
| School La, (Both.) G71 | 109 | CR43 |
| School La, (Camb.) G72 | 107 | CG41 |
| School Quad, Air. ML6 | 76 | DB27 |
| School Rd, (Stepps) G33 | 53 | CG23 |
| School Rd, (Torr.) G64 | 15 | BY12 |
| School Rd, (Newt. M.) G77 | 117 | BF49 |
| School Rd, Pais. PA1 | 64 | BA32 |
| School St, (Chap.) Air. ML6 | 97 | DF35 |
| School St, Coat. ML5 | 95 | CW33 |
| School St, Ham. ML3 | 140 | CT52 |
| School Wynd, Pais. PA1 | 62 | AU32 |
| Scioncroft Av, (Ruther.) G73 | 89 | BY38 |
| Scone Pl, (E.Kil.) G74 | 121 | BZ50 |
| Scone Pl, (Newt. M.) G77 | 118 | BK49 |
| Scone St, G21 | 50 | BS26 |
| Scone Wk, (Baill.) G69 | 92 | CJ34 |
| Sconser St, G23 | 31 | BN20 |
| Scorton Gdns, (Baill.) G69 off Danby Rd | 91 | CH33 |
| Scotia Cres, Lark. ML9 | 144 | DC60 |
| Scotia Gdns, Ham. ML3 | 140 | CS54 |
| Scotia St, Moth. ML1 | 127 | CY46 |
| Scotland St, G5 | 67 | BP32 |
| Scotland St W, G41 | 67 | BN32 |
| Scotsblair Av, (Kirk.) G66 | 17 | CE14 |
| Scotsburn Rd, G21 | 51 | BY25 |
| Scotstoun Mill Rd, G11 off Partick Br St | 66 | BL28 |
| Scotstoun Pl, G14 off Scotstoun St | 47 | BE26 |
| Scotstoun St, G14 | 47 | BE26 |
| Scott Av, John. PA5 | 79 | AG37 |
| Scott Cres, (Cumb.) G67 | 21 | CZ14 |
| Scott Dr, (Bears.) G61 | 29 | BE15 |
| Scott Dr, (Cumb.) G67 | 21 | CZ14 |
| Scott Gro, Ham. ML3 | 140 | CT51 |
| Scott Hill, (E.Kil.) G74 off Cantieslaw Dr | 122 | CC50 |
| Scott Pl, Bell. ML4 | 95 | CX38 |
| Scott Pl, John. PA5 | 79 | AG37 |
| Scott Rd, G52 | 64 | BB29 |
| Scott's Pl, Air. ML6 | 76 | DD29 |
| Scotts Rd, Pais. PA2 | 83 | AY34 |
| Scott St, G3 | 4 | BQ29 |
| Scott St, (Baill.) G69 | 92 | CK33 |
| Scott St, Clyde. G81 | 26 | AU17 |
| Scott St, Ham. ML3 | 140 | CT52 |
| Scott St, Lark. ML9 | 144 | DD59 |
| Scott St, Moth. ML1 | 128 | DA46 |
| Seafar Rd, (Cumb.) G67 | 22 | DA13 |
| Seafield Av, (Bears.) G61 | 11 | BH14 |
| Seafield Cres, (Cumb.) G68 | 20 | CU12 |
| Seafield Dr, (Ruther.) G73 | 105 | BZ42 |
| Seaforth Cres, (Barr.) G78 | 99 | AX40 |
| Seaforth La, (Mood.) G69 off Burnbrae Av | 37 | CQ19 |
| Seaforth Pl, Bell. ML4 | 110 | CV42 |
| Seaforth Rd, G52 | 64 | BC30 |
| Seaforth Rd, Clyde. G81 | 27 | AX20 |
| Seaforth Rd N, G52 | 64 | BC30 |
| Seaforth Rd S, G52 | 64 | BC30 |
| Seagrove St, G32 | 69 | BZ31 |
| Seamill Gdns, (E.Kil.) G74 | 135 | BZ51 |
| Seamill Path, G53 off Seamill St | 100 | BB40 |
| Seamill St, G53 | 100 | BB40 |
| Seamore St, G20 | 67 | BP27 |
| Seath Av, Air. ML6 | 76 | DA30 |
| Seath Rd, (Ruther.) G73 | 89 | BW36 |
| Seath St, G42 | 88 | BS35 |
| Seaton Ter, Ham. ML3 | 125 | CQ49 |
| Seaward La, G41 | 67 | BN32 |
| Seaward Pl, G41 | 87 | BN33 |
| Seaward St, G41 | 67 | BP32 |
| Second Av, (Millerston) G33 | 52 | CD24 |
| Second Av, G44 | 103 | BR39 |
| Second Av, (Bears.) G61 | 30 | BJ18 |
| Second Av, (Kirk.) G66 | 35 | CE20 |
| Second Av, (Udd.) G71 | 93 | CN36 |
| Second Av, Clyde. G81 | 26 | AV18 |
| Second Av, Renf. PA4 | 63 | AY27 |
| Second Gdns, G41 | 86 | BJ33 |
| Second Rd, (Blan.) G72 | 125 | CN48 |
| Second St, (Udd.) G71 | 93 | CP37 |
| Seedhill, Pais. PA1 | 82 | AV33 |
| Seedhill Rd, Pais. PA1 | 82 | AV33 |
| Seggielea La, G13 off Helensburgh Dr | 47 | BF23 |
| Seggielea Rd, G13 | 47 | BF23 |
| Seil Dr, G44 | 103 | BR41 |
| Selborne Pl, G13 off Selborne Rd | 47 | BG24 |
| Selborne Pl La, G13 | 47 | BG24 |

| Name | Page | Grid |
|------|------|------|
| Selborne Rd, G13 | 47 | BG24 |
| Selby Gdns, G32 | | |
| off Hailes Av | 71 | CF32 |
| Selby Pl, Coat. ML5 | 74 | CT27 |
| Selby St, Coat. ML5 | 74 | CT27 |
| Selkirk Av, G52 | 85 | BE33 |
| Selkirk Dr, (Ruther.) G73 | 89 | BY38 |
| Selkirk Pl, (E.Kil.) G74 | 123 | CD50 |
| Selkirk St, (Blan.) G72 | 124 | CM46 |
| Selkirk St, Ham. ML3 | 140 | CU51 |
| Selkirk Way, Bell. ML4 | | |
| off Bell St | 95 | CX38 |
| Selkirk Way, Coat. ML5 | 96 | DA34 |
| Sella Rd, (Bishop.) G64 | 33 | BZ19 |
| Selvieland Rd, G52 | 64 | BB32 |
| Semphill Gdns, (E.Kil.) G74 | 136 | CD51 |
| Sempie St, Ham. ML3 | 125 | CP49 |
| Sempill Av, Ersk. PA8 | 25 | AP19 |
| Semple Av, Bish. PA7 | 24 | AK18 |
| Semple Pl, (Linw.) Pais. PA3 | 60 | AK30 |
| Senga Cres, Bell. ML4 | | |
| off Oakdene Av | 95 | CW38 |
| Seres Rd, (Clark.) G76 | 118 | BM45 |
| Seton Ter, G31 | 68 | BV30 |
| Settle Gdns, (Baill.) G69 | | |
| off Danby Rd | 91 | CH33 |
| Seven Sisters, (Kirk.) G66 | 35 | CG16 |
| Seventh Av, (Udd.) G71 | 93 | CP37 |
| Seventh Rd, (Blan.) G72 | 125 | CN48 |
| Severn Rd, (E.Kil.) G75 | 134 | BV54 |
| Seymour Grn, (E.Kil.) G75 | 135 | BX53 |
| Seyton Av, (Giff.) G46 | 102 | BL44 |
| Seyton La, (E.Kil.) G74 | 122 | CA50 |
| Shaftesbury Ct, (E.Kil.) G74 | | |
| off Bosworth Rd | 123 | CE48 |
| Shaftesbury Cres, Moth. ML1 | 113 | DF42 |
| Shaftesbury St, G3 | 4 | BP29 |
| Shaftesbury St, Clyde. G81 | 26 | AV19 |
| Shafton Pl, G13 | 47 | BG21 |
| Shafton Rd, G13 | 47 | BG21 |
| Shakespeare Av, Clyde. G81 | 26 | AV17 |
| Shakespeare St, G20 | 49 | BN24 |
| Shamrock St, G4 | 4 | BQ28 |
| Shamrock St, (Kirk.) G66 | 17 | CF13 |
| Shandon Cres, Bell. ML4 | 95 | CW38 |
| Shandon Ter, Ham. ML3 | 139 | CP51 |
| Shandwick Sq, G34 | | |
| off Bogbain Rd | 72 | CJ29 |
| Shandwick Sq Shop Cen, G34 | 72 | CJ29 |
| Shandwick St, G34 | 72 | CJ29 |
| Shanks Av, (Barr.) G78 | 99 | AY43 |
| Shanks Cres, John. PA5 | 79 | AG35 |
| Shanks Ind Pk, (Barr.) G78 | 99 | AY40 |
| Shanks St, G20 | 49 | BN24 |
| Shanks St, Air. ML6 | 76 | DC28 |
| Shanks Way, (Barr.) G78 | | |
| off Blackbyres Rd | 99 | AY41 |
| Shannon St, G20 | 49 | BP24 |
| Shapinsay St, G22 | 50 | BT21 |
| Sharp Av, Coat. ML5 | 94 | CS33 |
| Sharp St, Moth. ML1 | 127 | CX46 |
| Shaw Av, Bish. PA7 | 24 | AL18 |
| Shawbridge Arc, G43 | | |
| off Ashtree Rd | 86 | BL37 |
| Shawbridge St, G43 | 86 | BK38 |
| Shawburn Cres, Ham. ML3 | | |
| off Shawburn St | 125 | CR49 |
| Shawburn St, Ham. ML3 | 125 | CQ49 |
| Shaw Ct, Ersk. PA8 | 25 | AP18 |
| Shaw Cres, Wis. ML2 | 143 | DF52 |
| Shawfield Dr, G5 | 88 | BU35 |
| Shawfield Ind Est, (Ruther.) G73 | 88 | BV35 |
| Shawfield Rd, G5 | 88 | BV34 |
| Shawhead Av, Coat. ML5 | 95 | CX33 |
| Shawhead Cotts, Coat. ML5 | | |
| off Dunottar Av | 95 | CX34 |
| Shawhead Ind Est, Coat. ML5 | 95 | CY35 |
| Shawhill Cres, (Newt. M.) G77 | 117 | BG50 |
| Shawhill Rd, G41 | 86 | BL37 |
| Shawhill Rd, G43 | 86 | BL37 |
| Shawholm Cres, G43 | 86 | BK38 |
| Shawlands Arc, G41 | 87 | BN37 |
| Shawlands Sq, G41 | 86 | BM37 |
| Shawmoss Rd, G41 | 86 | BL36 |
| Shawpark St, G20 | 49 | BN23 |
| Shaw Pl, (Linw.) Pais. PA3 | 60 | AK32 |
| Shawrigg Rd, Lark. ML9 | 145 | DE59 |
| Shaw Rd, (Miln.) G62 | 12 | BJ13 |
| Shaw Rd, (Newt. M.) G77 | 117 | BG49 |
| Shaws Rd, Lark. ML9 | 145 | DD61 |
| Shaw St, G51 | 66 | BJ29 |
| Shaw St, Lark. ML9 | 144 | DD61 |
| Shawwood Cres, (Newt. M.) G77 | 117 | BG50 |
| Shearer Dr, Ham. ML3 | 140 | CS54 |
| Shearers La, Renf. PA4 | | |
| off Fauldshead Rd | 45 | AZ26 |
| Shearer St, G5 | | |
| off Paisley Rd | 4 | BP31 |
| Sheddens Pl, G32 | 70 | CB32 |
| Sheddens Rbt, (Clark.) G76 | 119 | BN46 |
| Sheepburn Rd, (Udd.) G71 | 93 | CN38 |
| Sheila St, G33 | 52 | CA25 |
| Sheilinghill, Ham. ML3 | | |
| off Church St | 126 | CU49 |
| Shelley Ct, G12 | 48 | BJ24 |
| Shelley Dr, (Both.) G71 | 109 | CR42 |
| Shelley Dr, Clyde. G81 | 27 | AW17 |
| Shelley Rd, G12 | 47 | BH24 |
| Shells Rd, (Kirk.) G66 | 17 | CG12 |
| Sheppard St, G21 | | |
| off Cowlairs Rd | 50 | BU25 |
| Sherbrooke Av, G41 | 86 | BL34 |
| Sherbrooke Dr, G41 | 86 | BL33 |
| Sherbrooke Gdns, G41 | 86 | BL34 |
| Sherbrooke Pl, (E.Kil.) G75 | 135 | BY52 |
| Sherburn Gdns, (Baill.) G69 | 91 | CH33 |
| Sherdale Av, (Chap.) Air. ML6 | 97 | DF35 |
| Sheriff Pk Av, (Ruther.) G73 | 89 | BW38 |
| Sherry Av, Moth. ML1 | 112 | DB40 |
| Sherry Dr, Ham. ML3 | 139 | CP52 |
| Sherry Hts, (Camb.) G72 | 106 | CC39 |
| Sherwood Av, (Udd.) G71 | 109 | CQ40 |
| Sherwood Av, Pais. PA1 | 63 | AW31 |
| Sherwood Dr, (Thornlie.) G46 | 102 | BJ42 |
| Sherwood Pl, G15 | 28 | BD18 |
| Shetland Dr, G44 | 103 | BR41 |
| Shettleston Rd, G31 | 69 | BY31 |
| Shettleston Rd, G32 | 70 | CC32 |
| Shettleston Sheddings, G31 | 70 | CA32 |
| Shiel Ct, (E.Kil.) G74 | 122 | CB50 |
| Shielbridge Gdns, G23 | 31 | BN19 |
| Shiel Ct, (Barr.) G78 | 99 | AX40 |
| Shieldaig Dr, (Ruther.) G73 | 105 | BX41 |
| Shieldaig Rd, G22 | 49 | BR21 |
| Shieldburn Rd, G51 | 65 | BE30 |
| Shieldhall Gdns, G51 | 65 | BE30 |
| Shieldhall Rd, G51 | 64 | BD29 |
| Shieldhill, (E.Kil.) G75 | | |
| off Kelvin Dr | 136 | CB54 |
| Shieldmuir St, Wis. ML2 | 129 | DF49 |
| Shiel Dr, Lark. ML9 | 142 | DB56 |
| Shields Ct, Moth. ML1 | 128 | DD50 |
| Shields Dr, Moth. ML1 | 128 | DD50 |
| Shields Rd, G41 | 67 | BP32 |
| Shields Rd, Moth. ML1 | 143 | DE51 |
| Shiel Pl, (E.Kil.) G74 | 122 | CB50 |
| Shiel Pl, Coat. ML5 | 75 | CZ32 |
| Shiel Rd, (Bishop.) G64 | 33 | BX20 |
| Shilford Av, G13 | 46 | BC22 |
| Shillay St, G22 | 50 | BU21 |
| Shilton Dr, G53 | 101 | BE40 |
| Shilton La, Bish. PA7 | 24 | AN17 |
| Shinwell Av, Clyde. G81 | 27 | AZ20 |
| Shipbank La, G1 | | |
| off Clyde St | 5 | BS31 |
| Shira Ter, (E.Kil.) G74 | 136 | CD52 |
| Shirley Quad, Moth. ML1 | 127 | CZ50 |
| Shirrel Av, Bell. ML4 | | |
| off North Rd | 95 | CW38 |
| Shirrel Rd, Moth. ML1 | 112 | DD41 |
| Shirvalea, (Kilsyth) G65 | | |
| off Burnbrae | 19 | CP9 |
| Shiskine Dr, G20 | 48 | BL22 |
| Shiskine Pl, G20 | 48 | BL21 |
| Shiskine St, G20 | 48 | BL21 |
| Sholto Cres, (Righead Ind. Est.) | | |
| Bell. ML4 | 94 | CT38 |
| Shore St, G40 | 88 | BV35 |
| Shortridge St, G20 | 49 | BN24 |
| Shortroods Av, Pais. PA3 | 62 | AT30 |
| Shortroods Cres, Pais. PA3 | 62 | AT30 |
| Shortroods Rd, Pais. PA3 | 62 | AT30 |
| Shotts St, G33 | 71 | CF29 |
| Showcase Leisure Pk, (Baill.) G69 | 93 | CR33 |
| Shuna Cres, G20 | 49 | BN24 |
| Shuna Gdns, G20 | 49 | BN24 |
| Shuna Pl, G20 | 49 | BN24 |
| Shuna Pl, (Newt. M.) G77 | 116 | BD47 |
| Shuna St, G20 | 49 | BN23 |
| Shuttle La, G1 | | |
| off George St | 5 | BT30 |
| Shuttle St, G1 | 5 | BT30 |
| Shuttle St, (Kilsyth) G65 | 7 | CT5 |
| Shuttle St, (Kilb.) John. PA10 | 78 | AC33 |
| Shuttle St, Pais. PA1 | 82 | AU33 |
| Sidland Rd, G21 | 51 | BY24 |
| Sidlaw Av, (Barr.) G78 | | |
| off Ochil Dr | 99 | AY44 |
| Sidlaw Av, Ham. ML3 | 139 | CP51 |
| Sidlaw Dr, Wis. ML2 | 129 | DH50 |
| Sidlaw Rd, (Bears.) G61 | 28 | BD15 |
| Sidlaw Way, (Chap.) Air. ML6 | 97 | DH36 |
| Sidlaw Way, Lark. ML9 | | |
| off Pentland Cres | 142 | DB56 |
| Sielga Pl, G34 | 72 | CJ29 |
| Siemens Pl, G21 | 69 | BX27 |
| Siemens St, G21 | 69 | BX27 |
| Sievewright St, (Ruther.) G73 | | |
| off Hunter Rd | 89 | BY36 |
| Sighthill Ln, Lark. ML9 | | |
| off Muirshot Rd | 144 | DD57 |
| Sikeside Pl, Coat. ML5 | 75 | CZ32 |
| Sikeside St, Coat. ML5 | 75 | CZ32 |
| Silkin Av, Clyde. G81 | 27 | AZ20 |
| Silk St, Pais. PA1 | 62 | AV32 |
| Silvan Pl, (Clark.) G76 | 119 | BQ48 |
| Silver Birch Dr, G51 | 65 | BF30 |
| Silver Birch Gdns, G51 | 65 | BF30 |
| Silverburn Cen, G53 | 85 | BE38 |
| Silverburn Cres, Moth. ML1 | 113 | DF42 |
| Silverburn St, G33 | 70 | CA29 |
| Silverdale, (E.Kil.) G74 | 121 | BY50 |
| Silverdale St, G31 | 89 | BY33 |
| Silverdale Ter, (Plains) Air. ML6 | 59 | DH26 |
| Silverfir Ct, G5 | 88 | BT34 |
| Silverfir Pl, G5 | 88 | BT34 |

| | | | | | | | | | |
|---|---|---|---|---|---|---|---|---|---|
| Silver Firs, Moth. ML1 | 112 | DD42 | Skye Wynd, Ham. ML3 | 139 | CP52 | Southbank Rd, (Kirk.) G66 | 17 | CE14 |
| Silverfir St, G5 | 88 | BT34 | Skylands Gro, Ham. ML3 | 139 | CQ53 | Southbank St, G31 | 69 | BZ32 |
| Silvergrove St, G40 | 68 | BU32 | Skylands Pl, Ham. ML3 | 139 | CQ54 | South Bk St, Clyde. G81 | 45 | AY22 |
| Silvertonhill Av, Ham. ML3 | 140 | CU52 | Skylands Ri, Ham. ML3 | 139 | CQ53 | Southbar Av, G13 | 46 | BC22 |
| Silvertonhill Pl, Ham. ML3 | | | Slakiewood Av, (Gart.) G69 | 55 | CN22 | Southbar Rd, Ersk. PA8 | 43 | AQ23 |
| *off Chriss Av* | 140 | CT54 | Slatefield Ct, G31 | | | Southbar Rd, Renf. PA4 | 43 | AQ23 |
| Silverwells, (Both.) G71 | 109 | CR44 | *off Slatefield St* | 69 | BW31 | South Barrwood Rd, (Kilsyth) | | |
| Silverwells Ct, (Both.) G71 | 109 | CQ44 | Slatefield St, G31 | 69 | BW31 | G65 | 7 | CU6 |
| Silverwells Cres, (Both.) G71 | 109 | CQ44 | Sleaford Av, Moth. ML1 | 127 | CZ49 | South Biggar Rd, Air. ML6 | 76 | DD30 |
| Simons Cres, Renf. PA4 | 45 | AZ24 | Slenavon Av, (Ruther.) G73 | 105 | BZ42 | Southbrae Dr, G13 | 47 | BE24 |
| Simpson Ct, (Udd.) G71 | 109 | CP39 | Slessor Dr, (E.Kil.) G75 | 136 | CA54 | Southbrae Gdns, G13 | 47 | BF24 |
| Simpson Ct, Clyde. G81 | 27 | AW19 | Slioch Sq, Moth. ML1 | | | Southbrae La, G13 | | |
| Simpson Dr, (E.Kil.) G75 | 135 | BZ54 | *off Law Dr* | 113 | DE41 | *off Milner Rd* | 47 | BG24 |
| Simpson Gdns, (Barr.) G78 | 99 | AX43 | Sloy St, G22 | 50 | BT25 | South Br St, Air. ML6 | 76 | DC29 |
| Simpson Pl, (E.Kil.) G75 | | | Small Cres, (Blan.) G72 | 124 | CM46 | Southburn Rd, Air. ML6 | 75 | CZ30 |
| *off The Murray Rd* | 135 | BZ54 | Smeaton Av, (Torr.) G64 | 15 | BX13 | South Caldeen Rd, Coat. ML5 | 75 | CX32 |
| Simpson St, G20 | 49 | BP26 | Smeaton Dr, (Bishop.) G64 | 33 | BW17 | South Calder, Moth. ML1 | 128 | DB45 |
| Simpson Way, Bell. ML4 | 95 | CY38 | Smeaton Gro, G20 | 49 | BP23 | South Campbell St, Pais. PA2 | 82 | AU34 |
| Simshill Rd, G44 | 103 | BR42 | Smeaton St, G20 | 49 | BP23 | South Carbrain Rd, (Cumb.) G67 | 22 | DB13 |
| Sinclair Av, (Bears.) G61 | 29 | BG15 | Smith Cl, (Bishop.) G64 | 51 | BZ21 | South Chester St, G32 | 70 | CC32 |
| Sinclair Dr, G42 | 87 | BP38 | Smith Cres, Clyde. G81 | 27 | AX16 | South Circular Rd, Coat. ML5 | 75 | CW30 |
| Sinclair Dr, Coat. ML5 | 74 | CT30 | Smith Gdns, (Bishop.) G64 | 51 | BZ21 | South Commonhead Av, | | |
| Sinclair Gdns, (Bishop.) G64 | 51 | BW21 | Smith Gro, (Bishop.) G64 | 51 | BZ21 | Air. ML6 | 76 | DC28 |
| Sinclair Gro, Bell. ML4 | 110 | CV43 | Smithhills St, Pais. PA1 | 62 | AU32 | Southcroft Rd, (Ruther.) G73 | 88 | BU36 |
| Sinclair Pk, (E.Kil.) G75 | | | Smith Quad, Coat. ML5 | 75 | CV30 | Southcroft St, G51 | 66 | BK30 |
| *off Telford Rd* | 136 | CB53 | Smiths La, Pais. PA3 | 62 | AU31 | South Cft St, Pais. PA1 | | |
| Sinclair Pl, (E.Kil.) G75 | 136 | CB53 | Smithstone Cres, (Kilsyth) G65 | 7 | CU8 | *off Lawn St* | 62 | AV32 |
| Sinclair St, (Miln.) G62 | 12 | BJ11 | Smithstone Rd, (Cumb.) G68 | 20 | CV11 | South Crosshill Rd, (Bishop.) | | |
| Sinclair St, Clyde. G81 | 45 | AZ21 | Smith St, G14 | 65 | BG27 | G64 | 33 | BW20 |
| Singer Rd, (E.Kil.) G75 | 136 | CB55 | Smith Ter, (Ruther.) G73 | 89 | BX36 | South Dean Pk Av, (Both.) G71 | 109 | CQ43 |
| Singer Rd, Clyde. G81 | 26 | AV18 | Smith Way, (Bishop.) G64 | 51 | BZ21 | Southdeen Av, G15 | 28 | BD18 |
| Singer St, Clyde. G81 | 27 | AX18 | Smithycroft, Ham. ML3 | 141 | CW51 | Southdeen Gro, G15 | 28 | BD18 |
| Sir Michael Pl, Pais. PA1 | 82 | AT33 | Smithycroft Rd, G33 | 70 | CA28 | Southdeen Rd, G15 | 28 | BC18 |
| Sir Thomas Lipton Way, (Camb.) | | | Snaefell Av, (Ruther.) G73 | 105 | BY41 | South Douglas St, Clyde. G81 | 45 | AY21 |
| G72 *off Library Gdns* | 106 | CB39 | Snaefell Cres, (Ruther.) G73 | 105 | BY40 | South Dr, (Linw.) Pais. PA3 | 60 | AK31 |
| Sixth Av, Renf. PA4 | 63 | AY28 | Sneddon St, Ham. ML3 | 125 | CP47 | South Dumbreck Rd, (Kilsyth) | | |
| Sixth St, (Udd.) G71 | 93 | CN36 | Sneddon Ter, Ham. ML3 | 125 | CP47 | G65 | 7 | CR5 |
| Skaethorn Rd, G20 | 48 | BK22 | Snowdon Pl, G5 | | | South Elgin Pl, Clyde. G81 | 45 | AY22 |
| Skaterigg Dr, G13 | 47 | BH24 | *off Benthall St* | 88 | BT33 | South Elgin St, Clyde. G81 | 45 | AY22 |
| Skaterigg Gdns, G13 | 47 | BH24 | Snowdon St, G5 | | | Southend Pl, Bell. ML4 | 110 | CV41 |
| Skaterig La, G13 | 47 | BG24 | *off Benthall St* | 88 | BT33 | Southend Rd, Clyde. G81 | 27 | AX16 |
| Skelbo Path, G34 | | | Snuff Mill Rd, G44 | 103 | BR40 | Southern Av, (Ruther.) G73 | 105 | BX40 |
| *off Auchingill Rd* | 72 | CM28 | Society St, G31 | 69 | BX32 | Southerness Dr, (Cumb.) G68 | | |
| Skelbo Pl, G34 | 72 | CM28 | Solar Ct, Lark. ML9 | 144 | DD61 | *off Letham Gra* | 9 | DC8 |
| Skellyton Cres, Lark. ML9 | 144 | DD59 | Sollas Pl, G13 | 46 | BA21 | South Erskine Pk, (Bears.) G61 | 29 | BF16 |
| Skene Rd, G51 | 66 | BK32 | Solway Ct, Ham. ML3 | 139 | CR53 | Southesk Av, (Bishop.) G64 | 32 | BV18 |
| Skerne Rd, (E.Kil.) G75 | 134 | BX55 | Solway Pl, (Chry.) G69 | 36 | CM20 | Southesk Gdns, (Bishop.) G64 | 32 | BV18 |
| Skerray Quad, G22 | 50 | BS21 | Solway Rd, (Bishop.) G64 | 33 | BZ19 | South Ex Ct, G1 | 5 | BS30 |
| Skerray St, G22 | 50 | BS21 | Solway St, G40 | 88 | BV35 | Southfield Av, Pais. PA2 | 82 | AU37 |
| Skerryvore Pl, G33 | 70 | CD29 | Somerford Rd, (Bears.) G61 | 29 | BH20 | Southfield Cres, G53 | 85 | BE37 |
| Skerryvore Rd, G33 | 70 | CD29 | Somerled Av, Pais. PA3 | 62 | AV28 | Southfield Cres, Coat. ML5 | 75 | CY32 |
| Skibo Dr, (Thornlie.) G46 | 101 | BG42 | Somerset Av, Ham. ML3 | 125 | CR49 | Southfield Rd, (Cumb.) G68 | 21 | CY12 |
| Skibo La, (Thornlie.) G46 | 101 | BG42 | Somerset Pl, G3 | 4 | BP28 | South Frederick St, G1 | 5 | BS30 |
| Skimmers Hill, (M. of Cam.) G66 | 16 | CD9 | Somerset Pl Ms, G3 | 4 | BP28 | Southgate, (Miln.) G62 | | |
| Skipness Dr, G51 | 65 | BF29 | Somervell St, (Camb.) G72 | 106 | CB39 | *off Park Rd* | 12 | BJ12 |
| Skirsa Ct, G23 | | | Somerville Dr, G42 | 87 | BR37 | Southgate, (E.Kil.) G74 | | |
| *off Skirsa St* | 49 | BQ21 | Somerville Dr, (E.Kil.) G75 | 136 | CB54 | *off East Kilbride Shop Cen* | 136 | CA53 |
| Skirsa Pl, G23 | 49 | BP22 | Somerville La, (E.Kil.) G75 | 136 | CB54 | South Glassford St, (Miln.) G62 | 12 | BK12 |
| Skirsa Sq, G23 | 49 | BQ22 | Somerville Ter, (E.Kil.) G75 | | | South Hallhill Rd, G32 | 70 | CD32 |
| Skirsa St, G23 | 49 | BP21 | *off The Murray Rd* | 136 | CB54 | Southhill Av, (Ruther.) G73 | 105 | BY40 |
| Skirving St, G41 | 87 | BN37 | Sorby St, G31 | 69 | BZ32 | Southinch Av, G14 | 46 | BA23 |
| Skovlunde Way, (E.Kil.) G75 | 136 | CA55 | Sorley St, G11 | | | Southinch La, G14 | 46 | BA23 |
| Skye, (E.Kil.) G74 | 137 | CE52 | *off Dumbarton Rd* | 65 | BH27 | Southlea Av, (Thornlie.) G46 | 102 | BJ42 |
| Skye Av, Renf. PA4 | 63 | AY28 | Sorn St, G40 | 89 | BX34 | South Ln, (Chry.) G69 | 55 | CN21 |
| Skye Ct, (Cumb.) G67 | 21 | CZ13 | Souterhouse Rd, Coat. ML5 | 74 | CV32 | Southloch Gdns, G21 | 50 | BV26 |
| Skye Cres, (Old Kil.) G60 | 26 | AS16 | Southampton Dr, G12 | 48 | BK23 | Southloch St, G21 | 50 | BV26 |
| Skye Cres, Pais. PA2 | 82 | AT38 | Southampton La, G12 | 48 | BK23 | South Mains Rd, (Miln.) G62 | 11 | BH12 |
| Skye Dr, (Old Kil.) G60 | 26 | AS16 | South Annandale St, G42 | 87 | BR35 | South Medrox St, (Glenb.) | | |
| Skye Dr, (Cumb.) G67 | 21 | CZ13 | South Av, (Blan.) G72 | 124 | CM48 | Coat. ML5 | 56 | CS22 |
| Skye Gdns, (Bears.) G61 | 28 | BD15 | South Av, Clyde. G81 | 27 | AW19 | South Moraine La, G15 | | |
| Skye Pl, (Cumb.) G67 | 21 | CZ13 | South Av, Pais. PA2 | 82 | AV37 | *off Moraine Av* | 29 | BE19 |
| Skye Rd, (Cumb.) G67 | 21 | CZ13 | South Av, Renf. PA4 | 45 | AZ26 | South Muirhead Rd, (Cumb.) | | |
| Skye Rd, (Ruther.) G73 | 105 | BZ42 | Southbank Dr, (Kirk.) G66 | 17 | CE13 | G67 | 22 | DC11 |

| Name | Page | Grid |
|---|---|---|
| Southmuir Pl, G20 | 48 | BM24 |
| South Nimmo St, Air. ML6 | 76 | DD30 |
| South Nitshill Ind Est, G53 | 100 | BC40 |
| Southpark Av, G12 | 66 | BM27 |
| South Pk Av, (Barr.) G78 | 99 | AX42 |
| South Pk Dr, Pais. PA2 | 82 | AU35 |
| South Pk Gro, Ham. ML3 | 126 | CT50 |
| South Pk Rd, Ham. ML3 | 126 | CT50 |
| Southpark Ter, G12 | 67 | BN27 |
| off Southpark Av | 67 | BN27 |
| South Pl, Bell. ML4 | 110 | CV41 |
| South Portland St, G5 | 67 | BR32 |
| South Rd, (Clark.) G76 | 119 | BQ48 |
| South Robertson Pl, Air. ML6 | 76 | DA30 |
| South Scott St, (Baill.) G69 | 92 | CK33 |
| Southside Cres, G5 | 87 | BR33 |
| South St, G11 | 65 | BG27 |
| South St, G14 | 65 | BF27 |
| South St, (Inch.) Renf. PA4 | 43 | AR25 |
| South Vesalius St, G32 | | |
| off Shettleston Rd | 70 | CC32 |
| South Vw, (Blan.) G72 | 108 | CL44 |
| South Vw, Bell. ML4 | 110 | CU41 |
| South Vw, Clyde. G81 | 26 | AV18 |
| Southview Av, (Clark.) G76 | 119 | BN48 |
| Southview Ct, (Bishop.) G64 | | |
| off Southview Ter | 50 | BV22 |
| Southview Dr, (Bears.) G61 | 29 | BE16 |
| Southview Gro, (Bears.) G61 | 29 | BE16 |
| Southview Pl, (Gart.) G69 | 55 | CN23 |
| Southview Ter, (Bishop.) G64 | 50 | BV22 |
| South William St, John. PA5 | 79 | AH35 |
| Southwold Rd, Pais. PA1 | 64 | BA32 |
| Southwood Dr, G44 | 104 | BS40 |
| Southwood Pl, (Newt. M.) G77 | 131 | BF51 |
| South Woodside Rd, G4 | 67 | BN27 |
| South Woodside Rd, G20 | 49 | BP26 |
| Soutra Pl, G33 | 70 | CD29 |
| Spairdrum Rd, (Cumb.) G67 | 40 | DA17 |
| Spairdrum Rd, Air. ML6 | 40 | DC17 |
| Spalehall Dr, Moth. ML1 | 113 | DH42 |
| Spateston Rd, John. PA5 | 79 | AE38 |
| Spean Av, (E.Kil.) G74 | 136 | CD52 |
| Spean St, G44 | 103 | BQ39 |
| Speirsfield Ct, Pais. PA2 | 82 | AT34 |
| Speirsfield Gdns, Pais. PA2 | 82 | AT34 |
| Speirshall Cl, G14 | 46 | BB23 |
| Speirshall Ter, G14 | 46 | BA23 |
| Speirs Rd, (Bears.) G61 | 30 | BJ18 |
| Speirs Rd, John. PA5 | 80 | AK34 |
| Speirs Wf, G4 | 67 | BR27 |
| Spencer Cl, Pais. PA2 | 81 | AN37 |
| Spencer Dr, Pais. PA2 | 80 | AM37 |
| Spencerfield Gdns, Ham. ML3 | 126 | CV50 |
| Spencer Pl, Pais. PA2 | 81 | AN37 |
| Spencer St, G13 | 47 | BH22 |
| Spencer St, Clyde. G81 | 27 | AW18 |
| Spencer Vennel, Pais. PA2 | 81 | AN37 |
| Spence St, G20 | 48 | BL21 |
| Spey Av, Pais. PA2 | 81 | AN36 |
| Spey Ct, Air. ML6 | | |
| off Etive Dr | 77 | DE32 |
| Spey Dr, Coat. ML5 | 94 | CU33 |
| Spey Dr, Renf. PA4 | 64 | BA27 |
| Spey Gdns, Ham. ML3 | 139 | CR53 |
| Spey Gro, (E.Kil.) G75 | 134 | BU54 |
| Spey Pl, John. PA5 | 79 | AE37 |
| Spey Rd, (Bears.) G61 | 29 | BG16 |
| Spey St, G33 | 70 | CB29 |
| Spey Ter, (E.Kil.) G75 | 134 | BV54 |
| Spey Wk, (Cumb.) G67 | | |
| off Cumbernauld Shop Cen | 22 | DB12 |
| Spey Wk, Moth. ML1 | | |
| off Redwood Rd | 113 | DE39 |
| Spey Wynd, Lark. ML9 | | |
| off Riverside Rd | 144 | DC61 |
| Spiersbridge Av, (Thornlie.) G46 | 101 | BH42 |
| Spiersbridge La, (Thornlie.) G46 | 101 | BG42 |
| Spiersbridge Rd, (Thornlie.) G46 | 101 | BH42 |
| Spiersbridge Ter, (Thornlie.) | | |
| G46 | 101 | BG42 |
| Spiersbridge Toll, (Thornlie.) | | |
| G46 | 101 | BG43 |
| Spiersbridge Way, (Thornlie.) | | |
| G46 | 101 | BH42 |
| Spiers Gro, (Thornlie.) G46 | 101 | BH42 |
| Spiers Pl, (Linw.) Pais. PA3 | 60 | AL30 |
| Spindlehowe Rd, (Udd.) G71 | 109 | CP39 |
| Spinners Gdns, Pais. PA2 | 81 | AR34 |
| Spinners Row, John. PA5 | 79 | AF35 |
| Spittal Rd, (Ruther.) G73 | 104 | BV41 |
| Spittal Ter, (Camb.) G72 | 108 | CJ43 |
| Spoolers Rd, Pais. PA1 | 81 | AR34 |
| Spoutmouth, G1 | 5 | BT31 |
| Springbank Cres, Ham. ML3 | 139 | CQ54 |
| Springbank Rd, Pais. PA3 | 62 | AT30 |
| Springbank St, G20 | 49 | BP25 |
| Springbank Ter, Pais. PA3 | 62 | AT30 |
| Springbank Vw, (Plains) Air. ML6 | 59 | DH26 |
| Springboig Av, G32 | 71 | CE31 |
| Springboig Rd, G32 | 71 | CE30 |
| Springburn Pl, (E.Kil.) G74 | 121 | BW50 |
| Springburn Rd, G21 | 68 | BU27 |
| Springburn Rd, (Bishop.) G64 | 50 | BU24 |
| Springburn Shop Cen, G21 | 50 | BV25 |
| Springburn Way, G21 | 50 | BU25 |
| Springcroft Av, (Baill.) G69 | 72 | CK31 |
| Springcroft Cres, (Baill.) G69 | 72 | CK31 |
| Springcroft Dr, (Baill.) G69 | 72 | CJ31 |
| Springcroft Gdns, (Baill.) G69 | 72 | CL31 |
| Springcroft Gro, (Baill.) G69 | 72 | CK31 |
| Springcroft Rd, (Baill.) G69 | 72 | CK31 |
| Springcroft Wynd, (Baill.) G69 | 72 | CK31 |
| Springfield Av, (Bishop.) G64 | 51 | BW21 |
| Springfield Av, (Udd.) G71 | 109 | CP40 |
| Springfield Av, Pais. PA1 | 83 | AX33 |
| Springfield Ct, G1 | 5 | BS30 |
| Springfield Cres, (Bishop.) G64 | 51 | BW21 |
| Springfield Cres, (Udd.) G71 | 109 | CP40 |
| Springfield Cres, (Blan.) G72 | 124 | CL46 |
| Springfield Dr, (Barr.) G78 | 100 | BA44 |
| Springfield Gro, (Barr.) G78 | 115 | AZ45 |
| Springfield Pk, John. PA5 | 80 | AJ35 |
| Springfield Pk Rd, (Ruther.) | | |
| G73 | 105 | BY39 |
| Springfield Quay, G5 | 4 | BP31 |
| Springfield Rd, G31 | 89 | BY33 |
| Springfield Rd, G40 | 89 | BX34 |
| Springfield Rd, (Bishop.) G64 | 33 | BW20 |
| Springfield Rd, (Cumb.) G67 | 22 | DC9 |
| Springfield Rd, (Barr.) G78 | 115 | AY45 |
| Springfield Rd, Air. ML6 | 77 | DG30 |
| Springfield Sq, (Bishop.) G64 | 51 | BW21 |
| Springfield Wds, John. PA5 | | |
| off Springfield Pk | 80 | AJ35 |
| Springhall Ct, (Ruther.) G73 | | |
| off Cruachan Rd | 105 | BZ42 |
| Springhill Av, Air. ML6 | 76 | DD29 |
| Springhill Av, Coat. ML5 | 94 | CS33 |
| Springhill Dr N, (Baill.) G69 | 72 | CJ30 |
| Springhill Dr S, (Baill.) G69 | 72 | CJ30 |
| Springhill Fm Gro, (Baill.) G69 | 72 | CJ31 |
| Springhill Fm Pl, (Baill.) G69 | 72 | CJ31 |
| Springhill Fm Rd, (Baill.) G69 | 72 | CJ31 |
| Springhill Fm Way, (Baill.) G69 | 72 | CJ31 |
| Springhill Gdns, G41 | 87 | BN36 |
| Springhill Parkway, (Baill.) G69 | 72 | CJ31 |
| Springhill Pl, Coat. ML5 | 94 | CS33 |
| Springhill Rd, (Baill.) G69 | 71 | CH32 |
| Springhill Rd, (Clark.) G76 | 119 | BP46 |
| Springhill Rd, (Barr.) G78 | 99 | AX43 |
| Springholm Dr, Air. ML6 | 76 | DB27 |
| Springkell Av, G41 | 86 | BL34 |
| Springkell Dr, G41 | 86 | BK35 |
| Springkell Gdns, G41 | 86 | BL35 |
| Springkell Gate, G41 | 86 | BM35 |
| Spring La, G5 | | |
| off Lawmoor St | 88 | BS34 |
| Springside Gdns, G15 | 28 | BC16 |
| Springside Pl, G15 | 28 | BC17 |
| Springvale Dr, Pais. PA2 | 81 | AP35 |
| Springvale Ter, G21 | 50 | BU25 |
| Springwell Cres, (Blan.) G72 | 125 | CP46 |
| Springwells Av, Air. ML6 | 77 | DE29 |
| Springwells Cres, Air. ML6 | 77 | DE29 |
| Spring Wynd, G5 | 88 | BS33 |
| Spruce Av, (Blan.) G72 | 124 | CL45 |
| Spruce Av, Ham. ML3 | 140 | CU52 |
| Spruce Av, John. PA5 | 80 | AJ35 |
| Spruce Ct, Coat. ML5 | | |
| off Ailsa Rd | 94 | CV33 |
| Spruce Ct, Ham. ML3 | 140 | CU52 |
| Spruce Dr, (Kirk.) G66 | 34 | CC16 |
| Spruce Dr, (Camb.) G72 | 107 | CH41 |
| Spruce Rd, (Cumb.) G67 | 23 | DF9 |
| Spruce Rd, (Udd.) G71 | | |
| off Laburnum Rd | 94 | CS36 |
| Spruce St, G22 | 50 | BT24 |
| Spruce Way, (Camb.) G72 | | |
| off Spruce Dr | 107 | CH41 |
| Spruce Way, Moth. ML1 | | |
| off Shirrel Rd | 112 | DD41 |
| Spynie Pl, (Bishop.) G64 | 33 | BZ19 |
| Squire St, G14 | 65 | BF27 |
| Stable Gro, Pais. PA1 | 81 | AR33 |
| Stable Pl, (Miln.) G62 | 11 | BH10 |
| Stable Rd, (Miln.) G62 | 11 | BH10 |
| Stables, The, Pais. PA1 | 81 | AR33 |
| Staffa, (E.Kil.) G74 | 137 | CE53 |
| Staffa Av, Renf. PA4 | 63 | AY28 |
| Staffa Dr, (Kirk.) G66 | 18 | CK13 |
| Staffa Dr, Air. ML6 | 77 | DH30 |
| Staffa Dr, Pais. PA2 | 82 | AU38 |
| Staffa Rd, (Camb.) G72 | 106 | CB42 |
| Staffa St, G31 | 69 | BX29 |
| Staffa Ter, (Camb.) G72 | 106 | CB42 |
| Staffin Dr, G23 | 30 | BM20 |
| Staffin Path, G23 | 31 | BN20 |
| Staffin St, G23 | 31 | BN20 |
| Stafford St, G4 | 5 | BS28 |
| Stafford St, Bell. ML4 | 110 | CV41 |
| Stag St, G51 | 66 | BK30 |
| Staig Wynd, Moth. ML1 | | |
| off Dunbar Dr | 128 | DC49 |
| Staineybraes Pl, Air. ML6 | 76 | DB27 |
| Stair St, G20 | 49 | BP25 |
| Stamford Gate, G31 | 69 | BX32 |
| Stamford Pl, G31 | 69 | BX32 |
| Stamford Rd, G31 | 69 | BX32 |
| Stamford St, G31 | 69 | BX32 |
| Stamford St, G40 | 69 | BX32 |
| Stamperland Av, (Clark.) G76 | 119 | BP45 |
| Stamperland Cres, (Clark.) G76 | | |
| off Stamperland Hill | 119 | BN45 |
| Stamperland Dr, (Clark.) G76 | 119 | BP45 |
| Stamperland Gdns, (Clark.) | | |
| G76 | 103 | BP44 |
| Stamperland Hill, (Clark.) G76 | 119 | BN45 |

| | | |
|---|---|---|
| Stanalane St, (Thornlie.) G46 | 101 | BH41 |
| Standburn Rd, G21 | 51 | BY22 |
| Staneacre Pk, Ham. ML3 | 126 | CV50 |
| Stanefield Dr, Moth. ML1 | 113 | DG41 |
| Stanely Av, Pais. PA2 | 81 | AR36 |
| Stanely Cres, Pais. PA2 | 81 | AR37 |
| Stanely Dr, Pais. PA2 | 82 | AS36 |
| Stanely Gra, Pais. PA2 | 81 | AQ38 |
| Stanely Gro, Pais. PA2 | 81 | AR37 |
| Stanely Rd, Pais. PA2 | 82 | AS36 |
| Stanford St, Clyde. G81 | 27 | AY20 |
| Stanhope Dr, (Ruther.) G73 | 105 | BZ40 |
| Stanley Boul, (Blan.) G72 | 124 | CM49 |
| Stanley Dr, (Bishop.) G64 | 33 | BX19 |
| Stanley Dr, Bell. ML4 | 111 | CW39 |
| Stanley Pl, (Blan.) G72 | 108 | CM44 |
| Stanley St, G41 | 67 | BN32 |
| Stanley St, Ham. ML3 | 125 | CP49 |
| Stanley St La, G41 | 67 | BN32 |
| Stanmore Rd, G42 | 87 | BR37 |
| Stark Av, Clyde. G81 | 26 | AU15 |
| Starling Way, Bell. ML4 | 94 | CU37 |
| Startpoint St, G33 | 70 | CC29 |
| Station Brae, (Neil.) G78 | 114 | AS45 |
| Station Cres, Renf. PA4 | | |
| *off Station Rd* | 45 | AZ25 |
| Station Pk, (Baill.) G69 | 92 | CL33 |
| Station Rd, G20 | 48 | BL21 |
| Station Rd, (Millerston) G33 | 52 | CC24 |
| Station Rd, (Stepps) G33 | 53 | CF24 |
| Station Rd, (Giff.) G46 | | |
| *off Fenwick Rd* | 102 | BL42 |
| Station Rd, (Bears.) G61 | 29 | BE18 |
| Station Rd, (Bardowie) G62 | 13 | BQ14 |
| Station Rd, (Miln.) G62 | 12 | BJ12 |
| Station Rd, (Kilsyth) G65 | 7 | CT4 |
| Station Rd, (Lenz.) G66 | 35 | CE17 |
| Station Rd, (Baill.) G69 | 92 | CL33 |
| Station Rd, (Muir.) G69 | 54 | CL23 |
| Station Rd, (Both.) G71 | 109 | CQ43 |
| Station Rd, (Udd.) G71 | 109 | CN39 |
| Station Rd, (Blan.) G72 | 109 | CN44 |
| Station Rd, (Clark.) G76 | 119 | BQ48 |
| Station Rd, (Neil.) G78 | 114 | AT46 |
| Station Rd, Air. ML6 | 77 | DG29 |
| Station Rd, Bish. PA7 | 24 | AK19 |
| Station Rd, (Kilb.) John. PA10 | 78 | AC34 |
| Station Rd, Lark. ML9 | 144 | DD57 |
| Station Rd, Moth. ML1 | 112 | DC42 |
| Station Rd, Pais. PA1 | 81 | AQ34 |
| Station Rd, Renf. PA4 | 45 | AZ25 |
| Station Way, (Udd.) G71 | 109 | CP39 |
| Station Wynd, (Kilb.) | | |
| John. PA10 | 78 | AD35 |
| Staybrae Dr, G53 | 84 | BB36 |
| Staybrae Gro, G53 | 84 | BB36 |
| Steel St, G1 | 5 | BT31 |
| Steeple Sq, (Kilb.) John. PA10 | | |
| *off Ewing St* | 78 | AC34 |
| Steeple St, (Kilb.) John. PA10 | 78 | AC34 |
| Stenhouse Av, (Muir.) G69 | 54 | CL22 |
| Stenton Cres, Wis. ML2 | 143 | DF52 |
| Stenton Pl, Wis. ML2 | | |
| *off Carbarns Rd* | 143 | DF52 |
| Stenton St, G32 | 70 | CA30 |
| Stenzel Pl, (Stepps) G33 | 53 | CH24 |
| Stepford Pl, G33 | 71 | CH30 |
| Stepford Rd, G33 | 71 | CH30 |
| Stephen Cres, (Baill.) G69 | 71 | CH32 |
| Stephenson Pl, (E.Kil.) G75 | 135 | BZ53 |
| Stephenson Sq, (E.Kil.) G75 | | |
| *off Simpson Dr* | 135 | BZ53 |
| Stephenson St, G52 | 64 | BA29 |
| Stephenson Ter, (E.Kil.) G75 | 135 | BZ53 |
| Steppshill Ter, G33 | 53 | CE24 |
| Stepps Rd, G33 | 71 | CE28 |
| Stepps Rd, (Kirk.) G66 | 35 | CG19 |
| Stevens La, Moth. ML1 | | |
| *off Jerviston St* | 112 | DC42 |
| Stevenson Pl, Bell. ML4 | | |
| *off Kelvin Rd* | 95 | CX38 |
| Stevenson St, G40 | 5 | BU31 |
| Stevenson St, Clyde. G81 | 26 | AV17 |
| Stevenson St, Pais. PA2 | 82 | AU34 |
| Stevenston Ct, (New Stev.) | | |
| Moth. ML1 | 112 | DC41 |
| Stevenston St, Moth. ML1 | 112 | DC41 |
| Stewart Av, (Blan.) G72 | 124 | CL46 |
| Stewart Av, (Newt. M.) G77 | 117 | BG47 |
| Stewart Av, Ham. ML3 | 139 | CP53 |
| Stewart Av, Renf. PA4 | 63 | AX28 |
| Stewart Ct, (Ruther.) G73 | 89 | BY38 |
| Stewart Ct, (Barr.) G78 | | |
| *off Stewart St* | 99 | AY41 |
| Stewart Cres, (Barr.) G78 | 99 | AZ41 |
| Stewart Dr, (Baill.) G69 | 73 | CR31 |
| Stewart Dr, (Clark.) G76 | 118 | BM45 |
| Stewart Dr, Clyde. G81 | 27 | AX15 |
| Stewartfield Cres, (E.Kil.) G74 | 121 | BY49 |
| Stewartfield Dr, (E.Kil.) G74 | 121 | BZ49 |
| Stewartfield Gdns, (E.Kil.) G74 | 121 | BY49 |
| Stewartfield Gro, (E.Kil.) G74 | 121 | BX49 |
| Stewartfield Rd, (E.Kil.) G74 | 121 | BY50 |
| Stewartfield Way, (E.Kil.) G74 | 121 | BW49 |
| Stewartgill Pl, (Ashgill) Lark. | | |
| ML9 *off Auldton Ter* | 145 | DH60 |
| Stewarton Dr, (Camb.) G72 | 106 | CA40 |
| Stewarton Rd, (Thornlie.) G46 | 101 | BG43 |
| Stewarton Rd, (Newt. M.) G77 | 117 | BE46 |
| Stewart Pl, (Barr.) G78 | 99 | AZ41 |
| Stewart Rd, Pais. PA2 | 82 | AV37 |
| Stewart St, G4 | 4 | BR28 |
| Stewart St, (Miln.) G62 | 12 | BJ12 |
| Stewart St, (Barr.) G78 | 99 | AZ41 |
| Stewart St, Bell. ML4 | 111 | CY40 |
| Stewart St, Clyde. G81 | 26 | AU18 |
| Stewart St, Coat. ML5 | 75 | CW29 |
| Stewart St, Ham. ML3 | 125 | CQ48 |
| Stewartville St, G11 | 66 | BK27 |
| Stirling Av, (Bears.) G61 | 29 | BG19 |
| Stirling Av, (E.Kil.) G74 | 122 | CC50 |
| Stirling Dr, (Bears.) G61 | 29 | BE15 |
| Stirling Dr, (Bishop.) G64 | 32 | BU18 |
| Stirling Dr, (Ruther.) G73 | 105 | BX40 |
| Stirling Dr, Ham. ML3 | 125 | CN49 |
| Stirling Dr, John. PA5 | 79 | AF35 |
| Stirlingfauld Pl, G5 | 87 | BR33 |
| Stirling Gdns, (Bishop.) G64 | 32 | BU18 |
| Stirling Rd, G4 | 5 | BT29 |
| Stirling Rd, (Kilsyth) G65 | 8 | CV4 |
| Stirling Rd, (Cumb.) G67 | 40 | DC15 |
| Stirling Rd, Air. ML6 | 58 | DD26 |
| Stirling Rd, (Riggend) Air. ML6 | 40 | DC20 |
| Stirling Rd Ind Est, Air. ML6 | 59 | DE26 |
| Stirling St, (Cumb.) G67 | 22 | DD9 |
| Stirling St, Air. ML6 | 76 | DB30 |
| Stirling St, Coat. ML5 | 94 | CT33 |
| Stirling St, Moth. ML1 | 128 | DD49 |
| Stirling Way, (Baill.) G69 | | |
| *off Huntingtower Rd* | 92 | CJ33 |
| Stirling Way, Renf. PA4 | | |
| *off York Way* | 63 | AZ28 |
| Stirrat St, G20 | 48 | BL23 |
| Stirrat St, Pais. PA3 | 61 | AR30 |
| Stobcross Rd, G3 | 66 | BM29 |
| Stobcross St, G3 | 4 | BP30 |
| Stobcross St, Coat. ML5 | 75 | CW31 |
| Stobcross Wynd, G3 | 66 | BL29 |
| Stobhill Cotts, G21 | | |
| *off Stobhill Rd* | 51 | BW22 |
| Stobhill Rd, G21 | 50 | BV22 |
| Stobo, (E.Kil.) G74 | 123 | CE49 |
| Stobo Ct, (E.Kil.) G74 | 123 | CE49 |
| Stobs Dr, (Barr.) G78 | 99 | AX40 |
| Stobs Pl, G34 | 72 | CL28 |
| Stock Av, Pais. PA2 | 82 | AU34 |
| Stockholm Cres, Pais. PA2 | 82 | AU34 |
| Stockiemuir Av, (Bears.) G61 | 11 | BF14 |
| Stockiemuir Rd, (Bears.) G61 | 11 | BE12 |
| Stock St, Pais. PA2 | 82 | AU34 |
| Stockwell Pl, G1 | 5 | BS31 |
| Stockwell St, G1 | 5 | BS31 |
| Stoddard Sq, (Elder.) John. PA5 | 80 | AM34 |
| Stonebank Gro, G45 | 104 | BT42 |
| Stonebyres Ct, Ham. ML3 | 125 | CQ50 |
| Stonedyke Gro, G15 | 28 | BD19 |
| Stonefield Av, G12 | 48 | BK23 |
| Stonefield Av, Pais. PA2 | 82 | AV36 |
| Stonefield Cres, (Blan.) G72 | 124 | CK47 |
| Stonefield Cres, (Clark.) G76 | | |
| *off Dorian Dr* | 118 | BL45 |
| Stonefield Dr, Pais. PA2 | 82 | AV36 |
| Stonefield Gdns, Pais. PA2 | 82 | AV36 |
| Stonefield Grn, Pais. PA2 | 82 | AU36 |
| Stonefield Gro, Pais. PA2 | 82 | AU36 |
| Stonefield Pk, Pais. PA2 | 82 | AU37 |
| Stonefield Pk Gdns, (Blan.) | | |
| G72 | 124 | CM45 |
| Stonefield Pl, (Blan.) G72 | 124 | CK47 |
| Stonefield Rd, (Blan.) G72 | 124 | CL46 |
| Stonefield St, Air. ML6 | 76 | DC28 |
| Stonehall Av, Ham. ML3 | 139 | CR51 |
| Stonehaven Cres, Air. ML6 | 76 | DA32 |
| Stonelaw Dr, (Ruther.) G73 | 89 | BX38 |
| Stonelaw Rd, (Ruther.) G73 | 89 | BX38 |
| Stonelaw Twrs, (Ruther.) G73 | 105 | BY39 |
| Stoneside Dr, G43 | 102 | BJ39 |
| Stoneside Sq, G43 | 102 | BJ39 |
| Stoney Brae, Pais. PA1 | 62 | AU32 |
| Stoney Brae, Pais. PA2 | 82 | AU37 |
| Stoneyetts Cotts, (Chry.) G69 | 37 | CN17 |
| Stoneyetts Rd, (Mood.) G69 | 37 | CP18 |
| Stoneymeadow Rd, (Blan.) | | |
| G72 | 123 | CF48 |
| Stoneymeadow Rd, (E.Kil.) | | |
| G74 | 122 | CD49 |
| Stonyhurst St, G22 | 49 | BR25 |
| Stonylee Rd, (Cumb.) G67 | 22 | DC12 |
| Storie St, Pais. PA1 | 82 | AU33 |
| Stormyland Way, (Barr.) G78 | 99 | AY43 |
| Stornoway St, G22 | 50 | BS21 |
| Stow Brae, Pais. PA1 | 82 | AU33 |
| Stow St, Pais. PA1 | 82 | AU33 |
| Strachan St, Bell. ML4 | 111 | CW41 |
| Strachur Cres, G22 | 49 | BQ22 |
| Strachur Gdns, G22 | 49 | BQ22 |
| Strachur Pl, G22 | 49 | BQ22 |
| Strachur St, G22 | 49 | BQ22 |
| Strain Cres, Air. ML6 | 76 | DD31 |
| Straiton Dr, Ham. ML3 | 138 | CM51 |
| Straiton Pl, (Blan.) G72 | 124 | CM45 |
| Straiton St, G32 | 70 | CA30 |
| Stranka Av, Pais. PA2 | 82 | AS34 |
| Stranraer Dr, G15 | 29 | BE19 |
| Stratford, (E.Kil.) G74 | 123 | CF48 |
| Stratford St, G20 | 48 | BM24 |
| Strathallan Av, (E.Kil.) G75 | 135 | BW53 |

Strathallan Cres, Air. ML6 58 DC26
Strathallandale Ct, (E.Kil.) G75 134 BU53
Strathallan Gdns, (Kirk.) G66
  off Willowbank Gdns 17 CF13
Strathallan Gate, (E.Kil.) G75 134 BV52
Strathallan Wynd, (E.Kil.) G75 134 BV52
Strathallon Pl, (Ruther.) G73
  off Ranald Gdns 105 BZ42
Strathaven Rd, (E.Kil.) G75 136 CC53
Strathavon Cres, Air. ML6 76 DC27
Strathblane Cres, Air. ML6 58 DC26
Strathblane Dr, (E.Kil.) G75 134 BU53
Strathblane Gdns, G13 47 BH21
Strathblane Rd, (Miln.) G62 12 BL10
Strathbran St, G31 89 BZ33
Strathcairn Cres, Air. ML6 58 DC26
Strathcarron Cres, Pais. PA2 83 AX36
Strathcarron Dr, Pais. PA2 83 AX36
Strathcarron Pl, G20
  off Glenfinnan Rd 48 BM23
Strathcarron Pl, Pais. PA2 83 AX36
Strathcarron Rd, Pais. PA2 83 AX37
Strathcarron Way, Pais. PA2 83 AX36
Strathclyde Business Pk,
  Bell. ML4 94 CV37
Strathclyde Dr, (Ruther.) G73 89 BW38
Strathclyde Gdns, (Camb.) G72 107 CG42
Strathclyde Path, (Udd.) G71 109 CN39
Strathclyde Rd, Moth. ML1 127 CX47
Strathclyde St, G40 89 BW35
Strath Clyde Vw, (Both.) G71 109 CR44
Strathclyde Way, Bell. ML4
  off Clay Cres 95 CY38
Strathcona Dr, G13 47 BH22
Strathcona Gdns, G13 48 BJ22
Strathcona La, (E.Kil.) G75 136 CA54
Strathcona Pl, (Ruther.) G73
  off Ross Pl 105 BZ41
Strathcona Pl, (E.Kil.) G75 136 CA54
Strathcona St, G13 47 BH22
Strathconon Gdns, (E.Kil.) G75
  off Strathnairn Dr 134 BU53
Strathdearn Gro, (E.Kil.) G75 134 BU53
Strathdee Av, Clyde. G81 27 AX16
Strathdee Rd, G44 103 BN43
Strathdon Av, G44 103 BP43
Strathdon Av, Pais. PA2 82 AS35
Strathdon Dr, G44 103 BP43
Strathdon Pl, (E.Kil.) G75
  off Strathnairn Dr 134 BU53
Strathearn Gro, (Kirk.) G66 18 CK11
Strathearn Rd, (Clark.) G76 119 BN47
Strathendrick Dr, G44 103 BN41
Strathfillan Rd, (E.Kil.) G74 135 BZ51
Strathgoil Cres, Air. ML6 58 DC26
Strathkelvin Av, (Bishop.) G64
  off Southview Ter 50 BV22
Strathkelvin La, (E.Kil.) G75 134 BU53
Strathkelvin Pl, (Kirk.) G66 17 CE14
Strathkelvin Retail Pk, (Bishop.)
  G64 33 BY16
Strathmiglo Ct, (E.Kil.) G75 134 BU53
Strathmore Av, (Blan.) G72 108 CL44
Strathmore Av, Pais. PA1 83 AZ33
Strathmore Cres, Air. ML6
  off Broompark Cres 76 DC27
Strathmore Gdns, (Ruther.)
  G73 105 BZ41
Strathmore Gro, (E.Kil.) G75 134 BU53
Strathmore Ho, (E.Kil.) G74
  off Cornwall St 136 CA52
Strathmore Pl, Coat. ML5
  off Strathmore Wk 75 CZ32

Strathmore Rd, G22 49 BR22
Strathmore Rd, Ham. ML3 126 CU50
Strathmore Wk, Coat. ML5 75 CZ32
Strathmungo Cres, Air. ML6
  off Springholm Dr 76 DB27
Strathnairn Av, (E.Kil.) G75 134 BU53
Strathnairn Ct, (E.Kil.) G75
  off Strathnairn Dr 134 BU53
Strathnairn Dr, (E.Kil.) G75 134 BU53
Strathnairn Way, (E.Kil.) G75 134 BU53
Strathnaver Cres, Air. ML6 58 DC26
Strathnaver Gdns, (E.Kil.) G75
  off Strathnairn Av 134 BU53
Strathord Pl, (Mood.) G69 37 CQ18
Strathord St, G32 90 CC34
Strathpeffer Cres, Air. ML6 76 DC27
Strathpeffer Dr, (E.Kil.) G75
  off Strathnairn Dr 134 BU53
Strathrannoch Way, (E.Kil.)
  G75 134 BU53
Strathspey Av, (E.Kil.) G75 134 BU53
Strathspey Cres, Air. ML6 58 DC26
Strathtay Av, G44 103 BP43
Strathtay Av, (E.Kil.) G75 134 BU53
Strathtummel Cres, Air. ML6 58 DC26
Strathview Gdns, (Bears.) G61 29 BF17
Strathview Gro, G44 103 BN43
Strathview Pk, G44 103 BP43
Strathview Rd, Bell. ML4 110 CU42
Strathvithie Gro, (E.Kil.) G75 134 BU53
Strathwhillan Ct, (E.Kil.) G75 134 BU53
Strathwhillan Dr, (E.Kil.) G75 134 BV53
Strathy Pl, G20
  off Glenfinnan Rd 48 BM23
Strathyre Ct, (E.Kil.) G75 134 BU53
Strathyre Gdns, (Bears.) G61 30 BK16
Strathyre Gdns, (Mood.) G69
  off Heathfield Av 37 CQ18
Strathyre Gdns, (E.Kil.) G75 134 BU53
Strathyre Gdns, (Glenm.) Air.
  ML6 off Banchory Av 58 DB24
Strathyre Rd, (Blan.) G72 125 CP47
Strathyre St, G41 87 BN37
Stratton Dr, (Giff.) G46 102 BK43
Strauss Av, Clyde. G81 28 BA20
Stravaig Path, Pais. PA2 81 AQ38
Stravaig Wk, Pais. PA2 81 AQ38
Stravanan Av, G45 104 BU43
Stravanan Ct, G45 104 BU43
Stravanan Gdns, G45 104 BT43
Stravanan Pl, G51 104 BT43
Stravanan Rd, G45 104 BT43
Stravanan St, G45 104 BT43
Stravanan Ter, G45 104 BT43
Strawhill Rd, (Clark.) G76 119 BN46
Streamfield Gdns, G33 51 BZ22
Streamfield Gate, G33
  off Brookfield Dr 51 BZ22
Streamfield Lea, G33 51 BZ22
Streamfield Pl, G33 51 BZ22
Strenabey Av, (Ruther.) G73 105 BZ41
Striven Gdns, G20 49 BP26
Striven Ter, Ham. ML3 139 CQ52
Stroma St, G21 69 BX27
Stromness St, G5 87 BQ33
Strone Gdns, (Kilsyth) G65 7 CR5
Stronend St, G22 49 BR24
Strone Path, (Glenb.) Coat. ML5
  off Dinyra Pl 56 CS23
Strone Pl, Air. ML6 77 DE32
Strone Rd, G33 70 CD30
Stronsay Pl, (Bishop.) G64 33 BZ19
Stronsay St, G21 69 BX27

Stronvar Dr, G14 46 BD25
Stronvar La, G14
  off Larchfield Av 46 BD25
Stroud Rd, (E.Kil.) G75 135 BZ55
Strowan Cres, G32 90 CD33
Strowan St, G32 90 CD33
Struan Av, (Giff.) G46 102 BK42
Struan Gdns, G44 103 BQ40
Struan Rd, G44 103 BQ40
Struie St, G34 72 CJ29
Struma Dr, (Clark.) G76 118 BL45
Strutherhill Ind Est, Lark. ML9 145 DE61
Struthers Cres, (E.Kil.) G74 122 CD49
Struther St, Lark. ML9 144 DD61
Stuart Av, (Old Kil.) G60 25 AR16
Stuart Av, (Ruther.) G73 105 BX40
Stuart Dr, (Bishop.) G64 50 BU21
Stuart Dr, Lark. ML9 145 DE60
Stuarton Pk, (E.Kil.) G74 136 CA51
Stuart Quad, (Holytown)
  Moth. ML1 112 DD39
Stuart Quad, Wis. ML2 143 DF52
Stuart Rd, (Carm.) G76 120 BT45
Stuart Rd, Bish. PA7 24 AK17
Stuart St, (Old Kil.) G60 25 AR16
Stuart St, (E.Kil.) G74 136 CB51
Succoth St, G13 47 BH22
Sudbury Cres, (E.Kil.) G75 135 BX52
Suffolk St, G40
  off Kent St 5 BU31
Sugworth Av, (Baill.) G69 72 CK32
Suisnish, Ersk. PA8 44 AS22
Sumburgh St, G33 70 CB29
Summerfield Cotts, G14 65 BG27
Summerfield Rd, (Cumb.) G67 39 CW15
Summerfield St, G40 89 BX35
Summerhill & Garngibbock Rd,
  G67 39 CY18
Summerhill Av, Lark. ML9 144 DC59
Summerhill Dr, G15 28 BD17
Summerhill Gdns, G15 28 BD17
Summerhill Pl, G15 28 BD17
Summerhill Rd, G15 28 BC17
Summerhill Rd, (Clark.) G76 119 BP46
Summerhill Way, Bell. ML4 110 CV41
Summerlea Rd, (Thornlie.) G46 101 BH41
Summerlee Cotts, Coat. ML5
  off Melrose Pl 74 CV30
Summerlee Rd, Lark. ML9 142 DB56
Summerlee St, G33 71 CE29
Summerlee St, Coat. ML5 74 CV30
Summer St, G40 68 BV32
Summertown Rd, G51 66 BK30
Sunart Av, Renf. PA4 45 AX25
Sunart Ct, Ham. ML3
  off Etive Av 139 CQ52
Sunart Gdns, (Bishop.) G64 33 BY20
Sunart Rd, G52 65 BG32
Sunart Rd, (Bishop.) G64 33 BY20
Sunbury Av, (Clark.) G76 118 BL46
Sundale Av, (Clark.) G76 118 BM46
Sunflower Gdns, Moth. ML1
  off Park Neuk St 127 CZ45
Sunningdale Av, (Newt. M.)
  G77 117 BH48
Sunningdale Rd, G23 48 BM21
Sunningdale Wynd, (Both.)
  G71 109 CN42
Sunnybank Dr, (Clark.) G76 118 BM47
Sunnybank Gro, (Clark.) G76 118 BM47
Sunnybank St, G40 89 BX34
Sunnyhill, (Kilsyth) G65 19 CP10
Sunnylaw Dr, Pais. PA2 81 AQ35

| | | |
|---|---|---|
| Sunnylaw Pl, G22 | 49 | BR24 |
| Sunnylaw St, G22 | 49 | BR25 |
| Sunnyside Av, (Udd.) G71 | 109 | CP40 |
| Sunnyside Av, Moth. ML1 | 112 | DD40 |
| Sunnyside Cres, Moth. ML1 | 112 | DC40 |
| Sunnyside Dr, G15 | 28 | BC20 |
| Sunnyside Dr, (Baill.) G69 | 73 | CP32 |
| Sunnyside Dr, (Clark.) G76 | 118 | BM45 |
| Sunnyside Oval, Pais. PA2 | 82 | AU36 |
| Sunnyside Pl, G15 | 28 | BC20 |
| Sunnyside Pl, (Barr.) G78 | 99 | AX43 |
| Sunnyside Pl, Moth. ML1 | 112 | DC40 |
| Sunnyside Rd, Coat. ML5 | 75 | CW30 |
| Sunnyside Rd, Pais. PA2 | 82 | AT35 |
| Sunnyside St, Lark. ML9 | 144 | DB57 |
| Sunnyside Ter, Moth. ML1 | 112 | DC40 |
| Surrey St, G5 | 87 | BR33 |
| Sussex St, G41 | 67 | BN32 |
| Sutcliffe Ct, G13 | | |
| *off Sutcliffe Rd* | 47 | BG22 |
| Sutcliffe Rd, G13 | 47 | BG22 |
| Sutherland Av, G41 | 86 | BK34 |
| Sutherland Av, (Bears.) G61 | 11 | BG14 |
| Sutherland Cres, Ham. ML3 | 125 | CQ49 |
| Sutherland Dr, (Giff.) G46 | 102 | BM44 |
| Sutherland La, G12 | 66 | BL27 |
| Sutherland Pl, Bell. ML4 | 110 | CV43 |
| Sutherland Rd, Clyde. G81 | 27 | AX19 |
| Sutherland St, (Blan.) G72 | 124 | CL48 |
| Sutherland St, Pais. PA1 | 62 | AT32 |
| Sutherland Way, (E.Kil.) G74 | 123 | CE50 |
| Sutherness Dr, G33 | 70 | CC30 |
| Swaledale, (E.Kil.) G74 | 121 | BY50 |
| Swallow Gdns, G13 | 46 | BB22 |
| Swan Pl, John. PA5 | 79 | AE38 |
| Swanston St, G40 | 89 | BW35 |
| Swan St, G4 | 5 | BS28 |
| Swan St, Clyde. G81 | 26 | AV18 |
| Sween Av, G44 | 103 | BQ41 |
| Sween Dr, Ham. ML3 | 139 | CQ52 |
| Sween Path, Bell. ML4 | | |
| *off Millbank Av* | 111 | CY42 |
| Sweethill Ter, Coat. ML5 | | |
| *off Selkirk Way* | 95 | CZ34 |
| Sweethill Wk, Bell. ML4 | | |
| *off Harvey Way* | 95 | CX38 |
| Sweethope Gdns, (Both.) G71 | 109 | CR43 |
| Sweethope Pl, (Both.) G71 | 109 | CQ41 |
| Swift Bk, Ham. ML3 | 139 | CN52 |
| Swift Cres, G13 | 46 | BB22 |
| Swift Pl, (E.Kil.) G75 | 134 | BU55 |
| Swift Pl, John. PA5 | 79 | AF38 |
| Swindon St, Clyde. G81 | 26 | AU18 |
| Swinton Av, (Baill.) G69 | 72 | CL32 |
| Swinton Cres, (Baill.) G69 | 72 | CL32 |
| Swinton Cres, Coat. ML5 | 93 | CR33 |
| Swinton Dr, G52 | 64 | BD32 |
| Swinton Gdns, (Baill.) G69 | | |
| *off Swinton Av* | 72 | CM32 |
| Swinton Path, (Baill.) G69 | 72 | CM32 |
| Swinton Pl, G52 | 64 | BD32 |
| Swinton Pl, Coat. ML5 | | |
| *off Dunnachie Dr* | 93 | CR33 |
| Swinton Rd, (Baill.) G69 | 72 | CL32 |
| Swinton Vw, (Baill.) G69 | 72 | CL32 |
| Swisscot Av, Ham. ML3 | 139 | CR53 |
| Swisscot Wk, Ham. ML3 | | |
| *off Glencoe Pl* | 139 | CR53 |
| Switchback Rd, (Bears.) G61 | 29 | BH19 |
| Swordale Path, G34 | | |
| *off Swordale Pl* | 72 | CJ29 |
| Swordale Pl, G34 | 72 | CJ29 |

| | | |
|---|---|---|
| Sword St, G31 | 68 | BV31 |
| Sword St, Air. ML6 | 76 | DB30 |
| Sycamore Av, (Lenz.) G66 | 35 | CF15 |
| Sycamore Av, (Udd.) G71 | 94 | CS37 |
| Sycamore Av, John. PA5 | 80 | AJ36 |
| Sycamore Ct, (E.Kil.) G75 | 135 | BZ55 |
| Sycamore Ct, Coat. ML5 | | |
| *off Ailsa Rd* | 94 | CV33 |
| Sycamore Cres, (E.Kil.) G75 | 135 | BY55 |
| Sycamore Cres, Air. ML6 | 77 | DF31 |
| Sycamore Dr, Air. ML6 | 77 | DF31 |
| Sycamore Dr, Clyde. G81 | 26 | AV17 |
| Sycamore Dr, Ham. ML3 | 140 | CV51 |
| Sycamore Gro, (Blan.) G72 | 124 | CL45 |
| Sycamore Pl, (E.Kil.) G75 | 135 | BZ55 |
| Sycamore Pl, Moth. ML1 | 112 | DD42 |
| Sycamore Way, (Camb.) G72 | 107 | CH41 |
| Sycamore Way, (Carm.) G76 | | |
| *off Manse Rd* | 120 | BU46 |
| Sydenham La, G12 | | |
| *off Crown Rd S* | 48 | BK26 |
| Sydenham Rd, G12 | 48 | BL26 |
| Sydes Brae, (Blan.) G72 | 124 | CK49 |
| Sydney Dr, (E.Kil.) G75 | 135 | BY54 |
| Sydney Pl, (E.Kil.) G75 | 135 | BY53 |
| Sydney St, G31 | 5 | BU31 |
| Sydney St, Clyde. G81 | 26 | AT17 |
| Sykehead Av, Bell. ML4 | 111 | CX40 |
| Sykeside St, Air. ML6 | 96 | DA33 |
| Sykes Ter, (Neil.) G78 | 114 | AV46 |
| Sylvania Way, Clyde. G81 | 27 | AX19 |
| Sylvania Way S, Clyde. G81 | 27 | AX20 |
| Symington Dr, Clyde. G81 | 27 | AW19 |
| Symington Sq, (E.Kil.) G75 | | |
| *off Naysmyth Bk* | 136 | CB53 |
| Syriam Pl, G21 | | |
| *off Syriam St* | 50 | BV25 |
| Syriam St, G21 | 50 | BV25 |

**T**

| | | |
|---|---|---|
| Tabard Pl, G13 | 47 | BE21 |
| Tabard Pl N, G13 | | |
| *off Tabard Rd* | 47 | BE21 |
| Tabard Pl S, G13 | | |
| *off Tabard Rd* | 47 | BE21 |
| Tabard Rd, G13 | 47 | BE21 |
| Tabernacle La, (Camb.) G72 | 106 | CC40 |
| Tabernacle St, (Camb.) G72 | 106 | CC40 |
| Taggart Rd, (Kilsyth) G65 | 20 | CV10 |
| Taig Rd, (Kirk.) G66 | 18 | CK14 |
| Tain Pl, G34 | 72 | CM29 |
| Tait Av, (Barr.) G78 | 99 | AZ41 |
| Tak ma doon Rd, (Kilsyth) G65 | 7 | CU4 |
| Talbot, (E.Kil.) G74 | 123 | CE49 |
| Talbot Ct, G13 | 46 | BD24 |
| Talbot Dr, G13 | 46 | BD24 |
| Talbot Pl, G13 | 46 | BD24 |
| Talbot Ter, G13 | | |
| *off Kintillo Dr* | 46 | BD24 |
| Talbot Ter, (Udd.) G71 | 93 | CN37 |
| Talisman, Clyde. G81 | | |
| *off Onslow Rd* | 27 | AZ19 |
| Talisman Cres, Moth. ML1 | 111 | CZ43 |
| Talisman Rd, G13 | 47 | BD25 |
| Talisman Rd, Pais. PA2 | 81 | AN38 |
| Tallant Rd, G15 | 28 | BD18 |
| Tallant Ter, G15 | 29 | BE18 |
| Talla Rd, G52 | 64 | BD32 |
| Tamarack Cres, (Udd.) G71 | 94 | CS36 |
| Tamar Dr, (E.Kil.) G75 | 134 | BV55 |
| Tambowie Av, (Miln.) G62 | 11 | BH11 |
| Tambowie Cres, (Miln.) G62 | 11 | BH11 |

| | | |
|---|---|---|
| Tambowie St, G13 | 47 | BG22 |
| Tamshill St, G20 | 49 | BP23 |
| Tamworth St, G40 | | |
| *off Rimsdale St* | 69 | BW32 |
| Tanar Av, Renf. PA4 | 64 | BB28 |
| Tanar Way, Renf. PA4 | | |
| *off Afton Dr* | 64 | BA28 |
| Tandlehill Rd, (Kilb.) | | |
| John. PA10 | 78 | AD36 |
| Tanera Av, G44 | 104 | BS40 |
| Tanfield Pl, G32 | | |
| *off Tanfield St* | 71 | CE30 |
| Tanfield St, G32 | 71 | CE30 |
| Tankerland Rd, G44 | 103 | BQ39 |
| Tannadice Av, G52 | 85 | BE34 |
| Tannadice Path, G52 | | |
| *off Tannadice Av* | 85 | BE33 |
| Tanna Dr, G52 | 85 | BH34 |
| Tannahill Cres, John. PA5 | 79 | AG36 |
| Tannahill Dr, (E.Kil.) G74 | 123 | CE50 |
| Tannahill Rd, G43 | 103 | BP39 |
| Tannahill Rd, Pais. PA3 | 61 | AR31 |
| Tannahill Ter, Pais. PA3 | 61 | AR31 |
| Tannoch Dr, (Miln.) G62 | 12 | BK10 |
| Tannoch Dr, (Cumb.) G67 | 22 | DB14 |
| Tannoch Pl, (Cumb.) G67 | 22 | DB14 |
| Tannochside Business Pk, (Udd.) | | |
| G71 | 93 | CQ36 |
| Tannochside Dr, (Udd.) G71 | 93 | CQ36 |
| Tannock St, G22 | 49 | BR25 |
| Tantallon Dr, Coat. ML5 | 74 | CS28 |
| Tantallon Dr, Pais. PA2 | 81 | AQ36 |
| Tantallon Pk, (E.Kil.) G74 | 135 | BZ51 |
| Tantallon Rd, G41 | 87 | BN38 |
| Tantallon Rd, (Baill.) G69 | 92 | CJ34 |
| Tantallon Rd, (Both.) G71 | | |
| *off Olifard Av* | 109 | CR42 |
| Tanzieknowe Av, (Camb.) G72 | 106 | CD41 |
| Tanzieknowe Dr, (Camb.) G72 | 106 | CD42 |
| Tanzieknowe Pl, (Camb.) G72 | 106 | CD42 |
| Tanzieknowe Rd, (Camb.) G72 | 106 | CD42 |
| Taransay Ct, G22 | | |
| *off Liddesdale Sq* | 50 | BT22 |
| Taransay St, G51 | 66 | BJ29 |
| Tarbert Av, (Blan.) G72 | 108 | CL43 |
| Tarbert Ct, Ham. ML3 | 139 | CQ52 |
| Tarbert Way, Coat. ML5 | 94 | CU33 |
| Tarbolton, (E.Kil.) G74 | 123 | CF50 |
| Tarbolton Cres, (Chap.) Air. ML6 | 97 | DF37 |
| Tarbolton Dr, Clyde. G81 | 27 | AY18 |
| Tarbolton Path, Lark. ML9 | | |
| *off Annbank St* | 144 | DB58 |
| Tarbolton Rd, G43 | 102 | BM39 |
| Tarbolton Rd, (Cumb.) G67 | 22 | DD11 |
| Tarbolton Sq, Clyde. G81 | | |
| *off Tarbolton Dr* | 27 | AY18 |
| Tarbrax Way, Ham. ML3 | 125 | CQ50 |
| Tarff Av, (Eagle.) G76 | 133 | BN56 |
| Tarfside Av, G52 | 85 | BE33 |
| Tarfside Gdns, G52 | 85 | BF33 |
| Tarfside Oval, G52 | 85 | BF33 |
| Target Rd, Air. ML6 | 76 | DD31 |
| Tarland St, G51 | 65 | BH31 |
| Tarn Gro, G33 | 51 | BZ22 |
| Tarras Dr, Renf. PA4 | 64 | BA28 |
| Tarras Pl, (Camb.) G72 | 107 | CF40 |
| Tasman Dr, (E.Kil.) G75 | 135 | BX54 |
| Tassie Pl, (E.Kil.) G74 | 136 | CC51 |
| Tassie St, G41 | 86 | BM37 |
| Tattershall Rd, G33 | 71 | CE27 |
| Tavistock Dr, G43 | 102 | BM40 |
| Tay Av, Pais. PA2 | | |
| *off Don Dr* | 81 | AP36 |

| | | |
|---|---|---|
| Tay Av, Renf. PA4 | 46 | BA26 |
| Tay Ct, (Mood.) G69 | | |
| off Deepdene Rd | 37 | CQ19 |
| Tay Ct, (E.Kil.) G75 | 134 | BU54 |
| Tay Cres, G33 | 70 | CA28 |
| Tay Cres, (Bishop.) G64 | 33 | BX20 |
| Tay Gdns, Ham. ML3 | 139 | CR53 |
| Tay Gro, (Bish.) PA7 | 134 | BU54 |
| Tay Ln, Moth. ML1 | | |
| off Windsor Rd | 112 | DC40 |
| Taylor Av, (Kilb.) John. PA10 | 78 | AB34 |
| Taylor Av, Moth. ML1 | 113 | DF43 |
| Taylor Pl, G4 | 5 | BT29 |
| Taylor St, G4 | 5 | BT30 |
| Taylor St, Clyde. G81 | 45 | AY21 |
| Taymouth St, G32 | 90 | CD34 |
| Taynish Dr, G44 | 103 | BR41 |
| Tay Pl, (E.Kil.) G75 | 134 | BU54 |
| Tay Pl, John. PA5 | 79 | AE37 |
| Tay Pl, Lark. ML9 | 144 | DC61 |
| Tay Rd, (Bears.) G61 | 29 | BF19 |
| Tay Rd, (Bishop.) G64 | 33 | BX20 |
| Tayside, Air. ML6 | 76 | DB28 |
| Tay St, Coat. ML5 | 74 | CS28 |
| Tay Ter, (E.Kil.) G75 | 134 | BU53 |
| Tay Wk, (Cumb.) G67 | | |
| off Cumbernauld Shop Cen | 22 | DB11 |
| Teak Pl, (Udd.) G71 | 94 | CT36 |
| Teal Ct, (Strathclyde Bus. Pk.) | | |
| Bell. ML4 | 94 | CU37 |
| Teal Cres, (E.Kil.) G75 | 134 | BV56 |
| Teal Dr, G13 | 46 | BC22 |
| Tealing Av, G52 | 85 | BE33 |
| Tealing Cres, G52 | 85 | BE33 |
| Teasel Av, G53 | 100 | BD42 |
| Teawell Rd, (Newt. M.) G77 | 117 | BF48 |
| Technology Av, (Blan.) G72 | 124 | CL49 |
| Teesdale, (E.Kil.) G74 | 121 | BY50 |
| Teign Gro, (E.Kil.) G75 | 134 | BV55 |
| Teith Av, Renf. PA4 | 64 | BB27 |
| Teith Dr, (Bears.) G61 | 29 | BF18 |
| Teith Pl, (Camb.) G72 | 107 | CF40 |
| Teith St, G33 | 70 | CA28 |
| Telephone La, G12 | 48 | BL26 |
| Telford Av, (Strutherhill Ind. Est.) | | |
| Lark. ML9 | 145 | DE61 |
| Telford Ct, Clyde. G81 | 27 | AW19 |
| Telford Pl, (Cumb.) G67 | 22 | DC14 |
| Telford Rd, (Cumb.) G67 | 22 | DC13 |
| Telford Rd, (E.Kil.) G75 | 136 | CB53 |
| Telford St, Bell. ML4 | 111 | CW39 |
| Telford Ter, (E.Kil.) G75 | 136 | CB53 |
| Teme Pl, (E.Kil.) G75 | 134 | BV54 |
| Templar Av, G13 | 47 | BF21 |
| Temple Gdns, G13 | 47 | BH22 |
| Templeland Av, G53 | 85 | BE35 |
| Templeland Rd, G53 | 85 | BE35 |
| Temple Locks Ct, G13 | 48 | BJ22 |
| Temple Locks Pl, G13 | 47 | BH22 |
| Temple Rd, G13 | 48 | BJ22 |
| Templetons Business Cen, G40 | 68 | BU32 |
| Templeton St, G40 | 68 | BU32 |
| Tennant Av, (E.Kil.) G74 | 135 | BW51 |
| Tennant Rd, Pais. PA3 | 61 | AR31 |
| Tennant St, Renf. PA4 | 45 | AZ25 |
| Tennent St, Coat. ML5 | 75 | CX32 |
| Tennyson Dr, G31 | 90 | CA33 |
| Tenters Way, Pais. PA2 | 81 | AR34 |
| Tern Pl, John. PA5 | 79 | AF38 |
| Terrace Pl, (Camb.) G72 | 107 | CG40 |
| Terregles Av, G41 | 86 | BK35 |
| Terregles Cres, G41 | 86 | BK35 |
| Terregles Dr, G41 | 86 | BL35 |

| | | |
|---|---|---|
| Teviot Av, (Bishop.) G64 | 33 | BW18 |
| Teviot Av, Pais. PA2 | 81 | AN37 |
| Teviot Cres, (Bears.) G61 | 29 | BF19 |
| Teviot Dale, (E.Kil.) G74 | | |
| off Strathfillan Rd | 135 | BZ51 |
| Teviotdale, (Newt. M.) G77 | | |
| off Kirkvale Ct | 118 | BK48 |
| Teviot Dr, Bish. PA7 | 24 | AL19 |
| Teviot Pl, (Camb.) G72 | 107 | CF40 |
| Teviot Sq, (Cumb.) G67 | 22 | DB11 |
| Teviot St, G3 | 66 | BL29 |
| Teviot St, Coat. ML5 | 74 | CT27 |
| Teviot Ter, G20 | | |
| off Sanda St | 49 | BN25 |
| Teviot Ter, John. PA5 | 79 | AE37 |
| Teviot Wk, (Cumb.) G67 | | |
| off Cumbernauld Shop Cen | 22 | DB12 |
| Teviot Way, (Blan.) G72 | | |
| off Stonefield Rd | 124 | CL46 |
| Tewkesbury Rd, (E.Kil.) G74 | 123 | CF48 |
| Thane Rd, G13 | 47 | BE23 |
| Thanes Gate, (Udd.) G71 | 109 | CN40 |
| Thankerton Av, Moth. ML1 | 112 | DB40 |
| Thankerton Rd, Lark. ML9 | 144 | DD60 |
| Tharsis St, G21 | 68 | BV28 |
| Third Av, (Millerston) G33 | 52 | CD24 |
| Third Av, G44 | 87 | BR38 |
| Third Av, (Kirk.) G66 | 35 | CF20 |
| Third Av, Renf. PA4 | 63 | AY27 |
| Third Gdns, G41 | 86 | BJ33 |
| Thirdpart Cres, G13 | 46 | BA22 |
| Third Rd, (Blan.) G72 | 125 | CN48 |
| Third St, (Udd.) G71 | 93 | CP37 |
| Thirlmere, (E.Kil.) G75 | | |
| off Windermere | 134 | BV56 |
| Thistle Bk, (Lenz.) G66 | 35 | CF17 |
| Thistlebank Gro, Coat. ML5 | 94 | CU34 |
| Thistle Cres, Lark. ML9 | 144 | DD59 |
| Thistledown Gro, Coat. ML5 | 75 | CY32 |
| Thistle Gdns, Moth. ML1 | 112 | DC40 |
| Thistle Pl, (E.Kil.) G74 | 121 | BZ50 |
| Thistle Quad, Air. ML6 | | |
| off Thistle St | 76 | DD28 |
| Thistle Rd, Moth. ML1 | 112 | DC41 |
| Thistle St, G5 | 68 | BS32 |
| Thistle St, (Kirk.) G66 | 17 | CF13 |
| Thistle St, Air. ML6 | 76 | DD28 |
| Thistle St, Pais. PA2 | 82 | AS35 |
| Thistle Ter, G5 | 88 | BS33 |
| Thomas Muir Av, (Bishop.) G64 | 51 | BW21 |
| Thomas St, Pais. PA1 | 81 | AR33 |
| Thompson Brae, Pais. PA2 | 82 | AU34 |
| Thompson Pl, Clyde. G81 | 27 | AY15 |
| Thomson Av, (Kirk.) G66 | 17 | CG13 |
| Thomson Av, John. PA5 | 79 | AG34 |
| Thomson Av, Wis. ML2 | 143 | DF51 |
| Thomson Dr, (Bears.) G61 | 29 | BH15 |
| Thomson Dr, Air. ML6 | 76 | DB31 |
| Thomson Dr, Bell. ML4 | 110 | CT40 |
| Thomson Dr, Moth. ML1 | 127 | CZ48 |
| Thomson Gro, (Camb.) G72 | | |
| off Morrison Pk Dr | 90 | CC38 |
| Thomson St, G31 | 69 | BW31 |
| Thomson St, John. PA5 | 79 | AG35 |
| Thomson St, Renf. PA4 | 63 | AY27 |
| Thorn Av, (Thornton.) G74 | 120 | BS50 |
| Thornbank St, G3 | 66 | BL28 |
| Thorn Brae, John. PA5 | 80 | AJ34 |
| Thornbridge Av, G12 | | |
| off Balcarres Av | 48 | BL24 |
| Thornbridge Av, (Baill.) G69 | | |
| off Bannercross Dr | 72 | CK32 |
| Thornbridge Gdns, (Baill.) G69 | 72 | CJ32 |

| | | |
|---|---|---|
| Thornbridge Rd, (Baill.) G69 | 72 | CJ32 |
| Thorncliffe Gdns, G41 | 87 | BN35 |
| Thorncliffe La, G41 | 87 | BN35 |
| Thorn Ct, John. PA5 | | |
| off Thornhill | 80 | AK35 |
| Thorncroft Dr, G44 | 104 | BT41 |
| Thorndean Av, Bell. ML4 | 111 | CX41 |
| Thorndean Cres, Bell. ML4 | 111 | CX41 |
| Thorndene, (Elder.) John. PA5 | 80 | AK34 |
| Thorndene Av, Moth. ML1 | 113 | DE43 |
| Thornden La, G14 | 46 | BC25 |
| Thorn Dr, (Bears.) G61 | 29 | BF16 |
| Thorn Dr, (Ruther.) G73 | 105 | BY41 |
| Thorndyke, (E.Kil.) G74 | 123 | CE48 |
| Thorn Hts, (Bears.) G61 | 29 | BE17 |
| Thornhill, John. PA5 | 80 | AK35 |
| Thornhill Av, (Blan.) G72 | 124 | CM45 |
| Thornhill Av, (Elder.) John. PA5 | 80 | AK35 |
| Thornhill Dr, (Elder.) John. PA5 | 80 | AK35 |
| Thornhill Gdns, (Newt. M.) G77 | 131 | BF51 |
| Thornhill La, (Both.) G71 | | |
| off Churchill Cres | 109 | CR42 |
| Thornhill Path, G31 | | |
| off Crail St | 69 | BZ32 |
| Thornhill Rd, Ham. ML3 | 125 | CN49 |
| Thornhill Way, Coat. ML5 | 95 | CZ33 |
| Thorniecroft Dr, (Cumb.) G67 | 39 | CY15 |
| Thorniecroft Pl, (Cumb.) G67 | 39 | CY15 |
| Thornielee, (E.Kil.) G74 | 136 | CD51 |
| Thorniewood Gdns, (Udd.) G71 | 93 | CQ38 |
| Thorniewood Rd, (Udd.) G71 | 93 | CP37 |
| Thornkip Pl, Coat. ML5 | | |
| off Strathmore Wk | 75 | CZ32 |
| Thornlea Dr, (Giff.) G46 | 102 | BM41 |
| Thornley Av, G13 | 46 | BD23 |
| Thornliebank Ind Est, (Thornlie.) | | |
| G46 | 101 | BG42 |
| Thornliebank Rd, G43 | 102 | BJ40 |
| Thornliebank Rd, (Deac.) G46 | 117 | BF45 |
| Thornliebank Rd, (Thornlie.) | | |
| G46 | 102 | BJ41 |
| Thornly Pk Av, Pais. PA2 | 82 | AV37 |
| Thornly Pk Dr, Pais. PA2 | 82 | AV37 |
| Thornly Pk Gdns, Pais. PA2 | 82 | AU36 |
| Thornly Pk Rd, Pais. PA2 | 82 | AU36 |
| Thorn Rd, (Bears.) G61 | 29 | BE16 |
| Thorn Rd, Bell. ML4 | 111 | CX40 |
| Thornside Rd, John. PA5 | 80 | AJ34 |
| Thornton La, G20 | 49 | BN22 |
| Thornton Pl, Ham. ML3 | | |
| off High Parks Cres | 140 | CT55 |
| Thornton Rd, (Thornton.) G74 | 120 | BS50 |
| Thornton St, G20 | 49 | BN22 |
| Thornton St, Coat. ML5 | 74 | CT27 |
| Thorntree Av, Ham. ML3 | 125 | CP48 |
| Thorntree Way, (Both.) G71 | 109 | CR42 |
| Thornwood Av, G11 | 66 | BJ27 |
| Thornwood Av, (Kirk.) G66 | 34 | CC16 |
| Thornwood Cres, G11 | 47 | BH26 |
| Thornwood Dr, G11 | 65 | BH27 |
| Thornwood Dr, Pais. PA2 | 81 | AR35 |
| Thornwood Gdns, G11 | 65 | BH27 |
| Thornwood Pl, G11 | 47 | BH26 |
| Thornwood Quad, G11 | | |
| off Thornwood Dr | 47 | BH26 |
| Thornwood Rd, G11 | 65 | BH27 |
| Thornwood Ter, G11 | 65 | BH27 |
| Thornyburn Dr, (Baill.) G69 | 92 | CM33 |
| Thornyburn Pl, (Baill.) G69 | 92 | CL33 |
| Thrashbush La, Air. ML6 | | |
| off Thrashbush Rd | 76 | DD27 |
| Thrashbush Quad, Air. ML6 | 76 | DC27 |
| Thrashbush Rd, Air. ML6 | 76 | DC27 |

Threave Pl, (Newt. M.) G77 116 BD48
Three Rivers Wk, (E.Kil.) G75
   *off Hudson Ter* 135 BX53
Threestonehill Av, G32 70 CD31
Threshold, (E.Kil.) G74 136 CC51
Threshold Pk, (E.Kil.) G74 136 CC51
Thrums, (E.Kil.) G74 123 CF48
Thrums Av, (Bishop.) G64 33 BY20
Thrums Gdns, (Bishop.) G64 33 BY20
Thrushcraig Cres, Pais. PA2 82 AV35
Thrush Pl, John. PA5 79 AF38
Thurso St, G11 66 BL28
Thurston Rd, G52 64 BC32
Thyme Sq, Moth. ML1
   *off Alyssum Cres* 128 DA45
Tianavaig, Ersk. PA8 44 AS22
Tibbermore Rd, G11 48 BJ26
Tiber Av, Moth. ML1 111 CY44
Tighnasheen Way, (Blan.) G72 124 CM45
Tillanburn Rd, Moth. ML1 113 DH42
Tillet Oval, Pais. PA3 62 AT30
Tillie St, G20 49 BP26
Tillycairn Av, G33 71 CF27
Tillycairn Dr, G33 71 CF27
Tillycairn Pl, G33 71 CG27
Tillycairn Rd, G33 71 CG27
Tillycairn St, G33 71 CG27
Tilt St, G33 70 CA27
Time Capsule Leisure Cen,
   Coat. ML5 74 CV31
Timmons Gro, Bell. ML4 111 CZ40
Timmons Ter, (Chap.) Air. ML6 97 DF36
Tinkers La, Moth. ML1 127 CY47
Tintagel Gdns, (Chry.) G69 37 CP18
Tintock Dr, (Kirk.) G66 17 CH12
Tintock Pl, (Dullatur) G68 9 CZ7
Tintock Rd, G33 18 CK11
Tinto Dr, (Barr.) G78 99 AX44
Tinto Gro, (Baill.) G69 73 CR31
Tinto Rd, G43 102 BL40
Tinto Rd, (Bears.) G61 28 BD15
Tinto Rd, (Bishop.) G64 33 BY20
Tinto Rd, Air. ML6 76 DD31
Tinto Sq, Renf. PA4
   *off Ochil Rd* 63 AX28
Tinto Vw, Ham. ML3 140 CU53
Tinto Vw Rd, Lark. ML9 145 DG61
Tinto Way, (E.Kil.) G75 135 BX56
Tinwald Path, G52 64 BC32
Tiree, (E.Kil.) G74 137 CE54
Tiree Av, Pais. PA2 82 AT38
Tiree Av, Renf. PA4 63 AY29
Tiree Ct, (Cumb.) G67 21 CZ13
Tiree Dr, (Cumb.) G67 21 CZ13
Tiree Gdns, (Old Kil.) G60 26 AS15
Tiree Gdns, (Bears.) G61 28 BD15
Tiree Gdns, (Glenm.) Air. ML6
   *off Balmoral Av* 58 DB24
Tiree Gra, Ham. ML3 139 CP52
Tiree Pl, (Old Kil.) G60 26 AS15
Tiree Pl, (Newt. M.) G77 116 BD48
Tiree Pl, Coat. ML5
   *off Newton St* 94 CU33
Tiree Rd, (Cumb.) G67 21 CZ13
Tiree St, G21 69 BY27
Tirry Av, Renf. PA4 64 BB27
Tirry Way, Renf. PA4
   *off Morriston Cres* 64 BB27
Titwood Rd, G41 87 BN36
Titwood Rd, (Newt. M.) G77 131 BF52
Tiverton Av, G32 91 CF34
Tivoli Ct, (E.Kil.) G75 136 CA55
Tobago Pl, G40 68 BV32

Tobago Pl, (E.Kil.) G75 135 BW52
Tobago St, G40 68 BU32
Tobermory Rd, (Ruther.) G73 105 BZ42
Todburn Dr, Pais. PA2 82 AV37
Todd St, G31 69 BY30
Todhills, (E.Kil.) G75
   *off Todhills N* 136 CB53
Todhills N, (E.Kil.) G75 136 CB53
Todhills S, (E.Kil.) G75 136 CB53
Todholm Cres, Pais. PA2 83 AX35
Todholm Rd, Pais. PA2 83 AX35
Todholm Ter, Pais. PA2 83 AW35
Tofthill Av, (Bishop.) G64 32 BV19
Tofthill Gdns, (Bishop.) G64 32 BU19
Tollbrae Av, Air. ML6 76 DD30
Toll Ct, G51 67 BN31
Tollcross Pk Gdns, G32
   *off Tollcross Pk Vw* 90 CA34
Tollcross Pk Gro, G32
   *off Tollcross Pk Vw* 90 CB34
Tollcross Pk Vw, G32 90 CA34
Tollcross Rd, G31 69 BZ32
Tollcross Rd, G32 90 CA33
Tollhouse Gdns, Bell. ML4 111 CY42
Toll St, Moth. ML1 128 DB48
Toll Wynd, Ham. ML3 140 CS54
Tolsta St, G23 31 BN20
Tomtain Brae, (Cumb.) G68 20 CV14
Tomtain Ct, (Cumb.) G68 20 CV14
Tontine La, G1 5 BT31
Tontine Pl, (Ruther.) G73 106 CA41
Topaz Ter, Bell. ML4 111 CW42
Toppersfield, (Kilb.) John. PA10 79 AE35
Torbreck St, G52 65 BH32
Torbrex Rd, (Cumb.) G67 22 DC12
Torburn Av, (Giff.) G46 102 BK41
Tordene Path, (Cumb.) G68 21 CZ10
Torgyle St, G23 30 BM20
Tormeadow Rd, (Newt. M.)
   G77 117 BF48
Tormore St, G51 65 BF30
Tormusk Dr, G45 105 BW41
Tormusk Gdns, G45 105 BW41
Tormusk Gro, G45 105 BW41
Tormusk Rd, G45 105 BW41
Torness St, G11 66 BL27
Torogay Pl, G22 50 BU21
Torogay St, G22 50 BS22
Torogay Ter, G22 50 BS21
Toronto Wk, G32 91 CE37
Torphin Cres, G32 70 CC30
Torphin Wk, G32 70 CD31
Torrance Av, Air. ML6 77 DF30
Torrance Rd, (Torr.) G64 15 BY14
Torrance Rd, (E.Kil.) G74 136 CA51
Torrance St, G21 50 BV25
Torran Dr, Ersk. PA8 44 AU22
Torran Rd, G33 71 CH30
Torranyard Ter, Ham. ML3 139 CN52
Torr Gdns, G22 50 BT25
Torriden Ct, Coat. ML5
   *off Torriden St* 74 CU32
Torriden Pl, Coat. ML5 74 CU32
Torriden St, Coat. ML5 74 CU32
Torridon Av, G41 86 BK34
Torridon Av, Moth. ML1 113 DF42
Torridon Dr, Renf. PA4 64 BA27
Torridon Gdns, (Bears.) G61 11 BF14
Torridon Gdns, (Newt. M.) G77 118 BK49
Torridon Path, G41
   *off Dumbreck Av* 86 BJ34
Torrington Av, (Giff.) G46 118 BJ45
Torrington Cres, G32 91 CF34

Torrin Rd, G23 30 BM20
Torrisdale St, Coat. ML5 74 CU30
Torrisdale St, G42 87 BP35
Torrisdale St, Coat. ML5 74 CU30
Torr Pl, G22 50 BT25
Torr Rd, (Bishop.) G64 33 BZ20
Torr St, G22 50 BT25
Torryburn Rd, G21 51 BY25
Torwood Brae, Ham. ML3 139 CP51
Torwood La, (Mood.) G69
   *off Burnbrae Av* 37 CQ19
Toryglen Rd, (Ruther.) G73 88 BU37
Toryglen St, G5 88 BT35
Tourmaline Rd, Bell. ML4
   *off Sapphire Rd* 111 CX42
Tournai Path, (Blan.) G72
   *off Burnbrae Rd* 124 CM46
Toward Ct, (Blan.) G72 109 CN44
Toward Rd, G33 71 CE30
Tower Av, (Barr.) G78 99 AZ41
Tower Cres, Renf. PA4 63 AX27
Tower Dr, Renf. PA4 63 AX27
Towerhill Rd, G13 29 BE20
Tower Pl, (Miln.) G62 12 BK11
Tower Pl, John. PA5 79 AH36
Tower Rd, (Torr.) G64 14 BV11
Tower Rd, (Cumb.) G67 40 DC15
Tower Rd, John. PA5 79 AH36
Towerside Cres, G53 84 BC35
Towerside Rd, G53 84 BC35
Towers Pl, Air. ML6 77 DH30
Towers Rd, Air. ML6 77 DG29
Tower St, G41 67 BN32
Tower Ter, Pais. PA1 82 AT33
Towie Pl, G20
   *off Glenfinnan Dr* 48 BM23
Towie Pl, (Udd.) G71 109 CP39
Town Cen, (Cumb.) G67
   *off Cumbernauld Shop Cen* 22 DC12
Townhead, (Kirk.) G66 17 CF13
Townhead, (Holytown)
   Moth. ML1 96 DB38
Townhead Dr, Moth. ML1 113 DH42
Townhead Pl, (Udd.) G71 93 CQ37
Townhead Rd, (Newt. M.) G77 117 BF49
Townhead Rd, Coat. ML5 73 CQ28
Townhead St, (Kilsyth) G65 7 CT5
Townhead St, Ham. ML3 126 CV50
Townhead Ter, Pais. PA1 82 AT33
Townhill Rd, Ham. ML3 125 CN50
Townhill Ter, Ham. ML3
   *off Townhill Rd* 125 CN50
Townmill Rd, G31 68 BV29
Townsend St, G4 5 BS28
Tradeston St, G5 67 BQ32
Trafalgar Ct, (Dullatur) G68 9 CZ7
Trafalgar St, G40 88 BV34
Trafalgar St, Clyde. G81 26 AV18
Trainard Av, G32 90 CB33
Tranent Pl, G33 70 CA29
Traquair Av, Pais. PA2 81 AN37
Traquair Dr, G52 84 BD33
Traquair Wynd, (Blan.) G72
   *off Burnbrae Rd* 124 CM46
Treeburn Av, (Giff.) G46 102 BK42
Treemain Rd, (Giff.) G46 118 BJ45
Trees Pk Av, (Barr.) G78 99 AX41
Trefoil Av, G41 86 BM37
Trent Pl, (E.Kil.) G75 134 BU55
Trent St, Coat. ML5 74 CT27
Tresta Rd, G23 49 BP21
Tribboch St, Lark. ML9
   *off Watson St* 144 DB58

| | | |
|---|---|---|
| Trident Way, Renf. PA4 | | |
| off Newmains Rd | 63 | AY28 |
| Trinidad Grn, (E.Kil.) G75 | | |
| off Leeward Circle | 135 | BW52 |
| Trinidad Way, (E.Kil.) G75 | 135 | BW52 |
| Trinity Av, G52 | 85 | BE33 |
| Trinity Dr, (Camb.) G72 | 107 | CE42 |
| Trinity Way, Lark. ML9 | | |
| off Blair Atholl Dr | 145 | DE60 |
| Trinley Brae, G13 | 29 | BE20 |
| Trinley Rd, G13 | 29 | BF20 |
| Triton Pl, Bell. ML4 | 112 | DB40 |
| Trondra Path, G34 | 71 | CH29 |
| Trondra Pl, G34 | 71 | CH30 |
| Trondra Rd, G34 | 71 | CH29 |
| Trongate, G1 | 5 | BS31 |
| Troon Av, (E.Kil.) G75 | 135 | BW55 |
| Troon Ct, (E.Kil.) G75 | 135 | BX55 |
| Troon Gdns, (Cumb.) G68 | 9 | DB7 |
| Troon Pl, (Newt. M.) G77 | 118 | BJ49 |
| Troon St, G40 | 89 | BX34 |
| Trossachs Av, Moth. ML1 | | |
| off Howden Pl | 112 | DC40 |
| Trossachs Ct, G20 | | |
| off Trossachs St | 49 | BQ26 |
| Trossachs Rd, (Ruther.) G73 | 105 | BZ43 |
| Trossachs St, G20 | 49 | BQ26 |
| Troubridge Av, (Kilb.) | | |
| John. PA10 | 78 | AD36 |
| Troubridge Cres, (Kilb.) | | |
| John. PA10 | 78 | AD35 |
| Truce Rd, G13 | 46 | BD21 |
| Truro Av, (Chry.) G69 | 37 | CP18 |
| Tryst Rd, (Cumb.) G67 | 22 | DB12 |
| Tudor Rd, G14 | 47 | BG26 |
| Tudor St, (Baill.) G69 | 91 | CH34 |
| Tulley Wynd, Moth. ML1 | | |
| off Dinmont Cres | 111 | CZ43 |
| Tulliallan Pl, (E.Kil.) G74 | 136 | CC53 |
| Tullis Ct, G40 | 88 | BU33 |
| Tullis Gdns, G40 | 88 | BV33 |
| Tullis St, G40 | 88 | BU33 |
| Tulloch-Ard Pl, (Ruther.) G73 | | |
| off Lochbrae Dr | 105 | BZ42 |
| Tulloch Gdns, Moth. ML1 | 128 | DD49 |
| Tulloch St, G44 | 103 | BQ39 |
| Tullymet Rd, Ham. ML3 | 140 | CT53 |
| Tummel Dr, Air. ML6 | 76 | DB27 |
| Tummel Grn, (E.Kil.) G74 | 122 | CA50 |
| Tummell Way, Pais. PA2 | 81 | AP36 |
| Tummel St, G33 | 70 | CA27 |
| Tummel Wk, (Cumb.) G67 | | |
| off Cumbernauld Shop Cen | 22 | DB11 |
| Tunnel St, G3 | 67 | BN30 |
| Tuphall Rd, Ham. ML3 | 140 | CT51 |
| Tureen St, G40 | 68 | BV31 |
| Turnberry Av, G11 | | |
| off Turnberry Rd | 48 | BK26 |
| Turnberry Cres, (Chap.) Air. ML6 | | |
| off Honeywell Cres | 97 | DG36 |
| Turnberry Cres, Coat. ML5 | 94 | CU33 |
| Turnberry Dr, (Ruther.) G73 | 104 | BV41 |
| Turnberry Dr, (Newt. M.) G77 | 118 | BJ48 |
| Turnberry Dr, Ham. ML3 | 138 | CM51 |
| Turnberry Gdns, (Cumb.) G68 | 9 | DB8 |
| Turnberry Pl, (Ruther.) G73 | | |
| off Turnberry Dr | 104 | BV41 |
| Turnberry Pl, (E.Kil.) G75 | 135 | BX55 |
| Turnberry Rd, G11 | 48 | BJ26 |
| Turnberry Wynd, (Both.) G71 | 109 | CN42 |
| Turnbull St, G1 | 5 | BT31 |
| Turner Rd, G21 | 68 | BV27 |
| Turner Rd, Pais. PA3 | 62 | AV29 |
| Turners Av, Pais. PA1 | 81 | AR34 |
| Turner St, Coat. ML5 | 74 | CV31 |
| Turnhill Av, Ersk. PA8 | 43 | AR22 |
| Turnhill Cres, Ersk. PA8 | 43 | AR22 |
| Turnhill Dr, Ersk. PA8 | 43 | AR22 |
| Turnhill Gdns, Ersk. PA8 | 43 | AR22 |
| Turnlaw, (E.Kil.) G75 | 135 | BZ56 |
| Turnlaw Fm, (Camb.) G72 | 106 | CC44 |
| Turnlaw Rd, (Camb.) G72 | 106 | CC43 |
| Turnlaw St, G5 | 88 | BT33 |
| Turnyland Meadows, Ersk. PA8 | 43 | AR22 |
| Turnyland Way, Ersk. PA8 | 43 | AR22 |
| Turquoise Ter, Bell. ML4 | 111 | CX42 |
| Turret Cres, G13 | 47 | BE21 |
| Turret Rd, G13 | 47 | BE21 |
| Turriff St, G5 | 87 | BR33 |
| Twechar Enterprise Pk, (Kilsyth) | | |
| G65 | 19 | CP9 |
| Tweed Av, Pais. PA2 | 81 | AP35 |
| Tweed Ct, Air. ML6 | | |
| off Etive Dr | 77 | DE32 |
| Tweed Cres, G33 | 69 | BZ28 |
| Tweed Cres, Renf. PA4 | 46 | BA26 |
| Tweed Dr, (Bears.) G61 | 29 | BF18 |
| Tweed La, Moth. ML1 | | |
| off Redwood Rd | 112 | DD40 |
| Tweed Pl, John. PA5 | 79 | AE37 |
| Tweedsmuir, (Bishop.) G64 | 33 | BY19 |
| Tweedsmuir Cres, (Bears.) G61 | 11 | BG14 |
| Tweedsmuir Pk, Ham. ML3 | 140 | CS53 |
| Tweedsmuir Pl, Coat. ML5 | 95 | CY34 |
| Tweedsmuir Rd, G52 | 84 | BD33 |
| Tweed St, (E.Kil.) G75 | 134 | BV54 |
| Tweed St, Coat. ML5 | 95 | CW34 |
| Tweed St, Lark. ML9 | 144 | DC60 |
| Tweedvale Av, G14 | 46 | BA23 |
| Tweedvale Pl, G14 | | |
| off Tweedvale Av | 46 | BA23 |
| Tweed Wk, (Cumb.) G67 | | |
| off Cumbernauld Shop Cen | 22 | DB12 |
| Twinlaw St, G34 | 72 | CM28 |
| Tylney Rd, Pais. PA1 | 63 | AZ32 |
| Tyndrum Rd, (Bears.) G61 | | |
| off Rannoch Dr | 30 | BK16 |
| Tyndrum St, G4 | 5 | BS28 |
| Tynecastle Cres, G32 | 70 | CD30 |
| Tynecastle Path, G32 | | |
| off Lightburn Pl | 70 | CD30 |
| Tynecastle Pl, G32 | 70 | CD30 |
| Tynecastle St, G32 | 70 | CD30 |
| Tyne Pl, (E.Kil.) G75 | 134 | BU55 |
| Tyne St, G14 | 65 | BF27 |
| Tynron Ct, Ham. ML3 | 139 | CN52 |
| Tynwald Av, (Ruther.) G73 | 105 | BZ41 |
| **U** | | |
| Uddingston Rd, (Both.) G71 | 109 | CP42 |
| Udston Rd, Ham. ML3 | 125 | CN49 |
| Udston Ter, Ham. ML3 | 125 | CP48 |
| Uig Pl, G33 | 71 | CG32 |
| Uist Cres, (Stepps) G33 | 53 | CG25 |
| Uist Dr, (Kirk.) G66 | 18 | CJ13 |
| Uist Pl, Air. ML6 | 77 | DF31 |
| Uist St, G51 | 65 | BH30 |
| Ullswater, (E.Kil.) G75 | 134 | BV56 |
| Ulundi Rd, John. PA5 | 79 | AF35 |
| Ulva St, G52 | 65 | BH32 |
| Ulverston Ter, Ham. ML3 | 140 | CT55 |
| Umachan, Ersk. PA8 | 44 | AS22 |
| Underwood Ct, Pais. PA3 | 62 | AT32 |
| Underwood La, Pais. PA1 | 62 | AT32 |
| Underwood Rd, (Ruther.) G73 | 105 | BY39 |
| Underwood Rd, Pais. PA3 | 62 | AS32 |
| Underwood St, G41 | 87 | BN37 |
| Union Ct, Pais. PA2 | 82 | AU35 |
| Union Pl, G1 | | |
| off Gordon St | 4 | BR30 |
| Union St, G1 | 4 | BR30 |
| Union St, (Kirk.) G66 | 17 | CE13 |
| Union St, Clyde. G81 | 45 | AY21 |
| Union St, Ham. ML3 | 126 | CT49 |
| Union St, Lark. ML9 | 144 | DC58 |
| Union St, Moth. ML1 | 112 | DC41 |
| Union St, Pais. PA2 | 82 | AU35 |
| Unitas Rd, Bell. ML4 | 111 | CY40 |
| Unity Pl, G4 | 67 | BQ27 |
| University Av, G12 | 66 | BM27 |
| University Gdns, G12 | 66 | BM27 |
| University of Glasgow, G12 | 66 | BM27 |
| University Pl, G12 | 66 | BM27 |
| Unsted Pl, Pais. PA1 | 83 | AW33 |
| Unst La, (Camb.) G72 | 106 | CA43 |
| Unthank Rd, Bell. ML4 | 111 | CY40 |
| Uphall Pl, G33 | 70 | CA29 |
| Upland Rd, G14 | 47 | BE25 |
| Up La, (Kilsyth) G65 | | |
| off Up Rd | 7 | CT5 |
| Upper Bourtree Ct, (Ruther.) | | |
| G73 | 105 | BY41 |
| Upper Bourtree Dr, (Ruther.) | | |
| G73 | 105 | BX41 |
| Upper Glenburn Rd, (Bears.) | | |
| G61 | 29 | BE16 |
| Upper Mill St, Air. ML6 | 76 | DC29 |
| Up Rd, (Kilsyth) G65 | 7 | CT5 |
| Urquhart Cres, Renf. PA4 | 63 | AY27 |
| Urquhart Dr, (E.Kil.) G74 | 122 | CC50 |
| Urrdale Rd, G41 | 66 | BK32 |
| Usmore Pl, G33 | | |
| off Pendeen Cres | 71 | CG32 |
| **V** | | |
| Vaila La, (Camb.) G72 | 106 | CB42 |
| Vaila Pl, G23 | | |
| off Vaila St | 49 | BQ22 |
| Vaila St, G23 | 49 | BP22 |
| Valerio Ct, (Blan.) G72 | 124 | CM45 |
| Valetta Pl, Clyde. G81 | 26 | AT17 |
| Valeview Ter, G42 | | |
| off Battlefield Rd | 87 | BQ37 |
| Vale Wk, (Bishop.) G64 | 51 | BY21 |
| Vallantine Cres, (Udd.) G71 | 93 | CQ37 |
| Vallay St, G22 | 50 | BT21 |
| Valley Ct, Ham. ML3 | 140 | CS51 |
| Valleyfield, (E.Kil.) G75 | 135 | BZ52 |
| Valleyfield Av, Ham. ML3 | 141 | CY52 |
| Valleyfield Dr, (Cumb.) G68 | 20 | CU12 |
| Valleyfield St, G21 | | |
| off Ayr St | 50 | BU26 |
| Valley Vw, (Camb.) G72 | 107 | CE39 |
| Valley Vw, Moth. ML1 | 128 | DD50 |
| Vancouver Dr, (E.Kil.) G75 | 135 | BX52 |
| Vancouver La, G14 | | |
| off Vancouver Rd | 47 | BF25 |
| Vancouver Pl, Clyde. G81 | 26 | AT17 |
| Vancouver Rd, G14 | 47 | BE25 |
| Vanguard St, Clyde. G81 | 27 | AY19 |
| Vanguard Way, Renf. PA4 | 63 | AY28 |
| Vardar Av, (Clark.) G76 | 118 | BL45 |
| Vardon Lea, Moth. ML1 | 113 | DG44 |
| Varna La, G14 | 47 | BG26 |
| Varna Rd, G14 | 47 | BG25 |
| Varnsdorf Way, Air. ML6 | 77 | DG31 |
| Vasart Pl, G20 | 49 | BP24 |

Veitches Ct, Clyde. G81 — 27 AW15
Vennacher Rd, Renf. PA4 — 45 AW25
Vennard Gdns, G41 — 87 BN35
Vermont Av, (Ruther.) G73 — 89 BW38
Vermont St, G41 — 67 BN32
Vernon Bk, (E.Kil.) G74 — 122 CA50
Vernon Dr, (Linw.) Pais. PA3 — 60 AJ31
Verona Av, G14 — 47 BE25
Verona Gdns, G14 — 47 BE25
Verona La, G14 — 47 BE25
Vesalius St, G32 — 70 CC32
Veterans Cotts, (Erskine Hosp.) Bish. PA7 — 25 AP16
Viaduct Rd, (Clark.) G76 — 119 BP46
Vicarfield Pl, G51 — 66 BK30
Vicarfield St, G51 — 66 BK30
Vicarland Pl, (Camb.) G72 — 106 CC41
Vicarland Rd, (Camb.) G72 — 106 CC40
Vicars Wk, (Camb.) G72 — 106 CD40
Vickers St, Moth. ML1 — 127 CX45
Victoria Av, (Barr.) G78 — 99 AX41
Victoria Br, G1 — 5 BS31
Victoria Br, G5 — 5 BS31
Victoria Circ, G12 — 48 BL26
Victoria Ct, (Newt. M.) G77 — 131 BF51
Victoria Cres, G12
  off Downside Rd — 48 BL26
Victoria Cres, (Kilsyth) G65 — 7 CR5
Victoria Cres, (Clark.) G76 — 119 BP46
Victoria Cres, (Barr.) G78 — 99 AX41
Victoria Cres, Air. ML6 — 76 DA31
Victoria Cres, Wis. ML2
  off Shieldmuir St — 129 DF49
Victoria Cres La, G12 — 48 BL26
Victoria Cres Pl, G12
  off Bowmont Ter — 48 BL26
Victoria Cres Rd, G12 — 48 BL26
Victoria Cross, G42 — 87 BQ35
Victoria Dr, (Barr.) G78 — 99 AX41
Victoria Dr E, Renf. PA4 — 63 AY27
Victoria Dr W, Renf. PA4 — 45 AX26
Victoria Gdns, (Barr.) G78
  off Victoria Rd — 99 AX41
Victoria Gdns, Air. ML6 — 76 DB30
Victoria Gdns, Pais. PA2 — 82 AS35
Victoria Glade, (Dullatur) G68 — 9 CZ7
Victoria Gro, (Barr.) G78 — 99 AX41
Victoria La, (Newt. M.) G77 — 131 BF51
Victoria Pk, (Kilsyth) G65 — 7 CR5
Victoria Pk Cor, G14 — 47 BF25
Victoria Pk Dr N, G14 — 47 BF25
Victoria Pk Dr S, G14 — 47 BE26
Victoria Pk Gdns N, G11 — 47 BH26
Victoria Pk Gdns S, G11 — 47 BH26
Victoria Pk La N, G14 — 47 BF26
Victoria Pk La S, G14
  off Westland Dr — 47 BF26
Victoria Pk St, G14 — 47 BF26
Victoria Pl, (Miln.) G62
  off Glasgow Rd — 12 BK12
Victoria Pl, (Kilsyth) G65 — 7 CR5
Victoria Pl, (Ruther.) G73
  off Greenbank St — 89 BW37
Victoria Pl, (Barr.) G78 — 99 AY41
Victoria Pl, Air. ML6 — 76 DA31
Victoria Pl, Bell. ML4 — 110 CV41
Victoria Quad, Moth. ML1 — 112 DB40
Victoria Rd, (Stepps) G33 — 53 CF24
Victoria Rd, G42 — 87 BQ36
Victoria Rd, (Lenz.) G66 — 35 CE17
Victoria Rd, (Dullatur) G68 — 9 CZ7
Victoria Rd, (Ruther.) G73 — 105 BX39
Victoria Rd, (Barr.) G78 — 99 AX41

Victoria Rd, Pais. PA2 — 82 AS35
Victoria Sq, (Newt. M.) G77 — 131 BF51
Victoria St, (Kirk.) G66 — 17 CE13
Victoria St, (Blan.) G72 — 124 CM47
Victoria St, (Ruther.) G73 — 89 BW37
Victoria St, Ham. ML3 — 125 CR47
Victoria St, Lark. ML9 — 144 DC58
Victoria Ter, (Dullatur) G68 — 8 CY7
Victory Dr, (Kilb.) John. PA10 — 78 AC33
Victory Way, (Baill.) G69 — 92 CK33
Viewbank, (Thornlie.) G46 — 102 BJ42
Viewbank Av, (Calder.) Air. ML6 — 96 DD35
Viewbank St, (Glenb.) Coat. ML5 — 56 CV24
Viewfield, Air. ML6 — 76 DA30
Viewfield Av, (Bishop.) G64 — 50 BU21
Viewfield Av, (Lenz.) G66 — 35 CE16
Viewfield Av, (Baill.) G69 — 71 CH32
Viewfield Av, (Blan.) G72 — 109 CN44
Viewfield Dr, (Bishop.) G64 — 50 BU21
Viewfield Dr, (Baill.) G69 — 71 CH32
Viewfield La, G12 — 67 BN27
Viewfield Rd, (Bishop.) G64 — 50 BU21
Viewfield Rd, Bell. ML4 — 110 CV42
Viewfield Rd, Coat. ML5 — 93 CR33
Viewglen Ct, G45 — 104 BT44
Viewmount Dr, G20 — 48 BM22
Viewpark, (Miln.) G62
  off Crossveggate — 12 BK12
Viewpark Av, G31 — 69 BX29
Viewpark Dr, (Ruther.) G73 — 105 BX39
Viewpark Gdns, Renf. PA4 — 63 AX27
Viewpark Pl, Moth. ML1
  off Viewpark Rd — 127 CY47
Viewpark Rd, Moth. ML1 — 127 CY47
Viewpark Shop Cen, (Udd.) G71 — 94 CT38
Viewpoint Gate, G21 — 50 BV23
Viewpoint Pl, G21 — 50 BV23
Viewpoint Rd, G21 — 50 BV23
Viking Rd, (Thornlie.) G46 — 101 BH41
Viking Rd, Air. ML6 — 76 DD32
Viking Ter, (E.Kil.) G75 — 136 CA55
Viking Way, Renf. PA4
  off Vanguard Way — 63 AY28
Villafield Av, (Bishop.) G64 — 33 BW18
Villafield Dr, (Bishop.) G64 — 33 BW18
Villafield Ln, (Bishop.) G64
  off Villafield Av — 33 BW18
Village Gdns, (Blan.) G72 — 109 CN44
Village Rd, (Camb.) G72 — 107 CG40
Vincent Ct, Bell. ML4
  off Strachan St — 111 CW41
Vine St, G11 — 66 BK27
Vinicombe La, G12 — 48 BM26
Vinicombe St, G12 — 48 BM26
Vintner St, G4 — 68 BS27
Viola Pl, (Torr.) G64 — 15 BY13
Violet Pl, Moth. ML1 — 112 DD39
Violet St, Pais. PA1 — 83 AW33
Virginia Bldgs, G1
  off Virginia St — 5 BS30
Virginia Ct, G1
  off Virginia St — 5 BS30
Virginia Gdns, (Miln.) G62 — 12 BL13
Virginia Gro, Ham. ML3 — 139 CP53
Virginia Pl, G1 — 5 BS30
Virginia St, G1 — 5 BS30
Viscount Av, Renf. PA4 — 63 AY28
Viscount Gate, (Both.) G71 — 109 CN40
Vivian Av, (Miln.) G62 — 11 BH12
Voil Dr, G44 — 103 BQ41
Vorlich Ct, (Barr.) G78
  off Eildon Dr — 99 AY44

Vorlich Gdns, (Bears.) G61 — 11 BE14
Vorlich Wynd, Moth. ML1
  off Glenburn Av — 113 DE41
Vulcan St, G21
  off Springburn Way — 50 BU25
Vulcan St, Moth. ML1 — 128 DA45

# W

Waddell Av, (Glenm.) Air. ML6 — 57 CZ25
Waddell Ct, G5 — 68 BT32
Waddell St, G5 — 88 BT33
Waddell St, Air. ML6 — 76 DC28
Waid Av, (Newt. M.) G77 — 117 BE47
Waldemar Rd, G13 — 47 BE22
Waldo St, G13 — 47 BH22
Walkerburn Rd, G52 — 84 BD33
Walker Ct, G11 — 66 BK28
Walker Dr, (Elder.) John. PA5 — 80 AK35
Walker Path, (Udd.) G71 — 93 CQ37
Walker St, G11 — 66 BK28
Walker St, Pais. PA1 — 82 AT33
Walkinshaw Cres, Pais. PA2 — 61 AR31
Walkinshaw Rd, Renf. PA4 — 44 AS26
Walkinshaw St, G40 — 89 BW33
Walkinshaw St, John. PA5 — 79 AH34
Wallace Av, Bish. PA7 — 24 AK18
Wallace Av, (Elder.) John. PA5 — 80 AL34
Wallace Dr, (Bishop.) G64 — 51 BZ21
Wallace Dr, Lark. ML9 — 145 DE59
Wallace Gdns, (Torr.) G64 — 15 BX12
Wallace Gate, (Bishop.) G64 — 51 BZ21
Wallace Pl, (Bishop.) G64 — 51 BZ21
Wallace Pl, (Blan.) G72 — 109 CN44
Wallace Pl, Ham. ML3 — 141 CW51
Wallace Rd, Moth. ML1
  off Park Rd — 112 DD43
Wallace Rd, Renf. PA4 — 63 AW28
Wallace St, G5 — 4 BQ31
Wallace St, (Ruther.) G73 — 89 BW38
Wallace St, Clyde. G81 — 45 AX21
Wallace St, Coat. ML5 — 75 CW32
Wallace St, Moth. ML1 — 127 CZ46
Wallace St, Pais. PA3 — 62 AU31
Wallacewell Cres, G21 — 51 BX24
Wallacewell Pl, G21 — 51 BX24
Wallacewell Quad, G21 — 51 BY23
Wallacewell Rd, G21 — 51 BX24
Wallbrae Rd, (Cumb.) G67 — 22 DB13
Wallneuk, Pais. PA1
  off Incle St — 62 AV32
Wallneuk Rd, Pais. PA3 — 62 AV32
Walls St, G1 — 5 BT30
Walmer Cres, G51 — 66 BL31
Walnut Cl, (E.Kil.) G75 — 135 BY55
Walnut Cres, G22 — 50 BT24
Walnut Cres, John. PA5 — 80 AK36
Walnut Dr, (Kirk.) G66 — 34 CD15
Walnut Gate, (Camb.) G72 — 107 CH41
Walnut Gro, (E.Kil.) G75 — 135 BY55
Walnut Pl, G22
  off Walnut Cres — 50 BT24
Walnut Pl, (Udd.) G71 — 94 CS36
Walnut Rd, G22 — 50 BT24
Walpole La, (E.Kil.) G74 — 134 BT52
Walpole Pl, John. PA5
  off Hallhill Rd — 79 AF38
Walter St, G31 — 69 BX30
Walton Av, (Newt. M.) G77 — 117 BE47
Walton Ct, (Giff.) G46 — 102 BL43
Walton St, G41 — 87 BN37
Walton St, (Barr.) G78 — 99 AY42
Wamba Av, G13 — 47 BG21

| | | |
|---|---|---|
| Wamba Pl, G13 | | |
| *off Wamba Av* | 47 | BG21 |
| Wamphray Pl, (E.Kil.) G75 | 134 | BT54 |
| Wandilla Av, Clyde. G81 | 27 | AZ19 |
| Wanlock St, G51 | 66 | BJ29 |
| Wardend Rd, (Torr.) G64 | 15 | BX12 |
| Warden Rd, G13 | 47 | BF22 |
| Wardhill Rd, G21 | 51 | BX24 |
| Wardhouse Rd, Pais. PA2 | 82 | AS38 |
| Wardie Path, G33 | 71 | CH30 |
| Wardie Pl, G33 | 71 | CH30 |
| Wardie Rd, G33 | 71 | CH30 |
| Wardie Rd, G34 | 72 | CJ29 |
| Wardlaw Av, (Ruther.) G73 | 89 | BX38 |
| Wardlaw Cres, (E.Kil.) G75 | 136 | CB54 |
| Wardlaw Dr, (Ruther.) G73 | 89 | BX37 |
| Wardlaw Rd, (Bears.) G61 | 29 | BH20 |
| Wardrop Pl, (E.Kil.) G74 | 122 | CB50 |
| Wardrop St, G51 | 66 | BJ29 |
| Wardrop St, Pais. PA1 | 82 | AU33 |
| Wards Cres, Coat. ML5 | 74 | CU32 |
| Ware Path, G34 | 72 | CJ30 |
| Ware Rd, G34 | 71 | CH30 |
| Warilda Av, Clyde. G81 | 27 | AY19 |
| Warnock Cres, Bell. ML4 | 111 | CX41 |
| Warnock Rd, (Newt. M.) G77 | 117 | BE47 |
| Warnock St, G31 | 5 | BU29 |
| Warren Rd, Ham. ML3 | 140 | CT53 |
| Warren St, G42 | 87 | BR36 |
| Warriston Cres, G33 | 69 | BZ29 |
| Warriston Pl, G32 | | |
| *off Hermiston Rd* | 70 | CD30 |
| Warriston St, G33 | 69 | BZ29 |
| Warriston Way, (Ruther.) G73 | | |
| *off Lochaber Dr* | 105 | BZ41 |
| Warroch St, G3 | 4 | BP30 |
| Warwick, (E.Kil.) G74 | 123 | CE49 |
| Warwick Gro, Ham. ML3 | | |
| *off Stirling Dr* | 125 | CN48 |
| Washington Rd, (Kirk.) G66 | 16 | CD12 |
| Washington Rd, Pais. PA3 | 62 | AV29 |
| Washington St, G3 | 4 | BQ30 |
| Waterbank Rd, (Carm.) G76 | 120 | BT48 |
| Water Brae, Pais. PA1 | | |
| *off Forbes Pl* | 82 | AU33 |
| Waterfoot Av, G53 | 85 | BE37 |
| Waterfoot Rd, (Thornton.) G74 | 133 | BQ51 |
| Waterfoot Rd, (Clark.) G76 | 118 | BK50 |
| Waterfoot Rd, (Newt. M.) G77 | 117 | BH50 |
| Waterfoot Row, (Clark.) G76 | | |
| *off Waterfoot Rd* | 118 | BM50 |
| Waterfoot Ter, G53 | | |
| *off Waterfoot Av* | 85 | BE37 |
| Waterford Rd, (Giff.) G46 | 102 | BK42 |
| Waterhaughs Gdns, G33 | 51 | BZ22 |
| Waterhaughs Gro, G33 | 51 | BZ22 |
| Waterhaughs Pl, G33 | 51 | BZ22 |
| Waterloo Cl, (Kirk.) G66 | | |
| *off John St* | 17 | CF12 |
| Waterloo Gdns, (Kirk.) G66 | | |
| *off John St* | 17 | CF12 |
| Waterloo La, G2 | 4 | BR30 |
| Waterloo St, G2 | 4 | BQ30 |
| Watermill Av, (Lenz.) G66 | 35 | CF17 |
| Water Rd, (Barr.) G78 | 99 | AY42 |
| Water Row, G51 | 66 | BJ29 |
| Waterside Av, (Newt. M.) G77 | 117 | BE49 |
| Waterside Ct, (Clark.) G76 | | |
| *off Waterside Rd* | 120 | BT45 |
| Waterside Dr, (Newt. M.) G77 | 117 | BE49 |
| Waterside Gdns, (Camb.) G72 | 107 | CG42 |
| Waterside Gdns, (Carm.) G76 | 120 | BT46 |
| Waterside Gdns, Ham. ML3 | 140 | CU52 |

| | | |
|---|---|---|
| Waterside La, (Kilb.) John. PA10 | 79 | AE36 |
| Waterside Pl, G5 | 88 | BT33 |
| Waterside Rd, (Kirk.) G66 | 17 | CG14 |
| Waterside Rd, (Carm.) G76 | 120 | BT45 |
| Waterside St, G5 | 88 | BT33 |
| Waterside Ter, (Kilb.) John. PA10 | | |
| *off Kilbarchan Rd* | 79 | AE35 |
| Watling Pl, (E.Kil.) G75 | | |
| *off Leeward Circle* | 135 | BW52 |
| Watling St, (Udd.) G71 | 93 | CN37 |
| Watling St, Moth. ML1 | 111 | CX44 |
| Watson Av, (Ruther.) G73 | 88 | BV38 |
| Watson Av, (Linw.) Pais. PA3 | 60 | AK31 |
| Watson Cres, (Kilsyth) G65 | 7 | CU5 |
| Watson Pl, (Blan.) G72 | 124 | CK46 |
| Watson St, G1 | 5 | BT31 |
| Watson St, (Udd.) G71 | 109 | CP40 |
| Watson St, (Blan.) G72 | 124 | CK46 |
| Watson St, Lark. ML9 | 144 | DB58 |
| Watson St, Moth. ML1 | 128 | DA48 |
| Watsonville Pk, Moth. ML1 | | |
| *off Oakfield Rd* | 128 | DA47 |
| Watt Av, G33 | 53 | CH24 |
| Watt Cres, Bell. ML4 | 95 | CX38 |
| Watt Low Av, (Ruther.) G73 | 104 | BV39 |
| Watt Pl, (Miln.) G62 | 11 | BH10 |
| Watt Pl, (Blan.) G72 | 124 | CL49 |
| Watt Rd, G52 | 64 | BB30 |
| Watt St, G5 | 4 | BP31 |
| Watt St, Air. ML6 | 76 | DD28 |
| Waukglen Av, G53 | 100 | BD43 |
| Waukglen Cres, G53 | 101 | BE42 |
| Waukglen Dr, G53 | 100 | BD42 |
| Waukglen Gdns, G53 | 100 | BD42 |
| Waukglen Path, G53 | | |
| *off Waukglen Dr* | 100 | BD42 |
| Waukglen Pl, G53 | 100 | BD42 |
| Waukglen Rd, G53 | 100 | BD42 |
| Waulkmill Av, (Barr.) G78 | 99 | AZ41 |
| Waulkmill St, (Thornlie.) G46 | 101 | BG41 |
| Waulkmill Way, (Barr.) G78 | | |
| *off Waulkmill Av* | 99 | AZ41 |
| Waverley, (E.Kil.) G74 | 123 | CF49 |
| Waverley, Clyde. G81 | | |
| *off Onslow Rd* | 27 | AY19 |
| Waverley Ct, (Both.) G71 | 109 | CQ43 |
| Waverley Cres, (Kirk.) G66 | 17 | CG13 |
| Waverley Cres, (Cumb.) G67 | 21 | CZ14 |
| Waverley Cres, Ham. ML3 | 125 | CP49 |
| Waverley Dr, (Ruther.) G73 | 89 | BY38 |
| Waverley Gdns, G41 | 87 | BN36 |
| Waverley Gdns, (Elder.) John. PA5 | 80 | AM35 |
| Waverley Pk, (Kirk.) G66 | 17 | CF12 |
| Waverley Rd, Pais. PA2 | 81 | AP37 |
| Waverley St, G41 | 87 | BN36 |
| Waverley St, Coat. ML5 | 75 | CX28 |
| Waverley St, Ham. ML3 | 125 | CP49 |
| Waverley St, Lark. ML9 | 144 | DC61 |
| Waverley Ter, G31 | | |
| *off Whitevale St* | 69 | BW31 |
| Waverley Ter, (Blan.) G72 | 124 | CL48 |
| Waverley Way, Pais. PA2 | 81 | AP38 |
| Weardale La, G33 | 71 | CE29 |
| Weardale St, G33 | 71 | CE29 |
| Weaver Av, (Newt. M.) G77 | 117 | BE46 |
| Weaver Cres, Air. ML6 | 76 | DC32 |
| Weaver La, (Kilb.) John. PA10 | | |
| *off Glentyan Av* | 78 | AC33 |
| Weaver Pl, (E.Kil.) G75 | 134 | BU54 |
| Weavers Av, Pais. PA2 | 81 | AR34 |
| Weavers Gate, Pais. PA1 | 81 | AQ34 |

| | | |
|---|---|---|
| Weavers Rd, Pais. PA2 | 81 | AR34 |
| Weaver St, G4 | 5 | BT30 |
| Weaver Ter, Pais. PA2 | 83 | AW34 |
| Webster St, G40 | 89 | BW34 |
| Webster St, Clyde. G81 | 46 | BA21 |
| Wedderlea Dr, G52 | 64 | BC32 |
| Weensmoor Pl, G53 | | |
| *off Willowford Rd* | 100 | BC41 |
| Weensmoor Rd, G53 | 100 | BC40 |
| Weeple Dr, (Linw.) Pais. PA3 | 60 | AJ31 |
| Weighhouse Cl, Pais. PA1 | 82 | AU33 |
| Weir Av, (Barr.) G78 | 99 | AY43 |
| Weir St, Coat. ML5 | 75 | CW30 |
| Weir St, Pais. PA3 | 62 | AU32 |
| Weirwood Av, (Baill.) G69 | 91 | CH33 |
| Weirwood Gdns, (Baill.) G69 | 91 | CH33 |
| Welbeck Rd, G53 | 100 | BD40 |
| Weldon Pl, (Kilsyth) G65 | 20 | CV10 |
| Welfare Av, (Camb.) G72 | 107 | CF41 |
| Welland Pl, (E.Kil.) G75 | 134 | BU54 |
| Wellbank Pl, (Udd.) G71 | | |
| *off Church St* | 109 | CP40 |
| Well Brae, Lark. ML9 | 144 | DC59 |
| Wellbrae Rd, Ham. ML3 | 139 | CR52 |
| Wellbrae Ter, (Mood.) G69 | 37 | CP19 |
| Wellcroft Pl, G5 | 87 | BR33 |
| Wellcroft Rd, Ham. ML3 | 125 | CN50 |
| Wellcroft Ter, Ham. ML3 | 125 | CN50 |
| Wellesley Cres, (Cumb.) G68 | 20 | CU13 |
| Wellesley Cres, (E.Kil.) G75 | 134 | BV54 |
| Wellesley Dr, (Cumb.) G68 | 20 | CU12 |
| Wellesley Dr, (E.Kil.) G75 | 134 | BV53 |
| Wellesley Pl, (Cumb.) G68 | 20 | CT12 |
| Wellfield Av, (Giff.) G46 | 102 | BK42 |
| Wellfield Ct, (Giff.) G46 | | |
| *off Wellfield Av* | 102 | BK42 |
| Wellfield St, G21 | 50 | BV25 |
| Wellgate Ct, Lark. ML9 | | |
| *off Wellgate St* | 144 | DC57 |
| Wellgate St, Lark. ML9 | 144 | DC57 |
| Well Grn, G43 | 86 | BL37 |
| Wellgreen Ct, G43 | | |
| *off Well Grn* | 86 | BL37 |
| Wellhall Ct, Ham. ML3 | 125 | CR49 |
| Wellhall Rd, Ham. ML3 | 139 | CP51 |
| Wellhouse Cres, G33 | 71 | CG30 |
| Wellhouse Gdns, G33 | 71 | CG30 |
| Wellhouse Gro, G33 | 71 | CH30 |
| Wellhouse Path, G34 | 71 | CH30 |
| Wellhouse Rd, G33 | 71 | CH29 |
| Wellington, (E.Kil.) G75 | 135 | BX54 |
| Wellington La, G2 | 4 | BQ30 |
| Wellington Path, (Baill.) G69 | | |
| *off Nelson Pl* | 92 | CK33 |
| Wellington Pl, Clyde. G81 | 26 | AT17 |
| Wellington Pl, Coat. ML5 | 74 | CS32 |
| Wellington Rd, (Bishop.) G64 | 33 | BX17 |
| Wellington St, G2 | 4 | BR30 |
| Wellington St, Air. ML6 | 76 | DC28 |
| Wellington St, Pais. PA3 | 62 | AT32 |
| Wellington Way, Renf. PA4 | | |
| *off Tiree Av* | 63 | AY28 |
| Wellknowe Av, (Thornton.) G74 | 120 | BS50 |
| Wellknowe Pl, (Thornton.) G74 | 120 | BS50 |
| Wellknowe Rd, (Thornton.) G74 | 120 | BS50 |
| Wellmeadow Cl, (Newt. M.) G77 | 117 | BF48 |
| Wellmeadow Grn, (Newt. M.) G77 | 117 | BF47 |
| Wellmeadow Rd, G43 | 102 | BJ39 |
| Wellmeadows Ct, Ham. ML3 | 139 | CQ51 |
| Wellmeadows La, Ham. ML3 | 139 | CQ51 |
| Wellmeadow St, Pais. PA1 | 82 | AT33 |

Wellmeadow Way, (Newt. M.) G77 — 117 BF48
Wellpark Rd, Moth. ML1
 off Viewpark Rd — 127 CY47
Wellpark St, G31 — 5 BU30
Wellpark Ter, (Neil.) G78 — 114 AT47
Well Rd, (Kilb.) John. PA10 — 78 AC34
Wellshot Dr, (Camb.) G72 — 106 CB40
Wellshot Rd, G32 — 90 CB34
Wellside Av, Air. ML6 — 76 DC28
Wellside Dr, (Camb.) G72 — 107 CE41
Wellside La, Air. ML6 — 76 DD28
Wellside Quad, Air. ML6 — 76 DC28
Wellsquarry Rd, (Kittochside) G76 — 121 BY48
Wells St, Clyde. G81 — 26 AV18
Well St, Pais. PA1 — 62 AS32
Wellview Dr, Moth. ML1 — 127 CX47
Wellwynd, Air. ML6 — 76 DB29
Wellwynd Gdns, Air. ML6
 off Wellwynd — 76 DB29
Welsh Dr, (Blan.) G72 — 124 CM47
Welsh Dr, Ham. ML3 — 140 CS54
Welsh Row, (Calder.) Air. ML6 — 97 DE35
Wemyss Av, (Newt. M.) G77 — 117 BE46
Wemyss Dr, (Cumb.) G68 — 20 CU12
Wemyss Gdns, (Baill.) G69 — 92 CJ34
Wendur Way, Pais. PA3
 off Abbotsburn Way — 62 AU29
Wenlock Rd, Pais. PA2 — 82 AV35
Wensleydale, (E.Kil.) G74 — 121 BY50
Wentworth Dr, G23
 off Dougalston Rd — 31 BN20
Wentworth Gdns, (E.Kil.) G74 — 134 BT52
Wesley St, Air. ML6 — 76 DB30
Westacres Rd, (Newt. M.) G77 — 116 BD49
West Av, (Stepps) G33 — 53 CF24
West Av, (Udd.) G71 — 109 CR39
West Av, (Blan.) G72 — 125 CN48
West Av, Moth. ML1 — 112 DC43
West Av, Renf. PA4 — 45 AZ26
West Balgrochan Rd, (Torr.) G64 — 15 BX12
Westbank Ct, G12 — 67 BN27
Westbank La, G12 — 67 BN27
Westbank Quad, G12 — 67 BN27
Westbourne Cres, (Bears.) G61 — 29 BE16
Westbourne Dr, (Bears.) G61 — 29 BE16
Westbourne Gdns La, G12 — 48 BL25
Westbourne Gdns N, G12 — 48 BL25
Westbourne Gdns S, G12 — 48 BL25
Westbourne Gdns W, G12 — 48 BL25
Westbourne Rd, G12 — 48 BK25
Westbourne Shop Cen, (Barr.) G78 — 99 AX43
Westbourne Ter La, G12
 off Westbourne Rd — 48 BK25
West Brae, Pais. PA1 — 82 AT33
Westbrae Dr, G14 — 47 BG25
Westbrae Rd, (Newt. M.) G77 — 117 BH47
West Buchanan Pl, Pais. PA1
 off Sir Michael Pl — 82 AT33
Westburn Av, (Camb.) G72 — 107 CE39
Westburn Av, Pais. PA3 — 61 AQ32
Westburn Cres, (Ruther.) G73 — 88 BV38
Westburn Dr, (Camb.) G72 — 90 CD38
Westburn Fm Rd, (Camb.) G72 — 106 CD39
Westburn Rd, (Camb.) G72 — 107 CE39
West Burnside St, (Kilsyth) G65
 off Main St — 7 CT5
Westburn Way, Pais. PA3
 off Westburn Av — 61 AR32
West Campbell St, G2 — 4 BQ30
West Campbell St, Pais. PA1 — 81 AR33

West Canal St, Coat. ML5 — 74 CV31
Westcastle Ct, G45
 off Westcastle Cres — 104 BT42
Westcastle Cres, G45 — 104 BT42
Westcastle Gdns, G45 — 104 BT42
Westcastle Gro, G45
 off Westcastle Cres — 104 BT42
West Chapelton Av, (Bears.) G61 — 29 BH17
West Chapelton Cres, (Bears.) G61 — 29 BH17
West Chapelton Dr, (Bears.) G61 — 29 BH17
West Chapelton La, (Bears.) G61 — 29 BH17
West Clyde St, Lark. ML9 — 144 DD59
Westclyffe St, G41 — 87 BN36
West Coats Rd, (Camb.) G72 — 106 CB40
West Cotts, (Gart.) G69 — 54 CK26
West Ct, Clyde. G81 — 26 AU17
West Ct, Pais. PA1 — 81 AQ33
West Dr, Air. ML6 — 77 DG31
Westend, (Bears.) G61 — 30 BJ19
West End Dr, Bell. ML4 — 110 CV41
West End Pk St, G3 — 4 BP28
West End Pl, Bell. ML4 — 110 CV41
Westerburn St, G32 — 70 CB31
Wester Carriagehill, Pais. PA2 — 82 AU35
Wester Cleddens Rd, (Bishop.) G64 — 33 BW19
Wester Common Dr, G22 — 49 BQ24
Wester Common Rd, G22 — 49 BQ25
Wester Common Ter, G22 — 49 BR25
Westercraigs, G31 — 68 BV30
Westercraigs Ct, G31
 off Westercraigs — 68 BV30
Westerdale, (E.Kil.) G74 — 121 BY50
Westerfield Rd, (Cumb.) G68 — 38 CT15
Westerfield Rd, (Carm.) G76 — 120 BU48
Westergill Av, Air. ML6 — 77 DG31
Westergreens Av, (Kirk.) G66 — 35 CE15
Westerhill Rd, (Bishop.) G64 — 33 BY17
Westerhouse Path, G34
 off Kildermorie Rd — 71 CH29
Westerhouse Rd, G34 — 72 CJ28
Westerkirk Dr, G23 — 31 BN20
Westerlands, G12
 off Ascot Av — 47 BH23
Westerlands Dr, (Newt. M.) G77 — 116 BD49
Westerlands Gdns, (Newt. M.) G77 — 116 BD49
Westerlands Gro, (Newt. M.) G77 — 116 BD49
Westerlands Pl, (Newt. M.) G77 off Westacres Rd — 116 BD48
Westermains Av, (Kirk.) G66 — 16 CD14
Wester Mavisbank Av, Air. ML6 — 76 DA29
Wester Moffat Av, Air. ML6 — 77 DG30
Wester Moffat Cres, Air. ML6 — 77 DG30
Wester Myvot Rd, (Cumb.) G67 — 39 CW17
Western Av, (Ruther.) G73 — 88 BV37
Western Isles Rd, (Old Kil.) G60 — 26 AS16
Western Rd, (Camb.) G72 — 106 CA41
Wester Rd, G32 — 91 CF33
Westerton Av, (Bears.) G61 — 47 BH21
Westerton Av, (Clark.) G76 — 119 BQ48
Westerton Av, Lark. ML9 — 144 DC60
Westerton Ct, (Clark.) G76 — 119 BQ48
Westerton La, (Clark.) G76 — 119 BQ48
Westerton Rd, (Dullatur) G68 — 6 CY7
West Fairholm St, Lark. ML9 — 142 DB56
Westfarm Av, (Camb.) G72 — 107 CF39
Westfarm Ct, (Camb.) G72 — 91 CF38
Westfarm Cres, (Camb.) G72 — 107 CF39

Westfarm Dr, (Camb.) G72 — 91 CF38
Westfarm Gait, (Camb.) G72 — 107 CF39
Westfarm La, (Camb.) G72 — 91 CF38
Westfarm Wynd, (Camb.) G72 — 107 CF39
Westfield, (Cumb.) G68 — 38 CT15
Westfield Av, (Ruther.) G73 — 88 BV38
Westfield Cres, (Bears.) G61 — 29 BG19
Westfield Dr, G52 — 64 BC32
Westfield Dr, (Bears.) G61 — 29 BG19
Westfield Dr, (Cumb.) G68 — 20 CU14
Westfield Ind Est, (Cumb.) G68 — 38 CT15
Westfield Pl, (Cumb.) G68 — 38 CT15
Westfield Rd, (Thornlie.) G46 — 102 BJ43
Westfield Rd, (Kilsyth) G65 — 7 CR4
Westfields, (Bishop.) G64 — 32 BU18
Westfield Vil, (Ruther.) G73 — 88 BU38
Westgarth Pl, (E.Kil.) G74 — 121 BW50
Westgate Way, Bell. ML4
 off West End Dr — 110 CV40
West George La, G2 — 4 BQ29
West George St, G2 — 4 BQ29
West George St, Coat. ML5 — 75 CW29
West Glebe Ter, Ham. ML3
 off Glebe St — 140 CS51
West Graham St, G4 — 4 BQ28
West Greenhill Pl, G3 — 67 BN29
West Hamilton St, Moth. ML1 — 128 DA47
West High St, (Kirk.) G66 — 17 CE12
Westhorn Dr, G32 — 90 CC36
Westhouse Av, (Ruther.) G73 — 88 BU38
Westhouse Gdns, (Ruther.) G73 — 88 BU38
West Kirk St, Air. ML6 — 76 DB30
Westknowe Gdns, (Ruther.) G73 — 105 BX40
Westland Dr, G14 — 47 BF26
Westland Dr La, G14
 off Westland Dr — 47 BF26
Westlands Gdns, Pais. PA2 — 82 AT35
West La, Pais. PA1 — 81 AR33
Westlea Pl, Air. ML6 — 76 DC31
West Lo Rd, Renf. PA4 — 45 AX25
West Mains Rd, (E.Kil.) G74 — 135 BX51
West March Rd, Pais. PA3 — 61 AR30
Westminster Gdns, G12
 off Kersland St — 48 BM26
Westminster Ter, G3 — 67 BN29
Westmoreland St, G42 — 87 BQ35
Westmuir Pl, (Ruther.) G73 — 88 BU37
Westmuir St, G31 — 69 BZ32
West Nile St, G1 — 4 BR30
Westpark, (Miln.) G62 — 12 BJ13
Westpark Dr, Pais. PA3 — 61 AR32
Westport, (E.Kil.) G75 — 135 BW52
West Princes St, G4 — 67 BP27
Westray Av, (Newt. M.) G77 — 117 BE46
Westray Circ, G22 — 50 BS23
Westray Ct, (Cumb.) G67 — 21 CZ13
Westray Pl, G22 — 50 BT23
Westray Pl, (Bishop.) G64 — 33 BZ19
Westray Rd, (Cumb.) G67 — 22 DA13
Westray Sq, G22 — 50 BS22
Westray St, G22 — 50 BS22
West Regent La, G2 — 4 BR29
West Regent St, G2 — 4 BQ29
West Rd, (Torr.) G64 — 15 BX12
West Rd, (Kilb.) John. PA10 — 78 AC33
West Scott Ter, Ham. ML3 — 140 CT52
Westside Gdns, G11 — 66 BK27
West Stewart St, Ham. ML3 — 126 CS49
West St, G5 — 67 BQ32
West St, Clyde. G81 — 46 BA21
West St, Pais. PA1 — 82 AS33
West Thomson St, Clyde. G81 — 27 AW17

| | | |
|---|---|---|
| West Wellbrae Cres, Ham. ML3 | 139 | CR52 |
| West Whitby St, G31 | 89 | BY33 |
| Westwood Av, (Giff.) G46 | 102 | BK42 |
| Westwood Cres, Ham. ML3 | 140 | CS52 |
| Westwood Gdns, Pais. PA3 | 61 | AR32 |
| Westwood Hill, (E.Kil.) G75 | 135 | BX53 |
| Westwood Quad, Clyde. G81 | 27 | AZ20 |
| Westwood Rd, G43 | 102 | BK39 |
| Westwood Rd, (E.Kil.) G75 | 135 | BX53 |
| Westwood Sq, (E.Kil.) G75 | | |
| off Westwood Rd | 135 | BX53 |
| Weymouth Dr, G12 | 48 | BJ23 |
| Whamflet Av, (Baill.) G69 | 72 | CL30 |
| Wheatfield Rd, (Bears.) G61 | 29 | BF18 |
| Wheatholm Cres, Air. ML6 | | |
| off Wheatholm St | 76 | DD28 |
| Wheatholm St, Air. ML6 | 76 | DD28 |
| Wheatland Av, (Blan.) G72 | 124 | CL45 |
| Wheatlandhead Ct, (Blan.) G72 | 124 | CL45 |
| Wheatlands Dr, (Kilb.) | | |
| John. PA10 | 78 | AC33 |
| Wheatlands Fm Rd, (Kilb.) | | |
| John. PA10 | 78 | AC33 |
| Wheatley Ct, G32 | 70 | CC32 |
| Wheatley Cres, (Kilsyth) G65 | 7 | CT6 |
| Wheatley Dr, G32 | 70 | CC32 |
| Wheatley Ln, (Bishop.) G64 | 51 | BY21 |
| Wheatley Pl, G32 | 70 | CC32 |
| Wheatley Rd, G32 | 70 | CC32 |
| Whifflet Ct, Coat. ML5 | | |
| off Whifflet St | 95 | CX33 |
| Whifflet St, Coat. ML5 | 95 | CW34 |
| Whin Av, (Barr.) G78 | 99 | AW41 |
| Whinfell Dr, (E.Kil.) G75 | 135 | BW55 |
| Whinfell Gdns, (E.Kil.) G75 | 135 | BW55 |
| Whinfield Av, (Camb.) G72 | | |
| off Cambuslang Rd | 89 | BZ38 |
| Whinfield Path, G53 | | |
| off Parkhouse Rd | 100 | BC41 |
| Whinfield Rd, G53 | | |
| off Parkhouse Rd | 100 | BC41 |
| Whinhall Av, Air. ML6 | 76 | DB28 |
| Whinhall Rd, Air. ML6 | 76 | DA28 |
| Whin Hill, (E.Kil.) G74 | 122 | CD49 |
| Whinhill Gdns, G53 | 84 | BC34 |
| Whinhill Pl, G53 | 84 | BC34 |
| Whinhill Rd, G53 | 84 | BC34 |
| Whinhill Rd, Pais. PA2 | 83 | AX35 |
| Whinknowe, (Ashgill) Lark. ML9 | 145 | DH61 |
| Whin Ln, G65 | 6 | CM5 |
| Whinnie Knowe, Lark. ML9 | 144 | DB60 |
| Whinpark Av, Bell. ML4 | 110 | CV42 |
| Whin Pl, (E.Kil.) G74 | 122 | CD48 |
| Whins Rd, G41 | 86 | BL36 |
| Whin St, Clyde. G81 | 27 | AW17 |
| Whirlies Rbt, The, (E.Kil.) G74 | 122 | CC49 |
| Whirlow Gdns, (Baill.) G69 | 72 | CJ32 |
| Whirlow Rd, (Baill.) G69 | 72 | CJ32 |
| Whistleberry Cres, Ham. ML3 | 125 | CQ46 |
| Whistleberry Dr, Ham. ML3 | 125 | CQ46 |
| Whistleberry Ind Pk, Ham. ML3 | 125 | CQ46 |
| Whistleberry La, Ham. ML3 | 125 | CQ47 |
| Whistleberry Pk, Ham. ML3 | 125 | CQ46 |
| Whistleberry Retail Pk, (Blan.) | | |
| G72 | 125 | CP46 |
| Whistleberry Rd, (Blan.) G72 | 125 | CQ46 |
| Whistleberry Rd, Ham. ML3 | 125 | CQ46 |
| Whistleberry Wynd, Ham. ML3 | 125 | CQ46 |
| Whistlefield Ct, (Bears.) G61 | 29 | BH18 |
| Whitacres Path, G53 | | |
| off Wilton burn Rd | 100 | BC41 |
| Whitacres Pl, G53 | | |
| off Whitacres Rd | 100 | BC41 |

| | | |
|---|---|---|
| Whitacres Rd, G53 | 100 | BB41 |
| Whitburn St, G32 | 70 | CB30 |
| Whiteadder Pl, (E.Kil.) G75 | 134 | BT54 |
| White Cart Ct, G43 | 86 | BM38 |
| Whitecart Rd, (Abbots.) Pais. | | |
| PA3 off Sanderling Rd | 62 | AU29 |
| White Cart Twr, (E.Kil.) G74 | 136 | CD54 |
| Whitecraigs Ct, (Giff.) G46 | 118 | BJ45 |
| Whitecraigs Pl, G23 | | |
| off Fairhaven Rd | 49 | BN21 |
| Whitecrook St, Clyde. G81 | 45 | AX21 |
| Whitefield Av, (Camb.) G72 | 106 | CC41 |
| Whitefield Rd, G51 | 66 | BL32 |
| Whitefield Ter, (Camb.) G72 | | |
| off Croft Rd | 106 | CD40 |
| Whiteford Ct, Ham. ML3 | 140 | CS55 |
| Whiteford Rd, (Stepps) G33 | 53 | CH24 |
| Whiteford Rd, Pais. PA2 | 83 | AW35 |
| Whitehall St, G3 | 4 | BP30 |
| Whitehaugh Av, Pais. PA1 | 63 | AX32 |
| Whitehaugh Dr, Pais. PA1 | 63 | AX32 |
| Whitehaugh Path, G53 | | |
| off Wiltonburn Rd | 100 | BC40 |
| Whitehaugh Rd, G53 | 100 | BC41 |
| Whitehill Av, (Stepps) G33 | 53 | CF23 |
| Whitehill Av, (Kirk.) G66 | 17 | CH12 |
| Whitehill Av, (Cumb.) G68 | 21 | CZ11 |
| Whitehill Av, Air. ML6 | 76 | DC27 |
| Whitehill Ct, G31 | 69 | BW30 |
| Whitehill Ct, (Kirk.) G66 | 17 | CH12 |
| Whitehill Cres, (Kirk.) G66 | 17 | CH12 |
| Whitehill Cres, Clyde. G81 | 10 | BA14 |
| Whitehill Fm Rd, (Stepps) | | |
| G33 | 53 | CF24 |
| Whitehill Gdns, G31 | 69 | BW30 |
| Whitehill Gro, (Newt. M.) G77 | 131 | BH51 |
| Whitehill La, (Bears.) G61 | 29 | BF16 |
| Whitehill Pl, G31 | 69 | BW30 |
| Whitehill Rd, (Stepps) G33 | 53 | CF21 |
| Whitehill Rd, (Bears.) G61 | 29 | BF16 |
| Whitehill Rd, (Kirk.) G66 | 53 | CF22 |
| Whitehill Rd, Ham. ML3 | 125 | CR48 |
| Whitehills, Ersk. PA8 | 25 | AQ19 |
| Whitehills Dr, (E.Kil.) G75 | 136 | CA54 |
| Whitehills Pl, (E.Kil.) G75 | 136 | CA54 |
| Whitehills Ter, (E.Kil.) G75 | 136 | CA55 |
| Whitehill St, G31 | 69 | BW30 |
| Whitehill St La, G31 | 69 | BW30 |
| Whitehill Ter, (Gart.) G69 | 55 | CP25 |
| Whitehorse Wk, (E.Kil.) G75 | | |
| off Winnipeg Dr | 135 | BX53 |
| Whitehurst, (Bears.) G61 | 29 | BE15 |
| Whitehurst Pk, (Bears.) G61 | 29 | BE15 |
| Whitekirk Pl, G15 | 28 | BC19 |
| Whitelaw Av, (Glenb.) | | |
| Coat. ML5 | 56 | CV24 |
| Whitelaw Cres, Bell. ML4 | 111 | CZ41 |
| Whitelaw Gdns, (Bishop.) G64 | 33 | BW18 |
| Whitelaw St, G20 | 48 | BL22 |
| Whitelaw Ter, (Kilsyth) G65 | 19 | CP9 |
| Whitelee, (E.Kil.) G75 | 135 | BZ56 |
| Whitelee Cres, (Newt. M.) G77 | 116 | BD47 |
| Whitelee Gate, (Newt. M.) G77 | 116 | BD47 |
| Whiteloans, (Both.) G71 | 109 | CR42 |
| Whitemoss Av, G44 | 103 | BP41 |
| Whitemoss Av, (E.Kil.) G74 | 136 | CB52 |
| Whitemoss Gro, (E.Kil.) G74 | 136 | CC51 |
| Whitemoss Rd, (E.Kil.) G74 | 136 | CB52 |
| Whitemoss Rbt, (E.Kil.) G74 | 136 | CC52 |
| Whitepond Av, Bell. ML4 | | |
| off Footfield Rd | 110 | CV42 |
| Whiterigg Ct, Air. ML6 | | |
| off Monkscourt Av | 75 | CZ29 |

| | | |
|---|---|---|
| Whitesbridge Av, Pais. PA3 | 81 | AP33 |
| Whitesbridge Cl, Pais. PA3 | | |
| off Whitesbridge Av | 61 | AQ32 |
| Whitestone Av, (Cumb.) G68 | 21 | CX11 |
| White St, G11 | 66 | BK27 |
| White St, Clyde. G81 | 45 | AZ22 |
| Whitevale St, G31 | 69 | BW31 |
| Whithope Rd, G53 | 100 | BB40 |
| Whithope Ter, G53 | 100 | BB41 |
| Whithorn Cres, (Mood.) G69 | 37 | CP18 |
| Whitlawburn Av, (Camb.) G72 | 106 | CA41 |
| Whitlawburn Rd, (Camb.) G72 | 106 | CA41 |
| Whitlawburn Ter, (Camb.) G72 | 106 | CA41 |
| Whitriggs Rd, G53 | 100 | BB40 |
| Whitslade Pl, G34 | 71 | CH28 |
| Whitslade St, G34 | 72 | CJ28 |
| Whitsun Dale, (E.Kil.) G74 | 121 | BY50 |
| Whittagreen Av, Moth. ML1 | 113 | DF42 |
| Whittagreen Ct, Moth. ML1 | | |
| off Carfin Rd | 113 | DF42 |
| Whittagreen Cres, Moth. ML1 | 113 | DF42 |
| Whittingehame Dr, G12 | 47 | BH24 |
| Whittingehame Dr, G13 | 47 | BH24 |
| Whittingehame Gdns, G12 | 48 | BJ24 |
| Whittingehame La, G13 | 47 | BH24 |
| Whittingehame Pk, G12 | 47 | BH24 |
| Whittington St, Coat. ML5 | | |
| off Ellis St | 75 | CW31 |
| Whittliemuir Av, G44 | 103 | BP41 |
| Whitton Dr, (Giff.) G46 | 102 | BM41 |
| Whitton St, G20 | 48 | BL21 |
| Whitworth Dr, G20 | 49 | BQ23 |
| Whitworth Dr, Clyde. G81 | 27 | AW19 |
| Whitworth Gdns, G20 | 49 | BP23 |
| Whitworth Gate, G20 | 49 | BQ24 |
| Whyte Av, (Camb.) G72 | 106 | CA39 |
| Wick Av, Air. ML6 | 96 | DA33 |
| Wickets, The, Pais. PA1 | 83 | AW34 |
| Wickham Av, (Newt. M.) G77 | 117 | BF47 |
| Wigton Av, (Newt. M.) G77 | 117 | BE46 |
| Wigtoun Pl, (Cumb.) G67 | 22 | DD9 |
| Wilderness Brae, (Cumb.) G67 | 22 | DD9 |
| Wilfred Av, G13 | 47 | BF22 |
| Wilkie Cres, Lark. ML9 | 144 | DD59 |
| Wilkie Ln, Bell. ML4 | | |
| off Fleming Rd | 95 | CX38 |
| Wilkie Rd, (Udd.) G71 | 109 | CQ40 |
| William Dr, Ham. ML3 | 140 | CT54 |
| William Mann Dr, (Newt. M.) | | |
| G77 | 116 | BD49 |
| Williamsburgh Ct, Pais. PA1 | | |
| off Lacy St | 83 | AW33 |
| Williamsburgh Ter, Pais. PA1 | | |
| off Lacy St | 63 | AW32 |
| Williamson Pl, John. PA5 | 80 | AK35 |
| Williamson St, G31 | 89 | BY33 |
| Williamson St, Clyde. G81 | 27 | AX17 |
| William Spiers Pl, Lark. ML9 | 144 | DD60 |
| William St, G3 | 4 | BP29 |
| William St, (Kilsyth) G65 | | |
| off Backbrae St | 7 | CT5 |
| William St, Clyde. G81 | 27 | AW15 |
| William St, Coat. ML5 | 95 | CX33 |
| William St, Ham. ML3 | 125 | CR48 |
| William St, John. PA5 | 79 | AH34 |
| William St, Pais. PA1 | 82 | AS33 |
| William Ure Pl, (Bishop.) G64 | 33 | BX16 |
| Williamwood Dr, G44 | 103 | BP43 |
| Williamwood Pk, G44 | 103 | BP43 |
| Williamwood Pk W, G44 | 103 | BP43 |
| Willie Ross La, (Ruther.) G73 | 89 | BX36 |
| Willock Pl, G20 | 49 | BN22 |
| Willoughby Dr, G13 | 47 | BH23 |

Willoughby La, G13
*off Willoughby Dr* 47 BH23
Willow Av, (Bishop.) G64 51 BW21
Willow Av, (Lenz.) G66 35 CE15
Willow Av, (Elder.) John. PA5 80 AL35
Willow Av, (New Stev.)
Moth. ML1 112 DC43
Willowbank, Lark. ML9 142 DC56
Willowbank Cres, G3
*off Woodlands Rd* 67 BP27
Willowbank Gdns, (Kirk.) G66 17 CF13
Willowbank St, G3 67 BP27
Willow Ct, (E.Kil.) G75 135 BX55
Willow Cres, Coat. ML5 95 CW33
Willowdale Cres, (Baill.) G69 92 CJ33
Willowdale Gdns, (Baill.) G69 92 CJ33
Willow Dr, (Blan.) G72 124 CL45
Willow Dr, Air. ML6 77 DF30
Willow Dr, John. PA5 79 AH36
Willowford Rd, G53 100 BB41
Willow Gro, Moth. ML1 112 DD40
Willow La, G32 90 CD35
Willow Pl, (Udd.) G71
*off Laburnum Rd* 94 CT37
Willow Pl, John. PA5 80 AJ35
Willows, The, (Carm.) G76 120 BT45
Willow St, G13 47 BH22
Willow Way, Ham. ML3 140 CU52
Wilmot Rd, G13 47 BF23
Wilson Av, (Linw.) Pais. PA3 60 AJ31
Wilson Ct, Bell. ML4
*off Main St* 110 CV40
Wilson Pl, (E.Kil.) G74 122 CC49
Wilson Pl, (Newt. M.) G77 117 BE49
Wilsons Pl, Pais. PA1
*off Seedhill* 82 AV33
Wilson St, G1 5 BS30
Wilson St, Air. ML6 76 DB29
Wilson St, Coat. ML5 75 CY30
Wilson St, Ham. ML3 125 CQ48
Wilson St, Lark. ML9 144 DD60
Wilson St, Moth. ML1 128 DB46
Wilson St, Pais. PA1 82 AS33
Wilson St, Renf. PA4 45 AZ25
Wiltonburn Path, G53
*off Wiltonburn Rd* 100 BC41
Wiltonburn Rd, G53 100 BC41
Wilton Cres, G20 49 BP26
Wilton Cres La, G20 49 BP26
Wilton Dr, G20 49 BP26
Wilton Gdns, G20 49 BP26
Wilton St, G20 49 BN26
Wilton St, Coat. ML5 74 CT27
Wilverton Rd, G13 47 BG21
Winburne Cres, Ham. ML3
*off Clearfield Av* 125 CR49
Winchester Dr, G12 48 BK23
Windermere, (E.Kil.) G75 134 BV56
Windermere Gdns, Ham. ML3 140 CS55
Windermere St, Bell. ML4
*off West End Dr* 110 CV41
Windhill Cres, G43 102 BK40
Windhill Pk, (Eagle.) G76 133 BN51
Windhill Pl, G43
*off Windhill Rd* 102 BK40
Windhill Rd, G43 102 BK40
Windlaw Ct, G45 104 BT43
Windlaw Gdns, G44 103 BP42
Windlaw Pk Gdns, G44 103 BP41
Windlaw Rd, G45 104 BT44
Windlaw Rd, (Carm.) G76 120 BT45
Windmill Ct, Moth. ML1 128 DB47
Windmillcroft Quay, G5 4 BQ31

Windmillhill St, Moth. ML1 128 DB48
Windmill Rd, Ham. ML3 126 CT49
Windsor Av, (Newt. M.) G77 117 BH48
Windsor Cres, Clyde. G81 27 AW18
Windsor Cres, (Elder.)
John. PA5 80 AK36
Windsor Cres, Pais. PA1 63 AW31
Windsor Dr, (Glenm.) Air. ML6 58 DB25
Windsor Gdns, Ham. ML3 125 CQ48
Windsor Path, (Baill.) G69
*off Park Rd* 73 CP31
Windsor Path, Lark. ML9
*off Afton St* 145 DE59
Windsor Rd, Moth. ML1 112 DC40
Windsor Rd, Renf. PA4 63 AY27
Windsor St, G20 67 BQ27
Windsor St, G32 71 CE31
Windsor St, Coat. ML5 94 CU34
Windsor Ter, G20 67 BQ27
Windsor Wk, (Udd.) G71 93 CR38
Windward Rd, (E.Kil.) G75 135 BW52
Windyedge Cres, G13 47 BE24
Windyedge Pl, G13 47 BE24
Windyetts, (Kilsyth) G65 19 CP10
Windyridge, Ham. ML3
*off Chatelherault Cres* 140 CU52
Windyridge Pl, (Blan.) G72
*off Ansdell Av* 124 CL46
Wingate Cres, (E.Kil.) G74 123 CE49
Wingate Dr, (E.Kil.) G74 123 CE49
Wingate Pk, (E.Kil.) G74
*off Boswell Pk* 123 CE49
Wingate St, Wis. ML2 129 DF49
Wingfield Gdns, (Both.) G71
*off Blairston Av* 109 CR44
Winifred St, G33 51 BZ25
Winning Ct, (Blan.) G72 109 CN44
Winning Quad, Wis. ML2
*off English St* 129 DF50
Winning Row, G31 69 BZ32
Winnipeg Dr, (E.Kil.) G75 135 BX53
Wintergreen Ct, (E.Kil.) G74 121 BZ49
Wintergreen Dr, (E.Kil.) G74
*off Stewartfield Dr* 121 BZ49
Winton Av, (Giff.) G46 102 BL43
Winton Cres, (Blan.) G72 124 CM46
Winton Dr, G12 48 BL24
Winton Gdns, (Udd.) G71 93 CP38
Winton La, G12 48 BL24
Winton Pk, (E.Kil.) G75 135 BW52
Wirran Pl, G13 46 BA21
Wishart St, G31 5 BU30
Wishawhill St, Wis. ML2 129 DH50
Wiston St, (Camb.) G72 107 CF40
Witchwood Ct, Coat. ML5
*off Lomond Rd* 74 CT27
Witcutt Way, Wis. ML2 143 DG52
Woddrop St, G40 89 BX35
Wolcott Dr, (Blan.) G72
*off Ansdell Av* 124 CM45
Wolfe Av, (Newt. M.) G77 117 BE46
Wolseley St, G5 88 BT34
Woodale, Moth. ML1 127 CZ49
Wood Aven Dr, (E.Kil.) G74 121 BZ49
Woodbank Cres, (Clark.) G76 119 BN47
Woodbank Cres, John. PA5 79 AH35
Woodburn Av, (Blan.) G72 125 CN45
Woodburn Av, (Clark.) G76 119 BN47
Woodburn Av, Air. ML6 76 DB31
Woodburn Ct, (Ruther.) G73 105 BX39
Woodburn Rd, G43 102 BM40
Woodburn St, Moth. ML1 128 DA44

Woodburn Ter, Lark. ML9
*off Lansbury Ter* 145 DE59
Woodburn Way, (Cumb.) G68 21 CY11
Wood Cres, Moth. ML1 112 DA44
Woodcroft Av, G11 47 BH26
Woodend, (Blan.) G72
*off Muir St* 124 CM47
Woodend Ct, G32 91 CG35
Woodend Dr, G13 47 BG24
Woodend Dr, Air. ML6 77 DE28
Woodend Dr, Pais. PA1 83 AZ33
Woodend Gdns, G32 91 CF34
Woodend La, G13 47 BG24
Woodend La, Lark. ML9
*off Rannoch Dr* 145 DE60
Woodend Pl, (Elder.)
John. PA5 80 AK35
Woodend Rd, G32 91 CF35
Woodend Rd, (Ruther.) G73 105 BX41
Woodfarm Rd, (Thornlie.) G46 102 BJ43
Woodfield, (Udd.) G71 110 CS39
Woodfield Av, (Bishop.) G64 33 BX20
Woodfoot Path, G53
*off Whitehaugh Rd* 100 BC41
Woodfoot Pl, G53
*off Whitacres Rd* 100 BB41
Woodfoot Rd, Ham. ML3 139 CQ51
Woodford Pl, (Linw.) Pais. PA3 60 AJ31
Woodford St, G41 87 BN38
Woodgreen Av, G44 103 BR39
Woodhall Av, (Calder.)
Air. ML6 96 DD35
Woodhall Av, Coat. ML5 94 CU34
Woodhall Av, Ham. ML3 125 CR49
Woodhall Av, Moth. ML1 112 DB40
Woodhall Est, (Calder.)
Air. ML6 96 DD36
Woodhall Pl, Coat. ML5 94 CV34
Woodhall Rd, (Calder.)
Air. ML6 96 DD35
Woodhall St, G40 89 BX35
Woodhall St, (Chap.) Air. ML6 97 DF36
Woodhead Av, (Kirk.) G66 17 CF14
Woodhead Av, (Cumb.) G68 20 CV14
Woodhead Av, (Both.) G71 125 CR45
Woodhead Ct, (Cumb.) G68 20 CV14
Woodhead Cres, (Udd.) G71 93 CP38
Woodhead Cres, Ham. ML3 139 CR53
Woodhead Gdns, (Both.) G71 125 CR45
Woodhead Grn, Ham. ML3 139 CR53
Woodhead Gro, (Cumb.) G68 20 CV14
Woodhead Ind Est, (Chry.) G69 54 CK23
Woodhead Path, G53
*off Woodhead Rd* 100 BC40
Woodhead Pl, (Cumb.) G68 20 CV14
Woodhead Rd, G53 100 BB40
Woodhead Rd, (Cumb.) G68 20 CV14
Woodhead Rd, (Chry.) G69 54 CK24
Woodhead Ter, (Chry.) G69 54 CK22
Woodhead Vw, (Cumb.) G68 20 CV14
Woodhill Gro, (Bishop.) G64 51 BY21
Woodhill Rd, G21 51 BX23
Woodhill Rd, (Bishop.) G64 33 BY20
Woodholm Av, G44 104 BS39
Woodhouse Ct, (Clark.) G76
*off East Kilbride Rd* 119 BQ48
Woodhouse St, G13 47 BG22
Woodilee Cotts, (Kirk.) G66 35 CH15
Woodilee Ind Est, (Kirk.) G66 35 CG15
Woodilee Rd, (Kirk.) G66 35 CG16
Woodilee Rd, Moth. ML1 113 DG41
Woodland Av, (Kirk.) G66 16 CD13
Woodland Av, Air. ML6 97 DE33

| | | |
|---|---|---|
| Woodland Av, Pais. PA2 | 82 | AU37 |
| Woodland Cres, (Camb.) G72 | 106 | CD41 |
| Woodland Cres, (Eagle.) G76 | 132 | BM56 |
| Woodland Gdns, (Carm.) G76 | 120 | BT46 |
| Woodland Gdns, Ham. ML3 | 140 | CU51 |
| Woodlands, The, Bell. ML4 | | |
| off Forest Dr | 111 | CZ42 |
| Woodlands Av, (Gart.) G69 | 55 | CN22 |
| Woodlands Av, (Both.) G71 | 109 | CQ42 |
| Woodlands Ct, (Thornlie.) G46 | 101 | BH43 |
| Woodlands Ct, (Old Kil.) G60 | | |
| off Dumbarton Rd | 25 | AR16 |
| Woodlands Cres, (Thornlie.) G46 | 101 | BH42 |
| Woodlands Cres, (Both.) G71 | 109 | CP42 |
| Woodlands Cres, John. PA5 | 79 | AF36 |
| Woodlands Dr, G4 | 67 | BP27 |
| Woodlands Dr, Coat. ML5 | 74 | CT30 |
| Woodlands Dr, Moth. ML1 | 112 | DB40 |
| Woodlands Gdns, (Both.) G71 | 109 | CP42 |
| Woodlands Gate, G3 | 4 | BP28 |
| Woodlands Gate, (Thornlie.) G46 | 101 | BH42 |
| Woodlands Gro, (Miln.) G62 | 12 | BJ10 |
| Woodlands Pk, (Thornlie.) G46 | 101 | BH43 |
| Woodlands Pl, Coat. ML5 | 74 | CT30 |
| Woodlands Rd, G3 | 67 | BP27 |
| Woodlands Rd, (Thornlie.) G46 | 101 | BH43 |
| Woodlands Rd, Moth. ML1 | 128 | DB50 |
| Woodlands St, (Miln.) G62 | 12 | BJ11 |
| Woodlands St, Moth. ML1 | | |
| off Manse Rd | 128 | DB49 |
| Woodlands Ter, G3 | 67 | BN28 |
| Woodlands Ter, (Both.) G71 | 109 | CP42 |
| Woodland Ter, Lark. ML9 | 145 | DE60 |
| Woodland Way, (Cumb.) G67 | 22 | DD10 |
| Wood La, (Bishop.) G64 | 51 | BY21 |
| Woodlea Av, Air. ML6 | 97 | DE33 |
| Woodlea Dr, (Giff.) G46 | 102 | BM41 |
| Woodlea Dr, Ham. ML3 | 140 | CT53 |
| Woodlea Pl, Air. ML6 | 77 | DE28 |
| Woodlinn Av, G44 | 103 | BR40 |
| Woodmill Dr, (Torr.) G64 | 15 | BY12 |
| Woodmill Gdns, (Cumb.) G67 | 38 | CV15 |
| Woodneuk Ct, Pais. PA1 | 81 | AQ33 |
| Woodneuk La, (Gart.) G69 | 55 | CQ24 |
| Woodneuk Rd, G53 | 100 | BD41 |
| Woodneuk Rd, (Gart.) G69 | 55 | CP24 |
| Woodneuk St, (Chap.) Air. ML6 | 97 | DF36 |
| Woodneuk Ter, (Gart.) G69 | 55 | CP24 |
| Wood Quad, Clyde. G81 | 46 | BA21 |
| Woodrow Av, (Holytown) | | |
| Moth. ML1 | 112 | DD43 |
| Woodrow Circ, G41 | 86 | BM33 |
| Woodrow Pl, G41 | 86 | BL33 |
| Woodrow Rd, G41 | 86 | BM33 |
| Woodside Av, (Thornlie.) G46 | 102 | BJ42 |
| Woodside Av, (Kilsyth) G65 | 8 | CV5 |
| Woodside Av, (Lenz.) G66 | 35 | CF15 |
| Woodside Av, (Ruther.) G73 | 89 | BY38 |
| Woodside Av, Ham. ML3 | | |
| off Woodside Wk | 140 | CU51 |
| Woodside Ct, Coat. ML5 | | |
| off Torriden St | 74 | CT32 |
| Woodside Cres, G3 | 4 | BP28 |
| Woodside Cres, (Barr.) G78 | 99 | AZ43 |
| Woodside Cres, Pais. PA1 | 82 | AS33 |
| Woodside Dr, (Eagle.) G76 | 132 | BM51 |
| Woodside Dr, (Calder.) | | |
| Air. ML6 | 96 | DD35 |
| Woodside Gdns, (Carm.) G76 | 120 | BT46 |
| Woodside Gdns, (Clark.) G76 | 118 | BM46 |
| Woodside Gdns, Coat. ML5 | 94 | CT33 |

| | | |
|---|---|---|
| Woodside Gro, (Ruther.) G73 | 89 | BY38 |
| Woodside Pl, G3 | 4 | BP28 |
| Woodside Pl, (Udd.) G71 | 94 | CS37 |
| Woodside Pl La, G3 | 4 | BP28 |
| Woodside Rd, (Carm.) G76 | 120 | BT46 |
| Woodside St, (Chap.) Air. ML6 | 97 | DF35 |
| Woodside St, Coat. ML5 | 94 | CT33 |
| Woodside St, Moth. ML1 | 128 | DD49 |
| Woodside St, (Holytown) | | |
| Moth. ML1 | 96 | DA37 |
| Woodside St, (New Stev.) | | |
| Moth. ML1 | 112 | DC42 |
| Woodside Ter, G3 | 4 | BP28 |
| Woodside Ter La, G3 | 4 | BP28 |
| Woodside Wk, Ham. ML3 | 126 | CU50 |
| Woodstock Av, G41 | 86 | BM37 |
| Woodstock Av, (Kirk.) G66 | 17 | CH13 |
| Woodstock Av, Pais. PA2 | 81 | AN37 |
| Woodstock Way, Pais. PA2 | | |
| off Woodstock Av | 81 | AN37 |
| Wood St, G31 | 69 | BX29 |
| Wood St, Air. ML6 | 76 | DD28 |
| Wood St, Coat. ML5 | 74 | CU30 |
| Wood St, Moth. ML1 | 128 | DB45 |
| Wood St, Pais. PA2 | 83 | AX34 |
| Woodvale Av, (Giff.) G46 | 118 | BK45 |
| Woodvale Av, (Bears.) G61 | 30 | BK19 |
| Woodvale Av, Air. ML6 | 97 | DE33 |
| Woodvale Dr, Pais. PA3 | 61 | AQ32 |
| Woodview, (Udd.) G71 | 94 | CT37 |
| Wood Vw, Moth. ML1 | | |
| off Myrtle Dr | 112 | DD40 |
| Woodview Dr, Air. ML6 | 76 | DC32 |
| Woodview Dr, Bell. ML4 | 95 | CY38 |
| Woodview La, Air. ML6 | | |
| off Woodview Dr | 76 | DC32 |
| Woodview Rd, Lark. ML9 | 144 | DC61 |
| Woodview Ter, Ham. ML3 | 125 | CR49 |
| Woodville Pk, G51 | 66 | BK31 |
| Woodville St, G51 | 66 | BK31 |
| Woodyett Pk, (Clark.) G76 | 119 | BP48 |
| Woodyett Rd, (Clark.) G76 | 119 | BP48 |
| Wordsworth Way, (Both.) G71 | 109 | CR42 |
| Works Av, (Camb.) G72 | 107 | CG40 |
| Worsley Cres, (Newt. M.) G77 | 117 | BE47 |
| Wraes Av, (Barr.) G78 | 99 | AZ41 |
| Wraes Vw, (Barr.) G78 | 98 | AV44 |
| Wrangholm Cres, Moth. ML1 | 112 | DD42 |
| Wrangholm Dr, Moth. ML1 | 112 | DD42 |
| Wren Ct, (Strathclyde Bus. Pk.) | | |
| Bell. ML4 | 94 | CU37 |
| Wren Pl, John. PA5 | 79 | AF38 |
| Wright Av, (Barr.) G78 | 99 | AW43 |
| Wrightlands Cres, Ersk. PA8 | 44 | AU21 |
| Wright St, Renf. PA4 | 63 | AW28 |
| Wright Way, Moth. ML1 | | |
| off Woodside St | 112 | DC42 |
| Wye Cres, Coat. ML5 | 74 | CT27 |
| Wykeham Pl, G13 | 47 | BE23 |
| Wykeham Rd, G13 | 47 | BE23 |
| Wylie, (E.Kil.) G74 | 123 | CF48 |
| Wylie Av, (Newt. M.) G77 | 117 | BF46 |
| Wylie St, Ham. ML3 | 140 | CT51 |
| Wyndford Dr, G20 | 48 | BM24 |
| Wyndford Pl, G20 | | |
| off Wyndford Rd | 48 | BM24 |
| Wyndford Rd, G20 | 48 | BL24 |
| Wyndham Ct, G12 | | |
| off Wyndham St | 48 | BM25 |
| Wyndham St, G12 | 48 | BM25 |
| Wynford Ter, (Udd.) G71 | 93 | CR38 |
| Wynyard Grn, (E.Kil.) G75 | 135 | BX53 |
| Wyper Pl, G40 | 69 | BW31 |

| | | |
|---|---|---|
| Wyvil Av, G13 | 29 | BG20 |
| Wyvis Av, G13 | 46 | BA21 |
| Wyvis Av, (Bears.) G61 | 11 | BE14 |
| Wyvis Ct, (Newt. M.) G77 | 131 | BE51 |
| Wyvis Pl, G13 | 46 | BB21 |
| Wyvis Pl, (Newt. M.) G77 | 131 | BE51 |
| Wyvis Quad, G13 | 46 | BB21 |

**Y**

| | | |
|---|---|---|
| Yair Dr, G52 | 64 | BC31 |
| Yarrow Ct, (Camb.) G72 | | |
| off Gateside Av | 107 | CF40 |
| Yarrow Cres, Bish. PA7 | 24 | AL19 |
| Yarrow Gdns, G20 | 49 | BP26 |
| Yarrow Gdns La, G20 | | |
| off Yarrow Gdns | 49 | BP26 |
| Yarrow Pk, (E.Kil.) G74 | 136 | CC52 |
| Yarrow Rd, (Bishop.) G64 | 33 | BW17 |
| Yarrow Way, (Blan.) G72 | | |
| off Ennisfree Rd | 125 | CN45 |
| Yate Gro, G31 | 69 | BX32 |
| Yate Rd, G31 | 69 | BX32 |
| Yate St, G31 | 69 | BX32 |
| Yementry Ct, (Camb.) G72 | 106 | CB42 |
| Yetholm Gdns, (E.Kil.) G74 | 122 | CB49 |
| Yetholm St, G14 | | |
| off Speirshall Ter | 46 | BA23 |
| Yetholm Ter, Ham. ML3 | 125 | CN50 |
| Yett Rd, Moth. ML1 | 113 | DF42 |
| Yetts Cres, (Kirk.) G66 | 17 | CH13 |
| Yetts Hole Rd, G67 | 39 | CX20 |
| Yetts Hole Rd, Air. ML6 | 57 | CX26 |
| Yew Dr, G21 | 51 | BW26 |
| Yew Pl, John. PA5 | 79 | AH36 |
| Yews Cres, Ham. ML3 | 125 | CR48 |
| Yoker Burn Pl, G13 | | |
| off Yoker Mill Gdns | 46 | BA22 |
| Yokerburn Ter, Clyde. G81 | 45 | AZ22 |
| Yoker Ferry Rd, G14 | 46 | BA23 |
| Yoker Mill Gdns, G13 | 46 | BA22 |
| Yoker Mill Rd, G13 | 46 | BA22 |
| York Dr, (Ruther.) G73 | 105 | BZ40 |
| Yorkhill Par, G3 | 66 | BL28 |
| Yorkhill Quay, G3 | 66 | BK29 |
| Yorkhill St, G3 | 66 | BM29 |
| York Pl, Bell. ML4 | | |
| off Neilson St | 111 | CW40 |
| York Rd, (Chap.) Air. ML6 | 97 | DF37 |
| York St, G2 | 4 | BQ31 |
| York St, Clyde. G81 | 27 | AZ19 |
| York Way, Renf. PA4 | 63 | AZ28 |
| Younger Quad, (Bishop.) G64 | | |
| off Springfield Rd | 33 | BW20 |
| Young Pl, (Udd.) G71 | 93 | CQ37 |
| Young Pl, (E.Kil.) G75 | 136 | CC56 |
| Young St, Clyde. G81 | 27 | AX17 |
| Young Ter, G21 | 51 | BW25 |
| Young Wynd, Bell. ML4 | 95 | CW37 |
| Yukon Ter, (E.Kil.) G75 | 135 | BX53 |

**Z**

| | | |
|---|---|---|
| Zambesi Dr, (Blan.) G72 | 108 | CL44 |
| Zena Cres, G33 | 51 | BY25 |
| Zena Pl, G33 | 51 | BZ25 |
| Zena St, G33 | 51 | BZ25 |
| Zetland Rd, G52 | 64 | BB29 |